T0215514

Modern X86 Assembly Language Programming

Covers X86 64-bit, AVX, AVX2, and AVX-512

Third Edition

Daniel Kusswurm

Apress®

Modern X86 Assembly Language Programming: Covers X86 64-bit, AVX, AVX2, and AVX-512

Daniel Kusswurm
Geneva, IL, USA

ISBN-13 (pbk): 978-1-4842-9602-8   ISBN-13 (electronic): 978-1-4842-9603-5
https://doi.org/10.1007/978-1-4842-9603-5

Managing Director, Apress Media LLC: Welmoed Spahr
Acquisitions Editor: Celestin Suresh John
Development Editor: James Markham
Coordinating Editor: Mark Powers

Cover designed by eStudioCalamar

Cover image by Bolivia Inteligente on Unsplash (www.unsplash.com)

Distributed to the book trade worldwide by Apress Media, LLC, 1 New York Plaza, New York, NY 10004, U.S.A. Phone 1-800-SPRINGER, fax (201) 348-4505, e-mail orders-ny@springer-sbm.com, or visit www.springeronline.com. Apress Media, LLC is a California LLC and the sole member (owner) is Springer Science + Business Media Finance Inc (SSBM Finance Inc). SSBM Finance Inc is a **Delaware** corporation.

For information on translations, please e-mail booktranslations@springernature.com; for reprint, paperback, or audio rights, please e-mail bookpermissions@springernature.com.

Apress titles may be purchased in bulk for academic, corporate, or promotional use. eBook versions and licenses are also available for most titles. For more information, reference our Print and eBook Bulk Sales web page at http://www.apress.com/bulk-sales.

Any source code or other supplementary material referenced by the author in this book is available to readers on GitHub (https://github.com/Apress). For more detailed information, please visit https://www.apress.com/gp/services/source-code.

Paper in this product is recyclable

Table of Contents

About the Author

Daniel Kusswurm has 40+ years of professional experience as a software developer, computer scientist, and author. During his career, he has developed innovative software for medical devices, scientific instruments, and image processing applications. On many of these projects, he successfully employed x86 assembly language and the AVX, AVX2, and AVX-512 instruction sets to significantly improve the performance of computationally intense algorithms and solve unique programming challenges. His educational background includes a BS in electrical engineering technology from Northern Illinois University along with an MS and PhD in computer science from DePaul University.

Daniel is also the author of multiple computer programming books including *Modern Arm Assembly Language Programming* (ISBN: 9781484262665) and *Modern Parallel Programming with C++ and Assembly Language* (ISBN: 9781484279175), both published by Apress.

About the Technical Reviewer

 **Paul Cohen** retired from Intel after 26 years. After being hired as Intel's first Regional Software Specialist in New York, Paul spent his first 10 years at Intel in the sales force and won awards every year for being among the top performers. In 1990, Paul moved to Oregon to manage Intel's early software marketing efforts for operating systems including both real-time and Intel's UNIX. Following Intel's sale of this division, Paul joined the Intel Labs and was involved in the promotion of Native Signal Processing, which eventually became known as MMX/SSE. Before retiring, Paul managed Intel's performance tools marketing group.

Paul was an early member of the Intel startup team AnswerExpress, Intel's first attempt at consumer software. This product was sold on QVC, a first for Intel. Paul led the advanced research team, prototyping concepts of hosting an application on the Web (SaaS – something unheard of in 2000) that ended up in the first version of the product. When the team was sold, Paul led another Intel startup team involved in the definition of AdvancedTCA Blade Servers primarily used by telecom companies and patented many concepts in use today by the current Blade Servers manufacturer.

Paul has 18 patents and has a bachelor's degree in Computer Science and an MSEE from Stony Brook University.

Since retiring, Paul has traveled to over 75 countries and been on over 40 cruises.

Acknowledgments

It is impossible to write and publish a book without the dedication, expertise, and creativity of a professional behind-the-scenes team. This book is no exception. I would like to thank the talented editorial team at Apress including Celestin Suresh John, Nirmal Selvaraj, James Markham, and Mark Powers. I would also like to thank the entire production staff at Apress for their enthusiasm and hard work.

Paul Cohen merits a sincere thank-you for his thorough technical review and constructive comments. Ed Kusswurm is appreciatively acknowledged for his methodical scrutiny of each chapter and sensible suggestions. I accept full responsibility for any remaining imperfections.

Thanks to my professional colleagues for their support and encouragement. Finally, I would like to recognize parental nodes Armin (RIP) and Mary along with sibling nodes Mary, Tom, Ed, and John for their inspiration during the writing of this book.

Introduction

Since the publication of *Modern X86 Assembly Language Programming, First Edition*, I have been asked on numerous occasions, "Do programmers still use assembly language?" The answer to this question is a resounding yes, but with a few caveats.

Over the past several decades, software developers have used x86 assembly language to create innovative solutions for a wide variety of programming challenges. I can recall an era when it was common practice to code significant portions of a program (or even a complete application) using x86 assembly language. Nowadays, modern compilers can routinely generate machine code that is extremely efficient, both spatially and temporally, which means that the epoch of large assembly language programming projects is ancient history. However, use cases still exist where explicit assembly language coding is both feasible and computationally advantageous.

One scenario where assembly language programming is potentially beneficial is in an application that wants to fully exploit the single-instruction multiple-data (SIMD) capabilities of a modern x86 processor. A SIMD-capable x86 processor incorporates hardware components and instructions that perform simultaneous calculations using multiple data values, which can significantly improve the performance of a computationally intense function or algorithm. Unfortunately, many compilers are unable to wholly utilize the SIMD capabilities of an x86 processor. Assembly language programming, on the other hand, empowers the software developer to fully exploit these computational resources.

Modern X86 Assembly Language Programming

Modern X86 Assembly Language Programming, Third Edition is an instructional text that teaches you how to code x86-64 assembly language functions. It also explains how you can algorithmically exploit the SIMD capabilities of an x86-64 processor. The content of this book is organized to help you quickly understand x86-64 assembly language code. In addition, the accompanying source code is structured to accelerate comprehension of x86-64 assembly language instruction syntax, programming constructs, and data structures. After reading this book, you will be able to code performance-accelerated functions and algorithms using x86-64 assembly language and the AVX, AVX2, and AVX-512 instruction sets.

While it is still theoretically possible to write large sections or an entire application program using assembly language, the demanding requirements of contemporary software development mean that such an approach is both impractical and ill-advised. Instead, this book accentuates the coding x86-64 assembly language functions that are callable from C++. The downloadable software package for this book includes source code that works on both Windows (Visual C++ and MASM) and Linux (GNU C++ and NASM).

Before proceeding, it warrants mentioning that this edition of the *Modern X86 Assembly Language Programming* book doesn't cover x86-32 assembly language programming. It also doesn't discuss legacy x86 technologies such as the x87 floating-point unit, MMX, and X86-SSE (Streaming SIMD Extensions). The first edition of this text remains relevant if you're interested in learning about these topics. This book doesn't explain x86 architectural features or privileged instructions that are used in operating systems and device drivers. However, if your goal is to develop x86-64 assembly language code for these use cases, you'll need to thoroughly comprehend the material that's presented in this book.

While perusing *Modern X86 Assembly Language Programming, Third Edition*, you should keep in mind that explicit assembly language coding is often a trade-off between performance gains, development effort, and future maintainability. Perhaps the most important reason for writing this book is to impart the x86 programming savoir faire that you'll need to make informed decisions regarding these trade-offs.

Target Audience

The target audience for *Modern X86 Assembly Language Programming, Third Edition* includes:

- Software developers who are creating programs for x86 platforms and want to learn how to code performance-enhanced algorithms using the core x86-64 instruction set

- Software developers who need to learn how to write SIMD functions or accelerate the performance of new or existing code using the AVX, AVX2, and AVX-512 instruction sets

- Computer science/engineering students or hobbyists who want to learn or better understand x86-64 assembly language programming and the AVX, AVX2, and AVX-512 instruction sets

Readers of *Modern X86 Assembly Language Programming, Third Edition* should have previous programming experience with modern C++ (i.e., ISO C++11 or later). To run or modify the source code examples, some familiarity with Microsoft's Visual Studio or the GNU toolchain will be helpful.

Content Overview

The primary objective of this book is to teach you x86 64-bit assembly language programming and how to exploit AVX, AVX2, and AVX-512 instruction sets. Here's a brief overview of what you can expect to learn.

X86 Core Architecture – Chapter 1 explains the core architecture of an x86-64 processor. Topics discussed include fundamental data types, registers, status flags, memory addressing modes, and other important architectural details.

X86-64 Core Programming – Chapter 2 introduces the fundamentals of x86-64 assembly language programming. The source code examples illustrate essential x86-64 assembly language programming concepts including integer arithmetic, bitwise logical operations, and shift instructions. This chapter also explains basic assembler usage and assembly language syntax. Chapter 3 explores additional core x86-64 assembly language programming concepts including advanced integer arithmetic, memory addressing modes, and condition codes. This chapter also covers stack usage and for-loops. Chapter 4 explains x86-64 assembly language coding using arrays and structures. It also describes how to utilize x86-64 string processing instructions.

AVX Programming – Scalar Floating-Point – Chapter 5 explains scalar floating-point arithmetic and other operations using x86-64 assembly language and the AVX instruction set. It also outlines the C++ calling convention requirements for scalar floating-point arguments and return values.

Run-Time Calling Conventions – Chapter 6 formally describes the run-time calling conventions for x86-64 assembly language functions. The first section explains the requirements for Windows and Visual C++, while the second section covers Linux and GNU C++.

Introduction to x86-AVX – Chapter 7 introduces the SIMD capabilities of Advanced Vector Extensions (AVX). It includes a detailed discussion of AVX architecture and related topics. This chapter also explicates fundamental SIMD arithmetic and other SIMD programming concepts.

AVX Programming – Chapter 8 spotlights packed integer arithmetic and other operations using AVX. It also describes how to code packed integer calculating functions using arrays and the AVX instruction set. Chapter 9 illustrates packed floating-point arithmetic and other operations using AVX. This chapter also demonstrates how to use AVX instructions to perform calculations using floating-point arrays and matrices.

AVX2 Programming – Chapter 10 describes AVX2 packed integer programming. Additionally, it elucidates the coding of several image processing algorithms using the AVX2 instruction set. Chapter 11 teaches you how to enhance the performance of universal floating-point array and matrix calculations using x86-64 assembly language and the AVX2 instruction set. You'll also learn how to accelerate these types of calculations using fused-multiply-add (FMA) instructions. Chapter 12 explicates the coding of advanced algorithms including matrix inversions and convolutions using the AVX2 and FMA instruction sets.

AVX-512 Programming – Chapter 13 presents an overview of AVX-512. It also explains basic packed integer arithmetic using 512-bit wide operands. Chapter 14 explores AVX-512 packed floating-point arithmetic and other operations. Chapter 15 illustrates the use of AVX-512 instructions to accelerate the performance of common matrix and signal processing operations.

Advanced Topics – Chapter 16 demonstrates the use of the cpuid instruction. It also explains how to use non-temporal store instructions and perform SIMD text processing. Chapter 17 discusses guidelines that you can use to optimize the performance of your x86-64 assembly language code. This chapter also reviews several issues related to assembly language software development workflow.

Appendixes – Appendix A explains how to download, install, and execute the source code examples. This appendix additionally includes some brief usage notes about the software development tools that were used to create the source code examples. Appendix B contains a list of references that were consulted during the writing of this book. It also provides some supplemental resources that you can consult for additional x86-64 assembly language programming information.

Source Code

The source code published in this book is available on GitHub at https://github.com//apress/modern-x86-assembly-language-programming-3e.

■ **Caution**   The sole purpose of the source code is to elucidate programming topics that are directly related to the content of this book. Minimal attention is given to essential software engineering concerns such as robust error handling, security risks, numerical stability, rounding errors, or ill-conditioned functions. You are responsible for addressing these concerns should you decide to use any of the source code in your own programs.

The Windows source code examples were developed using Visual Studio 2022, MASM, and Windows 11. The source code examples will also work with Windows 10. The Linux source code examples were developed using GNU C++, Make, and NASM on Debian 11. They were also tested with Ubuntu 22.10. To execute the source code, the processor in your computer and its host operating system must support one or more of the following x86 instruction set extensions: AVX, AVX2, or AVX-512. Appendix A contains additional information about the source code and software development tools.

Terminology

Modern X86 Assembly Language Programming, Third Edition uses the expressions x86-64 and x86-32 to signify the 64-bit and 32-bit execution environments (i.e., registers, instructions, operands, memory addresses, data types, etc.) of an x86 processor. As mentioned earlier, the latter is not covered in this book, except for a few comparison references to aid those migrating from the 32-bit platform. The term x86 is employed for features that apply to both execution environments. The appellation x86-AVX is utilized as an umbrella expression for features that pertain to AVX, AVX2, and AVX-512. The individual acronyms are employed when discussing functional aspects or computational capabilities of a specific x86-AVX instruction set extension. Similarly, the terms x86-SSE or SSE, SSE2, SSE3, etc., are applied when describing similarities or differences between these legacy SIMD technologies and x86-AVX.

Additional Resources

An extensive set of x86-related programming documentation is available from both AMD and Intel. Appendix B lists several important resources that both aspiring and experienced x86 assembly language programmers will find useful. Of all the resources listed in Appendix B, the most valuable reference is Volume 2 of *Intel 64 and IA-32 Architectures Software Developer's Manual, Combined Volumes: 1, 2A, 2B, 2C, 2D, 3A, 3B, 3C, 3D, and 4* (www.intel.com/content/www/us/en/processors/architectures-software-developer-manuals.html). This tome contains comprehensive programming information for every x86 processor instruction including detailed operational descriptions, lists of valid operands, affected status flags, and potential exceptions. You are strongly encouraged to consult this indispensable resource when developing your own x86 assembly language code to verify correct instruction usage and execution outcomes.

CHAPTER 1

■ ■ ■

X86-64 Core Architecture

This chapter explores the core architecture of an x86-64 processor from the perspective of an application program. It begins with a brief historical overview of the x86 platform. The purpose of this overview is to provide a frame of reference for subsequent content. Next is a review of x86-64 fundamental, numeric, and SIMD (single instruction multiple data) data types. This is followed by an examination of x86-64 core architecture, which includes processor register sets, status flags, instruction operands, and memory addressing modes. The chapter concludes with a summary of important differences between x86-32 and x86-64 assembly language programming for the benefit of those migrating from the former.

Unlike languages such as C and C++, assembly language programming requires the software developer to comprehend specific architectural features of the target processor before attempting to write any code. The topics covered in this chapter will fulfill this requirement and provide a foundation for understanding the source code that's presented in subsequent chapters. Comprehension of this chapter's material is also necessary before you progress to the expositions that discuss AVX, AVX2, and AVX-512.

Historical Overview

Before examining the technical details of an x86-64 processor's core architecture, it can be constructive to understand how the architecture has evolved over the years. The short review that follows focuses on noteworthy processors and instruction set enhancements that have affected how software developers use x86-64 assembly language. Readers who are interested in a more comprehensive chronicle of x86-64 processor lineage can consult the resources listed in Appendix A.

The x86-64 processor platform is an extension of the original x86-32 platform. The first silicon embodiment of the x86-32 platform was the Intel 80386 microprocessor, which was introduced in 1985. The 80386 extended the architecture of the 16-bit 80286 to include 32-bit wide registers, native 32-bit arithmetic, flat memory model options, a 4 GB logical address space, and paged virtual memory. The 80486 processor improved the performance of the 80386 with the inclusion of on-chip memory caches and optimized instructions. Unlike the 80386 with its separate 80387 floating-point unit (FPU), most versions of the 80486 CPU included an integrated x87 FPU.

Expansion of the x86-32 platform continued with the introduction of the first Pentium brand processor in 1993. Known as the P5 microarchitecture, performance enhancements included a dual-instruction execution pipeline, 64-bit external data bus, and separate on-chip memory caches for both code and data. Later versions (1997) of the P5 microarchitecture incorporated a new computational resource called MMX technology, which supports SIMD operations (i.e., a single instruction that concurrently manipulates multiple data values) on packed integers using 64-bit wide registers. A packed integer is a collection of multiple data elements (e.g., eight 8-bit integers or four 16-bit integers) that enables the processor to perform various calculating operations (e.g., arithmetic, comparisons, conversions, etc.) on each independent element simultaneously.

© Daniel Kusswurm 2023
D. Kusswurm, *Modern X86 Assembly Language Programming*,
https://doi.org/10.1007/978-1-4842-9603-5_1

The P6 microarchitecture, first used on the Pentium Pro (1995) and Pentium II (1997), extended the x86-32 platform using a three-way superscalar design. This means that the processor is able (on average) to decode, dispatch, and execute three distinct instructions during each clock cycle. Other P6 augmentations included out-of-order instruction executions, improved branch prediction algorithms, and speculative executions. The Pentium III, also based on the P6 microarchitecture, was launched in 1999 and included a new SIMD technology called Streaming SIMD Extensions (SSE). SSE adds eight 128-bit wide registers to the x86-32 platform and instructions that perform packed single-precision floating-point arithmetic.

In 2000, Intel introduced a new microarchitecture called Netburst that included SSE2, which extended the floating-point capabilities of SSE to cover packed double-precision values. SSE2 also incorporated additional instructions that enabled the 128-bit SSE registers to be used for packed integer calculations and scalar floating-point operations. Processors based on the Netburst architecture included several variations of the Pentium 4. In 2004, the Netburst microarchitecture was upgraded to include SSE3 and hyper-threading technology. SSE3 adds new packed integer and packed floating-point instructions to the x86 platform, while hyper-threading technology parallelizes the processor's front-end instruction pipelines to improve performance. SSE3-capable processors include 90 nm (and smaller) versions of the Pentium 4 and Xeon product lines.

In 2006, Intel launched a new microarchitecture called Core. The Core microarchitecture included redesigns of many Netburst front-end pipelines and execution units to improve performance and reduce power consumption. It also incorporated several SIMD enhancements including SSSE3 and SSE4.1. These extensions added new packed integer and packed floating-point instructions to the platform but no new registers or data types. Processors based on the Core microarchitecture include CPUs from the Core 2 Duo and Core 2 Quad series and Xeon 3000/5000 series.

A microarchitecture called Nehalem followed Core in late 2008. The Nehalem microarchitecture incorporates SSE4.2. This final x86-SSE enhancement adds several application-specific accelerator instructions to the x86-SSE instruction set. SSE4.2 also incorporates new instructions that facilitate text string processing using 128-bit wide operands. Processors based on the Nehalem microarchitecture include first-generation Core i3, i5, and i7 CPUs. It also includes CPUs from the Xeon 3000, 5000, and 7000 series.

In 2011, Intel released its next-generation microarchitecture called Sandy Bridge. The Sandy Bridge microarchitecture introduced a new x86 SIMD technology called Advanced Vector Extensions (AVX). AVX adds packed floating-point operations (both single-precision and double-precision) using 256-bit wide registers and operands. AVX also supports a new three-operand instruction syntax, which improves code efficiency by reducing the number of register-to-register data transfers that a software function must perform. Processors based on the Sandy Bridge microarchitecture include second- and third-generation Core i3, i5, and i7 CPUs along with Xeon V2 series CPUs.

In 2013, Intel unveiled its Haswell microarchitecture. Haswell includes AVX2, which extends AVX to support packed integer operations using 256-bit wide registers and operands. AVX2 also supports enhanced data transfer capabilities with its broadcast, gather, and permute instructions. Another feature of the Haswell microarchitecture is its inclusion of fused-multiply-add (FMA) instructions. FMA enables software functions to perform product-sum (or dot product) calculations using a single floating-point rounding operation, which can improve both performance and accuracy. The Haswell microarchitecture also encompasses new general-purpose register instructions. Processors based on the Haswell microarchitecture include fourth-generation Core i3, i5, and i7 CPUs. AVX2 is also included in later generations of Core family CPUs and in Xeon V3, V4, and V5 series CPUs.

X86 platform extensions over the past few decades have not been limited to SIMD enhancements. In 2003, AMD introduced its Opteron processor, which extended the x86's execution environment from 32 bits to 64 bits. Intel followed suit in 2004 by adding essentially the same 64-bit extensions to its processors starting with certain versions of the Pentium 4. The x86-64 execution environment includes a larger address space, additional general-purpose registers, built-in 64-bit integer arithmetic, and other architectural extensions that improve processor performance.

Processors from AMD have also evolved over the past decades. In 2003, AMD introduced a series of processors based on its K8 microarchitecture. Original versions of the K8 included support for MMX, SSE, and SSE2, while later versions added SSE3. In 2007, the K10 microarchitecture was launched and included a SIMD enhancement called SSE4a. SSE4a contains several mask shift and streaming store instructions that are not available on processors from Intel. Following the K10, AMD introduced a new microarchitecture called Bulldozer in 2011. The Bulldozer microarchitecture includes SSSE3, SSE4.1, SSE4.2, SSE4a, and AVX. It also includes FMA4, which is a four-operand version of fused-multiply-add. Like SSE4a, processors marketed by Intel do not support FMA4 instructions. A 2012 update to the Bulldozer microarchitecture called Piledriver includes support for both FMA4 and the three-operand version of FMA, which is often called FMA3 by some CPU feature detection utilities (Appendix B lists some of these utilities). The first AMD microarchitecture to support AVX2, named Excavator, was launched in 2015. Processors based on the subsequent Zen (2017), Zen+ (2018), Zen 2 (2019), Zen 3 (2020), and Zen 4 (2022) microarchitectures also include AVX2; however, they do not support FMA4.

High-end desktop and server-oriented processors based on Intel's Skylake-X microarchitecture, first marketed during 2017, include a new SIMD extension called AVX-512. This architectural enhancement supports packed integer and floating-point operations using 512-bit wide registers and operands. AVX-512 also incorporates architectural additions that facilitate instruction-level masking and merging, floating-point rounding control, and broadcast operations. AMD processors based on the Zen 4 microarchitecture also support AVX-512.

Data Types

X86-64 assembly language functions can use a wide variety of data types. Most of these types originate from a small set of fundamental data types that are intrinsic to the x86 platform. A programmer can employ these fundamental data types to perform assorted arithmetic and data manipulation operations using signed and unsigned integers, single- and double-precision floating-point values, text strings, or SIMD values. The remainder of this section describes the x86 data types that are used in x86-64 assembly language functions.

Fundamental Data Types

A fundamental data type is an elementary unit of data that the processor manipulates during program execution. The x86-64 platform supports fundamental data types ranging from 8 bits (1 byte) to 128 bits (16 bytes). Table 1-1 shows these types along with typical usages.

Table 1-1. *Fundamental Data Types*

Data Type	Size (Bits)	Typical Use
Byte	8	Text characters, small integers
Word	16	Text characters, integers
Doubleword	32	Integers, single-precision floating-point
Quadword	64	Integers, double-precision floating-point, memory address
Double Quadword	128	Integers, packed integers, packed floating-point

The fundamental data types shown in Table 1-1 are, unsurprisingly, integer powers of two. The bits of a fundamental data type are numbered from right to left with 0 and *size – 1* used to identify the least and most significant bits, respectively. Fundamental data types larger than a single byte are stored in memory using little-endian byte ordering. In little-endian byte ordering, the processor stores the least significant byte of a multibyte value at the lowest memory address. Figure 1-1 illustrates the bit numbering and byte ordering schemes used by the fundamental data types shown in Table 1-1.

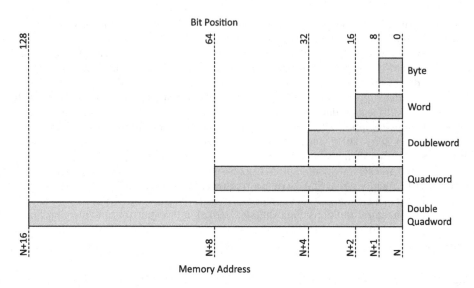

Figure 1-1. *Bit numbering and byte ordering schemes for x86-64 fundamental data types*

A fundamental data type is properly aligned in memory when its address is an integral multiple of its size in bytes. For example, a doubleword is properly aligned when it is stored at a memory address that is an integral multiple of four. Similarly, a quadword is properly aligned when it is stored at a memory address that is evenly divisible by eight. Unless enabled by the host operating system, an x86 processor does not require a fundamental data type to be properly aligned in memory. However, it is standard programming practice to properly align all values whenever possible to avoid potential performance penalties that can occur when the processor accesses an improperly aligned data value in memory.

Numerical Data Types

A numerical data type is an elementary scalar value such as an integer or floating-point number. All x86-64 numerical data types are represented using one of the fundamental data types discussed in the previous section. Table 1-2 shows valid x86-64 numerical data types and their corresponding C++ data types. The x86-64 instruction set supports arithmetic and logical operations using 8-, 16-, 32-, and 64-bit integers, both signed and unsigned. It also supports arithmetic calculations and data manipulation operations using scalar single-precision and double-precision floating-point values.

Table 1-2. *X86-64 Numeric Data Types*

Type	Size (Bits)	C++ Type	<cstdint>
Signed integer	8	char	int8_t
	16	short	int16_t
	32	int, long	int32_t
	64	long, long long	int64_t
Unsigned integer	8	unsigned char	uint8_t
	16	unsigned short	uint16_t
	32	unsigned int, unsigned long	uint32_t
	64	unsigned long, unsigned long long	uint64_t
Floating-point	32	float	n/a
	64	double	n/a

In Table 1-2, note that the size of a C++ long and unsigned long varies. 64-bit versions of Linux use 64-bit wide integers for both long and unsigned long, while 64-bit versions of Windows use 32-bit wide integers for these same types.

SIMD Data Types

A SIMD data type is a collection of bytes that the processor employs to perform an arithmetic calculation or data manipulation operation using multiple values. A SIMD data type can be regarded as a container object that holds multiple instances of the same fundamental data type (e.g., 8-, 16-, 32-, or 64-bit integers; half-, single-, or double-precision floating-point values). The bits of an x86 SIMD data type are numbered from right to left with *0* and *size – 1* denoting the least and most significant bits, respectively. X86 SIMD data types are also stored in memory using little-endian byte ordering as illustrated in Figure 1-2. In this figure, the terms xmmword, ymmword, and zmmword are expressions for 128-, 256-, and 512-bit wide SIMD data types, respectively.

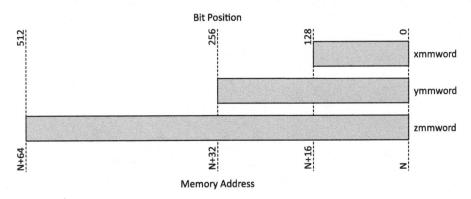

Figure 1-2. *X86 SIMD data types*

Programs can use x86 SIMD data types to perform simultaneous calculations using either packed integers or floating-point values. For example, a 128-bit wide packed data type can hold sixteen 8-bit integers, eight 16-bit integers, four 32-bit integers, or two 64-bit integers. A 256-bit wide packed data type can hold a variety of data elements including eight single-precision floating-point values or four double-precision floating-point values. Table 1-3 contains a complete list of the x86 SIMD data types and the maximum number of elements for various numerical data types.

Table 1-3. X86-64 SIMD Data Types and Element Capacities

Numerical Type	xmmword	ymmword	zmmword
8-bit integer	16	32	64
16-bit integer	8	16	32
32-bit integer	4	8	16
64-bit integer	2	4	8
Half-precision floating-point	8	16	32
Single-precision floating-point	4	8	16
Double-precision floating-point	2	4	8

Figure 1-3 highlights 128-bit and 256-bit wide x86-64 SIMD data types in greater detail. In this figure, the acronyms HPFP, SPFP, and DPFP denote half-, single-, and double-precision floating-point values, respectively. You'll learn more about x86-64 SIMD data types in Chapter 7.

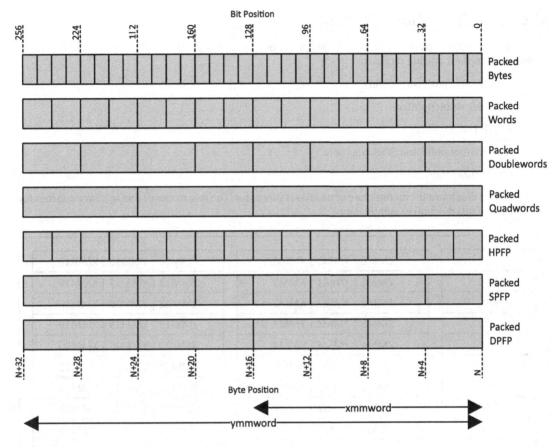

Figure 1-3. *128-bit and 256-bit wide x86-64 SIMD data types*

As mentioned earlier in this chapter, SIMD enhancements have been periodically added to the x86 platform starting in 1997 with MMX technology and most recently with the addition of AVX-512. This presents some challenges to the software developer who wants to exploit these technologies in that the packed data types described in Table 1-3 and Figure 1-3 and the corresponding AVX, AVX2, and AVX-512 instruction set extensions are not universally supported by all processors. Fortunately, methods are available to determine at run-time the specific x86 SIMD (and other) instruction set extensions that a processor supports. You'll learn more about this in Chapter 16.

Miscellaneous Data Types

The x86 platform also supports several miscellaneous data types including strings, bit fields, and bit strings. An x86 string is a contiguous block of bytes, words, doublewords, or quadwords. The core x86 instruction set includes instructions that perform string compare, load, move, scan, and store operations. X86 string instructions can also be used to perform these same operations using arrays of numerical values.

A bit field is a contiguous sequence of bits. Some x86 instructions extract bit fields for use in masking operations. A bit field can start at any bit position within a byte and contain up to 32 or 64 bits. A bit string is a contiguous sequence of bits. The x86 instruction set includes instructions that can clear, set, scan, and test individual bits within a bit string.

X86-64 Processor Architecture

From the perspective of an executing application program, the architecture of an x86-64 processor can be partitioned into the following sections:

- General-purpose registers
- Instruction pointer
- RFLAGS register
- Floating-point and SIMD registers
- MXCSR register

Figure 1-4 illustrates the architecture of an x86-64 processor. The remainder of this section examines the components of this diagram in greater detail.

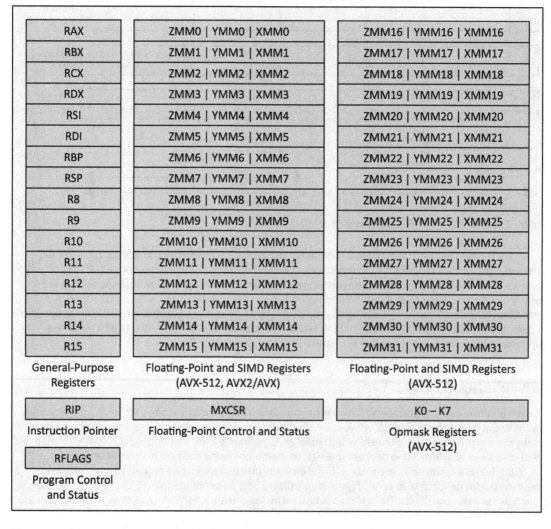

Figure 1-4. *X86-64 processor internal architecture*

General-Purpose Registers

All x86-64 processors contain 16 64-bit wide general-purpose registers. Functions use these registers to perform integer arithmetic, bitwise logical operations, comparisons, address calculations, and data transfers. A function can also store an intermediate or temporary result in a general-purpose register instead of saving it to memory. Figure 1-5 shows the complete set of x86-64 general-purpose registers along with their operand names.

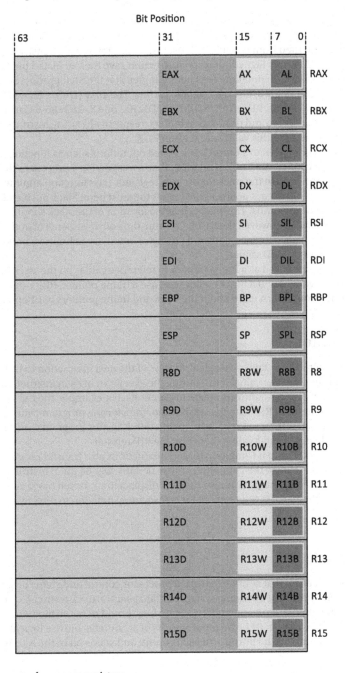

Figure 1-5. *X86-64 general-purpose registers*

The low-order byte, word, and doubleword of each 64-bit general-purpose register are independently accessible and can be employed to carry out operations using 8-, 16-, or 32-bit wide operands. For example, a function can use registers EAX, EBX, ECX, and EDX to perform 32-bit integer arithmetic in the low-order doublewords of RAX, RBX, RCX, and RDX, respectively. Similarly, registers AL, BL, CL, and DL can be used to carry out 8-bit calculations in the low-order bytes. Not shown in Figure 1-5 are the legacy byte registers AH, BH, CH, and DH. These registers are aliased to the high-order bytes of registers AX, BX, CX, and DX, respectively.

Despite their designation as general-purpose registers, the x86-64 instruction set imposes some notable restrictions on their use. Some instructions either require or implicitly use specific registers as operands. This is a legacy scheme inherited from the 8086 that ostensibly improves code density. For example, some variants of the imul (Multiply Signed Integers) instruction save the calculated product in RDX:RAX, EDX:EAX, DX:AX, or AX. The colon notation used here signifies that the final product is stored in two registers with the first register holding the most significant bits. The idiv (Divide Signed Integers) requires the integer dividend to be loaded in RDX:RAX, EDX:EAX, DX:AX, or AX. The x86-64 string instructions use registers RSI and RDI for the source and destination buffers, respectively; string instructions that employ a repeat (or length) count must load this value into register RCX.

The processor uses register RSP to support stack-based operations such as function calls and returns. The stack itself is simply a contiguous block of memory that is assigned to a process or thread by the operating system. Programs can use the stack to preserve registers, pass function arguments, and store temporary results. Register RSP always points to the stack's topmost item. Stack push and pop operations are performed using 64-bit wide operands. This means that the location of the stack should always be aligned on a quadword (8-byte) boundary. However, the 64-bit C++ run-time environments of both Windows and Linux align stack memory and RSP on a double quadword (16-byte) boundary to improve performance when loading or storing stack-based SIMD values.

Register RBP is sometimes used as a frame pointer to reference values on the stack including function arguments and local data variables. If a function does not use a frame pointer, RBP can be utilized as a general-purpose register. You'll learn more about the stack and frame pointers in Chapter 6.

Instruction Pointer

Instruction pointer register RIP contains the logical address of the next instruction to be executed. The processor automatically updates the value in RIP during the execution of each instruction. RIP is also modified during execution of some control-transfer instructions. For example, the call (Call Procedure) instruction pushes the contents of RIP onto the stack before transferring program control to the specified function address. The ret (Return from Procedure) instruction transfers program control by popping the topmost eight bytes off the stack and loading them into the RIP register.

The jmp (Jump) and jcc (Jump if Condition is Met) instructions also transfer program control by updating the contents of RIP. Unlike the call and ret instructions, x86-64 jump instructions are executed independent of the stack. The RIP register is also used for displacement-based operand memory addressing as explained later in this chapter. It is not possible for an executing function to directly read or modify the RIP register.

RFLAGS Register

RFLAGS is a 64-bit wide register that contains assorted processor control and status bits. Most of the control bits in RFLAGS are used by the host operating system to manage interrupts, restrict I/O operations, support program debugging, and handle virtual operations. These bits should *never* be modified by an application program. The status bits (or flags) in RFLAGS report results of arithmetic, bitwise logical, and compare operations. Table 1-4 summarizes the purpose of each control and status bit in the RFLAGS register.

Table 1-4. *RFLAGS Register*

Bit Position	Name	RFLAGS Symbol	Use
0	Carry Flag	CF	Status
1	Reserved		1
2	Parity Flag	PF	Status
3	Reserved		0
4	Auxiliary Carry Flag	AF	Status
5	Reserved		0
6	Zero Flag	ZF	Status
7	Sign Flag	SF	Status
8	Trap Flag	TF	System
9	Interrupt Enable Flag	IF	System
10	Direction Flag	DF	Control
11	Overflow Flag	OF	Status
12	I/O Privilege Level Bit 0	IOPL	System
13	I/O Privilege Level Bit 1	IOPL	System
14	Nested Task	NT	System
15	Reserved		0
16	Resume Flag	RF	System
17	Virtual 8086 Mode	VM	System
18	Alignment Check	AC	System
19	Virtual Interrupt Flag	VIF	System
20	Virtual Interrupt Pending	VIP	System
21	ID Flag	ID	System
22–63	Reserved		0

For application programs, the most important status bits in RFLAGS are the following flags: carry flag (RFLAGS.CF), overflow flag (RFLAGS.OF), parity flag (RFLAGS.PF), sign flag (RFLAGS.SF), and zero flag (RFLAGS.ZF). Some integer arithmetic instructions use the carry flag to signify an overflow condition when performing unsigned integer arithmetic. It is also used by some register rotate and shift instructions. The overflow flag signals that the result of a signed integer operation is too small or too large. The processor sets the parity flag to indicate whether the least significant byte of an arithmetic, compare, or logical operation contains an even number of "1" bits. Parity bits are used by some communication protocols to detect transmission errors. A few scalar floating-point compare instructions also use the parity flag to report results. The sign and zero flags are set by arithmetic and logical instructions to signify a negative, zero, or positive result.

RFLAGS contains a control bit called the direction flag (RFLAGS.DF) that is used by x86 string instructions. An application program can set or clear the direction flag, which defines the auto increment direction (0 = low to high addresses, 1 = high to low addresses) of the RDI and RSI registers during execution of a string instruction. Reserved bits in RFLAGS should never be modified, and no assumptions should ever be made regarding the state of any reserved bit.

Floating-Point and SIMD Registers

X86-64 processors that support AVX and AVX2 include 16 256-bit wide registers named YMM0–YMM15. The low-order 128 bits of each YMM register is aliased to a 128-bit wide XMM register as shown in Figure 1-6. The YMM and XMM registers can be used as operands with most AVX and AVX2 instructions to carry out SIMD operations using either packed integer or packed floating-point operands.

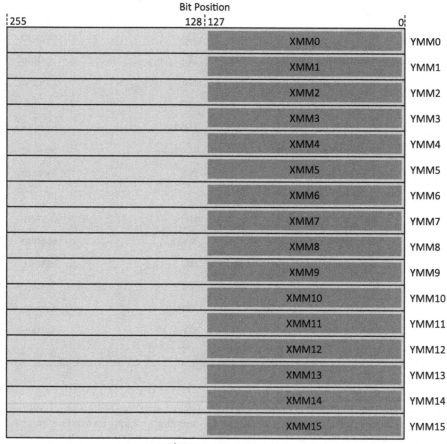

Figure 1-6. *AVX/AVX2 register set*

The XMM register set also supports scalar floating-point operations including basic arithmetic, comparisons, and type conversions. The processor uses the low-order 32 bits of an XMM register to perform scalar single-precision floating-point operations as illustrated in Figure 1-7. Similarly, the processor uses the low-order 64 bits of an XMM register to carry out scalar double-precision floating-point operations. When performing scalar floating-point operations, the processor does not directly manipulate the high-order 96 bits (single-precision) or 64 bits (double-precision) of an XMM register. However, some x86-AVX scalar floating-point instructions modify these bits in a destination operand. You'll learn more about this in Chapter 5.

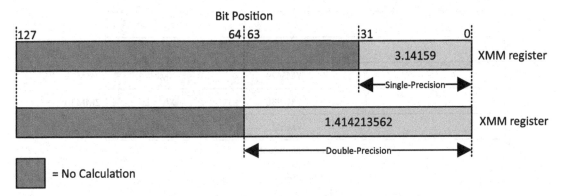

Figure 1-7. *Scalar floating-point values in an XMM register*

Not shown in Figure 1-5 is the legacy x87 FPU. An x86-64 program can still use the x87 FPU to perform scalar floating-point arithmetic. However, the x87 FPU is normally not used in x86-64 programs since it is more efficient code-wise to use the XMM register set to carry out scalar floating-point arithmetic and other operations.

AVX-512 extends the width of each YMM register from 256 bits to 512 bits. The 512-bit wide registers are named ZMM0–ZMM15. AVX-512 also adds 16 new SIMD registers named ZMM16–ZMM31. These new registers include aliased 256-bit wide YMM and 128-bit wide XMM registers as illustrated in Figure 1-8. Also shown in Figure 1-8 are eight opmask registers. AVX-512 instructions use these registers to perform merge masking and zero masking. The opmask registers are also employed to store the results of AVX-512 SIMD compare operations. You'll learn more about the ZMM and opmask register sets in Chapter 13.

Bit Position

511	256	255	128	127	0
	YMM0		XMM0		ZMM0
	YMM1		XMM1		ZMM1
	YMM2		XMM2		ZMM2
					.
					.
					.
	YMM29		XMM29		ZMM29
	YMM30		XMM30		ZMM30
	YMM31		XMM31		ZMM31

AVX-512 Register Set

Bit Position

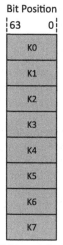

63   0

K0
K1
K2
K3
K4
K5
K6
K7

AVX-512 Opmask Register Set

Figure 1-8. *AVX-512 register set*

MXCSR Register

All x86-64 processors include a 32-bit control-status register named MXCSR. This register incorporates a collection of control flags that enable a program to configure options for floating-point operations and exceptions. It also includes a set of status flags that a program can test to detect floating-point error conditions. Table 1-5 describes the purpose of each MXCSR bit field.

Table 1-5. *MXCSR Register Bit Fields*

Bits	Symbol	Name	Description
0	IE	Invalid operation flag	Floating-point invalid operation error flag
1	DE	Denormal flag	Floating-point denormal error flag
2	ZE	Divide-by-zero flag	Floating-point division-by-zero error flag
3	OE	Overflow flag	Floating-point overflow error flag
4	UE	Underflow flag	Floating-point underflow error flag
5	PE	Precision flag	Floating-point precision error flag
6	DAZ	Denormals are zero	Enables automatic conversion of a denormal to zero
7	IM	Invalid operation mask	Floating-point invalid operation error exception mask
8	DM	Denormal mask	Floating-point denormal error exception mask
9	ZM	Divide-by-zero mask	Floating-point divide-by-zero error exception mask
10	OM	Overflow mask	Floating-point overflow error exception mask
11	UM	Underflow mask	Floating-point underflow error exception mask
12	PM	Precision mask	Floating-point precision error exception mask
13–14	RC	Rounding control	Specifies the method for rounding floating-point results; valid options include round to nearest (0b00), round down toward $-\infty$ (0b01), round up toward $+\infty$ (0b10), and round toward zero (0b11)
15	FZ	Flush to zero	Forces a zero result if the underflow exception is masked and a floating-point underflow error occurs
16–31	---	Reserved	Reserved for future use

Application programs normally do not directly modify the floating-point exception mask bits in MXCSR. However, most C++ run-time environments provide a library function that allows an application program to designate a callback function that gets invoked whenever a floating-point exception occurs. An application program can modify the MXCSR's rounding control bits (MXCSR.RC), and you'll learn how to do this in Chapter 5.

Instruction Operands

Nearly all x86-64 instructions use operands, which designate the specific values that an instruction will act upon. Most instructions require one or more source operands along with a single destination operand. Most instructions also require the programmer to explicitly specify the source and destination operands. There are, however, several instructions where register operands are either implicitly specified or required by an instruction as mentioned earlier in this chapter.

There are three basic types of operands: immediate, register, and memory. An immediate operand is a constant value that is explicitly coded. A register operand is the value in a general-purpose or SIMD register. A memory operand specifies a location in memory, which can contain any of the previously described data types. Most instructions can specify a memory location for either the source or destination operand but not both. Table 1-6 contains several examples of instructions that employ various x86-64 operand types.

Table 1-6. *Examples of x86-64 Instructions and Operands*

Type	Example	Analogous C++ Statement
Immediate	mov rax,42	rax = 42
	imul r12,-47	r12 *= -47
	shl r15,8	r15 <<= 8
	xor ecx,80000000h	ecx ^= 0x80000000
	sub r9b,14	r9b -= 14
Register	mov rax,rbx	rax = rbx
	add rbx,r10	rbx += r10
	mul rbx	rdx:rax = rax * rbx
	and r8w,0ff00h	r8w &= 0xff00
Memory	mov rax,[r13]	rax = *r13
	or rcx,[rbx+rsi*8]	rcx |= *(rbx+rsi*8)
	mov qword ptr [r8],17	*(long long*)r8 = 17
	shl word [r12],2	*(short*)r12 <<= 2

The mul rbx (Multiply Unsigned Integers) instruction that is shown in Table 1-6 is an example of an instruction that uses an implicit operand. In this example, implicit register RAX and explicit register RBX are used as the source operands, and implicit register pair RDX:RAX is the destination operand. The multiplicative product's high-order and low-order quadwords are stored in RDX and RAX, respectively.

The text qword ptr that's used in Table 1-6's penultimate example is a MASM size operator that acts like a C++ cast operator. In this instruction, 17 is subtracted from the 64-bit value whose memory location is specified by the contents of register R8. Without the qword ptr size operator, the assembly language statement is ambiguous since the assembler cannot ascertain the size of the operand pointed to by R8; the destination operand in memory could also be an 8-, 16-, or 32-bit value. The final example in Table 1-6 uses the NASM size operator word in a similar manner. You'll learn more about MASM and NASM directives and operators in subsequent chapters.

Memory Addressing

An x86 instruction requires up to four separate components to specify the location of an operand in memory. The four components include a constant displacement value, a base register, an index register, and a scale factor. Using these components, the processor calculates an effective address for a memory operand as follows:

```
EffectiveAddress = BaseReg + IndexReg * ScaleFactor + Disp
```

The base register (BaseReg) can be any general-purpose register. The index register (IndexReg) can be any general-purpose register except RSP. Valid scale factor (ScaleFactor) values include 1 (the default), 2, 4, and 8. Finally, the displacement (Disp) is an 8-, 16-, or 32-bit signed offset that is encoded within the instruction. Table 1-7 illustrates x86-64 memory addressing using different forms of the mov (Move) instruction. In these examples, register RAX (the destination operand) is loaded with the quadword value that is specified by the source operand. It is important to note that it is not necessary for an instruction to explicitly specify a complete set of effective address components. For example, a default value of zero is used for the displacement if an explicit value is not specified. The final size of an effective address calculation is always 64 bits.

Table 1-7. *Memory Operand Addressing*

Addressing Form	Example
RIP + Disp	mov rax,[Val]
BaseReg	mov rax,[rbx]
BaseReg + Disp	mov rax,[rbx+16]
IndexReg * SF + Disp	mov rax,[r15*8+48]
BaseReg + IndexReg	mov rax,[rbx+r15]
BaseReg + IndexReg + Disp	mov rax,[rbx+r15+32]
BaseReg + IndexReg * SF	mov rax,[rbx+r15*8]
BaseReg + IndexReg * SF + Disp	mov rax,[rbx+r15*8+64]

The memory addressing forms shown in Table 1-7 facilitate the referencing of simple variables, elements in an array, or specific members of a data structure. For example, the simple displacement form is often used to access a single global or static value. The base register form is analogous to a C++ pointer and is used to indirectly reference a single value. Individual members within a data structure can be retrieved using a base register and a displacement. The index register forms are useful for accessing a specific element in an array or matrix. Scale factors can reduce the amount code of needed to access elements in an array or matrix. Elements in more elaborate data structures can be referenced using a base register together with an index register, scale factor, and displacement.

The mov rax,[Val] instruction that's shown in the first row of Table 1-7 is an example of RIP-relative (or instruction pointer relative) addressing. With RIP-relative addressing, the processor calculates an effective address using the contents of the RIP register and a signed 32-bit displacement value that is encoded within the instruction. Figure 1-9 illustrates this calculation in greater detail. Note the little-endian ordering of the displacement value that's embedded in the machine encoding of the mov rax,[Val] instruction. RIP-relative addressing allows the processor to reference global or static operands using a 32-bit displacement instead of a 64-bit displacement, which reduces code space. It also facilitates position-independent code.

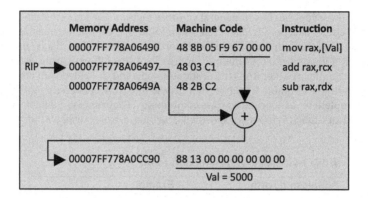

Figure 1-9. *RIP-relative effective address calculation*

One minor constraint of RIP-relative addressing is that the target memory operand must reside with a ± 2 GB address window of the value in RIP. For most programs, this limitation is rarely a concern. The calculation of a RIP-relative displacement value is usually determined automatically by the assembler or linker. This means that you can use a mov rax,[Val] or similar instruction without having to worry about the details of the displacement value calculation.

Condition Codes

Most x86-64 arithmetic, bitwise logical, shift, and rotate instructions update one or more of the status flags in the RFLAGS register. As discussed earlier in this chapter, the status flags provide additional information about the results of an operation. The jcc, cmovcc (Conditional Move), and setcc (Set Byte on Condition) instructions use what are called condition codes to test the status flags either individually or logically combined. Table 1-8 lists the condition codes, mnemonic suffixes, and the corresponding RFLAGS tested by these instructions.

Table 1-8. *Condition Codes, Mnemonic Suffixes, and Test Conditions*

Condition Code	Mnemonic Suffix	RFLAGS Test Condition
Above Neither below nor equal	A NBE	CF == 0 && ZF == 0
Above or equal Not Below	AE NB	CF == 0
Below Neither above nor equal	B NAE	CF == 1
Below or equal Not above	BE NA	CF == 1 || ZF == 1
Equal Zero	E Z	ZF == 1
Not equal Not zero	NE NZ	ZF == 0
Greater Neither less nor equal	G NLE	ZF == 0 && SF == OF
Greater or equal Not less	GE NL	SF == OF
Less Neither greater nor equal	L NGE	SF != OF
Less or equal Not greater	LE NG	ZF == 1 || SF != OF
Sign Not sign	S NS	SF == 1 SF == 0

(continued)

Table 1-8. (*continued*)

Condition Code	Mnemonic Suffix	RFLAGS Test Condition
Carry	C	CF == 1
Not carry	NC	CF == 0
Overflow	O	OF == 1
Not overflow	NO	OF == 0
Parity	P	PF == 1
Parity even	PE	
Not parity	NP	PF == 0
Parity odd	PO	

Note that Table 1-8 shows alternate forms for most mnemonic suffixes. These are defined to provide algorithmic flexibility or improve program readability. When using a conditional instruction such as jcc in source code, condition codes containing the words "above" and "below" are employed for unsigned integer operands, while the words "greater" and "less" are used for signed integer operands. If Table 1-8 seems a little confusing or abstract, don't worry. You will see a plethora of condition code examples in the programming chapters of this book.

Differences Between X86-64 and X86-32

There are some important differences between x86-64 and x86-32 assembly language programming. If you are learning x86 assembly language programming for the first time, you can either skim or skip this section since it discusses concepts that aren't fully explained until later in this book.

Most existing x86-32 instructions have an x86-64 equivalent instruction that enables a function to exploit 64-bit wide addresses and operands. X86-64 functions can also perform calculations using instructions that manipulate 8-bit, 16-bit, or 32-bit registers and operands. Except for the mov instruction, the maximum size of an x86-64 immediate value is 32 bits. If an instruction manipulates a 64-bit wide register or memory operand, any specified immediate (or effective address displacement) value is sign-extended to 64 bits prior to its use.

Table 1-9 contains some examples of x86-64 instructions using various operand sizes. Note that the memory operands in these example instructions are referenced using 64-bit registers, which is required to access the entire 64-bit linear address space. While it is possible for an x86-64 instruction to reference a memory operand using a 32-bit register (e.g., mov r10, [eax]), the location of the operand must reside in the low 4 GB portion of the 64-bit effective address space. Using 32-bit registers to access memory operands in x86-64 mode is not recommended since it introduces unnecessary and potentially dangerous code obfuscations. It also complicates software testing and debugging.

Table 1-9. *Examples of X86-64 Instructions Using Various Operand Sizes*

8-Bit	16-Bit	32-Bit	64-Bit
add al,bl	add ax,bx	add eax,ebx	add rax,rbx
cmp dl,[r15]	cmp dx,[r15]	cmp edx,[r15]	cmp rdx,[r15]
mul r10b	mul r10w	mul r10d	mul r10
or [r8+rdi],al	or [r8+rdi],ax	or [r8+rdi],eax	or [r8+rdi],rax
shl r9b,cl	shl r9w,cl	shl r9d,cl	shl r9,cl

The immediate value size limitation warrants some extra discussion since it sometimes affects the instruction sequences that a function must employ to carry out certain operations. Figure 1-10 contains a few examples of instructions that use a 64-bit register with an immediate operand. In the first example, the mov rax,100 instruction loads an immediate value into the RAX register. Note that the machine code uses only 32 bits to encode the immediate value 100, which is underlined. During instruction execution, this value is sign-extended to 64 bits and loaded into register RAX. The add rax,200 instruction that follows also sign-extends its immediate value prior to performing the addition. The next example opens with a mov rcx,-2000 instruction that loads a negative immediate value into RCX. The machine code for this instruction also uses 32 bits to encode the immediate value –2000, which is sign-extended to 64 bits and saved in RCX. The subsequent add rcx,1000 instruction yields a 64-bit result of –1000.

Machine Code	Instruction	DesOp Result
48 C7 C0 <u>64 00 00 00</u>	mov rax,100	0000000000000064h
48 05 C0 <u>C8 00 00 00</u>	add rax,200	000000000000012Ch
48 C7 C1 <u>30 F8 FF FF</u>	mov rcx,-2000	FFFFFFFFFFFFF830h
48 81 C1 <u>E8 03 00 00</u>	add rcx,1000	FFFFFFFFFFFFFC18h
48 C7 C2 <u>FF 00 00 00</u>	mov rdx,0ffh	00000000000000FFh
48 81 CA <u>00 00 00 80</u>	or rdx,80000000h	FFFFFFFF800000FFh
48 C7 C2 <u>FF 00 00 00</u>	mov rdx,0ffh	00000000000000FFh
49 B8 <u>00 00 00 80 00 00 00 00</u>	mov r8,80000000h	0000000080000000h
49 0B D0	or rdx,r8	00000000800000FFh

Figure 1-10. *Using 64-bit registers with immediate operands*

The third example employs a mov rdx,0ffh instruction to initialize register RDX. This is followed by an or rdx,80000000h instruction that sign-extends the immediate value 0x80000000 to 0xFFFFFFFF80000000 and then performs a bitwise inclusive OR operation. The value that's shown for RDX is almost certainly not the intended result. The final example illustrates how to carry out an operation that requires a 64-bit immediate value. A mov r8,80000000h instruction loads the 64-bit value 0x0000000080000000 into R8. As mentioned earlier in this section, the mov instruction is the only instruction that supports 64-bit immediate operands. Execution of the ensuing or rdx,r8 instruction yields the expected value.

The 32-bit size limitation for immediate values also applies to jmp and call instructions that specify relative-displacement targets. In these cases, the target (or location) of a jmp or call instruction must reside with a ± 2 GB address window of the current RIP register. Targets whose relative displacements exceed this window can only be accessed using a jmp or call instruction that employs an indirect operand (e.g., jmp rax or call [rax]). Like RIP-relative addressing, the size limitations described in this paragraph are unlikely to present significant obstacles for most assembly language functions.

Another difference between x86-32 and x86-64 assembly language programming is the effect that some instructions have on the upper 32 bits of a 64-bit general-purpose register. When using instructions that manipulate 32-bit registers and operands, the high-order 32 bits of the corresponding 64-bit general-purpose register are zeroed during execution. For example, assume that register RAX contains the value 0x8000000000000000. Execution of the instruction add eax,10 generates a result of 0x000000000000000A in RAX. However, when working with 8-bit or 16-bit registers and operands, the upper 56 or 48 bits of the corresponding 64-bit general-purpose register are *not* modified. Assuming again that RAX contains 0x8000000000000000, execution of the instructions add al,20 or add ax,40 would yield RAX values of 0x8000000000000014 or 0x8000000000000028, respectively.

The x86-64 platform imposes some restrictions on the use of legacy registers AH, BH, CH, and DH. These registers cannot be used with instructions that also reference one of the new 8-bit registers (i.e., SIL, DIL, BPL, SPL, and R8B–15B). Existing x86-32 instructions such as mov ah,bl and add dh,bl are still allowed. However, the instructions mov ah,r8b and add dh,r8b are invalid.

Finally, a handful of rarely used x86-32 instructions cannot be used in x86-64 programs. Table 1-10 lists these instructions. Somewhat surprisingly, early-generation x86-64 processors did not support the lahf (Load Status Flags into AH) and sahf (Store AH into Flags) instructions in x86-64 mode (they still worked in x86-32 code). Fortunately, these instructions were reinstated and should be available on most AMD and Intel processors marketed since 2006. A program can confirm processor support for the lahf and sahf instructions in x86-64 mode by using the cpuid (CPU Identification) instruction and testing the feature flag LAHF/SAHF.

Table 1-10. *X86-64 Invalid Instructions*

Mnemonic	Name
aaa	ASCII Adjust After Addition
aad	ASCII Adjust After Division
aam	ASCII Adjust After Multiplication
aas	ASCII Adjust After Subtraction
bound	Check Array Index Against Bounds
daa	Decimal Adjust After Addition
das	Decimal Adjust After Subtraction
into	Generate interrupt if RFLAGS.OF Equals 1
pop[a|ad]	Pop all General-Purpose Registers
push[a|ad]	Push all General-Purpose Registers

Legacy Instruction Sets

All x86-64 processors support the SSE2 instruction set. This means that x86-64 functions can safely use the packed integer instructions of SSE2 instead of MMX. It also means that x86-64 functions can use the scalar floating-point instructions of SSE2 (or AVX) instead of x87 FPU instructions. X86-64 functions can still utilize the MMX and x87 FPU instruction sets, and such use might be warranted when migrating x86-32 legacy code to x86-64. For new x86-64 software development, however, the use of the MMX and x87 FPU instruction sets is not recommended.

Summary

Here are the key learning points for Chapter 1:

- The fundamental data types of the x86-64 platform include byte (8-bit), word (16-bit), doubleword (32-bit), quadword (64-bit), and double quadword (128-bit). Programming language primitive data types such as characters, text strings, integers, and floating-point values are derived from the fundamental data types.

- An x86-64 processor includes 16 64-bit general-purpose registers that are used to perform arithmetic, logical, and data transfer operations using 8-, 16-, 32-, or 64-bit wide operands.

- An x86-64 processor also includes an instruction pointer (RIP) and control and status (RFLAGS) register. The former points to the next executable instruction; the latter contains processor control bits and status flags. Most arithmetic and logical instructions update one or more of the status flags in RFLAGS. These flags can be tested to alter program flow or conditionally assign values to variables.

- X86-64 processors that support AVX/AVX2 include 16 256-bit wide registers named YMM0–YMM15. The low-order 128 bits of each YMM register can be referenced as XMM0–XMM15.

- X86-64 processors that support AVX-512 include 32 512-bit wide registers named ZMM0–ZMM31. The low-order 256 bits/128 bits of each ZMM register are aliased to a corresponding YMM/XMM register. AVX-512-compliant processors also include eight opmask registers that facilitate merge masking and zero masking.

- A function can use the ZMM, YMM, and XMM registers to carry out SIMD operations using packed integers or packed floating-point values. The XMM registers can also be used to perform scalar floating-point arithmetic using single-precision or double-precision values.

- The MXCSR register contains control bits that select options for floating-point operations and exceptions. This register also contains status bits that report floating-point error conditions.

- An operand in memory can be referenced using a variety of addressing modes that include one or more of the following components: fixed displacement, base register, index register, and/or scale factor.

- Most x86-64 assembly language instructions can be used with the following explicit operand types: immediate, register, and memory. Some instructions use implicit register operands.

CHAPTER 2

■ ■ ■

X86-64 Core Programming – Part 1

In the previous chapter, you learned about the fundamentals of the x86-64 platform including its data types, register sets, and memory addressing modes. In this chapter, you'll discover how to code simple x86-64 assembly language functions that are callable from C++. You'll also master the semantics and syntax of an x86-64 assembly language source code file.

The content of Chapter 2 is organized as follows. The first section presents an overview of this book's source code. Next is a short passage that explains the basics of an assembler. The remaining sections explicate elementary x86-64 assembly language programming. Topics discussed include integer arithmetic, bitwise logical operations, shift operations, and conditional jump instructions. You'll also learn about run-time calling conventions and the requisite assembler directives needed to create executable code.

The primary purpose of the source code presented in this chapter is to elucidate proper use of the x86-64 instruction set and essential assembly language programming techniques. The assembly language code in each example is straightforward, but not necessarily optimal since understanding optimized assembly language code can be challenging especially for beginners. The source code examples in later chapters place more emphasis on efficient coding techniques.

Source Code Overview

As mentioned in the Introduction, the primary objective of this book is to help you learn x86-64 assembly language programming. The source code examples that you'll study in this and subsequent chapters are structured to help you achieve this goal.

Most of the source code examples published in this book follow the same design pattern. The first part of each example includes C++ code that performs test case initialization or other setup tasks. The second part contains the x86-64 assembly language code. For many examples, this part also includes some C++ code that performs the same calculation as the corresponding x86-64 assembly language function for result comparison or benchmarking purposes. The final component of each example contains C++ code that formats and displays the output. Given the variety and scope of the source code presented in this book, I decided to create a (hopefully) straightforward naming convention for both file and function names. These are outlined in Tables 2-1 and 2-2.

© Daniel Kusswurm 2023
D. Kusswurm, *Modern X86 Assembly Language Programming*,
https://doi.org/10.1007/978-1-4842-9603-5_2

Table 2-1. *Source Code File Name Suffixes*

File Name Suffix	Description
.h	C++ header file
.cpp	C++ source code file – function `main()`
_fcpp.cpp	C++ source code file – algorithm code
_misc.cpp	C++ source code – miscellaneous functions
_bm.cpp	C++ source code – benchmarking code
_fasm.asm	MASM x86-64 assembly language code
.asmh	MASM x86-64 assembly language header file
_fasm.s	NASM x86-64 assembly language code
.inc	NASM x86-64 assembly language header file

Table 2-2. *Source Code Function Name Suffixes*

Function Name Suffix	Description
_cpp (or no suffix)	C++ function
_a	X86-64 assembly language function (no x86-AVX instructions)
_avx	X86-64 assembly language function using AVX instructions
_avx2	X86-64 assembly language function using AVX2 instructions
_avx512	X86-64 assembly language function using AVX-512 instructions

The file and function naming conventions might appear unwarranted for the short source code examples in this chapter. However, they'll help you better understand the longer source code examples in later chapters, especially the ones that explicate the use of the x86-AVX instruction sets. Source code examples with function names incorporating the substrings _avx, _avx2, or _avx512 will only work on processors that support the AVX, AVX2, or AVX-512 instruction set extensions, respectively. You can use one of the free utilities listed in Appendix B to verify the processing capabilities of your computer. You'll also learn how to run-time detect the various x86-AVX instruction sets in Chapter 16. Appendix A contains additional information about the source code including download and setup instructions for both Windows and Linux. Depending on your personal preference, you may want to download and install the source code first before proceeding with the remaining sections of this chapter.

Finally, while reading this and subsequent chapters, I encourage you to scrutinize both the MASM (Windows) and NASM (Linux) source code even if you are currently interested in only one of the OS platforms. Studying a variety of assembly language source code examples will hasten the learning process, especially for novices. Doing this also prepares you, if necessary, to develop x86-64 assembly language code for a different OS platform.

Assembler Basics

An assembler is a software utility that translates assembly language source code into machine code. The output of an assembler is an object module that can be combined with other object modules (including C++ compiler–generated object modules) by a linker (or link editor) to create an executable file. Machine code is the unique sequence of zeros and ones that instruct the processor what to do. For example, the machine code for the x86-64 assembly language instruction add ecx,edx is 0x03CA. This bit pattern instructs the processor to add the 32-bit integer values in registers ECX and EDX and save the resultant sum in register ECX. The machine code for instruction add ecx,7 is 0x83C107, which adds seven to the value in register ECX. Note that the immediate constant seven is embedded in machine code bit pattern.

Unlike programming languages like C or C++, there are no ISO or other standards for assemblers. While there are often syntactical and semantical resemblances between assemblers for specific processor architectures, popular assemblers for x86 CPUs typically use distinct syntaxes, operators, directives, and macro processors. In other words, assembly language source code is principally assembler specific and nonportable.

The source code examples published in this book can be executed on either Windows or Linux. The Windows version of each source code example was developed using Visual C++ and MASM, while GNU C++ and NASM were used for the Linux version. MASM and NASM were chosen as the assemblers for this book's assembly language source code for a variety of reasons. MASM is included with Visual Studio, and NASM can be easily installed on a Linux computer. There is sufficient similarity between these two assemblers, which simplifies the source code explanations. Whenever possible, the source code examples avoid using features unique to MASM or NASM. Most importantly, both MASM and NASM use the same instruction mnemonics and operand orderings as those published in the AMD and Intel reference manuals.

Integer Arithmetic

In this section, you'll learn the basics of x86-64 assembly language programming. It begins with a simple program that demonstrates 32-bit integer addition and subtraction. This is followed by two source code examples that illustrate 32-bit integer bitwise logical and shift operations. The penultimate source code example of this section explains 64-bit integer addition and subtraction, while the final example covers integer multiplication and division.

■ **Note** Most of the examples in this and subsequent chapters combine multiple source code files into a single listing. This is done to minimize the number of listing references in the main text. The actual source code uses separate files for the C++ (.h, .cpp) and assembly language (.asmh, .asm, .inc, .s) code. The source code files also use the naming conventions described earlier in this chapter.

Integer Addition and Subtraction – 32-Bit

The first source code example is named Ch02_01. This example demonstrates how to use the x86-64 assembly language instructions add (Integer Add) and sub (Integer Subtract). It also illustrates important assembly language programming concepts including argument passing, returning values, and use of common assembler directives. Listing 2-1a shows the C++ source code for source code example Ch02_01.

Listing 2-1a. Example Ch02_01 C++ Code

```
//----------------------------------------------------------------------
// Ch02_01.h
//----------------------------------------------------------------------

#pragma once

// Ch02_01_fasm.asm, Ch02_01_fasm.s
extern "C" int AddSubI32_a(int a, int b, int c, int d);

// Ch02_01_misc.cpp
extern void DisplayResults(int a, int b, int c, int d, int r1, int r2);

//----------------------------------------------------------------------
// Ch02_01_misc.cpp
//----------------------------------------------------------------------

#include <iostream>
#include "Ch02_01.h"

void DisplayResults(int a, int b, int c, int d, int r1, int r2)
{
    constexpr char nl = '\n';

    std::cout << "----- Results for Ch02_01 -----\n";
    std::cout << "a =  " << a << nl;
    std::cout << "b =  " << b << nl;
    std::cout << "c =  " << c << nl;
    std::cout << "d =  " << d << nl;
    std::cout << "r1 = " << r1 << nl;
    std::cout << "r2 = " << r2 << nl;
    std::cout << nl;
}

//----------------------------------------------------------------------
// Ch02_01.cpp
//----------------------------------------------------------------------

#include "Ch02_01.h"

int main()
{
    int a = 10;
    int b = 40;
    int c = 9;
    int d = 6;

    int r1 = (a + b) - (c + d) + 7;
    int r2 = AddSubI32_a(a, b, c, d);
```

```
        DisplayResults(a, b, c, d, r1, r2);
        return 0;
}
```

Listing 2-1a starts with the header file Ch02_01.h, which contains the requisite function declarations for this example. Note that the declaration statement for assembly language function AddSubI32_a() includes a "C" modifier. This modifier instructs the C++ compiler to use C-style naming for this function instead of a C++ decorated name (a C++ decorated name incorporates extra characters added by the compiler that facilitate function overloading). The next file in Listing 2-1a is Ch02_01_misc.cpp. This file includes a single support function named DisplayResults(), which streams the results to std::cout. The final C++ file in Listing 2-1a, Ch02_01.cpp, contains main(). Function main() includes some elementary C++ code that initializes several integer variables and calculates (a + b) − (c + d) + 7. It then calls the assembly language function AddSubI32_a() to perform the same calculation. Function main() also employs DisplayResults() to display the calculated results in a console window.

Listing 2-1b shows the MASM code for file Ch02_01_fasm.asm, which contains the assembly language function AddSubI32_a(). The first thing to notice in Listing 2-1b is the topmost lines that begin with a semicolon. These are comment lines. MASM treats any text that follows a semicolon as comment text. The .code statement that follows is a MASM directive that signifies the beginning of a code section. An assembler directive is a statement that instructs the assembler to perform a particular action during assembly of the source code. Assembler directives do not directly generate executable code, but some directives (e.g., macro processor directives) can be employed to streamline code generation. You will learn how to use additional MASM and NASM directives throughout this book.

Listing 2-1b. Example Ch02_01 MASM Code

```
;-----------------------------------------------------------------------
; Ch02_01_fasm.asm
;-----------------------------------------------------------------------


;-----------------------------------------------------------------------
;int AddSubI32_a(int a, int b, int c, int d);
;-----------------------------------------------------------------------


        .code
AddSubI32_a proc

; Calculate (a + b) - (c + d) + 7
        add ecx,edx                     ;ecx = a + b
        add r8d,r9d                     ;r8d = c + d
        sub ecx,r8d                     ;ecx = (a + b) - (c + d)
        add ecx,7                       ;ecx = (a + b) - (c + d) + 7

        mov eax,ecx                     ;eax = final result

        ret                             ;return to caller

AddSubI32_a endp
        end
```

Following the .code directive is the statement AddSubI32_a proc. This statement signifies the start of a MASM function named AddSubI32_a(). Functions declared using the MASM proc directive are public (or global) by default. If you scan forward a few lines, you will notice the statement AddSubI32_a endp. This statement signifies the end of function AddSubI32_a().

Like many programming languages, the Visual C++ run-time environment uses a combination of processor registers and the stack when passing argument values to a function. In the current example, the Visual C++ compiler emitted code that loads argument values a, b, c, and d into registers ECX, EDX, R8D, and R9D, respectively, prior to calling AddSubI32_a(). Upon entry to function AddSubI32_a(), register ECX contains argument value a, register EDX contains argument value b, and so on. The specific registers used to pass arguments are defined by the Visual C++ run-time calling convention (also called an application binary interface or ABI). You will learn additional details about the Visual C++ run-time calling convention throughout this book.

The first executable instruction of AddSubI32_a(), add ecx,edx, calculates a + b and saves this sum in register ECX. Note the execution of this instruction does not alter the value in register EDX; it still contains b. The ensuing add r8d,r9d instruction calculates c + d and saves this sum in register R8D; the value in R9D remains the same. This is followed by a sub ecx,r8d instruction that computes (a + b) - (c + d). Note that the first three executable instructions of AddSubI32_a() used register operands. The next instruction, add ecx,7, completes the calculation of (a + b) - (c + d) + 7. This instruction uses an immediate operand to specify the constant value seven. Unlike some other assemblers, MASM doesn't require any special prefix symbols to signify a constant immediate operand.

The mov eax,ecx (Move) instruction that follows copies the value in register ECX to register EAX. An assembly language function that returns a 32-bit integer (or C++ int) value to its calling function must place this value in register EAX per the Visual C++ run-time calling convention. The final instruction of AddSubI32_a(), ret (Return from Procedure), returns program control to the calling function main(). The final statement in Listing 2-1b, end, is a required MASM directive that signifies the completion of assembly language statements. MASM ignores any text that appears after the end directive.

Listing 2-1c shows the NASM code for source code example Ch02_01. Like MASM, NASM assembly language source code files use semicolons to signify comment text. The statement %include "ModX86Asm3eNASM.inc" is a NASM directive that incorporates the contents of header file ModX86Asm3eNASM. inc during assembly of source code file Ch02_01_fasm.s. The NASM %include (and MASM include) directives are analogous to the C++ preprocessor #include directive. The motivations for using an include file here are explained later in this section.

Listing 2-1c. Example Ch02_01 NASM code

```
;-----------------------------------------------------------------------------
; Ch02_01_fasm.s
;-----------------------------------------------------------------------------

        %include "ModX86Asm3eNASM.inc"

;-----------------------------------------------------------------------------
; int AddSubI32_a(int a, int b, int c, int d);
;-----------------------------------------------------------------------------

        section .text

        global AddSubI32_a
AddSubI32_a:
```

```
; Calculate (a + b) - (c + d) + 7
        add edi,esi                    ;edi = a + b
        add edx,ecx                    ;edx = c + d
        sub edi,edx                    ;edi = (a + b) - (c + d)
        add edi,7                      ;edi = (a + b) - (c + d) + 7

        mov eax,edi                    ;eax = final result

        ret                            ;return to caller
```

Following the %include directive is the statement section .text. This statement is a NASM directive that defines the start of a code section. The ensuing statement, global AddSubI32_a, instructs NASM to export AddSubI32_a() as a public function, which means it can be called by functions defined in other modules. The AddSubI32_a: symbol that follows signifies the start of function AddSubI32_a(). Note that the trailing colon is required.

When passing arguments to a called function, the GNU C++ run-time calling convention specifies a different combination of registers compared to the Visual C++ calling convention. For NASM function AddSubI32_a(), argument values a, b, c, and d are passed via registers EDI, ESI, EDX, and ECX, respectively. Except for different registers, the NASM source code uses the same add and sub instructions as the MASM code to calculate (a + b) - (c + d) + 7. The GNU C++ run-time calling convention specifies the use of register EAX for a 32-bit integer return value, which is the reason for the mov eax,edi instruction. The final executable instruction in Listing 2-1c is ret. NASM assembly language source code files do not require an end or other directive to signify conclusion of the source code.

Listing 2-1d shows the contents of file ModX86Asm3eNASM.inc. Each NASM source code file in this book requires the same set of common directives, so it makes sense to place them in a single header file. The text default rel is a NASM directive that instructs the assembler to use RIP-relative addressing when emitting machine code for memory references. The NASM default is to apply absolute addressing, which is normally not used with x86-64 executable code. Using the default rel directive eliminates the need to explicitly override NASM's default behavior with the rel keyword in instructions that use memory operands. Function AnySubI32_a() doesn't include any memory operand instructions, but I think it's a good programming practice to always include a default rel statement in any NASM x86-64 assembly language source file (or shared header file) to prevent future maintenance issues.

Listing 2-1d. NASM Common Directives

```
;-----------------------------------------------------------------------------
; ModX86ASm3eNASM.inc
;-----------------------------------------------------------------------------

; Use RIP-relative memory addressing
        default rel

; Mark stack as non-executable for Binutils 2.39+
        section .note.GNU-stack noalloc noexec nowrite progbits
```

The second statement in file ModX86Asm3eNASM.inc, section .note.GNU-stack noalloc noexec nowrite progbits, instructs the GNU linker (ld) to mark the program's stack memory as non-executable. This statement is included to prevent the GNU linker from displaying a warning message when using GNU Binutils 2.39 or later. Here are the results for source code example Ch02_01:

```
----- Results for Ch02_01 -----
a =  10
b =  40
c =  9
d =  6
r1 = 42
r2 = 42
```

Bitwise Logical Operations

The next source code example, named Ch02_02, illustrates the use of the and (Logical Bitwise AND), or (Logical Bitwise Inclusive OR), xor (Logical Bitwise Exclusive OR), and not (Ones Complement Negation) instructions. Listing 2-2a shows the C++ source code for this example.

Listing 2-2a. Example Ch02_02 C++ Code

```
//-----------------------------------------------------------------------------
// Ch02_02.h
//-----------------------------------------------------------------------------

#pragma once

// Ch02_02_fasm.asm, Ch02_02_fasm.s
extern "C" unsigned int BitOpsU32_a(unsigned int a, unsigned int b,
    unsigned int c, unsigned int d);

// Ch02_02_fcpp.cpp
unsigned int BitOpsU32_cpp(unsigned int a, unsigned int b, unsigned int c,
    unsigned int d);

// Ch02_02_misc.cpp
extern void DisplayResults(unsigned int a, unsigned int b, unsigned int c,
    unsigned int d, unsigned int r1, unsigned int r2);

//-----------------------------------------------------------------------------
// Ch02_02_fcpp.cpp
//-----------------------------------------------------------------------------

#include "Ch02_02.h"

unsigned int BitOpsU32_cpp(unsigned int a, unsigned int b, unsigned int c,
    unsigned int d)
{
    // Calculate ~(((a & b) | c ) ^ d)
    unsigned int t1 = a & b;
    unsigned int t2 = t1 | c;
    unsigned int t3 = t2 ^ d;
    unsigned int result = ~t3;
```

```cpp
        return result;
}

//----------------------------------------------------------------------
// Ch02_02_misc.cpp
//----------------------------------------------------------------------

#include <iostream>
#include <iomanip>
#include "Ch02_02.h"

void DisplayResults(unsigned int a, unsigned int b, unsigned int c,
    unsigned int d, unsigned int r1, unsigned int r2)
{
    constexpr int w = 8;
    constexpr char nl = '\n';

    std::cout << "----- Results for Ch02_02 -----\n";

    std::cout << std::setfill('0');
    std::cout << "a =  0x" << std::hex << std::setw(w) << a << nl;
    std::cout << "b =  0x" << std::hex << std::setw(w) << b << nl;
    std::cout << "c =  0x" << std::hex << std::setw(w) << c << nl;
    std::cout << "d =  0x" << std::hex << std::setw(w) << d << nl;
    std::cout << "r1 = 0x" << std::hex << std::setw(w) << r1 << nl;
    std::cout << "r2 = 0x" << std::hex << std::setw(w) << r2 << nl;
    std::cout << nl;

    if (r1 != r2)
        std::cout << "Compare check failed" << nl;
}
//----------------------------------------------------------------------
// Ch02_02.cpp
//----------------------------------------------------------------------

#include "Ch02_02.h"

int main()
{
    unsigned int a = 0xffffffff;
    unsigned int b = 0x12345678;
    unsigned int c = 0x87654321;
    unsigned int d = 0x55555555;

    unsigned int r1 = BitOpsU32_cpp(a, b, c, d);
    unsigned int r2 = BitOpsU32_a(a, b, c, d);

    DisplayResults(a, b, c, d, r1, r2);
    return 0;
}
```

The organization of source code example Ch02_02 mimics example Ch02_01. In file Ch02_02.h, the function declaration for assembly language function BitOpsU32_a() employs the "C" modifier to compel C-style naming. Note that this function requires four arguments of type unsigned int (32-bit) and returns an unsigned int. The header file in Listing 2-2a also includes a declaration for the function BitOpsU32_cpp(). This C++ function performs the same calculation as its assembly language counterpart for comparison purposes. While overkill for this example, it is often useful to code C++ counterpart functions for result comparison purposes, especially for assembly language functions that carry out complicated arithmetic. The final function declaration in file Ch02_02.h is DisplayResults(). Listing 2-2a also includes the source code for files Ch02_02_fcpp.cpp and Ch02_02_misc.cpp. These files contain the definitions for functions BitOpsU32_cpp() and DisplayResults(), respectively.

File Ch02_02.cpp in Listing 2-2a includes function main(), which performs data initialization. It also calls the calculating functions BitOpsU32_cpp() and BitOpsU32_a(). Following execution of these functions, main() employs DisplayResults() to stream the results to std:cout.

Listing 2-2b shows the MASM source code for assembly language function BitOpsU32_a(). Like the previous example, the four 32-bit (unsigned int) argument values a, b, c, and d are passed to BitOpsU32_a() via registers ECX, EDX, R8D, and R9D, respectively. The first instruction of BitOpsU32_a(), and ecx,edx, performs a bitwise logical AND operation using the values in registers ECX and EDX; the result (a & b) is saved in ECX. The next instruction, or ecx,r8d, performs a bitwise logical OR using the values in registers ECX and R8D. Following execution of this instruction, register ECX contains (a & b) | c. This is followed by an xor ecx,r9d instruction that calculates ((a & b) | c) ^ d. The bitwise logical instruction, not ecx, completes the calculation of ~(((a & b) | c) ^ d). Note that the not instruction only requires a single operand (the source and destination operands are the same). The final two instructions of BitOpsU32_a(), mov eax,ecx and ret, copy the calculated value to register EAX and return program control to main().

Listing 2-2b. Example Ch02_02 MASM Code

```
;-----------------------------------------------------------------------------
; Ch02_02_fasm.asm
;-----------------------------------------------------------------------------


;-----------------------------------------------------------------------------
; unsigned int BitOpsU32_a(unsigned int a, unsigned int b, unsigned int c,
;    unsigned int d);
;-----------------------------------------------------------------------------

        .code
BitOpsU32_a proc

; Calculate ~(((a & b) | c ) ^ d)
        and ecx,edx                     ;ecx = a & b
        or ecx,r8d                      ;ecx = (a & b) | c
        xor ecx,r9d                     ;ecx = ((a & b) | c) ^ d
        not ecx                         ;ecx = ~(((a & b) | c ) ^ d)

        mov eax,ecx                     ;eax = final result
        ret                             ;return to caller

BitOpsU32_a endp
        end
```

Listing 2-2c shows the NASM code for function BitOpsU32_a(). This function exercises the same x86 bitwise logical instructions and the MASM code. Note that argument values a, b, c, and d are passed to BitOpsU32_a() using GNU C++ calling convention registers EDI, ESI, EDX, and ECX.

Listing 2-2c. Example Ch02_02 NASM Code

```
;-------------------------------------------------------------------------
; Ch02_02_fasm.asm
;-------------------------------------------------------------------------

        %include "ModX86Asm3eNASM.inc"

;-------------------------------------------------------------------------
; unsigned int BitOpsU32_a(unsigned int a, unsigned int b,, unsigned int c,
;   unsigned int d);
;-------------------------------------------------------------------------

        section .text

        global BitOpsU32_a
BitOpsU32_a:

; Calculate ~(((a & b) | c ) ^ d)
        and edi,esi                 ;edi = a & b
        or edi,edx                  ;edi = (a & b) | c
        xor edi,ecx                 ;edi = ((a & b) | c) ^ d
        not edi                     ;edi = ~(((a & b) | c ) ^ d)

        mov eax,edi                 ;eax = final result
        ret                         ;return to caller
```

Here are the results for source code example Ch02_02:

```
----- Results for Ch02_02 -----
a = 0xffffffff
b = 0x12345678
c = 0x87654321
d = 0x55555555
r1 = 0x3ddffdd3
r2 = 0x3ddffdd3
```

The x86-64 instruction set also includes a neg (Two's Complement Negation) instruction. This instruction performs a two's complement calculation. Like the not instruction, the neg instruction requires only a single operand.

Shift Operations

Source code example Ch02_03 illustrates the use of the shl (Shift Left) and shr (Shift Right) instructions. It also demonstrates the use of a C++ pointer argument in an assembly language function. Listing 2-3a shows the C++ source code for example Ch02_03.

Listing 2-3a. Example Ch02_03 C++ Code

```cpp
//-----------------------------------------------------------------------
// Ch02_03.h
//-----------------------------------------------------------------------

#pragma once

// Ch02_03_fasm.asm, Ch02_03_fasm.s
extern "C" int ShiftU32_a(unsigned int* a_shl, unsigned int* a_shr,
    unsigned int a, unsigned int count);

// Ch02_03_misc.cpp
extern void DisplayResults(const char* s, int rc, unsigned int a,
    unsigned int count, unsigned int a_shl, unsigned int a_shr);


//-----------------------------------------------------------------------
// Ch02_03_misc.cpp
//-----------------------------------------------------------------------

#include "Ch02_03.h"
#include <iostream>
#include <iomanip>
#include <bitset>

void DisplayResults(const char* s, int rc, unsigned int a, unsigned int count,
    unsigned int a_shl, unsigned int a_shr)
{
    constexpr int w = 10;
    constexpr char nl = '\n';

    std::bitset<32> a_bs(a);
    std::bitset<32> a_shl_bs(a_shl);
    std::bitset<32> a_shr_bs(a_shr);

    std::cout << s << nl;
    std::cout << "count: " << std::setw(w) << count << nl;
    std::cout << "a:     " << std::setw(w) << a << " (0b" << a_bs << ")" << nl;

    if (rc == 1)
    {
        std::cout << "shl:   " << std::setw(w) << a_shl;
        std::cout << " (0b" << a_shl_bs << ")" << nl;
        std::cout << "shr:   " << std::setw(w) << a_shr;
        std::cout << " (0b" << a_shr_bs << ")" << nl;
    }
}
```

```cpp
    else
        std::cout << "Invalid shift count" << nl;

    std::cout << nl;
}

//-----------------------------------------------------------------------------
// Ch02_03.cpp
//-----------------------------------------------------------------------------

#include <iostream>
#include "Ch02_03.h"

int main(void)
{
    int rc;
    unsigned int a, count, a_shl, a_shr;

    std::cout << "----- Results for Ch02_03 -----\n\n";

    a = 3119;
    count = 6;
    rc = ShiftU32_a(&a_shl, &a_shr, a, count);
    DisplayResults("Shift test #1", rc, a, count, a_shl, a_shr);

    a = 0x00800080;
    count = 4;
    rc = ShiftU32_a(&a_shl, &a_shr, a, count);
    DisplayResults("Shift test #2", rc, a, count, a_shl, a_shr);

    a = 0x80000001;
    count = 31;
    rc = ShiftU32_a(&a_shl, &a_shr, a, count);
    DisplayResults("Shift test #3", rc, a, count, a_shl, a_shr);

    a = 0x55555555;
    count = 32;
    rc = ShiftU32_a(&a_shl, &a_shr, a, count);
    DisplayResults("Shift test #4", rc, a, count, a_shl, a_shr);

    return 0;
}
```

Listing 2-3a opens with the C++ header file Ch02_03.h. Note that the declaration of assembly language function ShiftU32_a() contains two pointer arguments of type unsigned int. Function ShiftU32_a() employs pointer arguments so that it can pass multiple result values back to its caller. Also note that function ShiftU32_a() returns a result of type int, which signifies whether argument value count is valid. Listing 2-3a also shows the source code for function DisplayResults(), which formats and streams results to std::cout. Function main() includes C++ code that exercises ShiftU32_a() using several different test values.

Listing 2-3b shows the MASM code for function ShiftU32U_a(). The first executable instruction of this function, cmp r9d,32 (Compare Integer Operands), compares the value in register R9D (argument value count) with the constant value 32. During execution of this instruction, the processor subtracts 32 from R9D and sets the status flags in RFLAGS based on the result. The actual result of the subtraction is *not* saved in R9D but discarded. The next instruction, jae BadCnt (Jump if Condition Met), is a conditional jump instruction. In this instruction, the condition code suffix "ae" signifies above or equal (i.e., unsigned greater than or equal). The above or equal condition occurs when RFLAGS.CF == 0 is true (see Table 1-8). Thus, if count >= 32 is true, program control is transferred to the instruction location specified by the label BadCnt:. Note that MASM labels require a trailing colon. Toward the end of function ShiftU32_a() is the statement BadCnt: xor eax,eax. The xor eax,eax instruction performs an exclusive OR of register EAX with itself, which always yields a value of zero. This is the required return code when argument value count is invalid.

Listing 2-3b. Example Ch02_03 MASM Code

```
;-------------------------------------------------------------------------------
; Ch02_03_fasm.asm
;-------------------------------------------------------------------------------


;-------------------------------------------------------------------------------
; int ShiftU32_a(unsigned int* a_shl, unsigned int* a_shr, unsigned int a,
;    unsigned int count);
;
; returns:  0 = invalid shift count, 1 = valid shift count
;-------------------------------------------------------------------------------

        .code
ShiftU32_a proc
        cmp r9d,32                      ;is count >= 32
        jae BadCnt                      ;jump if count >= 32

        mov r10,rcx                     ;save a_shl
        mov ecx,r9d                     ;ecx = count

        mov eax,r8d                     ;eax = a
        shl eax,cl                      ;eax = a << count;
        mov [r10],eax                   ;save shl result

        shr r8d,cl                      ;r8d = a >> count
        mov [rdx],r8d                   ;save shr result

        mov eax,1                       ;valid shift count return code
        ret                             ;return to caller

BadCnt: xor eax,eax                     ;invalid shift count return code
        ret

ShiftU32_a endp
        end
```

If count >= 32 is false, program execution continues with the subsequent mov r10,rcx instruction. This instruction copies the value in 64-bit register RCX, which contains pointer argument a_shl, into register R10. The next instruction, mov ecx,r9d, copies argument value count into register ECX. The reason for these mov instructions will be explained shortly. For now, it's important to recognize that pointer argument a_shl was passed into ShiftU32_a() using register RCX. The Visual C++ run-time calling convention uses 64-bit registers when passing a 64-bit integer or pointer argument. Recapping Visual C++'s run-time argument registers, the first four 64-bit (32-bit) integer arguments are passed to a called function using registers RCX (ECX), RDX (EDX), R8 (R8D), and R9 (R9D). Additional arguments are passed via the stack, and you will learn how to do this in later chapters.

Returning to the assembly language code, the mov eax,r8d instruction copies argument value a into register EAX. A 32-bit register is used here since argument value a is an unsigned int. This is followed by a shl eax,cl instruction, which calculates a << count. The second operand of the shl instruction specifies the number of bits to shift; it can be either register CL, which contains the shift bit count value, or an immediate value. This is the reason for the earlier mov instructions using registers RCX and ECX; argument value a_shl must be preserved since it was passed via register RCX, and argument value count needs to be copied into register CL for the shl instruction. The final instruction of the current code block,[1] mov [r10],eax, saves a << count to the memory location pointed to by a_shl.

The next instruction pair, shr r8d,cl and mov [rdx],r8d, calculates a >> count and saves this result to the memory location pointed to by a_shr. The ensuing mov eax,1 sets a return code that signifies argument value count is valid. The x86-64 instruction set also includes a sar (Shift Arithmetic Right) instruction that performs arithmetic right shifts. During execution of a sar instruction, the processor fills open bit positions using the sign (most significant) bit of the original value. Both shr and shl fill open bit positions using zeros.

Listing 2-3c shows the NASM code for source code example Ch02_03. The code in this listing mimics the MASM code except for the register names. Note that argument value count was passed into ShiftU32_a() using register ECX, which means that the shift bit count is already loaded in the proper register for the shl and shr instructions. The GNU C++ run-time calling convention specifies that the first four 64-bit (32-bit) argument values are passed using registers RDI (EDI), RSI (ESI), RDX (EDX), and RCX (ECX). Additional integer arguments are passed via registers R8 (R8D), R9 (R9D), and the stack. You will learn more about this in later chapters.

Listing 2-3c. Example Ch02_03 NASM Code

```
;-------------------------------------------------------------------------------
; Ch02_03_fasm.s
;-------------------------------------------------------------------------------

        %include "ModX86Asm3eNASM.inc"


;-------------------------------------------------------------------------------
; int ShiftU32_asm(unsigned int* a_shl, unsigned int* a_shr, unsigned int a,
;   unsigned int count);
;
; returns:  0 = invalid shift count, 1 = valid shift count
;-------------------------------------------------------------------------------

        section .text
```

---

[1] A code block is an uninterrupted sequence (i.e., no blank lines) of assembly language instructions that perform a calculation or operation.

```
        global ShiftU32_a
ShiftU32_a:
        cmp ecx,32                      ;is count >= 32
        jae BadCnt                      ;jump if count >= 32

        mov eax,edx                     ;eax = a
        shl eax,cl                      ;eax = a << count;
        mov [rdi],eax                   ;save shl result

        shr edx,cl                      ;edx = a >> count
        mov [rsi],edx                   ;save shr result

        mov eax,1                       ;valid shift count return code
        ret                             ;return to caller

BadCnt: xor eax,eax                     ;invalid shift count return code
        ret
```

Here are the results for source code example Ch02_03:

```
----- Results for Ch02_03 -----

Shift test #1
count:          6
a:           3119 (0b00000000000000000000110000101111)
shl:       199616 (0b00000000000000110000101111000000)
shr:           48 (0b00000000000000000000000000110000)

Shift test #2
count:          4
a:        8388736 (0b00000000100000000000000010000000)
shl:    134219776 (0b00001000000000000000100000000000)
shr:       524296 (0b00000000000001000000000000001000)

Shift test #3
count:         31
a:     2147483649 (0b10000000000000000000000000000001)
shl:   2147483648 (0b10000000000000000000000000000000)
shr:            1 (0b00000000000000000000000000000001)

Shift test #4
count:         32
a:     1431655765 (0b01010101010101010101010101010101)
Invalid shift count
```

The x86-64 instruction set also includes the following instructions that perform rotate operations: rol (Rotate Left), ror (Rotate Right), rcl (Rotate Left Through Carry Flag), and rcr (Rotate Right Through Carry Flag). Like the shift instructions, the rotate instructions can be used with an immediate bit count operand or a variable bit count value in register CL.

Integer Addition and Subtraction – 64-bit

X86-64 processors can also perform 64-bit integer arithmetic using 64-bit registers. Source code example Ch02_04 demonstrates how to perform 64-bit integer addition and subtraction. It also highlights some issues that you need to be cognizant of when using immediate operands and 64-bit registers. Listing 2-4a shows the C++ source code for example Ch02_04.

Listing 2-4a. Example Ch02_04 C++ Code

```
//------------------------------------------------------------------------
// Ch02_04.h
//------------------------------------------------------------------------

#pragma once

// Ch02_04_fasm.asm, Ch02_04_fasm.s
extern "C" long long AddSubI64a_a(long long a, long long b, long long c,
    long long d);
extern "C" long long AddSubI64b_a(long long a, long long b, long long c,
    long long d);

// Ch02_04_misc.cpp
extern void DisplayResults(const char* msg, long long a, long long b, long long c,
    long long d, long long r1, long long r2);

//------------------------------------------------------------------------
// Ch02_04_misc.cpp
//------------------------------------------------------------------------

#include <iostream>
#include "Ch02_04.h"

void DisplayResults(const char* msg, long long a, long long b, long long c,
    long long d, long long r1, long long r2)
{
    constexpr char nl = '\n';

    std::cout << msg << nl;
    std::cout << "a = " << a << nl;
    std::cout << "b = " << b << nl;
    std::cout << "c = " << c << nl;
    std::cout << "d = " << d << nl;
    std::cout << "r1 = " << r1 << nl;
    std::cout << "r2 = " << r2 << nl;
    std::cout << nl;
}

//------------------------------------------------------------------------
// Ch02_04.cpp
//------------------------------------------------------------------------
```

```cpp
#include <iostream>
#include "Ch02_04.h"

int main()
{
    long long a = 10;
    long long b = 40;
    long long c = 9;
    long long d = 6;
    long long r1, r2;

    std::cout << "----- Results for Ch02_04 -----\n\n";

    r1 = (a + b) - (c + d) + 7;
    r2 = AddSubI64a_a(a, b, c, d);
    DisplayResults("Results for AddSubI64a_a()", a, b, c, d, r1, r2);

    b *= -10000000000;
    r1 = (a + b) - (c + d) + 12345678900;
    r2 = AddSubI64b_a(a, b, c, d);
    DisplayResults("Results for AddSubI64b_a()", a, b, c, d, r1, r2);

    return 0;
}
```

In Listing 2-4a, the header file Ch02_04.h includes function declarations for two assembly language functions: AddSubI64a_a() and AddSubI64b_a(). Note that both functions require arguments of type long long, which is a signed 64-bit integer on both Windows and Linux. The file Ch02_04_misc.cpp includes code that formats and streams the results to std::cout. In file Ch02_04.cpp, function main() contains code that performs test case initialization and exercises the previously mentioned assembly language functions.

Listing 2-4b shows the MASM code for example Ch02_04. The first function in this listing, AddSubI64_a(), is a 64-bit version of the same function that you saw in source code example Ch02_01 (Listing 2-1b). The only difference is that AddSubI64a_a() uses 64-bit instead of 32-bit registers. Also note that the calculated 64-bit return value is placed in register RAX per the Visual C++ calling convention.

Listing 2-4b. Example Ch02_04 MASM Code

```asm
;-------------------------------------------------------------------------------
; Ch02_04_fasm.asm
;-------------------------------------------------------------------------------


;-------------------------------------------------------------------------------
; long long AddSubI64a_a(long long a, long long b, long long c, long long d);
;-------------------------------------------------------------------------------

        .code
AddSubI64a_a proc

; Calculate (a + b) - (c + d) + 7
        add rcx,rdx                         ;rcx = a + b
        add r8,r9                           ;r8 = c + d
        sub rcx,r8                          ;rcx = (a + b) - (c + d)
```

```
        add rcx,7                       ;rcx = (a + b) - (c + d) + 7

        mov rax,rcx                     ;rax = final result

        ret                             ;return to caller
AddSubI64a_a endp


;-----------------------------------------------------------------------
; long long AddSubI64b_a(long long a, long long b, long long c, long long d);
;-----------------------------------------------------------------------

AddSubI64b_a proc

; Calculate (a + b) - (c + d) + 12345678900
        add rcx,rdx                     ;rcx = a + b
        add r8,r9                       ;r8 = c + d
        sub rcx,r8                      ;rcx = (a + b) - (c + d)

        mov rax,12345678900            ;rax = 12345678900
        add rax,rcx                     ;rax = (a + b) - (c + d) + 12345678900

        ret                             ;return to caller
AddSubI64b_a endp
        end
```

The next assembly language function in Listing 2-4b, AddSubI64b_a(), includes code that also uses the add and sub instructions with 64-bit registers. Note that the calculation performed by AddSubI64b_a() involves a large integer constant. Recall from the discussions in Chapter 1 that x86-64 machine language encodings do not support 64-bit immediate operands. The maximum size of an immediate operand is 32 bits, and this value is treated as a signed integer.

To perform integer arithmetic (or other) operations using a 64-bit immediate value, the constant must first be loaded into a 64-bit register using a mov instruction. The mov instruction is the only x86-64 instruction that can be used with a 64-bit immediate operand. This is the reason why AddSubI64_b() includes a mov rax,12345678900 instruction; add rcx,12345678900 is an invalid instruction.

Listing 2-4c shows the NASM code for example Ch02_04. Like the previous examples in this chapter, the primary difference between this code and the MASM code is the specific registers employed to carry out the required calculations.

Listing 2-4c. Example Ch02_04 NASM Code

```
;-----------------------------------------------------------------------
; Ch02_04_fasm.s
;-----------------------------------------------------------------------

        %include "ModX86Asm3eNASM.inc"


;-----------------------------------------------------------------------
; long long AddSubI64a_a(long long a, long long b, long long c, long long d);
;-----------------------------------------------------------------------
```

```nasm
        section .text

        global AddSubI64a_a
AddSubI64a_a:

; Calculate (a + b) - (c + d) + 7
        add rdi,rsi                     ;rdi = a + b
        add rdx,rcx                     ;rdx = c + d
        sub rdi,rdx                     ;rdi = (a + b) - (c + d)
        add rdi,7                       ;rdi = (a + b) - (c + d) + 7

        mov rax,rdi                     ;rax = final result

        ret                             ;return to caller

;-------------------------------------------------------------------------
; long long AddSubI64b_a(long long a, long long b, long long c, long long d);
;-------------------------------------------------------------------------

        global AddSubI64b_a
AddSubI64b_a:

; Calculate (a + b) - (c + d) + 12345678900
        add rdi,rsi                     ;rdi = a + b
        add rdx,rcx                     ;rdx = c + d
        sub rdi,rdx                     ;rdi = (a + b) - (c + d)

        mov rax,12345678900            ;rax = 12345678900
        add rax,rdi                     ;rax = (a + b) - (c + d) + 12345678900

        ret                             ;return to caller
```

Here are the results for source code example Ch02_04:

```
----- Results for Ch02_04 -----

Results for AddSubI64a_a()
a =   10
b =   40
c =   9
d =   6
r1 = 42
r2 = 42

Results for AddSubI64b_a()
a =   10
b =   -400000000000
c =   9
d =   6
r1 = -398765432115
r2 = -398765432115
```

Integer Multiplication and Division

The final source code example of this chapter, named Ch02_05, demonstrates the use of the imul (Signed Multiply) and idiv (Signed Divide) instructions. It also illustrates the use of the movsxd (Move with Sign Extension) and cdq (Convert Doubleword to Quadword) instructions. Listing 2-5a shows the C++ source code for this example.

Listing 2-5a. Example Ch02_05 C++ Code

```
//-----------------------------------------------------------------------------
// Ch02_05.h
//-----------------------------------------------------------------------------

#pragma once

// Ch02_05_fasm.asm, Ch02_05_fasm.s
extern "C" void MulI32_a(int* prod1, long long* prod2, int a, int b);
extern "C" int DivI32_a(int* quo, int* rem, int a, int b);

// Ch02_05_misc.cpp
extern void DisplayResults(int test_id, int a, int b, int prod1,
    long long prod2, int quo, int rem, int rc);

//-----------------------------------------------------------------------------
// Ch02_05_misc.cpp
//-----------------------------------------------------------------------------

#include <iostream>
#include "Ch02_05.h"

void DisplayResults(int test_id, int a, int b, int prod1,
    long long prod2, int quo, int rem, int rc)
{
    constexpr char nl = '\n';

    std::cout << "Mul/Div test case #" << test_id << nl;
    std::cout << "a = " << a << ", b = " << b << nl;
    std::cout << "prod1 = " << prod1 << ", prod2 = " << prod2 << nl;

    if (rc == 0)
        std::cout << "error: division by zero" << nl;
    else
        std::cout << "quo = " << quo << ", rem = " << rem << nl;

    std::cout << nl;
}

//-----------------------------------------------------------------------------
// Ch02_05.cpp
//-----------------------------------------------------------------------------
```

```
#include <iostream>
#include "Ch02_05.h"

int main()
{
    constexpr int a_vals[] {47, -291, 19, 247 };
    constexpr int b_vals[] {13, 7, 0, 85 };
    constexpr int n = sizeof(a_vals) / sizeof(int);

    std::cout << "----- Results for Ch02_05 -----\n\n";

    for (int i = 0; i < n; i++)
    {
        int a = a_vals[i];
        int b = b_vals[i];
        int prod1, quo, rem;
        long long prod2;

        MulI32_a(&prod1, &prod2, a, b);
        int rc = DivI32_a(&quo, &rem, a, b);
        DisplayResults(i, a, b, prod1, prod2, quo, rem, rc);
    }

    return 0;
}
```

Listing 2-5a shows the code for file Ch02_05.h, which contains the declarations for assembly language functions MulI32_a() and DivI32_a(). Also displayed in Listing 2-5a is file Ch02_05_misc.cpp. This file contains the code for the std::cout streaming output function DisplayResults(). Function main() includes code that performs test case initialization for the assembly language functions MulI32_a() and DivI32_a(). It also exercises these functions.

Listing 2-5b shows the MASM code for functions MulI32_a() and DivI32_a(). Function MulI32_a() begins its execution with a mov eax,r8d instruction that saves a copy of argument value a for later use. The next instruction, imul r8d,r9d, calculates a * b and saves the low-order 32 bits of the resultant 64-bit product in register R8D (recall that the product of two *n-bit* integers is always an integer of size *2n* bits). Whenever a full-size multiplicative product is not needed, it is usually more convenient to utilize the two-operand form of imul since it supports explicit source and destination operands. Note that the two-operand form of imul can also be used to perform multiplication using unsigned integers since the lower half of the full-size product is the same for both signed and unsigned integers.

Listing 2-5b. Example Ch02_05 MASM Code

```
;-----------------------------------------------------------------------------
; Ch02_05_fasm.asm
;-----------------------------------------------------------------------------


;-----------------------------------------------------------------------------
; void MulI32_a(int* prod1, long long* prod2, int a, int b);
;-----------------------------------------------------------------------------

        .code
```

```
MulI32_a proc
        mov eax,r8d                     ;eax = a
        imul r8d,r9d                    ;rd8 = a * b (32-bit product)
        mov [rcx],r8d                   ;save a * b to prod1

        mov r10,rdx                     ;r10 = prod2 pointer
        movsxd rax,eax                  ;rax = a (sign-extended)
        movsxd r11,r9d                  ;r11 = b (sign-extended)
        imul r11                        ;rdx:rax = a * b (128-bit product)
        mov [r10],rax                   ;save low-order qword to prod2
        ret                             ;return to caller
MulI32_a endp


;-------------------------------------------------------------------------
; int DivI32_a(int* quo, int* rem, int a, int b);
;
; returns: 0 = error (divisor equals zero), 1 = success
;-------------------------------------------------------------------------

DivI32_a proc
        or r9d,r9d                      ;is b == 0?
        jz InvalidDivisor               ;jump if yes

        mov r10,rdx                     ;r10 = rem pointer

        mov eax,r8d                     ;eax = a
        cdq                             ;sign-extend a to 64-bits (edx:eax)
        idiv r9d                        ;eax = quotient, edx = remainder

        mov [rcx],eax                   ;save quotient
        mov [r10],edx                   ;save remainder

        mov eax,1                       ;set success return code
        ret                             ;return to caller

InvalidDivisor:
        xor eax,eax                     ;set error return code
        ret
DivI32_a endp
        end
```

The next code block demonstrates the use of the single-operand form of the imul instruction. This form of imul employs register RAX (or EAX, AX, AL) as an implicit operand. The mov r10,rdx instruction saves a copy of argument value prod2 for later use. The next instruction, movsxd rax,eax, sign-extends the 32-bit value in EAX (argument value a) to 64 bits and saves this result in register RAX. The ensuing movsxd r11,r9d performs the same operation using argument value b. This is followed by an imul r11 instruction, which computes a * b using implicit register operand RAX and explicit register operand R11. The processor saves the resultant 128-bit product in register pair RDX:RAX. The mov [r10],rax instruction that follows saves the low-order 64 bits of a * b to the memory location pointed to by prod2. Note that prod2 is a pointer to a value of type long long.

Function DivI32_a() illustrates signed integer division using 32-bit integers. The first instruction of this function, or r9d,r9d, tests argument value b (the divisor) to see if it's equal to zero. During execution of this instruction, the processor sets RFLAGS.ZF to one if the result of the bitwise logical OR operation is zero. If b == 0 is true, the ensuing jz InvalidDivisor instruction skips over the division code. The code that follows label InvalidDivisor loads register EAX with an error return code and executes a ret instruction.

If b == 0 is false, execution continues with the mov r10,rdx instruction, which saves a copy of argument value rem for later use. The next instruction, mov eax,r8d, copies argument value a into register EAX. This is followed by a cdq instruction, which sign-extends the value in EAX to 64 bits and saves the resultant 64-bit value in register pair EDX:EAX. The cdq is often used to sign-extend a 32-bit integer to 64 bits before performing signed integer division. The next instruction, idiv r9d, divides the 64-bit signed integer value in register pair EDX:EAX (the dividend) by the 32-bit value in register R9D (the divisor). Following execution of this instruction, register EAX contains the quotient, and register EDX contains the remainder. These values are then saved using the instruction pair mov [rcx],eax and mov [r10],edx.

Listing 2-5c shows the NASM code for example Ch02_05. In this listing, function MulI32_a() uses different operand registers with the movsxd and imul instructions to carry out the required calculations. Function DivI32_a() also uses different operand registers.

Listing 2-5c. Example Ch02_05 NASM Code

```
;-------------------------------------------------------------------------------
; Ch02_05_fasm.s
;-------------------------------------------------------------------------------

        %include "ModX86Asm3eNASM.inc"


;-------------------------------------------------------------------------------
; void MulI32_a(int* prod1, long long* prod2, int a, int b);
;-------------------------------------------------------------------------------

        section .text

        global MulI32_a
MulI32_a:
        mov eax,edx                     ;eax = a
        imul edx,ecx                    ;ecx = a * b (32-bit product)
        mov [rdi],edx                   ;save a * b to prod1

        movsxd rax,eax                  ;rax = a (sign-extended)
        movsxd rcx,ecx                  ;rcx = b (sign-extended)
        imul rcx                        ;rdx:rax = a * b (128-bit product)
        mov [rsi],rax                   ;save low-order qword to prod2

        ret                             ;return to caller

;-------------------------------------------------------------------------------
; int DivI32_a(int* quo, int* rem, int a, int b);
;
; returns: 0 = error (divisior equals zero), 1 = success
;-------------------------------------------------------------------------------
```

```
        global DivI32_a
DivI32_a:
        or ecx,ecx                      ;is b == 0?
        jz InvalidDivisor               ;jump if yes

        mov eax,edx                     ;eax = a
        cdq                             ;sign-extend a to 64-bits (edx:eax)
        idiv ecx                        ;eax = quotient, edx = remainder

        mov [rdi],eax                   ;save quotient
        mov [rsi],edx                   ;save remainder

        mov eax,1                       ;set success return code
        ret                             ;return to caller

InvalidDivisor:
        xor eax,eax                     ;set error return code
        ret
```

The idiv instruction can also be used with 64-bit or 16-bit registers. Prior to performing a 64-bit or 16-bit division using idiv, the cqo (Convert Quadword to Double Quadword) or cwd (Convert Word to Doubleword) instructions are typically used to sign-extend the dividend value in register RAX or register AX. The cqo and cwd instructions save their sign-extended results in registers RDX:RAX or DX:AX. Finally, you can use the mul (Unsigned Multiply) and div (Unsigned Divide) instructions to perform unsigned multiplication and division. Unlike the imul instruction, the mul instruction can only be used with a single operand; the other operand is always implicit register operand RAX, EAX, AX, or AL. The resultant product is saved in registers RDX:RAX, EDX:EAX, DX:AX, or AX. The use of the div instruction mimics the idiv instruction except that the dividend value must be zero-extended instead of sign-extended. Here are the results for source code example Ch02_05:

```
----- Results for Ch02_05 -----

Mul/Div test case #0
a = 47, b = 13
prod1 = 611, prod2 = 611
quo = 3, rem = 8

Mul/Div test case #1
a = -291, b = 7
prod1 = -2037, prod2 = -2037
quo = -41, rem = -4

Mul/Div test case #2
a = 19, b = 0
prod1 = 0, prod2 = 0
error: division by zero

Mul/Div test case #3
a = 247, b = 85
prod1 = 20995, prod2 = 20995
quo = 2, rem = 77
```

You may have noticed that in Listings 2-5b and 2-5c, function DivI32_a() contains multiple ret instructions. Just like a C++ function that contains multiple return statements, an assembly language function can employ multiple ret instructions. For simple functions like DivI32_a(), using multiple ret instructions is often advantageous since it eliminates the need for extra jmp instructions. However, using multiple ret instructions in an assembly language function with a formal prologue and epilogue is more challenging and a potential source of programming errors. You will learn more about function prologues and epilogues in later chapters.

Summary

Here are the key learning points for Chapter 2:

- Assembly language functions should be declared using the extern "C" modifier, which instructs the C++ compiler to use C-style function names instead of C++ decorated names.

- The add and sub instructions perform integer (signed and unsigned) addition and subtraction.

- The imul and idiv instructions carry out signed integer multiplication and division. The corresponding instructions for unsigned integers are mul and div. The idiv and div instructions usually require the dividend to be sign- or zero-extended prior to use.

- The and, or, and xor instructions are used to perform bitwise AND, inclusive OR, and exclusive OR operations. The not and neg instructions perform one's and two's complement negation.

- The shl and shr instructions execute logical left and right shifts; sar is used for arithmetic right shifts.

- Nearly all x86-64 arithmetic, bitwise logical, shift, and rotate instructions set the status flags to indicate the results of an operation. The cmp instruction also sets the status flags. The jcc instruction can be used to alter program flows based on the state of one or more status flags.

- The Visual C++ run-time calling convention specifies that the first four 64-bit (32-bit) integer arguments are passed to a function using registers RCX (ECX), RDX (EDX), R8 (R8D), and R9 (R9D). Additional arguments are passed via the stack.

- The GNU C++ run-time calling convention specifies that the first four 64-bit (32-bit) integer arguments are passed to a function using registers RDI (EDI), RSI (ESI), RDX (EDX), and RCX (ECX). Additional arguments are passed via registers R8 (R8D), R9 (R9D), and the stack.

- MASM uses the directive .code to designate the start of a code section in an assembly language source code file. The directives proc and endp denote the beginning and end of an assembly language function.

- NASM uses the directive section .text to designate the start of a code section in an assembly language file. The global directive must also be used to make a function public. The directive default rel is also strongly recommended in all NASM source code files to avoid having to explicitly use the keyword rel for x86-64 RIP-relative memory addressing.

CHAPTER 3

■ ■ ■

X86-64 Core Programming – Part 2

The previous chapter introduced the fundamentals of x86-64 assembly language programming. You learned how to perform integer arithmetic using x86-64 assembly language instructions. You also studied the use of bitwise logical and shift instructions. Perhaps most importantly, your initiation to x86-64 assembly language programming has covered a slew of practical details including source code syntax, assembler directive usage, and calling convention requirements for function arguments and return values.

This chapter explores additional core x86-64 assembly language programming concepts. It begins with two source code examples that elucidate argument passing via the stack. These examples also provide additional details regarding the Visual C++ and GNU C++ calling conventions. The next source code example explains how to use various x86-64 memory addressing modes. This is followed by an example that illustrates the use of conditional jump and conditional move instructions. The final example explicates the coding of an assembly language for-loop.

Simple Stack Arguments

The first source code example of this chapter is named Ch03_01. This example demonstrates how to reference argument values passed via the stack. Listing 3-1a shows the C++ source code for example Ch03_01.

Listing 3-1a. Example Ch03_01 C++ Code

```
//-----------------------------------------------------------------------------
// Ch03_01.h
//-----------------------------------------------------------------------------

#pragma once
#include <cstdint>

// Ch03_01_fasm.asm, Ch03_01_fasm.s
extern "C" int32_t SumValsI32_a(int32_t a, int32_t b, int32_t c, int32_t d,
    int32_t e, int32_t f, int32_t g, int32_t h);

extern "C" uint64_t MulValsU64_a(uint64_t a, uint64_t b, uint64_t c, uint64_t d,
    uint64_t e, uint64_t f, uint64_t g, uint64_t h);

// Ch03_01_misc.cpp
void DisplayResults(int32_t a, int32_t b, int32_t c, int32_t d, int32_t e,
    int32_t f, int32_t g, int32_t h, int32_t result1, int32_t result2);
```

© Daniel Kusswurm 2023
D. Kusswurm, *Modern X86 Assembly Language Programming*,
https://doi.org/10.1007/978-1-4842-9603-5_3

```cpp
void DisplayResults(uint64_t a, uint64_t b, uint64_t c, uint64_t d, uint64_t e,
    uint64_t f, uint64_t g, uint64_t h, uint64_t result1, uint64_t result2);

//-----------------------------------------------------------------------------
// Ch03_01_misc.cpp
//-----------------------------------------------------------------------------

#include <iostream>
#include "Ch03_01.h"

void DisplayResults(int32_t a, int32_t b, int32_t c, int32_t d,
    int32_t e, int32_t f, int32_t g, int32_t h, int32_t result1, int32_t result2)
{
    constexpr char nl = '\n';

    std::cout << "\nStack Example #1\n";
    std::cout << "a = " << a << ", b = " << b << ", c = " << c << ' ';
    std::cout << "d = " << d << ", e = " << e << ", f = " << f << ' ';
    std::cout << "g = " << g << ", h = " << h << nl;
    std::cout << "result1 = " << result1 << ", result2 = " << result2 << nl;
}

void DisplayResults(uint64_t a, uint64_t b, uint64_t c, uint64_t d, uint64_t e,
    uint64_t f, uint64_t g, uint64_t h, uint64_t result1, uint64_t result2)
{
    constexpr char nl = '\n';

    std::cout << "\nStack Example #2\n";
    std::cout << "a = " << a << ", b = " << b << ", c = " << c << ' ';
    std::cout << "d = " << d << ", e = " << e << ", f = " << f << ' ';
    std::cout << "g = " << g << ", h = " << h << nl;
    std::cout << "result1 = " << result1 << ", result2 = " << result2 << nl;
}

//-----------------------------------------------------------------------------
// Ch03_01.cpp
//-----------------------------------------------------------------------------

#include <iostream>
#include "Ch03_01.h"

static void StackExample1(void)
{
    // Stack example #1 - 32-bit integers
    int32_t a = 2, b = -3, c = 8, d = 9;
    int32_t e = 3, f = -7, g = 5, h = -1000000;

    int32_t result1 = a + b + c + d + e + f + g + h;
    int32_t result2 = SumValsI32_a(a, b, c, d, e, f, g, h);
```

```
    DisplayResults(a, b, c, d, e, f, g, h, result1, result2);
}

static void StackExample2(void)
{
    // Stack example #2 - 64-bit integers
    uint64_t a = 10, b = 20, c = 30, d = 40;
    uint64_t e = 50, f = 60, g = 70, h = 80;

    uint64_t result1 = a * b * c * d * e * f * g * h;
    uint64_t result2 = MulValsU64_a(a, b, c, d, e, f, g, h);

    DisplayResults(a, b, c, d, e, f, g, h, result1, result2);
}

int main()
{
    std::cout << "----- Results for Ch03_01 ----\n";

    StackExample1();
    StackExample2();
}
```

Beginning with the header file Ch03_01.h in Listing 3-1a, note that the function declarations for SumValsI32_a() and MulValsU64_a() use fixed-size integer types, which are defined in the C++ header file <cstdint>. Many assembly language programmers prefer to use fixed-size integer types for assembly language function declarations since it eschews the size ambiguities of the standard C++ integer types short, int, long, etc. It also accentuates the exact size and type of the argument.

Also shown in Listing 3-1a is file Ch03_01_misc.cpp. Note that this file contains two overloaded versions of the function DisplayResults() that stream results to std::cout. Function main() in file Ch03_01.cpp includes the static functions StackExample1() and StackExample2(). These functions perform test case initializations and call assembly language functions SumValsI32_a() and MulValsU64_a(). Note that functions SumValsI32_a() and MulValsU64_a() require eight arguments of type int32_t and uint64_t, respectively.

Listing 3-1b shows the MASM source code for example Ch03_01.

Listing 3-1b. Example Ch03_01 MASM Code

```
;-----------------------------------------------------------------------------
; Ch03_01_fasm.asm
;-----------------------------------------------------------------------------


;-----------------------------------------------------------------------------
; int32_t SumValsI32_a(int32_t a, int32_t b, int32_t c, int32_t d, int32_t e,
;    int32_t f, int32_t g, int32_t h);
;-----------------------------------------------------------------------------

        .code
SumValsI32_a proc
```

```
; Calculate a + b + c + d
        add ecx,edx                     ;ecx = a + b
        add r8d,r9d                     ;r8d = c + d
        add ecx,r8d                     ;ecx = a + b + c + d

; Calculate e + f + g + h
        mov eax,[rsp+40]                ;eax = e
        add eax,[rsp+48]                ;eax = e + f
        add eax,[rsp+56]                ;eax = e + f + g
        add eax,[rsp+64]                ;eax = e + f + g + h

;Calculate a + b + c + d + e + f + g + h
        add eax,ecx                     ;eax = final sum
        ret
SumValsI32_a endp


;-------------------------------------------------------------------------
; uint64_t MulValsU64_a(uint64_t a, uint64_t b, uint64_t c, uint64_t d,
;   int64_t e, uint64_t f, uint64_t g, uint64_t h);
;-------------------------------------------------------------------------

MulValsU64_a proc

; Calculate a * b * c * d * e * f * g * h
        mov rax,rcx                     ;rax = a
        mul rdx                         ;rax = a * b
        mul r8                          ;rax = a * b * c
        mul r9                          ;rax = a * b * c * d

        mul qword ptr [rsp+40]          ;rax = a * b * c * d * e
        mul qword ptr [rsp+48]          ;rax = a * b * c * d * e * f
        mul qword ptr [rsp+56]          ;rax = a * b * c * d * e * f * g
        mul qword ptr [rsp+64]          ;rax = final product

        ret
MulValsU64_a endp
        end
```

Execution of function SumValsI32_a() begins with the instruction triplet add ecx,edx, add r8d,r9d, and add ecx,r8d. These instructions calculate a + b + c + d. Recall from the discussions in Chapter 2 that a Visual C++ function passes the first four 32-bit integer arguments to a called function using registers ECX, EDX, R8D, and R9D. The remaining arguments are passed via the stack as shown in Figure 3-1.

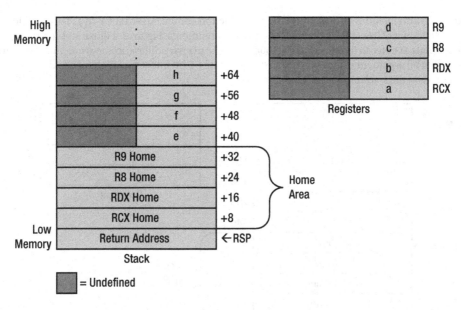

Figure 3-1. *Register and stack arguments for SumValsI32_a() (MASM version)*

In Figure 3-1, note that argument values a, b, c, and d are situated in the low-order doublewords (bits 31:0) of registers RCX, RDX, R8, and R9, respectively. These low-order doublewords can be referenced, as demonstrated in previous examples, using register names ECX, EDX, R8D, and R9D. It is also important to note that the high-order doublewords (bits 63:32) of RCX, RDX, R8, and R9 are undefined. This means that a function can't use register RCX, for example, as a 64-bit version of the 32-bit integer value in register ECX. An explicit zero or sign extension must be performed. You'll learn how to do this later in this chapter.

Also note in Figure 3-1 that upon entry to SumValsI32_a(), RSP points to the return address. Whenever a called function executes a ret instruction, the processor copies the quadword value pointed to by RSP into register RIP. It also adds eight to the value in RSP, which removes the return address from the stack. Immediately above the return address is the home area as shown in Figure 3-1. The Visual C++ run-time calling convention requires a calling function to allocate 32 bytes of data on the stack that a called function can use to temporarily save the values in registers RCX, RDX, R8, and R9. It is important to note that a called function is *not* required to save any register values in its home area. A function can optionally use its home area as intended to preserve registers RCX, RDX, R8, and R9; it can also use this area to temporarily store other data values. You'll learn more about the home area in later chapters.

In Figure 3-1, note that argument values e, f, g, and h are located on the stack above the home area. Each argument value is positioned at a known displacement from the current value in RSP. This facilitates easy access to these argument values when performing calculations. Also note that argument values e, f, g, and h are aligned on quadword (64-bit) boundaries. This is the default for x86-64 functions and creates areas on the stack that contain undefined values as shown in Figure 3-1.

Returning to the code in Listing 3-1b, the mov eax,[rsp+40] instruction loads register EAX with argument value e. In this instruction, register RSP acts as a base register, and the constant 40 is the displacement from the current value in RSP to argument value e on the stack. The next instruction, add eax,[rsp+48], calculates e + f. Note that the second operand of this instruction references argument value f on the stack; it doesn't need to be loaded into a register to perform the addition. The ensuing instruction pair, add eax,[rsp+56] and add eax,[rsp+64], completes the calculation of e + f + g + h. Just before the ret instruction is an add eax,ecx instruction that computes the final 32-bit sum.

Listing 3-1b also includes an assembly language function named MulValsU64_a(). This function calculates the product of its eight 64-bit unsigned integer arguments. Figure 3-2 illustrates the register and stack contents at entry to function MulValsU64_a(). The primary difference between this figure and Figure 3-1 is that all argument values for MulValsU64_a() are 64-bit integers, which means that there are no undefined areas on the stack or in an argument register.

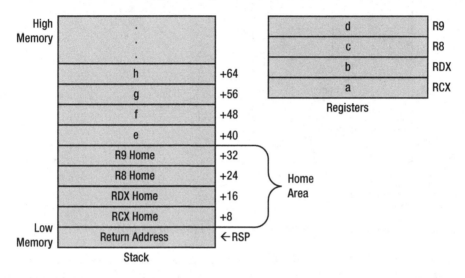

Figure 3-2. *Register and stack arguments for MulValsU64_a() (MASM version)*

Execution of function MulValsU64_a() begins with a mov rax,rcx instruction that copies argument value a into register RAX. The next instruction, mul rdx, multiplies the value in RAX with RDX (argument value b). Execution of this instruction yields a 128-bit product in register pair RDX:RAX. Note that in this example, the high-order quadword of each calculated product is ignored. The next two instructions, mul r8 and mul r9, complete the calculation of a * b * c * d.

The mul qword ptr [rsp+40] instruction multiplies the value in RAX by argument value e. The text qword ptr is a MASM size operator that denotes the size of argument value e. This operator is somewhat akin to a C-style cast operator. Without the qword ptr operator, the mul instruction is ambiguous since MASM can't ascertain which register (RAX, EAX, AX, or AL) should be used to perform the multiplication. Some assembly language programmers always include a size operator whenever an instruction references a memory operand since it improves readability. This book only employs size operators when required by an instruction or the assembler.[1]

The next three instructions, mul qword ptr [rsp+48], mul qword ptr [rsp+56], and mul qword ptr [rsp+64], complete the calculation of a * b * c * d * e * f * g * h. Note that since the computed product already resides in register RAX, no additional mov instructions are required before the ret instruction.

Listing 3-1c shows the NASM code for source code example Ch03_01. The arithmetic instructions used in the NASM version of AddValsI32_a() are the same ones that you saw in Listing 3-1b, albeit with different register operands.

---

[1] Previous editions of this book employed size operators for all instruction memory operands to improve readability. That style is not used in this edition to minimize differences between the MASM and NASM code.

Listing 3-1c. Example Ch03_01 NASM Code

```
;-------------------------------------------------------------------------------
; Ch03_01_fasm.s
;-------------------------------------------------------------------------------

        %include "ModX86Asm3eNASM.inc"

;-------------------------------------------------------------------------------
; int32_t SumValsI32_a(int32_t a, int32_t b, int32_t c, int32_t d,
;   int32_t e, int32_t f, int32_t g, int32_t h);
;-------------------------------------------------------------------------------

        section .text

        global SumValsI32_a
SumValsI32_a:

; Calculate a + b + c + d
        add edi,esi                     ;edi = a + b
        add edx,ecx                     ;edx = c + d
        add edi,edx                     ;edi = a + b + c + d

; Calculate e + f + g + h
        add r8d,r9d                     ;r8d = e + f
        mov eax,[rsp+8]                 ;eax = g
        add eax,[rsp+16]                ;eax = g + h
        add eax,r8d                     ;eax = e + f + g + h

;Calculate a + b + c + d + e + f + g + h
        add eax,edi                     ;eax = final sum
        ret


;-------------------------------------------------------------------------------
; uint64_t MulValsU64_a(uint64_t a, uint64_t b, uint64_t c, uint64_t d,
;   uint64_t e, uint64_t f, uint64_t g, uint64_t h);
;-------------------------------------------------------------------------------

        global MulValsU64_a
MulValsU64_a:

; Calculate a * b * c * d * e * f * g * h
        mov r10,rdx                     ;save copy of c
        mov rax,rdi                     ;rax = a
        mul rsi                         ;rax = a * b
        mul r10                         ;rax = a * b * c
        mul rcx                         ;rax = a * b * c * d
        mul r8                          ;rax = a * b * c * d * e
        mul r9                          ;rax = a * b * c * d * e * f
```

```
        mul qword [rsp+8]                    ;rax = a * b * c * d * e * f * g
        mul qword [rsp+16]                   ;rax = final product

        ret
```

Compared to Visual C++, the GNU C++ calling convention uses a different arrangement when passing argument values via the stack. Figure 3-3 shows the contents of the stack and argument registers upon entry to AddValsI32_a(). The first thing to notice is that argument values a, b, c, d, e, and f are passed using registers EDI, ESI, EDX, ECX, R8D, and R9D, respectively. Argument values g and h are passed via the stack as illustrated in Figure 3-3. Note that these values are located immediately above the return address since the GNU C++ calling convention doesn't implement a stack home area. However, the GNU C++ calling convention allows a leaf function (i.e., a function that doesn't call any other functions) to use the 128-byte area below the value in RSP as a temporary storage area. This area is called the red zone. You'll see examples of red zone use in later chapters.

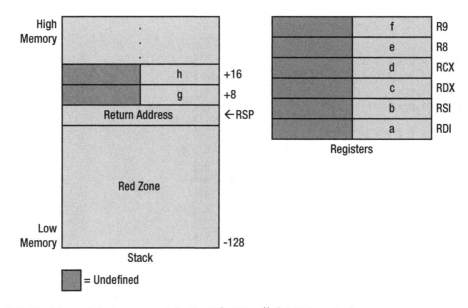

Figure 3-3. *Register and stack arguments for SumValsI32_a() (NASM version)*

Returning to Listing 3-1c, note the values of the displacements that are used in AddValsI32_a() to reference argument values g and h on the stack. Listing 3-1c also shows the NASM code for function MulValsU64_a(). Figure 3-4 shows the contents of the stack and registers upon entry to MulValsU64_a().

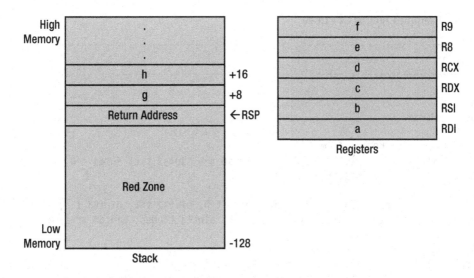

Figure 3-4. *Register and stack arguments for MulValsI64_a() (NASM version)*

Function MulValsU64_a() begins its execution with the instruction mov r10,rdx, which copies argument value c into register R10 for later use. The next instruction, mov rax,rdi, copies argument value a into register RAX. The ensuing five mul instructions calculate a * b * c * d * e * f. This is followed by a mul qword [rsp+8] that computes a * b * c * d * e * f * g. The qword size specifier is required and instructs NASM that it should perform the multiplication using register RAX and the quadword value located at [RSP+8]. The qword size specifier is also applied in the ensuing mul qword [rsp+16] instruction (RSP + 16 points to argument value h), which completes calculation of the required product. Here are the results for source code example Ch03_01:

```
----- Results for Ch03_01 ----

Stack Example #1
a = 2, b = -3, c = 8 d = 9, e = 3, f = -7 g = 5, h = -1000000
result1 = -999983, result2 = -999983

Stack Example #2
a = 10, b = 20, c = 30 d = 40, e = 50, f = 60 g = 70, h = 80
result1 = 4032000000000, result2 = 4032000000000
```

Mixed-Type Integer Arithmetic

In the source code examples presented thus far, only 32- and 64-bit wide integer argument values have been used. Real-world functions also use 8- and 16-bit integer arguments, and it's not uncommon for a function to employ a multiplicity of integer sizes as arguments. The next source code example, named Ch03_02, expounds on this. Listing 3-2a shows the C++ source code for example Ch03_02.

Listing 3-2a. Example Ch03_02 C++ Code

```cpp
//-----------------------------------------------------------------------------
// Ch03_02.h
//-----------------------------------------------------------------------------

#pragma once
#include <cstdint>

// Ch03_01_fasm.asm, Ch03_01_fasm.s
extern "C" int64_t CalcResultI64_a(int8_t a, int16_t b, int32_t c, int64_t d,
    int8_t e, int16_t f, int32_t g, int64_t h);

extern "C" void CalcResultU64_a(uint8_t a, uint16_t b, uint32_t c, uint64_t d,
    uint8_t e, uint16_t f, uint32_t g, uint64_t h, uint64_t* quo, uint64_t* rem);

// Ch03_02_misc.cpp
void DisplayResults(int8_t a, int16_t b, int32_t c, int64_t d,
    int8_t e, int16_t f, int32_t g, int64_t h, int64_t prod1, int64_t prod2);

void DisplayResults(uint8_t a, uint16_t b, uint32_t c, uint64_t d,
    uint8_t e, uint16_t f, uint32_t g, uint64_t h,
    uint64_t quo1, uint64_t rem1, uint64_t quo2, uint64_t rem2);

//-----------------------------------------------------------------------------
// Ch03_02_misc.cpp
//-----------------------------------------------------------------------------

#include <iostream>
#include "Ch03_02.h"

void DisplayResults(int8_t a, int16_t b, int32_t c, int64_t d,
    int8_t e, int16_t f, int32_t g, int64_t h, int64_t prod1, int64_t prod2)
{
    constexpr char nl = '\n';

    std::cout << "\nCalcResultI64 results\n";
    std::cout << "a = " << (int)a << ", b = " << b << ", c = " << c;
    std::cout << ", d = " << d << ", e = " << (int)e << ", f = " << f;
    std::cout << ", g = " << g << ", h = " << h << nl;
    std::cout << "prod1 = " << prod1 << nl;
    std::cout << "prod2 = " << prod2 << nl;
}

void DisplayResults(uint8_t a, uint16_t b, uint32_t c, uint64_t d,
    uint8_t e, uint16_t f, uint32_t g, uint64_t h,
    uint64_t quo1, uint64_t rem1, uint64_t quo2, uint64_t rem2)
{
    constexpr char nl = '\n';
```

```cpp
        std::cout << "\nCalcResultU64 results\n";
        std::cout << "a = " << (unsigned)a << ", b = " << b << ", c = " << c;
        std::cout << ", d = " << d << ", e = " << (unsigned)e << ", f = " << f;
        std::cout << ", g = " << g << ", h = " << h << nl;
        std::cout << "quo1 = " << quo1 << ", rem1 = " << rem1 << nl;
        std::cout << "quo2 = " << quo2 << ", rem2 = " << rem2 << nl;
}

//-------------------------------------------------------------------------
// Ch03_02.cpp
//-------------------------------------------------------------------------

#include <iostream>
#include "Ch03_02.h"

static void CalcResultI64(void)
{
    int8_t a = 2, e = 3;
    int16_t b = -3, f = -7;;
    int32_t c = 8, g = -5;
    int64_t d = 4, h = 10;

    // Calculate (a * b * c * d) + (e * f * g * h)
    int64_t prod1 = ((int64_t)a * b * c * d) + ((int64_t)e * f * g * h);
    int64_t prod2 = CalcResultI64_a(a, b, c, d, e, f, g, h);

    DisplayResults(a, b, c, d, e, f, g, h, prod1, prod2);
}

static void CalcResultU64(void)
{
    uint8_t a = 12, e = 101;
    uint16_t b = 17, f = 37;
    uint32_t c = 71000000, g =25;
    uint64_t d = 90000000000, h = 5;

    uint64_t quo1, rem1;
    uint64_t quo2, rem2;

    // Calculate quotient and remainder for (a + b + c + d) / (e + f + g + h)
    quo1 = ((uint64_t)a + b + c + d) / ((uint64_t)e + f + g + h);
    rem1 = ((uint64_t)a + b + c + d) % ((uint64_t)e + f + g + h);
    CalcResultU64_a(a, b, c, d, e, f, g, h, &quo2, &rem2);

    DisplayResults(a, b, c, d, e, f, g, h, quo1, rem1, quo2, rem2);
}
```

```
int main()
{
    std::cout << "----- Results for Ch03_02 -----\n";

    CalcResultI64();
    CalcResultU64();
    return 0;
}
```

In Listing 3-2a, header file Ch03_02.h includes declarations for assembly language functions CalcResultI64_a() and CalcResultU64_a(). The former expects a variety of signed integer arguments, while the latter makes use of unsigned integers. File Ch03_02_misc.cpp contains overloaded versions of DisplayResults(). Also shown in Listing 3-2a is file Ch03_02.cpp. This file opens with the static function CalcResultI64(). Following data initialization, function CalcResultI64() calculates prod1 = ((int64_t) a * b * c * d) + ((int64_t)e * f * g * h). CalcResultI64() also exercises the assembly language function CalcResultI64_a(), which computes the same value. The next function in file Ch03_02.cpp, CalcResultU64_a(), carries out its calculations using unsigned integers. Note that the C++ code in this function computes both a quotient (quo1) and a remainder (rem1). The assembly language code in function CalcResultU64_a() performs the same calculation.

Listing 3-2b shows the MASM code for example Ch03_02.

Listing 3-2b. Example Ch03_02 MASM Code

```
;-----------------------------------------------------------------------------
; Ch03_02_fasm.asm
;-----------------------------------------------------------------------------


;-----------------------------------------------------------------------------
; int64_t CalcResultI64_a(int8_t a, int16_t b, int32_t c, int64_t d,
;   int8_t e, int16_t f, int32_t g, int64_t h);
;-----------------------------------------------------------------------------

        .code
CalcResultI64_a proc

; Calculate a * b * c * d
        movsx rax,cl                    ;rax = a
        movsx r10,dx                    ;r10 = b
        imul rax,r10                    ;rax = a * b
        movsxd r10,r8d                  ;r10 = c
        imul r10,r9                     ;r10 = c * d
        imul rax,r10                    ;rax = a * b * c * d

; Calculate e * f * g * h
        movsx r10,byte ptr [rsp+40]     ;r10 = e
        movsx r11,word ptr [rsp+48]     ;r11 = f
        imul r10,r11                    ;r10 = e * f
        movsxd r11,dword ptr [rsp+56]   ;r11 = g
        imul r11,[rsp+64]               ;r11 = g * h
        imul r10,r11                    ;r10 = e * f * g * h
```

```
; Calculate (a * b * c * d) + (e * f * g * h)
        add rax,r10                             ;rax = final result
        ret
CalcResultI64_a endp

;-------------------------------------------------------------------------
; void CalcResultU64_a(uint8_t a, uint16_t b, uint32_t c, uint64_t d,
;   uint8_t e, uint16_t f, uint32_t g, uint64_t h, uint64_t* quo, uint64_t* rem);
;-------------------------------------------------------------------------

CalcResultU64_a proc

; Calculate a + b + c + d
        movzx rax,cl                            ;rax = a
        movzx r10,dx                            ;r10 = b
        add rax,r10                             ;rax = a + b
        mov r11d,r8d                            ;r11 = c
        add r11,r9                              ;r11 = c + d
        add rax,r11                             ;rax = a + b + c + d

; Calculate e + f + g + h
        movzx r10,byte ptr [rsp+40]             ;r10 = e
        movzx r11,word ptr [rsp+48]             ;r11 = f
        add r10,r11                             ;r10 = e + f
        mov r11d,[rsp+56]                       ;r11 = g
        add r11,[rsp+64]                        ;r11 = g + h;
        add r10,r11                             ;r10 = e + f + g + h

; Calculate (a + b + c + d) / (e + f + g + h)
; (no check for division by zero)
        xor edx,edx                             ;rdx:rax = a + b + c + d
        div r10                                 ;rdx:rax = rdx:rax / r10

; Save results
        mov rcx,[rsp+72]
        mov [rcx],rax                           ;save quotient
        mov rcx,[rsp+80]
        mov [rcx],rdx                           ;save remainder

        ret
CalcResultU64_a endp
        end
```

Figure 3-5 illustrates register and stack arguments upon entry to CalcResultI64_a(). The first executable instruction of this function, movsx rax,cl (Move with Sign Extension), sign-extends argument value a in register CL (CL is not altered) to 64 bits and saves this value in register RAX. Note in Figure 3-5 that the upper 56 bits of RCX are undefined. The ensuing movsx r10,dx instruction sign-extends argument value b to 64 bits and saves this value in R10. This is followed by an imul rax,r10 instruction, which calculates a * b. Recall that the two-operand variant of the 64-bit imul instruction only saves the low-order 64 bits of the 128-bit product. The ensuing instruction triplet, movsxd r10,r8d, imul r10,r9, and imul rax,r10, completes the calculation of a * b * c * d.

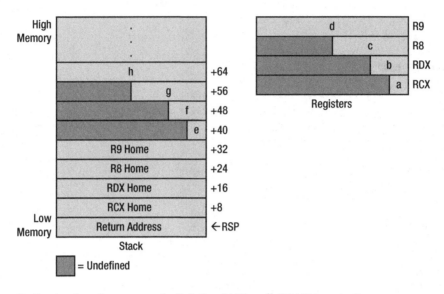

Figure 3-5. *Register and stack arguments for* CalcResultI64_a() *(MASM version)*

The second code block in CalcResultI64_a() calculates e * f * g * h. Note that the movsx and movsxd instructions use MASM size operators to signify the size of argument values e, f, and g on the stack. Also note in Figure 3-5 the undefined areas on the stack. The imul r11,[rsp+64] instruction doesn't require a size operator since the use of register operand R11 enables the assembler to correctly deduce the size of the memory operand at location RSP + 64.

Figure 3-6 shows register and stack arguments for function CalcResultU64_a(). Note again the undefined areas of each quadword register or memory location on the stack.

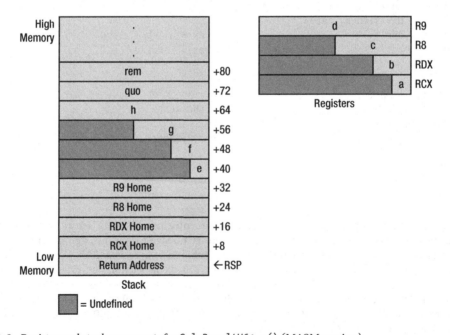

Figure 3-6. *Register and stack arguments for* CalcResultU64_a() *(MASM version)*

In Listing 3-2b, the layout of function CalcResultU64_a() is similar to CalcResultI64_a() but uses unsigned instead of signed 64-bit arithmetic. Note that CalcResultU64_a() uses the movzx (Move with Zero Extension) instruction to zero-extend unsigned 8- and 16-bit integers to 64 bits. A function can't use the movzx instruction with a 32-bit source operand. Instead, a simple mov can be employed to zero-extend an unsigned 32-bit integer to 64 bits. In function CalcResultU64_a(), the mov r11d,r8d performs this operation. Recall from earlier discussions that the processor zeros the upper 32 bits of a 64-bit register destination operand during execution of an instruction that employs 32-bit registers.

The third code block in CalcResultU64_a() exercises the div instruction to calculate (a + b + c + d) / (e + f + g + h). The xor edx,edx instruction that occurs just before the div r10 instruction is critical. The div r10 instruction uses register pair RDX:RAX as the dividend. Execution of the xor edx,edx instruction effectively zero-extends the 64-bit value in RAX to 128 bits in RDX:RAX (an xor rdx,rdx instruction could also be used here, but the machine encoding of xor edx,edx is one byte smaller). The final code block in CalcResultU64_a() saves the calculated quotient and remainder. Note that pointer arguments quo and rem are obtained from the stack.

Listing 3-2c shows the NASM code for source code example Ch03_02.

Listing 3-2c. Example Ch03_02 NASM Code

```
;-----------------------------------------------------------------------------
; Ch03_02_fasm.s
;-----------------------------------------------------------------------------

        %include "ModX86Asm3eNASM.inc"


;-----------------------------------------------------------------------------
; int64_t CalcResultI64_a(int8_t a, int16_t b, int32_t c, int64_t d,
;   int8_t e, int16_t f, int32_t g, int64_t h);
;-----------------------------------------------------------------------------

        section .text

        global CalcResultI64_a
CalcResultI64_a:

; Calculate a * b * c * d
        movsx rax,dil                   ;rax = a
        movsx r10,si                    ;r10 = b
        imul rax,r10                    ;rax = a * b
        movsxd r10,edx                  ;r10 = c
        imul r10,rcx                    ;r10 = c * d
        imul rax,r10                    ;rax = a * b * c * d

; Calculate e * f * g * h
        movsx r10,r8b                   ;r10 = e
        movsx r11,r9w                   ;r11 = f
        imul r10,r11                    ;r10 = e * f
        movsxd r11,dword [rsp+8]        ;r11 = g
        imul r11,[rsp+16]               ;r11 = g * h
        imul r10,r11                    ;r10 = e * f * g * h
```

```
; Calculate (a * b * c * d) + (e * f * g * h)
        add rax,r10                     ;rax = final result
        ret

;---------------------------------------------------------------------------
; void CalcResultU64_a(uint8_t a, uint16_t b, uint32_t c, uint64_t d,
;   uint8_t e, uint16_t f, uint32_t g, uint64_t h, uint64_t* quo, uint64_t* rem);
;---------------------------------------------------------------------------

        global CalcResultU64_a
CalcResultU64_a:

; Calculate a + b + c + d
        movzx rax,dil                   ;rax = a
        movzx r10,si                    ;r10 = b
        add rax,r10                     ;rax = a + b
        mov r11d,edx                    ;r11 = c
        add r11,rcx                     ;r11 = c + d
        add rax,r11                     ;rax = a + b + c + d

; Calculate e + f + g + h
        movzx r10,r8b                   ;r10 = e
        movzx r11,r9w                   ;r11 = f
        add r10,r11                     ;r10 = e + f
        mov r11d,[rsp+8]                ;r11 = g
        add r11,[rsp+16]                ;r11 = g + h;
        add r10,r11                     ;r10 = e + f + g + h

; Calculate (a + b + c + d) / (e + f + g + h)
; (no check for division by zero)
        xor edx,edx                     ;rdx:rax = a + b + c + d
        div r10                         ;rdx:rax = rdx:rax / r10

; Save results
        mov rcx,[rsp+24]
        mov [rcx],rax                   ;save quotient
        mov rcx,[rsp+32]
        mov [rcx],rdx                   ;save remainder

        ret
```

Figures 3-7 and 3-8 show register and stack arguments for the NASM versions of functions CalcResultsI64_a() and CalcResultsU64_a(), respectively. In Listing 3-2c, note the register names used for argument values a, b, e, and f. The names of these byte and word registers tend to be used less often than their doubleword and quadword counterparts. The calculating code in Listing 3-2c for NASM functions CalcResultsI64_a() and CalcResultsU64_a() is the same as the MASM versions in Listing 3-2b, but with different argument registers.

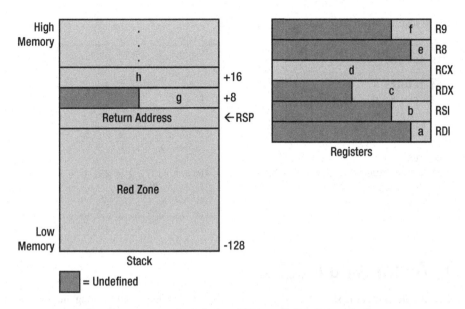

Figure 3-7. *Register and stack arguments for* `CalcResultI64_a()` *(NASM version)*

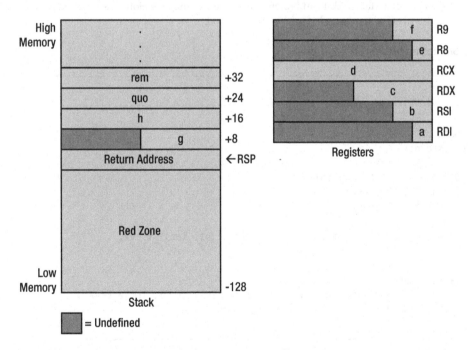

Figure 3-8. *Register and stack arguments for* `CalcResultU64_a()` *(NASM version)*

Here are the results for source code example Ch03_02:

```
----- Results for Ch03_02 -----

CalcResultI64 results
a = 2, b = -3, c = 8, d = 4, e = 3, f = -7, g = -5, h = 10
prod1 = 858
prod2 = 858

CalcResultU64 results
a = 12, b = 17, c = 71000000, d = 90000000000, e = 101, f = 37, g = 25, h = 5
quo1 = 536136904, rem1 = 157
quo2 = 536136904, rem2 = 157
```

Memory Addressing Modes

You learned in Chapter 1 that the x86-64 instruction set supports a variety of addressing modes that can be used to reference an operand in memory (see Table 1-7). In this section, you'll examine an assembly language function that illustrates how to use some of these modes. You'll also learn how to initialize an assembly language lookup table (LUT) and reference assembly language global variables in a C++ function. Listing 3-3a shows the C++ source code for example Ch03_03.

Listing 3-3a. Example Ch03_03 C++ Code

```cpp
//-------------------------------------------------------------------------
// Ch03_03.h
//-------------------------------------------------------------------------

#pragma once
#include <cstdint>

// Ch03_03_fasm.asm, Ch03_03_fasm.s
extern "C" int g_NumPrimes_a;
extern "C" int g_SumPrimes_a;

extern "C" int MemAddressing_a(int32_t i, int32_t* v1, int32_t* v2,
    int32_t* v3, int32_t* v4);

// Ch03_03_misc.cpp
extern void DisplayResults(int32_t i, int32_t rc, int32_t v1, int32_t v2,
    int32_t v3, int32_t v4);

//-------------------------------------------------------------------------
// Ch03_03_misc.cpp
//-------------------------------------------------------------------------

#include <iostream>
#include <iomanip>
#include "Ch03_03.h"
```

```cpp
void DisplayResults(int32_t i, int32_t rc, int32_t v1, int32_t v2,
    int32_t v3, int32_t v4)
{
    constexpr int w = 5;
    constexpr char nl = '\n';
    const char* delim = ", ";

    std::cout << "i  = " << std::setw(w - 1) << i << delim;
    std::cout << "rc = " << std::setw(w - 1) << rc << delim;
    std::cout << "v1 = " << std::setw(w) << v1 << delim;
    std::cout << "v2 = " << std::setw(w) << v2 << delim;
    std::cout << "v3 = " << std::setw(w) << v3 << delim;
    std::cout << "v4 = " << std::setw(w) << v4 << nl;

    if (!(v1 == v2 && v2 == v3 && v3 == v4))
        std::cout << "validation test failed, i = " << i << nl;
}

//-----------------------------------------------------------------------------
// Ch03_03.cpp
//-----------------------------------------------------------------------------

#include <iostream>
#include "Ch03_03.h"

int main()
{
    std::cout << "----- Results for Ch03_03 -----\n";

    // Initialize g_SumPrimes_a (defined in assembly langage file)
    g_SumPrimes_a = 0;

    for (int i = -1; i < g_NumPrimes_a + 1; i++)
    {
        int32_t v1 = -1, v2 = -1, v3 = -1, v4 = -1;
        int32_t rc = MemAddressing_a(i, &v1, &v2, &v3, &v4);

        DisplayResults(i, rc, v1, v2, v3, v4);
    }

    std::cout << "\ng_SumPrimes_a = " << g_SumPrimes_a << '\n';
    return 0;
}
```

Listing 3-3a begins with the C++ header file Ch03_03.h. The first two declarations in this file are global variables g_NumPrimes_a and g_SumPrimes_a. Note that both declaration statements include the "C" modifier, which instructs the C++ compiler to use C-style variable names instead of C++ decorated names. The reason for using the "C" modifier is that both g_NumPrimes_a and g_SumPrimes_a are defined in the assembly language files. More about this in a moment. Next in Listing 3-3a is the declaration of assembly language function MemAddressing_a().

The C++ code in main() includes a simple for-loop that exercises the assembly language function MemAddressing_a(). Note that for-loop index variable i is initialized to –1. This is done to test the invalid index check in MemAddressing_a(). Index variable i is also allowed to exceed the value of g_NumPrimes_a for the same reason. Function MemAddressing_a() uses argument value i as an index into a simple LUT of constant 32-bit integers, while the four pointer arguments are utilized to save values loaded from the LUT using different addressing modes.

Listing 3-3b shows the MASM code for source code example Ch03_03. Near the top of Listing 3-3b is a .const directive. This directive signifies the start of a block of memory that contains read-only data. Immediately following the .const directive is the definition of a LUT named PrimeNums. LUT PrimeNums contains 25 doubleword integer values. The text dd is a MASM synonym for the directive dword, which allocates storage space and optionally initializes a doubleword value. Other MASM memory space storage synonyms (directives) include db (byte), dw (word), and dq (qword). A MASM source code file can define and initialize a data variable using a memory storage directive or its corresponding synonym.

Listing 3-3b. Example Ch03_03 MASM Code

```
;-----------------------------------------------------------------------------
; Ch03_03_fasm.asm
;-----------------------------------------------------------------------------

; Simple LUT (.const section is read only)
                .const
PrimeNums       dd 2, 3, 5, 7, 11, 13, 17, 19, 23
                dd 29, 31, 37, 41, 43, 47, 53, 59
                dd 61, 67, 71, 73, 79, 83, 89, 97

                public g_NumPrimes_a
g_NumPrimes_a   dd ($ - PrimeNums) / sizeof dword

; Data section (.data section is read/write)
                .data
                public g_SumPrimes_a
g_SumPrimes_a   dd -9999


;-----------------------------------------------------------------------------
; int MemAddressing_a(int32_t i, int32_t* v1, int32_t* v2,
;   int32_t* v3, int32_t* v4);
;-----------------------------------------------------------------------------

        .code
MemAddressing_a proc

; Make sure 'i' is valid
        cmp ecx,-1
        jle InvalidIndex                ;jump if i <= -1
        cmp ecx,[g_NumPrimes_a]
        jge InvalidIndex                ;jump if i >= g_NumPrimes_a

; Initialize
        movsxd r10,ecx                  ;extend i to 64-bits
        lea r11,[PrimeNums]             ;r11 = address of PrimeNums
```

```
; Memory addressing - base register
        mov rcx,r10                      ;rcx = i
        shl rcx,2                        ;rcx = i * 4
        mov rax,r11                      ;rax = PrimeNums
        add rax,rcx                      ;rax = PrimeNums + i * 4
        mov eax,[rax]                    ;eax = PrimeNums[i]
        mov [rdx],eax                    ;save to v1

; Memory addressing - base register + index register
        mov rcx,r10                      ;rcx = i
        shl rcx,2                        ;rcx = i * 4
        mov eax,[r11+rcx]                ;eax = PrimeNums[i]
        mov [r8],eax                     ;save to v2

; Memory addressing - base register + index register * scale factor
        mov eax,[r11+r10*4]              ;eax = PrimeNums[i]
        mov [r9],eax                     ;save to v3

; Memory addressing - base register + index register * scale factor + disp
        sub r11,42                       ;r11 = PrimeNums - 42
        mov eax,[r11+r10*4+42]           ;eax = PrimeNums[i]
        mov r10,[rsp+40]                 ;r10 = v4 ptr
        mov [r10],eax                    ;save to v4

; Memory addressing - RIP relative
        add [g_SumPrimes_a],eax          ;update sum
        mov eax,1                        ;set success return code
        ret

InvalidIndex:
        xor eax,eax                      ;set error return code
        ret

MemAddressing_a endp
        end
```

The statement g_NumPrimes_a dd ($ - PrimeNums) / sizeof dword allocates storage space for a single doubleword value and initializes it with the number of doubleword elements in PrimeNums. The $ character is an assembler symbol that equals the current value of the location counter (or offset from the beginning of the current memory block). Subtracting the offset of PrimeNums from $ yields the size of the LUT in bytes. Dividing this result by the size in bytes of a doubleword (sizeof dword) value generates the correct number of LUT elements. These statements emulate a frequently used technique in C++ to define and initialize a variable with the number of elements in an array:

```
constexpr int Values[] = {10, 20, 30, 40, 50};
constexpr int NumValues = sizeof(Values) / sizeof(int);
```

The final statement of the .const section, public g_NumPrimes_a, declares g_NumPrimes_a as a public symbol so that it can be referenced in other functions. The .data directive that follows denotes the start of a memory block that contains modifiable (i.e., read/write) data. The statements public g_SumPrimes_a and g_SumPrimes_a dd -9999 define a publicly accessible doubleword variable with an initial value of –9999. The value –9999 is arbitrary and provides confirmation that the initialization of g_SumPrimes_a in main() is correct.

Upon entry into function MemAddressing_a(), argument value i is checked for validity since it will be used as an index into LUT PrimeNums. The cmp ecx,-1 instruction compares the contents of ECX, which contains i, to the immediate value –1. You learned in Chapter 2 that when the processor executes a cmp instruction, it subtracts the second operand from the first operand, sets the status flags based on the results of this operation, and discards the result. If i <= -1 is true, the ensuing jle InvalidIndex (Jump if Less or Equal) instruction transfers program control to the first instruction that follows the label InvalidIndex. A similar sequence of instructions is used to determine if i is too large. The cmp ecx,[g_NumPrimes_a] instruction compares ECX against the number of elements in the lookup table. If i >= g_NumPrimes_a is true, program control is transferred to the target location that is specified by the jge (Jump if Greater or Equal) instruction.

Immediately following the validation of i, the movsxd r10,ecx instruction sign-extends the table index value to 64 bits. Sign-extending or zero-extending a 32-bit integer to a 64-bit integer is often necessary when using an addressing mode that employs an index register as you'll soon see. The next instruction, lea r11,[PrimeNums] (Load Effective Address), loads the address of LUT PrimeNums into register R11. A function can also use the lea instruction to perform simple integer arithmetic, and you'll learn how to do this in later chapters.

The remaining code blocks in MemAddressing_a() illustrate accessing items in the LUT using various memory addressing modes. The first example uses BaseReg memory addressing to read an item from the LUT. To use a single base register, MemAddressing_a() must explicitly calculate the address of the *i-th* table element, which is achieved by adding the starting address of PrimeNums and the value i * 4. The mov rcx,r10 instruction copies i into register RCX. This is followed by a shl rcx,2 instruction that calculates i * 4 (i * 4 is calculated since each entry in PrimeNums is a doubleword value). The next two instructions, mov rax,r11 and add rax,rcx, calculate the required address. Following calculation of the required address, the specified LUT value is read using a mov eax,[rax] instruction. It is then saved to the memory location pointed to argument value v1.

In the second example, the LUT value is read using BaseReg + IndexReg memory addressing. This example is similar to the first one except that the processor computes the final effective address during execution of the mov eax,[r11+rcx] instruction. Note that in this example, recalculation of the LUT element offset using the instruction pair mov rcx,r10 and shl rcx,2 is superfluous but included to show the complete LUT address calculation.

The third example demonstrates the use of BaseReg + IndexReg * ScaleFactor memory addressing. The mov eax,[r11+r10*4] instruction loads the correct LUT value into register EAX. In the fourth (and somewhat contrived) example, BaseReg + IndexReg * ScaleFactor + Disp memory addressing is demonstrated. Note that argument value v4 was passed via the stack. The fifth and final memory addressing mode example uses an add [g_SumPrimes_A],eax instruction to highlight RIP-relative addressing. This instruction, which uses a memory location as a destination operand, updates a running sum of LUT values that is ultimately displayed by the C++ code.

Listing 3-3c shows the NASM code for source code example Ch03_03.

Listing 3-3c. Example Ch03_03 NASM Code

```
;-----------------------------------------------------------------------------
; Ch03_03_fasm.s
;-----------------------------------------------------------------------------

        %include "ModX86Asm3eNASM.inc"

; Simple LUT (section .rdata is read only)
                section .rdata
```

```
PrimeNums:      dd 2, 3, 5, 7, 11, 13, 17, 19, 23
                dd 29, 31, 37, 41, 43, 47, 53, 59
                dd 61, 67, 71, 73, 79, 83, 89, 97

                global g_NumPrimes_a
g_NumPrimes_a:  dd ($ - PrimeNums) / 4

; Data section (section .data is read/write)
                section .data
                global g_SumPrimes_a
g_SumPrimes_a:  dd -9999

;-----------------------------------------------------------------------------
; int MemAddressing_a(int32_t i, int32_t* v1, int32_t* v2,
;   int32_t* v3, int32_t* v4);
;-----------------------------------------------------------------------------

        section .text

        global MemAddressing_a
MemAddressing_a:

; Make sure 'i' is valid
        cmp edi,-1
        jle InvalidIndex                ;jump if i <= -1
        cmp edi,[g_NumPrimes_a]
        jge InvalidIndex                ;jump if i >= g_NumPrimes_a

; Initialize
        movsxd r10,edi                  ;extend i to 64-bits
        lea r11,[PrimeNums]             ;r11 = address of PrimeNums

; Memory addressing - base register
        mov rdi,r10                     ;rdi = i
        shl rdi,2                       ;rdi = i * 4
        mov rax,r11                     ;rax = PrimeNums
        add rax,rdi                     ;rax = PrimeNums + i * 4
        mov eax,[rax]                   ;eax = PrimeNums[i]
        mov [rsi],eax                   ;save to v1

; Memory addressing - base register + index register
        mov rdi,r10                     ;rdi = i
        shl rdi,2                       ;rdi = i * 4
        mov eax,[r11+rdi]               ;eax = PrimeNums[i]
        mov [rdx],eax                   ;save to v2

; Memory addressing - base register + index register * scale factor
        mov eax,[r11+r10*4]             ;eax = PrimeNums[i]
        mov [rcx],eax                   ;save to v3
```

```
; Memory addressing - base register + index register * scale factor + disp
        sub r11,42                      ;r11 = PrimeNums - 42
        mov eax,[r11+r10*4+42]          ;eax = PrimeNums[i]
        mov [r8],eax                    ;save to v4

; Memory addressing - RIP relative
        add [g_SumPrimes_a],eax         ;update sum
        mov eax,1                       ;set success return code
        ret

InvalidIndex:
        xor eax,eax                     ;set error return code
        ret
```

Source code example Ch03_03 exemplifies one noteworthy difference between MASM and NASM: the declaration and initialization of data values in an assembly language file. Near the top of Listing 3-3c is the statement section .rdata, which signifies the start of a read-only data section. Definition of LUT PrimeNums is next. NASM uses "pseudo instructions" db, dw, dd, and dq for byte, word, doubleword, and quadword storage allocation and initialization. Also note that the LUT name PrimeNums includes a trailing colon, which is required.

The next two statements, global g_NumPrimes_a and g_NumPrimes_a: dd ($ - PrimeNums) / 4, define a public variable named g_NumPrimes_a whose value equals the number of entries in PrimeNums. An explicit constant of four (size of a doubleword in bytes) is used here since there is no sizeof operator in NASM. Following the .rdata section is a .data section. NASM .data sections are used to allocate and initialize storage for read-write variables. The executable code for NASM function MemAddressing_a() mimics the MASM version with the only difference being the specific argument registers. Here are the results for source code example Ch03_03:

```
----- Results for Ch03_03 -----
i  =   -1, rc =    0, v1 =    -1, v2 =    -1, v3 =    -1, v4 =    -1
i  =    0, rc =    1, v1 =     2, v2 =     2, v3 =     2, v4 =     2
i  =    1, rc =    1, v1 =     3, v2 =     3, v3 =     3, v4 =     3
i  =    2, rc =    1, v1 =     5, v2 =     5, v3 =     5, v4 =     5
i  =    3, rc =    1, v1 =     7, v2 =     7, v3 =     7, v4 =     7
i  =    4, rc =    1, v1 =    11, v2 =    11, v3 =    11, v4 =    11
i  =    5, rc =    1, v1 =    13, v2 =    13, v3 =    13, v4 =    13
i  =    6, rc =    1, v1 =    17, v2 =    17, v3 =    17, v4 =    17
i  =    7, rc =    1, v1 =    19, v2 =    19, v3 =    19, v4 =    19
i  =    8, rc =    1, v1 =    23, v2 =    23, v3 =    23, v4 =    23
i  =    9, rc =    1, v1 =    29, v2 =    29, v3 =    29, v4 =    29
i  =   10, rc =    1, v1 =    31, v2 =    31, v3 =    31, v4 =    31
i  =   11, rc =    1, v1 =    37, v2 =    37, v3 =    37, v4 =    37
i  =   12, rc =    1, v1 =    41, v2 =    41, v3 =    41, v4 =    41
i  =   13, rc =    1, v1 =    43, v2 =    43, v3 =    43, v4 =    43
i  =   14, rc =    1, v1 =    47, v2 =    47, v3 =    47, v4 =    47
i  =   15, rc =    1, v1 =    53, v2 =    53, v3 =    53, v4 =    53
i  =   16, rc =    1, v1 =    59, v2 =    59, v3 =    59, v4 =    59
i  =   17, rc =    1, v1 =    61, v2 =    61, v3 =    61, v4 =    61
i  =   18, rc =    1, v1 =    67, v2 =    67, v3 =    67, v4 =    67
i  =   19, rc =    1, v1 =    71, v2 =    71, v3 =    71, v4 =    71
i  =   20, rc =    1, v1 =    73, v2 =    73, v3 =    73, v4 =    73
i  =   21, rc =    1, v1 =    79, v2 =    79, v3 =    79, v4 =    79
```

```
i  =   22, rc =    1, v1 =    83, v2 =    83, v3 =    83, v4 =    83
i  =   23, rc =    1, v1 =    89, v2 =    89, v3 =    89, v4 =    89
i  =   24, rc =    1, v1 =    97, v2 =    97, v3 =    97, v4 =    97
i  =   25, rc =    0, v1 =    -1, v2 =    -1, v3 =    -1, v4 =    -1

g_SumPrimes_a = 1060
```

Given the multiple addressing modes that are available on an x86 processor, you might wonder which mode should be used. The answer to this question depends on several factors including register availability, the number of times an instruction (or sequence of instructions) is expected to execute, instruction ordering, and memory space vs. execution time trade-offs. Hardware attributes such as the processor's underlying microarchitecture and cache sizes also play a role.

When coding an x86 assembly language function, one suggested guideline is to favor simpler forms of memory addressing (e.g., base register and displacement; base register, index register, and scale factor) whenever possible instead of a complex form (base register, index register, scale factor, and displacement). An instruction that references a memory operand using all four components of an effective address may execute slower on some processor microarchitectures (the lea instruction is one example of this). However, a complex form may be more efficient if it eliminates the need to preserve one or more non-volatile registers on the stack (non-volatile registers are explained in Chapter 4). You'll learn more about assembly language code efficiency and processor microarchitectures in Chapter 17.

Condition Codes

When developing code to implement a particular algorithm, it is often necessary to determine the minimum or maximum value of two numbers. The standard C++ library defines two template functions named std::min() and std::max() to perform these operations. Source code example Ch03_04 includes several three-argument versions of signed integer minimum and maximum functions. The purpose of these functions is to illustrate the use of the jcc (Conditional Jump) and cmovcc (Conditional Move) instructions. Listing 3-4a shows the C++ source code for example Ch03_04.

Listing 3-4a. Example Ch03_04 C++ Code

```
//-------------------------------------------------------------------------------
// Ch03_04.h
//-------------------------------------------------------------------------------

#pragma once
#include <cstdint>

// Ch03_04_fasm.asm, Ch03_04_fasm.s
extern "C" int32_t SignedMin1_a(int32_t a, int32_t b, int32_t c);
extern "C" int32_t SignedMin2_a(int32_t a, int32_t b, int32_t c);
extern "C" int32_t SignedMax1_a(int32_t a, int32_t b, int32_t c);
extern "C" int32_t SignedMax2_a(int32_t a, int32_t b, int32_t c);

// Ch03_04_misc.cpp
void DisplayResults(const char* s1, int32_t a, int32_t b, int32_t c, int32_t result);


//-------------------------------------------------------------------------------
// Ch03_04_misc.cpp
//-------------------------------------------------------------------------------
```

```cpp
#include <iostream>
#include <iomanip>
#include "Ch03_04.h"

void DisplayResults(const char* s1, int32_t a, int32_t b, int32_t c,
    int32_t result)
{
    constexpr int w = 4;

    std::cout << s1 << "(";
    std::cout << std::setw(w) << a << ", ";
    std::cout << std::setw(w) << b << ", ";
    std::cout << std::setw(w) << c << ") = ";
    std::cout << std::setw(w) << result << '\n';
}

//-----------------------------------------------------------------------------
// Ch03_04.cpp
//-----------------------------------------------------------------------------

#include <iostream>
#include "Ch03_04.h"

int main(void)
{
    constexpr int32_t a_vals[] { 2,   -3,  17, -47 };
    constexpr int32_t b_vals[] { 15, -22,  37, -16 };
    constexpr int32_t c_vals[] { 8,   28, -11,  -9 };
    constexpr int n = sizeof(a_vals) / sizeof(int32_t);

    std::cout << "----- Results for Ch03_04 -----\n";

    for (int i = 0; i < n; i++)
    {
        int32_t a = a_vals[i], b = b_vals[i], c = c_vals[i];

        int32_t smin1 = SignedMin1_a(a, b, c);
        int32_t smin2 = SignedMin2_a(a, b, c);
        int32_t smax1 = SignedMax1_a(a, b, c);
        int32_t smax2 = SignedMax2_a(a, b, c);

        std::cout << "\n------------- Example #" << i + 1 << " -------------\n";
        DisplayResults("SignedMin1_a", a, b, c, smin1);
        DisplayResults("SignedMin2_a", a, b, c, smin2);
        DisplayResults("SignedMax1_a", a, b, c, smax1);
        DisplayResults("SignedMax2_a", a, b, c, smax2);
    }

    return 0;
}
```

The C++ code in Listing 3-4a closely resembles the source code examples that you have already studied. C++ header file Ch03_04.h includes the requisite function declarations. File Ch03_04_misc.cpp contains code that formats and streams the results to std::cout. Function main(), located in file Ch03_04. cpp, performs test case initialization and exercises the assembly language functions SignedMin1_a(), SignedMin2_a(), SignedMax1_a(), and SignedMax2_a().

Listing 3-4b shows the MASM code for example Ch03_04. The second instruction of function SignedMin1_a(), cmp eax,edx, compares argument values a and b and sets the status flags in RFLAGS. The jle @F (Jump if Less Than or Equal) instruction that follows is a conditional jump instruction. If a <= b is true, the processor jumps forward to the first instruction that follows the label @@: (a conditional jump instruction can also use the symbol @B to perform a backward jump). If a <= b is false, the ensuing mov eax,edx instruction copies argument value b into register EAX. The next instruction, cmp eax,r8d, compares registers EAX (min(a, b)) and R8D (argument value c). If min(a,b) <= c is true, the jle @F skips over the subsequent mov eax,r8d instruction since EAX already contains min(a, b, c). Otherwise, the mov eax,r8d instruction gets executed, and it copies argument value c to register EAX.

Listing 3-4b. Example Ch03_04 MASM Code

```
;-------------------------------------------------------------------------------
; Ch03_04_fasm.asm
;-------------------------------------------------------------------------------


;-------------------------------------------------------------------------------
; int SignedMin1_a(int a, int b, int c);
;-------------------------------------------------------------------------------

        .code
SignedMin1_a proc
        mov eax,ecx
        cmp eax,edx                     ;compare a and b
        jle @F                          ;jump if a <= b
        mov eax,edx                     ;eax = b

@@:     cmp eax,r8d                     ;compare min(a, b) and c
        jle @F
        mov eax,r8d                     ;eax = min(a, b, c)
@@:     ret
SignedMin1_a endp


;-------------------------------------------------------------------------------
; int SignedMin2_a(int a, int b, int c);
;-------------------------------------------------------------------------------

SignedMin2_a proc
        cmp ecx,edx
        cmovg ecx,edx                   ;ecx = min(a, b)
        cmp ecx,r8d
        cmovg ecx,r8d                   ;ecx = min(a, b, c)
        mov eax,ecx
        ret
SignedMin2_a endp
```

```
;-------------------------------------------------------------------------------
; int SignedMax1_a(int a, int b, int c);
;-------------------------------------------------------------------------------

SignedMax1_a proc
        mov eax,ecx
        cmp eax,edx                     ;compare a and b
        jge @F                          ;jump if a >= b
        mov eax,edx                     ;eax = b

@@:     cmp eax,r8d                     ;compare max(a, b) and c
        jge @F
        mov eax,r8d                     ;eax = max(a, b, c)
@@:     ret
SignedMax1_a endp


;-------------------------------------------------------------------------------
; int SignedMax2_a(int a, int b, int c);
;-------------------------------------------------------------------------------

SignedMax2_a proc
        cmp ecx,edx
        cmovl ecx,edx                   ;ecx = max(a, b)
        cmp ecx,r8d
        cmovl ecx,r8d                   ;ecx = max(a, b, c)
        mov eax,ecx
        ret
SignedMax2_a endp
        end
```

Conditional jump instructions, especially data-dependent ones in a performance-critical for-loop, can adversely affect processor performance. Alternatively, a function can use the conditional move instruction cmovcc to circumvent the potential negative performance effects of a conditional jump. Function SignedMin2_a() illustrates the use of this instruction. The first executable instruction of SignedMin2_a(), cmp ecx,edx, compares argument values a and b. The next instruction, cmovg ecx,edx (Move if Greater), copies argument value b into register ECX if b > a is true. If b > a is false, the value in register RCX remains unaltered. The ensuing cmp ecx,r8d instruction compares min(a, b) and argument value c. If min(a,b) > c is false, instruction cmovg ecx,r8d copies c into register ECX.

Also shown in Listing 3-4b are the functions SignedMax1_a() and SignedMax2_a(). The only difference between these functions and SignedMin1_a() and SignedMin2_a() is the exercised condition codes. Function SignedMax1_a() uses jge (Jump if Greater or Equal) instead of jle, while SignedMax2_a() employs cmovl (Move if Less) instead of cmovg.

Listing 3-4c shows the NASM code for this source code example. This code mimics the MASM code except for register names and the use of the @@: label, which NASM does not support unless TASM (Turbo Assembler, an old x86 assembler once marketed by Borland) compatibility mode is enabled. Note that label names in a NASM source code file must be unique, which explains why different label names are used in functions SignedMin1_a() and SignedMax1_a().

Listing 3-4c. Example Ch03_04 NASM Code

```
;-------------------------------------------------------------------------------
; Ch03_04_fasm.s
;-------------------------------------------------------------------------------

        %include "ModX86Asm3eNASM.inc"

;-------------------------------------------------------------------------------
; int SignedMin1_a(int a, int b, int c);
;-------------------------------------------------------------------------------

        section .text

        global SignedMin1_a
SignedMin1_a:
        mov eax,esi
        cmp eax,edi                     ;compare a and b
        jle F1                          ;jump if a <= b
        mov eax,edi                     ;eax = b

F1:     cmp eax,edx                     ;compare min(a, b) and c
        jle F2
        mov eax,edx                     ;eax = min(a, b, c)
F2:     ret

;-------------------------------------------------------------------------------
; int SignedMin2_a(int a, int b, int c);
;-------------------------------------------------------------------------------

        global SignedMin2_a
SignedMin2_a:
        cmp edi,esi
        cmovg edi,esi                   ;edi = min(a, b)
        cmp edi,edx
        cmovg edi,edx                   ;edi = min(a, b, c)
        mov eax,edi
        ret

;-------------------------------------------------------------------------------
; int SignedMax1_a(int a, int b, int c);
;-------------------------------------------------------------------------------

        global SignedMax1_a
SignedMax1_a:
        mov eax,esi
        cmp eax,edi                     ;compare a and b
        jge F3                          ;jump if a >= b
        mov eax,edi                     ;eax = b
```

```
F3:     cmp eax,edx                      ;compare max(a, b) and c
        jge F4
        mov eax,edx                      ;eax = max(a, b, c)
F4:     ret


;-----------------------------------------------------------------------------
; int SignedMax2_a(int a, int b, int c);
;-----------------------------------------------------------------------------

        global SignedMax2_a
SignedMax2_a:
        cmp esi,edi
        cmovl esi,edi                    ;esi = max(a, b)
        cmp esi,edx
        cmovl esi,edx                    ;esi = max(a, b, c)
        mov eax,esi
        ret
```

Unsigned versions of this example's minimum and maximum functions can be easily created using the following instruction substitutions: jbe (Jump if Below or Equal) for jle, jae (Jump if Above or Equal) for jge, cmova (Move if Above) for cmovg, and cmovb (Move if Below) for cmovl. Here are the results for source code example Ch03_04:

```
----- Results for Ch03_04 -----

------------- Example #1 -------------
SignedMin1_a(   2,   15,    8) =    2
SignedMin2_a(   2,   15,    8) =    2
SignedMax1_a(   2,   15,    8) =   15
SignedMax2_a(   2,   15,    8) =   15

------------- Example #2 -------------
SignedMin1_a(  -3,  -22,   28) =  -22
SignedMin2_a(  -3,  -22,   28) =  -22
SignedMax1_a(  -3,  -22,   28) =   28
SignedMax2_a(  -3,  -22,   28) =   28

------------- Example #3 -------------
SignedMin1_a(  17,   37,  -11) =  -11
SignedMin2_a(  17,   37,  -11) =  -11
SignedMax1_a(  17,   37,  -11) =   37
SignedMax2_a(  17,   37,  -11) =   37

------------- Example #4 -------------
SignedMin1_a( -47,  -16,   -9) =  -47
SignedMin2_a( -47,  -16,   -9) =  -47
SignedMax1_a( -47,  -16,   -9) =   -9
SignedMax2_a( -47,  -16,   -9) =   -9
```

Assembly Language For-Loops

Perhaps the most important and functional construct in any programming language is the ubiquitous for-loop. The final source code example of this chapter, entitled Ch03_05, demonstrates how to code a simple x86-64 assembly language for-loop. Listing 3-5a shows the C++ source code for this example.

Listing 3-5a. Example Ch03_05 C++ Code

```
//-----------------------------------------------------------------------------
// Ch03_05.h
//-----------------------------------------------------------------------------

#pragma once
#include <cstdint>

// Ch03_05_fasm.asm, Ch03_05_fasm.s
extern "C" bool CalcSumCubes_a(int64_t* sum, int64_t n);

// Ch03_05_fcpp.cpp
extern bool CalcSumCubes_cpp(int64_t* sum, int64_t n);

// Ch03_05_misc.cpp
extern void DisplayResults(int id, int64_t n, int64_t sum1, bool rc1,
    int64_t sum2, bool rc2);

// Ch03_05.cpp
extern "C" int64_t g_ValMax;


//-----------------------------------------------------------------------------
// Ch03_05_misc.cpp
//-----------------------------------------------------------------------------

#include <iostream>
#include <iomanip>
#include "Ch03_05.h"

void DisplayResults(int id, int64_t n, int64_t sum1, bool rc1,
    int64_t sum2, bool rc2)
{
    constexpr char nl = '\n';
    const char* err_msg = "error: 'n' is out of range";

    std::cout << nl << "----- Test case #" << id << " -----\n";
    std::cout << "n = " << n << nl;

    std::cout << "sum1 = ";

    if (rc1)
        std::cout << sum1 << nl;
    else
        std::cout << err_msg << nl;
```

```cpp
    std::cout << "sum2 = ";

    if (rc2)
        std::cout << sum2 << nl;
    else
        std::cout << err_msg << nl;

    if (sum1 != sum2)
        std::cout << "Compare test failed!\n";
}

//-----------------------------------------------------------------------------
// Ch03_05_fcpp.cpp
//-----------------------------------------------------------------------------

#include "Ch03_05.h"

bool CalcSumCubes_cpp(int64_t* sum, int64_t  n)
{
    if (n <= 0 || n > g_ValMax)
    {
        *sum = 0;
        return false;
    }

    int64_t temp1 = n * (n + 1) / 2;

    *sum = temp1 * temp1;
    return true;
}

//-----------------------------------------------------------------------------
// Ch03_05.cpp
//-----------------------------------------------------------------------------

#include <iostream>
#include "Ch03_05.h"

constexpr int64_t c_ValMax = 77935;
int64_t g_ValMax = c_ValMax;

int main(void)
{
    constexpr int64_t n_vals[] { 3, 4, 21, 0,
        c_ValMax, c_ValMax + 1, 100, -42, };

    constexpr int64_t num_n_vals = sizeof(n_vals) / sizeof(int64_t);

    std::cout << "----- Results for Ch03_05 -----\n";
```

```
for (int i = 0; i < num_n_vals; i++)
{
    int64_t sum1, sum2;
    int64_t n = n_vals[i];

    bool rc1 = CalcSumCubes_cpp(&sum1, n);
    bool rc2 = CalcSumCubes_a(&sum2, n);

    DisplayResults(i, n, sum1, rc1, sum2, rc2);
}

return 0;
}
```

Listing 3-5a begins with the header file Ch03_05.h. Note that this file includes declarations for two calculating functions: CalcSumCubes_cpp() and CalcSumCubes_a(). Both functions calculate the sum of integer cubes between 1 and argument value n. However, they carry out their calculations differently. CalcSumCubes_cpp() uses a simple arithmetic expression to calculate sum1, while CalcSumCubes_a() uses an assembly language for-loop (for instructional purposes) to calculate sum2. Here are the equations:

$$sum_1 = \left(\frac{n(n+1)}{2} \right)^2$$

$$sum_2 = \sum_{i=1}^{n} i^3$$

Note in file Ch03_05.h that g_ValMax is declared using the "C" modifier since this value is referenced in the assembly language code.

In Listing 3-5a, file Ch03_05_fcpp.cpp contains the definition of CalcSumCubes_cpp(). Execution of this function begins with a validation check of argument value n to prevent an arithmetic overflow condition from occurring. The assembly language code that you will see shortly also performs this same check. The remaining code in CalcSumCubes_cpp calculates sum1. The C++ code in file Ch03_05.cpp includes function main(), which performs test case initialization and exercises the two sum calculating functions. Note that array n_vals in main() includes several illegal values (e.g., 0 and –42) for test purposes.

Listing 3-5b shows the MASM code for example Ch03_05. The extern g_ValMax:qword statement located near the top of file Ch03_05_fasm.asm is a MASM directive. This directive notifies the assembler that storage for global quadword value g_ValMax is defined in another module. The first code block in CalcSumCubes_a() verifies that argument n is valid. The test rdx,rdx (Logical Compare) instruction performs a bitwise logical AND of its two operands and sets the status flags in RFLAGS based on the result; the actual result is discarded. The ensuing jle BadArg instruction skips over the calculating code if n <= 0 is true. The next two instructions, cmp rdx,[g_ValMax] and jg BadArg, ensure that n > g_MaxVal is false. Note the use of the brackets in the cmp rdx,[g_ValMax] instruction, which as you saw earlier in this chapter signifies a memory operand. MASM also supports memory operand references sans the brackets (e.g., cmp rdx,g_ValMax). However, it is *strongly* recommended that brackets be used for all memory operands since they preclude potential syntactical and semantical ambiguities with other MASM symbolic names such as those defined in an equate (equ) statement. You'll learn how to use equate statements in Chapter 4.

Listing 3-5b. Example Ch03_05 MASM Code

```
;-----------------------------------------------------------------------
; Ch03_05_fasm.asm
;-----------------------------------------------------------------------


;-----------------------------------------------------------------------
; bool CalcSumCubes_a(int64_t* sum, int64_t n);
;-----------------------------------------------------------------------

        extern g_ValMax:qword

        .code
CalcSumCubes_a proc

; Make sure n is valid
        test rdx,rdx                    ;n <= 0?
        jle BadArg                      ;jump if yes
        cmp rdx,[g_ValMax]              ;n > g_ValMax?
        jg BadArg                       ;jump if yes

; Initialize
        xor r10,r10                     ;i = 0
        xor eax,eax                     ;sum = 0

; Calculate cube sum
Loop1:  add r10,1                       ;i += 1
        mov r11,r10                     ;r11 = i
        imul r11,r11                    ;r11 = i * i
        imul r11,r10                    ;r11 = i * i * i
        add rax,r11                     ;sum += i * i * i

        cmp r10,rdx                     ;i < n?
        jl Loop1                        ;jump if yes

Done:   mov [rcx],rax                   ;save final sum
        mov eax,1                       ;rc = true
        ret

BadArg: mov qword ptr [rcx],0           ;sum = 0 (error)
        xor eax,eax                     ;rc = false
        ret

CalcSumCubes_a endp
        end
```

The next code block in function CalcSumCubes_a(), xor r10,r10 and xor eax,eax, sets both i and sum equal to zero. Recall from earlier discussions that the xor eax,eax instruction sets register RAX to zero, but has a machine encoding that is one byte smaller than xor rax,rax. There is no space savings when performing operations like this using registers R8–R15; the machine encodings for both xor r10,r10 and xor r10d,r10d require three bytes.

The first instruction of for-loop Loop1, add r10,1, calculates i += 1. Loop index variable i is updated at the top of Loop1 since it precludes a loop-carried (or loop-carried data) dependency. A loop-carried dependency occurs when a for-loop uses a value calculated during a previous iteration (e.g., a[i] = a[i - 1] * 10). Avoiding loop-carried dependencies often results in faster code. It may also (depending on the processor's underlying microarchitecture) facilitate execution of multiple iterations of a for-loop simultaneously, especially in SIMD code. You'll see more examples of this in later chapters. Appendix B also contains some references that you can consult for more information about loop-carried dependencies.

Following execution of the add r10,1 instruction, CalcSumCubes_a() uses a mov r11,r10 instruction to copy i into register R11. The instruction pair that follows, imul r11,r11 and imul r11,r10, calculates i * i * i, and execution of the add rax,r11 instruction yields sum += i * i * i. The cmp r10,rdx instruction compares i against n. If i < n is true, the jl Loop1 instruction transfers program control back to the top of Loop1. Otherwise, the ensuing two instructions in CalcSumCubes_a(), mov [rcx],rax and mov eax,1, save the calculated sum value and set the return code to true.

Listing 3-5c shows the NASM code for example Ch03_05. Like most of the examples that you have already seen, the primary difference between this code and the MASM implementation is the specific register names. The other item of note is the cmp rsi,[g_ValMax] instruction. Recall the earlier recommendation that x86-64 NASM source code files always include a default rel directive to ensure RIP-relative memory addressing. Without this directive, the NASM keyword rel would be required in the cmp instruction (i.e., cmp rsi,[rel g_ValMax]). It also warrants mentioning here that NASM *requires* brackets for all instruction memory operands.

Listing 3-5c. Example Ch03_05 NASM Code

```
;-------------------------------------------------------------------------
; Ch03_05_fasm.s
;-------------------------------------------------------------------------

        %include "ModX86Asm3eNASM.inc"


;-------------------------------------------------------------------------
; bool CalcSumCubes_a(int64_t* sum, int64_t n);
;-------------------------------------------------------------------------

        section .text
        extern g_ValMax

        global CalcSumCubes_a
CalcSumCubes_a:

; Make sure n is valid
        test rsi,rsi                    ;n <= 0?
        jle BadArg                      ;jump if yes
        cmp rsi,[g_ValMax]              ;n > g_ValMax?
        jg BadArg                       ;jump if yes

; Initialize
        xor r10,r10                     ;i = 0
        xor eax,eax                     ;sum = 0

Loop1:  add r10,1                       ;i += 1
        mov r11,r10                     ;r11 = i
        imul r11,r11                    ;r11 = i * i
```

```
          imul r11,r10                  ;r11 = i * i * i
          add rax,r11                   ;sum += i * i * i

          cmp r10,rsi                   ;i < n?
          jl Loop1                      ;jump if yes

Done:     mov [rdi],rax                 ;save final sum
          mov eax,1                     ;rc = true
          ret

BadArg:   mov qword [rdi],0             ;sum = 0 (error)
          xor eax,eax                   ;rc = false
          ret
```

Here are the results for source code example Ch03_05:

```
----- Results for Ch03_05 -----

----- Test case #0 -----
n = 3
sum1 = 36
sum2 = 36

----- Test case #1 -----
n = 4
sum1 = 100
sum2 = 100

----- Test case #2 -----
n = 21
sum1 = 53361
sum2 = 53361

----- Test case #3 -----
n = 0
sum1 = error: 'n' is out of range
sum2 = error: 'n' is out of range

----- Test case #4 -----
n = 77935
sum1 = 9223193340756366400
sum2 = 9223193340756366400

----- Test case #5 -----
n = 77936
sum1 = error: 'n' is out of range
sum2 = error: 'n' is out of range
```

```
----- Test case #6 -----
n = 100
sum1 = 25502500
sum2 = 25502500

----- Test case #7 -----
n = -42
sum1 = error: 'n' is out of range
sum2 = error: 'n' is out of range
```

The x86-64 instruction set also includes the instructions inc (Increment by 1) and dec (Decrement by 1). These instructions add or subtract one from the specified operand. The machine encodings for both inc and dec are one byte smaller than an add or sub instruction with an immediate value of one. The drawback of using inc and dec is that they do not update RFLAGS.CF, which rules out their use in code that requires this flag. Both inc and dec update RFLAGS.OF, RFLAGS.SF, RFLAGS.ZF, RFLAGS.AF, and RFLAGS. PF according to the result. The add and sub instructions update these flags and RFLAGS.CF. The partial updating of the status flags in RFLAGS by inc and dec is slower on some processor microarchitectures. The use of an inc or dec instruction can also create an RFLAGS.CF data dependency if it's used before or after another instruction(s) that references or updates RFLAGS.CF. If speed is paramount, which is typically the principal reason for explicitly coding an assembly language function, a function should favor the use of an add or sub instruction with an immediate value of one instead of an inc or dec instruction.

Summary

Here are the key learning points for Chapter 3:

- A function can use the movsx and movsxd instructions to sign-extend an integer value. The movzx instruction can be used to zero-extend an integer value.

- A function can use the jcc conditional jump instruction to make run-time logic decisions. The cmovcc instruction can also be used to perform conditional moves.

- In MASM source code files, instructions that reference operands in memory should always use brackets around the memory operand (i.e., use mov eax,[MyVal] instead of mov eax,MyVal).

- The test instruction is often used as an alternative to the cmp instruction, especially when testing a value to ascertain if it's less than, equal to, or greater than zero.

- The x86-64 instruction set supports a variety of different address modes for accessing operands stored in memory. Computational requirements and register availability typically guide which mode is best to use.

- The Visual C++ run-time calling convention requires a calling function to pass the first four 64-bit integer arguments to function using registers RCX, RDX, R8, or R9. Small integer values are passed using the low-order bits of the corresponding 64-bit register (e.g., ECX, CX, or CL for a 32-, 16-, or 8-bit integer). Any additional arguments are passed via the stack.

- The Visual C++ run-time calling convention requires a calling function to allocate a 32-byte home area on the stack. The called function can use this space to save its argument register values or store other temporary data.

- The GNU C++ run-time calling convention requires a calling function to pass the first six 64-bit integer arguments to function using registers RDI, RSI, RDX, RCX, R8, or R9. Small integer values are passed using the low-order bits of the corresponding 64-bit register. Any additional arguments are passed via the stack.

- The GNU C++ run-time calling convention permits a leaf function to use the stack red zone area for temporary storage.

- The MASM directives .const and .data denote the start of memory section that contains read-only or read-write data. The corresponding NASM directives are section .rdata and section .data. Both assemblers support the use of the directives dq, dd, dw, and db to allocate and initialize data values in these sections.

- MASM functions can use the [qword | dword | word | byte] ptr operator to specify the size of a 64-, 32-, 16-, or 8-bit operand in memory. The corresponding NASM keywords are qword, dword, word, and byte.

- In performance-critical code, favor the use of an add or sub instruction with an immediate value of one when performing an increment or decrement operation. Minimize the use of the inc and dec instructions unless code space is a concern.

CHAPTER 4

■ ■ ■

X86-64 Core Programming – Part 3

In the previous chapter, you learned important new details regarding core x86-64 assembly language programming including memory addressing modes and argument passing via the stack. You also studied x86-64 conditional jump and move instructions. Perhaps most importantly, you learned how to code a basic for-loop using x86-64 assembly language.

The chapter that you are about to read completes your introduction to core x86-64 assembly language programming. It begins with a triplet of source code examples that illustrate operations and calculations using arrays and matrices. This is followed by several examples that demonstrate the use of x86-64 string instructions. The final example explains how to arrange and manipulate an x86-64 assembly language structure. Throughout this chapter, you'll also discover helpful particulars regarding the Visual C++ and GNU C++ calling conventions and how to employ additional x86-64 assembly language instructions and assembler directives.

Arrays

Arrays are an indispensable data construct in virtually all programming languages. In C++, there is an inherent connection between a built-in (C-style) array and a pointer since the name of an array is essentially a pointer to its first element. Moreover, whenever an array is used as a C++ function parameter, the compiler passes a pointer to the array instead of creating a duplicate copy on the stack or heap. Pointers are also utilized for arrays that are dynamically allocated at run-time. This section presents x86-64 assembly language code that processes arrays. The first two source code examples demonstrate common operations using one-dimensional arrays. This is followed by an example that explicates the techniques necessary to access the elements of a two-dimensional array.

One-Dimensional Arrays

In C++, one-dimensional arrays are stored in a contiguous block of memory that can be statically allocated at compile time or dynamically allocated during program execution. The elements of a C++ array are accessed using zero-based indexing, which means that valid indices for an array of size *N* range from *0* to *N – 1*.

Listing 4-1a shows the C++ source code for example Ch04_01. This listing includes a C++ function named SumElementsI32_cpp(), which sums the elements of an int32_t array. When developing assembly language code, it is often worthwhile (especially for complex calculations) to code both a C++ and an assembly language version of the same calculating function. The former can be used to confirm the correctness of the assembly language code. C++ function implementations can also be exploited for benchmarking purposes. You'll learn more about this in Chapter 10.

© Daniel Kusswurm 2023
D. Kusswurm, *Modern X86 Assembly Language Programming*,
https://doi.org/10.1007/978-1-4842-9603-5_4

Listing 4-1a. Example Ch04_01 C++ Code

```
//-----------------------------------------------------------------------------
// Ch04_01.h
//-----------------------------------------------------------------------------

#pragma once
#include <cstddef>
#include <cstdint>

// Ch04_01_fasm.asm, Ch04_01_fasm.s
extern "C" int64_t SumElementsI32_a(const int32_t* x, size_t n);

// Ch04_01_fcpp.cpp
extern int64_t SumElementsI32_cpp(const int32_t* x, size_t n);

// Ch04_01_misc.cpp
extern void FillArray(int32_t* x, size_t n);
extern void DisplayResults(const int32_t* x, size_t n, int64_t sum1, int64_t sum2);

//-----------------------------------------------------------------------------
// Ch04_01_misc.cpp
//-----------------------------------------------------------------------------

#include <iostream>
#include <iomanip>
#include "Ch04_01.h"
#include "MT.h"

void FillArray(int32_t* x, size_t n)
{
    constexpr int max_val = 1000;
    constexpr int min_val = -max_val;
    constexpr unsigned int rng_seed = 1337;

    MT::FillArray(x, n, min_val, max_val, rng_seed, true);
}

void DisplayResults(const int32_t* x, size_t n, int64_t sum1, int64_t sum2)
{
    constexpr char nl = '\n';

    std::cout << "----- Results for Ch04_01 -----\n";

    for (size_t i = 0; i < n; i++)
        std::cout << "x[" << i << "] = " << x[i] << nl;
    std::cout << nl;

    std::cout << "sum1 = " << sum1 << nl;
    std::cout << "sum2 = " << sum2 << nl;
}
```

```
//-----------------------------------------------------------------------------
// Ch04_01_fcpp.cpp
//-----------------------------------------------------------------------------

#include "Ch04_01.h"

int64_t SumElementsI32_cpp(const int32_t* x, size_t n)
{
    int64_t sum = 0;

    for (size_t i = 0; i < n; i++)
        sum += x[i];

    return sum;
}

//-----------------------------------------------------------------------------
// Ch04_01.cpp
//-----------------------------------------------------------------------------

#include "Ch04_01.h"

int main(void)
{
    constexpr size_t n = 20;
    int32_t x[n];

    FillArray(x, n);

    int64_t sum1 = SumElementsI32_cpp(x, n);
    int64_t sum2 = SumElementsI32_a(x, n);

    DisplayResults(x, n, sum1, sum2);
    return 0;
}
```

There are two other items in Listing 4-1a that warrant comments. First, note that size_t is used in the declarations of functions SumElementsI32_a() and SumElementsI32_cpp() for argument value n. For 64-bit executable files generated using Visual C++ and GNU C++, the size_t data type corresponds to an unsigned 64-bit integer. Second, examine the code for function FillArray() in file Ch04_01_misc.cpp. This function fills the specified array with random values. Function FillArray() uses template function MT::FillArray() to perform the actual fill. The source code for namespace MT (short for miscellaneous templates) is not shown in Listing 4-1a but is included in the downloadable software package. Other examples in this and subsequent chapters also make use of the helper template functions in namespace MT.

Listing 4-1b shows the MASM code for example Ch04_01. The opening code block of this function begins with an xor eax,eax instruction that initializes sum = 0. This is followed by a sub rcx,4 instruction, which loads the address of x[-1] into register RCX. The reason for doing this is that the first instruction of for-loop Loop1 updates register RCX so that it points to x[i]. Recall from the discussions in Chapter 3 that updating a pointer or index variable at the top of a for-loop precludes a loop-carried dependency condition. Following the requisite initializations, an or rdx,rdx instruction verifies that n == 0 is false. If n == 0 is true, the ensuing jz Done instruction skips over the code in Loop1.

Listing 4-1b. Example Ch04_01 MASM Code

```
;-----------------------------------------------------------------------
; Ch04_01_fasm.asm
;-----------------------------------------------------------------------


;-----------------------------------------------------------------------
; int64_t SumElementsI32_a(const int32_t* x, size_t n);
;-----------------------------------------------------------------------

            .code
SumElementsI32_a proc

; Perform required initializations
        xor eax,eax                     ;sum = 0
        sub rcx,4                       ;rcx = &x[-1]

; Make sure n is valid
        or rdx,rdx                      ;n == 0?
        jz Done                         ;jump if yes

; Sum the elements of x[]
Loop1:  add rcx,4                       ;rcx points to next element in x[]

        movsxd r11,dword ptr [rcx]      ;load (sign-extended) element from x[]
        add rax,r11                     ;update sum in rax

        sub rdx,1                       ;n -= 1
        jnz Loop1                       ;repeat until n is zero

Done:   ret                             ;return to caller

SumElementsI32_A endp
        end
```

Each iteration for Loop1 begins with an add rcx,4 instruction. Execution of this instruction points RCX to the next element in array x (i.e., x[i]). The add instruction uses an immediate value of four since the size of each int32_t element in array x is four bytes. The next instruction, movsxd r11,dword ptr [rcx], loads a sign-extended copy of x[i] into register R11. This is followed by an add rax,r11 instruction that calculates sum += x[i]. The subsequent sub rdx,1 instruction computes n -= 1, and the ensuing jnz Loop1 instruction ensures that Loop1 repeats until n == 0 is true. Note that following execution of Loop1, the calculated sum is already in register RAX, so an extra mov instruction is unnecessary.

Listing 4-1c shows the NASM code for example Ch04_01. The only difference between this code and the MASM code is the register names.

Listing 4-1c. Example Ch04_01 NASM Code

```
;-------------------------------------------------------------------------------
; Ch04_01_fasm.s
;-------------------------------------------------------------------------------

        %include "ModX86Asm3eNASM.inc"

;-------------------------------------------------------------------------------
; int64_t SumElementsI32_a(const int32_t* x, uint64_t n);
;-------------------------------------------------------------------------------

        section .text

        global SumElementsI32_a
SumElementsI32_a:

; Perform required initializations
        xor eax,eax                     ;sum = 0
        sub rdi,4                       ;rdi = &x[-1]

; Make sure n is valid
        or rsi,rsi                      ;n == 0?
        jz Done                         ;jump if yes

; Sum the elements of the array
Loop1:  add rdi,4                       ;rdi points to next element in x[]

        movsxd r11,dword [rdi]          ;load (sign-extended) element from x[]
        add rax,r11                     ;update sum in rax

        sub rsi,1                       ;n -= 1
        jnz Loop1                       ;repeat until n is zero

Done:   ret                             ;return to caller
```

Here are the results for source code example Ch04_01:

```
----- Results for Ch04_01 -----
x[0] = -476
x[1] = 121
x[2] = -683
x[3] = -575
x[4] = -444
x[5] = 86
x[6] = -81
x[7] = -933
x[8] = -358
x[9] = -529
x[10] = 37
x[11] = 184
```

```
x[12] = -476
x[13] = -330
x[14] = 953
x[15] = -459
x[16] = 466
x[17] = -385
x[18] = -770
x[19] = 605

sum1 = -4047
sum2 = -4047
```

You may have noticed that the C++ const modifier was used with array x in the declarations of both SumElementsI32_a() and SumElementsI32_cpp(). A C++ compiler will, of course, flag an error if it detects any code that attempts to modify a const value. An assembler, however, performs no such check. It is the programmer's responsibility to ensure that only non-constant variables are modified. Modifying a const data value in an assembly language program may cause a difficult-to-trace bug. It could also trigger a processor exception if the variable is allocated in a read-only section of memory.

Multiple One-Dimensional Arrays

It is often necessary to carry out a computation using multiple arrays. The next source code example, named Ch04_02, demonstrates how to do this. Listing 4-2a shows the C++ source code for example Ch04_02.

Listing 4-2a. Example Ch04_02 C++ Code

```
//-----------------------------------------------------------------------
// Ch04_02.h
//-----------------------------------------------------------------------

#pragma once
#include <cstddef>
#include <cstdint>

// Ch04_02_fasm.asm, Ch04_02_fasm.s
extern "C" void CalcArrayVals_a(int64_t* c, const int64_t* a, const int64_t* b,
    size_t n);

// Ch04_02_fcpp.cpp
extern void CalcArrayVals_cpp(int64_t* c, const int64_t* a, const int64_t* b,
    size_t n);

// Ch04_02_misc.cpp
extern void FillArrays(int64_t* c1, int64_t* c2, int64_t* a, int64_t* b, size_t n);

extern void DisplayResults(const int64_t* c1, const int64_t* c2, const int64_t* a,
    const int64_t* b, size_t n);
```

```cpp
//----------------------------------------------------------------------------
// Ch04_02_misc.cpp
//----------------------------------------------------------------------------

#include <iostream>
#include <iomanip>
#include <cstring>
#include "Ch04_02.h"
#include "MT.h"

void FillArrays(int64_t* c1, int64_t* c2, int64_t* a, int64_t* b, size_t n)
{
    constexpr int max_val = 1000;
    constexpr int min_val = -max_val;
    constexpr unsigned int rng_seed = 1001;

    MT::FillArray(a, n, min_val, max_val, rng_seed, true);
    MT::FillArray(b, n, min_val, max_val, rng_seed / 7, true);

    memset(c1, 0, sizeof(int64_t) * n);
    memset(c2, 0, sizeof(int64_t) * n);
}

void DisplayResults(const int64_t* c1, const int64_t* c2, const int64_t* a,
    const int64_t* b, size_t n)
{
    std::cout << "----- Results for Ch04_02 -----\n";

    for (size_t i = 0; i < n; i++)
    {
        std::cout << "a[" << std::setw(2) << i << "]: " << std::setw(8) << a[i];
        std::cout << "   ";
        std::cout << "b[" << std::setw(2) << i << "]: " << std::setw(8) << b[i];
        std::cout << "   ";
        std::cout << "c1[" << std::setw(2) << i << "]: " << std::setw(8) << c1[i];
        std::cout << "   ";
        std::cout << "c2[" << std::setw(2) << i << "]: " << std::setw(8) << c2[i];
        std::cout << '\n';

        if (c1[i] != c2[i])
        {
            std::cout << "array element compare failed\n";
            break;
        }
    }
}
```

```
//----------------------------------------------------------------------------
// Ch04_02_fcpp.cpp
//----------------------------------------------------------------------------

#include "Ch04_02.h"

void CalcArrayVals_cpp(int64_t* c, const int64_t* a, const int64_t* b, size_t n)
{
    for (size_t i = 0; i < n; i++)
        c[i] = (a[i] * 25) / (b[i] + 10);
}

//----------------------------------------------------------------------------
// Ch04_02.cpp
//----------------------------------------------------------------------------

#include "Ch04_02.h"

int main()
{
    constexpr size_t n = 20;
    int64_t a[n], b[n], c1[n], c2[n];

    FillArrays(c1, c2, a, b, n);

    CalcArrayVals_cpp(c1, a, b, n);
    CalcArrayVals_a(c2, a, b, n);

    DisplayResults(c1, c2, a, b, n);
    return 0;
}
```

In Listing 4-2a, C++ function CalcArrayVals_cpp() computes c[i] = (a[i] * 25) / (b[i] + 10). The arithmetic expression computed by this function is arbitrary and inconsequential. What is important is that the expression references the *i-th* element of three distinct arrays. The assembly language code that you'll see shortly performs the same calculation. The remaining C++ code in Listing 4-2a performs test case initializations, exercises the C++ and assembly language calculating functions, and streams results to std::cout.

Listing 4-2b shows the MASM code for example Ch04_02.

Listing 4-2b. Example Ch04_02 MASM Code

```
;----------------------------------------------------------------------------
; Ch04_02_fasm.asm
;----------------------------------------------------------------------------

;----------------------------------------------------------------------------
; void CalcArrayVals_a(int64_t* c, const int64_t* a, const int64_t* b, size_t n);
;----------------------------------------------------------------------------
```

```
        .code
CalcArrayVals_a proc frame
        push r12                         ;save non-volatile register r12
        .pushreg r12
        .endprolog

; Make sure n is valid
        or r9,r9                         ;n == 0?
        jz Done                          ;jump if yes

; Initialize
        mov r10,rdx                      ;r10 = ptr to a[]
        mov r11,-8                       ;r11 = common offset for arrays

; Calculate c[i] = a[i] * 25) / (b[i] + 10);
Loop1:  add r11,8                        ;r11 = offset for a[i], b[i], and c[i]

        mov rax,[r10+r11]                ;rax = a[i]
        imul rax,rax,25                  ;rax = a[i] * 25

        mov r12,[r8+r11]                 ;r12 = b[i]
        add r12,10                       ;r12 = b[i] + 10

        cqo                              ;rdx:rax = a[i] * 25
        idiv r12                         ;rax = (a[i] * 25) / (b[i] + 10)

        mov [rcx+r11],rax                ;save quotient to c[i]

        sub r9,1                         ;n -= 1
        jnz Loop1                        ;repeat until n == 0

        pop r12                          ;restore r12
Done:   ret                              ;return to caller

CalcArrayVals_a endp
        end
```

You may have noticed that in the source code examples presented thus far, the assembly language functions have used only a subset of the processor's general-purpose registers. The reason for this is that both the Visual C++ and GNU C++ run-time calling conventions designate each general-purpose register as either volatile or non-volatile. Functions are permitted to alter the contents of any volatile register but cannot modify a non-volatile register unless it preserves the caller's original value. The Visual C++ calling convention designates registers RSI, RDI, RBP, RSP, R12, R13, R14, and R15 as non-volatile; the remaining general-purpose registers are classified as volatile. The GNU C++ calling convention uses the same non-volatile registers except for RSI and RDI, which are classified as volatile.

Function CalcArrayVals_a() in Listing 4-2b uses non-volatile register R12, which means that its value must be preserved. A function typically saves the values of any non-volatile registers it uses on the stack in a section of code called the prologue. A function epilogue contains code that restores the values of any saved non-volatile registers. Function prologues and epilogues are also used to perform other calling convention-related tasks, and you'll learn more about these in Chapter 6.

In Listing 4-2b, the statement CalcArrayVals_a proc frame denotes the beginning of function CalcArrayValues_a(). Note that the proc directive includes a frame attribute. This attribute signifies that CalcArrayValues_a() utilizes a formal function prologue. It also enables additional MASM directives that must be used whenever a general-purpose register is saved on the stack or when a function employs a stack frame pointer. Chapter 6 discusses the frame attribute and stack frame pointers in greater detail.

The first x86-64 assembly language instruction of CalcArrayVal_a() is push r12 (Push Value onto Stack), which saves the current value in register R12 on the stack. Immediately following this is the MASM directive .pushreg r12. This directive instructs MASM to save information about the push r12 instruction in an assembler-maintained table that is used to unwind the stack during exception processing. Using exceptions with assembly language code is not discussed in this book; however, the Visual C++ calling convention requirements for saving registers on the stack must still be observed. The next statement, .endprolog, is another MASM directive that signifies the end of the prologue for CalcArrayVal_a(). Figure 4-1 shows the contents of the stack and argument registers following execution of the prologue code.

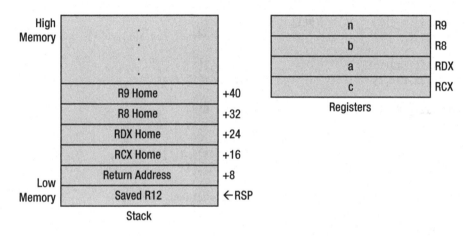

Figure 4-1. *Stack and register contents following execution of prologue in* CalcArrayVals_a()

In the first code block that follows the prologue, the instruction pair or r9,r9 and jz Done ensures that for-loop Loop1 is skipped if n == 0 is true. The next instruction, mov r10,rdx, copies argument value a into register R10 since RDX is needed to perform signed integer division later in Loop1. This is followed by a mov r11,-8 instruction. In Loop1, R11 is used as a common offset (i.e., index variable i) for arrays a, b, and c.

Each iteration of Loop1 begins with an add r11,8 instruction, which updates the common offset value in register R11 for the next set of elements from arrays a, b, and c. An immediate value of eight is used since the size of each int64_t array element value is eight bytes. The next instruction, mov rax,[r10+r11], loads argument value a[i] into register RAX. Recall that R10 points to the start of array a and R11 contains the offset to the current element. The ensuing imul rax,rax,25 instruction calculates a[i] * 25. This is followed by the instruction pair mov r12,[r8+r11] and add r12,10, which calculates b[i] + 10.

Execution continues with a cqo instruction. This instruction sign-extends the quadword value in RAX (a[i] * 25) to a double quadword value in register pair RDX:RAX. The subsequent idiv r12 instruction calculates (a[i] * 25) / (b[i] + 10). The idiv instruction saves the resultant quotient and remainder in registers RAX and RDX, respectively. The next instruction, mov [rcx+r11],rax, saves the calculated quotient to c[i]; the remainder is not saved. The final instruction pair of Loop1, sub r9,1 and jnz Loop1, guarantees that execution of Loop1 continues until n == 0 is true.

Just before the ret instruction is a pop r12 (Pop Value from Stack) instruction. Execution of a pop instruction copies the quadword value pointed by RSP into the specified operand register. It also adds eight to the value in RSP, which removes the just copied value from the stack. Following execution of the pop r12 instruction, RSP points to the return address. This is necessary for correct execution of the ensuing ret instruction. You'll see more examples of stack use later in this and subsequent chapters. Until then, it is important to always remember that stack operations are potentially hazardous. Failure to properly save or restore a non-volatile register is likely to cause a program crash (if the return address is invalid) or a subtle software bug that may be difficult to pinpoint.

Listing 4-2c shows the NASM code for example Ch04_02. The primary difference between this code and the MASM code in Listing 4-2b is the lack of a prologue. Recall the GNU C++ calling convention designates registers RSI and RDI as volatile. This means that enough volatile registers are available to carry out the required calculations without having to use any non-volatile registers.

Listing 4-2c. Example Ch04_02 NASM Code

```
;-----------------------------------------------------------------------
; Ch04_02_fasm.s
;-----------------------------------------------------------------------

        %include "ModX86Asm3eNASM.inc"

;-----------------------------------------------------------------------
; void CalcArrayVals_a(int64_t* c, const int64_t* a, const int64_t* b, size_t n);
;-----------------------------------------------------------------------

        section .text

        global CalcArrayVals_a
CalcArrayVals_a:

; Make sure n is valid
        or rcx,rcx                      ;n == 0?
        jz Done                         ;jump if yes

; Initialize
        mov r8,rdx                      ;r8 = ptr to b[]
        mov r11,-8                      ;r11 = common offset for arrays

; Calculate c[i] = a[i] * 25) / (b[i] + 10);
Loop1:  add r11,8                       ;r11 = offset for a[i], b[i], and c[i]

        mov rax,[rsi+r11]               ;rax = a[i]
        imul rax,rax,25                 ;rax = a[i] * 25

        mov r9,[r8+r11]                 ;r9 = b[i]
        add r9,10                       ;r9 = b[i] + 10

        cqo                             ;rdx:rax = a[i] * 25
        idiv r9                         ;rax = (a[i] * 25) / (b[i] + 10)

        mov [rdi+r11],rax               ;save quotient to c[i]

        sub rcx,1                       ;n -= 1
        jnz Loop1                       ;repeat until n == 0

Done:   ret                             ;return to caller
```

Here are the results for source code example Ch04_02:

```
----- Results for Ch04_02 -----
a[ 0]:    -388  b[ 0]:    476  c1[ 0]:    -19  c2[ 0]:    -19
a[ 1]:    -241  b[ 1]:    547  c1[ 1]:    -10  c2[ 1]:    -10
a[ 2]:    -470  b[ 2]:   -320  c1[ 2]:     37  c2[ 2]:     37
a[ 3]:     103  b[ 3]:    832  c1[ 3]:      3  c2[ 3]:      3
a[ 4]:    -608  b[ 4]:    -64  c1[ 4]:    281  c2[ 4]:    281
a[ 5]:    -545  b[ 5]:    677  c1[ 5]:    -19  c2[ 5]:    -19
a[ 6]:    -139  b[ 6]:   -152  c1[ 6]:     24  c2[ 6]:     24
a[ 7]:    -120  b[ 7]:   -456  c1[ 7]:      6  c2[ 7]:      6
a[ 8]:    -954  b[ 8]:    137  c1[ 8]:   -162  c2[ 8]:   -162
a[ 9]:    -131  b[ 9]:   -321  c1[ 9]:     10  c2[ 9]:     10
a[10]:    -609  b[10]:    763  c1[10]:    -19  c2[10]:    -19
a[11]:     652  b[11]:     25  c1[11]:    465  c2[11]:    465
a[12]:    -295  b[12]:   -934  c1[12]:      7  c2[12]:      7
a[13]:    -511  b[13]:    -91  c1[13]:    157  c2[13]:    157
a[14]:    -554  b[14]:   -983  c1[14]:     14  c2[14]:     14
a[15]:     262  b[15]:    375  c1[15]:     17  c2[15]:     17
a[16]:     227  b[16]:   -602  c1[16]:     -9  c2[16]:     -9
a[17]:     100  b[17]:   -873  c1[17]:     -2  c2[17]:     -2
a[18]:     161  b[18]:   -666  c1[18]:     -6  c2[18]:     -6
a[19]:     438  b[19]:    450  c1[19]:     23  c2[19]:     23
```

Table 4-1 summarizes what you have learned thus far regarding the x86-64 general-purpose registers and the two C++ calling conventions. You'll learn additional details about the calling convention requirements for general-purpose registers, including important usage deviations, in Chapters 5 and 6.

Table 4-1. *Summary of General-Purpose Registers and C++ Calling Conventions*

Register	VC++ Use	VC++ Type	GNU C++ Use	GNU C++ Type
RAX	Integer return value	Volatile	Integer return value	Volatile
RBX	-----	Non-volatile	-----	Non-volatile
RCX	Integer argument #1	Volatile	Integer argument #4	Volatile
RDX	Integer argument #2	Volatile	Integer argument #3	Volatile
RSI	-----	Non-volatile	Integer argument #2	Volatile
RDI	-----	Non-volatile	Integer argument #1	Volatile
RBP	Optional frame pointer	Non-volatile	Optional frame pointer	Non-volatile
RSP	Stack pointer	Non-volatile	Stack pointer	Non-volatile
R8	Integer argument #3	Volatile	Integer argument #5	Volatile
R9	Integer argument #4	Volatile	Integer argument #6	Volatile

(*continued*)

Table 4-1. (*continued*)

Register	VC++ Use	VC++ Type	GNU C++ Use	GNU C++ Type
R10	-----	Volatile	-----	Volatile
R11	-----	Volatile	-----	Volatile
R12	-----	Non-volatile	-----	Non-volatile
R13	-----	Non-volatile	-----	Non-volatile
R14	-----	Non-volatile	-----	Non-volatile
R15	-----	Non-volatile	-----	Non-volatile

Two-Dimensional Arrays

C++ also utilizes a contiguous block of memory to implement a two-dimensional array or matrix. The elements of a C++ matrix in memory are organized using row-major ordering. Row-major ordering arranges the elements of a matrix first by row and then by column. For example, elements of matrix int x[3][2] are stored in memory as follows: x[0][0], x[0][1], x[1][0], x[1][1], x[2][0], and x[2][1]. To access a specific element in a matrix, an assembly language function (or C++ compiler) must know the starting address of the matrix (i.e., the address of its first element), the row and column indices, the total number of columns, and the size in bytes of each element. Using this information, a function can use simple integer arithmetic to access a specific element in a matrix as exemplified by the source code example presented in this section.

Listing 4-3a shows the C++ source code for example Ch04_03, which demonstrates how to access the elements in a matrix of int32_t values. In this listing, file Ch04_03_fcpp.cpp contains a function named CalcMat2dSquares_cpp(). This function, and its counterpart assembly language function, calculates y[i][j] = x[j][i] * x[j][i]. Note that the indices in this expression for matrix x are intentionally reversed to make the code for this example a bit more interesting.

Listing 4-3a. Example Ch04_03 C++ Code

```
//-----------------------------------------------------------------------------
// Ch04_03.h
//-----------------------------------------------------------------------------

#pragma once
#include <cstddef>
#include <cstdint>

// Ch04_03_fasm.asm, Ch04_03_fasm.s
extern "C" void CalcMat2dSquares_a(int32_t* y, const int32_t* x, size_t m,
    size_t n);

// Ch04_03_fcpp.cpp
extern void CalcMat2dSquares_cpp(int32_t* y, const int32_t* x, size_t m,
    size_t n);

// Ch04_03_misc.cpp
extern void DisplayResults(const int32_t* y1, const int32_t* y2, const int32_t* x,
    size_t m, size_t n);
```

```cpp
//----------------------------------------------------------------------------
// Ch04_03_misc.cpp
//----------------------------------------------------------------------------

#include <iostream>
#include <iomanip>
#include "Ch04_03.h"

void DisplayResults(const int32_t* y1, const int32_t* y2, const int32_t* x,
    size_t m, size_t n)
{
    std::cout << "----- Results for Ch04_03 -----\n";

    for (size_t i = 0; i < m; i++)
    {
        for (size_t j = 0; j < n; j++)
        {
            size_t kx = j * m + i;
            size_t ky = i * n + j;

            std::cout << "x[" << std::setw(2) << j << "][" << std::setw(2) << i << "] = ";
            std::cout << std::setw(6) << x[kx] << "    ";

            std::cout << "y1[" << std::setw(2) << i << "][" << std::setw(2) << j << "] = ";
            std::cout << std::setw(6) << y1[ky] << "    ";

            std::cout << "y2[" << std::setw(2) << i << "][" << std::setw(2) << j << "] = ";
            std::cout << std::setw(6) << y2[ky] << '\n';

            if (y1[ky] != y2[ky])
            {
                std::cout << "\nmatrix element compare failed\n";
                break;
            }
        }
    }
}

//----------------------------------------------------------------------------
// Ch04_03_fcpp.cpp
//----------------------------------------------------------------------------

#include "Ch04_03.h"

void CalcMat2dSquares_cpp(int32_t* y, const int32_t* x, size_t m, size_t n)
{
    // Calculate y[i][i] = x[j][i] * x[j][i]

    for (size_t i = 0; i < m; i++)
    {
        for (size_t j = 0; j < n; j++)
```

```
        {
            size_t kx = j * m + i;
            size_t ky = i * n + j;

            y[ky] = x[kx] * x[kx];
        }
    }
}

//-----------------------------------------------------------------------
// Ch04_03.cpp
//-----------------------------------------------------------------------

#include <iostream>
#include "Ch04_03.h"

int main()
{
    constexpr size_t m = 6;
    constexpr size_t n = 3;
    constexpr int32_t x[n][m]
    {
      { 1, 2, 3, 4, 5, 6 },
      { 7, 8, 9, 10, 11, 12 },
      { 13, 14, 15, 16, 17, 18 }
    };

    int32_t y1[m][n], y2[m][n];

    CalcMat2dSquares_cpp(&y1[0][0], &x[0][0], m, n);
    CalcMat2dSquares_a(&y2[0][0], &x[0][0], m, n);

    DisplayResults(&y1[0][0], &y2[0][0], &x[0][0], m, n);
    return 0;
}
```

In function CalcMat2dSquares_cpp(), arguments x and y point the matrices in memory. The size of matrix x is n × m, while matrix y is m × n. Function CalcMat2dSquares_cpp() uses two nested for-loops to carry out the required calculation. Inside the inner for-loop, the expression kx = j * m + i calculates the offset for element x[j][i]. Similarly, the expression ky = i * n + j calculates the offset for element y[i][j].

Listing 4-3b shows the MASM code for example Ch04_03. Like the previous example, function CalcMat2dSquares_a() includes a function prologue that saves non-volatile register R12 on the stack. The next code block verifies that both m and n are not equal to zero, while the ensuing xor r10,r10 instruction sets i = 0.

Listing 4-3b. Example Ch04_03 MASM Code

```
;----------------------------------------------------------------------
; Ch04_03_fasm.asm
;----------------------------------------------------------------------


;----------------------------------------------------------------------
; void CalcMat2dSquares_a(int32_t* y, const int32_t* x, size_t m, size_t n);
;----------------------------------------------------------------------


        .code
CalcMat2dSquares_a proc frame
        push r12                         ;save caller's r12
        .pushreg r12
        .endprolog

; Make sure m and n are valid
        test r8,r8
        jz InvalidSize                   ;jump if m == 0
        test r9,r9
        jz InvalidSize                   ;jump if n == 0

;----------------------------------------------------------------------
; Register use in code below:
;
; rcx = y   rdx = x     r8 = m          r9 = n
; r10 = i   r11 = j     r12 = scratch   rax = scratch
;----------------------------------------------------------------------

; Initalize
        xor r10,r10                      ;i = 0

; Loop1 is outer for-loop, Loop2 is inner for-loop
Loop1:  xor r11,r11                      ;j = 0

; Calculate x[j][i] * x[j][i]
Loop2:  mov rax,r11                      ;rax = j
        imul rax,r8                      ;rax = j * m
        add rax,r10                      ;rax = j * m + i (kx)

        mov r12d,[rdx+rax*4]             ;r12d = x[j][i]
        imul r12d,r12d                   ;r12d = x[j][i] * x[j][i]

; Set y[i][j] = x[j][i] * x[j][i]
        mov rax,r10                      ;rax = i
        imul rax,r9                      ;rax = i * n
        add rax,r11                      ;rax = i * n + j (ky)

        mov [rcx+rax*4],r12d             ;save y[i][j]
```

```
; Update inner for-loop counter
        add r11,1                           ;j += 1
        cmp r11,r9
        jb Loop2                            ;jump if j < n

; Update outer for-loop counter
        add r10,1                           ;i += 1
        cmp r10,r8
        jb Loop1                            ;jump if i < m

InvalidSize:
        pop r12                             ;restore r12
        ret


CalcMat2dSquares_a endp
        end
```

The first instruction of for-loop Loop1, xor r11,r11, initializes j = 0. Each iteration of for-loop Loop2 begins with the instruction triplet mov rax,r11, imul rax,r8, and add rax,r10, which calculates kx = j * m + i. The next instruction, mov r12d,[rdx+rax*4], loads x[j][i] into register R12D. The mov instruction uses a scale factor of four since the size of each int32_t element in matrix x is four bytes. This is followed by an imul r12d,r12d instruction that calculates x[j][i] * x[j][i].

In the code block that follows, function CalcMat2dSquares_a() uses a similar sequence of instructions to calculate ky = i * n + j. It then executes a mov [rcx+rax*4],r12d instruction to complete the calculation of y[i][j] = x[j][i] * x[j][i]. The ensuing instruction triplet add r11,1, cmp r11,r9, and jb Loop2 updates index variable j and ensures that Loop2 repeats until j < n is false. A similar instruction triplet is employed for Loop1 index variable i.

Listing 4-3c shows the NASM code for example Ch04_03.

Listing 4-3c. Example Ch04_03 NASM Code

```
;-------------------------------------------------------------------------------
; Ch04_03_fasm.s
;-------------------------------------------------------------------------------

        %include "ModX86Asm3eNASM.inc"


;-------------------------------------------------------------------------------
; void CalcMat2dSquares_a(int32_t* y, const int32_t* x, size_t m, size_t n);
;-------------------------------------------------------------------------------

        section .text

        global CalcMat2dSquares_a
CalcMat2dSquares_a:

; Make sure m and n are valid
        test rdx,rdx
        jz InvalidSize                      ;jump if m == 0
        test rcx,rcx
        jz InvalidSize                      ;jump if n == 0
```

```
;----------------------------------------------------------------------
; Register use in code below:
;
; rdi = y    rsi = x      rdx = m        rcx = n
; r8 = i     r9 = j       r10 = tempval  rax = tempval
;----------------------------------------------------------------------

; Initalize
        xor r8,r8                        ;i = 0

; Loop1 is outer for-loop, Loop2 is inner for-loop
Loop1:  xor r9,r9                        ;j = 0

; Calculate x[j][i] * x[j][i]
Loop2:  mov rax,r9                       ;rax = j
        imul rax,rdx                     ;rax = j * m
        add rax,r8                       ;rax = j * m + i (kx)

        mov r10d,[rsi+rax*4]             ;r10d = x[j][i]
        imul r10d,r10d                   ;r10d = x[j][i] * x[j][i]

; Set y[i][j] = x[j][i] * x[j][i]
        mov rax,r8                       ;rax = i
        imul rax,rcx                     ;rax = i * n
        add rax,r9                       ;rax = i * n + j (ky)

        mov [rdi+rax*4],r10d             ;save y[i][j]

; Update inner for-loop counter
        add r9,1                         ;j += 1
        cmp r9,rcx
        jb Loop2                         ;jump if j < n

; Update outer for-loop counter
        add r8,1                         ;i += 1
        cmp r8,rdx
        jb Loop1                         ;jump if i < m

InvalidSize:
        ret
```

Other than different registers, the calculating code in Listing 4-3c matches the MASM code that's shown in Listing 4-3b. Note that the NASM version of CalcMat2dSquares_a() doesn't preserve any non-volatile register on the stack since enough volatile registers are available to carry out the required calculations. Here are the results for source code example Ch04_03:

```
----- Results for Ch04_03 -----
x[ 0][ 0] =       1   y1[ 0][ 0] =       1   y2[ 0][ 0] =       1
x[ 1][ 0] =       7   y1[ 0][ 1] =      49   y2[ 0][ 1] =      49
x[ 2][ 0] =      13   y1[ 0][ 2] =     169   y2[ 0][ 2] =     169
x[ 0][ 1] =       2   y1[ 1][ 0] =       4   y2[ 1][ 0] =       4
```

```
x[ 1][ 1] =      8   y1[ 1][ 1] =     64   y2[ 1][ 1] =     64
x[ 2][ 1] =     14   y1[ 1][ 2] =    196   y2[ 1][ 2] =    196
x[ 0][ 2] =      3   y1[ 2][ 0] =      9   y2[ 2][ 0] =      9
x[ 1][ 2] =      9   y1[ 2][ 1] =     81   y2[ 2][ 1] =     81
x[ 2][ 2] =     15   y1[ 2][ 2] =    225   y2[ 2][ 2] =    225
x[ 0][ 3] =      4   y1[ 3][ 0] =     16   y2[ 3][ 0] =     16
x[ 1][ 3] =     10   y1[ 3][ 1] =    100   y2[ 3][ 1] =    100
x[ 2][ 3] =     16   y1[ 3][ 2] =    256   y2[ 3][ 2] =    256
x[ 0][ 4] =      5   y1[ 4][ 0] =     25   y2[ 4][ 0] =     25
x[ 1][ 4] =     11   y1[ 4][ 1] =    121   y2[ 4][ 1] =    121
x[ 2][ 4] =     17   y1[ 4][ 2] =    289   y2[ 4][ 2] =    289
x[ 0][ 5] =      6   y1[ 5][ 0] =     36   y2[ 5][ 0] =     36
x[ 1][ 5] =     12   y1[ 5][ 1] =    144   y2[ 5][ 1] =    144
x[ 2][ 5] =     18   y1[ 5][ 2] =    324   y2[ 5][ 2] =    324
```

Strings

The x86-64 instruction set includes several useful instructions that process and manipulate strings. In x86 parlance, a string is a contiguous sequence of bytes, words, doublewords, or quadwords. Programs can use the x86-64 string instructions to process null-terminated C-style text strings (e.g., const char* str = "Hello, World!";). They also can be exploited to perform operations using the elements in an array. The source code examples in this section demonstrate x86-64 string instructions that carry out operations using conventional text strings and integer arrays.

Counting Characters

The first example of this section, named Ch04_04, uses the x86-64 string instruction lodsb (Load String Byte) to count the number of character occurrences in a text string. Listing 4-4a shows the C++ source code for this example.

Listing 4-4a. Example Ch04_04 C++ Code

```
//-----------------------------------------------------------------------------
// Ch04_04.h
//-----------------------------------------------------------------------------

#pragma once
#include <cstddef>
#include <cstdint>

// Ch04_04_fasm.asm, Ch04_04_fasm.s
extern "C" size_t CountChars_a(const char* s, char c);

// Ch04_04_fcpp.cpp
extern size_t CountChars_cpp(const char* s, char c);

// Ch04_04_misc.cpp
extern void DisplayResults(char sea_char, size_t n1, size_t n2);
```

```cpp
//-----------------------------------------------------------------------------
// Ch04_04_misc.cpp
//-----------------------------------------------------------------------------

#include <iostream>
#include "Ch04_04.h"

void DisplayResults(char sea_char, size_t n1, size_t n2)
{
    constexpr char nl = '\n';

    std::cout << "Search char: " << sea_char << " | ";
    std::cout << "Character counts: n1 = " << n1 << ", n2 = " << n2 << nl;

    if (n1 != n2)
        std::cout << "compare check failed!\n";
}

//-----------------------------------------------------------------------------
// Ch04_04_fcpp.cpp
//-----------------------------------------------------------------------------

#include "Ch04_04.h"

size_t CountChars_cpp(const char* s, char c)
{
    size_t num_chars = 0;

    for (size_t i = 0; s[i] != '\0'; i++)
    {
        if (s[i] == c)
            num_chars++;
    }

    return num_chars;
}

//-----------------------------------------------------------------------------
// Ch04_04.cpp
//-----------------------------------------------------------------------------

#include <iostream>
#include "Ch04_04.h"

int main()
{
    const char* test_string =
    {
        "azure, beige, black, blue, brown\n"
        "cyan, gold, gray, indigo, magenta\n"
        "maroon, orange, pink, purple, red\n"
```

```
        "teal, tan, violet, white, yellow\n"
    };

    constexpr char sea_chars[] {'a', 'e', 'i', 'm', 'o', 'r', 't', 'v', 'w', 'X'};
    constexpr size_t num_sea_chars = sizeof(sea_chars) / sizeof(char);

    std::cout << "----- Results for Ch04_04 -----\n\n";

    std::cout << "Test string:\n";
    std::cout << test_string << '\n';

    for (size_t j = 0; j < num_sea_chars; j++)
    {
        size_t n1 = CountChars_cpp(test_string, sea_chars[j]);
        size_t n2 = CountChars_a(test_string, sea_chars[j]);

        DisplayResults(sea_chars[j], n1, n2);
    }

    return 0;
}
```

In Listing 4-4a, function CountChars_cpp() in file Ch04_04_fcpp.cpp implements a straightforward character counting routine in C++. Function main() in Ch04_04.cpp defines a test string named test_string that it uses to exercise CountChars_cpp() and its counterpart assembly language function CountChars_a(). Also defined in main() is an array of search characters named sea_chars for test purposes.

Listing 4-4b shows the MASM code for CountChars_a(). This function requires two arguments: a pointer to test string s and search character c. Both arguments are of type char, which means that each character in string s and the search character c occupy one byte of storage. Execution of CountChars_a() begins with a mov r10,rsi instruction that copies RSI to R10. The reason for this mov instruction is that CountChars_a() utilizes the lodsb instruction, which uses register RSI as you'll soon see. Since RSI is a non-volatile register, its value must be preserved. The examples that you saw earlier in this chapter used the stack to preserve the value in a non-volatile register. In this example, we can use volatile register R11 to save RSI since CountChars_a() is a leaf function and R11 is not used elsewhere. If CountChars_a() were a non-leaf function, RSI would have been saved on the stack.

Listing 4-4b. Example Ch04_04 MASM Code

```
;-----------------------------------------------------------------------------
; Ch04_04_fasm.asm
;-----------------------------------------------------------------------------


;-----------------------------------------------------------------------------
; size_t CountChars_a(const char* s, char c);
;-----------------------------------------------------------------------------

        .code
CountChars_a proc
        mov r10,rsi                     ;save caller's rsi register
```

```
; Perform required initializations
        mov rsi,rcx                     ;rsi = s
        xor ecx,ecx                     ;num_chars = 0
        xor r8d,r8d                     ;r8 = 0 (required for add below)

; Repeat loop until the entire string has been scanned
Loop1:  lodsb                           ;load next char into register al
        test al,al                      ;test for end-of-string
        jz Done                         ;jump if end-of-string found
        cmp al,dl                       ;test current char
        sete r8b                        ;r8b = 1 if match, 0 otherwise
        add rcx,r8                      ;num_chars += r8
        jmp Loop1

Done:   mov rax,rcx                     ;rax = num_chars
        mov rsi,r10                     ;restore caller's rsi register
        ret

CountChars_a endp
        end
```

The next instruction in CountChars_a(), mov rsi,rcx, copies argument value s into register RSI for use by the lodsb instruction. Two xor instructions are then used to set RCX (num_chars) and R8 to zero. The reason for setting R8 to zero will be explained shortly. Execution of for-loop Loop1 begins with a lodsb instruction. This instruction copies the value pointed to by RSI into register AL. It also auto increments or decrements RSI based on the status of RFLAGS.DF. If RFLAGS.DF == 0 is true, which is the default for both Visual C++ and GNU C++, RSI is incremented by one; otherwise, RSI is decremented by one. Following execution of lodsb, register AL contains the current character of test string s, and RSI points to the next character in string s.

Occurring immediately after the loadsb instruction is the instruction pair test al,al and jz Done, which terminates Loop1 if the end-of-string character 0x00 is found. This is followed by a cmp al,dl instruction that compares the current string character to search character c. Execution of the ensuing sete r8b sets R8B to one if s[i] == c is true; otherwise, R8B is set to zero. Note that the sete instruction *does not* modify any of the high-order bits in R8, which clarifies why R8 was zeroed prior to the start of Loop1. The add rcx,r8 instruction that follows updates num_chars in register RCX. Following completion of Loop1, CountChars_a() copies num_chars into RAX using a mov rax,rcx instruction. The ensuing mov rsi,r10 instruction restores non-volatile register RSI.

Listing 4-4c shows the NASM code for example Ch04_04. In this listing, note that it is not necessary to preserve RSI since the GNU C++ calling convention designates it as a volatile register. The first two instructions of the initialization code block, mov dl,sil and mov rsi,rdi, load argument value c into register DL and pointer argument s into register RSI. The remaining code in Listing 4-4c is the same as the code in Listing 4-4b.

Listing 4-4c. Example Ch04_04 NASM Code

```
;-------------------------------------------------------------------------------
; Ch04_04_fasm.s
;-------------------------------------------------------------------------------

        %include "ModX86Asm3eNASM.inc"
```

```asm
;-------------------------------------------------------------------------------
; size_t CountChars_a(const char* s, char c);
;-------------------------------------------------------------------------------

        section .text

        global CountChars_a
CountChars_a:

; Perform required initializations
        mov dl,sil                      ;dl = c
        mov rsi,rdi                     ;rsi = s
        xor ecx,ecx                     ;num_chars = 0
        xor r8d,r8d                     ;r8 = 0 (required for add below)

; Repeat loop until the entire string has been scanned
Loop1:  lodsb                           ;load next char into register al
        test al,al                      ;test for end-of-string
        jz Done                         ;jump if end-of-string found
        cmp al,dl                       ;test current char
        sete r8b                        ;r8b = 1 if match, 0 otherwise
        add rcx,r8                      ;num_chars += r8
        jmp Loop1

Done:   mov rax,rcx                     ;rax = num_chars
        ret
```

Here are the results for source code example Ch04_04:

```
----- Results for Ch04_04 -----

Test string:
azure, beige, black, blue, brown
cyan, gold, gray, indigo, magenta
maroon, orange, pink, purple, red
teal, tan, violet, white, yellow

Search char: a | Character counts: n1 = 10, n2 = 10
Search char: e | Character counts: n1 = 12, n2 = 12
Search char: i | Character counts: n1 = 6, n2 = 6
Search char: m | Character counts: n1 = 2, n2 = 2
Search char: o | Character counts: n1 = 8, n2 = 8
Search char: r | Character counts: n1 = 7, n2 = 7
Search char: t | Character counts: n1 = 5, n2 = 5
Search char: v | Character counts: n1 = 1, n2 = 1
Search char: w | Character counts: n1 = 3, n2 = 3
Search char: X | Character counts: n1 = 0, n2 = 0
```

For other string or array element sizes, a function can use the lodsw (word), lodsd (doubleword), or lodsq (quadword) instructions.

Array Compare

The next source code example, named Ch04_05, exploits the cmpsd (Compare String Doubleword) instruction to compare elements in two int32_t arrays. This example also demonstrates the use of the repe (Repeat String) prefix. Listing 4-5a shows the C++ code for example Ch04_05.

Listing 4-5a. Example Ch04_05 C++ Code

```
//-----------------------------------------------------------------------
// Ch04_05.h
//-----------------------------------------------------------------------

#pragma once
#include <cstddef>
#include <cstdint>

// Ch04_05_fasm.asm, Ch04_05_fasm.s
extern "C" int64_t CompareArrays_a(const int32_t* x, const int32_t* y, int64_t n);

// Ch04_05_fcpp.cpp
extern int64_t CompareArrays_cpp(const int32_t* x, const int32_t* y, int64_t n);

// Ch04_05_misc.cpp
extern void InitArrays(int32_t* x, int32_t* y, int64_t n, unsigned int rng_seed);
extern void DisplayResult(const char* msg, int64_t expected, int64_t result1,
    int64_t result2);

//-----------------------------------------------------------------------
// Ch04_05_misc.cpp
//-----------------------------------------------------------------------

#include <iostream>
#include <cstring>
#include "Ch04_05.h"
#include "MT.h"

void InitArrays(int32_t* x, int32_t* y, int64_t n, unsigned int rng_seed)
{
    constexpr int min_val = 1;
    constexpr int max_val = 10000;

    MT::FillArray(x, n, min_val, max_val, rng_seed, true);
    memcpy(y, x, sizeof(int32_t) * n);
}

void DisplayResult(const char* msg, int64_t expected, int64_t result1, int64_t result2)
{
    std::cout << msg << " (index = " << expected << ")\n";
```

```
        std::cout << "  result1 = " << result1;
        std::cout << "  result2 = " << result2 << '\n';

        if (expected != result1 || expected != result2)
            std::cout << "  compare test failed\n";

        std::cout << '\n';
}

//-----------------------------------------------------------------------------
// Ch04_05_fcpp.cpp
//-----------------------------------------------------------------------------

#include "Ch04_05.h"

int64_t CompareArrays_cpp(const int32_t* x, const int32_t* y, int64_t n)
{
    if (n <= 0)
        return -1;

    int64_t i = 0;

    while (i < n)
    {
        if (x[i] != y[i])
            break;

        i++;
    }

    return i;
}
```

In file Ch04_05_fcpp.cpp, function CompareArrays_cpp() compares elements in two arrays of type int32_t. This function returns the index of the first mismatch it detects or argument value n if the two arrays are identical. It also returns a value of –1 to signify an illegal value for argument n. The remaining code in C++ code in Listing 4-5a performs test case initialization and formats the results for streaming to std::cout.

Listing 4-5b shows the MASM code for example Ch04_05. Execution of function CompareArrays_a() begins with two mov instructions, mov r10,rsi and mov r11,rdi. These instructions save non-volatile registers RSI and RDI in R10 and R11, respectively. Like the previous example, CompareArrays_a() preserves non-volatile RSI and RDI registers in this manner since it's a leaf function (they are restored just prior to execution of the ret instruction). Following non-volatile register preservation, the instruction pair test r8,r8 and jle Done confirms that argument value n is valid.

Listing 4-5b. Example Ch04_05 MASM Code

```
;------------------------------------------------------------------------
; Ch04_05_fasm.asm
;------------------------------------------------------------------------


;------------------------------------------------------------------------
; int64_t CompareArrays_a(const int32_t* x, const int32_t* y, int64_t n);
;
; Returns      -1          Value of n is invalid
;              0 <= i < n  Index of first non-matching element
;              n           All elements match
;------------------------------------------------------------------------

        .code
CompareArrays_a proc

; Save caller's non-volatile registers
        mov r10,rsi
        mov r11,rdi

; Validate n
        mov rax,-1                      ;rax = return code for invalid n
        test r8,r8
        jle Done                        ;jump if n <= 0

; Compare the arrays for equality
        mov rsi,rcx                     ;rsi = x
        mov rdi,rdx                     ;rdi = y
        mov rcx,r8                      ;rcx = n
        mov rax,r8                      ;rax = n

        repe cmpsd                      ;compare arrays

; Calculate index of first non-match
        jz Done                         ;jump if arrays are equal
        sub rax,rcx                     ;rax = index of mismatch + 1
        sub rax,1                       ;rax = index of mismatch

; Restore caller's non-volatile registers and return
Done:   mov rsi,r10
        mov rdi,r11
        ret
CompareArrays_a endp
        end
```

Following argument validation is the actual array element compare code. The mov rsi,rcx and mov rdi,rdx instructions copy array pointers x and y into registers RSI and RDI, respectively. The following instruction mov rcx,r8 copies argument value n into register RCX. More on this in a moment. The repe cmpsd instruction compares the two doubleword values pointed to by RSI and RDI and sets the status flags in RFLAGS according to the result. It also adds four (the size of a doubleword in bytes) to both RSI and RDI. The instruction prefix repe (Repeat While Equal) directs the processor to subtract one from RCX following execution of each cmpsd instruction; it also repeats execution of this instruction until either RCX == 0 or RFLAGS.ZF == 0 is true. Following execution of repe cmpsd, the index of the first mismatch is calculated. If the two arrays are equal, RFLAGS.ZF == 1 will be true, and the jz Done instruction skips over the subsequent two sub instructions since RAX already contains the correct return value (n). If RFLAGS.ZF == 0 is true, the instruction pair sub rax,rcx and sub rax,1 calculates the index of the first non-matching element.

Listing 4-5c shows the NASM code for example Ch04_05. Note that argument pointers x and y are already loaded in registers RDI and RSI, which means no additional mov instructions are necessary. Preservation of the values in these registers is also not needed since both RDI and RSI are volatile. The array comparison and index calculating code in Listing 4-5c matches the code in Listing 4-5b.

Listing 4-5c. Example Ch04_05 NASM Code

```
;-----------------------------------------------------------------------
; Ch04_05_fasm.s
;-----------------------------------------------------------------------

        %include "ModX86Asm3eNASM.inc"


;-----------------------------------------------------------------------
; int64_t CompareArrays_a(const int32_t* x, const int32_t* y, int64_t n);
;
; Returns         -1           Value of n is invalid
;                 0 <= i < n   Index of first non-matching element
;                 n            All elements match
;-----------------------------------------------------------------------

        section .text

        global CompareArrays_a
CompareArrays_a:

; Validate n
        mov rax,-1                      ;rax = return code for invalid n
        test rdx,rdx
        jle Done                        ;jump if n <= 0

; Compare the arrays for equality
; (rsi and rdi already contain pointers to arrays x and y)
        mov rcx,rdx                     ;rcx = n
        mov rax,rdx                     ;rax = n

        repe cmpsd                      ;compare arrays

; Calculate index of first non-match
        jz Done                         ;jump if arrays are equal
        sub rax,rcx                     ;rax = index of mismatch + 1
        sub rax,1                       ;rax = index of mismatch

Done:   ret
```

You can also use the cmpsb, cmpsw, and cmpsq for byte, word, and quadword comparisons. Other x86-64 string instruction repeat prefixes include rep (Repeat until RCX == 0) and repne (Repeat While Not Equal). The repne prefix terminates execution of its string instruction when either RCX == 0 or RFLAGS.ZF == 1 is true. Here are the results for example Ch04_05:

```
----- Results for Ch04_05 (array size = 10000) -----

Test using invalid array size (index = -1)
  result1 = -1   result2 = -1

Test using first element mismatch (index = 0)
  result1 = 0    result2 = 0

Test using middle element mismatch (index = 5000)
  result1 = 5000   result2 = 5000

Test using last element mismatch (index = 9999)
  result1 = 9999   result2 = 9999

Test with identical elements in each array (index = 10000)
  result1 = 10000   result2 = 10000
```

Array Copy and Fill

The next source code example, entitled Ch04_06, explains how to use the movsd (Move Data from String to String) and stosq (Store String) instructions to perform array copy and fill operations. Listing 4-6a shows the C++ source code for this example.

Listing 4-6a. Example Ch04_06 C++ Code

```cpp
//------------------------------------------------------------------------------
// Ch04_06.h
//------------------------------------------------------------------------------

#pragma once
#include <cstddef>
#include <cstdint>

// Ch04_06_fasm.asm, Ch04_06_fasm.s
extern "C" void CopyArrayI32_a(int32_t * b, const int32_t * a, size_t n);
extern "C" void FillArrayI64_a(const int64_t * a, int64_t fill_val, size_t n);

//------------------------------------------------------------------------------
// Ch04_06.cpp
//------------------------------------------------------------------------------

#include <iostream>
#include <iomanip>
#include <cstdint>
```

```cpp
#include "Ch04_06.h"

static void CopyArray(void)
{
    constexpr size_t n = 10;
    constexpr int32_t a[n] = { 10, -20, 30, 40, -50, 60, 70, -80, 90, 10 };
    int32_t b[n] = { 0, 0, 0, 0, 0, 0, 0, 0, 0, 0 };

    CopyArrayI32_a(b, a, n);

    std::cout << "\nCopyArrayI32_a() results:\n";

    for (size_t i = 0; i < n; i++)
    {
        std::cout << std::setw(5) << i << ": ";
        std::cout << std::setw(5) << a[i] << " ";
        std::cout << std::setw(5) << b[i] << '\n';
    }
}

static void FillArray(void)
{
    constexpr int64_t fill_val = -7;
    constexpr size_t n = 10;

    int64_t a[n] = {0, 0, 0, 0, 0, 0, 0, 0, 0, 0};
    FillArrayI64_a(a, fill_val, n);

    std::cout << "\nFillArrayI32_a() results:\n";

    for (size_t i = 0; i < n; i++)
    {
        std::cout << std::setw(5) << i << ": ";
        std::cout << std::setw(5) << a[i] << '\n';
    }
}

int main(void)
{
    std::cout << "----- Results for Ch04_06 -----\n";

    CopyArray();
    FillArray();
    return 0;
}
```

The purpose of the C++ code in Listing 4-6a should be readily apparent. The principal code for static functions CopyArray() and FillArray() is located in file Ch04_06.cpp. These C++ functions exercise the assembly language functions CopyArrayI32_a() and FillArrayI64_a(). Listing 4-6b shows the MASM code for example Ch04_06.

Listing 4-6b. Example Ch04_06 MASM Code

```
;-------------------------------------------------------------------------
; Ch04_06_fasm.asm
;-------------------------------------------------------------------------


;-------------------------------------------------------------------------
; void CopyArrayI32_a(int32_t* b, const int32_t* a, size_t n);
;-------------------------------------------------------------------------

        .code
CopyArrayI32_a proc

; Save non-volatile registers rsi and rdi
        mov r10,rsi
        mov r11,rdi

; Copy a[] to b[]
        mov rsi,rdx                     ;rsi = source array
        mov rdi,rcx                     ;rdi = destination array
        mov rcx,r8                      ;rcx = element count

        rep movsd                       ;copy elements from a[] to b[]

; Restore non-volatile registers and return
        mov rsi,r10
        mov rsi,r11
        ret
CopyArrayI32_a endp

;-------------------------------------------------------------------------
; void FillArrayI64_a(const int64_t* a, int64_t fill_val, size_t n);
;-------------------------------------------------------------------------

FillArrayI64_a proc

; Save non-volatile registers rsi and rdi
        mov r10,rsi
        mov r11,rdi

; Fill a[] with fill_val
        mov rdi,rcx                     ;rdi = destination array
        mov rax,rdx                     ;rax = fill value
        mov rcx,r8                      ;rcx = element count

        rep stosq                       ;set each element in a[] to fill_val

; Restore non-volatile registers and return
        mov rsi,r10
        mov rsi,r11
        ret
FillArrayI64_a endp
        end
```

The first assembly language function in Listing 4-6b, CopyArray_a(), copies n elements from source array a to destination array b. Following preservation of non-volatile registers RSI and RDI, CopyArrayI32_a() uses a mov rsi,rdx instruction to load argument pointer a into register RSI. This is followed by a mov rdi,rcx instruction that copies argument pointer b to register RDI. The mov rcx,r8 instruction loads the number of doubleword (int32_t) elements to copy into register RCX. This is followed by a rep movsd instruction. During each movsd instruction execution, the processor copies the doubleword value pointed to by RSI to the doubleword memory location pointed to by RDI. Registers RSI and RDI are both incremented by four (since RFLAGS.DF == 0), and RCX is decremented by one. This process continues until RCX == 0 is true. X86-64 processors also support byte, word, and quadword moves using the movsb, movsw, and movsq instructions, respectively.

Function FillArrayI64_a() uses rep stosq to fill an array of quadwords with the same value. Note that prior to execution of this instruction, FillArrayI64_a() loads destination array pointer a into register RDI, the quadword (int64_t) fill value into register RAX, and the number of quadword elements into register RCX. During execution of rep stosq, register RDI is incremented by eight and RCX decremented by one until the array fill is complete. Like other x86-64 string instructions, you can use other string store sizes including stosb (byte), stosw (word), and stosd (doubleword).

Listing 4-6c shows the NASM code for source code example Ch04_06. The code for NASM functions CopyArray_a() and FillArray_a() is shorter than the MASM versions since no non-volatile register saves and restores are necessary. Also, some registers already contain the correct values, which eliminate a few mov instructions.

Listing 4-6c. Example Ch04_06 NASM Code

```
;-------------------------------------------------------------------------
; Ch04_06_fasm.s
;-------------------------------------------------------------------------

        %include "ModX86Asm3eNASM.inc"


;-------------------------------------------------------------------------
; void CopyArrayI32_a(int32_t* b, const int32_t* a, size_t n);
;-------------------------------------------------------------------------

        section .text

        global CopyArrayI32_a
CopyArrayI32_a:

; Copy a[] to b[]
; (note: rsi and rdi already contain pointers to a[] and b[])
        mov rcx,rdx                     ;rcx = element count
        rep movsd                       ;copy elements in a[] to b[]
        ret


;-------------------------------------------------------------------------
; extern "C" void FillArrayI64_a(const int64_t* a, int64_t fill_val, size_t n);
;-------------------------------------------------------------------------

        global FillArrayI64_a
FillArrayI64_a:
```

```
; Fill a[] with fill_val
; (note: rdi already contains pointer to a[])
        mov rax,rsi                        ;rax = fill value
        mov rcx,rdx                        ;rcx = element count
        rep stosq                          ;set each element to fill_val
        ret
```

Here are the results for source code example Ch04_06:

```
----- Results for Ch04_06 -----

CopyArrayI32_a() results:
    0:    10    10
    1:   -20   -20
    2:    30    30
    3:    40    40
    4:   -50   -50
    5:    60    60
    6:    70    70
    7:   -80   -80
    8:    90    90
    9:    10    10

FillArrayI32_a() results:
    0:    -7
    1:    -7
    2:    -7
    3:    -7
    4:    -7
    5:    -7
    6:    -7
    7:    -7
    8:    -7
    9:    -7
```

Array Reversal

The final x86-64 string instruction example of this section, entitled Ch04_07, demonstrates how to reverse the elements of an integer array. It also illustrates the use of the pushfq (Push RFLAGS onto Stack), popfq (Pop RFLAGS from Stack), and std (Set Direction Flag) instructions. Listing 4-7a shows the C++ source code for this example.

Listing 4-7a. Example Ch04_07 C++ Code

```
//-----------------------------------------------------------------------------
// Ch04_07.h
//-----------------------------------------------------------------------------

#pragma once
#include <cstdint>
```

```cpp
// Ch04_07_fasm.asm, Ch04_07_fasm.s
extern "C" int ReverseArrayI32_a(int32_t* y, const int32_t* x, int32_t n);

// Ch04_07_misc.cpp
void InitArrays(int32_t* y, int32_t* x, int32_t n);
void DisplayResults(const int32_t* y, const int32_t* x, int32_t n, int rc);

//-----------------------------------------------------------------------------
// Ch04_07_misc.cpp
//-----------------------------------------------------------------------------

#include <iostream>
#include <iomanip>
#include <cstring>
#include "Ch04_07.h"
#include "MT.h"

void InitArrays(int32_t* y, int32_t* x, int32_t n)
{
    constexpr int max_val = 1000;
    constexpr int min_val = -max_val;
    constexpr unsigned int rng_seed = 17;

    MT::FillArray(x, n, min_val, max_val, rng_seed, true);
    memset(y, 0, sizeof(int32_t) * n);
}

void DisplayResults(const int32_t* y, const int32_t* x, int32_t n, int rc)
{
    if (rc != 0)
    {
        std::cout << "\n----- Results for Ch04_07 -----\n";

        constexpr int w = 5;

        for (int i = 0; i < n; i++)
        {
            std::cout << "  i: " << std::setw(w) << i;
            std::cout << "  y: " << std::setw(w) << y[i];
            std::cout << "  x: " << std::setw(w) << x[i] << '\n';

            if (x[i] != y[n - 1 - i])
            {
                std::cout << "ReverseArrayI32_a() element compare error\n";
                break;
            }
        }
    }
    else
        std::cout << "ReverseArrayI32_a() failed\n";
}
```

```cpp
//-----------------------------------------------------------------------------
// Ch04_07.cpp
//-----------------------------------------------------------------------------

#include "Ch04_07.h"

int main(void)
{
    constexpr int32_t n = 25;
    int32_t y[n], x[n];

    InitArrays(y, x, n);

    int rc = ReverseArrayI32_a(y, x, n);
    DisplayResults(y, x, n, rc);
    return 0;
}
```

In Listing 4-7a, function main() uses helper function InitArrays() in file Ch04_07_misc.cpp to initialize an array of int32_t elements. It then invokes the assembly language function ReverseArrayI32_a(), which copies the elements of array x to array y in reverse order.

Listing 4-7b shows the MASM code for example Ch04_07. Execution of ReverseArrayI32_a() begins with the preservation of non-volatile registers RSI and RDI in registers R10 and R11. Argument value n is then validated. The next two instructions, mov rsi,rdx and mov rdi,rcx, copy argument pointers x and y into registers RSI and RDI, respectively. This is followed by a mov ecx,r8d instruction that effectively copies argument value n to register RCX. The ensuing lea rsi,[rsi+rcx*4-4] instruction loads &x[n - 1] into register RSI. Note that this instruction incorporates all possible components of an x86-64 effective address. During execution of a lea instruction, the processor calculates the expression within the brackets and stores this value into the destination operand.

Listing 4-7b. Example Ch04_07 MASM Code

```asm
;-----------------------------------------------------------------------------
; Ch04_07_fasm.asm
;-----------------------------------------------------------------------------


;-----------------------------------------------------------------------------
; int ReverseArrayI32_a(int32_t* y, const int32_t* x, int32_t n);
;-----------------------------------------------------------------------------

        .code
ReverseArrayI32_a proc

; Save non-volatile registers
        mov r10,rsi
        mov r11,rdi

; Make sure n is valid
        xor eax,eax                     ;error return code
        test r8d,r8d                    ;is n <= 0?
        jle BadArg                      ;jump if n <= 0
```

```
; Initialize registers for reversal operation
        mov rsi,rdx                     ;rsi = x
        mov rdi,rcx                     ;rdi = y
        mov ecx,r8d                     ;rcx = n
        lea rsi,[rsi+rcx*4-4]           ;rsi = &x[n - 1]

; Save caller's RFLAGS.DF, then set RFLAGS.DF to 1
        pushfq                          ;save caller's RFLAGS.DF
        std                             ;RFLAGS.DF = 1

; Repeat loop until array reversal is complete
Loop1:  lodsd                           ;eax = *x--
        mov [rdi],eax                   ;*y = eax
        add rdi,4                        ;y++
        sub rcx,1                        ;n -= 1
        jnz Loop1                        ;jump if more elements

; Restore caller's RFLAGS.DF and set return code
        popfq                           ;restore caller's RFLAGS.DF
        mov eax,1                        ;set success return code

; Restore non-volatile registers and return
BadArg: mov rsi,r10
        mov rdi,r11
        ret
ReverseArrayI32_a endp
        end
```

A brief digression. A lea instruction with a memory operand that incorporates a base register, index register, and displacement may execute slower on some x86 processor microarchitectures compared to a lea instruction that encompasses fewer components. For a one-time initialization, the use of the lea instruction with all three components is still sensible, but such use should be minimized in performance-critical for-loops.

Returning to the code in Listing 4-7b, the processing loop of ReverseArrayI32_a() uses the lodsd instruction to traverse source array x starting from the final element x[n - 1] to the first element x[0]. To use the lodsb instruction in this manner, RFLAGS.DF must be set equal to one so that it performs an auto decrement of register RSI instead of an auto increment (recall that the default value for RFLAGS.DF is zero for both Visual C++ and GNU C++). Before changing the state of RFLAGS.DF, ReverseArrayI32_a() employs a pushfq instruction to save the current contents of RFLAGS (including the current state of RFLAGS.DF) on the stack. The ensuing std instruction sets RFLAGS.DF to one.

The next code block performs the actual array reversal. Each iteration of for-loop Loop1 begins with a lodsd instruction that loads the doubleword value pointed to by RSI into register EAX. Execution of this lodsd instruction also decrements RSI by four. This is followed by a mov [rdi],eax instruction that saves the just loaded value to destination array y. The ensuing instruction triplet, add rdi,4, sub rcx,1, and jnz Loop1, updates RDI (array y pointer), RCX (n), and repeats the execution of Loop1 until the array reversal operation is complete.

Following execution of Loop1, the popfq instruction restores the caller's original RFLAGS.DF to its original state. One question that might be asked at this point is if the C++ run-time environments assume that RFLAGS.DF is always cleared, why doesn't ReverseArrayI32_a() use a cld (Clear Direction Flag) instruction to restore RFLAGS.DF instead of a pushfq/popfq sequence? Yes, the C++ run-time environments assume that RFLAGS.DF is always cleared, but they cannot enforce this policy during program execution.

If a function like ReverseArrayI32_a() were to be included in a DLL (or shared library), it could conceivably be called by a function written in a programming language that uses a different default state for RFLAGS. DF. Using pushfq and popfq ensures that the caller's original RFLAGS.DF state is properly restored.

Listing 4-7c shows the NASM code for source code example Ch04_07. Like the previous example, the NASM code is somewhat shorter since some of the argument values are already loaded in the correct registers. The NASM version also uses the same sequence of pushfq and popfq instructions to preserve the caller's RFLAGS.DF state.

Listing 4-7c. Example Ch04_07 NASM Code

```
;-------------------------------------------------------------------------
; Ch04_07_fasm.s
;-------------------------------------------------------------------------

        %include "ModX86Asm3eNASM.inc"

;-------------------------------------------------------------------------
; int ReverseArrayI32_a(int32_t* y, const int32_t* x, int32_t n);
;-------------------------------------------------------------------------

        section .text

        global ReverseArrayI32_a
ReverseArrayI32_a:

; Make sure n is valid
        xor eax,eax                     ;error return code
        test edx,edx                    ;is n <= 0?
        jle BadArg                      ;jump if n <= 0

; Initialize registers for reversal operation
; (note: rsi and rdi already point to x[] and y[])
        mov ecx,edx                     ;rcx = n
        lea rsi,[rsi+rcx*4-4]           ;rsi = &x[n - 1]

; Save caller's RFLAGS.DF, then set RFLAGS.DF to 1
        pushfq                          ;save caller's RFLAGS.DF
        std                             ;RFLAGS.DF = 1

; Repeat loop until array reversal is complete
Loop1:  lodsd                           ;eax = *x--
        mov [rdi],eax                   ;*y = eax
        add rdi,4                       ;y++
        sub rcx,1                       ;n -= 1
        jnz Loop1                       ;jump if more elements

; Restore caller's RFLAGS.DF and set return code
        popfq                           ;restore caller's RFLAGS.DF
        mov eax,1                        ;set success return code

BadArg: ret
```

Here are the results for source code example Ch04_07:

```
----- Results for Ch04_07 -----
 i:    0  y:    728  x:   -411
 i:    1  y:    141  x:   -637
 i:    2  y:   -880  x:     61
 i:    3  y:    485  x:    689
 i:    4  y:    892  x:   -617
 i:    5  y:   -918  x:    778
 i:    6  y:   -285  x:   -865
 i:    7  y:    720  x:    614
 i:    8  y:   -922  x:    574
 i:    9  y:    260  x:   -180
 i:   10  y:    151  x:    313
 i:   11  y:   -561  x:   -794
 i:   12  y:    275  x:    275
 i:   13  y:   -794  x:   -561
 i:   14  y:    313  x:    151
 i:   15  y:   -180  x:    260
 i:   16  y:    574  x:   -922
 i:   17  y:    614  x:    720
 i:   18  y:   -865  x:   -285
 i:   19  y:    778  x:   -918
 i:   20  y:   -617  x:    892
 i:   21  y:    689  x:    485
 i:   22  y:     61  x:   -880
 i:   23  y:   -637  x:    141
 i:   24  y:   -411  x:    728
```

For assembly language programmers, the rep movs[b|w|d|q] and rep stos[b|w|d|q] instructions are probably the most useful for a couple of reasons. First, their usage is both convenient and straightforward. Second, modern x86 processors include enhanced implementations of these instructions that improve their performance compared to older processors. Appendix B contains some references that you can consult for more information regarding x86 string instructions.

Assembly Language Structures

A structure is a programming language construct that facilitates the definition of new data types using one or more existing data types. In this section, you'll learn how to define and use a common structure in both a C++ and x86-64 assembly language function. You'll also learn how to deal with potential semantic issues that can arise when working with a common structure that's manipulated by software functions written using different programming languages.

In C++, a structure is equivalent to a class. When a data type is defined using the keyword struct instead of class, all members are public by default. A C++ structure that's declared sans any member functions or operators is equivalent to a C-style structure such as typedef struct { ... } MyStruct;. C++ structure declarations are usually placed in a header file so they can be easily incorporated into multiple C++ files. The same technique also can be employed to declare and reference structures that are used in assembly language code. Unfortunately, it is not possible to declare a single structure in a header file and include this file in both C++ and assembly language source code files. If you want to use the "same" structure in both C++ and assembly language code, it must be declared twice, and both declarations must be semantically equivalent.

Listing 4-8a shows the C++ code for example Ch04_08, which demonstrates structure use in an assembly language function. In this listing, the header file Ch04_08.h includes a structure declaration named TestStruct. Note that this structure encompasses four integral types of varying sizes. When declaring a C++ structure, the default operation for most compilers is to properly align each structure member on its natural boundary. This means that there are often pad bytes between various structure members. More on this shortly.

Listing 4-8a. Example Ch04_08 C++ Code

```
//----------------------------------------------------------------------
// Ch04_08.h
//----------------------------------------------------------------------

#pragma once
#include <cstdint>

// Test structure

struct TestStruct
{
    int8_t  Val8;
    int64_t Val64;
    int16_t Val16;
    int32_t Val32;
};

// Ch04_08_fasm.asm, Ch04_08_fasm.s
extern "C" int64_t SumStructVals_a(const TestStruct* ts);

// Ch04_08_misc.cpp
extern void DisplayResults(const TestStruct& ts, int64_t sum1, int64_t sum2);

//----------------------------------------------------------------------
// Ch04_08_misc.cpp
//----------------------------------------------------------------------

#include <iostream>
#include <cstddef>
#include "Ch04_08.h"

void DisplayResults(const TestStruct& ts, int64_t sum1, int64_t sum2)
{
    constexpr char nl = '\n';

    std::cout << "----- Results for Ch04_08 -----\n";

    std::cout << "\n--- TestStruct Offsets ---\n";
    std::cout << "offsetof(ts.Val8):   " << offsetof(TestStruct, Val8) << nl;
    std::cout << "offsetof(ts.Val64):  " << offsetof(TestStruct, Val64) << nl;
    std::cout << "offsetof(ts.Val16):  " << offsetof(TestStruct, Val16) << nl;
    std::cout << "offsetof(ts.Val32):  " << offsetof(TestStruct, Val32) << nl;
```

```
    std::cout << "\n--- Calculated Results ---\n";
    std::cout << "ts1.Val8:    " << (int)ts.Val8 << nl;
    std::cout << "ts1.Val16:   " << ts.Val16 << nl;
    std::cout << "ts1.Val32:   " << ts.Val32 << nl;
    std::cout << "ts1.Val64:   " << ts.Val64 << nl;
    std::cout << "sum1:        " << sum1 << nl;
    std::cout << "sum2:        " << sum2 << nl;
}


//-----------------------------------------------------------------------
// Ch04_08.cpp
//-----------------------------------------------------------------------

#include "Ch04_08.h"

int main()
{
    TestStruct ts;

    ts.Val8 = -100;
    ts.Val16 = 2000;
    ts.Val32 = -300000;
    ts.Val64 = 40000000000;

    int64_t sum1 = ts.Val8 + ts.Val16 + ts.Val32 + ts.Val64;
    int64_t sum2 = SumStructVals_a(&ts);

    DisplayResults(ts, sum1, sum2);
    return 0;
}
```

In Listing 4-8a, file Ch04_08_misc.cpp contains a function named DisplayResults(). Note that this function employs the macro offsetof to display the offset of each member in struct TestStruct. Knowing this information is often helpful when creating a semantically equivalent assembly language structure. The code in function main() performs test case initialization. It also exercises the assembly language function SumStructVals_a(), which sums the elements of a TestStruct instance.

Listing 4-8b shows the MASM code for example Ch04_08. Near the top of this listing is the statement TestStruct struct, which signifies the start of a MASM structure. The next statement, Val8 db ?, declares structure member Val8, and it occupies one byte of storage. The ? symbol used here instructs MASM to perform storage allocation only. The next statement, PadA db 7 dup (?), adds seven bytes of padding to ensure that structure member Val64 is aligned on a quadword boundary. Unlike a C++ compiler, assemblers like MASM and NASM do not automatically align each structure member on its natural boundary. It is the responsibility of the programmer to manually perform this task. Note the PadB db 2 dup (?) statement that occurs later in TestStruct. This statement ensures doubleword alignment of structure member Val32. The statement TestStruct ends signifies the end of the structure declaration. Before continuing, it should be noted that the layout of TestStruct in this example is not optimal; the structure members are ordered for padding demonstration purposes. If TestStruct were to be used in production code, the structure members would most likely be arranged differently to minimize the size of each TestStruct instance.

Listing 4-8b. Example Ch04_08 MASM Code

```
;-------------------------------------------------------------------------------
; Ch04_08_fasm.asm
;-------------------------------------------------------------------------------

TestStruct struct
Val8     db ?
PadA     db 7 dup (?)
Val64    dq ?
Val16    dw ?
PadB     db 2 dup (?)
Val32    dd ?
TestStruct ends


;-------------------------------------------------------------------------------
; int64_t SumStructVals_a(const TestStruct* ts);
;-------------------------------------------------------------------------------

        .code
SumStructVals_a proc

; Compute ts->Val8 + ts->Val16, note sign extensions to 32-bits
        movsx eax,byte ptr [rcx+TestStruct.Val8]
        movsx edx,word ptr [rcx+TestStruct.Val16]
        add eax,edx

; Sign extend previous result to 64 bits
        movsxd rax,eax

; Add ts->Val32 to sum
        movsxd rdx,[rcx+TestStruct.Val32]
        add rax,rdx

; Add ts->Val64 to sum
        add rax,[rcx+TestStruct.Val64]
        ret

SumStructVals_a endp
        end
```

Returning to Listing 4-8b, the first executable instruction of SumStructVals_a(), movsx eax,byte ptr [rcx+TestStruct.Val8], loads a sign-extended copy of structure member Val8 into register EAX. Note the syntax that is used to reference Val8 (RCX points to the caller's TestStruct instance). This corresponds to BaseReg + Disp memory addressing. The remaining code in SumStructVals_a() contains various mov and add instructions that sum the elements of a TestStruct.

The NASM code for example Ch04_08, shown in Listing 4-8c, begins with the statement struc TestStruct that signifies the start of a NASM structure definition. The next statement, .Val8: resb 1, declares structure member Val8. The resb 1 text informs NASM that Val8 requires one byte of storage. Note that for each structure member name, the leading dot and trailing colon are required. The next statement, .PadA: resb 7, adds a seven-byte field named PadA to the structure. Like the MASM structure declaration that you saw earlier, doing this ensures that structure member Val64 is aligned on a quadword boundary. The remaining members of TestStruct are declared using the same syntax and storage keywords (res[b|w|d|q] for byte, word, doubleword, and quadword). The NASM keyword endstruc signifies the end of a structure declaration.

Listing 4-8c. Example Ch04_08 NASM Code

```
;-----------------------------------------------------------------------------
; Ch04_08_fasm.s
;-----------------------------------------------------------------------------

        %include "ModX86Asm3eNASM.inc"

; Test structure
struc TestStruct
.Val8:     resb   1
.PadA:     resb   7
.Val64:    resq   1
.Val16:    resw   1
.PadB      resb   2
.Val32:    resd   1
endstruc


;-----------------------------------------------------------------------------
; int64_t SumStructVals_a(const TestStruct* ts);
;-----------------------------------------------------------------------------

        section .text

        global SumStructVals_a
SumStructVals_a:

; Compute ts->Val8 + ts->Val16, note sign extensions to 32-bits
        movsx eax,byte [rdi+TestStruct.Val8]
        movsx edx,word [rdi+TestStruct.Val16]
        add eax,edx

; Sign extend previous result to 64 bits
        movsxd rax,eax

; Add ts->Val32 to sum
        movsxd rdx,[rdi+TestStruct.Val32]
        add rax,rdx

; Add ts->Val64 to sum
        add rax,[rdi+TestStruct.Val64]
        ret
```

The NASM assembly language source code in Listing 4-8c mimics the MASM source code except for a different register name for argument value ts. Here are the results for source code example Ch04_08:

```
----- Results for Ch04_08 -----

--- TestStruct Offsets ---
offsetof(ts.Val8):   0
offsetof(ts.Val64):  8
offsetof(ts.Val16):  16
offsetof(ts.Val32):  20

--- Calculated Results ---
ts1.Val8:    -100
ts1.Val16:   2000
ts1.Val32:   -300000
ts1.Val64:   40000000000
sum1:        39999701900
sum2:        39999701900
```

Summary

Here are the key learning points for Chapter 4:

- The address of an element in a one-dimensional array can be calculated using the base address (i.e., the address of the first element) of the array, the index of the element, and the size in bytes of each element.

- The address of an element in a two-dimensional array can be calculated using the base address of the array, the row and column indices, the number of columns, and the size in bytes of each element.

- The Visual C++ and GNU C++ calling conventions designate each general-purpose register as volatile or non-volatile. A function must preserve the contents of any non-volatile general-purpose register it uses.

- X86-64 assembly language code can define and use structures analogous to the way they're used in C++. An assembly language structure may require extra padding bytes to ensure that it's semantically equivalent to a corresponding C++ structure.

- The x86 string instructions cmpsx, lodsx, movsx, scasx, and stosx (where x = b (byte), w (word), d (doubleword), or q (quadword)) can be used to compare, load, copy, scan, or initialize text strings. They also can be used to perform operations on other contiguous data structures such as arrays and matrices.

- The prefixes rep, repe, repz, repne, and repnz can be used with a string instruction to repeat a string operation multiple times (RCX contains the count value) or until the specified zero flag (RFLAGS.ZF) condition occurs.

- A function can use the lea instruction to calculate the address of an object in memory. The use of a lea instruction with a memory operand that incorporates a base register, index register, and displacement may execute slower on some x86-64 processor microarchitectures and should be avoided in performance-critical for-loops.

- The pushfq and popfq instructions can be used to preserve values in the RFLAGS register.

- The direction flag (RFLAGS.DF) is considered non-volatile across function boundaries. A function must preserve and restore the caller's original value if it changes the state of RFLAGS.DF.

■ ■ ■

## CHAPTER 5

AVX Programming – Scalar Floating-Point

In the previous three chapters, you studied core x86-64 assembly language topics including integer arithmetic, bitwise logical operations, memory addressing modes, condition codes, and elementary programming constructs. You also learned essential details regarding assembly language source code semantics and syntax. In this chapter, you'll discover how to use the AVX instruction set to perform scalar floating-point calculations. The first section encompasses three source code examples that illustrate fundamental scalar floating-point arithmetic operations including addition, subtraction, multiplication, and division. In the next section, you'll study AVX scalar floating-point comparison and conversion instructions. The final section contains code that demonstrates operations using floating-point arrays.

The example code presented in this chapter requires a processor that supports AVX. You can use one of the freely available tools listed in Appendix B to determine whether your computer fulfills this requirement. In Chapter 16, you'll learn how to programmatically detect the presence of AVX and other x86 processor instruction set extensions.

■ **Note** Developing software that performs floating-point arithmetic always entails a few caveats. The purpose of the floating-point source code presented in this chapter and subsequent chapters is to illustrate the use of various x86-64 floating-point instructions. The source code does not address important floating-point concerns such as rounding errors, numerical stability, or ill-conditioned functions. Software developers must always be cognizant of these issues during the design and implementation of any algorithm that employs floating-point arithmetic. Appendix B contains a few references that you can consult to learn more about the potential pitfalls of floating-point arithmetic.

Floating-Point Programming Concepts

Before examining this chapter's source code, it makes sense to review a few underlying floating-point programming topics including data types, binary encodings, and special values. Software developers who understand these concepts are often able to improve the performance of algorithms that make heavy use of floating-point arithmetic and minimize potential floating-point errors.

© Daniel Kusswurm 2023
D. Kusswurm, *Modern X86 Assembly Language Programming*,
https://doi.org/10.1007/978-1-4842-9603-5_5

In mathematics, a real-number system depicts an infinite continuum of all possible positive and negative values including integers, rational numbers, and irrational numbers. Given their finite resources, modern computing architectures typically employ a floating-point system to approximate a real-number system. Like many other computing platforms, the x86's floating-point hardware is based on the IEEE 754 standard for binary floating-point arithmetic. This standard includes specifications that define binary encodings (or formats), range limits, and precisions for scalar floating-point values. The IEEE 754 standard also specifies important particulars related to floating-point arithmetic operations, rounding rules, and numerical exceptions.

The AVX instruction set supports common scalar floating-point operations using 32-bit single-precision (IEEE 754 binary32) and 64-bit double-precision (IEEE 754 binary64) values. Half-precision (IEEE 754 binary16) floating-point calculations can be performed on processors that support the AVX512-FP16 instruction set extension. Many C++ compilers including Visual C++ and GNU C++ use the x86's intrinsic single-precision and double-precision types to implement the C++ data types float and double. Figure 5-1 illustrates the memory organization for half-, single-, and double-precision floating-point values. This figure also includes common integer types for comparison purposes.

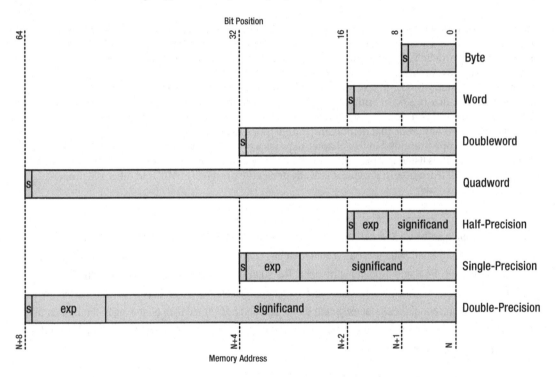

Figure 5-1. *Memory organization for half-, single-, and double-precision values*

The binary encoding of a floating-point value requires three distinct fields: a significand, an exponent, and a sign bit. The significand field represents a number's significant digits (or fractional part). The exponent specifies the location of the binary "decimal" point in the significand, which determines the magnitude. The sign (s) bit indicates whether the number is positive (s = 0) or negative (s = 1). Table 5-1 lists the various size parameters that are used to encode half-precision, single-precision, and double-precision floating-point values.

Table 5-1. *Floating-Point Size Parameters*

Field	Half-Precision	Single-Precision	Double-Precision
Sign	1 bit	1 bit	1 bit
Exponent	5 bits	8 bits	11 bits
Significand (stored bits)	10 bits	23 bits	52 bits
Total width	16 bits	32 bits	64 bits
Exponent bias	+15	+127	+1023

Figure 5-2 illustrates how to convert a decimal number into an IEEE 754–compliant floating-point value. In this example, the number 237.8125 is transformed from a decimal number to its single-precision floating-point binary encoding. The process starts by converting the number from base 10 to base 2. Next, the base 2 value is transformed to a binary scientific value. In Figure 5-2, the value to the right of the E_2 symbol is the binary exponent. A properly encoded floating-point value uses a biased exponent instead of the true exponent since this expedites floating-point compare operations. For a single-precision floating-point number, the bias value is +127. Adding the exponent bias value to the true exponent generates a binary scientific number with a biased exponent value. In the example that's shown in Figure 5-2, adding 111b (+7) to 1111111b (+127) yields a binary scientific with a biased exponent value of 10000110b (+134).

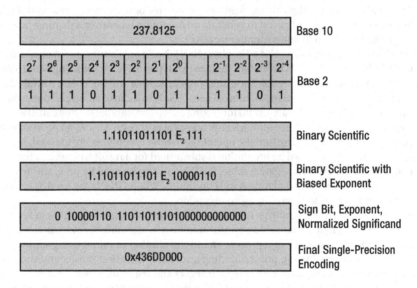

Figure 5-2. *Single-precision floating-point encoding process*

When encoding a half-, single-, or double-precision floating-point value, the leading 1 digit that's located to the left of the decimal point in Figure 5-2 is implied and not included in the final binary representation. Dropping the leading 1 digit forms a normalized significand. The three fields required for an IEEE 754–compliant encoding are now available, as shown in Table 5-2. A reading of the bit fields in this table from left to right yields the 32-bit value 0x436DD000, which is the final single-precision floating-point encoding of 237.8125.

Table 5-2. *Bit Fields for IEEE 754-Compliant Single-Precision Encoding of 237.8125*

Sign Bit	Biased Exponent	Normalized Significand
1	10000110	11011011101000000000000

The IEEE 754 binary encoding scheme reserves a small set of bit patterns for special values that are used to handle specific processing conditions. The first group of special values includes denormalized numbers (or denormal[1]). As shown in the earlier encoding example, the standard encoding of a floating-point number assumes that the leading digit of the significand is always a 1. One limitation of IEEE 754 floating-point encoding scheme is its inability to accurately represent numbers very close to zero. In these cases, values get encoded using a non-normalized format, which enables tiny numbers close to zero (both positive and negative) to be encoded using less precision. For many algorithms, denormal values are not a concern since the processor can still carry out floating-point calculations. In algorithms where the use of a denormal is problematic, a function can test a floating-point value to ascertain its denormal state, or the processor can be configured to generate an underflow or denormal exception.

Another application of special values involves the binary encodings that are used for floating-point zero. The IEEE 754 standard supports two different representations of floating-point zero: positive zero (+0.0) and negative zero (–0.0). A negative zero can be generated either algorithmically or as a side effect of the floating-point rounding mode. Computationally, the processor treats positive and negative zero the same, and the programmer typically does not need to be concerned.

The IEEE 754 encoding scheme also supports positive and negative representations of infinity. Infinities are produced by certain numerical algorithms, overflow conditions, or division by zero. As discussed later in this chapter, the processor can be configured to generate an exception whenever a floating-point overflow occurs or if a program attempts to divide a number by zero.

The final special value type is called Not a Number (NaN). NaNs are floating-point encodings that represent invalid numbers. The IEEE 754 standard defines two types of NaNs: signaling NaN (SNaN) and quiet NaN (QNaN). SNaNs are created by software; an x86-64 processor will not create a SNaN during any arithmetic operation. Any attempt by an instruction to use a SNaN will cause an invalid operation exception unless the exception is masked. SNaNs are useful for testing exception handlers. They can also be exploited by an application program for proprietary numerical-processing purposes. An x86-64 processor uses QNaNs as a default response to certain invalid arithmetic operations whose exceptions are masked. For example, one unique encoding of a QNaN, called an indefinite, is substituted for a result whenever a function uses a scalar square root instruction with a negative value. QNaNs can also be used by programs to signify algorithm-specific errors or other unusual numerical conditions. When QNaNs are used as operands, they enable continued processing without generating an exception.

When developing software that performs floating-point calculations, it is important to keep in mind that the IEEE 754 encoding scheme is simply an approximation of a real-number system. It is impossible for any floating-point encoding scheme to represent an infinite number of values using a finite number of bits. This limitation often causes floating-point rounding errors that can affect the accuracy of a calculation. Also, some mathematical properties that hold true for integers and real numbers are not necessarily true for floating-point numbers. For example, floating-point multiplication is not necessarily associative; $(a * b) * c$ may not equal $a * (b * c)$ depending on the values of a, b, and c. Developers of algorithms that require high levels of floating-point accuracy must be aware of these issues. You are encouraged to consult the floating-point references listed in Appendix B for more information regarding this topic.

---

[1] The IEEE 754-2008 standard uses the expression subnormal instead of denormal. This text utilizes denormal since this term is still used in the AMD and Intel programming reference manuals.

Scalar Floating-Point Registers

In Chapter 1, you learned that all x86-64 compatible processors include 16 XMM registers named XMM0–XMM15 (see Figures 1-6 and 1-7). Processors that support AVX-512 incorporate 16 additional XMM registers named XMM16–XMM31. A function can use these registers to perform scalar floating-point operations including fundamental arithmetic (e.g., addition, subtraction, multiplication, division, and square root), data transfers, comparisons, and type conversions. You'll learn how to perform these operations later in this chapter.

You also learned in Chapter 1 that an X86-64 processor contains a floating-point status-control register named MXCSR (see Figure 1-4 and Table 1-5). An application program can modify any of the MXCSR's control flags or status bits to accommodate its specific SIMD floating-point processing requirements. Any attempt to write a non-zero value to a reserved bit position will cause the processor to generate an exception. The processor sets an MXCSR error flag to 1 following the occurrence of an error condition. MXCSR error flags are not automatically cleared by the processor after an error is detected; they must be manually reset. The control flags and status bits of the MXCSR register can be modified using the vldmxcsr (Load MXCSR Register) instruction. Setting a mask bit to 1 disables the corresponding exception. The vstmxcsr (Store MXCSR Register) instruction can be used to save the current MXCSR state. An application program cannot directly access the internal processor tables that specify floating-point exception handlers. However, most C++ compilers provide a library function that allows an application program to designate a callback function that gets invoked whenever a floating-point exception occurs.

The MXCSR includes two control flags that can be used to speed up certain floating-point calculations. Setting the MXCSR.DAZ control flag to 1 can improve the performance of algorithms where the rounding of a denormal value to zero is acceptable. Similarly, the MXCSR.FZ control flag can be used to accelerate computations where floating-point underflows are common. The downside of enabling either of these options is noncompliance with the IEEE 754 floating-point standard.

Many modern programs use AVX scalar floating-point instructions instead of legacy SSE2 or x87 FPU instructions. The primary reason for this is that most AVX instructions employ three operands: two non-destructive source operands and one destination operand. The use of non-destructive source operands often reduces the number of register-to-register transfers that a function must perform, which yields more efficient code. The remaining sections of this chapter explain how to code assembly language functions that perform scalar floating-point operations using AVX. You'll also learn how to exchange floating-point arguments and return values between a C++ and assembly language function.

Single-Precision Floating-Point Arithmetic

In this section, you'll learn how to code assembly language functions that carry out elementary scalar floating-point arithmetic using AVX instructions. You'll also learn how to use a few floating-point assembler directives.

Temperature Conversions

The first source code example of this chapter illustrates how to perform temperature conversions between Fahrenheit and Celsius using AVX instructions and single-precision floating-point arithmetic. It also explains how to define and use floating-point constants in an assembly language function. Here are the equations that source code example Ch05_01 uses for temperature conversions:

$$C = (F - 32) * 5 / 9$$

$$F = (C * 9 / 5) + 32$$

Listing 5-1a shows the C++ source code for example Ch05_01. In this listing, header file Ch05_01.h contains declarations for the assembly language functions ConvertFtoC_avx() and ConvertCtoF_avx(). These functions perform temperature conversions between Fahrenheit and Celsius. Note that both functions require a single argument value of type float; they also return a value of type float. The _avx suffix used in the function names signifies that these functions require a processor that supports the AVX instruction set as explained in Chapter 2. Also shown in Listing 5-1a is the file Ch05_01.cpp, which contains code that performs test case initialization and exercises the temperature conversion functions.

Listing 5-1a. Example Ch05_01 C++ Code

```
//-----------------------------------------------------------------------
// Ch05_01.h
//-----------------------------------------------------------------------

#pragma once

// Ch05_01_fasm.asm, Ch05_01_fasm.s
extern "C" float ConvertFtoC_avx(float deg_f);
extern "C" float ConvertCtoF_avx(float deg_c);


//-----------------------------------------------------------------------
// Ch05_01.cpp
//-----------------------------------------------------------------------

#include <iostream>
#include <iomanip>
#include "Ch05_01.h"

static void ConvertFtoC(void)
{
    constexpr int w = 10;
    constexpr float deg_fvals[] =
    {
        -459.67f, -40.0f, 0.0f, 32.0f, 72.0f, 98.6f, 212.0f
    };
    constexpr size_t n = sizeof(deg_fvals) / sizeof(float);

    std::cout << "\n--- ConvertFtoC_avx() results ---\n";
    std::cout << std::fixed << std::setprecision(4);

    for (size_t i = 0; i < n; i++)
    {
        float deg_c = ConvertFtoC_avx(deg_fvals[i]);

        std::cout << "  i: " << i << "  ";
        std::cout << "f: " << std::setw(w) << deg_fvals[i] << "  ";
        std::cout << "c: " << std::setw(w) << deg_c << '\n';
    }
}
```

```cpp
static void ConvertCtoF(void)
{
    constexpr int w = 10;
    constexpr float deg_cvals[] =
    {
        -273.15f, -40.0f, -17.777778f, 0.0f, 25.0f, 37.0f, 100.0f
    };
    constexpr size_t n = sizeof(deg_cvals) / sizeof(float);

    std::cout << "\n--- ConvertCtoF_avx() results ---\n";
    std::cout << std::fixed << std::setprecision(4);

    for (size_t i = 0; i < n; i++)
    {
        float deg_f = ConvertCtoF_avx(deg_cvals[i]);

        std::cout << "  i: " << i << "   ";
        std::cout << "c: " << std::setw(w) << deg_cvals[i] << "   ";
        std::cout << "f: " << std::setw(w) << deg_f << '\n';
    }
}

int main()
{
    std::cout << "----- Results for Ch05_01 -----\n";

    ConvertFtoC();
    ConvertCtoF();
    return 0;
}
```

Listing 5-1b shows the MASM code for example Ch05_01. This listing begins with a .const section that defines the constants needed to convert a temperature value from Fahrenheit to Celsius and vice versa. The text real4 is a MASM directive that allocates storage space for single-precision floating-point value (the directive real8 can be used for double-precision floating-point values). MASM also supports the use of the dd (or dq) directive to define a floating-point constant (e.g., F32_32p0 dd 32.0). This text uses the former since it improves readability and reduces potential errors. Using dd without the decimal point would define an integer value.

Listing 5-1b. Example Ch05_01 MASM Code

```
;---------------------------------------------------------------------------
; Ch05_01_fasm.asm
;---------------------------------------------------------------------------

                .const
F32_ScaleFtoC   real4 0.55555556        ;5 / 9
F32_ScaleCtoF   real4 1.8               ;9 / 5
F32_32p0        real4 32.0
```

```
;--------------------------------------------------------------------
; float ConvertFtoC_avx(float deg_f);
;--------------------------------------------------------------------

        .code
ConvertFtoC_avx proc
        vmovss xmm1,[F32_32p0]           ;xmm1 = 32
        vsubss xmm2,xmm0,xmm1            ;xmm2 = f - 32

        vmovss xmm1,[F32_ScaleFtoC]     ;xmm1 = 5 / 9
        vmulss xmm0,xmm2,xmm1           ;xmm0 = (f - 32) * 5 / 9
        ret

ConvertFtoC_avx endp

;--------------------------------------------------------------------
; float ConvertCtoF_avx(float deg_c);
;--------------------------------------------------------------------

ConvertCtoF_avx proc
        vmulss xmm0,xmm0,[F32_ScaleCtoF]    ;xmm0 = c * 9 / 5
        vaddss xmm0,xmm0,[F32_32p0]         ;xmm0 = c * 9 / 5 + 32
        ret

ConvertCtoF_avx endp
        end
```

Immediately after the .const section in Listing 5-1b is the code for function ConvertFtoC_avx(). The first instruction of this function, vmovss xmm1,[F32_32p0] (Move or Merge Scalar SPFP Value), loads the single-precision floating-point value 32.0 from memory into register XMM1 (more precisely into XMM1[31:0]). A memory operand is used here since AVX scalar floating-point instructions cannot be used with an immediate operand (e.g., vmovss xmm1,32.0 is invalid).

Upon entry to function ConvertFtoC_avx(), register XMM0 contains argument value deg_f as specified by the Visual C++ calling convention. The particulars of floating-point argument passing will be explained later in this chapter. Following execution of the vmovss instruction, the vsubss xmm2,xmm0,xmm1 (Subtract Scalar SPFP Value) instruction calculates deg_f - 32.0 and saves the result in XMM2. Execution of this vsubss instruction *does not* modify the contents of source operands XMM0 and XMM1; however, it copies bits XMM0[127:32] (first source operand) to the same bit positions in destination operand XMM2. This copy operation can be exploited to merge floating-point values in a SIMD destination operand when the two source operands of an AVX scalar floating-point instruction are different. Other AVX scalar arithmetic instructions, both single- and double-precision, also carry out this bit copy operation, and it's usually ignored when performing ordinary scalar floating-point calculations.

The ensuing vmovss xmm1,[F32_ScaleFtoC] loads constant value 0.55555556 (or 5 / 9) into register XMM1. This is followed by a vmulss xmm0,xmm2,xmm1 (Multiply Scalar SPFP Value) instruction that computes (deg_f - 32.0) * 0.55555556 and saves the result (i.e., the converted temperature in Celsius) in XMM0. The Visual C++ calling convention designates register XMM0 for floating-point return values. Since the return value is already in XMM0, no additional vmovss instructions are necessary.

Next in Listing 5-1b is the assembly language function ConvertCtoF_avx(). The code for this function differs slightly from ConvertFtoC_avx() in that the AVX scalar floating-point arithmetic instructions use memory operands to reference the required conversion constants. At entry to ConvertCtoF_avx(), register XMM0 contains argument value deg_c. The instruction vmulss xmm0,xmm0,[F32_ScaleCtoF] calculates deg_c * 1.8. This is followed by a vaddss xmm0,xmm0,[F32_32p0] (Add Scalar SPFP Value) instruction that calculates deg_c * 1.8 + 32.0. It should be noted at this point that neither ConvertFtoC_avx() nor ConvertCtoF_avx() perform any validation checks for argument values that are physically impossible (e.g., a temperature of –1000 degrees Fahrenheit). Such checks require floating-point compare instructions, and you'll learn about these instructions later in this chapter.

Listing 5-1c shows the NASM code for this example. Like the MASM code, Listing 5-1c begins with a read-only section of single-precision floating-point constant values. The dd directive is used here since NASM doesn't support real4. Note that the arithmetic code in the NASM implementations of ConvertFtoC_avx() and ConvertCtoF_avx() is identical to the MASM versions including the use of XMM0 for the argument and return values.

Listing 5-1c. Example Ch05_01 NASM Code

```
;-------------------------------------------------------------------------------
; Ch05_01_fasm.s
;-------------------------------------------------------------------------------

        %include "ModX86Asm3eNASM.inc"

                section .rdata
F32_ScaleFtoC   dd 0.55555556               ;5 / 9
F32_ScaleCtoF   dd 1.8                      ;9 / 5
F32_32p0        dd 32.0


;-------------------------------------------------------------------------------
; float ConvertFtoC_avx(float deg_f);
;-------------------------------------------------------------------------------

        section .text

        global ConvertFtoC_avx
ConvertFtoC_avx:
        vmovss xmm1,[F32_32p0]              ;xmm1 = 32
        vsubss xmm2,xmm0,xmm1               ;xmm2 = f - 32

        vmovss xmm1,[F32_ScaleFtoC]         ;xmm1 = 5 / 9
        vmulss xmm0,xmm2,xmm1               ;xmm0 = (f - 32) * 5 / 9
        ret


;-------------------------------------------------------------------------------
; float ConvertCtoF_avx(float deg_c);
;-------------------------------------------------------------------------------

        global ConvertCtoF_avx
ConvertCtoF_avx:
        vmulss xmm0,xmm0,[F32_ScaleCtoF]    ;xmm0 = c * 9 / 5
        vaddss xmm0,xmm0,[F32_32p0]         ;xmm0 = c * 9 / 5 + 32
        ret
```

Here are the results for source code example Ch05_01:

```
----- Results for Ch05_01 -----

--- ConvertFtoC_avx() results ---
  i: 0  f:  -459.6700  c:  -273.1500
  i: 1  f:   -40.0000  c:   -40.0000
  i: 2  f:     0.0000  c:   -17.7778
  i: 3  f:    32.0000  c:     0.0000
  i: 4  f:    72.0000  c:    22.2222
  i: 5  f:    98.6000  c:    37.0000
  i: 6  f:   212.0000  c:   100.0000

--- ConvertCtoF_avx() results ---
  i: 0  c:  -273.1500  f:  -459.6700
  i: 1  c:   -40.0000  f:   -40.0000
  i: 2  c:   -17.7778  f:     0.0000
  i: 3  c:     0.0000  f:    32.0000
  i: 4  c:    25.0000  f:    77.0000
  i: 5  c:    37.0000  f:    98.6000
  i: 6  c:   100.0000  f:   212.0000
```

Cone Volume/Surface Area Calculation

The next source code example, named Ch05_02, demonstrates how to calculate the volume and surface area of a right-circular cone using AVX single-precision floating-point instructions. The volume and surface area of a right-circular cone can be calculated using the following equations:

$$V = \frac{\pi r^2 h}{3}$$

$$A = \pi r \left(r + \sqrt{r^2 + h^2} \right)$$

Listing 5-2a shows the C++ source code for example Ch05_02.

Listing 5-2a. Example Ch05_02 C++ Code

```cpp
//-----------------------------------------------------------------------------
// Ch05_02.h
//-----------------------------------------------------------------------------

#pragma once
#include <cstddef>

// Ch05_02_fasm.asm, Ch05_02_fasm.s
extern "C" void CalcConeVolSA_avx(float* vol, float* sa, float r, float h);
```

```cpp
// Ch05_02_fcpp.cpp
extern "C" float g_F32_PI;
extern void CalcConeVolSA_cpp(float* vol, float* sa, float r, float h);

// Ch05_02_misc.cpp
extern void DisplayResults(size_t i, float r, float h, float vol1, float sa1,
    float vol2, float sa2);

//-----------------------------------------------------------------------------
// Ch05_02_misc.cpp
//-----------------------------------------------------------------------------

#include <iostream>
#include <iomanip>
#include "Ch05_02.h"

void DisplayResults(size_t i, float r, float h, float vol1, float sa1, float vol2,
float sa2)
{
    constexpr int w1 = 4;
    constexpr int w2 = 8;
    constexpr char sp = ' ';

    std::cout << "i: " << i << sp;
    std::cout << "r: " << std::setw(w1) << r << sp;
    std::cout << "h: " << std::setw(w1) << h << sp;
    std::cout << "vol1: " << std::setw(w2) << vol1 << sp;
    std::cout << "vol2: " << std::setw(w2) << vol2 << sp;
    std::cout << "sa1: " << std::setw(w2) << sa1 << sp;
    std::cout << "sa2: " << std::setw(w2) << sa2 << '\n';
}

//-----------------------------------------------------------------------------
// Ch05_02_fcpp.cpp
//-----------------------------------------------------------------------------

#include <cmath>
#include <numbers>
#include "Ch05_02.h"

float g_F32_PI = std::numbers::pi_v<float>;      // used in asm code

void CalcConeVolSA_cpp(float* vol, float* sa, float r, float h)
{
    constexpr float pi = std::numbers::pi_v<float>;

    *vol = pi * r * r * h / 3.0f;
    *sa = pi * r * (r + sqrt(r * r + h * h));
}
```

```
//-----------------------------------------------------------------------------
// Ch05_02.cpp
//-----------------------------------------------------------------------------

#include <iostream>
#include <iomanip>
#include "Ch05_02.h"

int main()
{
    constexpr float r_vals[] { 1.0f, 2.0f, 3.0f, 4.0f, 5.0f };
    constexpr float h_vals[] { 1.0f, 3.5f, 4.0f, 6.5f, 8.0f };
    constexpr size_t n = sizeof(r_vals) / sizeof(float);

    std::cout << "----- Results for Ch05_02 -----\n";
    std::cout << std::fixed << std::setprecision(3);

    for (size_t i = 0; i < n; i++)
    {
        float vol1, sa1;
        float vol2, sa2;
        float r = r_vals[i];
        float h = h_vals[i];

        CalcConeVolSA_cpp(&vol1, &sa1, r, h);
        CalcConeVolSA_avx(&vol2, &sa2, r, h);
        DisplayResults(i, r, h, vol1, sa1, vol2, sa2);
    }

    return 0;
}
```

In Listing 5-2a, file Ch05_02.h contains the requisite function declarations for this example. Note that the "C" modifier is used in the declaration of g_F32_PI, which enables the assembly language code to reference this value. Example Ch05_02 uses a global variable for the transcendental constant π to ensure that both the C++ and assembly language code carry out their calculations using the exact same value. Function main() in file Ch05_02.cpp defines two arrays, r_vals and h_vals, of type float. These arrays hold test radii and heights. File Ch05_02_fcpp.cpp contains the definition of g_F32_PI. It also includes the definition of function CalcConeVolSA_cpp() for result comparison purposes.

Listing 5-2b shows the MASM code for example Ch05_02. Immediately after the .const section is the statement extern g_F32_PI:real4. Recall from the discussions in Chapter 3 that the MASM extern directive declares a variable whose definition is contained in another module.

Listing 5-2b. Example Ch05_02 MASM Code

```
;-----------------------------------------------------------------------------
; Ch05_02_fasm.asm
;-----------------------------------------------------------------------------

            .const
F32_3p0     real4 3.0

            extern g_F32_PI:real4
```

```
;-----------------------------------------------------------------------------
; void CalcConeVolSA_avx(float* vol, float* sa, float r, float h);
;-----------------------------------------------------------------------------

        .code
CalcConeVolSA_avx proc

; Calculate vol = pi * r * r * h / 3.0f;
        vmulss xmm0,xmm2,xmm2        ;xmm0 = r * r;
        vmulss xmm1,xmm0,[g_F32_PI]  ;xmm1 = r * r * pi
        vmulss xmm4,xmm1,xmm3        ;xmm4 = r * r * pi * h
        vdivss xmm5,xmm4,[F32_3p0]   ;xmm5 = r * r * pi * h / 3.0
        vmovss real4 ptr [rcx],xmm5  ;save volume

; Calculate sa = pi * r * (r + sqrt(r * r + h * h));
        vmulss xmm3,xmm3,xmm3        ;xmm3 = h * h
        vaddss xmm0,xmm0,xmm3        ;xmm0 = r * r + h * h
        vsqrtss xmm1,xmm0,xmm0       ;xmm1 = sqrt(r * r + h * h)
        vaddss xmm4,xmm1,xmm2        ;xmm4 = sqrt(r * r + h * h) + r
        vmulss xmm5,xmm2,[g_F32_PI]  ;xmm5 = r * pi
        vmulss xmm5,xmm5,xmm4        ;xmm5 = r * pi * (sqrt(r * r + h * h) + r)
        vmovss real4 ptr [rdx],xmm5  ;save surface area
        ret

CalcConeVolSA_avx endp
        end
```

Upon entry to function CalcConeVolSA_avx(), register RCX contains argument pointer vol, register RDX contains argument pointer sa, register XMM2 contains argument value r, and register XMM3 contains argument value h. The Visual C++ calling convention specifies a combination of general-purpose and XMM registers for functions that employ a mix of integer and floating-point arguments. Integer arguments are passed using the general-purpose registers, while floating-point arguments are passed using XMM registers. The first argument is passed in register RCX or XMM0, the second argument in register RDX or XMM1, the third argument in register R8 or XMM2, and the fourth argument in register R9 or XMM3. Any additional arguments are passed via the stack. Figure 5-3 illustrates register and stack contents for function CalcConeVolSA_avx(). You'll learn additional details about Visual C++'s calling convention requirements for floating-point values and registers in Chapter 6.

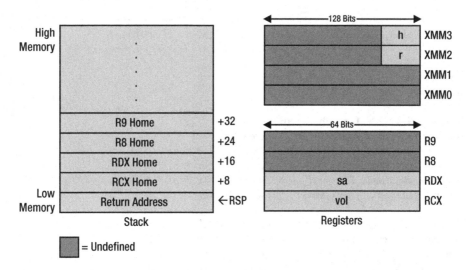

Figure 5-3. Argument register and stack contents for MASM function CalcConeVolSA_avx()

The first executable instruction of CalcConeVolSA_avx(), vmulss xmm0,xmm2,xmm2, calculates r * r. This is followed by a vmulss xmm1,xmm0,[g_F32_PI] instruction that computes r * r * g_F32_PI. The next two instructions, vmulss xmm4,xmm1,xmm3 and vdivss xmm5,xmm4,[F32_3p0], complete the cone volume calculation. The final instruction of the first code block, vmovss real4 ptr [rcx],xmm5, saves the calculated volume to the memory location pointed to by argument value vol. Note the use of the real4 ptr operator in the vmovss instruction, which MASM requires. You can also use operator dword ptr instead of real4 ptr with a vmovss instruction, but I prefer the latter since the former is also used with integer memory operands.

The second code block in function CalcConeVolSA_avx() calculates the cone surface area. Note that the vsqrtss (Compute Square Root of SPFP Value) requires three operands. During execution of this instruction, the processor calculates the square root of the single-precision floating-point value in bits 31:0 in the second source operand (XMM0) and saves this result in bits 31:0 of the destination operand (XMM1). The vsqrtss instruction also copies bits 127:32 of its first source operand to the same bit positions in the destination operand. Following calculation of the surface area, CalcConeVolSA_avx() employs a vmovss real4 ptr [rdx],xmm5 instruction to save the result.

Listing 5-2c shows the NASM code for example Ch05_02.

Listing 5-2c. Example Ch05_02 NASM Code

```
;-----------------------------------------------------------------------------
; Ch05_02_fasm.s
;-----------------------------------------------------------------------------

        %include "ModX86Asm3eNASM.inc"

            section .rdata
F32_3p0     dd 3.0


;-----------------------------------------------------------------------------
; void CalcConeVolSA_avx(float* vol, float* sa, float r, float h);
;-----------------------------------------------------------------------------
```

```
        section .text
        extern g_F32_PI

        global CalcConeVolSA_avx
CalcConeVolSA_avx:

; Calculate vol = pi * r * r * h / 3.0f;
        vmulss xmm2,xmm0,xmm0            ;xmm2 = r * r;
        vmulss xmm3,xmm2,[g_F32_PI]     ;xmm3 = r * r * pi
        vmulss xmm4,xmm3,xmm1           ;xmm4 = r * r * pi * h
        vdivss xmm5,xmm4,[F32_3p0]      ;xmm5 = r * r * pi * h / 3.0
        vmovss [rdi],xmm5               ;save volume

; Calculate sa = pi * r * (r + sqrt(r * r + h * h));
        vmulss xmm3,xmm1,xmm1           ;xmm3 = h * h
        vaddss xmm4,xmm2,xmm3           ;xmm4 = r * r + h * h
        vsqrtss xmm5,xmm4,xmm4          ;xmm5 = sqrt(r * r + h * h)
        vaddss xmm5,xmm0,xmm5           ;xmm5 = r + sqrt(r * r + h * h
        vmulss xmm2,xmm0,[g_F32_PI]     ;xmm2 = r * pi
        vmulss xmm5,xmm2,xmm5           ;xmm5 = r * pi * (r + sqrt(r * r + h * h))
        vmovss [rsi],xmm5               ;save surface area
        ret
```

Compared to the MASM implementation, the NASM code in Listing 5-2c uses different general-purpose and XMM registers since the calling convention requirements for argument values are different. In Chapter 2, you learned that the GNU C++ calling convention specifies the use of registers RDI, RSI, RDX, RCX, R8, and R9 for the first six integer argument values. The convention also specifies the use of registers XMM0–XMM7 for the first eight scalar floating-point arguments. Any additional arguments are passed via the stack. Unlike a Visual C++ function, a GNU C++ function *always* passes the first integer argument value in register RDI, the second integer argument value in register RSI, and so on. It also *always* passes the first scalar floating-point argument in register XMM0, the second scalar floating-point argument in register XMM1, and so on. Figure 5-4 shows stack and register contents upon entry to CalcConeVolSA_avx(). Chapter 6 discusses additional details regarding GNU C++'s calling convention requirements for floating-point values and registers.

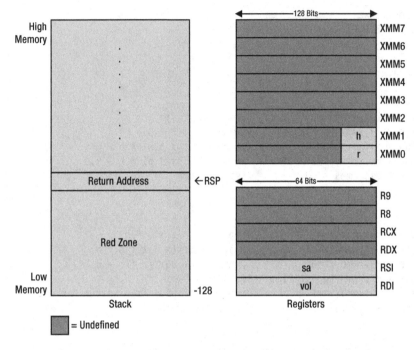

Figure 5-4. *Argument register and stack contents for NASM function* `CalcConeVolSA_avx()`

There are two other items to note in Listing 5-2c. First, the constant `F32_3p0` is defined using the `dd` operator since NASM doesn't support `real4`. Don't forget to include the decimal point when defining a floating-point constant since omitting it instructs NASM to generate an integer value instead. Second, note the two `vmovss` instructions. NASM doesn't require a size operator when using `vmovss` with a memory operand. Here are the results for source code example Ch05_02:

```
----- Results for Ch05_02 -----
i: 0 r: 1.000 h: 1.000 vol1:    1.047 vol2:    1.047 sa1:    7.584 sa2:    7.584
i: 1 r: 2.000 h: 3.500 vol1:   14.661 vol2:   14.661 sa1:   37.895 sa2:   37.895
i: 2 r: 3.000 h: 4.000 vol1:   37.699 vol2:   37.699 sa1:   75.398 sa2:   75.398
i: 3 r: 4.000 h: 6.500 vol1:  108.909 vol2:  108.909 sa1:  146.174 sa2:  146.174
i: 4 r: 5.000 h: 8.000 vol1:  209.440 vol2:  209.440 sa1:  226.728 sa2:  226.728
```

You may have noticed that all AVX scalar single-precision floating-point instruction mnemonics contain the suffix string `ss`. Similarly, AVX scalar double-precision floating-point instruction mnemonics use the suffix string `sd` as you'll see in the next section.

Double-Precision Floating-Point Arithmetic

The AVX instruction set also supports calculations using double-precision floating-point. The next source code example, named Ch05_03, calculates the surface area and volume of a sphere using double-precision floating-point arithmetic. Listing 5-3a shows the C++ source code for this example.

Listing 5-3a. Example Ch05_03 C++ Code

```
//-----------------------------------------------------------------------------
// Ch05_03.h
//-----------------------------------------------------------------------------

#pragma once
#include <cstddef>

// Ch05_03_fasm.asm, Ch05_03_fasm.s
extern "C" void CalcSphereVolSA_avx(double* vol, double* sa, double r);

// Ch05_03_fcpp.cpp
extern "C" double g_F64_PI;
extern void CalcSphereVolSA_cpp(double* vol, double* sa, double r);

// Ch05_03_misc.cpp
extern void DisplayResults(size_t i, double r, double vol1, double sa1,
    double vol2, double sa2);

//-----------------------------------------------------------------------------
// Ch05_03_misc.cpp
//-----------------------------------------------------------------------------

#include <iostream>
#include <iomanip>
#include "Ch05_03.h"

extern void DisplayResults(size_t i, double r, double vol1, double sa1,
    double vol2, double sa2)
{
    constexpr int w1 = 6;
    constexpr int w2 = 9;
    constexpr char sp = ' ';

    std::cout << "i: " << i << sp;
    std::cout << "r: " << std::setw(w1) << r << sp;
    std::cout << "vol1: " << std::setw(w2) << vol1 << sp;
    std::cout << "vol2: " << std::setw(w2) << vol2 << sp;
    std::cout << "sa1: " << std::setw(w2) << sa1 << sp;
    std::cout << "sa2: " << std::setw(w2) << sa2 << '\n';
}

//-----------------------------------------------------------------------------
// Ch05_03_fcpp.cpp
//-----------------------------------------------------------------------------

#include <numbers>
#include "Ch05_03.h"
```

149

```
double g_F64_PI = std::numbers::pi_v<double>;        // used in asm code

void CalcSphereVolSA_cpp(double* vol, double* sa, double r)
{
    double sa_temp = 4.0 * std::numbers::pi_v<double> * r * r;
    double vol_temp = sa_temp * r / 3.0;

    *sa = sa_temp;
    *vol = vol_temp;
}
//-----------------------------------------------------------------------
// Ch05_03.cpp
//-----------------------------------------------------------------------

#include <iostream>
#include <iomanip>
#include "Ch05_03.h"

int main()
{
    constexpr double r_vals[] = { 0.0, 1.0, 2.0, 3.0, 5.0, 10.0, 15.0, 20.0 };
    constexpr size_t n = sizeof(r_vals) / sizeof(double);

    std::cout << "----- Results for Ch05_03 -----\n";
    std::cout << std::fixed << std::setprecision(2);

    for (size_t i = 0; i < n; i++)
    {
        double vol1, sa1;
        double vol2, sa2;

        CalcSphereVolSA_cpp(&vol1, &sa1, r_vals[i]);
        CalcSphereVolSA_avx(&vol2, &sa2, r_vals[i]);
        DisplayResults(i, r_vals[i], vol1, sa1, vol2, sa2);
    }

    return 0;
}
```

Organization of the C++ code in Listing 5-3a resembles other examples that you have already seen. Note that the function declarations in file Ch05_03.h use the C++ type double. Also note that like the previous example, the declaration of g_F64_PI uses the "C" modifier since this global variable is referenced in the assembly language code. Functions CalcSphereVolSA_avx() and CalcSphereVolSA_cpp() use the following equations to calculate the surface area and volume of a sphere:

$$A = 4\pi r^2$$

$$V = \frac{4\pi r^3}{3} = \frac{Ar}{3}$$

Listing 5-3b shows the MASM code for example Ch05_03. Near the top of this listing is a .const section that defines two double-precision floating-point values named F64_3p0 and F64_4p0. The MASM directive real8 is the double-precision counterpart of the real4 directive that you saw in earlier examples. Execution of function CalcSphereVolSA_avx() begins with a vmulsd xmm1,xmm2,xmm2 (Multiply Scalar DPFP Value) instruction that calculates r * r. Note that argument value r was passed in register XMM2. The next two instructions, vmulsd xmm3,xmm1,[g_F64_PI] and vmulsd xmm4,xmm3,[F64_4p0], calculate the sphere's surface area (r * r * g_F64_PI * 4). This is followed by a vmovsd real8 ptr [rdx],xmm4 (Move or Merge Scalar DPFP Value) that saves the results to the memory location pointed to by argument value sa. Note that MASM requires use of the operator real8 ptr with a vmovsd instruction.

Listing 5-3b. Example Ch05_03 MASM Code

```
//----------------------------------------------------------------------------
// Ch05_03.cpp
//----------------------------------------------------------------------------

#include <iostream>
#include <iomanip>
#include "Ch05_03.h"

int main()
{
    constexpr double r_vals[] = { 0.0, 1.0, 2.0, 3.0, 5.0, 10.0, 15.0, 20.0 };
    constexpr size_t n = sizeof(r_vals) / sizeof(double);

    std::cout << "----- Results for Ch05_03 -----\n";
    std::cout << std::fixed << std::setprecision(2);

    for (size_t i = 0; i < n; i++)
    {
        double vol1, sa1;
        double vol2, sa2;

        CalcSphereVolSA_cpp(&vol1, &sa1, r_vals[i]);
        CalcSphereVolSA_avx(&vol2, &sa2, r_vals[i]);
        DisplayResults(i, r_vals[i], vol1, sa1, vol2, sa2);
    }

    return 0;
}
```

Following calculation of the surface area, the instruction pair vmulsd xmm5,xmm4,xmm2 and vdivsd xmm5,xmm5,[F64_3p0] (Divide Scalar DPFP Value) computes the sphere's volume. The ensuing vmovsd real8 ptr [rcx],xmm5 instruction saves the calculated volume.

Listing 5-3c contains the NASM code for example Ch05_03. This file begins with a .rdata section that defines the required constants. Note that double-precision floating-point values are defined using the dq specifier. The NASM implementation of CalcSphereVolSA_avx() uses the same AVX scalar floating-point instructions as the MASM version albeit with different registers. Note that argument value r is passed via register XMM0.

Listing 5-3c. Example Ch05_03 NASM Code

```
;------------------------------------------------------------------------
; Ch05_03_fasm.s
;------------------------------------------------------------------------

        %include "ModX86Asm3eNASM.inc"

        section .rdata
F64_3p0 dq 3.0
F64_4p0 dq 4.0


;------------------------------------------------------------------------
; void CalcSphereVolSA_avx(double* vol, double* sa, double r);
;------------------------------------------------------------------------

        section .text
        extern g_F64_PI

        global CalcSphereVolSA_avx
CalcSphereVolSA_avx:

; Calculate surface area = 4 * PI * r * r
        vmulsd xmm1,xmm0,xmm0          ;xmm1 = r * r
        vmulsd xmm3,xmm1,[g_F64_PI]    ;xmm3 = r * r * PI
        vmulsd xmm4,xmm3,[F64_4p0]     ;xmm4 = r * r * PI * 4
        vmovsd [rsi],xmm4              ;save surface area

; Calculate volume = sa * r / 3
        vmulsd xmm5,xmm4,xmm0          ;xmm4 = r * r * r * PI * 4
        vdivsd xmm5,xmm5,[F64_3p0]     ;xmm5 = r * r * r * PI * 4 / 3
        vmovsd [rdi],xmm5              ;save volume
        ret
```

Here are the results for source code example Ch05_03:

```
----- Results for Ch05_03 -----
i: 0 r:   0.00 vol1:      0.00 vol2:      0.00 sa1:     0.00 sa2:     0.00
i: 1 r:   1.00 vol1:      4.19 vol2:      4.19 sa1:    12.57 sa2:    12.57
i: 2 r:   2.00 vol1:     33.51 vol2:     33.51 sa1:    50.27 sa2:    50.27
i: 3 r:   3.00 vol1:    113.10 vol2:    113.10 sa1:   113.10 sa2:   113.10
i: 4 r:   5.00 vol1:    523.60 vol2:    523.60 sa1:   314.16 sa2:   314.16
i: 5 r:  10.00 vol1:   4188.79 vol2:   4188.79 sa1:  1256.64 sa2:  1256.64
i: 6 r:  15.00 vol1:  14137.17 vol2:  14137.17 sa1:  2827.43 sa2:  2827.43
i: 7 r:  20.00 vol1:  33510.32 vol2:  33510.32 sa1:  5026.55 sa2:  5026.55
```

Floating-Point Comparisons and Conversions

Functions that carry out floating-point arithmetic calculations are also likely to perform floating-point comparisons and conversions. The source code examples of this section demonstrate how to perform these operations. The first two examples illustrate floating-point comparisons using the vucomiss (Unordered Compare Scalar SPFP Values and Set RFLAGS) and vcmpss (Compare Scalar SPFP Values) instructions. The third example surveys several AVX floating-point conversion instructions. This example also explains how to modify the floating-point rounding control bits in the MXCSR register.

Floating-Point Comparisons

Listing 5-4a shows the C++ source code for example Ch05_04. This example illustrates the use of the vucomiss instruction, which performs a single-precision floating-point compare operation. The AVX instruction set also includes a vucomisd instruction that performs double-precision floating-point compare operation. Both instructions compare two floating-point values and set status flags in RFLAGS to signify a result of less than, equal, greater than, or unordered. An unordered result occurs if one of the compared values is a NaN. The explanations in this section apply to both vucomiss and vucomisd unless otherwise noted.

Listing 5-4a. Example Ch05_04 C++ Code

```
//-----------------------------------------------------------------------
// Ch05_04.h
//-----------------------------------------------------------------------

#pragma once
#include <cstddef>
#include <cstdint>

// Ch05_04_fasm.asm, Ch05_04_fasm.s
extern "C" void CompareF32_avx(uint8_t* cmp_results, float a, float b);

// Ch05_04_misc.cpp
extern void DisplayResults(const uint8_t* cmp_results, float a, float b);

// Miscellaenous constants
constexpr size_t c_NumCmpOps = 7;

//-----------------------------------------------------------------------
// Ch05_04_misc.cpp
//-----------------------------------------------------------------------

#include <iostream>
#include <iomanip>
#include "Ch05_04.h"

static const char* c_OpStrings[c_NumCmpOps] =
{
    "UO", "LT", "LE", "EQ", "NE", "GT", "GE"
};
```

```
void DisplayResults(const uint8_t* cmp_results, float a, float b)
{
    constexpr char nl = '\n';

    std::cout << std::fixed << std::setprecision(1);
    std::cout << "a = " << a << ", b = " << b << nl;

    for (size_t i = 0; i < c_NumCmpOps; i++)
    {
        std::cout << c_OpStrings[i] << '=';
        std::cout << std::boolalpha << std::left;
        std::cout << std::setw(6) << (cmp_results[i] != 0) << ' ';
    }

    std::cout << nl << nl;
}

//-----------------------------------------------------------------------
// Ch05_04.cpp
//-----------------------------------------------------------------------

#include <iostream>
#include <limits>
#include "Ch05_04.h"

int main()
{
    constexpr size_t n = 6;
    float a[n] { 120.0f, 250.0f, 300.0f, -18.0f,  -81.0f, 42.0f };
    float b[n] { 130.0f, 240.0f, 300.0f,  32.0f, -100.0f,  0.0f };

    // Set NAN test value
    b[n - 1] = std::numeric_limits<float>::quiet_NaN();

    std::cout << "\n----- Results for Ch05_04 -----\n";

    for (size_t i = 0; i < n; i++)
    {
        uint8_t cmp_results[c_NumCmpOps];

        CompareF32_avx(cmp_results, a[i], b[i]);
        DisplayResults(cmp_results, a[i], b[i]);
    }
}
```

In Listing 5-4a, function main() includes code that initializes test values in arrays a and b. Elements from these arrays are passed to the assembly language function CompareF32_avx(). Note that one of the values in test array b is set to a QNaN. Function CompareF32_avx() also requires an array argument of type uint8_t for its results.

Listing 5-4b shows the MASM code for function CompareF32_avx().

Listing 5-4b. Example Ch05_04 MASM Code

```
;----------------------------------------------------------------------------
; Ch05_04_fasm.asm
;----------------------------------------------------------------------------


;----------------------------------------------------------------------------
; void CompareF32_avx(uint8_t* cmp_results, float a, float b);
;----------------------------------------------------------------------------

        .code
CompareF32_avx proc

; Set result flags based on compare status
        vucomiss xmm1,xmm2
        setp byte ptr [rcx]             ;RFLAGS.PF = 1 if unordered
        jnp L1
        xor al,al
        mov [rcx+1],al                  ;set all other cmp_results[]
        mov [rcx+2],al                  ;values to 0
        mov [rcx+3],al
        mov [rcx+4],al
        mov [rcx+5],al
        mov [rcx+6],al
        ret

L1:     setb byte ptr [rcx+1]           ;set byte if a < b
        setbe byte ptr [rcx+2]          ;set byte if a <= b
        sete byte ptr [rcx+3]           ;set byte if a == b
        setne byte ptr [rcx+4]          ;set byte if a != b
        seta byte ptr [rcx+5]           ;set byte if a > b
        setae byte ptr [rcx+6]          ;set byte if a >= b
        ret

CompareF32_avx endp
        end
```

Execution of CompareF32_avx() begins with a vucomiss xmm1,xmm2 instruction that compares argument values a (XMM1) and b (XMM2). This instruction sets RFLAGS.ZF, RFLAGS.PF, and RFLAGS.CF as shown in Table 5-3. The setting of these status flags facilitates the use of the x86 conditional instructions cmovcc, jcc, and setcc as you'll soon see.

Table 5-3. *Status Flags Set During Execution of a vucomis[d|s] Instruction*

Condition	RFLAGS.ZF	RFLAGS.PF	RFLAGS.CF
XMM1 > XMM2	0	0	0
XMM1 == XMM2	1	0	0
XMM1 < XMM2	0	0	1
Unordered	1	1	1

It should be noted that the status flags shown in Table 5-3 are set only if floating-point exceptions are masked (the default state for Visual C++ and GNU C++) and neither vucomis[d|s] operand is a SNaN. If floating-point invalid operation exceptions are unmasked (MXCSR.IM = 0) and one of the vucomis[d|s] operands is a SNaN, the processor will generate an exception without updating the status flags in RFLAGS.

Following execution of the vucomiss xmm1,xmm2 instruction, CompareF32_avx() uses a series of setcc instructions to highlight the relational operators shown in Table 5-4. The setp byte ptr [rcx] instruction sets the destination operand byte pointed to by RCX (cmp_results) to 1 if the compare was unordered (RFLAGS.PF == 1 is true, which means at least one of the source operands is a NaN). Otherwise, the destination operand byte is set to 0. If the compare was ordered, the remaining setcc instructions in CompareF32_avx() save all possible compare outcomes by setting each entry in cmp_results to 0 or 1. As previously mentioned, a function can also use jcc or cmovcc following execution of a vucomis[d|s] instruction to perform conditional jumps or moves based on the outcome of a floating-point compare.

Table 5-4. *Condition Codes Following Execution of a* vucomis[d|s] *Instruction*

Relational Operator	Condition Code	RFLAGS Test Condition
XMM0 < XMM1	Below (b)	CF == 1
XMM0 <= XMM1	Below or equal (be)	CF == 1 || ZF == 1
XMM0 == XMM1	Equal (e or z)	ZF == 1
XMM0 != XMM1	Not Equal (ne or nz)	ZF == 0
XMM0 > XMM1	Above (a)	CF == 0 && ZF == 0
XMM0 >= XMM1	Above or Equal (ae)	CF == 0
Unordered	Parity (p)	PF == 1

Listing 5-4c shows the NASM code for example Ch05_04. This code is identical to the MASM code except for the specific register names.

Listing 5-4c. Example Ch05_04 NASM Code

```
;-------------------------------------------------------------------------------
; Ch05_04_fasm.s
;-------------------------------------------------------------------------------

        %include "ModX86Asm3eNASM.inc"


;-------------------------------------------------------------------------------
; void CompareF32_avx(uint8_t* cmp_results, float a, float b);
;-------------------------------------------------------------------------------

        section .text

        global CompareF32_avx
CompareF32_avx:

; Set result flags based on compare status
        vucomiss xmm0,xmm1
        setp [rdi]                      ;RFLAGS.PF = 1 if unordered
        jnp L1
```

```
        xor  al,al
        mov  [rdi+1],al                    ;set all other cmp_results[]
        mov  [rdi+2],al                    ;values to 0
        mov  [rdi+3],al
        mov  [rdi+4],al
        mov  [rdi+5],al
        mov  [rdi+6],al
        ret

L1:     setb  [rdi+1]                      ;set byte if a < b
        setbe [rdi+2]                      ;set byte if a <= b
        sete  [rdi+3]                      ;set byte if a == b
        setne [rdi+4]                      ;set byte if a != b
        seta  [rdi+5]                      ;set byte if a > b
        setae [rdi+6]                      ;set byte if a >= b
        ret
```

You can also use the vcomis[d|s] instruction to perform floating-point compare operations. The primary difference between this instruction and the vucomis[d|s] instruction used in example Ch05_04 is that the former signals an invalid operation exception (when enabled) for both SNaNs and QNaNs. Here are the results for source code example Ch05_04:

```
----- Results for Ch05_04 -----
a = 120.0, b = 130.0
UO=false  LT=true   LE=true   EQ=false  NE=true   GT=false  GE=false

a = 250.0, b = 240.0
UO=false  LT=false  LE=false  EQ=false  NE=true   GT=true   GE=true

a = 300.0, b = 300.0
UO=false  LT=false  LE=true   EQ=true   NE=false  GT=false  GE=true

a = -18.0, b = 32.0
UO=false  LT=true   LE=true   EQ=false  NE=true   GT=false  GE=false

a = -81.0, b = -100.0
UO=false  LT=false  LE=false  EQ=false  NE=true   GT=true   GE=true

a = 42.0, b = nan
UO=true   LT=false  LE=false  EQ=false  NE=false  GT=false  GE=false
```

The AVX instruction set includes another pair of scalar floating-point compare instructions named vcmps[d|s]. Unlike the vcomis[d|s] instructions, the vcmps[d|s] instructions do not modify any of the status bits in RFLAGS. They employ an immediate operand compare predicate and signify their results via doubleword (single-precision) or quadword (double-precision) mask of all zeros (compare predicate false) or all ones (compare predicate true). The next source code example, Ch05_05, demonstrates the use of the vcmpss instruction. The C++ source code for example Ch05_05 is almost identical to the C++ code used in the previous example except that it reports results for eight comparisons instead of seven. Given this, I'll omit the C++ code listing for this example and jump right into the assembly language code.

Listing 5-5a shows the source code for a MASM assembly language header file named cmpequ_fp.asmh. This file contains a series equ (equate) directives for the various floating-point compare predicates. Like the C++ preprocessor directive #define, you can employ the assembler directive equ to assign a symbolic name to a numeric value. The symbolic names defined in cmpequ_fp.asmh can be used with the vcmps[d|s] instructions as you'll soon see. The AVX SIMD floating-point compare instructions also use these same symbolic names. You'll learn more about this in Chapter 9. There is no standard filename extension for x86 assembly language header files. This text uses .asmh for MASM header files and .inc for NASM header files, respectively.

Listing 5-5a. Example Ch05_05 MASM Code (cmpequ_fp.asmh)

```
;-------------------------------------------------------------------
; cmpequ_fp.asmh
;-------------------------------------------------------------------


;-------------------------------------------------------------------
; See AMD & Intel programming references manuals for more information
; regarding compare predicates and invalid arithmetic (IA) exceptions.
;
; Compare predicate abbreviations
;   EQ = equal                NEQ = not equal
;   LT = less than            LE = less than or equal
;   NLT = not less than       NLE = not less than or equal
;   GT = greater than         GE = greater than or equal
;   NGT = not greater than    NGE = not greater than or equal
;   ORD = ordered             UNORD = unordered
;
; Compare predicate suffix letters
;   O = ordered               U = unordered
;   S = signaling             Q = non-signaling (quiet)
;-------------------------------------------------------------------


;-------------------------------------------------------------------
; Predicate      ImmVal     x > y   x < y   x == y   x or y     IA on
;                                                     is a NaN   QNAN
;-------------------------------------------------------------------

CMP_EQ_OQ        equ 00h  ;  F       F       T        F          N
CMP_LT_OS        equ 01h  ;  F       T       F        F          Y
CMP_LE_OS        equ 02h  ;  F       T       T        F          Y
CMP_UNORD_Q      equ 03h  ;  F       F       F        T          N
CMP_NEQ_UQ       equ 04h  ;  T       T       F        T          N
CMP_NLT_US       equ 05h  ;  T       F       T        T          Y
CMP_NLE_US       equ 06h  ;  T       F       F        T          Y
CMP_ORD_Q        equ 07h  ;  T       T       T        F          N

CMP_EQ_UQ        equ 08h  ;  F       F       T        T          N
CMP_NGE_US       equ 09h  ;  F       T       F        T          Y
CMP_NGT_US       equ 0ah  ;  F       T       T        T          Y
CMP_FALSE_OQ     equ 0bh  ;  F       F       F        F          N
CMP_NEQ_OQ       equ 0ch  ;  T       T       F        F          N
CMP_GE_OS        equ 0dh  ;  T       F       T        F          Y
```

```
CMP_GT_OS       equ 0eh  ;  T       F       F       F               Y
CMP_TRUE_UQ     equ 0fh  ;  T       T       T       T               N

CMP_EQ_OS       equ 10h  ;  F       F       T       F               Y
CMP_LT_OQ       equ 11h  ;  F       T       F       F               N
CMP_LE_OQ       equ 12h  ;  F       T       T       F               N
CMP_UNORD_S     equ 13h  ;  F       F       F       T               Y
CMP_NEQ_US      equ 14h  ;  T       T       F       T               Y
CMP_NLT_UQ      equ 15h  ;  T       F       T       T               N
CMP_NLE_UQ      equ 16h  ;  T       F       F       T               N
CMP_ORD_S       equ 17h  ;  T       T       T       F               Y

CMP_EQ_US       equ 18h  ;  F       F       T       T               Y
CMP_NGE_UQ      equ 19h  ;  F       T       F       T               N
CMP_NGT_UQ      equ 1ah  ;  F       T       T       T               N
CMP_FALSE_OS    equ 1bh  ;  F       F       F       F               Y
CMP_NEQ_OS      equ 1ch  ;  T       T       F       F               Y
CMP_GE_OQ       equ 1dh  ;  T       F       T       F               N
CMP_GT_OQ       equ 1eh  ;  T       F       F       F               N
CMP_TRUE_US     equ 1fh  ;  T       T       T       T               Y
```

You may have noticed that all of the symbolic names defined in cmpequ_fp.asmh include one or more suffix letters. These letters provide additional details regarding the type of compare being performed. The letters O and U signify ordered and unordered, while S and Q designate signaling and non-signaling (or quiet).

Listing 5-5b shows the MASM code for example Ch05_05. Near the top of file Ch05_05.asm is the statement include <cmpequ_fp.asmh>, which incorporates the contents of cmpequ_fp.asmh into file Ch05_05_fasm.asm during assembly. Using a MASM header file is analogous to using a C++ header file. The angled brackets surrounding the filename can be omitted if the filename doesn't contain any backslashes or MASM special characters, but it's usually simpler and more consistent to just always use them. Besides equ statements, assembly language header files often contain macro definitions. You'll learn about macros later in this chapter.

Listing 5-5b. Example Ch05_05 MASM Code

```
;-------------------------------------------------------------------------------
; Ch05_05_fasm.asm
;-------------------------------------------------------------------------------

        include <cmpequ_fp.asmh>


;-------------------------------------------------------------------------------
; void CompareF32_avx(uint8_t* cmp_results, float a, float b);
;-------------------------------------------------------------------------------

        .code
CompareF32_avx proc

; Perform compare for equality
        vcmpss xmm5,xmm1,xmm2,CMP_EQ_OQ     ;perform compare operation
        vmovd eax,xmm5                      ;eax = compare result (all 1s or 0s)
        and al,1                            ;mask out unneeded bits
        mov [rcx],al                        ;save result
```

```
; Perform compare for inequality
        vcmpss xmm5,xmm1,xmm2,CMP_NEQ_OQ
        vmovd eax,xmm5
        and al,1
        mov [rcx+1],al

; Perform compare for less than
        vcmpss xmm5,xmm1,xmm2,CMP_LT_OQ
        vmovd eax,xmm5
        and al,1
        mov [rcx+2],al

; Perform compare for less than or equal
        vcmpss xmm5,xmm1,xmm2,CMP_LE_OQ
        vmovd eax,xmm5
        and al,1
        mov [rcx+3],al

; Perform compare for greater than
        vcmpss xmm5,xmm1,xmm2,CMP_GT_OQ
        vmovd eax,xmm5
        and al,1
        mov [rcx+4],al

; Perform compare for greater than or equal
        vcmpss xmm5,xmm1,xmm2,CMP_GE_OQ
        vmovd eax,xmm5
        and al,1
        mov [rcx+5],al

; Perform compare for ordered
        vcmpss xmm5,xmm1,xmm2,CMP_ORD_Q
        vmovd eax,xmm5
        and al,1
        mov [rcx+6],al

; Perform compare for unordered
        vcmpss xmm5,xmm1,xmm2,CMP_UNORD_Q
        vmovd eax,xmm5
        and al,1
        mov [rcx+7],al
        ret

CompareF32_avx endp
        end
```

In Listing 5-5b, the first executable instruction of function CompareF32_avx(), vcmpss
xmm5,xmm1,xmm2,CMP_EQ_OQ, performs a compare for equality using argument values a (XMM1) and b
(XMM2). If a == b is true, the processor sets bits XMM5[31:0] to all ones; otherwise, these same bits are set
to all zeros. Execution of a vcmpss instruction also copies bits 127:32 of the first source operand to the same
bit positions of the destination operand. The next instruction, vmovd eax,xmm5 (Move Doubleword), copies

the low-order doubleword of register XMM5 (i.e., XMM5[31:0]) to register EAX. Execution of the ensuing and al,1 instruction yields a value of 0 (a == b is false) or 1 (a == b is true) in register AL. The final instruction in the first code block, mov [rcx],al, saves this value to cmp_results. The remaining code blocks in function CompareF32_avx() demonstrate the use of other common floating-point compare predicates.

Listing 5-5c shows the NASM code for example Ch05_05. File Ch05_05_fasm.s uses the NASM statement %include "cmpequ_fp.inc" to include the NASM header file cmpequ_fp.inc. This file contains the same compare predicate definitions as the MASM header file cmpequ_fp.asmh that's shown in Listing 5-5a. MASM and NASM both use the same syntax for equ statements. However, they use different directives and syntax for other common header file content, which is why this book uses different filename extensions for MASM and NASM header files.

Listing 5-5c. Example Ch05_05 NASM Code

```
;-----------------------------------------------------------------------------
; Ch05_05_fasm.s
;-----------------------------------------------------------------------------

        %include "ModX86Asm3eNASM.inc"
        %include "cmpequ_fp.inc"


;-----------------------------------------------------------------------------
; void CompareF32_avx(uint8_t* cmp_results, float a, float b);
;-----------------------------------------------------------------------------

        section .text

        global CompareF32_avx
CompareF32_avx:

; Perform compare for equality
        vcmpss xmm5,xmm0,xmm1,CMP_EQ_OQ         ;perform compare operation
        vmovd eax,xmm5                          ;eax = compare result (all 1s or 0s)
        and al,1                                ;mask out unneeded bits
        mov [rdi],al                            ;save result

; Perform compare for inequality
        vcmpss xmm5,xmm0,xmm1,CMP_NEQ_OQ
        vmovd eax,xmm5
        and al,1
        mov [rdi+1],al

; Perform compare for less than
        vcmpss xmm5,xmm0,xmm1,CMP_LT_OQ
        vmovd eax,xmm5
        and al,1
        mov [rdi+2],al

; Perform compare for less than or equal
        vcmpss xmm5,xmm0,xmm1,CMP_LE_OQ
        vmovd eax,xmm5
        and al,1
        mov [rdi+3],al
```

```
; Perform compare for greater than
        vcmpss xmm5,xmm0,xmm1,CMP_GT_OQ
        vmovd eax,xmm5
        and al,1
        mov [rdi+4],al

; Perform compare for greater than or equal
        vcmpss xmm5,xmm0,xmm1,CMP_GE_OQ
        vmovd eax,xmm5
        and al,1
        mov [rdi+5],al

; Perform compare for ordered
        vcmpss xmm5,xmm0,xmm1,CMP_ORD_Q
        vmovd eax,xmm5
        and al,1
        mov [rdi+6],al

; Perform compare for unordered
        vcmpss xmm5,xmm0,xmm1,CMP_UNORD_Q
        vmovd eax,xmm5
        and al,1
        mov [rdi+7],al
        ret
```

Except for different register names, the NASM version of function CompareF32_avx() in Listing 5-5c is the same as the MASM version in Listing 5-5b. Here are the results for source code example Ch05_05:

```
----- Results for Ch05_05 -----
a = 120.0
b = 130.0
cmp_eq  = false  cmp_ne  = true   cmp_lt  = true   cmp_le  = true
cmp_gt  = false  cmp_ge  = false  cmp_ord = true   cmp_uno = false

a = 250.0
b = 240.0
cmp_eq  = false  cmp_ne  = true   cmp_lt  = false  cmp_le  = false
cmp_gt  = true   cmp_ge  = true   cmp_ord = true   cmp_uno = false

a = 300.0
b = 300.0
cmp_eq  = true   cmp_ne  = false  cmp_lt  = false  cmp_le  = true
cmp_gt  = false  cmp_ge  = true   cmp_ord = true   cmp_uno = false

a = -18.0
b = 32.0
cmp_eq  = false  cmp_ne  = true   cmp_lt  = true   cmp_le  = true
cmp_gt  = false  cmp_ge  = false  cmp_ord = true   cmp_uno = false

a = -81.0
b = -100.0
```

```
cmp_eq  = false  cmp_ne  = true   cmp_lt  = false  cmp_le  = false
cmp_gt  = true   cmp_ge  = true   cmp_ord = true   cmp_uno = false

a = 42.0
b = nan
cmp_eq  = false  cmp_ne  = false  cmp_lt  = false  cmp_le  = false
cmp_gt  = false  cmp_ge  = false  cmp_ord = false  cmp_uno = true
```

Many x86 assemblers, including MASM and NASM, support pseudo-op forms of the vcmps[d|s] instructions. Pseudo-ops are simulated instruction mnemonics with the compare predicate embedded within the mnemonic text. In Listing 5-5b, for example, the pseudo-op vcmpeqss xmm5,xmm1,xmm2 could have been used instead of the instruction vcmpss xmm5,xmm1,xmm2,CMP_EQ_OQ. This book uses the four-operand instruction variant since it's much easier (IMHO) to read an explicit compare predicate operand instead of text that's buried within the pseudo-op mnemonic.

Floating-Point Conversions

Most C++ programs perform type conversions. For example, it is often necessary to cast a single-precision or double-precision floating-point value to an integer or vice versa. A function may also need to size-promote a single-precision floating-point value to double-precision or narrow a double-precision floating-point value to single-precision. AVX includes several instructions that perform conversions using either scalar or packed operands.

Listing 5-6a shows the C++ source code for example Ch05_06. This example illustrates the use of AVX scalar floating-point conversion instructions. Source code example Ch05_06 also introduces macros and explains how to change the rounding control bits in the MXCSR register.

Listing 5-6a. Example Ch05_06 C++ Code

```
//-----------------------------------------------------------------------------
// Ch05_06.h
//-----------------------------------------------------------------------------

#pragma once
#include <cstddef>
#include <cstdint>

// Simple union for data exchange
union Uval
{
    int32_t m_I32;
    int64_t m_I64;
    float m_F32;
    double m_F64;
};

// The order of values in enum CvtOp must match the jump table
// that's defined in the .asm or .s file.
enum class CvtOp : unsigned int
{
    I32_F32,        // int32_t to float
```

```
    F32_I32,        // float to int32_t
    I32_F64,        // int32_t to double
    F64_I32,        // double to int32_t
    I64_F32,        // int64_t to float
    F32_I64,        // float to int64_t
    I64_F64,        // int64_t to double
    F64_I64,        // double to int64_t
    F32_F64,        // float to double
    F64_F32,        // double to float
};

// Enumerated type for rounding control
enum class RC : unsigned int
{
    Nearest, Down, Up, Zero      // Do not change order
};

// Ch05_06_fasm.asm, Ch05_06_fasm.s
extern "C" bool ConvertScalar_avx(Uval* a, Uval* b, CvtOp cvt_op, RC rc);


//----------------------------------------------------------------------------
// Ch05_06.cpp
//----------------------------------------------------------------------------

#include <iostream>
#include <iomanip>
#include <string>
#include <limits>
#include <numbers>
#include "Ch05_06.h"

const std::string c_RcStrings[] = { "Nearest", "Down", "Up", "Zero" };
constexpr RC c_RcVals[] = { RC::Nearest, RC::Down, RC::Up, RC::Zero };
constexpr size_t c_NumRC = sizeof(c_RcVals) / sizeof(RC);

int main(void)
{
    constexpr char nl = '\n';
    Uval src1, src2, src3, src4, src5, src6, src7;

    src1.m_F32 = std::numbers::pi_v<float>;
    src2.m_F32 = -std::numbers::e_v<float>;
    src3.m_F64 = std::numbers::sqrt2_v<double>;
    src4.m_F64 = 1.0 / std::numbers::sqrt2_v<double>;
    src5.m_F64 = std::numeric_limits<double>::epsilon();
    src6.m_I32 = std::numeric_limits<int>::max();
    src7.m_I64 = std::numeric_limits<long long>::max();

    std::cout << "----- Results for Ch05_06 -----\n";
```

```cpp
    for (size_t i = 0; i < c_NumRC; i++)
    {
        RC rc = c_RcVals[i];
        Uval des1, des2, des3, des4, des5, des6, des7;

        ConvertScalar_avx(&des1, &src1, CvtOp::F32_I32, rc);
        ConvertScalar_avx(&des2, &src2, CvtOp::F32_I64, rc);
        ConvertScalar_avx(&des3, &src3, CvtOp::F64_I32, rc);
        ConvertScalar_avx(&des4, &src4, CvtOp::F64_I64, rc);
        ConvertScalar_avx(&des5, &src5, CvtOp::F64_F32, rc);
        ConvertScalar_avx(&des6, &src6, CvtOp::I32_F32, rc);
        ConvertScalar_avx(&des7, &src7, CvtOp::I64_F64, rc);

        std::cout << std::fixed;
        std::cout << "\nRounding control = " << c_RcStrings[(int)rc] << nl;

        std::cout << "  F32_I32: " << std::setprecision(8);
        std::cout << src1.m_F32 << " --> " << des1.m_I32 << nl;

        std::cout << "  F32_I64: " << std::setprecision(8);
        std::cout << src2.m_F32 << " --> " << des2.m_I64 << nl;

        std::cout << "  F64_I32: " << std::setprecision(8);
        std::cout << src3.m_F64 << " --> " << des3.m_I32 << nl;

        std::cout << "  F64_I64: " << std::setprecision(8);
        std::cout << src4.m_F64 << " --> " << des4.m_I64 << nl;

        std::cout << "  F64_F32: ";
        std::cout << std::setprecision(16) << src5.m_F64 << " --> ";
        std::cout << std::setprecision(8) << des5.m_F32 << nl;

        std::cout << "  I32_F32: " << std::setprecision(8);
        std::cout << src6.m_I32 << " --> " << des6.m_F32 << nl;

        std::cout << "  I64_F64: " << std::setprecision(8);
        std::cout << src7.m_I64 << " --> " << des7.m_F64 << nl;
    }

    return 0;
}
```

Near the top of Listing 5-6a is the definition of a union named Uval. Source code example Ch05_06 uses this union to simplify data exchange between the C++ and assembly language code. Following the declaration of Uval is an enum named CvtOp, which defines symbolic names for various conversion operations. Also included in file Ch05_06.h is the enum RC. This type defines symbolic names for the floating-point rounding modes. Recall from the discussions in Chapter 1 that the MXCSR register contains a two-bit field that specifies the rounding method for AVX floating-point operations (see Table 1-5).

Function main() in Listing 5-6a includes code that performs Uval test case initialization and streams results to std::cout. Note that each use of the assembly language function ConvertScalar_avx() requires two argument values of type Uval, one argument of type CvtOp, and one argument of type RC.

Listing 5-6b shows the MASM code for example Ch05_06. As mentioned earlier in this chapter, assembly language source code files often employ the equ directive to define symbolic names for numerical constants. The first non-comment statement in file Ch05_06_fasm.asm, MxcsrRcMask equ 9fffh, defines a symbolic name for a mask that will be used to modify the bits in MXCSR.RC. This is followed by another equ directive MxcsrRcShift equ 13 that defines a shift count for MXCSR.RC. The final equ directive, MxcsrRSP equ 8, defines an offset for a memory location on the stack that's used by the vldmxcsr and vstmxcsr instructions.

Listing 5-6b. Example Ch05_06 MASM Code

```
;-------------------------------------------------------------------------
; Ch05_06_fasm.asm
;-------------------------------------------------------------------------


MxcsrRcMask        equ 9fffh                 ;bit mask for MXCSR.RC
MxcsrRcShift       equ 13                    ;shift count for MXCSR.RC
MxcsrRSP           equ 8                     ;stack offset for vstmxcsr & vldmxcsr


;-------------------------------------------------------------------------
; Macro GetRC_M - copies MXCSR.RC to r10d[1:0]
;-------------------------------------------------------------------------


GetRC_M macro
        vstmxcsr dword ptr [rsp+MxcsrRSP]    ;save mxcsr register
        mov r10d,[rsp+MxcsrRSP]

        shr r10d,MxcsrRcShift                ;r10d[1:0] = MXCSR.RC
        and r10d,3                           ;clear unused bits
        endm


;-------------------------------------------------------------------------
; Macro SetRC_M - sets MXCSR.RC to RcReg[1:0]  (RcReg must be 32-bit register)
;-------------------------------------------------------------------------


SetRC_M macro RcReg
        vstmxcsr dword ptr [rsp+MxcsrRSP]    ;save current MXCSR
        mov eax,[rsp+MxcsrRSP]

        and RcReg,3                          ;clear unusned bits
        shl RcReg,MxcsrRcShift               ;RcReg[14:13] = rc

        and eax,MxcsrRcMask                  ;clear non MXCSR.RC bits
        or eax,RcReg                         ;insert new MXCSR.RC

        mov [rsp+MxcsrRSP],eax
        vldmxcsr dword ptr [rsp+MxcsrRSP]    ;load updated MXCSR
        endm
```

```
;-----------------------------------------------------------------------------
; bool ConvertScalar_avx(Uval* des, const Uval* src, CvtOp cvt_op, RC rc)
;-----------------------------------------------------------------------------

        .code
ConvertScalar_avx proc

; Make sure cvt_op is valid
        cmp r8d,CvtOpTableCount             ;is cvt_op >= CvtOpTableCount
        jae BadCvtOp                        ;jump if cvt_op is invalid

; Save current MSCSR.RC
        GetRC_M                             ;r10d = current RC

; Set new rounding mode
        SetRC_M r9d                         ;set new MXCSR.RC

; Jump to target conversion code block
        mov eax,r8d                         ;rax = cvt_op
        lea r11,[CvtOpTable]                ;r11 = address of CvtOpTable
        lea r11,[r11+rax*8]                 ;r11 = address of entry in CvtOpTable
        jmp qword ptr [r11]                 ;jump to selected code block

; Conversions between int32_t and float/double

I32_F32:
        mov eax,[rdx]                       ;load integer value
        vcvtsi2ss xmm0,xmm0,eax             ;convert to float
        vmovss real4 ptr [rcx],xmm0         ;save result
        jmp Done

F32_I32:
        vmovss xmm0,real4 ptr [rdx]         ;load float value
        vcvtss2si eax,xmm0                  ;convert to integer
        mov [rcx],eax                       ;save result
        jmp Done

I32_F64:
        mov eax,[rdx]                       ;load integer value
        vcvtsi2sd xmm0,xmm0,eax             ;convert to double
        vmovsd real8 ptr [rcx],xmm0         ;save result
        jmp Done

F64_I32:
        vmovsd xmm0,real8 ptr [rdx]         ;load double value
        vcvtsd2si eax,xmm0                  ;convert to integer
        mov [rcx],eax                       ;save result
        jmp Done

; Conversions between int64_t and float/double
```

167

```
I64_F32:
        mov rax,[rdx]                    ;load integer value
        vcvtsi2ss xmm0,xmm0,rax          ;convert to float
        vmovss real4 ptr [rcx],xmm0      ;save result
        jmp Done

F32_I64:
        vmovss xmm0,real4 ptr [rdx]      ;load float value
        vcvtss2si rax,xmm0               ;convert to integer
        mov [rcx],rax                    ;save result
        jmp Done

I64_F64:
        mov rax,[rdx]                    ;load integer value
        vcvtsi2sd xmm0,xmm0,rax          ;convert to double
        vmovsd real8 ptr [rcx],xmm0      ;save result
        jmp Done

F64_I64:
        vmovsd xmm0,real8 ptr [rdx]      ;load double value
        vcvtsd2si rax,xmm0               ;convert to integer
        mov [rcx],rax                    ;save result
        jmp Done

; Conversions between float and double

F32_F64:
        vmovss xmm0,real4 ptr [rdx]      ;load float value
        vcvtss2sd xmm1,xmm1,xmm0         ;convert to double
        vmovsd real8 ptr [rcx],xmm1      ;save result
        jmp Done

F64_F32:
        vmovsd xmm0,real8 ptr [rdx]      ;load double value
        vcvtsd2ss xmm1,xmm1,xmm0         ;convert to float
        vmovss real4 ptr [rcx],xmm1      ;save result
        jmp Done

BadCvtOp:
        xor eax,eax                      ;set error return code
        ret

Done:   SetRC_M r10d                     ;restore original MXCSR.RC
        mov eax,1                        ;set success return code
        ret

; The order of values in following table must match enum CvtOp
; that's defined in the .h file.

        align 8
CvtOpTable  equ $
```

```
            dq I32_F32, F32_I32
            dq I32_F64, F64_I32
            dq I64_F32, F32_I64
            dq I64_F64, F64_I64
            dq F32_F64, F64_F32
CvtOpTableCount equ ($ - CvtOpTable) / size qword

ConvertScalar_avx endp
        end
```

Immediately following the three equ statements is the definition of a MASM macro named GetRC_M. A macro is a text substitution mechanism that enables a programmer to represent a sequence of assembly language instructions, data, or other statements using a single text string. Assembly language macros are typically employed to generate sequences of instructions that will be used more than once. Macros are also frequently exploited to avoid the performance overhead of a function call.

Macro GetRC_M emits a sequence of assembly language instructions that obtain the current value of MXCSR.RC. The first instruction of this macro, vstmxcsr dword ptr [rsp+MxcsrRSP], saves the contents of register MXCSR on the stack. The reason for saving MXCSR on the stack is that vstmxcsr only supports memory operands. The location used here corresponds to the home area for register RCX. Recall that the Visual C++ run-time calling convention permits a called function to use its home area to store temporary values. The next instruction, mov r10d,[rsp+MxcsrRSP], copies this value from the stack and loads it into register R10D. The ensuing instruction pair, shr r10d,MxcsrRcShift and and r10d,3, relocates the rounding control bits to bits 1:0 of register R10D; all other bits in R10D are set to zero. The text endm is a MASM assembler directive that signifies the end of macro GetRC_M.

Following the definition of macro GetRC_M is another macro named SetRC_M. This macro emits instructions that modify MXCSR.RC. Note that macro SetRC_M includes an argument named RcReg. This is a symbolic name for the general-purpose register that contains the new value for MXCSR.RC. More on this in a moment. Macro SetRC_M also begins with the instruction sequence vstmxcsr dword ptr [rsp+MxcsrRSP] and mov eax,[rsp+MxcsrRSP] to obtain the current contents of MXCSR. It then employs the instruction pair and RcReg,3 and shl RcReg,MxcsrRcShift. These instructions shift the new bits for MXCSR.RC into the correct position. During macro expansion, the assembler replaces macro argument RcReg with the actual register name as you'll soon see. The ensuing and eax,MxcsrRcMask and or eax,RcReg instructions update MXCSR.RC with the new rounding mode. The next instruction pair, mov [rsp+MxcsrRSP],eax and vldmxcsr dword ptr [rsp+MxcsrRSP], loads the new RC control bits into MXCSR.RC. Note that the instruction sequence used in SetRC_M preserves all other bits in the MXCSR register.

Function ConvertScalar_avx() begins its execution with the instruction pair cmp r8d,CvtOpTableCount and jae BadCvtOp that validates argument value cvt_op. If cvt_op is valid, ConvertScalar_avx() uses macros GetRC_M and SetRC_M r9d to modify MXCSR.RC. Note that register R9D contains the new rounding mode. Figure 5-5 contains a portion of the MASM listing file (with some minor edits to improve readability) that shows the expansion of macros GetRC_M and SetRC_M. The MASM listing file denotes macro expanded instructions with a "1" in a column located to the left of each instruction mnemonic. Note that in the expansion of macro SetRC_M, register R9D is substituted for macro argument RcReg.

```
00000000                            .code
00000000                   ConvertScalar_avx proc

                  ; Make sure cvt_op is valid
00000000  41/ 81 F8              cmp r8d,CvtOpTableCount          ;is cvt_op >=
CvtOpTableCount
      0000000A
00000007  0F 83 000000CC         jae BadCvtOp                     ;jump if cvt_op is invalid

                  ; Save current MSCSR.RC
                                  GetRC_M                          ;r10d = current RC
0000000D  C5 F8/ AE 5C 24    1    vstmxcsr dword ptr [rsp+MxcsrRSP] ;save mxcsr register
      08
00000013  44/ 8B 54 24       1    mov r10d,[rsp+MxcsrRSP]
      08
00000018  41/ C1 EA 0D       1    shr r10d,MxcsrRcShift            ;r10d[1:0] = MXCSR.RC
0000001C  41/ 83 E2 03       1    and r10d,3                       ;clear unused bits

                  ; Set new rounding mode
                                  SetRC_M r9d                      ;set new MXCSR.RC
00000020  C5 F8/ AE 5C 24    1    vstmxcsr dword ptr [rsp+MxcsrRSP] ;save current MXCSR
      08
00000026  8B 44 24 08        1    mov eax,[rsp+MxcsrRSP]
0000002A  41/ 83 E1 03       1    and r9d,3                        ;clear unusned bits
0000002E  41/ C1 E1 0D       1    shl r9d,MxcsrRcShift             ;RcReg[14:13] = rc
00000032  25 00009FFF        1    and eax,MxcsrRcMask              ;clear non MXCSR.RC bits
00000037  41/ 0B C1          1    or eax,r9d                       ;insert new MXCSR.RC
0000003A  89 44 24 08        1    mov [rsp+MxcsrRSP],eax
0000003E  C5 F8/ AE 54 24    1    vldmxcsr dword ptr [rsp+MxcsrRSP] ;load updated MXCSR
      08

                  ; Jump to target conversion code block
00000044  41/ 8B C0              mov eax,r8d                       ;rax = cvt_op
00000047  4C/ 8D 1D              lea r11,[CvtOpTable]              ;r11 = address of
CvtOpTable
      00000108 R
0000004E  4D/ 8D 1C C3          lea r11,[r11+rax*8]               ;r11 = address of entry in
CvtOpTable
00000052  41/ FF 23             jmp qword ptr [r11]               ;jump to selected code
block
```

Figure 5-5. *Expansion of macros GetRC_M and SetRC_M*

Function ConvertScalar_avx() uses argument value cvt_op and a jump table to select a conversion code block. This construct is akin to a C++ switch statement. Immediately after the ret instruction is a jump table named CvtOpTable. The align 8 statement that appears just before the start of CvtOpTable is an assembler directive that instructs MASM to align the start of CvtOpTable on a quadword boundary. The align 8 directive is used here since CvtOpTable contains quadword elements of labels defined in ConvertScalar_avx(). The labels correspond to code blocks that perform a specific numerical conversion. The instruction jmp [r11+rax*8] transfers program control to the code block specified by cvt_op, which was copied into RAX. More specifically, execution of the jmp [r11+rax*8] instruction loads RIP with the quadword value stored in memory location R11 + RAX * 8. You may have noticed that jump table CvtOpTable is located within the .code section. The reason for this is that the scope of a MASM function label is local to that function.

Each conversion code block in ConvertScalar_avx() uses a different AVX instruction to carry out a specific conversion operation. For example, the code block that follows label I32_F32 uses the instruction vcvtsi2ss (Convert Doubleword Integer to SPFP Value) to convert a 32-bit signed integer to single-precision floating-point. Table 5-5 summarizes the scalar floating-point conversion instructions used in example Ch05_06.

Table 5-5. *AVX Scalar Floating-Point Instructions*

Instruction Mnemonic	Description
vcvtsi2ss	Convert 32- or 64-bit signed integer to SPFP
vcvtsi2sd	Convert 32- or 64-bit signed integer to DPFP
vcvtss2si	Convert SPFP to 32- or 64-bit signed integer
vcvtsd2si	Convert DPFP to 32- or 64-bit signed integer
vcvtss2sd	Convert SPFP to DPFP
vcvtsd2ss	Convert DPFP to SPFP

The last instruction of each conversion code block is a jmp Done instruction. The label Done is located near the end of function ConvertScalar_avx(). At label Done, function ConvertScalar_avx() uses SetRC_M r10d to restore the original value of MXCSR.RC. The Visual C++ calling convention classifies MXCSR.RC as non-volatile, which means that a called function must preserve the caller's original value. You'll learn more about this later in Chapter 6.

Listing 5-6c shows the NASM code for example Ch05_06. Near the top of this listing are the same three equ statements that you saw in Listing 5-6b. However, note that the value for MxcsrRSP is different. In the NASM code, RSP + MxcsrRSP (RSP – 8) points to a stack memory location in the red zone. Recall from the discussions in Chapter 3 that the GNU C++ calling convention allows a leaf function to use the red zone for temporary storage (see Figure 3-3).

Listing 5-6c. Example Ch05_06 NASM Code

```
;-------------------------------------------------------------------------
; Ch05_06_fasm.s
;-------------------------------------------------------------------------

        %include "ModX86Asm3eNASM.inc"

MxcsrRcMask     equ 9fffh                   ;bit mask for MXCSR.RC
MxcsrRcShift    equ 13                      ;shift count for MXCSR.RC
MxcsrRSP        equ -8                      ;stack offset for vstmxcsr & vldmxcsr


;-------------------------------------------------------------------------
; Macro GetRC_M - copies MXCSR.RC to r10d[1:0]
;-------------------------------------------------------------------------

%macro GetRC_M 0
        vstmxcsr [rsp+MxcsrRSP]             ;save mxcsr register
        mov r10d,[rsp+MxcsrRSP]

        shr r10d,MxcsrRcShift               ;r10d[1:0] = MXCSR.RC
        and r10d,3                          ;clear unused bits
%endmacro
```

```
;--------------------------------------------------------------------
; Macro SetRC_M - sets MXCSR.RC to %1[1:0] (%1 must be 32-bit register)
;--------------------------------------------------------------------

%macro SetRC_M 1
        vstmxcsr [rsp+MxcsrRSP]             ;save current MXCSR
        mov eax,[rsp+MxcsrRSP]

        and %1,3                            ;clear unusned bits
        shl %1,MxcsrRcShift                 ;%1[14:13] = rc

        and eax,MxcsrRcMask                 ;clear non MXCSR.RC bits
        or eax,%1                           ;insert new MXCSR.RC

        mov [rsp+MxcsrRSP],eax
        vldmxcsr [rsp+MxcsrRSP]             ;load updated MXCSR
%endmacro

;--------------------------------------------------------------------
; bool ConvertScalar_avx(Uval* des, const Uval* src, CvtOp cvt_op, RC rc)
;--------------------------------------------------------------------

        section .text

        global ConvertScalar_avx
ConvertScalar_avx:

; Make sure cvt_op is valid
        cmp edx,CvtOpTableCount             ;is cvt_op >= CvtOpTableCount
        jae BadCvtOp                        ;jump if cvt_op is invalid

; Save current MSCSR.RC
        GetRC_M                             ;r10d = current RC

; Set new rounding mode
        SetRC_M ecx                         ;set new MXCSR.RC

; Jump to target conversion code block
        mov eax,edx                         ;rax = cvt_op
        lea r11,[CvtOpTable]                ;r11 = address of CvtOpTable
        lea r11,[r11+rax*8]                 ;r11 = address of entry in CvtOpTable
        jmp qword [r11]                     ;jump to selected code block

; Conversions between int32_t and float/double

I32_F32:
        mov eax,[rsi]                       ;load integer value
        vcvtsi2ss xmm0,xmm0,eax             ;convert to float
        vmovss [rdi],xmm0                   ;save result
        jmp Done
```

```
F32_I32:
        vmovss xmm0,[rsi]                      ;load float value
        vcvtss2si eax,xmm0                     ;convert to integer
        mov [rdi],eax                          ;save result
        jmp Done

I32_F64:
        mov eax,[rsi]                          ;load integer value
        vcvtsi2sd xmm0,xmm0,eax                ;convert to double
        vmovsd [rdi],xmm0                      ;save result
        jmp Done

F64_I32:
        vmovsd xmm0,[rsi]                      ;load double value
        vcvtsd2si eax,xmm0                     ;convert to integer
        mov [rdi],eax                          ;save result
        jmp Done

; Conversions between int64_t and float/double

I64_F32:
        mov rax,[rsi]                          ;load integer value
        vcvtsi2ss xmm0,xmm0,rax                ;convert to float
        vmovss [rdi],xmm0                      ;save result
        jmp Done

F32_I64:
        vmovss xmm0,[rsi]                      ;load float value
        vcvtss2si rax,xmm0                     ;convert to integer
        mov [rdi],rax                          ;save result
        jmp Done

I64_F64:
        mov rax,[rsi]                          ;load integer value
        vcvtsi2sd xmm0,xmm0,rax                ;convert to double
        vmovsd [rdi],xmm0                      ;save result
        jmp Done

F64_I64:
        vmovsd xmm0,[rsi]                      ;load double value
        vcvtsd2si rax,xmm0                     ;convert to integer
        mov [rdi],rax                          ;save result
        jmp Done

; Conversions between float and double

F32_F64:
        vmovss xmm0,[rsi]                      ;load float value
        vcvtss2sd xmm1,xmm1,xmm0               ;convert to double
        vmovsd [rdi],xmm1                      ;save result
        jmp Done
```

173

```
F64_F32:
        vmovsd xmm0,[rsi]               ;load double value
        vcvtsd2ss xmm1,xmm1,xmm0        ;convert to float
        vmovss [rdi],xmm1               ;save result
        jmp Done

BadCvtOp:
        xor eax,eax                     ;set error return code
        ret

Done:   SetRC_M r10d                    ;restore original MXCSR.RC
        mov eax,1                       ;set success return code
        ret

; The order of values in following table must match enum CvtOp
; that's defined in the .h file.

        section .data align = 8

CvtOpTable equ $
        dq I32_F32, F32_I32
        dq I32_F64, F64_I32
        dq I64_F32, F32_I64
        dq I64_F64, F64_I64
        dq F32_F64, F64_F32
CvtOpTableCount equ ($ - CvtOpTable) / 8
```

Following the equ definitions in Listing 5-6c is the statement %macro GetRC_M 0, which denotes the start of a NASM macro named GetRC_M. The 0 text that follows the macro name signifies the number of macro parameters. The NASM version of GetRC_M uses the same instructions as the MASM version in Listing 5-6b. The NASM directive %endmacro denotes the end of macro GetRC_M.

Next in Listing 5-6c is the definition of macro SetRC_M. This macro requires one parameter, which must be a 32-bit register name. Within the macro definition, note the use of the symbol %1. During macro expansion, NASM replaces this symbol with the text corresponding to the first macro parameter. While not used in this example, NASM macros also support multiple parameters; additional parameters are referenced using the symbols %2, %3, etc.

The executable code in the NASM version of ConvertScalar_avx() is basically the same as the NASM version except for the argument registers. Near the end of Listing 5-6c is the statement section .data align = 8, which signifies the start of a data section that is aligned on a quadword boundary. Located in this section is the LUT CvtOpTable. Here are the results for source code example Ch05_06:

```
----- Results for Ch05_06 -----

Rounding control = Nearest
  F32_I32: 3.14159274 --> 3
  F32_I64: -2.71828175 --> -3
  F64_I32: 1.41421356 --> 1
  F64_I64: 0.70710678 --> 1
  F64_F32: 0.0000000000000002 --> 0.00000000
  I32_F32: 2147483647 --> 2147483648.00000000
  I64_F64: 9223372036854775807 --> 9223372036854775808.00000000
```

```
Rounding control = Down
  F32_I32: 3.14159274 --> 3
  F32_I64: -2.71828175 --> -3
  F64_I32: 1.41421356 --> 1
  F64_I64: 0.70710678 --> 0
  F64_F32: 0.0000000000000002 --> 0.00000000
  I32_F32: 2147483647 --> 2147483520.00000000
  I64_F64: 9223372036854775807 --> 9223372036854774784.00000000

Rounding control = Up
  F32_I32: 3.14159274 --> 4
  F32_I64: -2.71828175 --> -2
  F64_I32: 1.41421356 --> 2
  F64_I64: 0.70710678 --> 1
  F64_F32: 0.0000000000000002 --> 0.00000000
  I32_F32: 2147483647 --> 2147483648.00000000
  I64_F64: 9223372036854775807 --> 9223372036854775808.00000000

Rounding control = Zero
  F32_I32: 3.14159274 --> 3
  F32_I64: -2.71828175 --> -2
  F64_I32: 1.41421356 --> 1
  F64_I64: 0.70710678 --> 0
  F64_F32: 0.0000000000000002 --> 0.00000000
  I32_F32: 2147483647 --> 2147483520.00000000
  I64_F64: 9223372036854775807 --> 9223372036854774784.00000000
```

Before moving on to the next section, it warrants mentioning that there are no calling conventions or protocols that specify how to utilize parameters, registers, instructions, or data allocations within a macro. The programmer is responsible for handling these items. This absence of formal standards means that macros must be judiciously employed since it's very easy to create convoluted code that's difficult to maintain, especially when using nested macros. You'll see more examples of macro use in later chapters.

Floating-Point Arrays

In Chapter 4, you learned how to perform simple calculations using the elements of an integer array. In this section, you'll study a source code example that calculates the mean and sample standard deviation of a double-precision floating-point array. Here are the equations used in example Ch05_07 to calculate the mean and standard deviation:

$$\bar{x} = \frac{1}{n}\sum_i x_i$$

$$s = \sqrt{\frac{1}{n-1}\sum_i \left(x_i - \bar{x}\right)^2}$$

Listing 5-7a shows the C++ code for source code example Ch05_07. In this listing, header file Ch05_07.h contains the requisite function declarations for this example. Note that distinct C++ and assembly language functions are declared to calculate the mean and standard deviation.

Listing 5-7a. Example Ch05_07 C++ Code

```
//------------------------------------------------------------------------------
// Ch05_07.h
//------------------------------------------------------------------------------

#pragma once
#include <cstddef>

// Ch05_07_fasm.asm, Ch05_07_fasm.s
extern "C" bool CalcMeanF64_avx(double* mean, const double* x, size_t n);
extern "C" bool CalcStDevF64_avx(double* st_dev, const double* x, size_t n,
    double mean);

// Ch05_07_fcpp.cpp
extern bool CalcMeanF64_cpp(double* mean, const double* x, size_t n);
extern bool CalcStDevF64_cpp(double* st_dev, const double* x, size_t n,
    double mean);

// Ch05_07_misc.cpp
extern void InitArray(double* x, size_t n);

// Miscellaneous constants
constexpr size_t c_NumElements = 91;
constexpr double c_RngMin = 1.0;
constexpr double c_RngMax = 100.0;
constexpr unsigned int c_RngSeed = 13;

//------------------------------------------------------------------------------
// Ch05_07_misc.cpp
//------------------------------------------------------------------------------

#include "Ch05_07.h"
#include "MT.h"

void InitArray(double* x, size_t n)
{
    MT::FillArrayFP(x, n, c_RngMin, c_RngMax, c_RngSeed);
}

//------------------------------------------------------------------------------
// Ch05_07_fcpp.cpp
//------------------------------------------------------------------------------

#include <cmath>
#include "Ch05_07.h"

bool CalcMeanF64_cpp(double* mean, const double* x, size_t n)
{
    if (n < 2)
        return false;
```

```
    double sum = 0.0;

    for (size_t i = 0; i < n; i++)
        sum += x[i];

    *mean = sum / n;
    return true;
}

bool CalcStDevF64_cpp(double* st_dev, const double* x, size_t n, double mean)
{
    if (n < 2)
        return false;

    double sum_squares = 0.0;

    for (size_t i = 0; i < n; i++)
    {
        double temp = x[i] - mean;
        sum_squares += temp * temp;
    }

    *st_dev = sqrt(sum_squares / (n - 1));
    return true;
}

//-----------------------------------------------------------------------------
// Ch05_07.cpp
//-----------------------------------------------------------------------------

#include <iostream>
#include <iomanip>
#include <vector>
#include "Ch05_07.h"

static void CalcMeanStDevF64(void)
{
    constexpr size_t n = c_NumElements;
    std::vector<double> x_v(n);
    double* x = x_v.data();

    InitArray(x, n);

    double mean1, mean2, st_dev1, st_dev2;

    bool rc1 = CalcMeanF64_cpp(&mean1, x, n);
    bool rc2 = CalcMeanF64_avx(&mean2, x, n);
    bool rc3 = CalcStDevF64_cpp(&st_dev1, x, n, mean1);
    bool rc4 = CalcStDevF64_avx(&st_dev2, x, n, mean2);
```

```cpp
    std::cout << "----- Results for Ch05_07 -----\n";
    std::cout << std::fixed << std::setprecision(6);

    if (rc1 && rc2 && rc3 && rc4)
    {
        constexpr int w = 10;
        constexpr char nl = '\n';

        std::cout << "n:       " << std::setw(w) << n << nl;
        std::cout << "mean1:   " << std::setw(w) << mean1 << "  ";
        std::cout << "st_dev1: " << std::setw(w) << st_dev1 << nl;
        std::cout << "mean2:   " << std::setw(w) << mean2 << "  ";
        std::cout << "st_dev2: " << std::setw(w) << st_dev2 << nl;
    }
    else
        std::cout << "Invalid return code\n";
}

int main(void)
{
    CalcMeanStDevF64();
    return 0;
}
```

The C++ calculating functions CalcMeanF64_cpp() and CalcStDevF64_cpp() shown in Listing 5-7a are straightforward. The code in file Ch05_07.cpp performs test case initialization and exercises the C++ and assembly language mean and standard deviation calculating functions.

Listing 5-7b shows the MASM code for example Ch05_07. Upon entry to the assembly language function CalcMeanF64_avx(), argument value n is validated. Note that the number of array elements must be greater than one to calculate a sample standard deviation. Following validation of n, the vxorpd,xmm0,xmm0,xmm0 instruction (Bitwise XOR of Packed Double-Precision Floating-Point Values) initializes sum to 0.0. This instruction performs a bitwise logical XOR using all 128 bits of both source operands. The vxorpd instruction is technically an AVX SIMD instruction; the mnemonic suffix pd signifies packed double-precision. It's used here since AVX does not include explicit logical bitwise instructions for scalar floating-point operands. The vcvtsi2sd xmm1,xmm1,r8 instruction converts argument value n to double-precision floating-point and saves this value in register XMM1 for later use.

Listing 5-7b. Example Ch05_07 MASM Code

```
;-----------------------------------------------------------------------------
; Ch05_07_fasm.asm
;-----------------------------------------------------------------------------


;-----------------------------------------------------------------------------
; bool CalcMeanF64_avx(double* mean, const double* x, size_t n);
;-----------------------------------------------------------------------------

        .code
CalcMeanF64_avx proc
```

```
; Make sure n is valid
        cmp r8,1                                ;is n <= 1?
        jbe BadArg                              ;jump if yes

; Initialize
        sub rdx,8                               ;rdx = &x[-1]
        vxorpd xmm0,xmm0,xmm0                    ;sum = 0.0
        vcvtsi2sd xmm1,xmm1,r8                   ;convert n to DPFP

; Sum the elements of x[]
Loop1:  add rdx,8                               ;rdx = &x[i]
        vaddsd xmm0,xmm0,real8 ptr [rdx]         ;sum += x[i]
        sub r8,1                                 ;n -= 1
        jnz Loop1                                ;repeat until n == 0

; Calculate and save the mean
        vdivsd xmm2,xmm0,xmm1                     ;xmm2 = mean = sum / n
        vmovsd real8 ptr [rcx],xmm2               ;save mean

        mov eax,1                                ;set success return code
        ret

BadArg: xor eax,eax                              ;set error return code
        ret

CalcMeanF64_avx endp

;-----------------------------------------------------------------------------
; bool CalcStDevF64_avx(double* st_dev, const double* x, size_t n, double mean);
;-----------------------------------------------------------------------------

CalcStDevF64_avx proc

; Make sure n is valid
        cmp r8,1                                ;is n <= 1?
        jbe BadArg                              ;jump if yes

; Initialize
        sub rdx,8                               ;rdx = &x[-1]
        mov r9,r8                               ;r9 = n
        sub r9,1                                ;r9 = n - 1 (for SD calculation)
        vcvtsi2sd xmm4,xmm4,r9                   ;convert n - 1 to DPFP
        vxorpd xmm0,xmm0,xmm0                    ;sum_squares = 0.0

; Sum the elements of x
Loop2:  add rdx,8                               ;rdx = &x[i]
        vmovsd xmm1,real8 ptr [rdx]               ;xmm1 = x[i]
        vsubsd xmm2,xmm1,xmm3                     ;xmm2 = x[i] - mean
        vmulsd xmm2,xmm2,xmm2                     ;xmm2 = (x[i] - mean) ** 2
        vaddsd xmm0,xmm0,xmm2                     ;sum_squares += (x[i] - mean) ** 2
```

```
        sub r8,1                        ;n -= 1
        jnz Loop2                       ;repeat until done

; Calculate and save standard deviation
        vdivsd xmm0,xmm0,xmm4           ;xmm0 = sum_squares / (n - 1)
        vsqrtsd xmm0,xmm0,xmm0          ;xmm0 = st_dev
        vmovsd real8 ptr [rcx],xmm0     ;save st_dev

        mov eax,1                       ;set success return code
        ret

BadArg: xor eax,eax                     ;set error return code
        ret


CalcStDevF64_avx endp
        end
```

In Listing 5-7b, the code block that calculates the sample mean requires only seven instructions. The first instruction of summing for-loop Loop1, add rdx,8 updates register RDX so that it points to the next element in array x. This is followed by the vaddsd xmm0,xmm0,real8 ptr [rdx] instruction that calculates sum += x[i]. The ensuing sub r8,1 instruction computes n -= 1, and the subsequent jnz Loop1 instruction ensures that Loop1 repeats until n == 0 is true. Following execution of Loop1, CalcMeanF64_avx() uses the instruction pair vdivsd xmm2,xmm0,xmm1 and vmovsd real8 ptr [rcx],xmm2 to calculate and save the mean.

The code in Listing 5-7b for function CalcStDevF64_avx() is also succinct. Following validation of argument value n, the instruction triplet mov r9,r8, sub r9,1, and vcvtsi2sd xmm4,xmm4,r9 convert n - 1 to a double-precision floating-point value for later use. The vxorpd xmm0,xmm0,xmm0 instruction sets sum_squares = 0.0. In for-loop Loop2, function CalcStDevF64_avx() uses the same basic for-loop construct that you saw in Loop1 to calculate sum_squares. Note that the code in Loop2 calculates sum_squares per the previously described equation for sample standard deviation. Following completion of Loop2, CalcStDevF64_avx() employs the instruction pair vdivsd xmm0,xmm0,xmm4 and vsqrtsd xmm0,xmm0,xmm0 to calculate the final standard deviation. The ensuing vmovsd real8 ptr [rcx],xmm0 instruction saves this result.

Listing 5-7c shows the NASM code for example Ch05_07. The code in this listing is basically the same as the MASM code presented in Listing 5-7b with the principal modification being different argument registers.

Listing 5-7c. Example Ch05_07 NASM Code

```
;-------------------------------------------------------------------------
; Ch05_07_fasm.s
;-------------------------------------------------------------------------

        %include "ModX86Asm3eNASM.inc"


;-------------------------------------------------------------------------
; bool CalcMeanF64_avx(double* mean, const double* x, size_t n);
;-------------------------------------------------------------------------

        section .text

        global CalcMeanF64_avx
CalcMeanF64_avx:
```

```
; Make sure n is valid
        cmp rdx,1                       ;is n <= 1?
        jbe BadAr1                      ;jump if yes

; Initialize
        sub rsi,8                       ;rsi = &x[-1]
        vxorpd xmm0,xmm0,xmm0           ;sum = 0.0
        vcvtsi2sd xmm1,xmm1,rdx         ;convert n to DPFP

; Sum the elements of x
Loop1:  add rsi,8                       ;rsi = &x[i]
        vaddsd xmm0,xmm0,[rsi]          ;sum += x[i]
        sub rdx,1                       ;n -= 1
        jnz Loop1                       ;repeat until n == 0

; Calculate and save the mean
        vdivsd xmm1,xmm0,xmm1           ;xmm2 = mean = sum / n
        vmovsd [rdi],xmm1               ;save mean

        mov eax,1                       ;set success return code
        ret

BadAr1: xor eax,eax                     ;set error return code
        ret


;-------------------------------------------------------------------------------
; bool CalcStDevF64_avx(double* st_dev, const double* x, size_t n, double mean);
;-------------------------------------------------------------------------------

        global CalcStDevF64_avx
CalcStDevF64_avx:

; Make sure n is valid
        cmp rdx,1                       ;is n <= 1?
        jbe BadAr2                      ;jump if yes

; Initialize
        sub rsi,8                       ;rsi = &x[-1]
        mov r9,rdx                      ;r9 = n
        sub r9,1                        ;r9 = n - 1 (for SD calculation)
        vcvtsi2sd xmm4,xmm4,r9          ;convert n - 1 to DPFP
        vmovsd xmm3,xmm0,xmm0           ;xmm3 = mean
        vxorpd xmm0,xmm0,xmm0           ;sum_squares = 0.0

; Sum the elements of x
Loop2:  add rsi,8                       ;rsi = &x[i]
        vmovsd xmm1,[rsi]               ;xmm1 = x[i]
        vsubsd xmm2,xmm1,xmm3           ;xmm2 = x[i] - mean
        vmulsd xmm2,xmm2,xmm2           ;xmm2 = (x[i] - mean) ** 2
        vaddsd xmm0,xmm0,xmm2           ;sum_squares += (x[i] - mean) ** 2
```

```
        sub rdx,1                      ;n -= 1
        jnz Loop2                      ;repeat until done

; Calculate and save standard deviation
        vdivsd xmm0,xmm0,xmm4          ;xmm0 = sum_squares / (n - 1)
        vsqrtsd xmm0,xmm0,xmm0         ;xmm0 = st_dev
        vmovsd [rdi],xmm0              ;save st_dev

        mov eax,1                      ;set success return code
        ret

BadAr2: xor eax,eax                    ;set error return code
        ret
```

Here are the results for source code example Ch05_07:

```
----- Results for Ch05_07 -----
n:              91
mean1:    49.602157  st_dev1:   27.758245
mean2:    49.602157  st_dev2:   27.758245
```

The assembly language code presented in example Ch05_07 can easily be adapted to perform single-precision instead of double-precision arithmetic. To do this, first change the double-precision scalar floating-point arithmetic instructions to their single-precision counterparts (e.g., vaddsd to vaddss, vsubsd to vsubss, etc.). Next, modify the pointer update instructions in the for-loops to use an immediate value of four instead of eight. Finally, convert all memory operand size modifiers (e.g., real8 ptr to real4 ptr).

Summary

Here are the key learning points for Chapter 5:

- The vadds[d|s], vsubs[d|s], vmuls[d|s], vdivs[d|s], and vsqrts[d|s] instructions perform basic double-precision and single-precision floating-point arithmetic.

- The vmovs[d|s] instructions copy a scalar floating-point value from one XMM register to another; they are also used to load/store scalar floating-point values from/ to memory.

- The vcoms[d|s] instructions compare two scalar floating-point values and set the status flags in RFLAGS to signify the result.

- The vcmps[d|s] instructions compare two scalar floating-point values using a compare predicate. If the compare predicate is true, the destination operand is set to all ones; otherwise, it is set to all zeros.

- The vcvts[d|s]2si instructions convert a scalar floating-point value to a signed integer value; the vcvtsi2s[d|s] instructions perform the opposite conversion.

- The vcvtsd2ss instruction converts a scalar double-precision floating-point value to single-precision; the vcvtss2sd instruction performs the opposite conversion.

- The `vldmxcsr` instruction loads a value into the MXCSR register; the `vstmxcsr` instruction saves the current contents of the MXCSR register.

- The Visual C++ calling convention specifies the use of registers XMM0–XMM3 for floating-point arguments. Additional arguments are passed via the stack. Floating-point return values are passed back to the calling function using register XMM0.

- The GNU C++ calling convention specifies the use of registers XMM0–XMM7 for floating-point arguments. Additional arguments are passed via the stack. Floating-point return values are passed back to the calling function using register XMM0.

- To define a scalar floating-point constant data value, use the `dd` (single-precision) or `dq` (double-precision) directive. In MASM source code files, you can also use the directives `real4` or `real8`.

CHAPTER 6

■ ■ ■

Run-Time Calling Conventions

In the previous five chapters, you studied numerous code examples that informally discussed various aspects of the Visual C++ (Windows) and GNU C++ (Linux) run-time calling conventions. In this chapter, the calling conventions are formally explained. The discussions reiterate some earlier elucidations and introduce new requirements not already examined. A solid understanding of these calling conventions is essential since they're used extensively in subsequent chapters that explain x86-AVX SIMD programming.

The remainder of this chapter is partitioned into three sections. The first section covers calling convention terminology and topics common to both Visual C++ and GNU C++. The second section dives into the details of the Visual C++ calling convention. The final section describes the calling convention requirements for GNU C++.

Calling Convention Overview

A run-time calling convention is a specification that describes data exchange between a calling function and called function. More specifically, a calling convention specifies how a calling function should pass argument values to a called function. This includes which registers to use, when to use the stack, function prologue and epilogue requisites, plus any requirements imposed by the host OS or C++ compiler. A calling convention also dictates how a called function should return a value to its caller.

An x86-64 assembly language (or C++) function can be logically partitioned into three distinct sections. The first section is called the prologue. A function prologue contains code that preserves non-volatile registers, establishes a stack frame, and allocates storage on the stack for local variables. It is important to note that depending on its computational requirements, a function prologue may incorporate some, all, or none of these elements. The middle section of a function contains the code that carries out the desired computation. The final section is called the epilogue. This section includes code that releases any previously allocated stack storage, deconstructs the stack frame, and restores non-volatile registers. Like a prologue, the specific actions (if any) performed by a function in its epilogue will vary depending on its computation requirements.

As you have already seen, there are some similarities between the Visual C++ and GNU C++ calling conventions. Both conventions classify each general-purpose register as volatile or non-volatile. A called function can modify the value in a volatile general-purpose register. However, it must not alter the value in a non-volatile register. If a called function requires a non-volatile register to perform a calculation, it must preserve the caller's original value. As mentioned in the previous paragraph, the code that performs non-volatile register preservation and restoration is usually located in a function's prologue and epilogue, respectively.

The actions that a function performs in its prologue and epilogue also depend somewhat on whether the function is a leaf or non-leaf function. A leaf function is a function that does not call any other functions. Leaf functions often contain code that carry out straightforward calculations using only volatile registers.

© Daniel Kusswurm 2023
D. Kusswurm, *Modern X86 Assembly Language Programming*,
https://doi.org/10.1007/978-1-4842-9603-5_6

185

Many leaf functions do not require an explicit prologue and epilogue. A non-leaf function is a function that calls one or more other functions. These functions are frequently more complex, utilize both volatile and non-volatile registers, and consume stack space for local variable storage. A non-leaf function is also responsible for ensuring that RSP and the stack itself are properly arranged for any called functions. You'll learn more about the non-leaf function requirements for RSP and the stack later in this chapter.

The remainder of this chapter contains code that expounds various aspects of the Visual C++ and GNU C++ calling conventions. It should be noted that the examples presented in this chapter only consider calling convention specifications related to this book's source code. It does not discuss nonrelated calling convention topics such as the requirements for variadic functions, bit fields, passing of structures or unions by value, or returning structures or unions by value. Appendix B contains a list of references that you can consult for more information about these topics.

Calling Convention Requirements for Visual C++

In this section, you'll examine four MASM source code examples. The first three examples illustrate how to code functions that preserve and restore non-volatile general-purpose and XMM registers using explicit x86-64 assembly language instructions and MASM assembler directives. These examples also convey critical programming information regarding the use of function-local stack memory and the organization of a stack frame. The fourth explains how to call a C++ library function from a MASM coded assembly language function. This example also demonstrates how to use several prologue and epilogue macros, which help automate most of the programming labor associated with a non-leaf MASM function.

Stack Frames

The first example of this section, named Ch06_01, demonstrates how to initialize and use a stack frame pointer in a MASM assembly language function. Source code example Ch06_01 also illustrates some of the programming protocols that a MASM assembly language function prologue and epilogue must observe. Listing 6-1a shows the C++ source code for example Ch06_01.

Listing 6-1a. Example Ch06_01 C++ Code

```
//-----------------------------------------------------------------------
// Ch06_01.h
//-----------------------------------------------------------------------

#pragma once
#include <cstdint>

// Ch06_01_fasm.asm
extern "C" int64_t SumIntegers_a(int8_t a, int16_t b, int32_t c, int64_t d,
    int8_t e, int16_t f, int32_t g, int64_t h);

//-----------------------------------------------------------------------
// Ch06_01.cpp
//-----------------------------------------------------------------------

#include <iostream>
#include <iomanip>
#include "Ch06_01.h"
```

```
int main()
{
    int8_t a = 10, e = -20;
    int16_t b = -200, f = 400;
    int32_t c = -300, g = -600;
    int64_t d = 4000, h = -8000;

    int64_t sum1 = a + b + c + d + e + f + g + h;
    int64_t sum2 = SumIntegers_a(a, b, c, d, e, f, g, h);

    constexpr int w = 7;
    constexpr char nl = '\n';

    std::cout << "----- Results for Ch06_01 -----\n";
    std::cout << "a:    " << std::setw(w) << (int)a << nl;
    std::cout << "b:    " << std::setw(w) << b << nl;
    std::cout << "c:    " << std::setw(w) << c << nl;
    std::cout << "d:    " << std::setw(w) << d << nl;
    std::cout << "e:    " << std::setw(w) << (int)e << nl;
    std::cout << "f:    " << std::setw(w) << f << nl;
    std::cout << "g:    " << std::setw(w) << g << nl;
    std::cout << "h:    " << std::setw(w) << h << nl;
    std::cout << "sum1: " << std::setw(w) << sum1 << nl;
    std::cout << "sum2: " << std::setw(w) << sum2 << nl;

    std::cout << "\nsum1/sum2 compare check ";

    if (sum1 == sum2)
        std::cout << "passed\n";
    else
        std::cout << "failed!\n";

    return 0;
}
```

The C++ code in Listing 6-1a prepares a simple test case for the assembly language function SumIntegers_a(), which sums a series of eight signed integers. Listing 6-1b shows the MASM code for example Ch06_01.

Listing 6-1b. Example Ch06_01 MASM Code

```
;-------------------------------------------------------------------------------
; Ch06_01_fasm.asm
;-------------------------------------------------------------------------------


;-------------------------------------------------------------------------------
; int64_t SumIntegers_a(int8_t a, int16_t b, int32_t c, int64_t d,
;   int8_t e, int16_t f, int32_t g, int64_t h);
;-------------------------------------------------------------------------------
```

```
RBP_RA      equ 24        ;number of bytes between RBP and return address on stack
STK_LOCAL   equ 16        ;size in bytes of local stack space

        .code
SumIntegers_a proc frame

; Function prologue
        push rbp                            ;save caller's rbp register
        .pushreg rbp
        sub rsp,STK_LOCAL                   ;allocate local stack space
        .allocstack STK_LOCAL
        mov rbp,rsp                         ;set frame pointer
        .setframe rbp,0
        .endprolog                          ;mark end of prologe

; Save argument registers to home area (optional)
        mov [rbp+RBP_RA+8],rcx
        mov [rbp+RBP_RA+16],rdx
        mov [rbp+RBP_RA+24],r8
        mov [rbp+RBP_RA+32],r9

; Calculate a + b + c + d
        movsx rcx,cl                        ;rcx = a
        movsx rdx,dx                        ;rdx = b
        movsxd r8,r8d                       ;r8 = c;
        add rcx,rdx                         ;rcx = a + b
        add r8,r9                           ;r8 = c + d
        add r8,rcx                          ;r8 = a + b + c + d
        mov [rbp],r8                        ;save sum on stack to LocalVar1

; Calculate e + f + g + h
        movsx rcx,byte ptr [rbp+RBP_RA+40]  ;rcx = e
        movsx rdx,word ptr [rbp+RBP_RA+48]  ;rdx = f
        movsxd r8,dword ptr [rbp+RBP_RA+56] ;r8 = g
        add rcx,rdx                         ;rcx = e + f
        add r8,[rbp+RBP_RA+64]              ;r8 = g + h
        add r8,rcx                          ;r8 = e + f + g + h

; Compute final sum
        mov rax,[rbp]                       ;rax = a + b + c + d (LocalVar1)
        add rax,r8                          ;rax = final sum

; Function epilogue
        add rsp,16                          ;release local stack space
        pop rbp                             ;restore caller's rbp register
        ret

SumIntegers_a endp
        end
```

Functions that need to reference both argument values and local variables on the stack often include prologue code that creates a stack frame. Register RBP is customarily used as the stack frame pointer. Following stack frame initialization, the remaining code in a function can access items on the stack using RBP as a base register. Near the top of file Ch06_01_fasm.asm in Listing 6-1b are the equ statements RBP_RA equ 24 and STK_LOCAL equ 16. Symbolic name RBP_RA denotes the number of bytes between RBP and the return address on stack. It also equals the number of extra bytes needed to reference the stack home area. STK_LOCAL represents the number of bytes allocated on the stack for local storage. More on these values in a moment.

Following definition of RBP_RA and STK_LOCAL is the statement SumIntegers_a proc frame, which defines the beginning of function SumIntegers_a(). The frame attribute notifies MASM that the function SumIntegers_a() uses a stack frame pointer. It also instructs MASM to generate static table data that the Visual C++ run-time environment uses to process exceptions. The ensuing push rbp instruction saves the caller's RBP register on the stack since function SumIntegers_a() uses this register as its stack frame pointer. The .pushreg rbp statement that follows is a MASM directive that saves stack offset information about the push rbp instruction in an exception handling table. Using exceptions with assembly language code is not discussed in this book, but the Visual C++ calling convention requirements for saving registers on the stack must still be observed. Keep in mind that MASM (and NASM) directives are not executable instructions; they are directions to the assembler on how to perform specific actions during assembly of the source code.

The sub rsp,STK_LOCAL instruction allocates STK_LOCAL bytes of space on the stack for local variables. Function SumIntegers_a() only uses eight bytes of this space, but the Visual C++ calling convention requires functions to maintain double quadword (16-byte) alignment of the stack pointer outside of the prologue. You'll learn more about stack pointer alignment requirements later in this section. The next statement, .allocstack STK_LOCAL, is a MASM directive that saves local stack size allocation information in the Visual C++ run-time exception handling tables.

The mov rbp,rsp instruction initializes register RBP as the stack frame pointer, and the .setframe rbp,0 directive notifies the assembler of this action. The offset value zero that is included in the .setframe directive is the difference in bytes between RSP and RBP. In function SumIntegers_a(), the values in registers RSP and RBP are identical, so the offset value is zero. Later in this section, you'll learn more about the .setframe directive. It should be noted that a MASM function can use any non-volatile register as its stack frame pointer. Using RBP maintains consistency between x86-64 and x86-32 assembly language code, which uses register EBP. The final assembler directive, .endprolog, signifies the end of the prologue for function SumIntegers_a(). Figure 6-1 shows the stack layout and argument registers following execution of the prologue's mov rbp,rsp instruction.

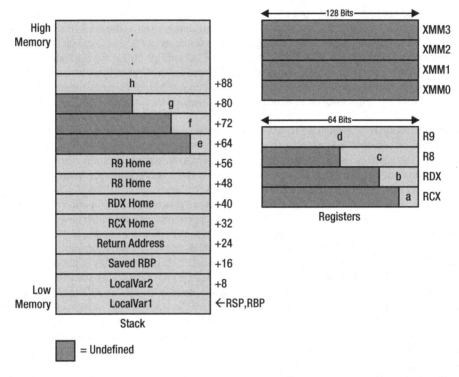

Figure 6-1. *Stack layout and registers in function SumIntegers_a() following execution of prologue* mov rsp,rsp *instruction*

The next code block contains a series of mov instructions that save registers RCX, RDX, R8, and R9 to their respective home areas on this stack. This step is optional and included in SumIntegers_a() for demonstration purposes. Note that the offset value in each mov instruction memory operand includes the symbolic constant RBP_RA. Another option allowed by the Visual C++ calling convention is to save an argument register to its corresponding home area prior to the push rbp instruction using RSP as a base register (e.g., mov [rsp+8],rcx, mov [rsp+16],rdx, and so on). Also keep in mind that a function can use its home area to store other temporary values. When used for alternative storage purposes, the home area should not be referenced by an assembly language instruction until after the .endprolog directive.

Following the home area save operation, function SumIntegers_a() sums argument values a, b, c, and d. It then saves this intermediate sum to LocalVar1 on the stack using a mov [rbp],r8 instruction. Note that the summation calculation sign-extends argument values a, b, and c using a movsx or movsxd instruction. A similar sequence of instructions is used to sum argument values e, f, g, and h, which are located on the stack and referenced using the stack frame pointer RBP and a constant offset. The symbolic name RBP_RA is also used here to account for the extra stack space needed to reference argument values on the stack. The two intermediate sums are then added to produce the final sum in register RAX.

A function epilogue must release any local stack storage space that was allocated in the prologue, restore any non-volatile registers that were saved on the stack, and execute a function return. The add rsp,16 instruction releases the 16 bytes of stack space that SumIntegers_a() allocated in its prologue. This is followed by a pop rbp instruction, which restores the caller's RBP register. The obligatory ret instruction is next. Note that the epilogue doesn't require any MASM directives. Here are the results for source code example Ch06_01:

```
----- Results for Ch06_01 -----
a:         10
b:       -200
c:       -300
d:       4000
e:        -20
f:        400
g:       -600
h:      -8000
sum1:   -4710
sum2:   -4710

sum1/sum2 compare check passed
```

Using Non-volatile General-Purpose Registers

The next source code example, Ch06_02, demonstrates how to exploit non-volatile general-purpose registers in a MASM function. It also provides additional programming details regarding stack frames and the use of local variables. Listing 6-2a shows the C++ code for this example, which includes the code that perform test case initialization for assembly language function CalSumProd_avx().

Listing 6-2a. Example Ch06_02 C++ Code

```cpp
//-----------------------------------------------------------------------
// Ch06_02.h
//-----------------------------------------------------------------------

#pragma once
#include <cstdint>

// Ch06_02_fasm.asm
extern "C" void CalcSumProd_avx(const int64_t* a, const int64_t* b, int32_t n,
    int64_t* sum_a, int64_t* sum_b, int64_t* prod_a, int64_t* prod_b);

//-----------------------------------------------------------------------
// Ch06_02.cpp
//-----------------------------------------------------------------------

#include <iostream>
#include <iomanip>
#include "Ch06_02.h"

int main()
{
    constexpr int n = 6;
    constexpr int64_t a[n] = { 2, -2, -6, 7, 12, 5 };
    constexpr int64_t b[n] = { 3, 5, -7, 8, 4, 9 };
    int64_t sum_a, sum_b, prod_a, prod_b;
```

```
    CalcSumProd_avx(a, b, n, &sum_a, &sum_b, &prod_a, &prod_b);

    constexpr int w = 6;
    constexpr char nl = '\n';
    const char* sp = "    ";

    std::cout << "----- Results for Ch06_02 -----\n";

    for (int i = 0; i < n; i++)
    {
        std::cout << "i: " << std::setw(w) << i << sp;
        std::cout << "a: " << std::setw(w) << a[i] << sp;
        std::cout << "b: " << std::setw(w) << b[i] << nl;
    }

    std::cout << nl;
    std::cout << "sum_a = " << std::setw(w) << sum_a << sp;
    std::cout << "sum_b = " << std::setw(w) << sum_b << nl;
    std::cout << "prod_a = " << std::setw(w) << prod_a << sp;
    std::cout << "prod_b = " << std::setw(w) << prod_b << nl;
}
```

Listing 6-2b shows the MASM code for example Ch06_02. Toward the top of this code is a series of equ statements that control how much local stack space is allocated in the prologue of function CalcSumProd_avx(). Like the previous example, the function CalcSumProd_avx() includes the frame attribute as part of its proc statement to indicate that it employs a stack frame pointer. A sequence of push instructions saves non-volatile registers RBP, RBX, R12, and R13 on the stack. Note that a .pushreg directive follows each push instruction, which instructs MASM to add information about each push instruction to the Visual C++ run-time exception handling tables.

Listing 6-2b. Example Ch06_02 MASM Code

```
;-------------------------------------------------------------------------------
; Ch06_02_fasm.asm
;-------------------------------------------------------------------------------


;-------------------------------------------------------------------------------
; void CalcSumProd_avx(const int64_t* a, const int64_t* b, int32_t n,
;     int64_t* sum_a, int64_t* sum_b, int64_t* prod_a, int64_t* prod_b);
;
; Named expressions for constant values:
;
; NUM_PUSHREG    number of prologue non-volatile register pushes
; STK_LOCAL1     size in bytes of STK_LOCAL1 area (see figure in text)
; STK_LOCAL2     size in bytes of STK_LOCAL2 area (see figure in text)
; STK_PAD        extra bytes (0 or 8) needed to 16-byte align RSP
; STK_TOTAL      total size in bytes of local stack
; RBP_RA         number of bytes between RBP and return address on stack
;-------------------------------------------------------------------------------
```

```
NUM_PUSHREG        equ 4
STK_LOCAL1         equ 32
STK_LOCAL2         equ 16
STK_PAD            equ ((NUM_PUSHREG AND 1) XOR 1) * 8
STK_TOTAL          equ STK_LOCAL1 + STK_LOCAL2 + STK_PAD
RBP_RA             equ NUM_PUSHREG * 8 + STK_LOCAL1 + STK_PAD

; Test SIMD values. Note that TestVal1 is Intentionally misaligned
                   .const
                   align 4
TestVal0           db 0ffh
TestVal1           db 0, 1, 2, 3, 4, 5, 6, 7, 8, 9, 10, 11, 12, 13, 14, 15


        .code
CalcSumProd_avx proc frame

; Function prologue
        push rbp                            ;save non-volatile register RBP
        .pushreg rbp
        push rbx                            ;save non-volatile register RBX
        .pushreg rbx
        push r12                            ;save non-volatile register R12
        .pushreg r12
        push r13                            ;save non-volatile register R13
        .pushreg r13

        sub rsp,STK_TOTAL                   ;allocate local stack space
        .allocstack STK_TOTAL
        lea rbp,[rsp+STK_LOCAL2]            ;set frame pointer
        .setframe rbp,STK_LOCAL2
        .endprolog                          ;end of prologue

; Initialize local variables on the stack (demonstration only)
        vmovdqu xmm5,xmmword ptr [TestVal1]
        vmovdqa xmmword ptr [rbp-16],xmm5   ;save xmm5 to LocalVar2A/2B
        mov qword ptr [rbp],0aah            ;save 0xaa to LocalVar1A
        mov qword ptr [rbp+8],0bbh          ;save 0xbb to LocalVar1B
        mov qword ptr [rbp+16],0cch         ;save 0xcc to LocalVar1C
        mov qword ptr [rbp+24],0ddh         ;save 0xdd to LocalVar1D

; Save argument values to home area (optional)
        mov [rbp+RBP_RA+8],rcx
        mov [rbp+RBP_RA+16],rdx
        mov [rbp+RBP_RA+24],r8
        mov [rbp+RBP_RA+32],r9

; Perform required initializations for processing loop
        test r8d,r8d                        ;is n <= 0?
        jle Done                            ;jump if n <= 0
```

```
        mov  rbx,-8                          ;rbx = offset to array elements
        xor  r10,r10                         ;r10 = sum_a
        xor  r11,r11                         ;r11 = sum_b
        mov  r12,1                           ;r12 = prod_a
        mov  r13,1                           ;r13 = prod_b

; Compute the array sums and products
@@:     add  rbx,8                           ;rbx = offset to next elements
        mov  rax,[rcx+rbx]                   ;rax = a[i]
        add  r10,rax                         ;update sum_a
        imul r12,rax                         ;update prod_a
        mov  rax,[rdx+rbx]                   ;rax = b[i]
        add  r11,rax                         ;update sum_b
        imul r13,rax                         ;update prod_b

        sub  r8d,1                           ;n -= 1
        jnz  @B                              ;repeat until done

; Save the final results
        mov  [r9],r10                        ;save sum_a
        mov  rax,[rbp+RBP_RA+40]             ;rax = ptr to sum_b
        mov  [rax],r11                       ;save sum_b
        mov  rax,[rbp+RBP_RA+48]             ;rax = ptr to prod_a
        mov  [rax],r12                       ;save prod_a
        mov  rax,[rbp+RBP_RA+56]             ;rax = ptr to prod_b
        mov  [rax],r13                       ;save prod_b

; Function epilogue
Done:   lea  rsp,[rbp+STK_LOCAL1+STK_PAD]    ;restore rsp
        pop  r13                             ;restore non-volatile GP registers
        pop  r12
        pop  rbx
        pop  rbp
        ret


CalcSumProd_avx endp
        end
```

The sub rsp,STK_TOTAL instruction allocates space on the stack for local variables, and the mandatory .allocstack STK_TOTAL MASM directive follows next. Register RBP is then initialized as the function's stack frame pointer using a lea rbp,[rsp+STK_LOCAL2] instruction, which loads RSP + STK_LOCAL2 into register RBP. Figure 6-2 illustrates the layout of the stack following execution of this lea instruction. Positioning RBP so that it "splits" the local stack area into two sections often enables the assembler to generate machine code that is slightly more efficient since a larger portion of the local stack area can be referenced using 8-bit signed instead of 32-bit signed displacements. It also simplifies the saving and restoring of non-volatile XMM registers, which is discussed in the next section. Following the lea instruction is a .setframe rbp,STK_LOCAL2 directive that properly configures the Visual C++ run-time exception handling tables. The size parameter of a .setframe directive must be an even multiple of 16 and less than or equal to 240. The .endprolog directive signifies the end of the prologue for function CalcSumProd_avx().

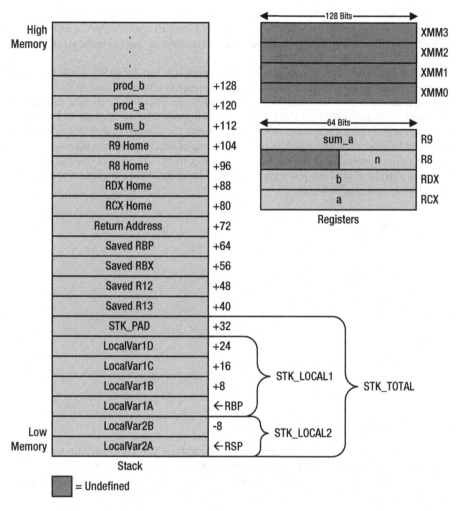

Figure 6-2. *Stack layout and argument registers following execution of* lea rbp,[rsp+STK_LOCAL2] *in function* CalcSumProd_avx()

The next code block contains instructions that initialize several local variables on the stack. These instructions are for demonstration purposes only. The vmovdqu xmm5,xmmword ptr [TestVal1] (Move Unaligned Packed Integer Values) loads 16 bytes of data from memory location TestVal1 into register XMM5. The ensuing vmovdqa [rbp-16],xmm5 (Move Aligned Packed Integer Values) saves this data on the stack. Both vmovdqu and vmovdqa are AVX SIMD instructions; they are used to perform moves of unaligned and aligned SIMD data values, respectively. The processor will generate an exception if vmovdqa is used with an XMM (YMM) register and a memory operand that is not properly aligned on a 16-byte (32-byte) boundary. You'll learn more about these instructions in later chapters. Following initialization of the local variables, the argument registers are saved to their home locations, also just for demonstration purposes.

Function CalcSumProd_avx() computes sums and products using the elements of two integer arrays. Prior to the start of the for-loop, the instruction pair test r8d,r8d and jle Done skips over the for-loop if n <= 0 is true. Recall that the test instruction performs a bitwise logical AND of its two operands and updates the status flags in RFLAGS; the result of the bitwise logical AND operation is discarded. Following validation of argument value n, the function CalcSumProd_avx() initializes the intermediate values sum_a (R10) and

195

sum_b (R11) to zero, and prod_a (R12) and prod_b (R13) to one. It then calculates the sum and product of the input arrays a and b. The results are saved to the memory locations specified by the caller. Note that the pointers for sum_b, prod_a, and prod_b were passed to CalcSumProd_avx() via the stack as shown in Figure 6-2.

The epilogue of function CalcSumProd_avx() begins with a lea rsp,[rbp+STK_LOCAL1+STK_PAD] instruction that restores register RSP to the value it had immediately after execution of the push r13 instruction in the prologue. When restoring RSP in an epilogue, the Visual C++ run-time calling convention specifies that either a lea rsp,[RFP+X] or add rsp,X instruction must be used, where RFP denotes the stack frame pointer register and X is a constant value. This limits the number of instruction patterns that the run-time exception handler must identify. The subsequent pop instructions restore the non-volatile general-purpose registers prior to execution of the ret instruction. According to the Visual C++ calling convention, function epilogues must be void of any processing logic including the setting of a return value. Here are the results for source code example Ch06_02:

```
----- Results for Ch06_02 -----
i:    0   a:    2   b:    3
i:    1   a:   -2   b:    5
i:    2   a:   -6   b:   -7
i:    3   a:    7   b:    8
i:    4   a:   12   b:    4
i:    5   a:    5   b:    9

sum_a =     18   sum_b =     22
prod_a =  10080   prod_b = -30240
```

Using Non-volatile XMM Registers

In Chapter 5, you learned how to use volatile XMM registers (XMM0–XMM5) to perform scalar floating-point arithmetic. The next source code example, named Ch06_03, illustrates the prologue and epilogue conventions that must be observed before a MASM function can utilize a non-volatile XMM register (XMM6–XMM15). Listing 6-3a shows the C++ source code for example Ch06_03.

Listing 6-3a. Example Ch06_03 C++ Code

```
//------------------------------------------------------------------------------
// Ch06_03.h
//------------------------------------------------------------------------------

#pragma once

// Ch06_03_fasm.asm
extern "C" bool CalcConeAreaVol_avx(const double* r, const double* h, int n,
    double* sa_cone, double* vol_cone);

// Ch06_03_fcpp.cpp
extern "C" double g_F64_PI;

extern bool CalcConeAreaVol_cpp(const double* r, const double* h, int n,
    double* sa_cone, double* vol_cone);
```

```cpp
//-----------------------------------------------------------------------
// Ch06_03_fcpp.cpp
//-----------------------------------------------------------------------

#include <cmath>
#include <numbers>
#include "Ch06_03.h"

double g_F64_PI = std::numbers::pi_v<double>;      // used in asm code

bool CalcConeAreaVol_cpp(const double* r, const double* h, int n,
    double* sa_cone, double* vol_cone)
{
    constexpr double pi = std::numbers::pi_v<double>;

    if (n <= 0)
        return false;

    for (int i = 0; i < n; i++)
    {
        sa_cone[i] = pi * r[i] * (r[i] + sqrt(r[i] * r[i] + h[i] * h[i]));
        vol_cone[i] = pi * r[i] * r[i] * h[i] / 3.0;
    }

    return true;
}

//-----------------------------------------------------------------------
// Ch06_03.cpp
//-----------------------------------------------------------------------

#include <iostream>
#include <iomanip>
#include "Ch06_03.h"

int main()
{
    constexpr int n = 7;
    constexpr double r[n] = { 1.0, 1.0, 2.0, 2.0, 3.0, 3.0, 4.25 };
    constexpr double h[n] = { 1.0, 2.0, 3.0, 4.0, 5.0, 10.0, 12.5 };
    double sa_cone1[n], sa_cone2[n], vol_cone1[n], vol_cone2[n];

    CalcConeAreaVol_cpp(r, h, n, sa_cone1, vol_cone1);
    CalcConeAreaVol_avx(r, h, n, sa_cone2, vol_cone2);

    std::cout << "----- Results for Ch06_03 -----\n";
    std::cout << std::fixed;

    constexpr int w = 14;
    constexpr char nl = '\n';
    constexpr char sp = ' ';
```

197

```cpp
    for (int i = 0; i < n; i++)
    {
        std::cout << std::setprecision(2);
        std::cout << "r/h: " << std::setw(w) << r[i] << sp;
        std::cout << std::setw(w) << h[i] << nl;

        std::cout << std::setprecision(6);
        std::cout << "sa:   " << std::setw(w) << sa_cone1[i] << sp;
        std::cout << std::setw(w) << sa_cone2[i] << nl;

        std::cout << "vol: " << std::setw(w) << vol_cone1[i] << sp;
        std::cout << std::setw(w) << vol_cone2[i] << nl;
        std::cout << nl;
    }

    return 0;
}
```

Functions CalcConeAreaVol_cpp() and CalcConeAreaVol_avx() calculate surface areas and volumes of right-circular cones using the following formulas:

$$sa = \pi \, r \left(r + \sqrt{r^2 + h^2} \right)$$

$$vol = \frac{\pi r^2 h}{3}$$

Listing 6-3b shows the MASM code for example Ch06_03.

Listing 6-3b. Example Ch06_03 MASM Code

```asm
;-----------------------------------------------------------------------------
; Ch06_03_fasm.asm
;-----------------------------------------------------------------------------


;-----------------------------------------------------------------------------
; bool CalcConeAreaVol_A(const double* r, const double* h, int n,
;   double* sa_cone, double* vol_cone);
;
; Named expressions for constant values
;
; NUM_PUSHREG    number of prolog non-volatile register pushes
; STK_LOCAL1     size in bytes of STK_LOCAL1 area (see figure in text)
; STK_LOCAL2     size in bytes of STK_LOCAL2 area (see figure in text)
; STK_PAD        extra bytes (0 or 8) needed to 16-byte align RSP
; STK_TOTAL      total size in bytes of local stack
; RBP_RA         number of bytes between RBP and ret addr on stack
;-----------------------------------------------------------------------------

NUM_PUSHREG    equ 7
STK_LOCAL1     equ 16
```

```
STK_LOCAL2          equ 64
STK_PAD             equ ((NUM_PUSHREG AND 1) XOR 1) * 8
STK_TOTAL           equ STK_LOCAL1 + STK_LOCAL2 + STK_PAD
RBP_RA              equ NUM_PUSHREG * 8 + STK_LOCAL1 + STK_PAD

            extern g_F64_PI:real8

            .const
F64_3p0     real8 3.0

        .code
CalcConeAreaVol_avx proc frame

; Save non-volatile general-purpose registers
        push rbp
        .pushreg rbp
        push rbx
        .pushreg rbx
        push rsi
        .pushreg rsi
        push r12
        .pushreg r12
        push r13
        .pushreg r13
        push r14
        .pushreg r14
        push r15
        .pushreg r15

; Allocate local stack space and initialize frame pointer
        sub rsp,STK_TOTAL               ;allocate local stack space
        .allocstack STK_TOTAL
        lea rbp,[rsp+STK_LOCAL2]        ;rbp = stack frame pointer
        .setframe rbp,STK_LOCAL2

; Save non-volatile registers XMM12 - XMM15. Note that STK_LOCAL2 must
; be greater than or equal to the number of XMM register saves times 16.
        vmovdqa xmmword ptr [rbp-STK_LOCAL2+48],xmm12
        .savexmm128 xmm12,48
        vmovdqa xmmword ptr [rbp-STK_LOCAL2+32],xmm13
        .savexmm128 xmm13,32
        vmovdqa xmmword ptr [rbp-STK_LOCAL2+16],xmm14
        .savexmm128 xmm14,16
        vmovdqa xmmword ptr [rbp-STK_LOCAL2],xmm15
        .savexmm128 xmm15,0
        .endprolog

; Access local variables on the stack (demonstration only)
        mov qword ptr [rbp],-1          ;LocalVar1A = -1
        mov qword ptr [rbp+8],-2        ;LocalVar1B = -2
```

```
; Initialize the processing loop variables. Note that many of the
; register initializations below are performed merely to illustrate
; use of the non-volatile GP and XMM registers.
        mov esi,r8d                     ;esi = n
        test esi,esi                    ;is n <= 0?
        jle BadVal                      ;jump if yes

        mov rbx,-8                      ;rbx = offset to array elements
        mov r12,rcx                     ;r12 = ptr to r
        mov r13,rdx                     ;r13 = ptr to h
        mov r14,r9                      ;r14 = ptr to sa_cone
        mov r15,[rbp+RBP_RA+40]         ;r15 = ptr to vol_cone
        vmovsd xmm14,real8 ptr [g_F64_PI]  ;xmm14 = pi
        vmovsd xmm15,real8 ptr [F64_3p0]   ;xmm15 = 3.0

; Calculate cone surface areas and volumes
; sa = pi * r * (r + sqrt(r * r + h * h))
; vol = pi * r * r * h / 3
@@:     add rbx,8                       ;rbx = offset to next elements
        vmovsd xmm0,real8 ptr [r12+rbx]  ;xmm0 = r
        vmovsd xmm1,real8 ptr [r13+rbx]  ;xmm1 = h
        vmovsd xmm12,xmm12,xmm0         ;xmm12 = r
        vmovsd xmm13,xmm13,xmm1         ;xmm13 = h

        vmulsd xmm0,xmm0,xmm0           ;xmm0 = r * r
        vmulsd xmm1,xmm1,xmm1           ;xmm1 = h * h
        vaddsd xmm0,xmm0,xmm1           ;xmm0 = r * r + h * h

        vsqrtsd xmm0,xmm0,xmm0          ;xmm0 = sqrt(r * r + h * h)
        vaddsd xmm0,xmm0,xmm12          ;xmm0 = r + sqrt(r * r + h * h)
        vmulsd xmm0,xmm0,xmm12          ;xmm0 = r * (r + sqrt(r * r + h * h))
        vmulsd xmm0,xmm0,xmm14          ;xmm0 = pi * r * (r + sqrt(r * r + h * h))

        vmulsd xmm12,xmm12,xmm12        ;xmm12 = r * r
        vmulsd xmm13,xmm13,xmm14        ;xmm13 = h * pi
        vmulsd xmm13,xmm13,xmm12        ;xmm13 = pi * r * r * h
        vdivsd xmm13,xmm13,xmm15        ;xmm13 = pi * r * r * h / 3

        vmovsd real8 ptr [r14+rbx],xmm0  ;save surface area
        vmovsd real8 ptr [r15+rbx],xmm13 ;save volume

        sub esi,1                       ;update counter
        jnz @B                          ;repeat until done

        mov eax,1                       ;set success return code

; Restore non-volatile XMM registers
Done:   vmovdqa xmm12,xmmword ptr [rbp-STK_LOCAL2+48]
        vmovdqa xmm13,xmmword ptr [rbp-STK_LOCAL2+32]
        vmovdqa xmm14,xmmword ptr [rbp-STK_LOCAL2+16]
        vmovdqa xmm15,xmmword ptr [rbp-STK_LOCAL2]
```

```
; Restore non-volatile general-purpose registers
        lea rsp,[rbp+STK_LOCAL1+STK_PAD]      ;restore rsp
        pop r15
        pop r14
        pop r13
        pop r12
        pop rsi
        pop rbx
        pop rbp
        ret

BadVal: xor eax,eax                           ;set error return code
        jmp Done

CalcConeAreaVol_avx endp
        end
```

In Listing 6-3b, function CalcConeAreaVol_avx() begins its execution by saving the non-volatile general-purpose registers that it uses on the stack. It then allocates the specified amount of local stack space and initializes RBP as the stack frame pointer. The next code block saves non-volatile registers XMM12–XMM15 on the stack using a series of vmovdqa instructions. A .savexmm128 directive must be employed after each vmovdqa instruction. Like the other prologue directives, the .savexmm128 directive instructs MASM to store information regarding the preservation of a non-volatile XMM register in the run-time exception handling tables. The offset argument of a .savexmm128 directive represents the displacement of the saved XMM register on the stack relative to register RSP. Note that the size of STK_LOCAL2 must be greater than or equal to the number of saved XMM registers multiplied by 16. Figure 6-3 illustrates the layout of the stack following execution of the prologue's vmovdqa xmmword ptr [rbp-STK_LOCAL2],xmm15 instruction.

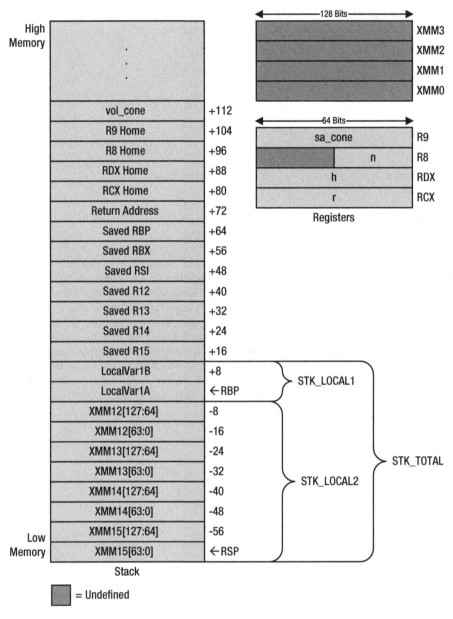

Figure 6-3. *Stack layout and argument registers following execution of* `vmovdqa xmmword ptr [rbp-STK_ LOCAL2],xmm15` *in function* `CalcConeAreaVol_avx()`

Following its prologue, `CalcConeAreaVol()` accesses local variables `LocalVar1A` and `LocalVar1B` for demonstration purposes. Initialization of registers used in the main for-loop occurs next. Note that many of these initializations are either suboptimal or superfluous; they are performed merely to highlight the use of non-volatile registers, both general-purpose and XMM. Calculation of the cone surface areas and volumes is then carried out using AVX scalar double-precision floating-point arithmetic instructions that you have already seen.

202

Upon completion of the processing loop, the non-volatile XMM registers are restored using a series of vmovdqa instructions. The function CalcConeAreaVol_avx() then releases its local stack space and restores the previously saved non-volatile general-purpose registers that it used. Here are the results for source code example Ch06_03:

```
----- Results for Ch06_03 -----
r/h:            1.00              1.00
sa:         7.584476          7.584476
vol:        1.047198          1.047198

r/h:            1.00              2.00
sa:        10.166407         10.166407
vol:        2.094395          2.094395

r/h:            2.00              3.00
sa:        35.220717         35.220717
vol:       12.566371         12.566371

r/h:            2.00              4.00
sa:        40.665630         40.665630
vol:       16.755161         16.755161

r/h:            3.00              5.00
sa:        83.229761         83.229761
vol:       47.123890         47.123890

r/h:            3.00             10.00
sa:       126.671905        126.671905
vol:       94.247780         94.247780

r/h:            4.25             12.50
sa:       233.025028        233.025028
vol:      236.437572        236.437572
```

The Visual C++ calling convention designates registers XMM0–XMM5 as volatile; registers XMM6–XMM15 are classified as non-volatile. Bits 255:128 of registers YMM0–YMM15 are designated as volatile. On systems that support AVX-512, bits 511:128 of registers ZMM0–ZMM15 and bits 511:0 of registers ZMM16–ZMM31 are classified as volatile.

Calling External Functions

The purpose of the three previous source code examples was to explicate the requirements of the Visual C++ run-time calling convention for x86-64 MASM functions. The calling convention's rigid requisites for function prologues and epilogues are somewhat lengthy and a potential source of programming errors. It is important to recognize that the stack layout of a function is primarily determined by the number of non-volatile (both general-purpose and XMM) registers that must be preserved and the amount of local stack space that's needed. A method is needed to automate most of the coding drudgery associated with the calling convention.

Listing 6-4a shows the C++ code for example Ch06_04. This code example demonstrates how to use several macros that I've written to simplify prologue and epilogue coding in a MASM function. This example also illustrates how to call a C++ library function from a MASM function.

Listing 6-4a. Example Ch06_04 C++ Code

```
//-----------------------------------------------------------------------------
// Ch06_04.h
//-----------------------------------------------------------------------------

#pragma once

// Ch06_04_fasm.asm
extern "C" bool CalcBSA_avx(const double* ht, const double* wt, int n,
    double* bsa1, double* bsa2, double* bsa3, double* bsa_mean);

// Ch06_04_fcpp.cpp
extern bool CalcBSA_cpp(const double* ht, const double* wt, int n,
    double* bsa1, double* bsa2, double* bsa3, double* bsa_mean);

//-----------------------------------------------------------------------------
// Ch06_04_fcpp.cpp
//-----------------------------------------------------------------------------

#include <cmath>
#include "Ch06_04.h"

bool CalcBSA_cpp(const double* ht, const double* wt, int n, double* bsa1,
    double* bsa2, double* bsa3, double* bsa_mean)
{
    if (n <= 0)
        return false;

    for (int i = 0; i < n; i++)
    {
        bsa1[i] = 0.007184 * pow(ht[i], 0.725) * pow(wt[i], 0.425);
        bsa2[i] = 0.0235 * pow(ht[i], 0.42246) * pow(wt[i], 0.51456);
        bsa3[i] = sqrt(ht[i] * wt[i] / 3600.0);

        bsa_mean[i] = (bsa1[i] + bsa2[i] + bsa3[i]) / 3.0;
    }

    return true;
}

//-----------------------------------------------------------------------------
// Ch06_04.cpp
//-----------------------------------------------------------------------------

#include <iostream>
#include <iomanip>
#include "Ch06_04.h"
```

```cpp
int main(void)
{
    constexpr int n = 6;
    constexpr double ht[n] = { 150, 160, 170, 180, 190, 200 };
    constexpr double wt[n] = { 50.0, 60.0, 70.0, 80.0, 90.0, 100.0 };
    double bsa1_a[n], bsa1_b[n];
    double bsa2_a[n], bsa2_b[n];
    double bsa3_a[n], bsa3_b[n];
    double bsa_mean_a[n], bsa_mean_b[n];

    CalcBSA_cpp(ht, wt, n, bsa1_a, bsa2_a, bsa3_a, bsa_mean_a);
    CalcBSA_avx(ht, wt, n, bsa1_b, bsa2_b, bsa3_b, bsa_mean_b);

    constexpr int w1 = 6;
    constexpr int w2 = 7;
    constexpr char sp = ' ';

    std::cout << std::fixed;
    std::cout << "----- Results for Ch06_04 -----\n";

    for (int i = 0; i < n; i++)
    {
        std::cout << std::setprecision(1);
        std::cout << "height: " << std::setw(w1) << ht[i] << " (cm)  ";
        std::cout << "weight: " << std::setw(w1) << wt[i] << " (kg)\n";
        std::cout << std::setprecision(4);

        std::cout << "C++ | ";
        std::cout << "bas1: " << std::setw(w2) << bsa1_a[i] << sp;
        std::cout << "bas2: " << std::setw(w2) << bsa2_a[i] << sp;
        std::cout << "bsa3: " << std::setw(w2) << bsa3_a[i] << sp;
        std::cout << "bsa_mean: ";
        std::cout << std::setw(w2) << bsa_mean_a[i] << " (sq. m)\n";

        std::cout << "ASM | ";
        std::cout << "bsa1: " << std::setw(w2) << bsa1_b[i] << sp;
        std::cout << "bsa2: " << std::setw(w2) << bsa2_b[i] << sp;
        std::cout << "bsa3: " << std::setw(w2) << bsa3_b[i] << sp;
        std::cout << "bsa_mean: ";
        std::cout << std::setw(w2) << bsa_mean_b[i] << " (sq. m)\n\n";
    }
}
```

Healthcare professionals often use the body surface area (BSA) to establish chemotherapy dosages for cancer patients. Table 6-1 lists three well-known equations that calculate BSA. In this table, each equation uses the symbol H for patient height in centimeters, W for patient weight in kilograms, and BSA for patient surface area in square meters. Functions CalcBSA_cpp() and CalcBSA_avx() compute the body surface area using equations shown in Table 6-1.

Table 6-1. *Body Surface Area Equations*

Method	Equation
DuBois and DuBois	$BSA = 0.007184 \times H^{0.725} \times W^{0.425}$
Gehan and George	$BSA = 0.0235 \times H^{0.42246} \times W^{0.51456}$
Mosteller	$BSA = \sqrt{H \times W / 3600}$

Listing 6-4b shows the MASM code for example Ch06_04. The code in Listing 6-4b begins with the statement include <MacrosX86-64-AVX.asmh>, which incorporates the contents of file MacrosX86-64-AVX.asmh into Ch06_04_fasm.asm during assembly. This file (source code not shown but included with the software download package) contains several macros that help automate much of the coding grunt work associated with the Visual C++ calling convention. As you have already seen, using an assembly language include file is analogous to using a C++ include file.

Listing 6-4b. Example Ch06_04 MASM Code

```
;-----------------------------------------------------------------------------
; Ch06_04_fasm.asm
;-----------------------------------------------------------------------------

        include <MacrosX86-64-AVX.asmh>


;-----------------------------------------------------------------------------
; bool CalcBSA_avx(const double* ht, const double* wt, int n,
;   double* bsa1, double* bsa2, double* bsa3, double* bsa_mean);
;-----------------------------------------------------------------------------


; Constants required for BSA calculations


                .const
F64_0p007184    real8 0.007184
F64_0p725       real8 0.725
F64_0p425       real8 0.425
F64_0p0235      real8 0.0235
F64_0p42246     real8 0.42246
F64_0p51456     real8 0.51456
F64_3600p0      real8 3600.0
F64_3p0         real8 3.0

        .code
        extern pow:proc

CalcBSA_avx proc frame
        CreateFrame_M BSA_,16,64,rbx,rsi,rdi,r12,r13,r14,r15
        SaveXmmRegs_M xmm6,xmm7,xmm8,xmm9
        EndProlog_M

; Save argument registers to home area (optional). Note that the home
; area can also be used to store other transient data values.
        mov [rbp+BSA_OffsetHomeRCX],rcx
```

```
        mov [rbp+BSA_OffsetHomeRDX],rdx
        mov [rbp+BSA_OffsetHomeR8],r8
        mov [rbp+BSA_OffsetHomeR9],r9

; Perform required initializations and error checks. Note that the
; various array pointers are maintained in non-volatile registers, which
; eliminates the need to perform reloads after the calls to pow().
        test r8d,r8d                            ;is n <= 0?
        jle BadVal                              ;jump if yes

        mov [rbp],r8d                           ;save n to local var
        mov r12,rcx                             ;r12 = ptr to ht
        mov r13,rdx                             ;r13 = ptr to wt
        mov r14,r9                              ;r14 = ptr to bsa1
        mov r15,[rbp+BSA_OffsetStackArgs]       ;r15 = ptr to bsa2
        mov rbx,[rbp+BSA_OffsetStackArgs+8]     ;rbx = ptr to bsa3
        mov rdi,[rbp+BSA_OffsetStackArgs+16]    ;rdi = ptr to bsa_mean
        mov rsi,-8                              ;common array offset

; Allocate home space on stack for use by pow()
        sub rsp,32

; Calculate bsa1 = 0.007184 * pow(ht, 0.725) * pow(wt, 0.425);
@@:     add rsi,8                               ;update array offset
        vmovsd xmm0,real8 ptr [r12+rsi]         ;xmm0 = ht
        vmovsd xmm8,xmm8,xmm0
        vmovsd xmm1,real8 ptr [F64_0p725]
        call pow                                ;xmm0 = pow(ht, 0.725)
        vmovsd xmm6,xmm6,xmm0

        vmovsd xmm0,real8 ptr [r13+rsi]         ;xmm0 = wt
        vmovsd xmm9,xmm9,xmm0
        vmovsd xmm1,real8 ptr [F64_0p425]
        call pow                                ;xmm0 = pow(wt, 0.425)
        vmulsd xmm6,xmm6,real8 ptr [F64_0p007184]
        vmulsd xmm6,xmm6,xmm0                   ;xmm6 = bsa1

; Calculate bsa2 = 0.0235 * pow(ht, 0.42246) * pow(wt, 0.51456);
        vmovsd xmm0,xmm0,xmm8                   ;xmm0 = ht
        vmovsd xmm1,real8 ptr [F64_0p42246]
        call pow                                ;xmm0 = pow(ht, 0.42246)
        vmovsd xmm7,xmm7,xmm0

        vmovsd xmm0,xmm0,xmm9                   ;xmm0 = wt
        vmovsd xmm1,real8 ptr [F64_0p51456]
        call pow                                ;xmm0 = pow(wt, 0.51456)
        vmulsd xmm7,xmm7,real8 ptr [F64_0p0235]
        vmulsd xmm7,xmm7,xmm0                   ;xmm7 = bsa2
```

```
; Calculate bsa3 = sqrt(ht * wt / 3600.0);
        vmulsd xmm8,xmm8,xmm9                    ;xmm8 = ht * wt
        vdivsd xmm8,xmm8,real8 ptr [F64_3600p0]  ;xmm8 = ht * wt / 3600
        vsqrtsd xmm8,xmm8,xmm8                   ;xmm8 = bsa3

; Calculate bsa_mean = (bas1 + bas2 + bas3) / 3.0
        vaddsd xmm0,xmm6,xmm7                    ;xmm0 = bsa1 + bsa2
        vaddsd xmm1,xmm0,xmm8                    ;xmm1 = bsa1 + bsa2 + bsa3
        vdivsd xmm2,xmm1,real8 ptr [F64_3p0]    ;xmm2 = (bsa3 + bsa1 + bsa2) / 3.0

; Save BSA results
        vmovsd real8 ptr [r14+rsi],xmm6         ;save bsa1
        vmovsd real8 ptr [r15+rsi],xmm7         ;save bsa2
        vmovsd real8 ptr [rbx+rsi],xmm8         ;save bsa3
        vmovsd real8 ptr [rdi+rsi],xmm2         ;save bsa_mean

        sub dword ptr [rbp],1                   ;n -= 1
        jnz @B

        mov eax,1                               ;set success return code

Done:   RestoreXmmRegs_M xmm6,xmm7,xmm8,xmm9
        DeleteFrame_M rbx,rsi,rdi,r12,r13,r14,r15
        ret

BadVal: xor eax,eax                             ;set error return code
        jmp Done

CalcBSA_avx endp
        end
```

Figure 6-4 shows a generic stack layout diagram for a non-leaf MASM function. Note the similarities between this figure and the more detailed stack layouts of Figures 6-2 and 6-3. The macros defined in MacrosX86-64-AVX.asmh assume that a function's stack layout will conform to what is shown in Figure 6-4. They enable a function to tailor a custom stack frame by specifying the amount of local stack space that is needed and which non-volatile registers must be preserved. The macros also perform most of the critical stack offset calculations, which significantly reduces the risk of a programming error in a function prologue or epilogue.

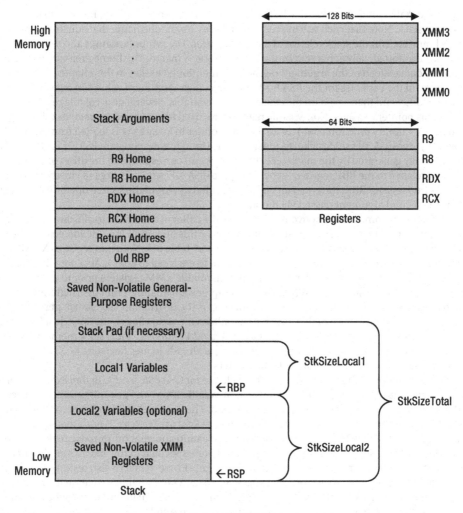

Figure 6-4. *Generic stack layout for a non-leaf x86-64 MASM function*

Following the include statement in Listing 6-4b is a .const section that contains definitions for the various floating-point constant values used in the BSA equations. The line extern pow:proc facilitates the use of the C++ library function pow(). Following the CalcBSA_avx proc frame statement, the macro CreateFrame_M emits assembly language code that initializes the stack frame. It also saves the specified non-volatile general-purpose registers on the stack. Macro CreateFrame_M requires several parameters including a prefix string and the size in bytes of StkSizeLocal1 and StkSizeLocal2 (see Figure 6-4). Macro CreateFrame_M uses the specified prefix string to generate symbolic names that can be employed to reference items on the stack. It is somewhat convenient to use a shortened version of the function name as the prefix string, but any file-unique text string can be used. Note that both StkSizeLocal1 and StkSizeLocal2 must be evenly divisible by 16. StkSizeLocal2 must also be less than or equal to 240 and greater than or equal to the number of saved XMM registers multiplied by 16.

The next statement makes use of the SaveXmmRegs_M macro to save the specified non-volatile XMM registers to the XMM save area on the stack. This is followed by the EndProlog_M macro, which signifies the end of a function's prologue. At this point, register RBP is configured as the function's stack frame pointer. It is also safe to use any of the saved non-volatile general-purpose or XMM registers.

The code block that follows EndProlog_M saves argument registers RCX, RDX, R8, and R9 to their home locations on the stack. Note that each mov instruction includes a symbolic name that equates to the offset of the register's home area on the stack relative to the RBP register. The symbolic names and the corresponding offset values were automatically generated by the CreateFrame_M macro. The home area can also be used to store temporary data instead of the argument registers, as mentioned earlier in this chapter.

Initialization of the variables for the BSA for-loop occurs next. Argument value n in register R8D is checked for validity and then saved on the stack as a local variable. Several non-volatile registers are then initialized as pointer registers. Non-volatile registers are used to avoid register reloads following each call to the C++ library function pow(). Note that the pointer to array bsa2 is loaded from the stack using a mov r15,[rbp+BSA_OffsetStackArgs] instruction. The symbolic constant BSA_OffsetStackArgs is also automatically generated by the macro CreateFrame_M and corresponds to the offset of the first stack argument relative to the RBP register. A mov rbx,[rbp+BSA_OffsetStackArgs+8] instruction loads argument bsa3 into register RBX; the constant eight is included as part of the source operand displacement since bsa3 is the second argument passed via the stack.

The Visual C++ run-time calling convention requires the caller of a function to allocate the callee's home area on the stack. The sub rsp,32 instruction performs this operation for function pow(). The ensuing code block calculates BSA values using the equations shown in Table 6-1. Note that registers XMM0 and XMM1 are loaded with the necessary argument values prior to each call to pow(). Also note that some of the return values from pow() are temporarily preserved in non-volatile XMM registers prior to their actual use.

The code in the BSA for-loop uses AVX scalar double-precision floating-point instructions to carry out the required calculations. Toward the bottom of the for-loop is the instruction sub dword ptr [rbp],1, which calculates n -= 1. Execution of this instruction updates the status flags in RFLAGS just like a sub instruction that uses register operands. Function CalcBSA_avx() employs a local stack memory location for variable n since all non-volatile general-purpose registers are already in use. Registers RCX, RDX, R8, and R9 can't be used for variable n since these are volatile registers.

Following completion of the BSA for-loop is the epilogue for CalcBSA_avx(). Before execution of the ret instruction, function CalcBSA_avx() must restore all non-volatile XMM and general-purpose registers that it saved in the prologue. The stack frame must also be deleted. The RestoreXmmRegs_M macro restores the non-volatile XMM registers. The order of the register list for macro RestoreXmmRegs_M *must* match the register list that was used with the SaveXmmRegs_M macro. Stack frame cleanup and general-purpose register restores are handled by the DeleteFrame_M macro. The order of the registers specified in this macro's argument list *must* be identical to the prologue's CreateFrame_M macro. The DeleteFrame_M macro also restores RSP from RBP, which means that it is not necessary to code an explicit add rsp,32 instruction to release the home area that was allocated on the stack for pow(). You'll see additional examples of function prologue and epilogue macro usage in subsequent chapters. Here are the results for source code example Ch06_04:

```
----- Results for Ch06_04 -----
height:  150.0 (cm)  weight:   50.0 (kg)
C++ | bas1:  1.4325 bas2:  1.4608 bsa3:  1.4434 bsa_mean:  1.4456 (sq. m)
ASM | bsa1:  1.4325 bsa2:  1.4608 bsa3:  1.4434 bsa_mean:  1.4456 (sq. m)

height:  160.0 (cm)  weight:   60.0 (kg)
C++ | bas1:  1.6221 bas2:  1.6489 bsa3:  1.6330 bsa_mean:  1.6346 (sq. m)
ASM | bsa1:  1.6221 bsa2:  1.6489 bsa3:  1.6330 bsa_mean:  1.6346 (sq. m)

height:  170.0 (cm)  weight:   70.0 (kg)
C++ | bas1:  1.8097 bas2:  1.8313 bsa3:  1.8181 bsa_mean:  1.8197 (sq. m)
ASM | bsa1:  1.8097 bsa2:  1.8313 bsa3:  1.8181 bsa_mean:  1.8197 (sq. m)
```

```
height:  180.0 (cm)  weight:   80.0 (kg)
C++ | bas1:  1.9964 bas2:  2.0095 bsa3:  2.0000 bsa_mean:  2.0020 (sq. m)
ASM | bsa1:  1.9964 bsa2:  2.0095 bsa3:  2.0000 bsa_mean:  2.0020 (sq. m)

height:  190.0 (cm)  weight:   90.0 (kg)
C++ | bas1:  2.1828 bas2:  2.1844 bsa3:  2.1794 bsa_mean:  2.1822 (sq. m)
ASM | bsa1:  2.1828 bsa2:  2.1844 bsa3:  2.1794 bsa_mean:  2.1822 (sq. m)

height:  200.0 (cm)  weight:  100.0 (kg)
C++ | bas1:  2.3693 bas2:  2.3566 bsa3:  2.3570 bsa_mean:  2.3610 (sq. m)
ASM | bsa1:  2.3693 bsa2:  2.3566 bsa3:  2.3570 bsa_mean:  2.3610 (sq. m)
```

Calling Convention Requirements for GNU C++

In this section, you'll study three NASM source code examples. The first example illustrates argument passing using general-purpose registers and the stack. The second example explicates non-volatile general-purpose register usage. This example also explains how to initialize and use a stack frame pointer. The final source code example details how to call a C++ library function from a NASM coded assembly language function.

Stack Arguments

Listing 6-5a shows the C++ code for example Ch06_05. This example demonstrates argument passing via general-purpose registers and the stack. It also illustrates the use of the stack red zone for temporary storage.

Listing 6-5a. Example Ch06_05 C++ Code

```
//-----------------------------------------------------------------------------
// Ch06_05.h
//-----------------------------------------------------------------------------

#pragma once
#include <cstdint>

// Ch06_05_fasm.asm
extern "C" int64_t MulIntegers_a(int8_t a, int16_t b, int32_t c, int64_t d,
    int8_t e, int16_t f, int32_t g, int64_t h);

// Ch06_05_fcpp.cpp
extern int64_t MulIntegers_cpp(int8_t a, int16_t b, int32_t c, int64_t d,
    int8_t e, int16_t f, int32_t g, int64_t h);

//-----------------------------------------------------------------------------
// Ch06_05_fcpp.cpp
//-----------------------------------------------------------------------------

#include "Ch06_05.h"
```

```cpp
int64_t MulIntegers_cpp(int8_t a, int16_t b, int32_t c, int64_t d,
    int8_t e, int16_t f, int32_t g, int64_t h)
{
    return a * b * c * d * e * f * g * h;
}

//----------------------------------------------------------------------------
// Ch06_05.cpp
//----------------------------------------------------------------------------

#include <iostream>
#include <iomanip>
#include "Ch06_05.h"

int main()
{
    int8_t a = 10, e = -51;
    int16_t b = -21, f = 68;
    int32_t c = -37, g = -73;
    int64_t d = 49, h = -82;

    int64_t prod1 = MulIntegers_cpp(a, b, c, d, e, f, g, h);
    int64_t prod2 = MulIntegers_a(a, b, c, d, e, f, g, h);

    constexpr int w = 14;
    constexpr char nl = '\n';

    std::cout << "----- Results for Ch06_05 -----\n";
    std::cout << "a:     " << std::setw(w) << (int)a << nl;
    std::cout << "b:     " << std::setw(w) << b << nl;
    std::cout << "c:     " << std::setw(w) << c << nl;
    std::cout << "d:     " << std::setw(w) << d << nl;
    std::cout << "e:     " << std::setw(w) << (int)e << nl;
    std::cout << "f:     " << std::setw(w) << f << nl;
    std::cout << "g:     " << std::setw(w) << g << nl;
    std::cout << "h:     " << std::setw(w) << h << nl;
    std::cout << "prod1: " << std::setw(w) << prod1 << nl;
    std::cout << "prod2: " << std::setw(w) << prod2 << nl;

    return 0;
}
```

Source code example Ch06_05 includes two functions, MulIntegers_cpp() and MulIntegers_a(), that calculate integer products. Note in Listing 6-5a that both function declarations include eight signed integer arguments of various widths. Function main() contains code that exercises the product calculating functions. It also formats the results for streaming to std::cout.

Listing 6-5b shows the NASM code for example Ch06_05.

Listing 6-5b. Example Ch06_05 NASM Code

```nasm
;-------------------------------------------------------------------------
; Ch06_05_fasm.s
;-------------------------------------------------------------------------

        %include "ModX86Asm3eNASM.inc"

;-------------------------------------------------------------------------
; int64_t MulIntegers_a(int8_t a, int16_t b, int32_t c, int64_t d,
;   int8_t e, int16_t f, int32_t g, int64_t h);
;-------------------------------------------------------------------------

; Offsets for red zone variables
RZ_A    equ -8
RZ_B    equ -16
RZ_C    equ -120
RZ_D    equ -128

; Offsets for stack arguments
ARG_G   equ 8
ARG_H   equ 16

        section .text

        global MulIntegers_a
MulIntegers_a:

; Sign-extend and save a, b, c, and d to red zone
        movsx rdi,dil                   ;rdi = a
        mov [rsp+RZ_A],rdi              ;save sign-extended a
        movsx rsi,si                    ;rsi = b
        mov [rsp+RZ_B],rsi              ;save sign-extended b
        movsxd rdx,edx                  ;rdx = c;
        mov [rsp+RZ_C],rdx              ;save sign-extended c
        mov [rsp+RZ_D],rcx              ;save d

; Calculate a * b * c * d * e * f * g * h
        movsx r8,r8b                    ;r8 = e
        movsx r9,r9w                    ;r9 = f
        movsxd r10,[rsp+ARG_G]          ;r10 = g
        mov r11,[rsp+ARG_H]             ;r11 = h

        imul r8,[rsp+RZ_A]             ;r8 = e * a
        imul r9,[rsp+RZ_B]             ;r9 = f * b
        imul r10,[rsp+RZ_C]            ;r10 = g * c
        imul r11,[rsp+RZ_D]            ;r11 = h * d
        imul r8,r9                      ;r8 = e * a * f * b
        imul r10,r11                    ;r10 = g * c * h * d
        imul r8,r10                     ;r8 = e * a * f * b * g * c * h * d

        mov rax,r8                      ;rax = final product
        ret
```

Toward the top of Listing 6-5b is a sequence of four equ statements that define (arbitrary) red zone offsets relative to register RSP for argument values a, b, c, and d. Recall that the GNU C++ calling convention designates the 128-byte area below the value in RSP as the red zone. A leaf function can use this area to temporarily store intermediate results or other data. Immediately following the red zone equ statements are two additional equates that signify the location of argument values g and h on the stack. Figure 6-5 shows the layout of the stack and register contents upon entry to function MulIntegers_a().

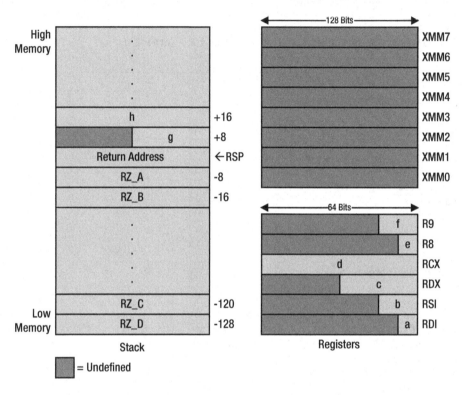

Figure 6-5. *Stack layout and register contents upon entry to* MulIntegers_a()

The opening code block in function MulIntegers_a() contains instructions that temporarily save argument values a, b, c, and d to their designated red zone locations. Note that these saves are for demonstration purposes only; different instructions could have been employed here to carry out the required product calculations sans use of the red zone. However, the sign extensions of argument values a, b, and c are required. The second code block in MulIntegers_a() exploits additional movsx and movsxd instructions to sign-extend argument values e, f, and g. Also note in this code block that argument values g and h are loaded into their respective registers from the stack.

Function MulIntegers_a()'s penultimate code block exercises a series of imul instructions that calculate the product of all eight signed integer arguments. Note that the first four imul instructions use red zone memory operands for a, b, c, and d. The mov rax,r8 instruction copies the calculated product into register RAX so that it can be passed back to the calling function. Here are the results for source code example Ch06_05:

```
----- Results for Ch06_05 -----
a:                   10
b:                  -21
c:                  -37
d:                   49
e:                  -51
f:                   68
g:                  -73
h:                  -82
prod1: -7903744637040
prod2: -7903744637040
```

Using Non-volatile General-Purpose Registers and Stack Frames

The next source code example, Ch06_06, explains how to initialize and use a NASM stack frame pointer. It also demonstrates preservation of non-volatile general-purpose registers on the stack. Listing 6-6a shows the C++ code for example Ch06_06.

Listing 6-6a. Example Ch06_06 C++ Code

```cpp
//-----------------------------------------------------------------------
// Ch06_06.h
//-----------------------------------------------------------------------

#pragma once
#include <cstdint>

// Ch06_06_fasm.asm
extern "C" int64_t AddIntegers_a(int8_t a, int16_t b, int32_t c, int64_t d,
    int8_t e, int16_t f, int32_t g, int64_t h);

// Ch06_06_fcpp.cpp
extern int64_t AddIntegers_cpp(int8_t a, int16_t b, int32_t c, int64_t d,
    int8_t e, int16_t f, int32_t g, int64_t h);

//-----------------------------------------------------------------------
// Ch06_06_fcpp.cpp
//-----------------------------------------------------------------------

#include "Ch06_06.h"

int64_t AddIntegers_cpp(int8_t a, int16_t b, int32_t c, int64_t d,
    int8_t e, int16_t f, int32_t g, int64_t h)
{
    return a + b + c + d + e + f + g + h;
}
```

```cpp
//-----------------------------------------------------------------------------
// Ch06_06.cpp
//-----------------------------------------------------------------------------

#include <iostream>
#include <iomanip>
#include "Ch06_06.h"

int main()
{
    int8_t a = 10, e = -51;
    int16_t b = -21, f = 68;
    int32_t c = -37, g = -73;
    int64_t d = 49, h = -82;

    int64_t sum1 = AddIntegers_cpp(a, b, c, d, e, f, g, h);
    int64_t sum2 = AddIntegers_a(a, b, c, d, e, f, g, h);

    constexpr  int w = 6;
    constexpr char nl = '\n';

    std::cout << "----- Results for Ch06_06 -----\n";
    std::cout << "a:     " << std::setw(w) << (int)a << nl;
    std::cout << "b:     " << std::setw(w) << b << nl;
    std::cout << "c:     " << std::setw(w) << c << nl;
    std::cout << "d:     " << std::setw(w) << d << nl;
    std::cout << "e:     " << std::setw(w) << (int)e << nl;
    std::cout << "f:     " << std::setw(w) << f << nl;
    std::cout << "g:     " << std::setw(w) << g << nl;
    std::cout << "h:     " << std::setw(w) << h << nl;
    std::cout << "sum1: " << std::setw(w) << sum1 << nl;
    std::cout << "sum2: " << std::setw(w) << sum2 << nl;

    return 0;
}
```

The C++ code in Listing 6-6a mimics the previous example with the primary difference being that functions AddIntegers_cpp() and AddIntegers_a() calculate sums instead of products. Note that a variety of integer sizes are used for the arguments and that these values are sign-extended when necessary. Also shown in Listing 6-6a is the function main(), which contains the now familiar test case initialization and display output code.

Listing 6-6b presents the NASM code for example Ch06_06. The first four equ statements in this listing, TEMP_A, TEMP_B, TEMP_C, and TEMP_D, define offsets for temporary variables on the stack relative to frame pointer RBP. More on this in a moment. The equ definition of STK_LOCAL signifies the number of bytes that AddIntegers_a() will allocate on the stack for temporary storage. The final two equate symbols, ARG_G and ARG_H, represent offsets relative to RBP for argument values g and h, which are passed via the stack.

Listing 6-6b. Example Ch06_06 NASM Code

```nasm
;-----------------------------------------------------------------------
; Ch06_06_fasm.s
;-----------------------------------------------------------------------

        %include "ModX86Asm3eNASM.inc"

;-----------------------------------------------------------------------
; int64_t AddIntegers_a(int8_t a, int16_t b, int32_t c, int64_t d,
;    int8_t e, int16_t f, int32_t g, int64_t h);
;-----------------------------------------------------------------------

; RBP offsets for temp variables on stack
TEMP_A      equ -8
TEMP_B      equ -16
TEMP_C      equ -24
TEMP_D      equ -32

STK_LOCAL   equ 32      ;storage space allocated on stack for temp variables

; RBP offsets for stack arguments
ARG_G   equ 32
ARG_H   equ 40

        section .text

        global AddIntegers_a
AddIntegers_a:

; Function prologue
        push rbp                    ;save callers RBP
        push r14                    ;r14, r15 pushes for demo only
        push r15
        mov rbp,rsp
        sub rsp,STK_LOCAL           ;allocate STK_LOCAL bytes on stack

; Sign-extend and save a, b, c, and d on stack
        movsx rdi,dil               ;rdi = a
        mov [rbp+TEMP_A],rdi         ;save sign-extended a
        movsx rsi,si                ;rsi = b
        mov [rbp+TEMP_B],rsi         ;save sign-extended b
        movsxd rdx,edx              ;rdx = c;
        mov [rbp+TEMP_C],rdx         ;save sign-extended c
        mov [rbp+TEMP_D],rcx         ;save d

; Sign-extend e, f, and g
        movsx rcx,r8b               ;rcx = e
        movsx rdx,r9w               ;rdx = f
        movsxd r8,[rbp+ARG_G]        ;r8 = g
        mov r9,[rbp+ARG_H]           ;r9 = h
```

```
; Calculate a + b + c + d + e + f + g + h
        add rcx,[rbp+TEMP_A]                 ;rcx = e + a
        add rdx,[rbp+TEMP_B]                 ;rdx = f + b
        add r8,[rbp+TEMP_C]                  ;rdx = g + c
        add r9,[rbp+TEMP_D]                  ;rdx = h + d
        add rcx,rdx                          ;rcx = e + a + f + b
        add r8,r9                            ;r8 = g + c + h + d
        add rcx,r8                           ;rcx = e + a + f + b + g + c + h + d
        mov rax,rcx                          ;rax = final product

; Function epilogue
        mov rsp,rbp                          ;release local storage
        pop r15
        pop r14
        pop rbp                              ;restore non-volatile GPRs
        ret
```

Function AddIntegers_a() opens with a code block that implements a formal function prologue. It begins with the instruction triplet push rbp, push r14, and push r15. These instructions save registers RBP, R14, and R15 on the stack. Note that the push r14 and push r15 instructions are exercised here solely to demonstrate non-volatile general-purpose register preservation. Following the push instructions, the mov rbp,rsp instruction copies RSP into RBP, which initializes it for use as a stack frame pointer. The final instruction of the prologue code block, sub rsp,STK_LOCAL, allocates STK_LOCAL bytes on the stack for temporary storage. Figure 6-6 illustrates the layout of the stack and argument register values following execution of this instruction.

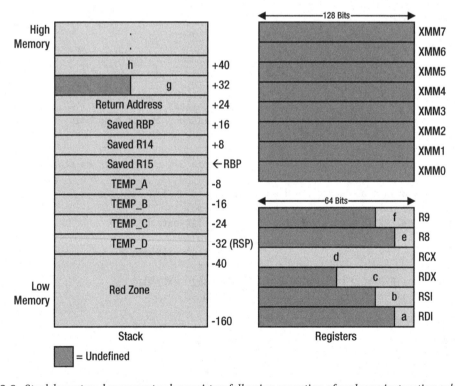

Figure 6-6. *Stack layout and argument value registers following execution of prologue instruction* sub rsp,STK_LOCAL *in* AddIntegers_a()

Note in Figure 6-6 that argument values g and h have positive displacements relative to RBP, but local variables TEMP_A–TEMP_D have negative displacements. This "splitting" of argument and local variables into two areas on the stack is potentially advantageous. The machine code encodings of x86-64 instructions that reference memory operands using a displacement (e.g., mov rcx,[RBP+TEMP_A] or add rcx,[RBP+TEMP_A]) encode the displacement value using a signed 8- or 32-bit integer. Using a stack frame pointer often means that memory operands for stack arguments and local variables can be encoded using 8-bit instead of 32-bit displacements, which reduces code size. Another perceived advantage of stack frame pointer usage is that new arguments or local values can usually be added without changing the displacements of any existing values. The drawback of using a stack frame pointer is that it consumes a general-purpose register that might be more valuable for other calculations.

Returning to the code in Listing 6-6b, function AddIntegers_a() uses a series of movsx, movsxd, and mov instructions to save sign-extended copies of argument values a, b, c, and d on the stack. Note that these instructions use RBP as a base register. The next code block contains instructions that create sign-extended copies of argument values e, f, and g while the mov r9,[rbp+ARG_H] instruction copies argument value h into register R9. This is followed by a code block that sums all eight argument values using 64-bit integer arithmetic.

The final code block of function AddIntegers_a() is its epilogue. The first epilogue instruction, mov rsp,rbp, releases the local stack storage space that was allocated in the prologue. Note that execution of this instruction also properly positions register RSP for the ensuing pop and ret instructions. This means that it is *not* necessary to include an explicit add RSP,STK_LOCAL instruction in the epilogue. Here are the results for source code example Ch06_06:

```
----- Results for Ch06_06 -----
a:          10
b:         -21
c:         -37
d:          49
e:         -51
f:          68
g:         -73
h:         -82
sum1:     -137
sum2:     -137
```

Calling External Functions

The final example of this section, dubbed Ch06_07, is a NASM implementation of example Ch06_04. The C++ source code for example Ch06_07 is identical to the C++ source code for example Ch06_04. Before continuing with this section, you may want to review the C++ code in Listing 6-4a and the three BSA equations in Table 6-1. Listing 6-7 shows the NASM code for example Ch06_07.

Listing 6-7. Example Ch06_07 NASM Code

```
;-----------------------------------------------------------------------
; Ch06_07_fasm.s
;-----------------------------------------------------------------------

        %include "ModX86Asm3eNASM.inc"

                section .rdata
F64_0p007184    dq 0.007184
F64_0p725       dq 0.725
F64_0p425       dq 0.425
F64_0p0235      dq 0.0235
F64_0p42246     dq 0.42246
F64_0p51456     dq 0.51456
F64_3600p0      dq 3600.0
F64_3p0         dq 3.0


;-----------------------------------------------------------------------
; bool CalcBSA_avx(const double* ht, const double* wt, int n,
;    double* bsa1, double* bsa2, double* bsa3, double* bsa_mean);
;-----------------------------------------------------------------------

; Offsets (relative to rsp) for stack local variables
STK_BSA3        equ 16
STK_TEMP1_F64   equ 8
STK_TEMP2_F64   equ 0

STK_LOCAL       equ 24          ;stack storage space in bytes for local variables
STK_PAD         equ 0           ;extra pad bytes for rsp 16-byte alignment

; Offsets for stack arguments
ARG_BSA_MEAN    equ 80

        section .text
        extern pow

        global CalcBSA_avx
CalcBSA_avx:
; Function prologue
        push rbp                            ;save non-volatile GPRs
        push rbx
        push r12
        push r13
        push r14
        push r15

        sub rsp,STK_LOCAL+STK_PAD           ;allocate local storage space

; Perform required error checks and initializations. Note that
; most arguments are copied to non-volatile registers to preserve
; their values across function boundaries.
```

```
        Test edx,edx                    ;is n <= 0?
        Jle BadVal                      ;jump if yes

        mov ebp,edx                     ;ebp = n
        mov r12,rdi                     ;r12 = ht ptr
        mov r13,rsi                     ;r13 = wt ptr
        mov r14,rcx                     ;r14 = bsa1 ptr
        mov r15,r8                      ;r15 = bsa2 ptr
        mov [rsp+STK_BSA3],r9           ;save bsa3 on stack
        mov rbx,-8                      ;common array offset

; Calculate bsa1 = 0.007184 * pow(ht, 0.725) * pow(wt, 0.425);
Loop1:  add rbx,8                       ;update array offset
        vmovsd xmm0,[r12+rbx]           ;xmm0 = ht
        vmovsd xmm1,[F64_0p725]         ;xmm1 = 0.754
        call pow wrt ..plt              ;xmm0 = pow(ht, 0.725)
        vmovsd [rsp+STK_TEMP1_F64],xmm0 ;save intermediate result on stack

        vmovsd xmm0,[r13+rbx]           ;xmm0 = wt
        vmovsd xmm1,[F64_0p425]         ;xmm1 = 0.425
        call pow wrt ..plt              ;xmm0 = pow(wt, 0.425)

        vmulsd xmm1,xmm0,[rsp+STK_TEMP1_F64]   ;xmm1 = pow(ht, 0.725) * pow(wt, 0.425)
        vmulsd xmm2,xmm1,[F64_0p007184]        ;xmm2 = bsa1
        vmovsd [r14+rbx],xmm2                  ;save bsa1

; Calculate bsa2 = 0.0235 * pow(ht, 0.42246) * pow(wt, 0.51456);
        vmovsd xmm0,[r12+rbx]           ;xmm0 = ht
        vmovsd xmm1,[F64_0p42246]       ;xmm1 = 0.42246
        call pow wrt ..plt              ;xmm0 = pow(ht, 0.42246)
        vmovsd [rsp+STK_TEMP2_F64],xmm0 ;save intermediate result on stack

        vmovsd xmm0,[r13+rbx]           ;xmm0 = wt
        vmovsd xmm1,[F64_0p51456]       ;xmm1 = 0.51456
        call pow wrt ..plt              ;xmm0 = pow(wt, 0.51456)

        vmulsd xmm1,xmm0,[rsp+STK_TEMP2_F64]   ;xmm1 = pow(wt, 0.51456) * pow(ht, 0.42246)
        vmulsd xmm5,xmm1,[F64_0p0235]          ;xmm5 = bsa2
        vmovsd [r15+rbx],xmm5                  ;save bsa2

; Calculate bsa3 = sqrt(ht * wt / 3600.0);
        vmovsd xmm0,[r12+rbx]           ;xmm0 = ht
        vmulsd xmm1,xmm0,[r13+rbx]      ;xmm1 = ht * wt
        vdivsd xmm2,xmm1,[F64_3600p0]   ;xmm2 = ht * wt / 3600
        vsqrtsd xmm3,xmm2,xmm2          ;xmm3 = bsa3
        mov rax,[rsp+STK_BSA3]          ;rax = bsa3 array pointer
        vmovsd [rax+rbx],xmm3           ;save bsa3

; Calculate bsa_mean = (bsa1 + bsa2 + bsa3) / 3.0
        vaddsd xmm0,xmm3,[r14+rbx]      ;xmm0 = bsa3 + bsa1
        vaddsd xmm1,xmm0,xmm5           ;xmm1 = bsa3 + bsa1 + bsa2
```

```
            vdivsd xmm2,xmm1,[F64_3p0]          ;xmm2 = (bsa3 + bsa1 + bsa2) / 3.0
            mov rax,[rsp+ARG_BSA_MEAN]          ;rax = bsa_mean array pointer
            vmovsd [rax+rbx],xmm2               ;save bsa mean

            sub ebp,1                           ;n -= 1
            jnz Loop1                           ;repeat loop until done

            mov eax,1                           ;set success return code

; Function epilogue
Done:       add rsp,STK_LOCAL+STK_PAD           ;release local storage space
            pop r15                             ;restore NV GPRs
            pop r14
            pop r13
            pop r12
            pop rbx
            pop rbp
            ret

BadVal: xor eax,eax                             ;set error return code
        jmp Done
```

Listing 6-7 opens with an .rdata section that contains definitions of the required double-precision floating-point constants for this example. This is followed by a series of equ statements. STK_BSA3, STK_TEMP1_F64, and STK_TEMP2_F64 represent offsets relative to RSP for local variables used in CalcBSA_avx(). The next equ symbol, STK_LOCAL, defines the number of bytes needed for local variables on the stack.

The GNU C++ calling convention requires RSP to be aligned on a 16-byte boundary before calling an external function. This requirement means that it is sometimes necessary to add extra pad bytes so that RSP is properly aligned. In Listing 6-7, symbol STK_PAD defines the number of required pad bytes. Note that this value is zero for function CalcBSA_avx(). Defining symbol STK_PAD, even though its value is zero, provides an important reminder that STK_PAD may need to be modified if the stack layout changes during future maintenance (the value of STK_PAD is normally zero or eight).

Function CalcBSA_avx() opens with a prologue that employs several push instructions to save registers RBP, RBX, and R12-R15 on the stack. The ensuing sub rsp,STK_LOCAL+STK_PAD instruction allocates stack space for the local variables. Figure 6-7 shows the layout of the stack following execution of the sub rsp,STK_LOCAL+STK_PAD instruction. In this figure, note that there is no red zone for CalcBSA_avx() since it's a non-leaf function. Also note that the number of quadwords between STK_TEMP2_F64 and the return address (inclusive) is 10, which means that RSP is properly aligned on a 16-byte boundary since $((8 * 10) \% 16) == 0$ is true.

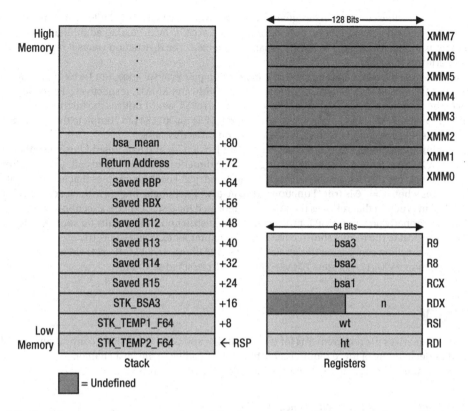

Figure 6-7. *Stack layout and argument registers following execution of instruction* sub rsp,STK_LOCAL+STK_ *PAD in function* CalcBSA_avx()

Following execution of the prologue, argument n is tested to confirm that it's greater than zero. The subsequent code block contains a series of mov instructions that copy most argument values from volatile general-purpose registers into non-volatile registers. The reason for this is that CalcBSA_avx() calls the C++ library function pow(). Transferring these arguments to non-volatile registers guarantees that their values are preserved across a function boundary. Note that argument value n is copied into register EBP, which is available since CalcBSA_avx() does not use a stack frame pointer. Also note that argument value bsa3 is temporarily saved on the stack since all other non-volatile registers are already in use.

Execution of for-loop Loop1 begins with an add rbx,8 instruction that updates register RBX, which contains a common offset for various data arrays used in CalcBSA_avx(). The next instruction, vmovsd xmm0,[r12+rbx], loads ht[i] into register XMM0. This is followed by a vmovsd xmm1,[F64_Op725] instruction that loads the double-precision floating-point constant value 0.725 into register XMM1. The ensuing call pow wrt ..plt instruction calls the C++ library function pow() to calculate pow(ht[i], 0.725). The text wrt ..plt (with respect to Procedure Link Table[1]) is a NASM special symbol that instructs the assembler to use the entry for pow() in the linker's PLT when emitting machine code for the call instruction.

---

[1] The PLT contains function addresses that can't be resolved until run-time, such as the address of a function in a shared object library.

The GNU C++ calling convention designates registers XMM0–XMM15 as volatile, which means their values are not preserved across function boundaries. Since CalcBSA_avx() makes additional calls to pow(), the current return value from pow() in XMM0 must be protected. The instruction vmovsd [rsp+STK_TEMP1_F64],xmm0 performs this task.

The second code block in Loop1 employs the instruction pair vmovsd xmm0,[r13+rbx] and vmovsd xmm1,[F64_Op425] to load wt[i] and 0.425 into registers XMM0 and XMM1, respectively. Following execution of the second call pow wrt ..plt instruction, CalcBSA_avx() utilizes the instruction pair vmulsd xmm1,xmm0,[rsp+STK_TEMP1_F64] and vmulsd xmm2,xmm1,[F64_Op007184] to complete the calculation of bsa1[i]. The ensuing vmovsd [r14+rbx],xmm2 instruction saves this value.

The remaining code blocks in Loop1 compute bsa2[i], bsa3[i], and bsa_mean[i] using similar sequences of AVX scalar double-precision floating-point arithmetic instructions and calls to pow(). Toward the bottom of Loop1, the instruction sequence sub ebp,1 and jnz Loop1 guarantees that execution of Loop1 terminates when n == 0 is true. Function CalcBSA_avx()'s epilogue begins with an add rsp,STK_LOCAL+STK_PAD instruction that releases the prologue-allocated local stack space. Execution of this instruction also properly positions RSP for the ensuing pop instructions. The results for source code example Ch06_07 are identical to the results shown earlier in this chapter for example Ch06_04.

The GNU C++ calling convention designates bits 255:128 of registers YMM0–YMM15 as volatile. On systems that support AVX-512, registers ZMM0–ZMM31 are classified as volatile.

Summary

This section summarizes the requirements for the Visual C++ and GNU C++ calling conventions. You should have a solid understanding of these requirements before proceeding to the next chapter.

Table 6-2 summarizes register usage for the Visual C++ calling convention.

Table 6-2. *Visual C++ Calling Convention Register Usage*

Register	Type	Usage
RAX	Volatile	Integer return value
RBX	Non-volatile	Scratch
RCX	Volatile	Integer argument
RDX	Volatile	Integer argument
RSI	Non-volatile	Scratch
RDI	Non-volatile	Scratch
RBP	Non-volatile	Stack frame pointer or scratch
RSP	Non-volatile	Stack pointer
R8	Volatile	Integer argument
R9	Volatile	Integer argument
R10	Volatile	Scratch
R11	Volatile	Scratch
R12–R15	Non-volatile	Scratch

(*continued*)

Table 6-2. (*continued*)

Register	Type	Usage
XMM0	Volatile	Floating-point argument, floating-point return value
XMM1	Volatile	Floating-point argument
XMM2	Volatile	Floating-point argument
XMM3	Volatile	Floating-point argument
XMM4	Volatile	Scratch
XMM5	Volatile	Scratch
XMM6–XMM15	Non-volatile	Scratch

The following bullet list summarizes other important Visual C++ calling convention requirements:

- The first function argument is passed using register RCX (integer) or XMM0 (floating-point). The second, third, and fourth arguments are passed via registers RDX or XMM1, R8 or XMM2, and R9 or XMM3. Any additional arguments are passed via the stack.

- 8-, 16-, and 32-bit wide integer argument values are passed in the low-order byte, word, or doubleword of the corresponding quadword register (or stack memory location). The high-order bits are undefined.

- Single-precision and double-precision floating-point register arguments are passed using XMM register bits 31:0 or 63:0, respectively. All other XMM register bits are undefined.

- Register RAX/EAX/AX/AL is used for an integer return value.

- Register XMM0 is used for a single- or double-precision floating-point return value.

- Bits 255:128 of registers YMM0–YMM15 are classified as volatile.

- On systems that support AVX-512, bits 511:256 of registers ZMM0–ZMM15 are classified as volatile. Registers ZMM16–ZMM31 are also classified as volatile.

- A function prologue must employ the MASM directives `.pushreg`, `.setframe`, `.savexmm128`, and `.endprolog` where required.

Table 6-3 summarizes register usage for the GNU calling convention.

Table 6-3. *GNU C++ Calling Convention Register Usage*

Register	Type	Usage
RAX	Volatile	Integer return value
RBX	Non-volatile	Scratch
RCX	Volatile	Fourth integer argument
RDX	Volatile	Third integer argument
RSI	Volatile	Second integer argument
RDI	Volatile	First integer argument
RBP	Non-volatile	Stack frame pointer or scratch
RSP	Non-volatile	Stack pointer
R8	Volatile	Fifth integer argument
R9	Volatile	Sixth integer argument
R10	Volatile	Scratch
R11	Volatile	Scratch
R12–R15	Non-volatile	Scratch
XMM0	Volatile	First floating-point argument, floating-point return value
XMM1	Volatile	Second floating-point argument
XMM2	Volatile	Third floating-point argument
XMM3	Volatile	Fourth floating-point argument
XMM4	Volatile	Fifth floating-point argument
XMM5	Volatile	Sixth floating-point argument
XMM6	Volatile	Seventh floating-point argument
XMM7	Volatile	Eighth floating-point argument
XMM8–XMM15	Volatile	Scratch

The following bullet list summarizes other important GNU C++ calling convention requirements:

- The first six integer arguments are passed using the general-purpose registers shown in Table 6-3. The first eight floating-point arguments are passed using the XMM registers shown in Table 6-3. Any additional arguments are passed via the stack.

- 8-, 16-, and 32-bit wide integer argument values are passed in the low-order byte, word, or doubleword of the corresponding quadword register (or stack memory location). The high-order bits are undefined.

- Single-precision and double-precision floating-point register arguments are passed using XMM register bits 31:0 or 63:0, respectively. All other XMM register bits are undefined.

- Register RAX/EAX/AX/AL is used for an integer return value.

- Register XMM0 is used for a single- or double-precision floating-point return value.

- Bits 255:128 of registers YMM0–YMM15 are classified as volatile.

- On systems that support AVX-512, registers ZMM16–ZMM31 are classified as volatile.

Both calling conventions designate RFLAGS.DF and MXCSR.RC as non-volatile. Failure to preserve these values may cause some C++ library functions to perform erratically or fail completely.

■ ■ ■

## CHAPTER 7

Introduction to X86-AVX SIMD Programming

In the first six chapters of this book, you learned essential details about an x86-64 processor including its data types, general-purpose registers, and memory addressing modes. You also examined a variety of source code examples that illustrated the fundamentals of x86-64 assembly language programming. At this point, you should have a solid understanding of the x86-64 assembly language instructions that perform integer arithmetic, compare operations, conditional jumps, and scalar floating-point arithmetic. You should also comprehend basic assembler usage (instruction syntax, data storage directives, operators, etc.) and the protocol requirements for calling an x86-84 assembly language function from C++.

The chapter you are about to read introduces x86-AVX SIMD programming. It begins with a brief synopsis of SIMD programming concepts. Next is an overview of the functional capabilities of x86-AVX. This is followed by an examination of the AVX and AVX2 execution environment, which covers register sets, SIMD data types, and instruction syntax.

Most of the topics presented in this chapter are applicable to both AVX and AVX2. They also provide the contextual foundation necessary to master AVX-512, which is covered in later chapters. As a reminder, this book uses the term x86-AVX as an umbrella expression to describe common characteristics and shared computing resources of Advanced Vector Extensions. The acronyms AVX, AVX2, and AVX-512 are employed when discussing features, attributes, or instructions connected to a specific x86-AVX instruction set extension.

SIMD Programming Concepts

The following section introduces SIMD programming concepts. It begins with a section that formally defines SIMD. This is followed by a few sections that explain fundamental SIMD arithmetic and data manipulation operations.

What Is SIMD?

SIMD (single instruction multiple data) is a parallel computing technique whereby a CPU (or processing element incorporated within a CPU) performs a single operation using multiple data items concurrently. For example, a SIMD-capable CPU can execute a single arithmetic operation (e.g., addition, subtraction, multiplication, etc.) using several elements of a floating-point array simultaneously. SIMD operations are frequently employed to accelerate the performance of computationally intense algorithms and functions in machine learning, image processing, audio/video encoding and decoding, matrix and vector computations, data mining, and computer graphics.

D. Kusswurm, *Modern X86 Assembly Language Programming*,
https://doi.org/10.1007/978-1-4842-9603-5_7

The underlying principles behind a SIMD arithmetic calculation are best illustrated by a simple source code example. Listing 7-1a shows a portion of the C++ source code for example Ch07_01. In this listing, note that function CalcZ_cpp() calculates z[i] = x[i] + y[i] using single-precision floating-point arrays.

Listing 7-1a. Example Ch07_01 C++ Code

```
//----------------------------------------------------------------------
// Ch07_01_fcpp.cpp
//----------------------------------------------------------------------

#include "Ch07_01.h"

void CalcZ_cpp(float* z, const float* x, const float* y, size_t n)
{
    for (size_t i = 0; i < n; i++)
        z[i] = x[i] + y[i];
}
```

Listing 7-1b shows the MASM code for example Ch07_01. In this listing, function CalcZ_avx() performs the same array calculation as CalcZ_cpp() but employs SIMD (or packed) AVX single-precision floating-point instructions to carry out the computations.

Listing 7-1b. Example Ch07_01 MASM Code

```
;----------------------------------------------------------------------
; Ch07_01_fasm.asm
;----------------------------------------------------------------------


;----------------------------------------------------------------------
; void CalcZ_avx(float* z, const float* x, const float* x, size_t n);
;----------------------------------------------------------------------

NSE     equ 8                           ;num_simd_elements

        .code
CalcZ_avx proc
        test r9,r9                      ;n == 0?
        jz Done                         ;jump if yes

; Initialize
        mov rax,-1                      ;rax = array offset for Loop2
        cmp r9,NSE                      ;n < NSE?
        jb Loop2                        ;jump if yes
        mov rax,-NSE                    ;rax = array offset for Loop1

; Calculate z[i:i+7] = x[i:i+7] + y[i:i+7]
Loop1:  add rax,NSE                     ;update offset for next SIMD group
        vmovups ymm0,ymmword ptr [rdx+rax*4]     ;ymm0 = x[i:i+7]
        vaddps ymm1,ymm0,ymmword ptr [r8+rax*4]  ;z[i:i+7] = x[i:i+7] + y[i:i+7]
        vmovups ymmword ptr [rcx+rax*4],ymm1     ;save z[i:i+7]
```

```
        sub r9,NSE                               ;n -= NSE
        cmp r9,NSE                               ;n >= NSE?
        jae Loop1                                ;jump if yes

        test r9,r9                               ;n == 0?
        jz Done                                  ;jump if yes
        add rax,NSE-1                            ;adjust offset for Loop2

; Calculate z[i] = x[i] + y[i] (num residual elements = [1, NSE - 1])
Loop2:  add rax,1                                ;i += 1
        vmovss xmm0,real4 ptr [rdx+rax*4]        ;xmm0 = x[i]
        vaddss xmm1,xmm0,real4 ptr [r8+rax*4]    ;z[i] = x[i] + y[i]
        vmovss real4 ptr [rcx+rax*4],xmm1        ;save z[i]

        sub r9,1                                 ;n -= 1
        jnz Loop2                                ;repeat Loop2 until done

Done:   vzeroupper                               ;clear upper bits of ymm regs
        ret                                      ;return to caller
CalcZ_avx endp
        end
```

The particulars of x86-AVX assembly language instruction syntax and SIMD arithmetic are explained later in this and subsequent chapters. For now, just take note of the AVX instruction vaddps ymm1,ymm0,ymmword ptr [r8+rax*4] (Add Packed Single-Precision Floating-Point Values) in Loop1. This instruction calculates $z[i:i+7] = x[i:i+7] + y[i:i+7]$. What differentiates the vaddps instruction from normal scalar floating-point arithmetic (e.g., vaddss) is that the processor performs eight array element additions simultaneously. The other item of note in Listing 7-1b is the AVX scalar arithmetic in for-loop Loop2. This for-loop handles any residual elements when n is not evenly divisible by eight.

The NASM code for example Ch07_01 is essentially the same as the MASM code in Listing 7-1b except for different argument registers. It is included with the software download package. Don't worry if you're somewhat perplexed by the source code in Listing 7-1b. Perhaps the most important purpose of this book is to teach you how to code functions like this using x86-64 assembly language and the AVX, AVX2, and AVX-512 instruction sets.

One final note regarding the code in example Ch07_01. Recent versions of mainstream C++ compilers such as Visual C++ and GNU C++ are often capable of automatically generating efficient x86-AVX code for trivial arithmetic functions like CalcZ_cpp(). However, these compilers still struggle sometimes to generate efficient x86-AVX code for more complicated functions, especially ones that employ nested for-loops or nontrivial decision logic. In these cases, manually coded x86-64 assembly language functions can frequently outperform the SIMD code generated by a modern C++ compiler.

SIMD Integer Arithmetic

As implied by the words of the acronym, a SIMD computing element executes the same operation on multiple data items simultaneously. Universal SIMD operations include basic arithmetic such as addition, subtraction, multiplication, and division. SIMD processing techniques can also be applied to a variety of other computational tasks including data comparisons, conversions, shifts, Boolean operations, and permutations. Processors facilitate SIMD operations by reinterpreting the bits of an operand in a register or memory location. For example, a 128-bit wide SIMD operand can hold two independent 64-bit integer values. It is also capable of accommodating four 32-bit integers, eight 16-bit integers, or sixteen 8-bit integers as illustrated in Figure 7-1.

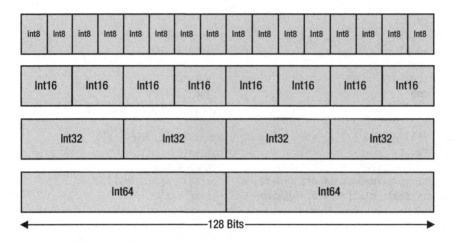

Figure 7-1. *128-bit wide SIMD operands using various integer types*

Figure 7-2 illustrates SIMD integer additions using 128-bit wide operands with eight 16-bit integers, four 32-bit integers, and two 64-bit integers. Like the floating-point example that you saw earlier, faster processing takes place when using SIMD arithmetic since the processor can perform the required calculations in parallel. For example, when 16-bit integer elements are used in a SIMD operand, the processor performs all eight 16-bit additions simultaneously.

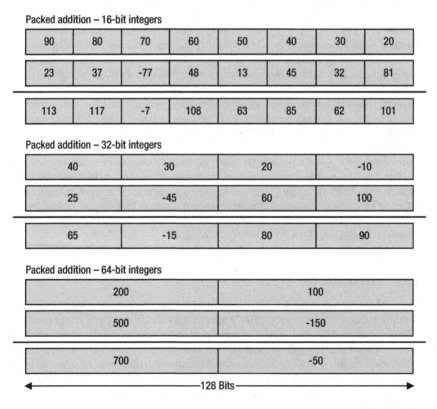

Figure 7-2. *SIMD integer addition using 16-, 32-, and 64-bit wide elements*

Besides packed integer addition, x86-AVX includes instructions that perform other common arithmetic calculations with packed integers including subtraction, multiplication, shifts, and bitwise logical operations. Figure 7-3 illustrates various packed shift operations using 32-bit wide integer elements.

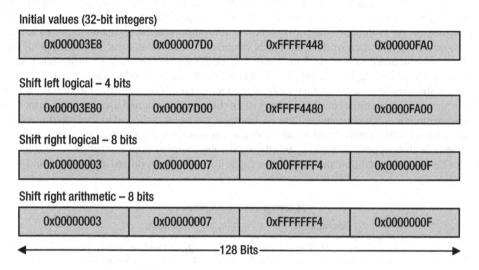

Figure 7-3. *SIMD shift operations*

Figure 7-4 demonstrates bitwise logical operations using packed 32-bit integers. Note that when performing a SIMD bitwise logical operation, distinct elements are usually irrelevant since the logical operation is carried out using the corresponding bit positions of each SIMD operand. In other words, the outcome of a SIMD bitwise logical operation is not determined by the element type (e.g., byte, word, doubleword, or quadword) since resultant SIMD bit pattern is the same.

Initial values (32-bit integers)

0xAAAAAAAA	0x89ABCDEF	0x12345678	0x55555555

0xFF0000FF	0x80808080	0x12345678	0x0F0F0F0F

Bitwise logical AND

0xAA0000AA	0x80808080	0x12345678	0x05050505

Bitwise logical OR

0xFFAAAAFF	0x89ABCDEF	0x12345678	0x5F5F5F5F

Bitwise logical XOR

0x55AAAA55	0x092B4D6F	0x00000000	0x5A5A5A5A

◄————————————128 Bits————————————►

Figure 7-4. *SIMD bitwise logical operations*

Wraparound vs. Saturated Arithmetic

One useful computational capability of x86-AVX is its support for saturated integer arithmetic. When performing saturated integer arithmetic, the processor automatically clips the elements of a SIMD operand to prevent an arithmetic overflow or underflow condition from occurring. This is different from normal (or wraparound) integer arithmetic where an overflow or underflow result is retained. Saturated integer arithmetic is advantageous when working with pixel values since it eliminates the need to explicitly check each pixel value for an overflow or underflow. X86-AVX includes instructions that perform packed saturated addition and subtraction using 8- or 16-bit wide integer elements, both signed and unsigned.

Figure 7-5 shows an example of packed 16-bit signed integer addition using both wraparound and saturated arithmetic. An overflow condition occurs when the two 16-bit signed integers are summed using wraparound arithmetic. With saturated arithmetic, however, the result is clipped to the largest possible 16-bit signed integer value. Figure 7-6 illustrates a similar example using 8-bit unsigned integers. Besides addition, x86-AVX also supports saturated packed integer subtraction as shown in Figure 7-7. Table 7-1 summarizes the saturated addition and subtraction range limits for all supported integer sizes and sign types.

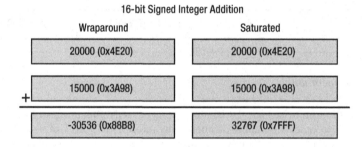

Figure 7-5. *16-bit signed integer addition using wraparound and saturated arithmetic*

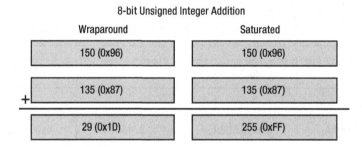

Figure 7-6. *8-bit unsigned integer addition using wraparound and saturated arithmetic*

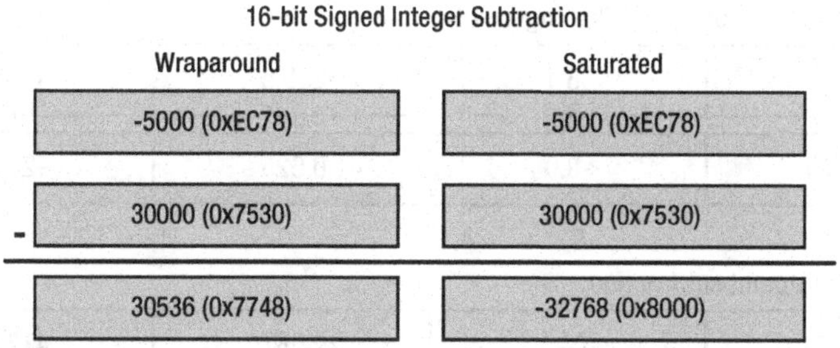

16-bit Signed Integer Subtraction

Wraparound	Saturated
-5000 (0xEC78)	-5000 (0xEC78)
30000 (0x7530)	30000 (0x7530)
30536 (0x7748)	-32768 (0x8000)

Figure 7-7. *16-bit signed integer subtraction using wraparound and saturated arithmetic*

Table 7-1. *Range Limits for Saturated Arithmetic*

Integer Type	Lower Limit	Upper Limit
8-bit signed	–128	127
8-bit unsigned	0	255
16-bit signed	–32768	32767
16-bit unsigned	0	65535

SIMD Floating-Point Arithmetic

X86-AVX supports SIMD floating-point arithmetic operations using single-precision or double-precision elements. This includes addition, subtraction, multiplication, division, and square root. Figures 7-8 and 7-9 illustrate a few common SIMD floating-point arithmetic operations.

Initial values (single-precision floating-point)

12.0	17.5	37.25	18.9	20.2	-23.75	0.125	47.5
88.0	17.5	28.0	100.5	5.625	33.0	-0.5	0.1

Packed floating-point addition

100.0	35.0	65.25	119.4	25.825	9.25	-0.375	47.6

Packed floating-point multiplication

1056.0	306.25	1043.0	1899.45	113.625	-783.75	-0.0625	4.75

◄─────────────────256 Bits─────────────────►

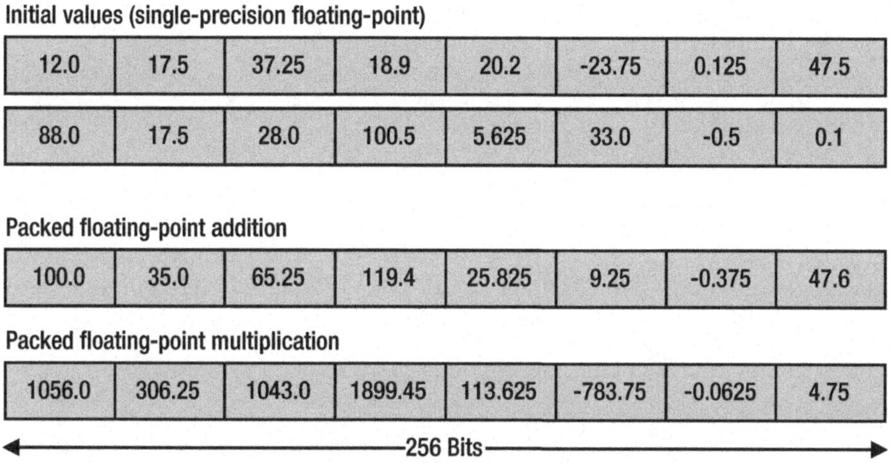

Figure 7-8. *SIMD single-precision floating-point addition and multiplication*

235

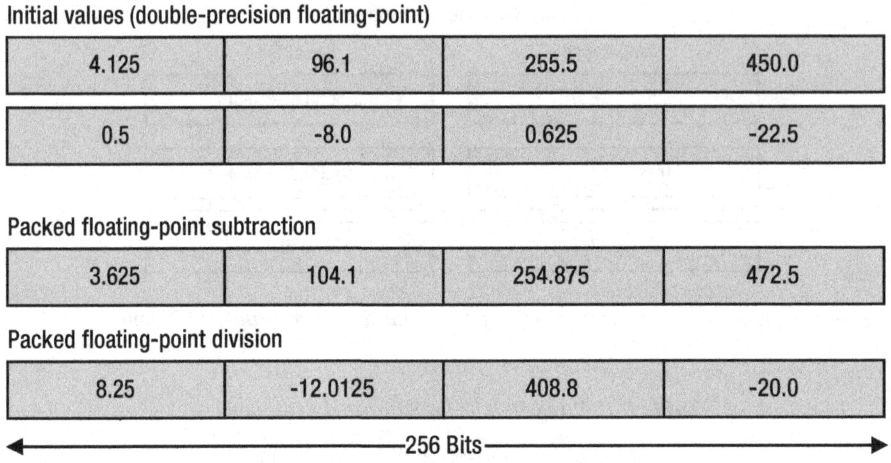

Initial values (double-precision floating-point)

4.125	96.1	255.5	450.0
0.5	-8.0	0.625	-22.5

Packed floating-point subtraction

3.625	104.1	254.875	472.5

Packed floating-point division

8.25	-12.0125	408.8	-20.0

◄───────────────256 Bits───────────────►

Figure 7-9. *SIMD double-precision floating-point subtraction and division*

The SIMD arithmetic operations that you have seen thus far perform their calculations using corresponding elements of the two source operands. These types of operations are usually called vertical arithmetic. X86-AVX also includes arithmetic instructions that carry out operations using the adjacent elements of a SIMD operand. Adjacent element calculations are termed horizontal arithmetic. Horizontal arithmetic is frequently used to perform a reduction, which arithmetically fuses the distinct elements of a SIMD operand to a single value. Figure 7-10 illustrates horizontal addition using packed single-precision floating-point elements and horizontal subtraction using packed double-precision floating-point elements. X86-AVX also supports integer horizontal addition and subtraction using packed 16- or 32-bit wide integers.

Horizontal addition – single-precision floating-point

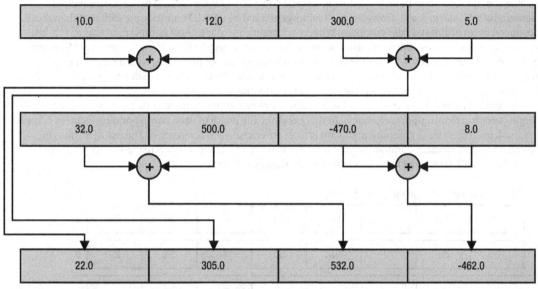

Horizontal subtraction – double-precision floating-point

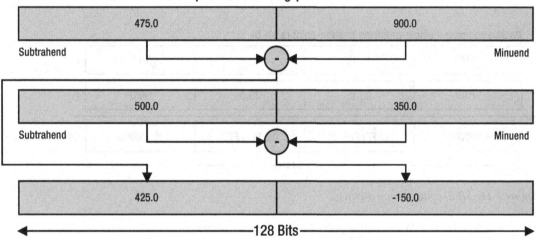

Figure 7-10. Floating-point horizontal addition and subtraction

SIMD Data Manipulation Operations

Besides arithmetic calculations, algorithms often need to perform data manipulation operations using SIMD operands. X86-AVX SIMD data manipulation operations include element comparisons, shuffles, permutations, blends, conditional moves, broadcasts, size promotions/reductions, and type conversions. You'll learn more about these operations in the x86-AVX programming chapters of this book. However, a few common SIMD data manipulation operations are employed repeatedly to warrant a few preliminary comments in this chapter.

One indispensable SIMD data manipulation operation is a data compare. Like a SIMD arithmetic calculation, the operation performed during a SIMD comparison is carried out using the individual elements of a SIMD operand. However, the results generated by a SIMD compare are different than those produced by an ordinary scalar compare. When performing a scalar integer compare such as a > b, an x86-64 processor conveys the result using status bits in RFLAGS as you have already seen. A SIMD compare is different in that it needs to report the results of multiple compare operations, which means a single set of status bits in RFLAGS is inadequate. To overcome this limitation, SIMD comparisons return a mask value that signifies the result of each SIMD element compare operation.

Figure 7-11 illustrates a couple of SIMD compare operations using packed 16-bit integers and packed single-precision floating-point elements. In this example, the result of each corresponding element compare is a mask of all ones if the compare predicate is true; otherwise, zero is returned. The use of all ones or all zeros for each element compare result facilitates subsequent computations using simple Boolean operations. You'll learn how to do this in the programming chapters.

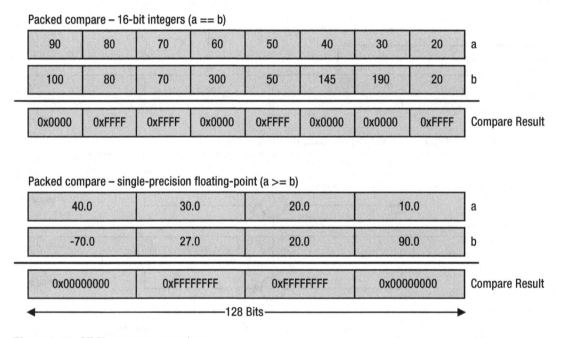

Packed compare – 16-bit integers (a == b)

| 90 | 80 | 70 | 60 | 50 | 40 | 30 | 20 | a |
| 100 | 80 | 70 | 300 | 50 | 145 | 190 | 20 | b |

| 0x0000 | 0xFFFF | 0xFFFF | 0x0000 | 0xFFFF | 0x0000 | 0x0000 | 0xFFFF | Compare Result |

Packed compare – single-precision floating-point (a >= b)

| 40.0 | 30.0 | 20.0 | 10.0 | a |
| -70.0 | 27.0 | 20.0 | 90.0 | b |

| 0x00000000 | 0xFFFFFFFF | 0xFFFFFFFF | 0x00000000 | Compare Result |

◄─────────────128 Bits─────────────►

Figure 7-11. *SIMD compare operations*

Another common SIMD data manipulation operation is a permutation. SIMD permutations are employed to rearrange the elements of a SIMD operand. They are often applied prior to a particular calculation or to accelerate the performance of a SIMD arithmetic operation. A permutation generally requires two SIMD operands: a source operand of elements to permute and a set of integer indices. Figure 7-12 illustrates an x86-AVX permutation using single-precision floating-point elements. In this example, the elements in the topmost SIMD operand are reordered using the element indices specified by the middle SIMD operand. Note that the same source operand element can be copied to multiple destination elements by simply specifying the appropriate index.

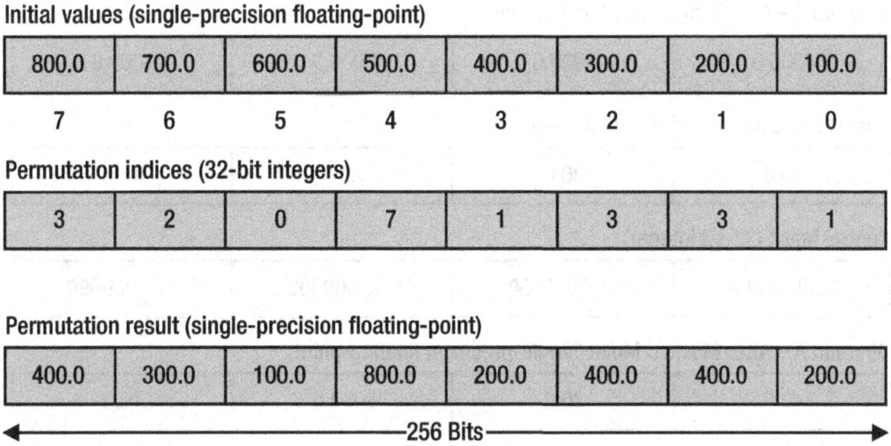

Initial values (single-precision floating-point)

800.0	700.0	600.0	500.0	400.0	300.0	200.0	100.0
7	6	5	4	3	2	1	0

Permutation indices (32-bit integers)

3	2	0	7	1	3	3	1

Permutation result (single-precision floating-point)

400.0	300.0	100.0	800.0	200.0	400.0	400.0	200.0

◄─────────────────────256 Bits─────────────────────►

***Figure 7-12.** SIMD permutation operation*

A broadcast operation copies a single value (or several values) to multiple locations in a SIMD operand. Broadcasts are often employed to load a scalar constant into each element of a SIMD operand. X86-AVX supports broadcast operations using either integer or floating-point values. Figure 7-13 shows the workings of a broadcast operation using single-precision floating-point values.

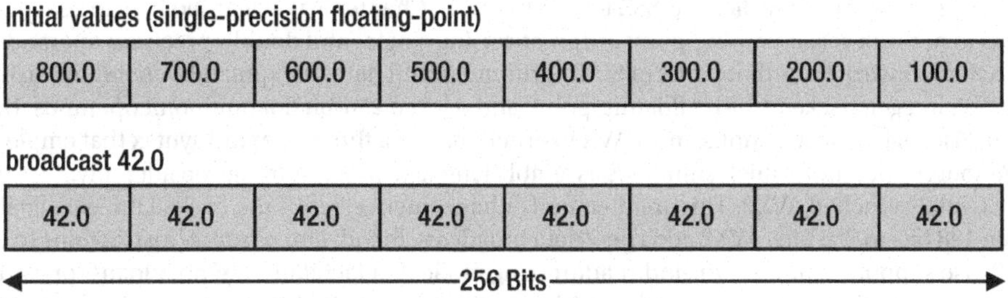

Initial values (single-precision floating-point)

800.0	700.0	600.0	500.0	400.0	300.0	200.0	100.0

broadcast 42.0

42.0	42.0	42.0	42.0	42.0	42.0	42.0	42.0

◄─────────────────────256 Bits─────────────────────►

***Figure 7-13.** Single-precision floating-point broadcast of constant 42.0*

Figure 7-14 shows one more common data manipulation operation. A masked move conditionally copies the elements from one SIMD operand to another SIMD operand based on the values in a control mask. In Figure 7-14, elements from Operand B are conditionally copied to Operand A if the most significant bit of the corresponding control mask is set to 1; otherwise, the element value in Operand A remains unaltered. Both AVX and AVX2 support masked moves using SIMD control masks. On processors that support AVX-512, an opmask register is utilized to carry out a masked move.

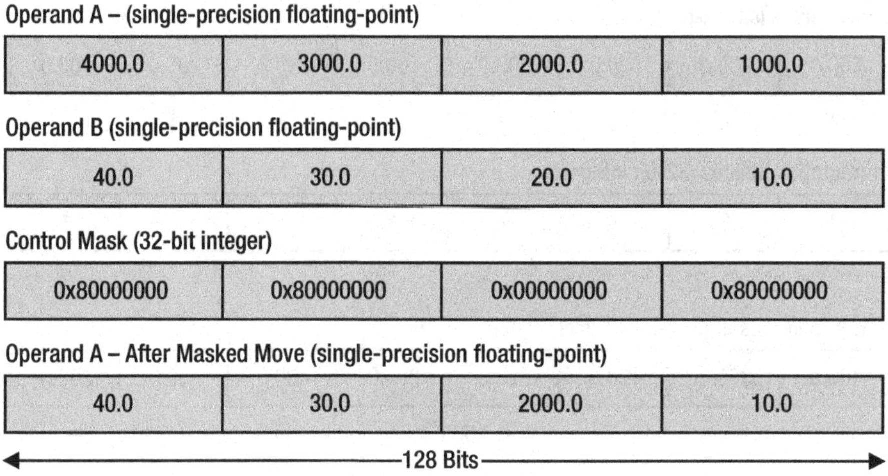

Operand A – (single-precision floating-point)

4000.0	3000.0	2000.0	1000.0

Operand B (single-precision floating-point)

40.0	30.0	20.0	10.0

Control Mask (32-bit integer)

0x80000000	0x80000000	0x00000000	0x80000000

Operand A – After Masked Move (single-precision floating-point)

40.0	30.0	2000.0	10.0

◀──────────────128 Bits──────────────▶

Figure 7-14. *Masked move operation*

X86-AVX Overview

AMD and Intel first incorporated AVX into their CPUs starting in 2011. AVX significantly expands the computational capabilities of earlier x86-SSE technologies. In Chapter 5, you learned how to use AVX instructions to perform scalar floating-point arithmetic using single- and double-precision operands. AVX also includes instructions that perform SIMD arithmetic and data manipulation operations using packed 128-bit integer, packed 128-bit floating-point, and packed 256-bit floating-point operands. Unlike general-purpose register instructions, most AVX instructions use a three-operand syntax that employs non-destructive source operands, which simplifies assembly language programming considerably.

In 2013, Intel launched AVX2. This architectural enhancement extends the packed integer capabilities of AVX from 128 bits to 256 bits. AVX2 adds new data broadcast, blend, and permute instructions to the x86 platform. It also supports a new vector-index addressing mode that facilitates memory loads (or gathers) of data elements from noncontiguous locations. The most recent x86-AVX extension is called AVX-512, which expands the maximum SIMD operand width from 256 bits to 512 bits. Table 7-2 summarizes the fundamental capabilities of x86-AVX. In this table, the acronyms SPFP and DPFP are used to signify single-precision floating-point and double-precision floating-point, respectively.

Table 7-2. *Summary of X86-AVX Fundamental Capabilities*

Feature	AVX	AVX2	AVX-512
Three-operand syntax; non-destructive source operands	Yes	Yes	Yes
SIMD operations using 128-bit packed integers	Yes	Yes	Yes
SIMD operations using 256-bit packed integers	No	Yes	Yes
SIMD operations using 512-bit packed integers	No	No	Yes
SIMD operations using 128-bit packed SPFP, DPFP	Yes	Yes	Yes
SIMD operations using 256-bit packed SPFP, DPFP	Yes	Yes	Yes
SIMD operations using 512-bit packed SPFP, DPFP	No	No	Yes
Scalar SPFP, DPFP arithmetic	Yes	Yes	Yes
Enhanced SPFP, DPFP compare operations	Yes	Yes	Yes
Basic SPFP, DPFP broadcast and permute	Yes	Yes	Yes
Enhanced SPFP, DPFP broadcast and permute	No	Yes	Yes
Packed integer broadcast	No	Yes	Yes
Enhanced packed integer broadcast, compare, permute, conversions	No	No	Yes
Instruction-level broadcast and rounding control	No	No	Yes
Fused-multiply-add	No	Yes	Yes
Data gather	No	Yes	Yes
Data scatter	No	No	Yes
Merge masking and zero masking using opmask registers	No	No	Yes

Table 7-2 includes fused-multiply-add (FMA) as an AVX2 feature since it's closely aligned with it. However, it is important to note that FMA is a distinct x86 instruction set extension. A program must confirm the presence of this feature set extension by testing the cpuid instruction FMA feature flag before using any of the corresponding instructions. You'll learn how to do this in Chapter 16. It should also be noted that other feature extensions besides the principal ones listed in Table 7-2 are included in recent processors from both AMD and Intel, especially extensions that augment the fundamental capabilities of AVX-512. You'll learn more about some of these extensions in later chapters.

The remainder of this chapter explains principal aspects of x86-AVX technologies including noteworthy particulars of AVX and AVX2. Some of this material has already been briefly mentioned in earlier chapters but warrants repetition given its importance. Comprehensive details regarding the specifics of AVX-512 are discussed in Chapter 13.

AVX/AVX2 SIMD Architecture Overview

This section presents an overview of AVX/AVX2 SIMD architecture. It begins with an explanation of SIMD registers. This is followed by a description of AVX/AVX2 SIMD data types. The section concludes with a synopsis of AVX/AVX2 instruction syntax.

SIMD Registers

X86-64 processors that support AVX incorporate 16 256-bit wide registers named YMM0–YMM15. The low-order 128 bits of each YMM register are aliased to a corresponding XMM register as illustrated in Figure 7-15. Most AVX instructions can use any of the XMM or YMM registers as SIMD operands. You learned in Chapter 5 that the XMM registers can also be employed to carry out scalar floating-point calculations using either single-precision or double-precision values. Programmers with assembly language experience using x86-SSE need to be aware of some minor execution differences between this legacy technology and x86-AVX. These differences are explained later in this chapter.

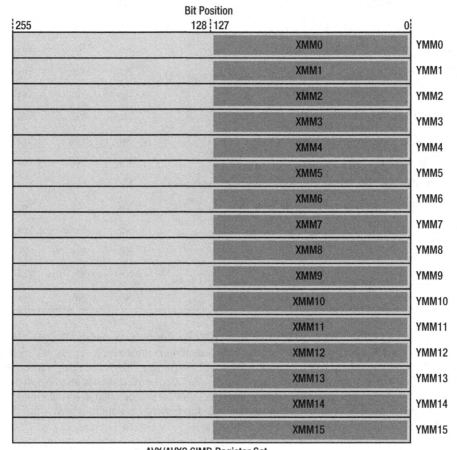

Figure 7-15. AVX register set

AVX2 extends the packed integer processing capabilities of AVX to the YMM register set and 256-bit wide operands in memory. It also includes expanded computational resources as outlined in Table 7-2.

Chapter 1 introduced the x86 MXCSR control-status register. This register contains status flags that report floating-point error conditions. MXCSR also includes control bits that specify the default rounding mode for most x86-AVX scalar and SIMD floating-point arithmetic instructions (see example Ch05_06). Table 1-5 in Chapter 1 describes the function of each MXCSR status flag and control bit.

SIMD Data Types

Figure 7-16 shows the scalar and SIMD data types supported by AVX and AVX2.

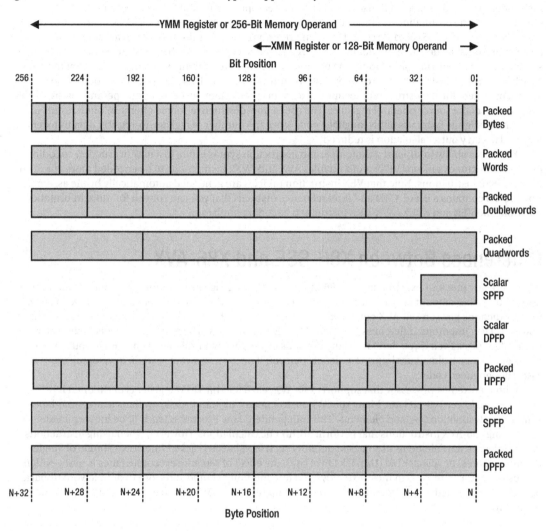

Figure 7-16. *AVX and AVX2 data types*

The HPFP item in Figure 7-16 signifies half-precision floating-point. Processors that support AVX may also support another x86 instruction set extension termed F16C. The F16C extension includes instructions that convert packed single-precision floating-point values to half-precision and vice versa. The F16C extension does not support half-precision arithmetic or other operations using scalar or SIMD operands.

Instruction Syntax

Perhaps the most noteworthy programming facet of x86-AVX is its use of a contemporary assembly language instruction syntax. Most x86-AVX instructions use a three-operand format that consists of two source operands and one destination operand. The general syntax that's employed for x86-AVX instructions is InstrMnemonic DesOp,SrcOp1,SrcOp2. Here, InstrMnemonic signifies the x86-AVX instruction mnemonic, DesOp represents the destination operand, and SrcOp1 and SrcOp2 denote the two source operands. A small subset of x86-AVX instructions employ one or three source operands along with a destination operand. Nearly all x86-AVX instruction source operands are non-destructive. This means that the source operands are not modified during instruction execution, except in cases where the destination operand register is the same as one of the source operand registers. The use of non-destructive source operands often results in simpler and slightly faster assembly language code since the number of register-to-register data transfers required to carry out a calculation is reduced.

X86-AVX's ability to support a three-operand instruction syntax is due to a new instruction encoding prefix. The vector extension (VEX) prefix enables AVX and AVX2 instructions to be encoded more efficiently than x86-SSE instructions. Note that VEX instruction prefixes are generated automatically by the assembler. Appendix B contains a list of AMD and Intel reference manuals that you can consult for more information regarding the VEX and EVEX (AVX-512) instruction encoding prefixes.

Differences Between X86-SSE and X86-AVX

If you have any previous experience with x86-SSE assembly language programming, you have undoubtedly noticed that a fair amount of symmetry exists between this execution environment and x86-AVX. Most x86-SSE instructions have an x86-AVX equivalent that can use either 256-bit or 128-bit wide operands. There are, however, a few important differences between x86-SSE and x86-AVX. The remainder of this section clarifies these differences. Even if you don't have any previous experience with x86-SSE, I encourage you to read this section since it elucidates important details that you'll need to be aware of when developing x86-AVX assembly language code.

Within an x86-64 processor that supports x86-AVX, each 256-bit YMM register is partitioned into an upper and lower 128-bit lane. Many x86-AVX instructions carry out their operations using same-lane source and destination operand elements. This independent lane execution tends to be inconspicuous when using x86-AVX instructions that perform arithmetic calculations. However, when using instructions that reorder the data elements of a packed quantity such as vshufps (Packed Interleave Shuffle of Single-Precision Values) or vpunpcklwd (Unpack Low Data), the effect of separate execution lanes is more evident as illustrated in Figure 7-17. In these examples, the floating-point shuffle and word to doubleword unpack operations are carried out independently in both the upper (bits 255:128) and lower (bits 127:0) double quadwords.

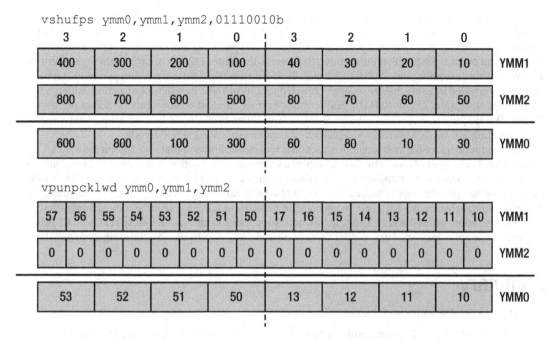

Figure 7-17. Examples of x86-AVX instruction execution using independent lanes

The aliasing of the XMM and YMM register sets introduces a few programming issues that software developers need to keep in mind. The first issue relates to the processor's handling of a YMM register's high-order 128 bits when the corresponding XMM register is used as a destination operand. When executed on a processor that supports x86-AVX, an x86-SSE instruction that uses an XMM register as a destination operand will never modify the upper 128 bits of the corresponding YMM register. However, the equivalent x86-AVX instruction will zero the upper 128 bits of the respective YMM register. Consider, for example, the following instances of the (v)cvtps2pd (Convert Packed Single-Precision to Packed Double-Precision) instruction:

```
cvtps2pd xmm0,xmm1
vcvtps2pd xmm0,xmm1
vcvtps2pd ymm0,ymm1
```

The x86-SSE cvtps2pd instruction converts the two packed single-precision floating-point values in the low-order quadword (bits 63:0) of XMM1 to double-precision floating-point and saves the result in register XMM0. This instruction does not modify bits YMM0[255:128]. The first vcvtps2pd instruction performs the same packed single-precision to packed double-precision conversion operation; it also zeroes bits YMM0[255:128]. The second vcvtps2pd instruction converts the four packed single-precision floating-point values in the low-order 128 bits of YMM1 to packed double-precision floating-point values and saves the result to YMM0. On processors that support AVX-512, the two vcvtps2pd instructions also zero bits ZMM0[511:256].

Compared to x86-SSE, x86-AVX relaxes the alignment requirements for SIMD operands in memory. Except for instructions that explicitly require an aligned operand (e.g., vmovdqa, vmovap[d|s], etc.), proper alignment of a 128-bit or 256-bit wide operand in memory is not mandatory. However, 128-bit and 256-bit wide operands should *always* be properly aligned on a 16-bit or 32-byte boundary whenever possible to prevent processing delays that can occur when the processor accesses unaligned operands in memory.

The last issue that programmers need to be aware of involves the intermixing of x86-AVX and x86-SSE code. Programs are allowed to intermix x86-AVX and x86-SSE instructions, but any intermixing should be kept to a minimum to avoid internal processor state transition penalties that can affect performance. These penalties can occur if the processor is required to preserve the upper 128 bits of each YMM register during a transition from executing x86-AVX to executing x86-SSE instructions. State transition penalties can be completely avoided by using the vzeroupper (Zero Upper Bits of YMM Registers) instruction, which zeroes bits 255:128 of registers YMM0–YMM15. The vzeroupper instruction also zeroes bits 511:256 of registers ZMM0–ZMM15 on processors that support AVX-512. This instruction should be used prior to any transition from executing 256-bit AVX/AVX2 or 512-bit AVX-512 code to executing x86-SSE code.

One common use of the vzeroupper instruction is by a public function that uses 256-bit x86-AVX instructions. These types of functions should employ a vzeroupper instruction before any ret instruction since this prevents processor state transition penalties from occurring in any high-level language code that uses x86-SSE instructions. The vzeroupper instruction should also be utilized prior to calling any C++ library functions that might contain legacy x86-SSE code. In later chapters, you'll see numerous source code examples that demonstrate proper use of the vzeroupper instruction. Functions can also use the vzeroall (Zero All YMM Registers) instruction instead of vzeroupper to avoid potential x86-AVX to x86-SSE state transition penalties.

Summary

Here are the key learning points for Chapter 7:

- SIMD is a parallel computing technique that carries out simultaneous calculations using multiple data items.

- AVX supports SIMD operations using 128-bit and 256-bit wide packed floating-point operands, both single-precision and double-precision.

- AVX also supports SIMD operations using 128-bit wide packed integer and scalar floating-point operands. AVX2 extends the AVX instruction set to support SIMD operations using 256-bit wide packed integer operands.

- The x86-AVX execution environment includes 16 YMM (256-bit) and XMM (128-bit) registers. Each XMM register is aliased with the low-order 128 bits of its corresponding YMM register.

- The x86-AVX execution environment also contains a status-control register named MXCSR. This register contains status flags that report floating-point error conditions. MXCSR also includes control bits for setting the default rounding mode for floating-point arithmetic operations.

- Most x86-AVX instructions use a three-operand syntax that includes two non-destructive source operands, except when the same register is used as both a source and destination operand.

- X86-AVX supports both wraparound and saturated arithmetic for packed 8- and 16-bit integers, both signed and unsigned.

- Except for instructions that explicitly specify aligned operands, 128-bit and 256-bit wide operands in memory need not be properly aligned. However, SIMD operands in memory should always be properly aligned whenever possible to avoid delays that can occur when the processor accesses an unaligned operand in memory.

- A vzeroupper or vzeroall instruction should be used in any function that executes a 256-bit or 512-bit x86-AVX instruction to avoid potential x86-AVX to x86-SSE state transition performance penalties.

■ ■ ■

## CHAPTER 8

AVX Programming – Packed Integers

The focus of this chapter is AVX integer programming using 128-bit wide SIMD operands. The first section examines several concise source code examples that illustrate packed integer arithmetic including addition, subtraction, and multiplication. This section also explains AVX bitwise logical operations and shifts. The second section contains two source code examples that demonstrate elementary SIMD calculations using integer arrays. Integer arrays are frequently utilized to maintain the pixels of a digital image. As you'll soon see, AVX is ideally suited for many types of image processing algorithms.

Performing packed integer operations using 256-bit wide operands requires a processor that supports AVX2. Chapter 10 covers AVX2 packed integer programming, which builds on the topics and examples presented in this chapter.

Integer Arithmetic

This section contains four source code examples that exemplify basic AVX instruction usage with 128-bit wide packed integer operands. The first two examples cover elementary packed integer arithmetic including addition, subtraction, and multiplication. The second two examples demonstrate packed integer bitwise logical and shift (both logical and arithmetic) operations.

Addition and Subtraction

Listing 8-1a shows the C++ source code for example Ch08_01. This example explicates AVX packed integer addition and subtraction using word (16-bit) elements and 128-bit wide SIMD operands.

Listing 8-1a. Example Ch08_01 C++ Code

```
struct alignas(16) XmmVal
{
public:
    union
    {
        int8_t m_I8[16];
        int16_t m_I16[8];
        int32_t m_I32[4];
        int64_t m_I64[2];
```

© Daniel Kusswurm 2023
D. Kusswurm, *Modern X86 Assembly Language Programming*,
https://doi.org/10.1007/978-1-4842-9603-5_8

```
            uint8_t m_U8[16];
            uint16_t m_U16[8];
            uint32_t m_U32[4];
            uint64_t m_U64[2];
            float m_F32[4];
            double m_F64[2];
        };

    // ...

    //---------------------------------------------------------------------
    // Ch08_01.h
    //---------------------------------------------------------------------

    #pragma once
    #include "XmmVal.h"

    // Ch08_01_fasm.asm, Ch08_01_fasm.s
    extern "C" void AddI16_avx(XmmVal* c1, XmmVal* c2, const XmmVal* a,
        const XmmVal* b);

    extern "C" void SubI16_avx(XmmVal* c1, XmmVal* c2, const XmmVal* a,
        const XmmVal* b);

    //---------------------------------------------------------------------
    // Ch08_01.cpp
    //---------------------------------------------------------------------

    #include <iostream>
    #include "Ch08_01.h"

    static void AddI16(void)
    {
        constexpr char nl = '\n';
        XmmVal a, b, c1, c2;

        // Packed int16_t addition
        a.m_I16[0] = 10;          b.m_I16[0] = 100;
        a.m_I16[1] = 200;         b.m_I16[1] = -200;
        a.m_I16[2] = 30;          b.m_I16[2] = 32760;
        a.m_I16[3] = -32766;      b.m_I16[3] = -400;
        a.m_I16[4] = 50;          b.m_I16[4] = 500;
        a.m_I16[5] = 60;          b.m_I16[5] = -600;
        a.m_I16[6] = 32000;       b.m_I16[6] = 1200;
        a.m_I16[7] = -32000;      b.m_I16[7] = -950;

        AddI16_avx(&c1, &c2, &a, &b);

        std::cout << "\nAddI16_avx() results - Wraparound Addition\n";
        std::cout << "a:  " << a.ToStringI16() << nl;
        std::cout << "b:  " << b.ToStringI16() << nl;
        std::cout << "c1: " << c1.ToStringI16() << nl;
```

```
        std::cout << "\nAddI16_avx() results - Saturated Addition\n";
        std::cout << "a:  " << a.ToStringI16() << nl;
        std::cout << "b:  " << b.ToStringI16() << nl;
        std::cout << "c2: " << c2.ToStringI16() << nl;
}

static void SubI16(void)
{
        constexpr char nl = '\n';
        XmmVal a, b, c1, c2;

        a.m_I16[0] = 10;            b.m_I16[0] = 100;
        a.m_I16[1] = 200;           b.m_I16[1] = -200;
        a.m_I16[2] = -30;           b.m_I16[2] = 32760;
        a.m_I16[3] = -32766;        b.m_I16[3] = 400;
        a.m_I16[4] = 50;            b.m_I16[4] = 500;
        a.m_I16[5] = 60;            b.m_I16[5] = -600;
        a.m_I16[6] = 32000;         b.m_I16[6] = 1200;
        a.m_I16[7] = -32000;        b.m_I16[7] = 950;

        SubI16_avx(&c1, &c2, &a, &b);

        std::cout << "\nSubI16_avx() results - Wraparound Subtraction\n";
        std::cout << "a:  " << a.ToStringI16() << nl;
        std::cout << "b:  " << b.ToStringI16() << nl;
        std::cout << "c1: " << c1.ToStringI16() << nl;
        std::cout << "\nSubI16_avx() results - Saturated Subtraction\n";
        std::cout << "a:  " << a.ToStringI16() << nl;
        std::cout << "b:  " << b.ToStringI16() << nl;
        std::cout << "c2: " << c2.ToStringI16() << nl;
}

int main()
{
        std::cout << "----- Results for Ch08_01 -----\n";

        AddI16();
        SubI16();
        return 0;
}
```

Listing 8-1a begins with the declaration of a C++ structure named XmmVal, which is declared in the header file XmmVal.h. This structure contains a publicly accessible anonymous union whose members correspond to the packed data types that can be used with a 128-bit wide x86-AVX operand. Note that XmmVal is declared using the C++ alignas(16) specifier. This specifier instructs the C++ compiler to align each instance of an XmmVal on a 16-byte boundary. When a processor executes an x86-AVX instruction that references a SIMD operand in memory, maximum performance is achieved when the operand is aligned on its natural boundary (e.g., 16-, 32-, or 64-byte boundaries for 128-, 256-, or 512-bit wide operands, respectively). Some x86-AVX instructions require their operands to be properly aligned, and these instructions will trigger a processor exception if they attempt to access a misaligned operand in memory. The structure XmmVal also defines several member functions that format the contents of an XmmVal instance for streaming to std::cout. The source code for these member functions is not shown in Listing 8-1a but is included in the software download package.

The next file in Listing 8-1a is the C++ header file Ch08_01.h, which contains the function declarations for this example. Note that functions AddI16_avx() and SubI16_avx() both require pointer arguments of type XmmVal. It should be noted that structure XmmVal is used in this and subsequent examples to illustrate SIMD data exchange between a C++ and assembly language function. In later examples, you'll learn how to use standard C++ arrays and matrices.

The file Ch08_01.cpp follows next in Listing 8-1a. This file contains function main() along with two static functions named AddI16() and AddU16(). Function AddI16() begins its execution by initializing two XmmVal variables with packed 16-bit signed integer data. This is followed by a call to function AddI16_avx(), which performs packed 16-bit signed integer addition. The remaining code in AddI16() displays the results calculated by AddI16_avx(). The function SubI16() is almost identical to AddI16() except that it exercises SubI16_avx() to perform packed 16-bit integer subtraction.

Listing 8-1b shows the MASM code for example Ch08_01. In this listing, file Ch08_01_fasm.asm opens with the definition of a function named AddI16_avx(). The first executable instruction of this function, vmovdqa xmm0,xmmword ptr [r8] (Move Aligned Packed Integers), loads XmmVal value a into register XMM0. The vmovdqa instruction that's used here requires the specified memory operand to be aligned on a 16-byte boundary. Recall that the definition of XmmVal included the alignas(16) specifier, which compels the C++ compiler to properly align each XmmVal instance. The text xmmword ptr is a MASM operator that signifies the size (16 bytes) of the SIMD operand in memory. The ensuing vmovdqa xmm1,xmmword ptr [r9] instruction loads XmmVal value b into register XMM1.

Listing 8-1b. Example Ch08_01 MASM Code

```
;-------------------------------------------------------------------------------
; Ch08_01_fasm.asm
;-------------------------------------------------------------------------------


;-------------------------------------------------------------------------------
; void AddI16_avx(XmmVal* c1, XmmVal* c2, const XmmVal* a, const XmmVal* b);
;-------------------------------------------------------------------------------

        .code
AddI16_avx proc
        vmovdqa xmm0,xmmword ptr [r8]        ;xmm0 = a
        vmovdqa xmm1,xmmword ptr [r9]        ;xmm1 = b

        vpaddw xmm2,xmm0,xmm1                ;packed add - wraparound
        vpaddsw xmm3,xmm0,xmm1               ;packed add - saturated

        vmovdqa xmmword ptr [rcx],xmm2       ;save c1
        vmovdqa xmmword ptr [rdx],xmm3       ;save c2
        ret
AddI16_avx endp


;-------------------------------------------------------------------------------
; void SubI16_avx(XmmVal* c1, XmmVal* c2, const XmmVal* a, const XmmVal* b);
;-------------------------------------------------------------------------------

SubI16_avx proc
        vmovdqa xmm0,xmmword ptr [r8]        ;xmm0 = a
```

```
        vmovdqa xmm1,xmmword ptr [r9]         ;xmm1 = b

        vpsubw xmm2,xmm0,xmm1                 ;packed sub - wraparound
        vpsubsw xmm3,xmm0,xmm1                ;packed sub - saturated

        vmovdqa xmmword ptr [rcx],xmm2        ;save c1
        vmovdqa xmmword ptr [rdx],xmm3        ;save c2
        ret
SubI16_avx endp
        end
```

The next executable instruction in function AddI16_avx(), vpaddw xmm2,xmm0,xmm1 (Add Packed Integers), performs packed integer addition using word elements. More specifically, this instruction performs integer addition using the corresponding word element positions in registers XMM0 and XMM1; the results are saved in the corresponding word element positions of register XMM2. The ensuing vpaddsw xmm3,xmm0,xmm1 (Add Packed Signed Integers with Signed Saturation) also performs packed word addition but uses saturated arithmetic. Recall from the discussions in Chapter 7 that when performing saturated addition, the processor clips the result of each SIMD element sum to prevent arithmetic underflows or overflows from occurring. The final two instructions of AddI16_avx(), vmovdqa xmmword ptr [rcx],xmm2 and vmovdqa xmmword ptr [rdx],xmm3, save the calculated results.

Function SubI16_avx() is similar to AddI16_avx() but employs the instructions vpsubw xmm2,xmm0,xmm1 and vpsubsw xmm3,xmm0,xmm1 to perform wraparound and saturated subtraction instead of addition.

Listing 8-1c shows the NASM code for example Ch08_01. The assembly language code in this listing utilizes the same AVX instructions as its MASM counterpart albeit with different argument registers. Note that NASM code does not require a size operator with the vmovdqa instructions.

Listing 8-1c. Example Ch08_01 NASM Code

```
;-----------------------------------------------------------------------------
; Ch08_01_fasm.s
;-----------------------------------------------------------------------------

        %include "ModX86Asm3eNASM.inc"

;-----------------------------------------------------------------------------
; void AddI16_avx(XmmVal* c1, XmmVal* c2, const XmmVal* a, const XmmVal* b);
;-----------------------------------------------------------------------------

        section .text

        global AddI16_avx
AddI16_avx:

        vmovdqa xmm0,[rdx]                    ;xmm0 = a
        vmovdqa xmm1,[rcx]                    ;xmm1 = b

        vpaddw xmm2,xmm0,xmm1                 ;packed add - wraparound
        vpaddsw xmm3,xmm0,xmm1                ;packed add - saturated

        vmovdqa [rdi],xmm2                    ;save c1
```

```
        vmovdqa [rsi],xmm3                      ;save c2
        ret


;-------------------------------------------------------------------
; void SubI16_avx(XmmVal* c1, XmmVal* c2, const XmmVal* a, const XmmVal* b);
;-------------------------------------------------------------------

        global SubI16_avx
SubI16_avx:

        vmovdqa xmm0,[rdx]                      ;xmm0 = a
        vmovdqa xmm1,[rcx]                      ;xmm1 = b

        vpsubw  xmm2,xmm0,xmm1                  ;packed sub - wraparound
        vpsubsw xmm3,xmm0,xmm1                  ;packed sub - saturated

        vmovdqa [rdi],xmm2                      ;save c1
        vmovdqa [rsi],xmm3                      ;save c2
        ret
```

AVX also includes the instructions vpadd[b|d|q] and vpsub[b|d|q], which perform addition and subtraction using byte, doubleword, and quadword integers. Saturated addition and subtraction using signed byte values can be performed using vpaddsb and vpsubsb, respectively. For unsigned byte and word elements, the instructions vpaddu[b|w] and vpsubu[b|w] are available. You'll see examples of these instructions later in this book. Here are the results for source code example Ch08_01:

```
----- Results for Ch08_01 -----

AddI16_avx() results - Wraparound Addition
a:        10       200        30    -32766  |      50       60     32000    -32000
b:       100      -200     32760      -400  |     500     -600      1200      -950
c1:      110         0    -32746     32370  |     550     -540    -32336     32586

AddI16_avx() results - Saturated Addition
a:        10       200        30    -32766  |      50       60     32000    -32000
b:       100      -200     32760      -400  |     500     -600      1200      -950
c2:      110         0     32767    -32768  |     550     -540     32767    -32768

SubI16_avx() results - Wraparound Subtraction
a:        10       200       -30    -32766  |      50       60     32000    -32000
b:       100      -200     32760       400  |     500     -600      1200       950
c1:      -90       400     32746     32370  |    -450      660     30800     32586

SubI16_avx() results - Saturated Subtraction
a:        10       200       -30    -32766  |      50       60     32000    -32000
b:       100      -200     32760       400  |     500     -600      1200       950
c2:      -90       400    -32768    -32768  |    -450      660     30800    -32768
```

Multiplication

AVX also supports packed integer multiplication using 128-bit wide SIMD operands. However, the AVX instructions that perform packed integer multiplication are somewhat different than packed addition and subtraction. The reason for this is that the product of two n bit integers always yields a result that is $2n$ bits wide. The next source code example, Ch08_02, demonstrates packed integer multiplication using several different techniques. Listing 8-2a shows the C++ source code for this example.

Listing 8-2a. Example Ch08_02 C++ Code

```
//------------------------------------------------------------
// Ch08_02.h
//------------------------------------------------------------

#pragma once
#include "XmmVal.h"

// Ch08_02_fasm.asm
extern "C" void MulI16_avx(XmmVal c[2], const XmmVal* a, const XmmVal* b);
extern "C" void MulI32a_avx(XmmVal* c, const XmmVal* a, const XmmVal* b);
extern "C" void MulI32b_avx(XmmVal c[2], const XmmVal* a, const XmmVal* b);


//------------------------------------------------------------
// Ch08_02.cpp
//------------------------------------------------------------

#include <iostream>
#include <iomanip>
#include "Ch08_02.h"

static void MulI16(void)
{
    constexpr char nl = '\n';
    XmmVal a, b, c[2];

    a.m_I16[0] = 10;        b.m_I16[0] = -5;
    a.m_I16[1] = 3000;      b.m_I16[1] = 100;
    a.m_I16[2] = -2000;     b.m_I16[2] = -9000;
    a.m_I16[3] = 42;        b.m_I16[3] = 1000;
    a.m_I16[4] = -5000;     b.m_I16[4] = 25000;
    a.m_I16[5] = 8;         b.m_I16[5] = 16384;
    a.m_I16[6] = 10000;     b.m_I16[6] = 3500;
    a.m_I16[7] = -60;       b.m_I16[7] = 6000;

    MulI16_avx(c, &a, &b);

    std::cout << "\nMulI16_avx() results:\n";
    for (size_t i = 0; i < 8; i++)
    {
        std::cout << "a[" << i << "]: " << std::setw(8) << a.m_I16[i] << "  ";
        std::cout << "b[" << i << "]: " << std::setw(8) << b.m_I16[i] << "  ";
```

```cpp
        if (i < 4)
        {
            std::cout << "c[0][" << i << "]: ";
            std::cout << std::setw(12) << c[0].m_I32[i] << nl;
        }
        else
        {
            std::cout << "c[1][" << i - 4 << "]: ";
            std::cout << std::setw(12) << c[1].m_I32[i - 4] << nl;
        }
    }
}

static void MulI32a(void)
{
    constexpr char nl = '\n';
    XmmVal a, b, c;

    a.m_I32[0] = 10;         b.m_I32[0] = -500;
    a.m_I32[1] = 3000;       b.m_I32[1] = 100;
    a.m_I32[2] = -2000;      b.m_I32[2] = -12000;
    a.m_I32[3] = 4200;       b.m_I32[3] = 1000;

    MulI32a_avx(&c, &a, &b);

    std::cout << "\nMulI32a_avx() results:\n";
    for (size_t i = 0; i < 4; i++)
    {
        std::cout << "a[" << i << "]: " << std::setw(10) << a.m_I32[i] << "   ";
        std::cout << "b[" << i << "]: " << std::setw(10) << b.m_I32[i] << "   ";
        std::cout << "c[" << i << "]: " << std::setw(10) << c.m_I32[i] << nl;
    }
}

static void MulI32b(void)
{
    constexpr char nl = '\n';
    XmmVal a, b, c[2];

    a.m_I32[0] = 10;         b.m_I32[0] = -500;
    a.m_I32[1] = 3000;       b.m_I32[1] = 100;
    a.m_I32[2] = -40000;     b.m_I32[2] = -1200000;
    a.m_I32[3] = 4200;       b.m_I32[3] = 1000;

    MulI32b_avx(c, &a, &b);

    std::cout << "\nMulI32b_avx() results:\n";
    for (size_t i = 0; i < 4; i++)
    {
        std::cout << "a[" << i << "]: " << std::setw(10) << a.m_I32[i] << "   ";
        std::cout << "b[" << i << "]: " << std::setw(10) << b.m_I32[i] << "   ";
```

```
        if (i < 2)
        {
            std::cout << "c[0][" << i << "]: ";
            std::cout << std::setw(14) << c[0].m_I64[i] << nl;
        }
        else
        {
            std::cout << "c[1][" << i - 2 << "]: ";
            std::cout << std::setw(14) << c[1].m_I64[i - 2] << nl;
        }
    }
}

int main()
{
    std::cout << "----- Results for Ch08_02 -----\n";

    MulI16();
    MulI32a();
    MulI32b();
    return 0;
}
```

The header file Ch08_02.h in Listing 8-2a contains declarations for three AVX assembly language functions, MulI16_avx(), MulI32a_avx(), and MulI32b_avx(), that perform packed integer multiplication. Note that like the previous example, these functions utilize instances of XmmVal for data exchange between the C++ and assembly language code. The C++ code in file Ch08_02.cpp includes three static functions, MulI16(), MulI32a(), and MulI32b(), that perform test case initialization for the previously mentioned AVX assembly language functions. These C++ functions also format and stream results to std::cout.

Listing 8-2b shows the MASM code for example Ch08_02.

Listing 8-2b. Example Ch08_02 MASM Code

```
;-----------------------------------------------------------------------------
; Ch08_02_fasm.asm
;-----------------------------------------------------------------------------


;-----------------------------------------------------------------------------
; void MulI16_avx(XmmVal c[2], const XmmVal* a, const XmmVal* b);
;-----------------------------------------------------------------------------

        .code
MulI16_avx proc
        vmovdqa xmm0,xmmword ptr [rdx]      ;xmm0 = a
        vmovdqa xmm1,xmmword ptr [r8]       ;xmm1 = b

        vpmullw xmm2,xmm0,xmm1              ;packed mul - low result
        vpmulhw xmm3,xmm0,xmm1              ;packed mul - high result

        vpunpcklwd xmm4,xmm2,xmm3           ;packed low-order dwords
        vpunpckhwd xmm5,xmm2,xmm3           ;packed high-order dwords
```

```
        vmovdqa xmmword ptr [rcx],xmm4      ;save c[0]
        vmovdqa xmmword ptr [rcx+16],xmm5   ;save c[1]
        ret
MulI16_avx endp

;----------------------------------------------------------------
; void MulI32a_avx(XmmVal* c, const XmmVal* a, const XmmVal* b);
;----------------------------------------------------------------

MulI32a_avx proc
        vmovdqa xmm0,xmmword ptr [rdx]      ;xmm0 = a
        vmovdqa xmm1,xmmword ptr [r8]       ;xmm1 = b

        vpmulld xmm2,xmm0,xmm1              ;packed mul - low result

        vmovdqa xmmword ptr [rcx],xmm2      ;save c
        ret
MulI32a_avx endp

;----------------------------------------------------------------
; void MulI32b_avx(XmmVal c[2], const XmmVal* a, const XmmVal* b);
;----------------------------------------------------------------

MulI32b_avx proc
        vmovdqa xmm0,xmmword ptr [rdx]      ;xmm0 = a
        vmovdqa xmm1,xmmword ptr [r8]       ;xmm1 = b

        vpmuldq xmm2,xmm0,xmm1              ;packed mul - a & b even dwords
        vpsrldq xmm3,xmm0,4                 ;shift a_vals right 4 bytes
        vpsrldq xmm4,xmm1,4                 ;shift b_vals right 4 bytes
        vpmuldq xmm5,xmm3,xmm4              ;packed mul - a & b odd dwords

        vpextrq qword ptr [rcx],xmm2,0      ;save qword product 0
        vpextrq qword ptr [rcx+8],xmm5,0    ;save qword product 1
        vpextrq qword ptr [rcx+16],xmm2,1   ;save qword product 2
        vpextrq qword ptr [rcx+24],xmm5,1   ;save qword product 3
        ret
MulI32b_avx endp
        end
```

In Listing 8-2b, the file Ch08_02_fasm.asm contains three functions that perform packed integer multiplication. The first function, MulI16_avx(), begins its execution with two vmovdqa instructions that load argument values a and b into registers XMM0 and XMM1, respectively. This is followed by a vpmullw xmm2,xmm0,xmm1 (Multiply Packed Signed Integers and Store Low Result) instruction that performs packed signed integer multiplication using the 16-bit wide elements of XMM0 and XMM1. The vpmullw instruction saves the low-order 16 bits of each 32-bit product in register XMM2. The vpmulhw xmm3,xmm0,xmm1 (Multiply Packed Signed Integers and Store High Result) that follows calculates and saves the high-order 16 bits of each 32-bit product in register XMM3. The ensuing instruction pair, vpunpcklwd xmm4,xmm2,xmm3 (Unpack Low Data) and vpunpckhwd xmm5,xmm2,xmm3 (Unpack High Data), interleaves the low- and high-order word elements of their respective source operands to form the final doubleword products as shown in Figure 8-1. The last two AVX instructions of function MulI16_avx(), vmovdqa xmmword ptr [rcx],xmm4 and vmovdqa xmmword ptr [rcx+16],xmm5, save the calculated products to c[0] and c[1]. Note that the second vmovdqa instruction uses a displacement value of 16 since each XmmVal instance in array c is 16 bytes wide.

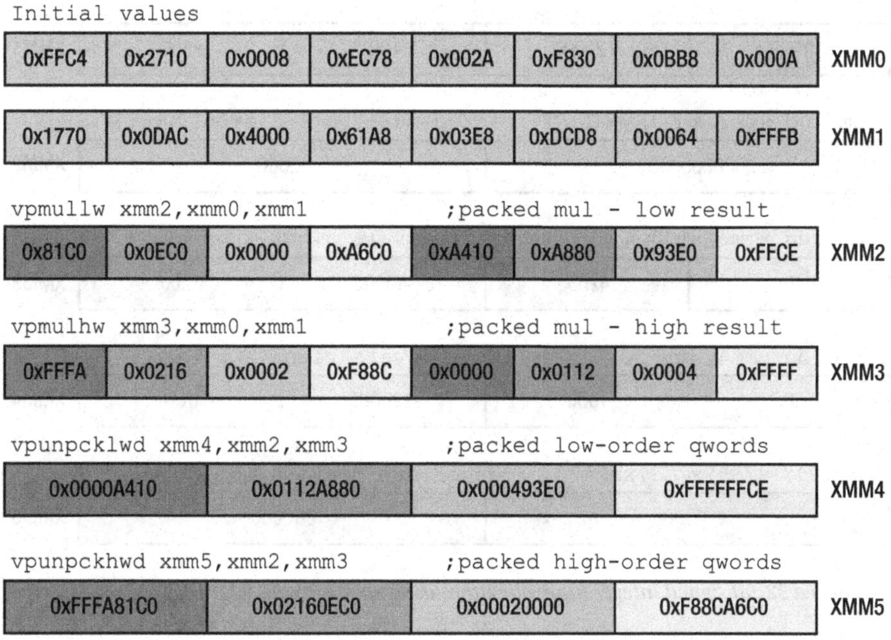

Initial values

0xFFC4	0x2710	0x0008	0xEC78	0x002A	0xF830	0x0BB8	0x000A	XMM0

0x1770	0x0DAC	0x4000	0x61A8	0x03E8	0xDCD8	0x0064	0xFFFB	XMM1

vpmullw xmm2,xmm0,xmm1   ;packed mul - low result

0x81C0	0x0EC0	0x0000	0xA6C0	0xA410	0xA880	0x93E0	0xFFCE	XMM2

vpmulhw xmm3,xmm0,xmm1   ;packed mul - high result

0xFFFA	0x0216	0x0002	0xF88C	0x0000	0x0112	0x0004	0xFFFF	XMM3

vpunpcklwd xmm4,xmm2,xmm3   ;packed low-order qwords

0x0000A410	0x0112A880	0x000493E0	0xFFFFFFCE	XMM4

vpunpckhwd xmm5,xmm2,xmm3   ;packed high-order qwords

0xFFFA81C0	0x02160EC0	0x00020000	0xF88CA6C0	XMM5

Figure 8-1. *Packed 16-bit signed integer multiplication using* vpmullw, vpmulhw, vpunpcklwd, *and* vpunpckhwd

The next function in Listing 8-2b, MulI32a_avx(), performs packed signed integer multiplication using 32-bit wide elements. In this function, the vpmulld xmm2,xmm0,xmm1 instruction saves only the low-order 32 bits of each 64-bit product.

The final function in Listing 8-2b, MulI32b_avx(), performs packed signed integer multiplication using 32-bit wide elements and saves complete 64-bit products. Function MulI32b_avx() begins its execution with two vmovdqa instructions that load argument values a and b into registers XMM0 and XMM1. The next instruction, vpmuldq xmm2,xmm0,xmm1 (Multiple Packed Doubleword Integers), performs packed 32-bit signed integer multiplication using the even-numbered elements of XMM0 and XMM1 and saves the resultant 64-bit products in register XMM2. The ensuing vpsrldq xmm3,xmm0,4 (Shift Double Quadword Right) and vpsrldq xmm4,xmm1,4 instructions right shift registers XMM0 (a) and XMM1 (b) by four bytes. This facilitates the use of the next instruction, vpmuldq xmm5,xmm3,xmm4, which calculates products using the odd-numbered elements of a and b as illustrated in Figure 8-2.

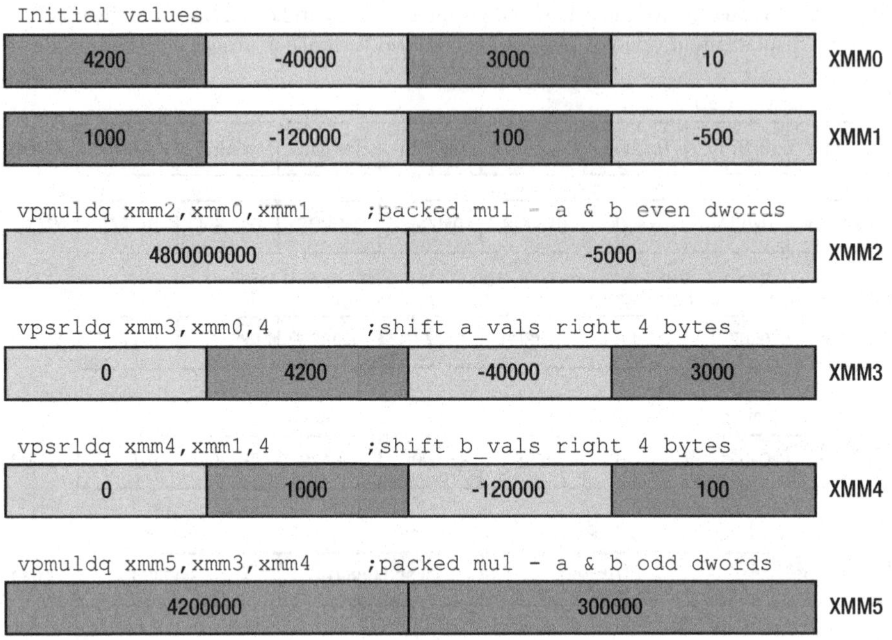

Initial values

| 4200 | -40000 | 3000 | 10 | XMM0 |

| 1000 | -120000 | 100 | -500 | XMM1 |

vpmuldq xmm2,xmm0,xmm1   ;packed mul - a & b even dwords

| 4800000000 | -5000 | XMM2 |

vpsrldq xmm3,xmm0,4   ;shift a_vals right 4 bytes

| 0 | 4200 | -40000 | 3000 | XMM3 |

vpsrldq xmm4,xmm1,4   ;shift b_vals right 4 bytes

| 0 | 1000 | -120000 | 100 | XMM4 |

vpmuldq xmm5,xmm3,xmm4   ;packed mul - a & b odd dwords

| 4200000 | 300000 | XMM5 |

Figure 8-2. *Packed 32-bit signed integer multiplication using* vpmuldq *and* vpsrldq

Following calculation of the quadword products, MulI32b_avx() uses four vpextrq (Extract Quadword) instructions to save the results. Note that the immediate constant used with each vpextrq instruction selects which quadword element to extract from the first source operand. Also note that each vpextrq instruction specifies a destination operand in memory. Most x86-AVX instructions require the destination operand to be an XMM, YMM, or ZMM register.

Listing 8-2c shows the NASM code for example Ch08_02. Except for different argument registers, the code in this listing is the same as the MASM code. Note that in Listing 8-2c, the vmovdqa or vpextrq instructions do not require a size operator.

Listing 8-2c. Example Ch08_02 NASM CODE

```
;-------------------------------------------------------------------------
; Ch08_02_fasm.s
;-------------------------------------------------------------------------

        %include "ModX86Asm3eNASM.inc"

;-------------------------------------------------------------------------
; void MulI16_avx(XmmVal c[2], const XmmVal* a, const XmmVal* b);
;-------------------------------------------------------------------------

        section .text

        global MulI16_avx
MulI16_avx:
```

```
        vmovdqa xmm0,[rsi]                      ;xmm0 = a
        vmovdqa xmm1,[rdx]                      ;xmm1 = b

        vpmullw xmm2,xmm0,xmm1                  ;packed mul - low result
        vpmulhw xmm3,xmm0,xmm1                  ;packed mul - high result

        vpunpcklwd xmm4,xmm2,xmm3               ;packed low-order dwords
        vpunpckhwd xmm5,xmm2,xmm3               ;packed high-order dwords

        vmovdqa [rdi],xmm4                      ;save c[0]
        vmovdqa [rdi+16],xmm5                   ;save c[1]
        ret

;-------------------------------------------------------------------------------
; void MulI32a_avx(XmmVal* c, const XmmVal* a, const XmmVal* b);
;-------------------------------------------------------------------------------

        global MulI32a_avx
MulI32a_avx:

        vmovdqa xmm0,[rsi]                      ;xmm0 = a
        vmovdqa xmm1,[rdx]                      ;xmm1 = b

        vpmulld xmm2,xmm0,xmm1                  ;packed mul - low result

        vmovdqa [rdi],xmm2                      ;save c
        ret

;-------------------------------------------------------------------------------
; void MulI32b_avx(XmmVal c[2], const XmmVal* a, const XmmVal* b);
;-------------------------------------------------------------------------------

        global MulI32b_avx
MulI32b_avx:

        vmovdqa xmm0,[rsi]                      ;xmm0 = a
        vmovdqa xmm1,[rdx]                      ;xmm1 = b

        vpmuldq xmm2,xmm0,xmm1                  ;packed mul - a & b even dwords
        vpsrldq xmm3,xmm0,4                     ;shift a_vals right 4 bytes
        vpsrldq xmm4,xmm1,4                     ;shift b_vals right 4 bytes
        vpmuldq xmm5,xmm3,xmm4                  ;packed mul - a & b odd dwords

        vpextrq [rdi],xmm2,0                    ;save qword product 0
        vpextrq [rdi+8],xmm5,0                  ;save qword product 1
        vpextrq [rdi+16],xmm2,1                 ;save qword product 2
        vpextrq [rdi+24],xmm5,1                 ;save qword product 3
        ret
```

Here are the results for source code example Ch08_02:

```
----- Results for Ch08_02 -----

MulI16_avx() results:
a[0]:       10  b[0]:       -5  c[0][0]:           -50
a[1]:     3000  b[1]:      100  c[0][1]:        300000
a[2]:    -2000  b[2]:    -9000  c[0][2]:      18000000
a[3]:       42  b[3]:     1000  c[0][3]:         42000
a[4]:    -5000  b[4]:    25000  c[1][0]:    -125000000
a[5]:        8  b[5]:    16384  c[1][1]:        131072
a[6]:    10000  b[6]:     3500  c[1][2]:      35000000
a[7]:      -60  b[7]:     6000  c[1][3]:       -360000

MulI32a_avx() results:
a[0]:       10  b[0]:     -500  c[0]:        -5000
a[1]:     3000  b[1]:      100  c[1]:       300000
a[2]:    -2000  b[2]:   -12000  c[2]:     24000000
a[3]:     4200  b[3]:     1000  c[3]:      4200000

MulI32b_avx() results:
a[0]:       10  b[0]:     -500  c[0][0]:          -5000
a[1]:     3000  b[1]:      100  c[0][1]:         300000
a[2]:   -40000  b[2]:  -1200000  c[1][0]:    48000000000
a[3]:     4200  b[3]:     1000  c[1][1]:        4200000
```

Bitwise Logical Operations

The next source code example, named Ch08_03, highlights the use of AVX bitwise logical instructions including vpand (Bitwise Logical AND), vpor (Bitwise Logical OR), and vpxor (Bitwise Logical Exclusive OR). Listing 8-3a shows the C++ source code for this example.

Listing 8-3a. Example Ch08_03 C++ Code

```
//------------------------------------------------------------------------
// Ch08_03.h
//------------------------------------------------------------------------

#pragma once
#include "XmmVal.h"

// Ch08_03_fasm.asm, Ch08_03_fasm.s
extern "C" void AndU16_avx(XmmVal* c, const XmmVal* a, const XmmVal* b);
extern "C" void OrU16_avx(XmmVal* c, const XmmVal* a, const XmmVal* b);
extern "C" void XorU16_avx(XmmVal* c, const XmmVal* a, const XmmVal* b);

//------------------------------------------------------------------------
// Ch08_03.cpp
//------------------------------------------------------------------------
```

```cpp
#include <iostream>
#include "Ch08_03.h"

static void BitwiseLogical(void)
{
    XmmVal a, b, c;
    constexpr char nl = '\n';

    a.m_U16[0] = 0x1234;        b.m_U16[0] = 0xFF00;
    a.m_U16[1] = 0xABDC;        b.m_U16[1] = 0x00FF;
    a.m_U16[2] = 0xAA55;        b.m_U16[2] = 0xAAAA;
    a.m_U16[3] = 0x1111;        b.m_U16[3] = 0x5555;
    a.m_U16[4] = 0xFFFF;        b.m_U16[4] = 0x8000;
    a.m_U16[5] = 0x7F7F;        b.m_U16[5] = 0x7FFF;
    a.m_U16[6] = 0x9876;        b.m_U16[6] = 0xF0F0;
    a.m_U16[7] = 0x7F00;        b.m_U16[7] = 0x0880;

    AndU16_avx(&c, &a, &b);
    std::cout << "\nAndU16_avx() results:\n";
    std::cout << "a: " << a.ToStringX16() << nl;
    std::cout << "b: " << b.ToStringX16() << nl;
    std::cout << "c: " << c.ToStringX16() << nl;

    OrU16_avx(&c, &a, &b);
    std::cout << "\nOrU16_avx() results:\n";
    std::cout << "a: " << a.ToStringX16() << nl;
    std::cout << "b: " << b.ToStringX16() << nl;
    std::cout << "c: " << c.ToStringX16() << nl;

    XorU16_avx(&c, &a, &b);
    std::cout << "\nXorU16_avx() results:\n";
    std::cout << "a: " << a.ToStringX16() << nl;
    std::cout << "b: " << b.ToStringX16() << nl;
    std::cout << "c: " << c.ToStringX16() << nl;
}

int main()
{
    std::cout << "----- Results for Ch08_03 -----\n";

    BitwiseLogical();
    return 0;
}
```

The C++ source code in Listing 8-3a performs test case initialization for the assembly language functions AndU16_avx(), OrU16_avx(), and XorU16_avx(). These functions carry out bitwise logical operations using the supplied XmmVal arguments. Function main() in Listing 8-3a also formats and streams the calculated results to std::cout.

Listing 8-3b shows the MASM code for example Ch08_03. In this listing, function AndU16_avx() begins its execution with a vmovdqa xmm0,xmmword ptr [rdx] instruction that loads XmmVal a into register XMM0. The next instruction, vpand xmm1,xmm0,[r8], calculates a & b. In this instruction, note the use of source operand register R8, which points to XmmVal b in memory. Most AVX SIMD arithmetic instructions can reference a single source operand in memory, which eliminates the need to code an explicit vmovdqa or other AVX move instructions. Also note that the vpand instruction mnemonic does not include a size suffix letter. Recall that when performing AVX (or AVX2) packed integer bitwise logical operations, the notion of distinct SIMD elements (e.g., byte, word, doubleword, or quadword) is usually inapplicable.

Listing 8-3b. Example Ch08_03 MASM Code

```
;-----------------------------------------------------------------------
; Ch08_03_fasm.asm
;-----------------------------------------------------------------------


;-----------------------------------------------------------------------
; void AndU16_avx(XmmVal* c, const XmmVal* a, const XmmVal* b);
;-----------------------------------------------------------------------

        .code
AndU16_avx proc
        vmovdqa xmm0,xmmword ptr [rdx]          ;xmm0 = a
        vpand xmm1,xmm0,[r8]                    ;xmm1 = a & b
        vmovdqa xmmword ptr [rcx],xmm1          ;save result
        ret
AndU16_avx endp


;-----------------------------------------------------------------------
; void OrU16_avx(XmmVal* c, const XmmVal* a, const XmmVal* b);
;-----------------------------------------------------------------------

OrU16_avx proc
        vmovdqa xmm0,xmmword ptr [rdx]          ;xmm0 = a
        vpor xmm1,xmm0,[r8]                     ;xmm1 = a | b
        vmovdqa xmmword ptr [rcx],xmm1          ;save result
        ret
OrU16_avx endp


;-----------------------------------------------------------------------
; void XorU16_avx(XmmVal* c, const XmmVal* a, const XmmVal* b);
;-----------------------------------------------------------------------

XorU16_avx proc
        vmovdqa xmm0,xmmword ptr [rdx]          ;xmm0 = a
        vpxor xmm1,xmm0,[r8]                    ;xmm1 = a ^ b
        vmovdqa xmmword ptr [rcx],xmm1          ;save result
        ret
XorU16_avx endp
        end
```

Also shown in Listing 8-3b are functions OrU16_avx() and XorU16_avx(), which demonstrate the use of the vpor and vpxor instructions.

Listing 8-3c shows the NASM code for example Ch08_03. Like the earlier examples of this section, different argument registers are the primary distinction between this code and the MASM code.

Listing 8-3c. Example Ch08_03 NASM Code

```nasm
;-------------------------------------------------------------------------
; Ch08_03.fasm.s
;-------------------------------------------------------------------------

        %include "ModX86Asm3eNASM.inc"

;-------------------------------------------------------------------------
; void AndU16_avx(XmmVal* c, const XmmVal* a, const XmmVal* b);
;-------------------------------------------------------------------------

        section .text

        global AndU16_avx
AndU16_avx:

        vmovdqa xmm0,[rsi]              ;xmm0 = a
        vpand xmm1,xmm0,[rdx]          ;xmm1 = a & b
        vmovdqa [rdi],xmm1            ;save result
        ret


;-------------------------------------------------------------------------
; void OrU16_avx(XmmVal* c, const XmmVal* a, const XmmVal* b);
;-------------------------------------------------------------------------

        global OrU16_avx
OrU16_avx:

        vmovdqa xmm0,[rsi]              ;xmm0 = a
        vpor xmm1,xmm0,[rdx]          ;xmm1 = a | b
        vmovdqa [rdi],xmm1            ;save result
        ret


;-------------------------------------------------------------------------
; void XorU16_avx(XmmVal* c, const XmmVal* a, const XmmVal* b);
;-------------------------------------------------------------------------

        global XorU16_avx
XorU16_avx:

        vmovdqa xmm0,[rsi]              ;xmm0 = a
        vpxor xmm1,xmm0,[rdx]          ;xmm1 = a ^ b
        vmovdqa [rdi],xmm1            ;save result
        ret
```

Here are the results for source code example Ch08_03:

```
----- Results for Ch08_03 -----

AndU16_avx() results:
a:    1234    ABDC    AA55    1111    |    FFFF    7F7F    9876    7F00
b:    FF00    00FF    AAAA    5555    |    8000    7FFF    F0F0    0880
c:    1200    00DC    AA00    1111    |    8000    7F7F    9070    0800

OrU16_avx() results:
a:    1234    ABDC    AA55    1111    |    FFFF    7F7F    9876    7F00
b:    FF00    00FF    AAAA    5555    |    8000    7FFF    F0F0    0880
c:    FF34    ABFF    AAFF    5555    |    FFFF    7FFF    F8F6    7F80

XorU16_avx() results:
a:    1234    ABDC    AA55    1111    |    FFFF    7F7F    9876    7F00
b:    FF00    00FF    AAAA    5555    |    8000    7FFF    F0F0    0880
c:    ED34    AB23    00FF    4444    |    7FFF    0080    6886    7780
```

Arithmetic and Logical Shifts

The final source code example of this section, Ch08_04, highlights the use of the AVX instructions vpsllw (Shift Packed Data Left Logical), vpsrlw (Shift Packed Data Right Logical), and vpsraw (Shift Packed Data Right Arithmetic). Listing 8-4a shows the C++ source code for this example.

Listing 8-4a. Example Ch08_04 C++ Code

```
//-----------------------------------------------------------------------------
// Ch08_04.h
//-----------------------------------------------------------------------------

#pragma once
#include <cstdint>
#include "XmmVal.h"

// Ch08_04_fasm.asm, Ch08_04_fasm.s
extern "C" void SllU16_avx(XmmVal* c, const XmmVal* a, uint32_t count);
extern "C" void SrlU16_avx(XmmVal* c, const XmmVal* a, uint32_t count);
extern "C" void SraU16_avx(XmmVal* c, const XmmVal* a, uint32_t count);

//-----------------------------------------------------------------------------
// Ch08_04.cpp
//-----------------------------------------------------------------------------

#include <iostream>
#include "Ch08_04.h"

static void ShiftU16(void)
{
    XmmVal a, c;
```

```
    constexpr char nl = '\n';
    constexpr uint32_t count_l = 8;
    constexpr uint32_t count_r = 4;

    a.m_U16[0] = 0x1234;
    a.m_U16[1] = 0xFFB0;
    a.m_U16[2] = 0x00CC;
    a.m_U16[3] = 0x8080;
    a.m_U16[4] = 0x00FF;
    a.m_U16[5] = 0xAAAA;
    a.m_U16[6] = 0x0F0F;
    a.m_U16[7] = 0x0101;

    SllU16_avx(&c, &a, count_l);
    std::cout << "\nSllU16_avx() results ";
    std::cout << "(count = " << count_l << "):\n";
    std::cout << "a: " << a.ToStringX16() << nl;
    std::cout << "c: " << c.ToStringX16() << nl;

    SrlU16_avx(&c, &a, count_r);
    std::cout << "\nSrlU16_avx() results ";
    std::cout << "(count = " << count_r << "):\n";
    std::cout << "a: " << a.ToStringX16() << nl;
    std::cout << "c: " << c.ToStringX16() << nl;

    SraU16_avx(&c, &a, count_r);
    std::cout << "\nSraU16_avx() results";
    std::cout << "(count = " << count_r << "):\n";
    std::cout << "a: " << a.ToStringX16() << nl;
    std::cout << "c: " << c.ToStringX16() << nl;
}

int main()
{
    std::cout << "----- Results for Ch08_04 -----\n";

    ShiftU16();
    return 0;
}
```

In Listing 8-4a, note that the declarations for functions SllU16_avx(), SrlU16_avx(), and SraU16_avx() include an argument value named count. This value signifies the shift bit count as you'll soon see. Also note in function main() that XmmVal a is initialized using 16-bit wide integer elements.

Listing 8-4b shows the MASM code for example Ch08_04. Function SllU16_avx() begins its execution with a vmovdqa xmm0,xmmword ptr [rdx] instruction that loads XmmVal a into register XMM0. The next instruction, vmovd xmm1,r8d (Move Doubleword), copies the doubleword value in register R8D (argument value count) to XMM1[31:0]. Execution of this instruction also zeroes bits YMM1[255:32]; bits ZMM1[511:256] are likewise zeroed if the processor supports AVX-512. The ensuing vpsllw xmm2,xmm0,xmm1 instruction left shifts each word element in XMM0 using the shift count in XMM1[31:0].

Listing 8-4b. Example Ch08_04 MASM Code

```
;-----------------------------------------------------------------------
; Ch08_04_fasm.asm
;-----------------------------------------------------------------------


;-----------------------------------------------------------------------
; void SllU16_avx(XmmVal* c, const XmmVal* a, uint32_t count);
;-----------------------------------------------------------------------

        .code
SllU16_avx proc
        vmovdqa xmm0,xmmword ptr [rdx]      ;xmm0 = a
        vmovd xmm1,r8d                      ;xmm1[31:0] = count

        vpsllw xmm2,xmm0,xmm1               ;left shift word elements of a

        vmovdqa xmmword ptr [rcx],xmm2      ;save result
        ret
SllU16_avx endp


;-----------------------------------------------------------------------
; void SrlU16_Aavx(XmmVal* c, const XmmVal* a, uint32_t count);
;-----------------------------------------------------------------------

SrlU16_avx proc
        vmovdqa xmm0,xmmword ptr [rdx]      ;xmm0 = a
        vmovd xmm1,r8d                      ;xmm1[31:0] = count

        vpsrlw xmm2,xmm0,xmm1               ;right shift word elements of a

        vmovdqa xmmword ptr [rcx],xmm2      ;save result
        ret
SrlU16_avx endp


;-----------------------------------------------------------------------
; void SraU16_Aavx(XmmVal* c, const XmmVal* a, uint32_t count);
;-----------------------------------------------------------------------

SraU16_avx proc
        vmovdqa xmm0,xmmword ptr [rdx]      ;xmm0 = a
        vmovd xmm1,r8d                      ;xmm1[31:0] = count

        vpsraw xmm2,xmm0,xmm1               ;right shift word elements of a

        vmovdqa xmmword ptr [rcx],xmm2      ;save result
        ret
SraU16_avx endp
        end
```

Functions SrlU16_avx() and SraU16_avx() use a code arrangement that's similar to SllU16_avx(). Function SrlU16_avx() demonstrates the use of the vpsrlw instruction, while SraU16_avx() highlights the use of the vpsraw instruction. The AVX instructions vpsllw, vpsrlw, and vpsraw can also be used with an immediate operand that specifies the shift bit count.

Listing 8-4c shows the NASM code for example Ch08_04.

Listing 8-4c. Example Ch08_04 NASM Code

```
;-------------------------------------------------------------------------
; Ch08_04.fasm.s
;-------------------------------------------------------------------------

        %include "ModX86Asm3eNASM.inc"

;-------------------------------------------------------------------------
; void SllU16_avx(XmmVal* c, const XmmVal* a, uint32_t count);
;-------------------------------------------------------------------------

        section .text

        global SllU16_avx
SllU16_avx:
        vmovdqa xmm0,[rsi]                  ;xmm0 = a
        vmovd xmm1,edx                      ;xmm1[31:0] = count

        vpsllw xmm2,xmm0,xmm1               ;left shift word elements of a

        vmovdqa [rdi],xmm2                  ;save result
        ret


;-------------------------------------------------------------------------
; void SrlU16_Aavx(XmmVal* c, const XmmVal* a, uint32_t count);
;-------------------------------------------------------------------------

        global SrlU16_avx
SrlU16_avx:
        vmovdqa xmm0,[rsi]                  ;xmm0 = a
        vmovd xmm1,edx                      ;xmm1[31:0] = count

        vpsrlw xmm2,xmm0,xmm1               ;right shift word elements of a

        vmovdqa [rdi],xmm2                  ;save result
        ret


;-------------------------------------------------------------------------
; void SraU16_Aavx(XmmVal* c, const XmmVal* a, uint32_t count);
;-------------------------------------------------------------------------

        global SraU16_avx
SraU16_avx:
        vmovdqa xmm0,[rsi]                  ;xmm0 = a
        vmovd xmm1,edx                      ;xmm1[31:0] = count
```

```
        vpsraw xmm2,xmm0,xmm1              ;right shift word elements of a

        vmovdqa [rdi],xmm2                 ;save result
        ret
```

AVX also supports SIMD element shifts using doubleword and quadword elements (e.g., vpsll[d|q], vpsrl[d|q], and vpsra[d|q]). You'll see other examples of AVX shift instruction use in later chapters. Here are the results for source code example Ch08_04:

```
----- Results for Ch08_04 -----

SllU16_avx() results (count = 8):
a:   1234    FFB0    00CC    8080   |   00FF    AAAA    0F0F    0101
c:   3400    B000    CC00    8000   |   FF00    AA00    0F00    0100

SrlU16_avx() results (count = 4):
a:   1234    FFB0    00CC    8080   |   00FF    AAAA    0F0F    0101
c:   0123    0FFB    000C    0808   |   000F    0AAA    00F0    0010

SraU16_avx() results(count = 4):
a:   1234    FFB0    00CC    8080   |   00FF    AAAA    0F0F    0101
c:   0123    FFFB    000C    F808   |   000F    FAAA    00F0    0010
```

Integer Arrays

The first set of source code examples in this chapter were designed to familiarize you with AVX packed integer programming and instructions. Each example included a simple assembly language function that demonstrated execution of multiple AVX instructions using instances of the structure XmmVal. For some real-world applications, it may be appropriate to create a small set of functions like the ones you've seen thus far. However, to fully exploit the benefits of the AVX, you need to code functions that perform computations using conventional programming data structures such as arrays or matrices.

The source code examples in this section spotlight algorithms that process arrays of unsigned 8-bit integers using the AVX instruction set. In the first example, you'll learn how to determine the minimum and maximum value of an array. This example has a certain practicality to it since digital images are often stored in memory using arrays of unsigned 8-bit integers. Moreover, many image-processing algorithms (e.g., contrast enhancement) often need to determine the minimum (darkest) and maximum (lightest) pixels in an image. The second source code example illustrates how to calculate the mean value of an array of unsigned 8-bit integers. This is another instance of a realistic algorithm that is directly relevant to the province of image processing.

Pixel Minimum and Maximum

Source code example Ch08_05 demonstrates how to find the minimum and maximum value in an array of unsigned 8-bit integers. This example also illustrates the use of dynamically allocated arrays that are properly aligned for use in an x86-AVX calculating function. Listing 8-5a shows the C++ code for example Ch08_05.

Listing 8-5a. Example Ch08_05 C++ Code

```
//----------------------------------------------------------------------
// Ch08_05.h
//----------------------------------------------------------------------

#pragma once
#include <cstddef>
#include <cstdint>

// Ch08_05_fasm.asm, Ch08_05_fasm.s
extern "C" bool CalcMinMaxU8_avx(uint8_t* x_min, uint8_t* x_max,
    const uint8_t* x, size_t n);

// Ch08_05_fcpp.cpp
extern bool CalcMinMaxU8_cpp(uint8_t* x_min, uint8_t* x_max,
    const uint8_t* x, size_t n);

// Ch08_05_misc.cpp
extern void InitArray(uint8_t* x, size_t n, unsigned int rng_seed);

// c_NumElements must be > 0 and even multiple of 16
constexpr size_t c_NumElements = 10000000;
constexpr unsigned int c_RngSeedVal = 23;

//----------------------------------------------------------------------
// Ch08_05_misc.cpp
//----------------------------------------------------------------------

#include "Ch08_05.h"
#include "MT.h"

void InitArray(uint8_t* x, size_t n, unsigned int rng_seed)
{
    int rng_min_val = 5;
    int rng_max_val = 250;
    MT::FillArray(x, n, rng_min_val, rng_max_val, rng_seed);

    // Use known min & max values for validation purposes
    x[(n / 4) * 3 + 1] = 2;
    x[n / 4 + 11] = 3;
    x[n / 2] = 252;
    x[n / 2 + 13] = 253;
    x[n / 8 + 5] = 4;
    x[n / 8 + 7] = 254;
}

//----------------------------------------------------------------------
// Ch08_05_fcpp.cpp
//----------------------------------------------------------------------
```

```cpp
#include "Ch08_05.h"
#include "AlignedMem.h"

bool CalcMinMaxU8_cpp(uint8_t* x_min, uint8_t* x_max, const uint8_t* x, size_t n)
{
    // Validate argument value n
    if (n == 0 || (n % 16) != 0)
        return false;

    // Make sure array x is properly aligned
    if (!AlignedMem::IsAligned(x, 16))
        return false;

    // Find pixel minimum and maximum
    uint8_t min_val = 0xff;
    uint8_t max_val = 0;

    for (size_t i = 0; i < n; i++)
    {
        uint8_t val = *x++;

        if (val < min_val)
            min_val = val;
        else if (val > max_val)
            max_val = val;
    }

    *x_min = min_val;
    *x_max = max_val;
    return true;
}
//------------------------------------------------------------------------------
// Ch08_05.cpp
//------------------------------------------------------------------------------

#include <iostream>
#include "Ch08_05.h"
#include "AlignedMem.h"

static void CalcMinMaxU8()
{
    constexpr char nl = '\n';
    constexpr size_t n = c_NumElements;

    AlignedArray<uint8_t> x_aa(n, 16);
    uint8_t* x = x_aa.Data();

    InitArray(x, n, c_RngSeedVal);

    uint8_t x_min1 = 0, x_max1 = 0;
    uint8_t x_min2 = 0, x_max2 = 0;
```

```
    bool rc0 = CalcMinMaxU8_cpp(&x_min1, &x_max1, x, n);
    bool rc1 = CalcMinMaxU8_avx(&x_min2, &x_max2, x, n);

    std::cout << "\nCalcMinMaxU8_cpp() results:\n";
    std::cout << "rc0: " << rc0 << "  x_min1: " << (int)x_min1;
    std::cout << "  x_max1: " << (int)x_max1 << nl;

    std::cout << "\nCalcMinMaxU8_avx() results:\n";
    std::cout << "rc1: " << rc1 << "  x_min2: " << (int)x_min2;
    std::cout << "  x_max2: " << (int)x_max2 << nl;
}

int main(void)
{
    std::cout << "----- Results for Ch08_05 -----\n";

    CalcMinMaxU8();
    return 0;
}
```

Listing 8-5a opens with the C++ header file Ch08_05.h, which contains the requisite function declarations for this example. Note that the value of c_NumElements must be greater than zero and an integral multiple of 16. Doing this simplifies the assembly language code. Requiring c_NumElements, which signifies the number of integer elements in the test array, to be an even multiple of 16 is not as restrictive as it might appear since the number of pixels in a digital camera image is often an integral multiple of 64 due to the processing requirements of the JPEG algorithms. Later examples will include additional code that can process arrays and pixel buffers of any size.

Next in Listing 8-5a is the file Ch08_05_misc.cpp. In this file, function InitArray() incorporates code that fills test array x using random values. The majority of the array initialization code is handled by a C++ template function named MT::FillArray(), which is defined in the header file MT.h (MT stands for miscellaneous templates). The source code for MT.h is not shown in Listing 8-5a; however, this file is included as part of the software download package in subfolder Include. The Include subfolder also contains several other shared header files that will be used extensively in this and subsequent x86-AVX programming examples to carry out test case initializations, result comparisons, and performance benchmarking.

Also shown in Listing 8-5a is the file Ch08_05_fcpp.cpp, which contains the function CalcMinMaxU8_cpp(). This function is a C++ implementation of the array minimum-maximum algorithm and will be used for result comparison purposes. Function CalcMinMaxU8_cpp() begins its execution with two argument checks. First, it confirms that both n > 0 and (n % 16) == 0 are true. It then utilizes function AlignedMem::IsAligned() (see AlignedMem.h) to ensure that array x is properly aligned on a 16-byte boundary. The remaining code in CalcMinMaxU8_cpp() harnesses a crude for-loop to find the minimum and maximum pixel values.

Near the top of function CalcMinMaxU8() in Listing 8-5a is the statement AlignedArray<uint8_t> x_aa(n, 16). This statement dynamically allocates an array of type uint8_t that is aligned on a 16-byte boundary.[1] The reason for aligning x_aa on a 16-byte boundary is that the assembly language code uses the vmovdqa instruction. Recall that this instruction requires proper alignment of a source operand in memory. The next statement, uint8_t* x = x_aa.Data(), initializes a standard C++ pointer to the allocated array.

---

[1] Template class AlignedArray<> uses static function OS::AlignedMalloc() (see OS.h) to dynamically allocate a memory block that is aligned on a specific boundary. Class OS contains operating system helper functions that work on both Windows and Linux.

Following array initialization, CalcMinMaxU8() exercises the minimum-maximum functions CalcMinMaxU8_cpp() and CalcMinMaxU8_avx().

Listing 8-5b shows the MASM code for example Ch08_05. Near the top of this listing is the statement NSE equ 16. NSE (num_simd_elements) is a symbolic constant that represents the number of array (pixel) elements processed during each iteration of for-loop Loop1. More on this shortly.

Listing 8-5b. Example Ch08_05 MASM Code

```
;-----------------------------------------------------------------------
; Ch08_05_fasm.asm
;-----------------------------------------------------------------------


;-----------------------------------------------------------------------
; bool CalcMinMaxU8_avx(uint8_t* x_min, uint8_t* x_max,
;   const uint8_t* x, size_t n);
;-----------------------------------------------------------------------


NSE     equ 16                          ;num_simd_elements
                                        ;(num pixels per iteration of Loop1)


        .code
CalcMinMaxU8_avx proc

; Make sure n and x are valid
        test r9,r9                      ;is n == 0?
        jz BadArg                       ;jump if yes

        test r9,0fh                     ;is n even multiple of 16?
        jnz BadArg                      ;jump if no

        test r8,0fh                     ;is x aligned to 16b boundary?
        jnz BadArg                      ;jump if no

; Initialize packed min and max values
        vpcmpeqb xmm4,xmm4,xmm4          ;packed minimums (all 0xff)
        vpxor xmm5,xmm5,xmm5             ;packed maximums (all 0x00)
        sub r8,NSE                       ;adjust pointer for Loop1

; Find packed min-max values in x[]
Loop1:  add r8,NSE                       ;r8 points to x[i:i+NSE-1]
        vmovdqa xmm0,xmmword ptr [r8]    ;xmm0 = block of 16 pixels
        vpminub xmm4,xmm4,xmm0           ;update packed min values
        vpmaxub xmm5,xmm5,xmm0           ;update packed max values

        sub r9,NSE                       ;n -= NSE
        jnz Loop1                        ;repeat until done

; Reduce packed min values
        vpsrldq xmm0,xmm4,8
        vpminub xmm0,xmm0,xmm4           ;xmm0[63:0] = final 8 min vals
        vpsrldq xmm1,xmm0,4
        vpminub xmm1,xmm0,xmm1           ;xmm1[31:0] = final 4 min vals
```

```
        vpsrldq xmm2,xmm1,2
        vpminub xmm2,xmm2,xmm1          ;xmm2[15:0] = final 2 min vals
        vpsrldq xmm3,xmm2,1
        vpminub xmm3,xmm3,xmm2          ;xmm3[7:0] = final min val
        vpextrb byte ptr [rcx],xmm3,0   ;save final min val

; Reduce packed max values
        vpsrldq xmm0,xmm5,8
        vpmaxub xmm0,xmm0,xmm5          ;xmm0[63:0] = final 8 max vals
        vpsrldq xmm1,xmm0,4
        vpmaxub xmm1,xmm0,xmm1          ;xmm1[31:0] = final 4 max vals
        vpsrldq xmm2,xmm1,2
        vpmaxub xmm2,xmm2,xmm1          ;xmm2[15:0] = final 2 max vals
        vpsrldq xmm3,xmm2,1
        vpmaxub xmm3,xmm3,xmm2          ;xmm3[7:0] = final max val
        vpextrb byte ptr [rdx],xmm3,0   ;save final max val

        mov eax,1                       ;set success return code
        ret

BadArg: xor eax,eax                     ;set error return code
        ret

CalcMinMaxU8_avx endp
        end
```

Function CalcMinMaxU8_avx() begins its execution with two test instructions that confirm argument value n is not equal to zero and an integral multiple of 16. The third test instruction verifies that array x is aligned on a 16-byte boundary. Following argument validation, CalcMinMaxU8_avx() uses a vpcmpeqb xmm4,xmm4,xmm4 (Compare Packed Data for Equal) instruction to load 0xFF into each byte element of register XMM4. More specifically, vpcmpeqb performs byte element compares using its two source operands and sets the corresponding byte element in the destination operand to 0xFF if source operand elements are equal. Function CalcMinMaxU8_avx() uses vpcmpeqb xmm4,xmm4,xmm4 to set each byte element in register XMM4 to 0xFF since this is somewhat faster than using a vmovdqa instruction to load a 128-bit wide constant of all ones from memory. The ensuing vpxor xmm5,xmm5,xmm5 instruction sets each byte element in register XMM5 to 0x00. The final initialization code block instruction, sub r8,NSE, adjusts R8 (array x) to prevent a loop-carried dependency in Loop1. Recall that a loop-carried dependency condition arises when calculations in a for-loop are dependent on values computed during a prior iteration. Having a loop-carried dependency in a for-loop, especially one that performs SIMD operations, sometimes results in slower performance.

Each iteration of for-loop Loop1 begins with an add r8,NSE instruction that points R8 to the next block of elements in array x. The next instruction, vmovdqa xmm0,xmmword ptr [r8], loads array elements x[i:i+NSE-1] into register XMM0. This is followed by a vpminub xmm4,xmm4,xmm0 (Minimum of Packed Unsigned Integers) instruction that updates the packed minimum values in XMM4. The ensuing vpmaxub xmm5,xmm5,xmm0 (Maximum of Packed Unsigned Integers) instruction updates the packed maximum values in XMM5. Execution of Loop1 repeats until n == 0 is true. Figure 8-3 illustrates execution of vpminub and vpmaxub in Loop1.

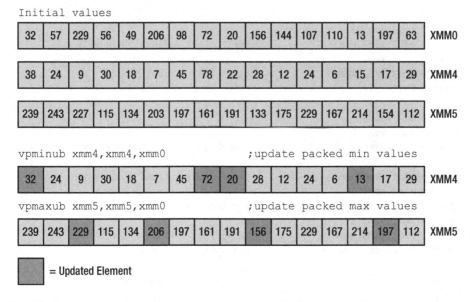

Figure 8-3. *Pixel minimum and maximum compares using* vpminub *and* vpmaxub

Following execution of Loop1, registers XMM4 and XMM5 contain the final 16 minimum and maximum values, respectively. The true minimum (maximum) value is one of the sixteen unsigned 8-bit integer elements in register XMM4 (XMM5). To find the true minimum (maximum) value, the elements in XMM4 (XMM5) must be reduced to a single scalar value. This action is called a reduction. Figure 8-4 illustrates the reduction of XMM4 using a series of vpsrldq (Shift Double Quadword Right Logical) and vpminub instructions. Note that execution of vpsrldq performs right byte shifts of its first source operand; the number of bytes to shift is specified by the second (immediate) source operand.

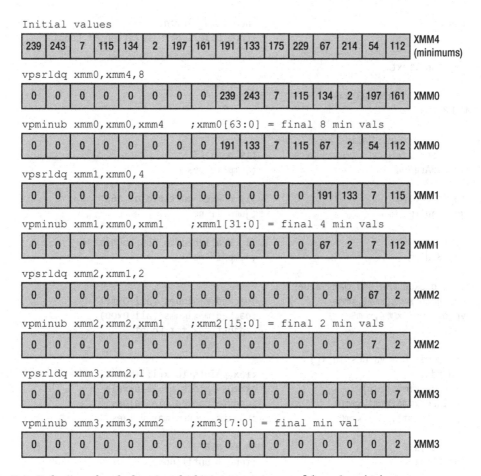

Figure 8-4. *Reduction of packed unsigned 8-bit integers using* vpsrldq *and* vpminub

The final instruction in the minimum reduction code block, vpextrb byte ptr [rcx],xmm3,0 (Extract Byte), copies the minimum pixel value in XMM3[7:0] to the buffer pointed to by x_min. The next code block in function CalcMinMaxU8_avx() uses the same reduction technique to determine the maximum pixel value. Note that this code block employs vpmaxub instead of vpminub.

Listing 8-5c shows the NASM code for example Ch08_05. Except for different argument registers, this code is equivalent to its MASM counterpart.

Listing 8-5c. Example Ch08_05 NASM Code

```
;------------------------------------------------------------------------------
; Ch08_05.fasm.s
;------------------------------------------------------------------------------

        %include "ModX86Asm3eNASM.inc"


;------------------------------------------------------------------------------
; bool CalcMinMaxU8_avx(uint8_t* x_min, uint8_t* x_max,
;   const uint8_t* x, size_t n);
;------------------------------------------------------------------------------
```

```
NSE     equ 16                              ;num_simd_elements
                                            ;(num pixels per iteration of Loop1)

        section .text

        global CalcMinMaxU8_avx
CalcMinMaxU8_avx:

; Make sure n and x are valid
        test rcx,rcx                        ;is n == 0?
        jz BadArg                           ;jump if yes

        test rcx,0fh                        ;is n even multiple of 16?
        jnz BadArg                          ;jump if no

        test rdx,0fh                        ;is x aligned to 16b boundary?
        jnz BadArg                          ;jump if no

; Initialize packed min and max values
        vpcmpeqb xmm4,xmm4,xmm4             ;packed minimums (all 0xff)
        vpxor xmm5,xmm5,xmm5               ;packed maximums (all 0x00)
        sub rdx,NSE                         ;adjust rdx for Loop1

; Find packed min-max values in x[]
Loop1:  add rdx,NSE                         ;rdx points to x[i:i+NSE-1]
        vmovdqa xmm0,[rdx]                  ;xmm0 = block of 16 pixels
        vpminub xmm4,xmm4,xmm0             ;update packed min values
        vpmaxub xmm5,xmm5,xmm0             ;update packed max values

        sub rcx,NSE                         ;n -= NSE
        jnz Loop1                           ;repeat until done

; Reduce packed min values
        vpsrldq xmm0,xmm4,8
        vpminub xmm0,xmm0,xmm4             ;xmm0[63:0] = final 8 min vals
        vpsrldq xmm1,xmm0,4
        vpminub xmm1,xmm0,xmm1             ;xmm1[31:0] = final 4 min vals
        vpsrldq xmm2,xmm1,2
        vpminub xmm2,xmm2,xmm1             ;xmm2[15:0] = final 2 min vals
        vpsrldq xmm3,xmm2,1
        vpminub xmm3,xmm3,xmm2             ;xmm3[7:0] = final min val
        vpextrb [rdi],xmm3,0               ;save final min val

; Reduce packed max values
        vpsrldq xmm0,xmm5,8
        vpmaxub xmm0,xmm0,xmm5             ;xmm0[63:0] = final 8 max vals
        vpsrldq xmm1,xmm0,4
        vpmaxub xmm1,xmm0,xmm1             ;xmm1[31:0] = final 4 max vals
        vpsrldq xmm2,xmm1,2
```

```
        vpmaxub xmm2,xmm2,xmm1          ;xmm2[15:0] = final 2 max vals
        vpsrldq xmm3,xmm2,1
        vpmaxub xmm3,xmm3,xmm2          ;xmm3[7:0] = final max val
        vpextrb [rsi],xmm3,0            ;save final max val

        mov eax,1                       ;set success return code
        ret

BadArg: xor eax,eax                     ;set error return code
        ret
```

Here are the results for example Ch08_05:

```
----- Results for Ch08_05 -----

CalcMinMaxU8_cpp() results:
rc0: 1  x_min1: 2  x_max1: 254

CalcMinMaxU8_avx() results:
rc1: 1  x_min2: 2  x_max2: 254
```

Pixel Mean

Another common image processing technique is to compute the mean intensity of an image's pixels. The final source example of this chapter, Ch08_06, demonstrates how to do this using AVX instructions and SIMD arithmetic. Listing 8-6a shows the C++ source code for example Ch08_06.

Listing 8-6a. Example Ch08_06 C++ Code

```
//----------------------------------------------------------------------------
// Ch08_06.h
//----------------------------------------------------------------------------

#pragma once
#include <cstddef>
#include <cstdint>

// Ch08_06_fasm.asm, Ch08_06_fasm.s
extern "C" bool CalcMeanU8_avx(double* mean_x, uint64_t* sum_x, const uint8_t* x,
    uint32_t n);

// Ch08_06_fcpp.cpp
extern bool CalcMeanU8_cpp(double* mean_x, uint64_t* sum_x, const uint8_t* x,
    uint32_t n);

// Ch08_06_misc.cpp
extern void InitArray(uint8_t* x, uint32_t n, unsigned int seed);

// Miscellaneous constants
```

```cpp
constexpr size_t c_Alignment = 16;
constexpr uint32_t c_NumElements = 10000000;
constexpr unsigned int c_RngSeedVal = 29;

//----------------------------------------------------------------------
// Ch08_06_misc.cpp
//----------------------------------------------------------------------

#include "Ch08_06.h"
#include "MT.h"

void InitArray(uint8_t* x, uint32_t n, unsigned int rng_seed)
{
    constexpr int rng_min_val = 0;
    constexpr int rng_max_val = 255;
    MT::FillArray(x, n, rng_min_val, rng_max_val, rng_seed);
}

//----------------------------------------------------------------------
// Ch08_06_fcpp.cpp
//----------------------------------------------------------------------

#include "Ch08_06.h"
#include "AlignedMem.h"

bool CalcMeanU8_cpp(double* mean_x, uint64_t* sum_x, const uint8_t* x,
    uint32_t n)
{
    // Validate arguments
    if (n <= 0 || (n % 64) != 0)
        return false;

    if (!AlignedMem::IsAligned(x, c_Alignment))
        return false;

    // Calculate pixel mean
    uint64_t sum_x_temp = 0;

    for (size_t i = 0; i < n; i++)
        sum_x_temp += x[i];

    *sum_x = sum_x_temp;
    *mean_x = (double)sum_x_temp / n;
    return true;
}

//----------------------------------------------------------------------
// Ch08_06.cpp
//----------------------------------------------------------------------
```

```
#include <iostream>
#include <iomanip>
#include "Ch08_06.h"
#include "AlignedMem.h"

static void CalcMeanU8(void)
{
    constexpr char nl = '\n';
    constexpr uint32_t n = c_NumElements;

    AlignedArray<uint8_t> x_aa(n, c_Alignment);
    uint8_t* x = x_aa.Data();

    InitArray(x, n, c_RngSeedVal);

    bool rc0, rc1;
    uint64_t sum_x0, sum_x1;
    double mean_x0, mean_x1;

    rc0 = CalcMeanU8_cpp(&mean_x0, &sum_x0, x, n);
    rc1 = CalcMeanU8_avx(&mean_x1, &sum_x1, x, n);

    std::cout << std::fixed << std::setprecision(6);

    std::cout << "\nCalcMeanU8_cpp() results:\n";
    std::cout << "rc0:      " << rc0 << nl;
    std::cout << "sum_x0:   " << sum_x0 << nl;
    std::cout << "mean_x0:  " << mean_x0 << nl;

    std::cout << "\nCalcMeanU8_avx() results:\n";
    std::cout << "rc1:      " << rc1 << nl;
    std::cout << "sum_x1:   " << sum_x1 << nl;
    std::cout << "mean_x1:  " << mean_x1 << nl;
}

int main(void)
{
    std::cout << "----- Results for Ch08_06 -----\n";

    CalcMeanU8();
    return 0;
}
```

The layout of the C++ code in Listing 8-6a closely resembles the previous example. File Ch08_06_misc.cpp contains function InitArray(), which fills the specified test array using random values. Function CalcMeanU8_cpp() in file Ch08_06_fcpp.cpp incorporates C++ code that calculates the mean of values in array x. Note that argument value n must be an integral multiple of 64. More on this later. Function CalcMeanU8() in file Ch08_06.cpp performs test case initialization. It also exercises the mean calculating functions CalcMeanU8_cpp() and CalcMeanU8_avx(). Note that template class AlignedArray<> is used to allocate storage for the test array on a c_Alignment (16-byte) boundary.

Listing 8-6b contains the MASM code for example Ch08_06. Function CalcMeanU8_avx() opens with an explicit prologue that utilizes macros CreateFrame_M and SaveXmmRegs_M (see Chapter 6) to create a stack frame and preserve the value of non-volatile register XMM15 on the stack. Following its prologue, CalcMeanU8_avx() uses two test instructions to validate argument n. It also uses a test instruction to ensure that array x is aligned on a 16-byte boundary.

Listing 8-6b. Example Ch08_06 MASM Code

```
;------------------------------------------------------------------------------
; Ch08_06_fasm.asm
;------------------------------------------------------------------------------

        include <MacrosX86-64-AVX.asmh>

;------------------------------------------------------------------------------
; bool CalcMeanU8_avx(double* mean_x, uint64_t* sum_x, const uint8_t* x,
;   uint32_t n);
;------------------------------------------------------------------------------

NSE     equ 64                          ;num pixels per iteration of Loop1

        .code
CalcMeanU8_avx proc frame

; Prologue
        CreateFrame_M MeanU8_,0,16
        SaveXmmRegs_M xmm15
        EndProlog_M

; Make sure n and x are valid
        test r9d,r9d                    ;is n <= 0?
        jz BadArg                       ;jump if yes

        test r9d,3fh                    ;is n even multiple of 64?
        jnz BadArg                      ;jump if no

        test r8,0fh                     ;is x aligned on a 16-byte boundary?
        jnz BadArg                      ;jump if no

; Initialize
        vpxor xmm5,xmm5,xmm5            ;packed sums (2 qwords)
        vpxor xmm15,xmm15,xmm15        ;packed zero for size promotions
        mov r10d,r9d                   ;r10d = n (for use in Loop1)
        sub r8,NSE                      ;adjust x for Loop1

; Calculate sum of all pixels
Loop1:  add r8,NSE                      ;r8 = &x[i]
        vpxor xmm0,xmm0,xmm0           ;initialize loop packed sums (16 words)
        vpxor xmm1,xmm1,xmm1

        vmovdqa xmm2,xmmword ptr [r8]   ;load pixel block x[i:i+15]
        vpunpcklbw xmm3,xmm2,xmm15     ;promote x[i:i+7] to words
```

```
        vpaddw  xmm0,xmm0,xmm3               ;update sums[0:7]
        vpunpckhbw xmm4,xmm2,xmm15           ;promote x[i+8:i+15] to words
        vpaddw  xmm1,xmm1,xmm4               ;update sums[8:15]

        vmovdqa xmm2,xmmword ptr [r8+16]     ;load pixel block x[i+16:i+31]
        vpunpcklbw xmm3,xmm2,xmm15           ;promote x[i+16:i+23] to words
        vpaddw  xmm0,xmm0,xmm3               ;update sums[0:7]
        vpunpckhbw xmm4,xmm2,xmm15           ;promote x[i+24:i+31] to words
        vpaddw  xmm1,xmm1,xmm4               ;update sums[8:15]

        vmovdqa xmm2,xmmword ptr [r8+32]     ;load pixel block x[i+32:i+47]
        vpunpcklbw xmm3,xmm2,xmm15           ;promote x[i+32:i+39] to words
        vpaddw  xmm0,xmm0,xmm3               ;update sums[0:7]
        vpunpckhbw xmm4,xmm2,xmm15           ;promote x[i+40:i+47] to words
        vpaddw  xmm1,xmm1,xmm4               ;update sums[8:15]

        vmovdqa xmm2,xmmword ptr [r8+48]     ;load pixel block x[i+48:i+63]
        vpunpcklbw xmm3,xmm2,xmm15           ;promote x[i+48:i+55] to words
        vpaddw  xmm0,xmm0,xmm3               ;update sums[0:7]
        vpunpckhbw xmm4,xmm2,xmm15           ;promote x[i+56:i+63] to words
        vpaddw  xmm1,xmm1,xmm4               ;update sums[8:15]

        vpaddw  xmm0,xmm0,xmm1               ;loop packed sums (8 words)
        vpunpcklwd xmm1,xmm0,xmm15           ;promote loop packed sums to dwords
        vpunpckhwd xmm2,xmm0,xmm15
        vpaddd  xmm3,xmm1,xmm2               ;loop packed sums (4 dwords)

        vpunpckldq xmm0,xmm3,xmm15           ;promote loop packed sums to qwords
        vpunpckhdq xmm1,xmm3,xmm15
        vpaddq  xmm5,xmm5,xmm0               ;update packed sums (2 qwords)
        vpaddq  xmm5,xmm5,xmm1

        sub     r10d,NSE                     ;n -= NSE
        jnz     Loop1                        ;repeat until done

; Reduce packed sums (2 qwords) to single qword
        vpextrq rax,xmm5,0                   ;rax = xmm5[63:0]
        vpextrq r10,xmm5,1                   ;r10 = xmm5[127:64]
        add     rax,r10                      ;rax = final pixel sum
        mov     qword ptr [rdx],rax          ;save final pixel sum

; Calculate mean
        vcvtsi2sd xmm0,xmm0,rax              ;convert sum to DPFP
        vcvtsi2sd xmm1,xmm1,r9d              ;convert n to DPFP
        vdivsd  xmm2,xmm0,xmm1               ;mean = sum / n
        vmovsd  real8 ptr [rcx],xmm2         ;save mean

        mov     eax,1                        ;set success return code

; Epilogue
Done:   RestoreXmmRegs_M xmm15
```

```
        DeleteFrame_M
        ret

BadArg: xor eax,eax                      ;set error return code
        jmp Done

CalcMeanU8_avx endp
        end
```

The initialization code block in CalcMeanU8_avx() begins with a vpxor xmm5,xmm5,xmm5 instruction that sets the lower and upper quadwords of register XMM5 to zero. These quadwords are used later in for-loop Loop1 to maintain packed pixel sums. The next instruction, vpxor xmm15,xmm15,xmm15, zeroes register XMM15 so that it can be used to perform unsigned integer size promotions (e.g., byte to word, word to doubleword, and doubleword to quadword) in Loop1. The final two initialization code block instructions, mov r10d,r9d and sub r8,NSE, load argument value n into register R10D and adjust R8 (array x pointer) for use in Loop1.

Each iteration of Loop1 begins with an add r8,NSE instruction that loads &x[i] into R8. Note in this example that the value for equate symbol NSE is 64, which means that Loop1 will process 64 array elements (or pixel values) during each iteration. More about this in a moment. The ensuing instruction pair, vpxor xmm0,xmm0,xmm0 and vpxor xmm1,xmm1,xmm1, sets registers XMM0 and XMM1 to zero; these registers are used to maintain intermediate packed word sums as you'll soon see.

The next code block opens with a vmovdqa xmm2,xmmword ptr [r8] instruction that loads byte elements x[i:i+15] into register XMM2. The next instruction, vpunpcklbw xmm3,xmm2,xmm15 (Unpack Low Data Byte to Word), interleaves the low-order bytes of registers XMM2 and XMM15; it saves the interleaved values in XMM3. More specifically, the vpunpcklbw performs XMM3[7:0] = XMM2[7:0], XMM3[15:7] = XMM15[7:0], XMM3[23:16] = XMM2[15:8], XMM3[31:24] = XMM15[15:8], etc., which effectively zero-extends the eight low-order bytes (x[i:i+7]) in register XMM2 to words. The zero-extended word values are saved in XMM3. Execution of the ensuing vpaddw xmm0,xmm0,xmm3 instruction updates the intermediate word sums in register XMM0. The next two instructions, vpunpckhbw xmm4,xmm2,xmm15 (Unpack High Data Byte to Word) and vpaddw xmm1,xmm1,xmm4, carry out the same operation using the eight high-order bytes (x[i+8:i+15]) of register XMM2. Figure 8-5 illustrates execution of this instruction sequence in greater detail.

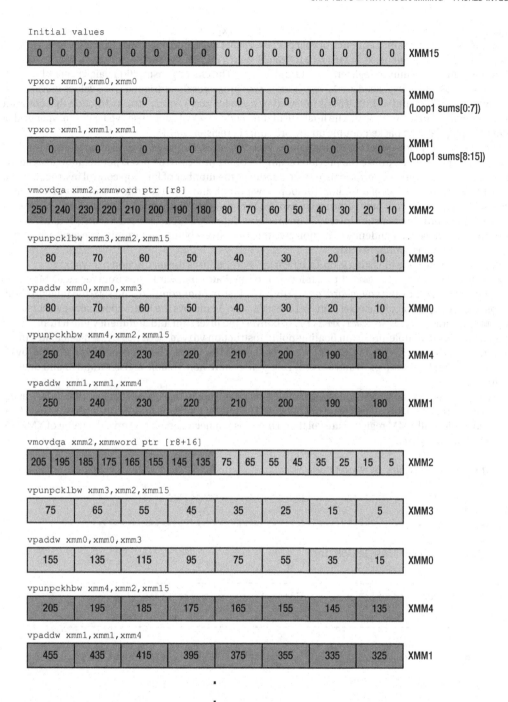

Figure 8-5. *Summing of pixel values using vpunpcklbw, vpunpckhbw, and vpaddw in Loop1 of CalcMeanU8_avx( )*

The next three code blocks in Loop1 sum pixel elements x[i+16:i+31], x[i+32:i+47], and x[i+48:i+63] using the same sequence of vpunpcklbw, vpunpckhbw, and vpaddw instructions. Following the summing of pixel elements x[i:i+63], CalcMeanU8_avx() employs vpaddw xmm0,xmm0,xmm1 to total the intermediate word sums in registers XMM0 and XMM1. The ensuing instruction pair, vpunpcklwd xmm1,xmm0,xmm15 and vpunpckhwd xmm2,xmm0,xmm15, size-promotes the unsigned word values in XMM0 to doublewords in XMM1 and XMM2. This is followed by a vpaddd xmm3,xmm1,xmm2 instruction that combines the intermediate doubleword sums. The final calculating code block of Loop1 uses vpunpckldq, vpunpckhdq, and vpaddq to update the packed double quadword sums in register XMM5.

The SIMD code in for-loop Loop1 incorporates a few assembly language optimization strategies that warrant a closer look. First, unlike the previous example, Loop1 processes 64 pixels per iteration instead of 16. Doing this often improves performance since it reduces the number of for-loop control instructions that get executed. This is called loop unrolling[2] (or loop unwinding), and you'll see other examples of it in later chapters. The second item to note is the use of two XMM registers to maintain the intermediate word sums. The use of dual word sum registers instead of one reduces data dependencies between instructions. Both loop unrolling and data dependency reduction give the processor a better opportunity to execute multiple AVX SIMD instructions simultaneously.

Returning to the code in Listing 8-6b, CalcMeanU8_avx() utilizes the instruction pair vpextrq rax,xmm5,0 and vpextrq r10,xmm5,1 to extract the intermediate quadword sums from register XMM5. The subsequent add rax,r10 and mov qword ptr [rdx],rax instructions compute and save the final pixel sum.

Following calculation of the pixel sum, CalcMeanU8_avx() employs the instruction pair vcvtsi2sd xmm0,xmm0,rax and vcvtsi2sd xmm1,xmm1,r9d to convert the pixel sum and argument value n from unsigned integers to double-precision floating-point. Instruction vdivsd xmm2,xmm0,xmm1 calculates the mean, and the ensuing vmovsd real8 ptr [rcx],xmm2 saves this value. The epilogue of CalcMeanU8_avx() utilizes macros RestoreXmmRegs_M and DeleteFrame_M to restore non-volatile register XMM15 and delete the stack frame.

Listing 8-6c shows the NASM code for example Ch08_06. Note in this listing that function CalcMeanU8_avx() does not require a formal prologue or epilogue. The reason for this is that according to the GNU C++ calling convention, all XMM registers are volatile. Thus, it is not necessary to preserve the value of XMM15 or any other XMM register.

Listing 8-6c. Example Ch08_06 NASM Code

```
;-----------------------------------------------------------------------------
; Ch08_06.fasm.s
;-----------------------------------------------------------------------------

        %include "ModX86Asm3eNASM.inc"

;-----------------------------------------------------------------------------
; bool CalcMeanU8_avx(double* mean_x, uint64_t* sum_x, const uint8_t* x,
;    uint32_t n);
;-----------------------------------------------------------------------------

NSE     equ 64                          ;num pixels per iteration of Loop1

        section .text
```

---

[2] In this example, Loop1 is partially unrolled.

```
        global CalcMeanU8_avx
CalcMeanU8_avx:

; Make sure n and x are valid
        test ecx,ecx                    ;is n <= 0?
        jz BadArg                       ;jump if yes

        test ecx,3fh                    ;is n even multiple of 64?
        jnz BadArg                      ;jump if no

        test rdx,0fh                    ;is x aligned on a 16-byte boundary?
        jnz BadArg                      ;jump if no

; Initialize
        vpxor xmm5,xmm5,xmm5             ;packed sums (2 qwords)
        vpxor xmm15,xmm15,xmm15          ;packed zero for size promotions
        mov r10d,ecx                    ;r10d = n (for use in Loop1)
        sub rdx,NSE                     ;adjust x for Loop1

; Calculate sum of all pixels
Loop1:  add rdx,NSE                     ;r8 = &x[i]
        vpxor xmm0,xmm0,xmm0            ;initialize loop packed sums (16 words)
        vpxor xmm1,xmm1,xmm1

        vmovdqa xmm2,[rdx]              ;load pixel block x[i:i+15]
        vpunpcklbw xmm3,xmm2,xmm15      ;promote x[i:i+7] to words
        vpaddw xmm0,xmm0,xmm3           ;update sums[0:7]
        vpunpckhbw xmm4,xmm2,xmm15      ;promote x[i+8:i+15] to words
        vpaddw xmm1,xmm1,xmm4           ;update sums[8:15]

        vmovdqa xmm2,[rdx+16]           ;load pixel block x[i+16:i+31]
        vpunpcklbw xmm3,xmm2,xmm15      ;promote x[i+16:i+23] to words
        vpaddw xmm0,xmm0,xmm3           ;update sums[0:7]
        vpunpckhbw xmm4,xmm2,xmm15      ;promote x[i+24:i+31] to words
        vpaddw xmm1,xmm1,xmm4           ;update sums[8:15]

        vmovdqa xmm2,[rdx+32]           ;load pixel block x[i+32:i+47]
        vpunpcklbw xmm3,xmm2,xmm15      ;promote x[i+32:i+39] to words
        vpaddw xmm0,xmm0,xmm3           ;update sums[0:7]
        vpunpckhbw xmm4,xmm2,xmm15      ;promote x[i+40:i+47] to words
        vpaddw xmm1,xmm1,xmm4           ;update sums[8:15]

        vmovdqa xmm2,[rdx+48]           ;load pixel block x[i+48:i+63]
        vpunpcklbw xmm3,xmm2,xmm15      ;promote x[i+48:i+55] to words
        vpaddw xmm0,xmm0,xmm3           ;update sums[0:7]
        vpunpckhbw xmm4,xmm2,xmm15      ;promote x[i+56:i+63] to words
        vpaddw xmm1,xmm1,xmm4           ;update sums[8:15]

        vpaddw xmm0,xmm0,xmm1           ;loop packed sums (8 words)
        vpunpcklwd xmm1,xmm0,xmm15      ;promote loop packed sums to dwords
        vpunpckhwd xmm2,xmm0,xmm15
```

```
        vpaddd xmm3,xmm1,xmm2                  ;loop packed sums (4 dwords)

        vpunpckldq xmm0,xmm3,xmm15             ;promote loop packed sums to qwords
        vpunpckhdq xmm1,xmm3,xmm15
        vpaddq xmm5,xmm5,xmm0                  ;update packed sums (2 qwords)
        vpaddq xmm5,xmm5,xmm1

        sub r10d,NSE                           ;n -= NSE
        jnz Loop1                              ;repeat until done

; Reduce packed sums (2 qwords) to single qword
        vpextrq rax,xmm5,0                     ;rax = xmm5[63:0]
        vpextrq r10,xmm5,1                     ;r10 = xmm5[127:64]
        add rax,r10                            ;rax = final pixel sum
        mov [rsi],rax                          ;save final pixel sum

; Calculate mean
        vcvtsi2sd xmm0,xmm0,rax                ;convert sum to DPFP
        vcvtsi2sd xmm1,xmm1,ecx                ;convert n to DPFP
        vdivsd xmm2,xmm0,xmm1                  ;mean = sum / n
        vmovsd [rdi],xmm2                      ;save mean

        mov eax,1                              ;set success return code
        ret

BadArg: xor eax,eax                            ;set error return code
        ret
```

Here are the results for source code example Ch08_06:

```
----- Results for Ch08_06 -----

CalcMeanU8_cpp() results:
rc0:       1
sum_x0:  2098086
mean_x0: 128.057007

CalcMeanU8_avx() results:
rc1:       1
sum_x1:  2098086
mean_x1: 128.057007
```

Summary

Here are the key learning points for Chapter 8:

- The vpadd[b|w|d|q] instructions perform packed addition. The vpadds[b|w] and vpaddus[b|w] instructions perform packed signed and unsigned saturated addition.

- The vpsub[b|w|d|q] instructions perform packed subtraction. The vpsubs[b|w] and vpsubus[b|w] instructions perform packed signed and unsigned saturated subtraction.

- The vpmul[h|l]w instructions carry out multiplication using packed word operands. The vpmuldq and vpmulld instructions carry out multiplication using packed doubleword operands.

- The vpsll[w|d|q] and vpsrl[w|d|q] instructions execute logical left and right shifts using packed operands. The vpsra[w|d|q] instructions execute arithmetic right shifts using packed operands. The vps[l|r]dq instructions execute logical left and right shifts using 128-bit wide operands.

- Assembly language functions can use the vpand, vpor, and vpxor instructions to perform bitwise AND, inclusive OR, and exclusive OR operations using packed integer operands.

- The instructions vpextr[b|w|d|q] extract an element value from a packed integer operand.

- The vpunpckl[bw|dw|dq] and vpunpckh[bw|dw|dq] instructions unpack and interleave the contents of their two source operands. These instructions are frequently used to size-promote packed integer operands.

- The vpminu[b|w|d] and vpmaxu[b|w|d] instructions perform packed unsigned integer minimum-maximum compares.

- Packed integer memory operands referenced by a vmovdqa instruction must be properly aligned on a 16-byte (XMM register), 32-byte (YMM register), or 64-byte (ZMM register) boundary. The vmovdqu instruction can be used for unaligned packed integer operands in memory.

- Partially unrolling for-loops to reduce the number of executed loop control instructions often results in faster code. Minimizing or eliminating data dependencies between instructions also yields improved performance.

## CHAPTER 9

AVX Programming – Packed Floating-Point

The source code examples of the previous chapter elucidated the fundamentals of AVX programming using packed integer operands. In this chapter, you'll learn how to use the AVX instruction set to perform SIMD operations using packed floating-point operands. The chapter begins with three source code examples that demonstrate common packed floating-point operations including basic arithmetic, data comparisons, and data conversions. The next two source code examples elucidate SIMD mathematics using floating-point arrays. The final example of this chapter spotlights SIMD computations using a floating-point matrix.

Packed Floating-Point Arithmetic

In this section, you'll study three source code examples that illustrate the use of AVX packed floating-point instructions using single-precision and double-precision values. The first example explains basic packed floating-point arithmetic. The second source code example expounds packed floating-point comparisons. The final source code example of this section describes packed floating-point conversions. Each source code example in this section uses 256-bit wide operands and the YMM register set. You'll also learn how and when to use the vzeroupper (Zero Upper Bits of YMM and ZMM Registers) instruction.

Elementary Operations

Listing 9-1a shows the C++ code for example Ch09_01. This example highlights elementary floating-point arithmetic operations including addition, subtraction, multiplication, division, and square roots using 256-bit wide packed operands.

Listing 9-1a. Example Ch09_01 C++ Code

```
struct alignas(32) YmmVal
{
public:
    union
    {
        int8_t m_I8[32];
        int16_t m_I16[16];
        int32_t m_I32[8];
        int64_t m_I64[4];
```

© Daniel Kusswurm 2023
D. Kusswurm, *Modern X86 Assembly Language Programming*,
https://doi.org/10.1007/978-1-4842-9603-5_9

```
        uint8_t m_U8[32];
        uint16_t m_U16[16];
        uint32_t m_U32[8];
        uint64_t m_U64[4];
        float m_F32[8];
        double m_F64[4];
    };

// ...

//-------------------------------------------------------------------------
// Ch09_01.h
//-------------------------------------------------------------------------

#pragma once
#include "YmmVal.h"

// Ch09_01_fasm.asm, Ch09_01_fasm.s
extern "C" void PackedMathF32_avx(YmmVal* c, const YmmVal* a, const YmmVal* b);
extern "C" void PackedMathF64_avx(YmmVal* c, const YmmVal* a, const YmmVal* b);

//-------------------------------------------------------------------------
// Ch09_01.cpp
//-------------------------------------------------------------------------

#include <iostream>
#include <iomanip>
#include <string>
#include <numbers>
#include "Ch09_01.h"

static const char* c_OprStr[8] =
{
    "Add", "Sub", "Mul", "Div", "Min", "Max", "Sqrt a", "Abs b"
};

constexpr size_t c_NumOprStr = sizeof(c_OprStr) / sizeof(char*);

static void PackedMathF32(void)
{
    using namespace std::numbers;
    constexpr char nl = '\n';

    YmmVal a, b, c[c_NumOprStr];

    a.m_F32[0] = 36.0f;                 b.m_F32[0] = -(float)(1.0f / 9.0f);
    a.m_F32[1] = (float)(1.0 / 32.0);   b.m_F32[1] = 64.0f;
    a.m_F32[2] = 2.0f;                  b.m_F32[2] = -0.0625f;
    a.m_F32[3] = 42.0f;                 b.m_F32[3] = 8.666667f;
    a.m_F32[4] = (float)pi;             b.m_F32[4] = -4.0;
```

```
    a.m_F32[5] = 18.6f;                b.m_F32[5] = -64.0f;
    a.m_F32[6] = 3.0f;                 b.m_F32[6] = -5.95f;
    a.m_F32[7] = 142.0f;               b.m_F32[7] = (float)sqrt2;

    PackedMathF32_avx(c, &a, &b);

    std::cout << ("\nPackedMathF32_avx() results:\n");

    for (size_t i = 0; i < 2; i++)
    {
        std::string s0 = (i == 0) ? "a lo:     " : "a hi:     ";
        std::string s1 = (i == 0) ? "b lo:     " : "b hi:     ";

        std::cout << s0 << a.ToStringF32(i) << nl;
        std::cout << s1 << b.ToStringF32(i) << nl;

        for (size_t j = 0; j < c_NumOprStr; j++)
        {
            std::cout << std::setw(9) << std::left << c_OprStr[j];
            std::cout << c[j].ToStringF32(i) << nl;
        }

        if (i == 0)
            std::cout << nl;
    }
}

static void PackedMathF64(void)
{
    using namespace std::numbers;
    constexpr char nl = '\n';

    YmmVal a, b, c[c_NumOprStr];

    a.m_F64[0] = 2.0;         b.m_F64[0] = pi;
    a.m_F64[1] = 4.0;         b.m_F64[1] = e;
    a.m_F64[2] = 7.5;         b.m_F64[2] = -9.125;
    a.m_F64[3] = 3.0;         b.m_F64[3] = -pi;

    PackedMathF64_avx(c, &a, &b);

    std::cout << ("\nPackedMathF64_avx() results:\n");

    for (size_t i = 0; i < 2; i++)
    {
        std::string s0 = (i == 0) ? "a lo:     " : "a hi:     ";
        std::string s1 = (i == 0) ? "b lo:     " : "b hi:     ";

        std::cout << s0 << a.ToStringF64(i) << nl;
        std::cout << s1 << b.ToStringF64(i) << nl;
```

```cpp
        for (size_t j = 0; j < c_NumOprStr; j++)
        {
            std::cout << std::setw(9) << std::left << c_OprStr[j];
            std::cout << c[j].ToStringF64(i) << nl;
        }

        if (i == 0)
            std::cout << nl;
    }
}

int main(void)
{
    std::cout << "----- Results for Ch09_01 -----\n";

    PackedMathF32();
    PackedMathF64();
    return 0;
}
```

Listing 9-1a begins with the declaration of a C++ structure named YmmVal. Like the XmmVal structure that you saw in Chapter 8, this structure contains a publicly accessible anonymous union whose members correspond to the packed data types that can be used with a 256-bit wide x86-AVX operand. Note that YmmVal is declared using the alignas(32) specifier, which instructs the C++ compiler to align each YmmVal instance on a 32-byte boundary. This is done to improve performance as explained in Chapter 7. Structure YmmVal also defines several member functions that format the contents of a YmmVal variable for display purposes. The source code for these member functions is not shown in Listing 9-1a but is included in the software download package.

The next C++ file in Listing 9-1a, Ch09_01.h, incorporates the function declarations for this example. Note that both PackedMathF32_avx() and PackedMathF64_avx() require pointer arguments of type YmmVal. Next in Listing 9-1a is file Ch09_01.cpp. This file contains two static functions named PackedMathF32() and PackedMathF64(). These functions perform test case initialization for the AVX assembly language functions PackedMathF32_avx() and PackedMathF64_avx(), respectively. They also format and stream the results to std::cout.

File Ch09_01_fasm.asm, shown in Listing 9-1b, contains the MASM code for example Ch09_01. This file begins with a .const section that defines integer masks for calculating floating-point absolute values. Note that the most significant bits of both F64_AbsMask and F32_AbsMask are set to zero, while all other bits are set to one. The most significant bit in each mask corresponds to the floating-point sign bit. Also note that both F64_AbsMask and F32_AbsMask are properly aligned since MASM automatically aligns the start of each .const section on a double quadword boundary.

Listing 9-1b. Example Ch09_01 MASM Code

```asm
;-----------------------------------------------------------------------------
; Ch09_01_fasm.asm
;-----------------------------------------------------------------------------

            .const
F64_AbsMask   dq 07fffffffffffffffh
F32_AbsMask   dd 07fffffffh
```

```
;-----------------------------------------------------------------------------
; void PackedMathF32_avx(YmmVal* c, const YmmVal* a, const YmmVal* b);
;-----------------------------------------------------------------------------

        .code
PackedMathF32_avx proc
        vmovaps ymm0,ymmword ptr [rdx]          ;ymm0 = a
        vmovaps ymm1,ymmword ptr [r8]           ;ymm1 = b

        vaddps ymm2,ymm0,ymm1                   ;SPFP addition
        vmovaps ymmword ptr[rcx],ymm2

        vsubps ymm2,ymm0,ymm1                   ;SPFP subtraction
        vmovaps ymmword ptr[rcx+32],ymm2

        vmulps ymm2,ymm0,ymm1                   ;SPFP multiplication
        vmovaps ymmword ptr[rcx+64],ymm2

        vdivps ymm2,ymm0,ymm1                   ;SPFP division
        vmovaps ymmword ptr[rcx+96],ymm2

        vminps ymm2,ymm0,ymm1                   ;SPFP min
        vmovaps ymmword ptr[rcx+128],ymm2

        vmaxps ymm2,ymm0,ymm1                   ;SPFP max
        vmovaps ymmword ptr[rcx+160],ymm2

        vsqrtps ymm2,ymm0                       ;SPFP sqrt(a)
        vmovaps ymmword ptr[rcx+192],ymm2

        vbroadcastss ymm3,real4 ptr [F32_AbsMask] ;load abs mask
        vandps ymm2,ymm3,ymm1                      ;SPFP abs(b)
        vmovaps ymmword ptr[rcx+224],ymm2

        vzeroupper                              ;clear upper YMM/ZMM bits
        ret
PackedMathF32_avx endp

;-----------------------------------------------------------------------------
; void PackedMathF64_avx(YmmVal* c, const YmmVal* a, const YmmVal* b);
;-----------------------------------------------------------------------------

PackedMathF64_avx proc
        vmovapd ymm0,ymmword ptr [rdx]          ;ymm0 = a
        vmovapd ymm1,ymmword ptr [r8]           ;ymm1 = b

        vaddpd ymm2,ymm0,ymm1                   ;DPFP addition
        vmovapd ymmword ptr[rcx],ymm2

        vsubpd ymm2,ymm0,ymm1                   ;DPFP subtraction
        vmovapd ymmword ptr[rcx+32],ymm2
```

```
        vmulpd ymm2,ymm0,ymm1              ;DPFP multiplication
        vmovapd ymmword ptr[rcx+64],ymm2


        vdivpd ymm2,ymm0,ymm1              ;DPFP division
        vmovapd ymmword ptr[rcx+96],ymm2


        vminpd ymm2,ymm0,ymm1              ;DPFP min
        vmovapd ymmword ptr[rcx+128],ymm2


        vmaxpd ymm2,ymm0,ymm1              ;DPFP max
        vmovapd ymmword ptr[rcx+160],ymm2


        vsqrtpd ymm2,ymm0                  ;DPFP sqrt(a)
        vmovapd ymmword ptr[rcx+192],ymm2


        vbroadcastsd ymm3,real8 ptr [F64_AbsMask] ;load abs mask
        vandpd ymm2,ymm3,ymm1                      ;DPFP abs(b)
        vmovapd ymmword ptr[rcx+224],ymm2


        vzeroupper                         ;clear upper YMM/ZMM bits
        ret
PackedMathF64_avx endp
        end
```

Function PackedMathF32_avx() begins with a vmovaps ymm0,ymmword ptr [rdx] (Move Aligned Packed SPFP Values) instruction that loads argument value a into register YMM0. This is followed by a vmovaps ymm1,ymmword ptr [r8] instruction that loads argument value b into YMM1. When used to load (or store) a YMM register, the vmovaps instruction requires its source operand in memory to be aligned on a 32-byte boundary (recall that the declaration of YmmVal included an alignas(32) specifier). The next instruction, vaddps ymm2,ymm0,ymm1 (Add Packed SPFP Values), adds the floating-point elements in registers YMM0 (a) and YMM1 (b) and saves the result in register YMM2. The vmovaps ymmword ptr[rcx],ymm2 instruction that follows saves the resultant packed sums in YMM2 to c[0].

The ensuing code blocks illustrate other packed arithmetic operations using 256-bit wide operands and single-precision floating-point elements. The vsubps (Subtract Packed SPFP Values), vmulps (Multiply Packed SPFP Values), and vdivps (Divide Packed SPFP Values) perform packed subtraction, multiplication, and division. The instructions vminps (Minimum of SPFP Values), vmaxps (Maximum of SPFP Values), and vsqrtps (Square Root of SPFP values) calculate packed minimums, maximums, and square roots, respectively.

Following calculation of the square roots, PackedMathF32_avx() uses a vbroadcastss ymm3,real4 ptr [F32_AbsMask] (Load with Broadcast Floating-Point Data) instruction, which loads F32_AbsMask (0x7FFFFFFF) into each doubleword element of YMM3. The next instruction, vandps ymm2,ymm3,ymm1 (Bitwise Logical AND of Packed SPFP Values), performs a bitwise logical AND of registers YMM3 and YMM1 and saves the result in YMM2. This operation zeroes the sign bit of each single-precision floating-point element in YMM1, which yields the absolute values.

Prior to its ret instruction, function PackedMathF32_avx() utilizes a vzeroupper instruction. Operationally, this instruction zeroes the upper 128 (384) bits of registers YMM0–YMM15 (ZMM0–ZMM15). Execution of a vzeroupper does not modify registers XMM0–XMM15. The real reason for using vzeroupper here is to preclude potential performance delays that can occur whenever the processor transitions from executing x86-AVX instructions to executing legacy x86-SSE instructions. Any x86-64 assembly language function that uses registers YMM0–YMM15 (or ZMM0–ZMM15) should always include a vzeroupper instruction prior to executing a ret instruction. A vzeroupper instruction should also be used before calling another function that might use x86-SSE legacy instructions including C++ library functions. A function can also employ the vzeroall (Zero XMM, YMM, and ZMM Registers) instruction as an alternative to vzeroupper. The vzeroall instruction zeroes all bits in registers XMM0–XMM15, YMM0–YMM15, and ZMM0–ZMM15; it does not modify any bits in registers ZMM16–ZMM31. Execution of a vzeroall instruction is usually slower than a vzeroupper instruction, so the latter is typically used.

Following PackedMathF32_avx() in Listing 9-1b is the function PackedMathF64_avx(). This function illustrates common arithmetic operations using 256-bit wide operands and double-precision floating-point elements. Note that the double-precision AVX instruction mnemonics use a pd suffix instead of ps.

Listing 9-1c shows the NASM code for example Ch09_01. This listing opens with an .rdata section that defines the absolute value masks F64_AbsMask and F32_AbsMask. Unless otherwise specified, NASM aligns the start of an .rdata section on a quadword boundary. This is why the definition of F64_AbsMask is positioned before F32_AbsMask.

Listing 9-1c. Example Ch09_01 NASM Code

```
;-------------------------------------------------------------------------
; Ch09_01 fasm.s
;-------------------------------------------------------------------------

        %include "ModX86Asm3eNASM.inc"

        section .rdata
F64_AbsMask   dq 07fffffffffffffffh
F32_AbsMask   dd 07fffffffh


;-------------------------------------------------------------------------
; void PackedMathF32_avx(YmmVal* c, const YmmVal* a, const YmmVal* b);
;-------------------------------------------------------------------------

        section .text

        global PackedMathF32_avx
PackedMathF32_avx:

        vmovaps ymm0,[rsi]              ;ymm0 = a
        vmovaps ymm1,[rdx]              ;ymm1 = b

        vaddps ymm2,ymm0,ymm1          ;SPFP addition
        vmovaps [rdi],ymm2

        vsubps ymm2,ymm0,ymm1          ;SPFP subtraction
        vmovaps [rdi+32],ymm2

        vmulps ymm2,ymm0,ymm1          ;SPFP multiplication
        vmovaps [rdi+64],ymm2

        vdivps ymm2,ymm0,ymm1          ;SPFP division
        vmovaps [rdi+96],ymm2

        vminps ymm2,ymm0,ymm1          ;SPFP min
        vmovaps [rdi+128],ymm2
```

```
        vmaxps  ymm2,ymm0,ymm1                  ;SPFP max
        vmovaps [rdi+160],ymm2

        vsqrtps ymm2,ymm0                       ;SPFP sqrt(a)
        vmovaps [rdi+192],ymm2

        vbroadcastss ymm3,[F32_AbsMask]         ;load abs mask
        vandps  ymm2,ymm3,ymm1                   ;SPFP abs(b)
        vmovaps [rdi+224],ymm2

        vzeroupper                              ;clear upper YMM/ZMM bits
        ret

;-------------------------------------------------------------------------------
; void PackedMathF64_avx(YmmVal c[8], const YmmVal* a, const YmmVal* b);
;-------------------------------------------------------------------------------

        global PackedMathF64_avx
PackedMathF64_avx:

        vmovapd ymm0,[rsi]                      ;ymm0 = a
        vmovapd ymm1,[rdx]                      ;ymm1 = b

        vaddpd  ymm2,ymm0,ymm1                  ;DPFP addition
        vmovapd [rdi],ymm2

        vsubpd  ymm2,ymm0,ymm1                  ;DPFP subtraction
        vmovapd [rdi+32],ymm2

        vmulpd  ymm2,ymm0,ymm1                  ;DPFP multiplication
        vmovapd [rdi+64],ymm2

        vdivpd  ymm2,ymm0,ymm1                  ;DPFP division
        vmovapd [rdi+96],ymm2

        vminpd  ymm2,ymm0,ymm1                  ;DPFP min
        vmovapd [rdi+128],ymm2

        vmaxpd  ymm2,ymm0,ymm1                  ;DPFP max
        vmovapd [rdi+160],ymm2

        vsqrtpd ymm2,ymm0                       ;DPFP sqrt(a)
        vmovapd [rdi+192],ymm2

        vbroadcastsd ymm3,[F64_AbsMask]         ;load abs mask
        vandpd  ymm2,ymm3,ymm1                   ;DPFP abs(b)
        vmovapd [rdi+224],ymm2

        vzeroupper                              ;clear upper YMM/ZMM bits
        ret
```

The remaining code in Listing 9-1c mimics the code in Listing 9-1b except for the argument value registers. Note that NASM does not require a size operator with the vmovaps and vmovapd instructions. Here are the results for source code example Ch09_01:

```
----- Results for Ch09_01 -----

PackedMathF32_avx() results:
a lo:        36.000000        0.031250   |      2.000000       42.000000
b lo:        -0.111111       64.000000   |     -0.062500        8.666667
Add          35.888889       64.031250   |      1.937500       50.666668
Sub          36.111111      -63.968750   |      2.062500       33.333332
Mul          -4.000000        2.000000   |     -0.125000      364.000000
Div         -324.000000       0.000488   |    -32.000000        4.846154
Min          -0.111111        0.031250   |     -0.062500        8.666667
Max          36.000000       64.000000   |      2.000000       42.000000
Sqrt a        6.000000        0.176777   |      1.414214        6.480741
Abs b         0.111111       64.000000   |      0.062500        8.666667

a hi:         3.141593       18.600000   |      3.000000      142.000000
b hi:        -4.000000      -64.000000   |     -5.950000        1.414214
Add          -0.858407      -45.400002   |     -2.950000      143.414215
Sub           7.141593       82.599998   |      8.950000      140.585785
Mul         -12.566371    -1190.400024   |    -17.849998      200.818329
Div          -0.785398       -0.290625   |     -0.504202      100.409164
Min          -4.000000      -64.000000   |     -5.950000        1.414214
Max           3.141593       18.600000   |      3.000000      142.000000
Sqrt a        1.772454        4.312772   |      1.732051       11.916375
Abs b         4.000000       64.000000   |      5.950000        1.414214

PackedMathF64_avx() results:
a lo:                   2.000000000000   |           4.000000000000
b lo:                   3.141592653590   |           2.718281828459
Add                     5.141592653590   |           6.718281828459
Sub                    -1.141592653590   |           1.281718171541
Mul                     6.283185307180   |          10.873127313836
Div                     0.636619772368   |           1.471517764686
Min                     2.000000000000   |           2.718281828459
Max                     3.141592653590   |           4.000000000000
Sqrt a                  1.414213562373   |           2.000000000000
Abs b                   3.141592653590   |           2.718281828459

a hi:                   7.500000000000   |           3.000000000000
b hi:                  -9.125000000000   |          -3.141592653590
Add                    -1.625000000000   |          -0.141592653590
Sub                    16.625000000000   |           6.141592653590
Mul                   -68.437500000000   |          -9.424777960769
Div                    -0.821917808219   |          -0.954929658551
Min                    -9.125000000000   |          -3.141592653590
Max                     7.500000000000   |           3.000000000000
Sqrt a                  2.738612787526   |           1.732050807569
Abs b                   9.125000000000   |           3.141592653590
```

Packed Comparisons

In Chapter 5, you learned how to compare scalar single-precision and double-precision floating-point values using the vcmps[d|s] instructions. In this section, you'll learn how to compare packed single-precision and double-precision floating-point values using the vcmpp[d|s] instructions. Like their scalar counterparts, these packed compare instructions require four operands: a destination operand, two source operands, and an immediate compare predicate. The packed compare instructions vcmppd and vcmpps signify their results using quadword or doubleword masks, respectively, of all zeros (false compare result) or all ones (true compare result). Listing 9-2a shows the C++ code for example Ch09_02.

Listing 9-2a. Example Ch09_02 C++ Code

```
//--------------------------------------------------------------------------
// Ch09_02.h
//--------------------------------------------------------------------------

#pragma once
#include "YmmVal.h"

// Ch09_02_fasm.asm, Ch09_02_fasm.s
extern "C" void PackedCompareF32_avx(YmmVal* c, const YmmVal* a, const YmmVal* b);
extern "C" void PackedCompareF64_avx(YmmVal* c, const YmmVal* a, const YmmVal* b);


//--------------------------------------------------------------------------
// Ch09_02.cpp
//--------------------------------------------------------------------------

#include <iostream>
#include <iomanip>
#include <string>
#include <limits>
#include <numbers>
#include "Ch09_02.h"

static const char* c_CmpStr[8] =
{
    "EQ", "NE", "LT", "LE", "GT", "GE", "ORDERED", "UNORDERED"
};

constexpr size_t c_NumCmpStr = sizeof(c_CmpStr) / sizeof(char*);

static void PackedCompareF32()
{
    using namespace std::numbers;

    constexpr char nl = '\n';
    constexpr float qnan_f32 = std::numeric_limits<float>::quiet_NaN();
    YmmVal a, b, c[c_NumCmpStr];

    a.m_F32[0] = 2.0f;              b.m_F32[0] = 1.0f;
    a.m_F32[1] = 7.0f;              b.m_F32[1] = 12.0f;
    a.m_F32[2] = -6.0f;             b.m_F32[2] = -6.0f;
```

```cpp
    a.m_F32[3] = 3.0f;              b.m_F32[3] = 8.0f;
    a.m_F32[4] = -16.0f;           b.m_F32[4] = -36.0f;
    a.m_F32[5] = 3.5f;             b.m_F32[5] = 3.5f;
    a.m_F32[6] = (float)pi;        b.m_F32[6] = -6.0f;
    a.m_F32[7] = (float)sqrt2;     b.m_F32[7] = qnan_f32;

    PackedCompareF32_avx(c, &a, &b);

    std::cout << ("\nPackedCompareF32_avx() results:\n");

    for (size_t i = 0; i < 2; i++)
    {
        std::string s0 = (i == 0) ? "a lo:    " : "a hi:    ";
        std::string s1 = (i == 0) ? "b lo:    " : "b hi:    ";

        std::cout << s0 << a.ToStringF32(i) << nl;
        std::cout << s1 << b.ToStringF32(i) << nl;

        for (size_t j = 0; j < c_NumCmpStr; j++)
        {
            std::cout << std::setw(9) << std::left << c_CmpStr[j];
            std::cout << c[j].ToStringX32(i) << nl;
        }

        if (i == 0)
            std::cout << nl;
    }
}

static void PackedCompareF64()
{
    using namespace std::numbers;

    constexpr char nl = '\n';
    constexpr double qnan_f64 = std::numeric_limits<double>::quiet_NaN();
    YmmVal a, b, c[c_NumCmpStr];

    a.m_F64[0] = 2.0;       b.m_F64[0] = e;
    a.m_F64[1] = pi ;       b.m_F64[1] = -1.0 / pi;
    a.m_F64[2] = 12.0;      b.m_F64[2] = 42.0;
    a.m_F64[3] = qnan_f64;  b.m_F64[3] = sqrt2;

    PackedCompareF64_avx(c, &a, &b);

    std::cout << ("\nPackedCompareF64_avx() results:\n");

    for (size_t i = 0; i < 2; i++)
    {
        std::string s0 = (i == 0) ? "a lo:    " : "a hi:    ";
        std::string s1 = (i == 0) ? "b lo:    " : "b hi:    ";
```

```
        std::cout << s0 << a.ToStringF64(i) << nl;
        std::cout << s1 << b.ToStringF64(i) << nl;

        for (size_t j = 0; j < c_NumCmpStr; j++)
        {
            std::cout << std::setw(9) << std::left << c_CmpStr[j];
            std::cout << c[j].ToStringX64(i) << nl;
        }

        if (i == 0)
            std::cout << nl;
    }
}

int main(void)
{
    std::cout << "----- Results for Ch09_02 -----\n";

    PackedCompareF32();
    PackedCompareF64();
    return 0;
}
```

In Listing 9-2a, file Ch09_02.cpp opens with a static function named PackedCompareF32(). This function performs test case initialization for the assembly language function PackedCompareF32_avx(). It also formats and stream results to std::cout. In function PackedCompareF32_avx(), note that one of the elements in YmmVal b is initialized to a QNaN (Quiet NaN). Recall from the discussions in Chapter 7 that a QNaN is a type of NaN that the processor propagates through most arithmetic operations without raising an exception. Also shown in Listing 9-2a is the static function PackedCompareF64(). This function resembles PackedCompareF32() except that it utilizes double-precision instead of single-precision values. Listing 9-2b shows the MASM code for example Ch09_02.

Listing 9-2b. Example Ch09_02 MASM Code

```
;-----------------------------------------------------------------------------
; Ch09_02_fasm.asm
;-----------------------------------------------------------------------------

        include <cmpequ_fp.asmh>


;-----------------------------------------------------------------------------
; void PackedCompareF32_avx(YmmVal* c, const YmmVal* a, const YmmVal* b);
;-----------------------------------------------------------------------------

        .code
PackedCompareF32_avx proc
        vmovaps ymm0,ymmword ptr [rdx]          ;ymm0 = a
        vmovaps ymm1,ymmword ptr [r8]           ;ymm1 = b

        vcmpps ymm2,ymm0,ymm1,CMP_EQ_OQ         ;packed compare for EQ
        vmovaps ymmword ptr[rcx],ymm2
```

```asm
        vcmpps ymm2,ymm0,ymm1,CMP_NEQ_OQ      ;packed compare for NEQ
        vmovaps ymmword ptr[rcx+32],ymm2

        vcmpps ymm2,ymm0,ymm1,CMP_LT_OQ       ;packed compare for LT
        vmovaps ymmword ptr[rcx+64],ymm2

        vcmpps ymm2,ymm0,ymm1,CMP_LE_OQ       ;packed compare for LE
        vmovaps ymmword ptr[rcx+96],ymm2

        vcmpps ymm2,ymm0,ymm1,CMP_GT_OQ       ;packed compare for GT
        vmovaps ymmword ptr[rcx+128],ymm2

        vcmpps ymm2,ymm0,ymm1,CMP_GE_OQ       ;packed compare for GE
        vmovaps ymmword ptr[rcx+160],ymm2

        vcmpps ymm2,ymm0,ymm1,CMP_ORD_Q       ;packed compare for ORD
        vmovaps ymmword ptr[rcx+192],ymm2

        vcmpps ymm2,ymm0,ymm1,CMP_UNORD_Q     ;packed compare for UNORD
        vmovaps ymmword ptr[rcx+224],ymm2


        vzeroupper
        ret
PackedCompareF32_avx endp


;-----------------------------------------------------------------------------
; void PackedCompareF64_avx(YmmVal* c, const YmmVal* a, const YmmVal* b);
;-----------------------------------------------------------------------------


PackedCompareF64_avx proc
        vmovapd ymm0,ymmword ptr [rdx]        ;ymm0 = a
        vmovapd ymm1,ymmword ptr [r8]         ;ymm1 = b

        vcmppd ymm2,ymm0,ymm1,CMP_EQ_OQ       ;packed compare for EQ
        vmovapd ymmword ptr[rcx],ymm2

        vcmppd ymm2,ymm0,ymm1,CMP_NEQ_OQ      ;packed compare for NEQ
        vmovapd ymmword ptr[rcx+32],ymm2

        vcmppd ymm2,ymm0,ymm1,CMP_LT_OQ       ;packed compare for LT
        vmovapd ymmword ptr[rcx+64],ymm2

        vcmppd ymm2,ymm0,ymm1,CMP_LE_OQ       ;packed compare for LE
        vmovapd ymmword ptr[rcx+96],ymm2

        vcmppd ymm2,ymm0,ymm1,CMP_GT_OQ       ;packed compare for GT
        vmovapd ymmword ptr[rcx+128],ymm2

        vcmppd ymm2,ymm0,ymm1,CMP_GE_OQ       ;packed compare for GE
        vmovapd ymmword ptr[rcx+160],ymm2
```

```
        vcmppd ymm2,ymm0,ymm1,CMP_ORD_Q        ;packed compare for ORD
        vmovapd ymmword ptr[rcx+192],ymm2

        vcmppd ymm2,ymm0,ymm1,CMP_UNORD_Q      ;packed compare for UNORD
        vmovapd ymmword ptr[rcx+224],ymm2

        vzeroupper
        ret
PackedCompareF64_avx endp
        end
```

In Listing 9-2b, file Ch09_02_fasm.asm opens with the line include <cmpequ_fp.asmh>. Recall from the discussions in Chapter 5 that file cmpequ_fp.asmh contains a series of equ statements that define symbolic names for x86-AVX floating-point compare predicates (see Listing 5-5a). Execution of function PackedCompareF32_avx() begins with two vmovaps instructions that load argument values a and b into registers YMM0 and YMM1, respectively. The next instruction, vcmpps ymm2,ymm0,ymm1,CMP_EQ_OQ, compares corresponding single-precision floating-point elements in YMM0 and YMM1 for equality. If the elements are equal, the corresponding element position in YMM2 is set to 0xFFFFFFFF; otherwise, it's set to 0x00000000 as shown in Figure 9-1. The ensuing vmovaps ymmword ptr[rcx],ymm2 instruction saves the mask result to c[0].

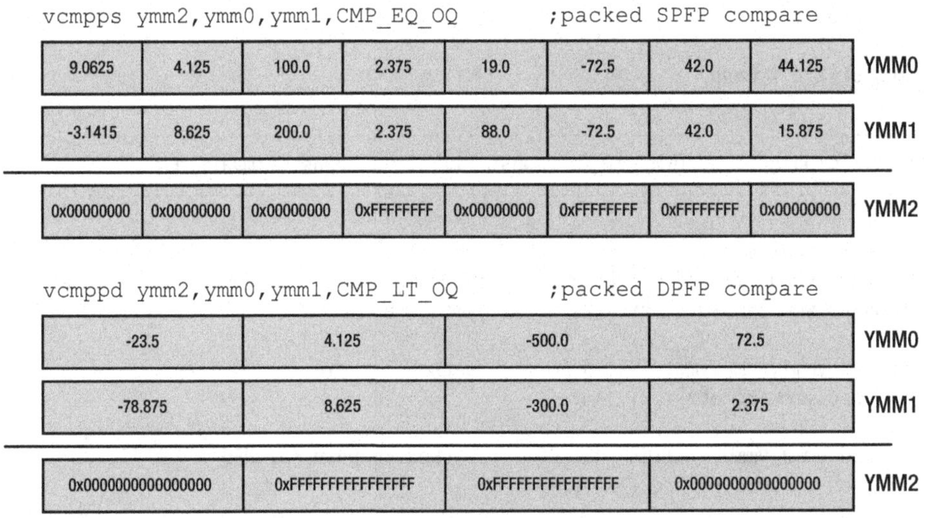

Figure 9-1. *Execution examples of AVX instructions* vcmpps *and* vcmppd

The subsequent code blocks in PackedCompareF32_avx() demonstrate the use of the vcmpps instruction with different compare predicates. Note that the displacement employed in each vmovaps instruction is an even multiple of 32, which corresponds to the width in bytes of a YMM register. Also note that PackedCompareF32_avx() employs a vzeroupper instruction prior to its ret instruction. The next function in Listing 9-2b, PackedCompareF64_avx(), illustrates packed double-precision floating-point comparisons using the AVX instruction vcmppd. Figure 9-1 contains an execution example of vcmppd using compare predicate CMP_LT_OQ.

Listing 9-2c shows the NASM code for example Ch09_02. The code in this listing matches the MASM code in Listing 9-2b, except for different argument value registers.

Listing 9-2c. Example Ch09_02 NASM Code

```
;-------------------------------------------------------------------------------
; Ch09_02 fasm.s
;-------------------------------------------------------------------------------

        %include "ModX86Asm3eNASM.inc"
        %include "cmpequ_fp.inc"


;-------------------------------------------------------------------------------
; void PackedCompareF32_avx(YmmVal* c, const YmmVal* a, const YmmVal* b);
;-------------------------------------------------------------------------------

        section .text

        global PackedCompareF32_avx
PackedCompareF32_avx:
        vmovaps ymm0,[rsi]                  ;ymm0 = a
        vmovaps ymm1,[rdx]                  ;ymm1 = b

        vcmpps ymm2,ymm0,ymm1,CMP_EQ_OQ     ;packed compare for EQ
        vmovaps [rdi],ymm2

        vcmpps ymm2,ymm0,ymm1,CMP_NEQ_OQ    ;packed compare for NEQ
        vmovaps [rdi+32],ymm2

        vcmpps ymm2,ymm0,ymm1,CMP_LT_OQ     ;packed compare for LT
        vmovaps [rdi+64],ymm2

        vcmpps ymm2,ymm0,ymm1,CMP_LE_OQ     ;packed compare for LE
        vmovaps [rdi+96],ymm2

        vcmpps ymm2,ymm0,ymm1,CMP_GT_OQ     ;packed compare for GT
        vmovaps [rdi+128],ymm2

        vcmpps ymm2,ymm0,ymm1,CMP_GE_OQ     ;packed compare for GE
        vmovaps [rdi+160],ymm2

        vcmpps ymm2,ymm0,ymm1,CMP_ORD_Q     ;packed compare for ORD
        vmovaps [rdi+192],ymm2

        vcmpps ymm2,ymm0,ymm1,CMP_UNORD_Q   ;packed compare for UNORD
        vmovaps [rdi+224],ymm2

        vzeroupper
        ret
```

```
;------------------------------------------------------------------------
; void PackedCompareF64_avx(YmmVal* c, const YmmVal* a, const YmmVal* b);
;------------------------------------------------------------------------

        global PackedCompareF64_avx
PackedCompareF64_avx:
        vmovapd ymm0,[rsi]                  ;ymm0 = a
        vmovapd ymm1,[rdx]                  ;ymm1 = b

        vcmppd ymm2,ymm0,ymm1,CMP_EQ_OQ     ;packed compare for EQ
        vmovapd [rdi],ymm2

        vcmppd ymm2,ymm0,ymm1,CMP_NEQ_OQ    ;packed compare for NEQ
        vmovapd [rdi+32],ymm2

        vcmppd ymm2,ymm0,ymm1,CMP_LT_OQ     ;packed compare for LT
        vmovapd [rdi+64],ymm2

        vcmppd ymm2,ymm0,ymm1,CMP_LE_OQ     ;packed compare for LE
        vmovapd [rdi+96],ymm2

        vcmppd ymm2,ymm0,ymm1,CMP_GT_OQ     ;packed compare for GT
        vmovapd [rdi+128],ymm2

        vcmppd ymm2,ymm0,ymm1,CMP_GE_OQ     ;packed compare for GE
        vmovapd [rdi+160],ymm2

        vcmppd ymm2,ymm0,ymm1,CMP_ORD_Q     ;packed compare for ORD
        vmovapd [rdi+192],ymm2

        vcmppd ymm2,ymm0,ymm1,CMP_UNORD_Q   ;packed compare for UNORD
        vmovapd [rdi+224],ymm2

        vzeroupper
        ret
```

Like the scalar floating-point compare instructions vcmps[d|s], both MASM and NASM support pseudo-op forms of the vcmpp[d|s] instructions. Recall from Chapter 5 that pseudo-op forms are simulated instructions that contain an embedded compare predicate in the mnemonic. For example, function PackedCompareF32_avx() could have used vcmpeqps ymm2,ymm0,ymm1 instead of vcmpps ymm2,ymm0,ymm1,CMP_EQ_OQ. I personally prefer the latter style since it is much easier to read the compare predicate. Here are the results for source code example Ch09_02:

```
----- Results for Ch09_02 -----

PackedCompareF32_avx() results:
a lo:          2.000000      7.000000   |    -6.000000      3.000000
b lo:          1.000000     12.000000   |    -6.000000      8.000000
EQ             00000000     00000000   |    FFFFFFFF     00000000
NE             FFFFFFFF     FFFFFFFF   |    00000000     FFFFFFFF
LT             00000000     FFFFFFFF   |    00000000     FFFFFFFF
LE             00000000     FFFFFFFF   |    FFFFFFFF     FFFFFFFF
```

GT	FFFFFFFF	00000000		00000000	00000000
GE	FFFFFFFF	00000000		FFFFFFFF	00000000
ORDERED	FFFFFFFF	FFFFFFFF		FFFFFFFF	FFFFFFFF
UNORDERED	00000000	00000000		00000000	00000000
a hi:	-16.000000	3.500000		3.141593	1.414214
b hi:	-36.000000	3.500000		-6.000000	nan
EQ	00000000	FFFFFFFF		00000000	00000000
NE	FFFFFFFF	00000000		FFFFFFFF	00000000
LT	00000000	00000000		00000000	00000000
LE	00000000	FFFFFFFF		00000000	00000000
GT	FFFFFFFF	00000000		FFFFFFFF	00000000
GE	FFFFFFFF	FFFFFFFF		FFFFFFFF	00000000
ORDERED	FFFFFFFF	FFFFFFFF		FFFFFFFF	00000000
UNORDERED	00000000	00000000		00000000	FFFFFFFF

```
PackedCompareF64_avx() results:
```

a lo:	2.000000000000		3.141592653590
b lo:	2.718281828459		-0.318309886184
EQ	0000000000000000		0000000000000000
NE	FFFFFFFFFFFFFFFF		FFFFFFFFFFFFFFFF
LT	FFFFFFFFFFFFFFFF		0000000000000000
LE	FFFFFFFFFFFFFFFF		0000000000000000
GT	0000000000000000		FFFFFFFFFFFFFFFF
GE	0000000000000000		FFFFFFFFFFFFFFFF
ORDERED	FFFFFFFFFFFFFFFF		FFFFFFFFFFFFFFFF
UNORDERED	0000000000000000		0000000000000000
a hi:	12.000000000000		nan
b hi:	42.000000000000		1.414213562373
EQ	0000000000000000		0000000000000000
NE	FFFFFFFFFFFFFFFF		0000000000000000
LT	FFFFFFFFFFFFFFFF		0000000000000000
LE	FFFFFFFFFFFFFFFF		0000000000000000
GT	0000000000000000		0000000000000000
GE	0000000000000000		0000000000000000
ORDERED	FFFFFFFFFFFFFFFF		0000000000000000
UNORDERED	0000000000000000		FFFFFFFFFFFFFFFF

Packed Conversions

A common operation in many algorithms that perform SIMD floating-point arithmetic is to cast a packed single-precision or double-precision floating-point value to packed integers or vice versa. It is also often necessary for a function to size-promote packed single-precision floating-point value to packed double-precision or size-narrow a packed double-precision floating-point value to single-precision. The next source code example, named Ch09_03, illustrates the use of the AVX instructions that perform these types of conversions. Listing 9-3a shows the C++ source code for example Ch09_03.

Listing 9-3a. Example Ch09_03 C++ Code

```
//----------------------------------------------------------------------
// Ch09_03.h
//----------------------------------------------------------------------

#pragma once
#include "XmmVal.h"

// The order of values in the following enum must match the jump
// tables defined in the assembly langage files.

enum CvtOp : unsigned int
{
    I32_F32, F32_I32, I32_F64, F64_I32, F32_F64, F64_F32,
};

// Ch09_03_fasm.asm, Ch09_03_fasm.s
extern "C" bool PackedConvertFP_avx(const XmmVal& a, XmmVal& b, CvtOp cvt_op);

//----------------------------------------------------------------------
// Ch09_03.cpp
//----------------------------------------------------------------------

#include <iostream>
#include <numbers>
#include "Ch09_03.h"
#include "XmmVal.h"

static void PackedConvertF32(void)
{
    XmmVal a, b;
    constexpr char nl = '\n';

    a.m_I32[0] = 10;
    a.m_I32[1] = -500;
    a.m_I32[2] = 600;
    a.m_I32[3] = -1024;
    PackedConvertFP_avx(a, b, CvtOp::I32_F32);
    std::cout << "\nCvtOp::I32_F32 results:\n";
    std::cout << "a: " << a.ToStringI32() << nl;
    std::cout << "b: " << b.ToStringF32() << nl;

    a.m_F32[0] = 1.0f / 3.0f;
    a.m_F32[1] = 2.0f / 3.0f;
    a.m_F32[2] = -a.m_F32[0] * 2.0f;
    a.m_F32[3] = -a.m_F32[1] * 2.0f;
    PackedConvertFP_avx(a, b, CvtOp::F32_I32);
    std::cout << "\nCvtOp::F32_I32 results:\n";
    std::cout << "a: " << a.ToStringF32() << nl;
    std::cout << "b: " << b.ToStringI32() << nl;
```

```
    // F32_F64 converts the two low-order SPFP values of 'a'
    a.m_F32[0] = 1.0f / 7.0f;
    a.m_F32[1] = 2.0f / 9.0f;
    a.m_F32[2] = 0;
    a.m_F32[3] = 0;
    PackedConvertFP_avx(a, b, CvtOp::F32_F64);
    std::cout << "\nCvtOp::F32_F64 results:\n";
    std::cout << "a: " << a.ToStringF32() << nl;
    std::cout << "b: " << b.ToStringF64() << nl;
}

static void PackedConvertF64(void)
{
    using namespace std::numbers;

    XmmVal a, b;
    constexpr char nl = '\n';

    // I32_F64 converts the two low-order doubleword integers of 'a'
    a.m_I32[0] = 10;
    a.m_I32[1] = -20;
    a.m_I32[2] = 0;
    a.m_I32[3] = 0;
    PackedConvertFP_avx(a, b, CvtOp::I32_F64);
    std::cout << "\nCvtOp::I32_F64 results:\n";
    std::cout << "a: " << a.ToStringI32() << nl;
    std::cout << "b: " << b.ToStringF64() << nl;

    // F64_I32 sets the two high-order doublewords of 'b' to zero
    a.m_F64[0] = pi;
    a.m_F64[1] = e;
    PackedConvertFP_avx(a, b, CvtOp::F64_I32);
    std::cout << "\nCvtOp::F64_I32 results:\n";
    std::cout << "a: " << a.ToStringF64() << nl;
    std::cout << "b: " << b.ToStringI32() << nl;

    // F64_F32 sets the two high-order SPFP values of 'b' to zero
    a.m_F64[0] = sqrt2;
    a.m_F64[1] = 1.0 / sqrt2;
    PackedConvertFP_avx (a, b, CvtOp::F64_F32);
    std::cout << "\nCvtOp::F64_F32 results:\n";
    std::cout << "a: " << a.ToStringF64() << nl;
    std::cout << "b: " << b.ToStringF32() << nl;
}

int main(void)
{
    std::cout << "----- Results for Ch09_03 -----\n";

    PackedConvertF32();
    PackedConvertF64();
    return 0;
}
```

The C++ code in Listing 9-3a begins with an enum named CvtOp that defines the conversion operations supported by the assembly language function PackedConvertFP_avx(). Note that the numeric value assigned to each CvtOp identifier (I32_F32 = 0, F32_I32 = 1, etc.) is critical since the assembly language code uses them as indices into a lookup table (LUT). In file Ch09_03.cpp, static function PackedConvertF32() exercises some test cases using packed single-precision floating-point operands. Similarly, static function PackedConvertF64() contains test cases for packed double-precision floating-point operands.

Listing 9-3b shows the MASM code for example Ch09_03. Toward the bottom of this listing is the previously mentioned LUT. CvtOpTable contains a list of labels that are defined within PackedConvertFP_avx(). The target of each label is a short code block that performs a specific packed floating-point conversion. The equate CvtOpTableCount defines the number of items in the LUT and is used to validate argument value cvt_op. The align 8 directive instructs the assembler to align CvtOpTable on a quadword boundary to avoid unaligned memory accesses when referencing elements in the LUT. Note that CvtOpTable is defined inside the assembly language function PackedConvertFP_avx() (i.e., between the MASM proc and endp directives), which means that storage for the LUT is allocated in a .code section. Clearly, the LUT does not contain any executable instructions, and this is why the table is positioned after the ret instruction. This also means that the data in CvtOpTable is read-only; the processor will generate an exception on any write attempt to LUT CvtOpTable.

Listing 9-3b. Example Ch09_03 MASM Code

```
;-------------------------------------------------------------------
; Ch09_03_fasm.asm
;-------------------------------------------------------------------


;-------------------------------------------------------------------
; bool PackedConvertFP_avx(const XmmVal& a, XmmVal& b, CvtOp cvt_op);
;-------------------------------------------------------------------

        .code
PackedConvertFP_avx proc

; Make sure cvt_op is valid
        cmp r8d,CvtOpTableCount          ;is cvt_op valid?
        jae InvalidCvtOp                 ;jmp if cvt_op is invalid

; Jump to code block specfied by cvt_op
        mov eax,1                        ;set valid cvt_op return code
        mov r8d,r8d                      ;r8 = cvt_op (zero extended)
        lea r9,[CvtOpTable]              ;r9 = address of CvtOpTable
        mov r10,[r9+r8*8]                ;r10 = address of entry in CvtOpTable
        jmp qword ptr r10                ;jump to conversion code block

; Convert packed signed doubleword integers to packed SPFP values
I32_F32:
        vmovdqa xmm0,xmmword ptr [rcx]
        vcvtdq2ps xmm1,xmm0
        vmovaps xmmword ptr [rdx],xmm1
        ret
```

```
; Convert packed SPFP values to packed signed doubleword integers
F32_I32:
        vmovaps xmm0,xmmword ptr [rcx]
        vcvtps2dq xmm1,xmm0
        vmovdqa xmmword ptr [rdx],xmm1
        ret

; Convert packed signed doubleword integers to packed DPFP values
I32_F64:
        vmovdqa xmm0,xmmword ptr [rcx]
        vcvtdq2pd xmm1,xmm0
        vmovapd xmmword ptr [rdx],xmm1
        ret

; Convert packed DPFP values to packed signed doubleword integers
F64_I32:
        vmovapd xmm0,xmmword ptr [rcx]
        vcvtpd2dq xmm1,xmm0
        vmovdqa xmmword ptr [rdx],xmm1
        ret

; Convert packed SPFP to packed DPFP
F32_F64:
        vmovaps xmm0,xmmword ptr [rcx]
        vcvtps2pd xmm1,xmm0
        vmovapd xmmword ptr [rdx],xmm1
        ret

; Convert packed DPFP to packed SPFP
F64_F32:
        vmovapd xmm0,xmmword ptr [rcx]
        vcvtpd2ps xmm1,xmm0
        vmovaps xmmword ptr [rdx],xmm1
        ret

InvalidCvtOp:
        xor eax,eax                     ;set invalid cvt_op return code
        ret

; The order of values in the following table must match the enum CvtOp
; that's defined in Ch09_03.h.

        align 8
CvtOpTable    equ $
        dq I32_F32, F32_I32
        dq I32_F64, F64_I32
        dq F32_F64, F64_F32
CvtOpTableCount equ ($ - CvtOpTable) / size qword

PackedConvertFP_avx endp
        end
```

The assembly language function PackedConvertFP_avx() commences its execution by validating argument value cvt_op. Following argument validation, PackedConvertFP_avx() employs the instruction triplet mov r8d,r8d, lea r9,[CvtOpTable], and mov r10,[r9+r8*8] to load the address of the conversion code block specified by cvt_op into register R10. The ensuing jmp qword ptr r10 transfers program control to this code block.

The conversion code blocks in PackedConvertFP_avx() utilize the aligned move instructions vmovaps, vmovapd, and vmovdqa to transfer packed operands to and from memory. Specific AVX conversion instructions carry out the requested operations. For example, the vcvtps2dq and vcvtdq2ps instructions perform conversions between packed single-precision floating-point and signed doubleword integer values and vice versa. When used with 128-bit wide operands, these instructions convert four values simultaneously. The counterpart double-precision instructions, vcvtpd2dq and vcvtdq2pd, are slightly different in that only two values are converted due to the element size differences (32 and 64 bits). The vcvtps2pd and vcvtpd2ps instructions perform their conversions in a similar manner. Note that the vcvtpd2dq and vcvtpd2ps instructions set the high-order 64 bits of the destination operand to zero. AVX packed conversion instructions use the floating-point rounding mode that's specified by MXCSR.RC as described in Chapter 5. The default rounding mode for Visual C++ and GNU C++ is round to nearest.

Listing 9-3c shows the NASM code for example Ch09_03. Note that the definition of LUT CvtOpTable is situated in a .data section that follows the ret instruction. Also note the use of the align = 8 parameter, which ensures that each quadword value in CvtOpTable is properly aligned in memory.

Listing 9-3c. Example Ch09_03 NASM Code

```
;-----------------------------------------------------------------------
; Ch09_03 fasm.s
;-----------------------------------------------------------------------

        %include "ModX86Asm3eNASM.inc"

;-----------------------------------------------------------------------
; bool PackedConvertFP_avx(const XmmVal& a, XmmVal& b, CvtOp cvt_op);
;-----------------------------------------------------------------------

        section .text

        global PackedConvertFP_avx
PackedConvertFP_avx:

; Make sure cvt_op is valid
        cmp edx,CvtOpTableCount          ;is cvt_op valid?
        jae InvalidCvtOp                 ;jmp if cvt_op is invalid

; Jump to code block specfied by cvt_op
        mov eax,1                        ;set valid cvt_op return code
        mov edx,edx                      ;rdx = cvt_op (zero extended)
        lea r9,[CvtOpTable]              ;r9 = address of CvtOpTable
        mov r10,[r9+rdx*8]               ;r10 = address of entry in CvtOpTable
        jmp qword r10                    ;jump to conversion code block

; Convert packed signed doubleword integers to packed SPFP values
I32_F32:
        vmovdqa xmm0,[rdi]               ;load a
        vcvtdq2ps xmm1,xmm0              ;perform conversion
```

```
        vmovaps [rsi],xmm1                         ;save to b
        ret

; Convert packed SPFP values to packed signed doubleword integers
F32_I32:
        vmovaps xmm0,[rdi]
        vcvtps2dq xmm1,xmm0
        vmovdqa [rsi],xmm1
        ret

; Convert packed signed doubleword integers to packed DPFP values
I32_F64:
        vmovdqa xmm0,[rdi]
        vcvtdq2pd xmm1,xmm0
        vmovapd [rsi],xmm1
        ret

; Convert packed DPFP values to packed signed doubleword integers
F64_I32:
        vmovapd xmm0,[rdi]
        vcvtpd2dq xmm1,xmm0
        vmovdqa [rsi],xmm1
        ret

; Convert packed SPFP to packed DPFP
F32_F64:
        vmovaps xmm0,[rdi]
        vcvtps2pd xmm1,xmm0
        vmovapd [rsi],xmm1
        ret

; Convert packed DPFP to packed SPFP
F64_F32:
        vmovapd xmm0,[rdi]
        vcvtpd2ps xmm1,xmm0
        vmovaps [rsi],xmm1
        ret

InvalidCvtOp:
        xor eax,eax                        ;set invalid cvt_op return code
        ret

; The order of values in the following table must match the enum CvtOp
; that's defined in Ch09_03.h.

        section .data align = 8

CvtOpTable equ $
        dq I32_F32, F32_I32
        dq I32_F64, F64_I32
        dq F32_F64, F64_F32
CvtOpTableCount equ ($ - CvtOpTable) / 8
```

Here are the results for source code example Ch09_03:

```
----- Results for Ch09_03 -----

CvtOp::I32_F32 results:
a:              10           -500  |             600          -1024
b:       10.000000     -500.000000  |      600.000000    -1024.000000

CvtOp::F32_I32 results:
a:        0.333333       0.666667  |       -0.666667       -1.333333
b:               0              1  |              -1             -1

CvtOp::F32_F64 results:
a:        0.142857       0.222222  |        0.000000        0.000000
b:            0.142857149243  |           0.222222223878

CvtOp::I32_F64 results:
a:              10            -20  |               0               0
b:           10.000000000000  |       -20.000000000000

CvtOp::F64_I32 results:
a:          3.141592653590  |           2.718281828459
b:               3              3  |               0               0

CvtOp::F64_F32 results:
a:          1.414213562373  |           0.707106781187
b:        1.414214       0.707107  |        0.000000        0.000000
```

Packed Floating-Point Arithmetic – Arrays

AVX floating-point SIMD instructions are ideally suited for performing packed arithmetic operations using arrays and matrices. In this section, you'll examine two source examples that use AVX SIMD instructions to carry out calculations using double-precision floating-point arrays. The third source code example elucidates the use of AVX SIMD instructions using a matrix of double-precision floating-point values.

Mean and Standard Deviation

In Chapter 5, you learned how to calculate the mean and standard deviation of a double-precision floating-point array using AVX scalar instructions (see example Ch05_07). In this section, you'll learn how to perform these same calculations using AVX SIMD instructions. The equations used in this example to calculate the mean and standard deviation are identical to the equations used in example Ch05_07; they're repeated as follows for convenience:

$$\bar{x} = \frac{1}{n} \sum_i x_i$$

$$s = \sqrt{\frac{1}{n-1} \sum_i (x_i - \bar{x})^2}$$

The C++ code for example Ch09_04 is identical to the code that you saw in example Ch05_07 (see Listing 5-7a).

Listing 9-4a shows the MASM code for example Ch09_04. Function CalcMeanF64_avx() starts with a code block that validates argument value n (R8) for size and array pointer x (RDX) for proper alignment on a 32-byte boundary. In the initialization code block that follows, CalcMeanF64_avx() uses a vxorpd ymm5,ymm5,ymm5 instruction to set sums = 0.0. It should be noted that register YMM5 contains four double-precision intermediate sums as you'll soon see. In the initialization code block, also note the use of the instructions cmp r8,NSE and jb Loop2. These instructions skip over the SIMD arithmetic in for-loop Loop1 if n >= NSE (NSE equals 4) is false.

Listing 9-4a. Example Ch09_04 MASM Code

```
;-------------------------------------------------------------------------
; Ch09_04_fasm.asm
;-------------------------------------------------------------------------


;-------------------------------------------------------------------------
; bool CalcMeanF64_avx(double* mean, const double* x, size_t n);
;-------------------------------------------------------------------------

NSE     equ 4                           ;number of SIMD elements per iteration

        .code
CalcMeanF64_avx proc

; Validate arguments
        cmp r8,2                        ;is n >= 2?
        jb BadArg                       ;jump if no
        test rdx,01fh                   ;is x 32b aligned?
        jnz BadArg                      ;jump if no

; Initialize
        mov r9,r8                       ;save copy of n
        vxorpd ymm5,ymm5,ymm5           ;packed (4 DPFP) sums = 0.0

        lea r10,[rdx-8]                 ;r10 = &x[i - 1] for Loop2
        cmp r8,NSE                      ;is n >= NSE?
        jb Loop2                        ;jump if no (n >= 2 from first cmp)
        lea r10,[rdx-NSE*8]             ;r10 = &x[i - NSE] for Loop1

; Calculate packed sums using SIMD addition
Loop1:  add r10,NSE*8                   ;r10 = &x[i]
        vaddpd ymm5,ymm5,[r10]          ;update packed sums
        sub r8,NSE                      ;n -= NSE
        cmp r8,NSE                      ;is n >= NSE?
        jae Loop1                       ;jump if yes

; Reduce packed sums to scalar value
        vextractf128 xmm1,ymm5,1        ;extract upper 2 packed sums
        vaddpd xmm2,xmm1,xmm5           ;xmm2 = 2 packed sums
        vhaddpd xmm5,xmm2,xmm2          ;xmm5[63:0] = scalar sum
```

313

```
        test r8,r8                          ;is n == 0?
        jz CalcMN                           ;jump if yes
        add r10,NSE*8-8                     ;r10 = &x[i - 1]

; Add remaining elements in x[] to sum
Loop2:  add r10,8                           ;r10 = &x[i]
        vaddsd xmm5,xmm5,real8 ptr [r10]    ;sum += x[i]
        sub r8,1                            ;n -= 1
        jnz Loop2                           ;repeat until n == 0 is true

; Calculate mean
CalcMN: vcvtsi2sd xmm0,xmm0,r9              ;convert n to SPFP
        vdivsd xmm1,xmm5,xmm0               ;mean = sum / n
        vmovsd real8 ptr [rcx],xmm1         ;save mean

        mov eax,1                           ;set success code
        vzeroupper                          ;clear upper YMM/ZMM bits
        ret

BadArg: xor eax,eax                         ;set error return code
        ret


CalcMeanF64_avx endp

;-----------------------------------------------------------------------------
; bool CalcStDevF64_avx(double* st_dev, const double* x, size_t n, double mean);
;-----------------------------------------------------------------------------


CalcStDevF64_avx proc

; Validate arguments
        cmp r8,2                            ;is n >= 2?
        jb BadArg                           ;jump if no
        test rdx,01fh                       ;is x 32b aligned?
        jnz BadArg                          ;jump if no

; Initialize
        mov r9,r8                           ;save copy of n
        vxorpd ymm5,ymm5,ymm5               ;packed (4 doubles) sums_sqs = 0.0

        vmovsd real8 ptr [rsp+8],xmm3       ;save mean for broadcast
        vbroadcastsd ymm4,real8 ptr [rsp+8] ;ymm4 = packed mean

        lea r10,[rdx-8]                     ;r10 = &x[i - 1] for Loop2
        cmp r8,NSE                          ;is n >= NSE?
        jb Loop4                            ;jump if no (n >= 2 from first cmp)
        lea r10,[rdx-NSE*8]                 ;r10 = &x[i - NSE] for Loop1

; Calculate packed sums-of-squares using SIMD arithmetic
Loop3:  add r10,NSE*8                       ;r10 = &x[i]
        vmovapd ymm0,ymmword ptr [r10]      ;load elements x[i:i+7]
        vsubpd ymm1,ymm0,ymm4               ;ymm1 = packed x[i] - mean
```

```
        vmulpd ymm1,ymm1,ymm1              ;ymm1 = packed (x[i] - mean) ** 2
        vaddpd ymm5,ymm5,ymm1              ;update packed sum_sqs

        sub r8,NSE                         ;n -= NSE
        cmp r8,NSE                         ;n >= NSE?
        jae Loop3                          ;jump if yes

; Reduce packed sum_sqs to single value
        vextractf128 xmm1,ymm5,1           ;extract upper 2 packed sum_sqs
        vaddpd xmm2,xmm1,xmm5              ;xmm2 = 2 packed sum_sqs
        vhaddpd xmm5,xmm2,xmm2            ;xmm3[63:0] = sum_sqs

        test r8,r8                         ;is n >= 0?
        jz CalcSD                          ;jump if yes
        add r10,NSE*8-8                     ;r10 = &x[i - 1]

; Add remaining elements in x[] to sum_sqs
Loop4:  add r10,8                          ;r10 = &x[i]
        vmovsd xmm0,real8 ptr [r10]        ;load x[i]
        vsubsd xmm1,xmm0,xmm4              ;xmm1 = x[i] - mean
        vmulsd xmm2,xmm1,xmm1              ;xmm2 = (x[i] - mean) ** 2
        vaddsd xmm5,xmm5,xmm2              ;update sum_sqs

        sub r8,1                           ;n -= 1
        jnz Loop4                          ;repeat until n == 0 is true

; Calculate standard deviation
CalcSD: sub r9,1                           ;r9 = n - 1
        vcvtsi2sd xmm0,xmm0,r9             ;convert n - 1 to SPFP
        vdivsd xmm1,xmm5,xmm0             ;var = sum_sqs / (n - 1)
        vsqrtsd xmm2,xmm2,xmm1           ;sd = sqrt(var)
        vmovsd real8 ptr [rcx],xmm2       ;save sd

        mov eax,1                          ;set success code
        vzeroupper                         ;clear upper YMM/ZMM bits
        ret

BadArg: xor eax,eax                        ;set error return code
        ret


CalcStDevF64_avx endp
        end
```

Execution of Loop1 commences with an add r10,NSE*8 instruction that points R10 to the next set of elements in array x. The vaddpd ymm5,ymm5,[r10] instruction that follows adds elements x[i:i+NSE-1] to the intermediate sums maintained in register YMM5. Following execution of Loop1, the four intermediate double-precision sums in register YMM5 are reduced to a scalar value using the instruction triplet vextractf128 xmm1,ymm5,1, vaddpd xmm2,xmm1,xmm5, and vhaddpd xmm5,xmm2,xmm2. The vextractf128 (Extract Floating-Point Values) instruction copies 128 bits of packed floating-point data from its first source operand to the destination operand. The immediate operand specifies which bits (0 = bits 127:0, 1 = bits 255:128) should be copied. Figure 9-2 illustrates the sequence of instruction that CalcMeanF64_avx() uses to reduce the packed double-precision intermediate sums in register YMM5 to a scalar value.

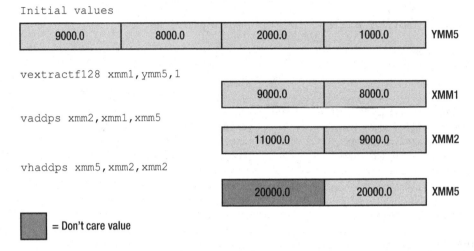

Initial values

Figure 9-2. Reduction of four double-precision floating-point values to a scalar in `CalcMeanF64_avx()`

Following the reduction operation, `CalcMeanF64_avx()` executes Loop2, which adds any residual elements from array x to the scalar double-precision sum in register XMM5. The ensuing instruction triplet `vcvtsi2sd xmm0,xmm0,r9`, `vdivsd xmm1,xmm5,xmm0`, and `vmovsd real8 ptr [rcx],xmm1` calculates and saves the mean value.

Also shown in Listing 9-4a is function `CalcStDevF64_avx()`, which computes the standard deviation. The code arrangement of this function is similar to `CalcMeanF64_avx()` but with a few minor changes. In the initialization code block, `CalcStDevF64_avx()` employs the instruction pair `vmovsd real8 ptr [rsp+8],xmm3` and `vbroadcastsd ymm4,real8 ptr [rsp+8]` to copy argument value mean (XMM3) into each element position of YMM4. The reason for temporarily copying mean onto the stack (in the home area) prior to the broadcast operation is that the AVX `vbroadcastsd` instruction requires a source operand in memory. (On processors that support AVX2, the source operand for a `vbroadcastsd` instruction can also be an XMM register.)

In function `CalcStDevF64_avx()`, each iteration of for-loop Loop3 calculates packed sums-of-squares using elements x[i:i+NSE-1]. Following execution of Loop3, the packed sums-of-squares in YMM5 are reduced to a scalar value using the same sequence of `vextractf128`, `vaddpd`, and `vhaddpd` instructions that you saw in `CalcMeanF64_avx()`. For-loop Loop4 processes any residual elements. The final code block in `CalcStDevF64_avx()` calculates and saves the standard deviation.

Listing 9-4b shows the NASM code for example Ch09_04. This code closely resembles the MASM code except for the specific argument registers used. Note that in function `CalcStDevF64_avx()`, argument value mean is passed via register XMM0. Also note in the initialization code block that argument value mean is copied to the stack's red zone so that it can be used as a source operand with the `vbroadcastsd` instruction.

Listing 9-4b. Example Ch09_04 NASM Code

```
;---------------------------------------------------------------------------
; Ch09_04 fasm.s
;---------------------------------------------------------------------------

        %include "ModX86Asm3eNASM.inc"


;---------------------------------------------------------------------------
; bool CalcMeanF64_avx(float* mean, const float* x, size_t n);
;---------------------------------------------------------------------------
```

```
NSE       equ 4                                 ;number of SIMD elements per iteration

          section .text

          global CalcMeanF64_avx
CalcMeanF64_avx:

; Validate arguments
          cmp rdx,2                             ;is n >= 2?
          jb BadAr1                             ;jump if no
          test rsi,01fh                         ;is x 32b aligned?
          jnz BadAr1                            ;jump if no

; Initialize
          mov r9,rdx                            ;save copy of n
          vxorpd ymm5,ymm5,ymm5                 ;packed (4 DPFP) sums = 0.0

          lea r10,[rsi-8]                       ;r10 = &x[i - 1] for Loop2
          cmp rdx,NSE                           ;is n >= NSE?
          jb Loop2                              ;jump if no (n >= 2 from first cmp)
          lea r10,[rsi-NSE*8]                   ;r10 = &x[i - NSE] for Loop1

; Calculate packed sums using SIMD addition
Loop1:    add r10,NSE*8                         ;r10 = &x[i]
          vaddpd ymm5,ymm5,[r10]                ;update packed sums
          sub rdx,NSE                           ;n -= NSE
          cmp rdx,NSE                           ;is n >= NSE?
          jae Loop1                             ;jump if yes

; Reduce packed sums to scalar value
          vextractf128 xmm1,ymm5,1              ;extract upper 2 packed sums
          vaddpd xmm2,xmm1,xmm5                 ;xmm2 = 2 packed sums
          vhaddpd xmm5,xmm2,xmm2                ;xmm5[63:0] = scalar sum

          test rdx,rdx                          ;is n == 0?
          jz CalcMN                             ;jump if yes
          add r10,NSE*8-8                       ;r10 = &x[i - 1]

; Add remaining elements in x[] to sum
Loop2:    add r10,8                             ;r10 = &x[i]
          vaddsd xmm5,xmm5,[r10]                ;sum += x[i]
          sub rdx,1                             ;n -= 1
          jnz Loop2                             ;repeat until n == 0 is true

; Calculate mean
CalcMN:   vcvtsi2sd xmm0,xmm0,r9                ;convert n to SPFP
          vdivsd xmm1,xmm5,xmm0                 ;mean = sum / n
          vmovsd [rdi],xmm1                     ;save mean

          mov eax,1                             ;set success code
          vzeroupper                            ;clear upper YMM/ZMM bits
          ret
```

```
BadAr1: xor eax,eax                       ;set error return code
        ret


;-------------------------------------------------------------------------
; bool CalcStDevF64_avx(float* st_dev, const float* x, size_t n, float mean);
;-------------------------------------------------------------------------

        global CalcStDevF64_avx
CalcStDevF64_avx:

; Validate arguments
        cmp rdx,2                         ;is n >= 2?
        jb BadAr2                         ;jump if no
        test rsi,01fh                     ;is x 32b aligned?
        jnz BadAr2                        ;jump if no

; Initialize
        mov r9,rdx                        ;save copy of n
        vxorpd ymm5,ymm5,ymm5             ;packed (4 doubles) sums_sqs = 0.0

        vmovsd [rsp-8],xmm0               ;save mean for broadcast
        vbroadcastsd ymm4,[rsp-8]         ;ymm4 = packed mean

        lea r10,[rsi-8]                   ;r10 = &x[i - 1] for Loop2
        cmp rdx,NSE                       ;is n >= NSE?
        jb Loop4                          ;jump if no (n >= 2 from first cmp)
        lea r10,[rsi-NSE*8]               ;r10 = &x[i - NSE] for Loop1

; Calculate packed sums-of-squares using SIMD arithmetic
Loop3:  add r10,NSE*8                     ;r10 = &x[i]
        vmovapd ymm0,[r10]                ;load elements x[i:i+7]
        vsubpd ymm1,ymm0,ymm4             ;ymm1 = packed x[i] - mean
        vmulpd ymm1,ymm1,ymm1             ;ymm1 = packed (x[i] - mean) ** 2
        vaddpd ymm5,ymm5,ymm1             ;update packed sum_sqs

        sub rdx,NSE                       ;n -= NSE
        cmp rdx,NSE                       ;n >= NSE?
        jae Loop3                         ;jump if yes

; Reduce packed sum_sqs to single value
        vextractf128 xmm1,ymm5,1          ;extract upper 2 packed sum_sqs
        vaddpd xmm2,xmm1,xmm5             ;xmm2 = 2 packed sum_sqs
        vhaddpd xmm5,xmm2,xmm2            ;xmm3[63:0] = sum_sqs

        test rdx,rdx                      ;is n >= 0?
        jz CalcSD                         ;jump if yes
        add r10,NSE*8-8                   ;r10 = &x[i - 1]

; Add remaining elements in x[] to sum_sqs
Loop4:  add r10,8                         ;r10 = &x[i]
        vmovsd xmm0,[r10]                 ;load x[i]
```

```
        vsubsd xmm1,xmm0,xmm4          ;xmm1 = x[i] - mean
        vmulsd xmm2,xmm1,xmm1          ;xmm2 = (x[i] - mean) ** 2
        vaddsd xmm5,xmm5,xmm2          ;update sum_sqs

        sub rdx,1                      ;n -= 1
        jnz Loop4                      ;repeat until n == 0 is true

; Calculate standard deviation
CalcSD: sub r9,1                       ;r9 = n - 1
        vcvtsi2sd xmm0,xmm0,r9         ;convert n - 1 to SPFP
        vdivsd xmm1,xmm5,xmm0          ;var = sum_sqs / (n - 1)
        vsqrtsd xmm2,xmm2,xmm1         ;sd = sqrt(var)
        vmovsd [rdi],xmm2              ;save sd

        mov eax,1                      ;set success code
        vzeroupper                     ;clear upper YMM/ZMM bits
        ret

BadAr2: xor eax,eax                    ;set error return code
        ret
```

You may recall from example Ch08_06 (Listings 8-6b and 8-6c) that the primary calculating loop was partially unrolled, which often results in improved performance. The same optimization strategy also could be employed in functions CalcMeanF64_avx() and CalcStDev_avx(). For this example, I decided against doing this to simplify the code. You'll see examples of partial loop unrolls using floating-point SIMD arithmetic in later chapters. Here are the results for source code example Ch09_04:

```
----- Results for Ch09_04 -----
n:              91
mean1:    49.602157  st_dev1:  27.758245
mean2:    49.602157  st_dev2:  27.758245
```

Distance Calculations

The next source code example, named Ch09_05, demonstrates how to calculate 2D Euclidean distances using double-precision floating-point arrays of coordinate points. It also illustrates how to implement a SIMD ternary operator using AVX instructions. Listing 9-5a shows the C++ code for example Ch09_05.

Listing 9-5a. Example Ch09_05 C++ Code

```cpp
//-----------------------------------------------------------------------------
// Ch09_05.h
//-----------------------------------------------------------------------------

#pragma once
#include <cstddef>

// Ch09_05_fasm.asm, Ch09_05_fasm.s
extern "C" bool CalcDistances_avx(double* d, const double* x1, const double* y1,
    const double* x2, const double* y2, size_t n, double thresh);
```

319

```cpp
// Ch09_05_fcpp.cpp
extern bool CalcDistances_cpp(double* d, const double* x1, const double* y1,
    const double* x2, const double* y2, size_t n, double thresh);

// Ch09_05_misc.cpp
extern "C" bool CheckArgs(const double* d, const double* x1, const double* y1,
    const double* x2, const double* y2, size_t n);

extern void DisplayResults(const double* d1, const double* d2, const double* x1,
    const double* y1, const double* x2, const double* y2, size_t n, double thresh);

extern void InitArrays(double* x1, double* y1, double* x2, double* y2, size_t n);

// Miscellaneous constants
constexpr size_t c_Alignment = 32;
constexpr size_t c_NumPoints = 20;        // Must be > 0 and evely divisble by 4
constexpr double c_Thresh = 25.0;

//----------------------------------------------------------------------------
// Ch09_05_misc.cpp
//----------------------------------------------------------------------------

#include <iostream>
#include <iomanip>
#include <string>
#include <cmath>
#include <random>
#include "Ch09_05.h"
#include "AlignedMem.h"

bool CheckArgs(const double* d, const double* x1, const double* y1,
    const double* x2, const double* y2, size_t n)
{
    if (n == 0 || (n % 4) != 0)
        return false;

    if (!AlignedMem::IsAligned(d, c_Alignment))
        return false;
    if (!AlignedMem::IsAligned(x1, c_Alignment))
        return false;
    if (!AlignedMem::IsAligned(y1, c_Alignment))
        return false;
    if (!AlignedMem::IsAligned(x2, c_Alignment))
        return false;
    if (!AlignedMem::IsAligned(y2, c_Alignment))
        return false;

    return true;
}
```

```cpp
void DisplayResults(const double* d1, const double* d2, const double* x1,
    const double* y1, const double* x2, const double* y2, size_t n, double thresh)
{
    constexpr int w = 9;
    constexpr char nl = '\n';

    std::cout << std::fixed << std::setprecision(4);
    std::cout << "----- Results for Ch09_05 (thresh = " << thresh;
    std::cout << ") -----\n\n";

    std::cout << std::setw(w) << "x1" << " ";
    std::cout << std::setw(w) << "y1" << " ";
    std::cout << std::setw(w) << "x2" << " ";
    std::cout << std::setw(w) << "y2" << " |";
    std::cout << std::setw(w) << "d1" << " ";
    std::cout << std::setw(w) << "d2" << nl;
    std::cout << std::string(60, '-') << nl;

    for (size_t i = 0; i < n; i++)
    {
        std::cout << std::setw(w) << x1[i] << " ";
        std::cout << std::setw(w) << y1[i] << " ";
        std::cout << std::setw(w) << x2[i] << " ";
        std::cout << std::setw(w) << y2[i] << " |";
        std::cout << std::setw(w) << d1[i] << " ";
        std::cout << std::setw(w) << d2[i] << nl;

        if (fabs(d1[i] - d2[i]) > 1.0e-9)
        {
            std::cout << "compare check failed\n";
            break;
        }
    }
}


void InitArrays(double* x1, double* y1, double* x2, double* y2, size_t n)
{
    constexpr unsigned int rng_seed = 39;
    constexpr double min_val = 1.0;
    constexpr double max_val = 75.0;

    std::mt19937 rng {rng_seed};
    std::uniform_real_distribution<double> dist {min_val, max_val};

    for (size_t i = 0; i < n; i++)
    {
        x1[i] = dist(rng);
        y1[i] = dist(rng);
        x2[i] = dist(rng);
        y2[i] = dist(rng);
    }
}
```

```cpp
//-------------------------------------------------------------------------
// Ch09_05.cpp
//-------------------------------------------------------------------------

#include "Ch09_05.h"
#include "AlignedMem.h"

static void CalcDistances(void)
{
    // Allocate and initialize test arrays
    constexpr size_t n = c_NumPoints;

    AlignedArray<double> x1_aa(n, c_Alignment);
    AlignedArray<double> y1_aa(n, c_Alignment);
    AlignedArray<double> x2_aa(n, c_Alignment);
    AlignedArray<double> y2_aa(n, c_Alignment);
    AlignedArray<double> d1_aa(n, c_Alignment);
    AlignedArray<double> d2_aa(n, c_Alignment);

    double* x1 = x1_aa.Data();
    double* y1 = y1_aa.Data();
    double* x2 = x2_aa.Data();
    double* y2 = y2_aa.Data();
    double* d1 = d1_aa.Data();
    double* d2 = d2_aa.Data();

    InitArrays(x1, y1, x2, y2, n);

    // Calculate distances
    CalcDistances_cpp(d1, x1, y1, x2, y2, n, c_Thresh);
    CalcDistances_avx(d2, x1, y1, x2, y2, n, c_Thresh);

    // Display results
    DisplayResults(d1, d2, x1, y1, x2, y2, n, c_Thresh);
}

int main(void)
{
    CalcDistances();
    return 0;
}
```

Listing 9-5a starts with the C++ header file Ch09_05.h. Note that function CheckArgs() is declared using the "C" modifier since it's called from the assembly language code. The definition of CheckArgs() is located in file Ch09_05_misc.cpp along with two other miscellaneous functions: DisplayResults() and InitArrays().

The Euclidean distance between two coordinate positions on a 2D grid can be calculated using the following formula:

$$dist = \sqrt{\left(x_1 - x_2\right)^2 + \left(y_1 - y_2\right)^2}$$

In Listing 9-5a, file Ch09_05_fcpp.cpp contains a function named CalcDistances_cpp(). This function contains C++ code that computes 2D Euclidean distance values. Note that CalcDistances_cpp() utilizes CheckArgs() for argument validation. Also note in the for-loop that each calculated distance is compared to a threshold value. If dist >= thresh is true, then d[i] = dist * -1.0; otherwise, d[i] = dist. This ternary expression is included for demonstration purposes. The assembly language function CalcDistances_avx() performs the same computation using AVX SIMD instructions.

Also shown in Listing 9-5a is file Ch09_05.cpp. In this file, the static function CalcDistances() uses template class AlignedArray<> to allocate aligned arrays for the 2D coordinate and distance values. Note that raw C++ pointers are passed to the distance calculating functions CalcDistances_cpp() and CalcDistances_avx().

Listing 9-5b shows the MASM code for example Ch09_05. In this file, function CalcDistances_avx() opens with a formal prologue that exploits macros CreateFrame_M and SaveXmmRegs_M to create a stack frame and preserve values in non-volatile general-purpose and XMM registers. A stack frame is created here since CalcDistances_avx() is a non-leaf function. Following its prologue, CalcDistances_avx() employs a series of mov instructions that copy argument values d, x1, x2, y1, and y2 to non-volatile registers RBX, R12, R13, R14, and R15. The mov instructions are necessary to preserve any argument values passed via volatile registers prior to calling CheckArgs().

Listing 9-5b. Example Ch09_05 MASM Code

```
;-----------------------------------------------------------------------------
; Ch09_05_fasm.asm
;-----------------------------------------------------------------------------

        include <cmpequ_fp.asmh>
        include <MacrosX86-64-AVX.asmh>


        .const
F64_minus1   real8 -1.0


;-----------------------------------------------------------------------------
; bool CalcDistances_avx(double* d, const double* x1, const double* y1,
;    const double* x2, const double* y2, size_t n, double thresh);
;-----------------------------------------------------------------------------


NSE      equ 4                       ;num simd elements per iteration

        extern CheckArgs:proc

        .code
CalcDistances_avx proc frame

; Function prologue
        CreateFrame_M CD_,0,32,rbx,r12,r13,r14,r15
        SaveXmmRegs_M xmm14,xmm15
        EndProlog_M

; Copy arguments in volatile registers to non-volatile registers
        mov rbx,rcx                         ;rbx = d
        mov r12,rdx                         ;r12 = x1
        mov r13,r8                          ;r13 = y1
```

```
        mov r14,r9                                      ;r14 = x2
        mov r15,[rbp+CD_OffsetStackArgs]                ;r15 = y2

; Make sure the arguments are valid. Note that arguments d, x1, y1, and x2 are
; already in the correct registers for CheckArgs().
        mov rax,[rbp+CD_OffsetStackArgs+8]              ;rax = n
        push rax                                        ;copy n to stack
        push r15                                        ;copy y2 to stack
        sub rsp,32                                      ;create home area
        call CheckArgs
        or eax,eax                                      ;valid arguments?
        jz BadArg                                       ;jump if CheckArgs() failed


;-----------------------------------------------------------------------------
; Registers used in code below:
;
; rax = array offset       rbx = d          r10 = n          r12 = x1
; r13 = y1                  r14 = x2         r15 = y2
;
; ymm14 = packed thresh     ymm15 = packed -1.0
;-----------------------------------------------------------------------------

; Initialize
        mov rax,-NSE*8                                  ;array offset
        mov r10,[rbp+CD_OffsetStackArgs+8]              ;r10 = n
        vbroadcastsd ymm14,real8 ptr [rbp+CD_OffsetStackArgs+16]  ;packed thresh
        vbroadcastsd ymm15,real8 ptr [F64_minus1]       ;packed -1.0

; Calculate distances using SIMD arithmetic
Loop1:  add rax,NSE*8                                   ;rax = offset to next elements

        vmovapd ymm0,ymmword ptr [r12+rax]              ;ymm0 = x1[i:i+NSE-1]
        vsubpd ymm1,ymm0,[r14+rax]                      ;ymm1 = x1 - x2
        vmulpd ymm1,ymm1,ymm1                           ;ymm1 = (x1 - x2) ** 2

        vmovapd ymm2,ymmword ptr [r13+rax]              ;ymm2 = y1[i:i+NSE-1]
        vsubpd ymm3,ymm2,[r15+rax]                      ;ymm3 = y1 - y2
        vmulpd ymm3,ymm3,ymm3                           ;ymm3 = (y1 - y1) ** 2

        vaddpd ymm4,ymm1,ymm3                           ;(x1 - x2) ** 2 + (y1 - y1) ** 2
        vsqrtpd ymm0,ymm4                               ;distance (dist in C++ code)

; Calculate d = (temp3 >= thresh) ? temp3 * -1.0 : temp3; using SIMD arithmetic
        vcmppd ymm1,ymm0,ymm14,CMP_GE_OQ                ;compare raw dist to thresh
        vandpd ymm2,ymm1,ymm15                          ;ymm2 = -1.0 (compare true) or 0.0
        vmulpd ymm3,ymm2,ymm0                           ;ymm3 = -1.0 * dist or 0.0
        vandnpd ymm4,ymm1,ymm0                          ;ymm4 = 0.0 or dist
        vorpd ymm5,ymm3,ymm4                            ;ymm5 = final result
        vmovapd ymmword ptr [rbx+rax],ymm5              ;save result to d[i:i+NSE-1]
```

```
        sub r10,NSE                          ;n -= NSE
        jnz Loop1                            ;jump if yes

        mov eax,1                            ;set success return code

; Function epilogue
Done:   vzeroupper
        RestoreXmmRegs_M xmm14,xmm15
        DeleteFrame_M rbx,r12,r13,r14,r15    ;delete stack frame and restore regs
        ret

BadArg: xor eax,eax                          ;set errror return code
        jmp Done


CalcDistances_avx endp
        end
```

The next code block in CalcDistances_avx() includes instructions that call CheckArgs() to perform argument validation. Note that prior to the call CheckArgs instruction, argument values n and y2 are pushed onto the stack; the other argument values for CheckArgs() are already loaded in the correct registers. Also note the sub rsp,32 instruction, which allocates the stack home area for CheckArgs(). Following execution of CheckArgs(), CalcDistances_avx() skips over the calculating code if CheckArgs() returned an error code. You may have noticed that CalcDistances_avx() does not include any RSP adjustment instructions following the call to CheckArgs(). This is one advantage of using a stack frame pointer. Macro DeleteFrame_M, employed in the epilogue, uses the value in register RBP to ensure that RSP is properly set prior to restoring the specified non-volatile general-purpose registers as explained in Chapter 6 (see Figure 6-4 and the code for macro DeleteFrame_M in file MacrosX86-64-AVX.asmh).

Located above the start of Loop1 is an initialization code block. Note the use of the vbroadcastsd instructions that create packed versions of argument value thresh and floating-point constant –1.0 in registers YMM14 and YMM15, respectively. Each iteration of Loop1 begins with an add rax,NSE*8 instruction that updates the common array offset value in register RAX for the next set of coordinate calculations. The ensuing three code blocks calculate dist[i:i+3] using AVX packed double-precision floating-point instructions. Note that following these calculations, register YMM0 contains four distance values.

Figure 9-3 illustrates execution of the AVX instructions that perform the SIMD ternary operation in for-loop Loop1. Looking at the code in Listing 9-5b, the SIMD ternary operation starts with a vcmppd ymm1,ymm0,ymm14,CMP_GE_OQ instruction that compares each element in YMM0 to thresh. Execution of this instruction sets the corresponding element in YMM1 to 0xFFFFFFFFFFFFFFFF if dist >= thresh is true; otherwise, the element is set to 0x0000000000000000. The vandpd ymm2,ymm1,ymm15 instruction loads –1.0 or 0.0 into each element of YMM2, and the subsequent vmulpd ymm3,ymm2,ymm0 instruction loads -1.0 * dist or 0.0 into each element of YMM3. Execution of the vandnpd ymm4,ymm1,ymm0 (Bitwise Logical AND NOT of Packed DPFP Values) instruction loads 0.0 or dist into each element of YMM4 (the vandnpd instruction calculates ~ymm1 & ymm0). This is followed by a vorpd ymm5,ymm3,ymm4 instruction that completes the SIMD ternary calculation. An important takeaway point from the code in CalcDistances_avx() is that a function can carry out data-dependent SIMD logic decisions using common Boolean operations. You'll see additional examples of this in later chapters.

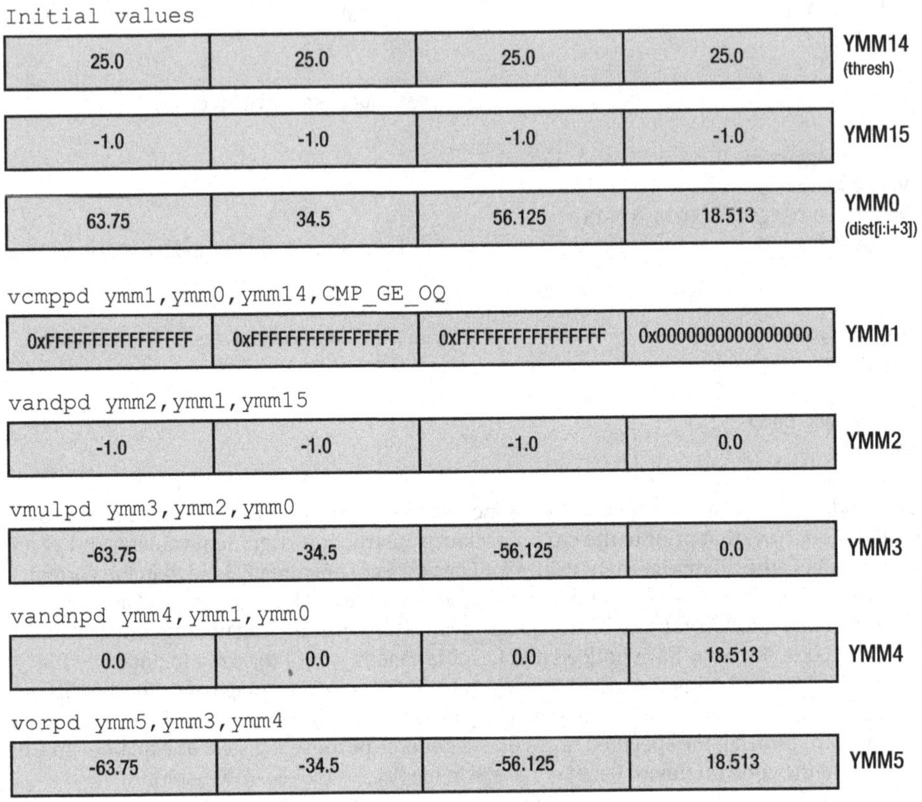

Initial values

| 25.0 | 25.0 | 25.0 | 25.0 | YMM14
(thresh) |

| -1.0 | -1.0 | -1.0 | -1.0 | YMM15 |

| 63.75 | 34.5 | 56.125 | 18.513 | YMM0
(dist[i:i+3]) |

vcmppd ymm1,ymm0,ymm14,CMP_GE_OQ

| 0xFFFFFFFFFFFFFFFF | 0xFFFFFFFFFFFFFFFF | 0xFFFFFFFFFFFFFFFF | 0x0000000000000000 | YMM1 |

vandpd ymm2,ymm1,ymm15

| -1.0 | -1.0 | -1.0 | 0.0 | YMM2 |

vmulpd ymm3,ymm2,ymm0

| -63.75 | -34.5 | -56.125 | 0.0 | YMM3 |

vandnpd ymm4,ymm1,ymm0

| 0.0 | 0.0 | 0.0 | 18.513 | YMM4 |

vorpd ymm5,ymm3,ymm4

| -63.75 | -34.5 | -56.125 | 18.513 | YMM5 |

Figure 9-3. *SIMD ternary calculation used in* CalcDistances_avx()

Listing 9-5c shows the NASM code for example Ch09_05. In this listing, execution of function CalcDistances_avx() opens with a prologue that employs a series of push instructions to preserve non-volatile registers RBX, R12, R13, R14, and R15 on the stack. The ensuing sub rsp,16 instruction allocates 16 bytes of stack space for temporary storage. An explicit instruction is used here to adjust RSP since the red zone is not available (CheckDistances_avx() is a non-leaf function). Following the saving of argument values n and thresh on the stack (these values are in volatile registers), CheckDistances_avx() calls CheckArgs() to perform argument validation. Note that argument values d, x1, x2, y1, y2, and n are already loaded in the correct registers for CheckArgs().

Listing 9-5c. Example Ch09_05 NASM Code

```
;-----------------------------------------------------------------------
; Ch09_05 fasm.s
;-----------------------------------------------------------------------

        %include "ModX86Asm3eNASM.inc"
        %include "cmpequ_fp.inc"

        section .rdata
F64_minus1  dq  -1.0
```

```
;------------------------------------------------------------------------------
; bool CalcDistances_avx(double* d, const double* x1, const double* y1,
;    const double* x2, const double* y2, size_t n, double thresh);
;------------------------------------------------------------------------------

NSE        equ 4                               ;num simd elements per iteration

           section .text
           extern CheckArgs

           global CalcDistances_avx
CalcDistances_avx:
           push rbx                            ;save non-volatile GPRs
           push r12
           push r13
           push r14
           push r15
           sub rsp,16                          ;stack space arg saves

; Copy arguments in volatile registers to non-volatile registers.
; Also save args n and thresh on stack.
           mov rbx,rdi                         ;rbx = d
           mov r12,rsi                         ;r12 = x1
           mov r13,rdx                         ;r13 = y1
           mov r14,rcx                         ;r14 = x2
           mov r15,r8                          ;r15 = y2
           mov [rsp],r9                        ;save n on stack
           vmovsd [rsp+8],xmm0                 ;save thresh on stack

; Make sure the arguments are valid. Note that arguments d, x1, y1, x2,
; y2, and n are already in the correct registers for CheckArgs().
           call CheckArgs
           or eax,eax                          ;valid arguments?
           jz BadArg                           ;jump if CheckArgs() failed

;------------------------------------------------------------------------------
; Registers used in code below:
;
; rax = array offset       rbx = d        r10 = n          r12 = x1
; r13 = y1                  r14 = x2       r15 = y2
;
; ymm14 = packed thresh     ymm15 = packed -1.0
;------------------------------------------------------------------------------

; Initialize
           mov rax,-NSE*8                      ;rax = array offset
           mov r10,[rsp]                       ;r10 = n
           vbroadcastsd ymm14,[rsp+8]          ;packed thresh
           vbroadcastsd ymm15,[F64_minus1]     ;packed -1.0

; Calculate distances using SIMD arithmetic
Loop1:  add rax,NSE*8                          ;rax = offset to next elements
```

```
        vmovapd ymm0,[r12+rax]               ;ymm0 = x1[i:i+NSE-1]
        vsubpd ymm1,ymm0,[r14+rax]           ;ymm1 = x1 - x2
        vmulpd ymm1,ymm1,ymm1                 ;ymm1 = (x1 - x2) ** 2

        vmovapd ymm2,[r13+rax]               ;ymm2 = y1[i:i+NSE-1]
        vsubpd ymm3,ymm2,[r15+rax]           ;ymm3 = y1 - y2
        vmulpd ymm3,ymm3,ymm3                 ;ymm3 = (y1 - y1) ** 2

        vaddpd ymm4,ymm1,ymm3                 ;(x1 - x2) ** 2 + (y1 - y1) ** 2
        vsqrtpd ymm0,ymm4                     ;raw dist (dist in C++ code)

; Calculate d = (temp3 >= thresh) ? temp3 * -1.0 : temp3;
        vcmppd ymm1,ymm0,ymm14,CMP_GE_OQ     ;compare raw dist to thresh
        vandpd ymm2,ymm1,ymm15               ;ymm2 = -1.0 (compare true) or 0.0
        vmulpd ymm3,ymm2,ymm0                 ;ymm3 = -1.0 * dist or 0.0
        vandnpd ymm4,ymm1,ymm0               ;ymm4 = 0.0 or dist
        vorpd ymm5,ymm3,ymm4                  ;ymm5 = final result
        vmovapd [rbx+rax],ymm5               ;save result to d[i:i+NSE-1]

        sub r10,NSE                           ;n -= NSE
        jnz Loop1                             ;jump if yes

        mov eax,1                             ;set success return code

Done:   vzeroupper
        add rsp,16                            ;release local stack space
        pop r15                               ;restore non-volatile registers
        pop r14
        pop r13
        pop r12
        pop rbx
        ret

BadArg: xor eax,eax                           ;set errror return code
        jmp Done
```

The NASM version of CalcDistances_avx() uses the same AVX SIMD instructions as its MASM counterpart in for-loop Loop1. Following execution of Loop1, CalcDistances_avx() employs a formal function epilogue to release the previously allocated local stack space and perform non-volatile general-purpose register restoration. Note the inclusion of the add rsp,16 instruction, which releases the stack storage space and ensures that RSP contains the correct value for the ensuing pop instructions. Here are the results for source code example Ch09_05:

```
----- Results for Ch09_05 (thresh = 25.0000) -----

        x1       y1       x2       y2 |      d1        d2
--------------------------------------------------------------
    1.4193   60.9381   28.1498   62.3203 |  -26.7662  -26.7662
   45.6211   31.3445   17.8668   52.2026 |  -34.7183  -34.7183
   19.3088   69.7241   40.1756   18.2590 |  -55.5345  -55.5345
   35.7644   74.3092   25.8307   19.3251 |  -55.8742  -55.8742
```

26.5019	28.6746	27.3385	51.6712	23.0119	23.0119
22.4397	68.9241	8.9053	19.0044	-51.7219	-51.7219
64.0793	12.0018	37.2446	66.0294	-60.3248	-60.3248
25.2135	24.3822	53.2614	18.4492	-28.6685	-28.6685
33.6993	39.2796	15.6201	56.1528	24.7298	24.7298
51.2222	26.2416	21.9895	17.1022	-30.6281	-30.6281
49.3491	62.0335	37.7140	10.1119	-53.2093	-53.2093
67.8222	21.8987	19.2436	59.0732	-61.1704	-61.1704
38.9824	32.9499	34.2359	56.1616	23.6920	23.6920
36.6898	63.5419	36.8821	74.6301	11.0899	11.0899
26.4318	3.7547	40.6940	32.9107	-32.4574	-32.4574
17.2157	29.4545	12.5259	29.1989	4.6967	4.6967
17.4332	16.3869	58.3692	31.8759	-43.7684	-43.7684
35.8889	17.8839	16.9624	65.8577	-51.5722	-51.5722
50.4938	43.9717	61.8307	24.9722	22.1248	22.1248
10.0090	42.7649	25.1586	61.5460	24.1297	24.1297

Packed Floating-Point Arithmetic – Matrices

In Chapter 4, you studied a source code example that illustrated how to reference the elements of an integer matrix using x86-64 assembly language (see example Ch04_03). Recall that the elements of a C++ matrix in memory are organized using row-major ordering. For example, elements of the C++ matrix double x[3][3] are stored in memory as follows: x[0][0], x[0][1], x[0][2], x[1][0], x[1][1], x[1][2], x[2][0], x[2][1], and x[2][2]. To access a specific element in a matrix, a function (or C++ compiler) must know the starting address of the matrix (i.e., the address of its first element), the row and column indices, the total number of columns, and the size in bytes of each element. Using this information, a function can use simple integer arithmetic to calculate the unique address of a specific matrix element.

Column Means

The final source code example of this chapter, named Ch09_06, uses AVX SIMD instructions to calculate column means of a double-precision floating-point matrix. Listing 9-6a shows the C++ source code for example Ch09_06.

Listing 9-6a. Example Ch09_06 C++ Code

```
//-------------------------------------------------------------------------
// Ch09_06.h
//-------------------------------------------------------------------------

#pragma once
#include <cstddef>
#include <vector>

// Ch09_06_fasm.asm, Ch09_06_fasm.s
extern "C" void CalcColMeansF64_avx(double* col_means, const double* x,
    size_t nrows, size_t ncols);
```

```cpp
// Ch09_06_fcpp.cpp
extern void CalcColMeansF64_cpp(double* col_means, const double* x,
    size_t nrows, size_t ncols);

// Ch09_06_misc.cpp
extern void DisplayResults(std::vector<double>& col_means1,
    std::vector<double>& col_means2, std::vector<double>& x, size_t nrows,
    size_t ncols);

extern void InitMatrix(std::vector<double>& x, size_t nrows, size_t ncols);

// Miscellaneous constants
constexpr size_t c_NumRows = 21;
constexpr size_t c_NumCols = 15;
constexpr unsigned int c_RngSeed = 41;
constexpr double c_MatrixFillMin = 1.0;
constexpr double c_MatrixFillMax = 80.0;

//-----------------------------------------------------------------------
// Ch09_06_misc.cpp
//-----------------------------------------------------------------------

#include <iostream>
#include <iomanip>
#include "Ch09_06.h"
#include "MT.h"

void DisplayResults(std::vector<double>& col_means1,
    std::vector<double>& col_means2, std::vector<double>& x, size_t nrows,
    size_t ncols)
{
    constexpr int w = 5;
    constexpr char nl = '\n';

    std::cout << std::fixed << std::setprecision(1);
    std::cout << "----- Results for Ch09_06 -----\n";

    for (size_t i = 0; i < nrows; i++)
    {
        for (size_t j = 0; j < ncols; j++)
            std::cout << std::setw(w) << x[i * ncols + j] << " ";
        std::cout << nl;
    }

    std::cout << nl;

    for (size_t j = 0; j < ncols; j++)
        std::cout << std::setw(w) << col_means1[j] << " ";
    std::cout << nl;
```

```
    for (size_t j = 0; j < ncols; j++)
        std::cout << std::setw(w) << col_means2[j] << " ";
    std::cout << nl;

    if (!MT::CompareVectorsFP(col_means1, col_means2, 1.0e-6))
        std::cout << "MT::CompareVectorsFP() failed\n";
}

void InitMatrix(std::vector<double>& x, size_t nrows, size_t ncols)
{
    MT::FillMatrixFP(x.data(), nrows, ncols, c_MatrixFillMin, c_MatrixFillMax, c_RngSeed);
}

//----------------------------------------------------------------------------
// Ch09_06_fcpp.cpp
//----------------------------------------------------------------------------

#include "Ch09_06.h"

void CalcColMeansF64_cpp(double* col_means, const double* x, size_t nrows,
    size_t ncols)
{
    // Initialize col_means
    for (size_t j = 0; j < ncols; j++)
        col_means[j] = 0.0;

    // Calculate column sums
    for (size_t i = 0; i < nrows; i++)
    {
        for (size_t j = 0; j < ncols; j++)
            col_means[j] += x[i * ncols + j];
    }

    // Calculate column means
    for (size_t j = 0; j < ncols; j++)
        col_means[j] /= (double)nrows;
}
```

Most of the C++ code in Listing 9-6a is mundane, but a few particulars warrant some comments. File Ch09_06_fcpp.cpp contains a function named CalcColMeansF64_cpp(). This function calculates column means for matrix x using elementary for-loops. Note that the middle two for-loops use col_means to compute sums for each column in matrix x. Following calculation of the column sum, each entry in col_means is divided by nrows to determine the correct column mean. In file Ch09_06.cpp, static function CalcColMeansF64() uses C++ STL class std::vector to instantiate storage for matrix x, col_means1, and col_means2. However, raw C++ pointers are passed to the column mean calculating functions CalcColMeansF64_cpp() and CalcColMeansF64_avx().

Listing 9-6b shows the MASM code for example Ch09_06. Function CalcColMeansF64_avx() begins with a short prologue that preserves non-volatile registers RSI and RDI on the stack. Note that the prologue uses MASM directives .pushreg and .endprolog instead of macro CreateFrame_M since CalcColMeansF64_avx() doesn't require a frame pointer. Following its prologue, CalcColMeansF64_avx() validates argument values nrows and ncols for size. It then sets each element in col_means to 0.0 using a rep stosq instruction. Note that registers RDI, RCX, and RAX are initialized with col_means, ncols, and 0x0000000000000000 (which corresponds to 0.0) prior to execution of the stosq instruction.

Listing 9-6b. Example Ch09_06 MASM Code

```
;-------------------------------------------------------------------------
; Ch09_06_fasm.asm
;-------------------------------------------------------------------------


;-------------------------------------------------------------------------
; void CalcColMeansF64_avx(double* col_means, const double* x,
;   size_t nrows, size_t ncols);
;-------------------------------------------------------------------------

NSE     equ 4                           ;num_simd_elements
NSE2    equ 2                           ;num_simd_elements2

        .code
CalcColMeansF64_avx proc frame

; Function prologue
        push rsi
        .pushreg rsi
        push rdi
        .pushreg rdi
        .endprolog

; Validate nrows and ncols
        test r8,r8
        jz Done                         ;jump if nrows == 0
        test r9,r9
        jz Done                         ;jump if ncols == 0

; Initialize all elements in col_means to 0.0
        mov r10,rcx                     ;save col_means for later
        mov rdi,rcx                     ;rdi = col_means
        mov rcx,r9                      ;number of elements in ncol_means
        xor eax,eax                     ;rax = fill value
        rep stosq                       ;fill col_means with 0

;-------------------------------------------------------------------------
; Registers used in code below:
;
; rsi = &x[i][j]           r8  = nrows       rax = scratch register
; rcx = &x[0][0]           r9  = ncols
; rdx = &col_means[j]      r10 = i
; rdi = &col_means[0]      r11 = j
;-------------------------------------------------------------------------
```

```
; Initialize
        mov rcx,rdx                             ;rcx = &x[0][0]
        mov rdi,r10                             ;rdi = &col_means[0]
        xor r10,r10                             ;i = 0

; Repeat Loop1 while i < nrows
Loop1:  cmp r10,r8
        jae CalcCM                              ;jump if i >= nrows

        xor r11,r11                             ;j = 0

; Repeat Loop2 while j < ncols
Loop2:  cmp r11,r9
        jb F1                                   ;jump if j < ncols

        add r10,1                               ;i += 1
        jmp Loop1

; Calculate &x[i][j] and &col_means[j]
F1:     mov rax,r10                             ;rax = i
        mul r9                                  ;rax = i * ncols
        add rax,r11                             ;rax = i * ncols + j
        lea rsi,[rcx+rax*8]                     ;rsi = &x[i][j]
        lea rdx,[rdi+r11*8]                     ;rdx = &col_means[j]

        mov rax,r11                             ;rax = j
        add rax,NSE                             ;rax = j + NSE
        cmp rax,r9
        ja F2                                   ;jump if j + NSE > ncols

; Update sums (4 columns)
        vmovupd ymm0,ymmword ptr [rdx]          ;ymm0 = col_means[j:j+3]
        vaddpd ymm1,ymm0,[rsi]                  ;col_means[j:j+3] += x[i][j:j+3]
        vmovupd ymmword ptr [rdx],ymm1          ;save result

        add r11,NSE                             ;j += NSE
        jmp Loop2

F2:     mov rax,r11                             ;rax = j
        add rax,NSE2                            ;rax = j + NSE2
        cmp rax,r9
        ja F3                                   ;jump if j + NSE2 > ncols

; Update sums (2 columns)
        vmovupd xmm0,xmmword ptr [rdx]          ;xmm0 = col_means[j:j+1]
        vaddpd xmm1,xmm0,[rsi]                  ;col_means[j:j+1] += x[i][j:j+1]
        vmovupd xmmword ptr [rdx],xmm1          ;save result

        add r11,NSE2                            ;j += NSE2
        jmp Loop2
```

```
; Update sums (1 column)
F3:     vmovsd xmm0,real8 ptr [rdx]         ;xmm0 = col_means[j]
        vaddsd xmm1,xmm0,real8 ptr [rsi]    ;col_means[j] += x[i][j]
        vmovsd real8 ptr [rdx],xmm1         ;save result

        add r11,1                           ;j += 1
        jmp Loop2

; Calculate column means
CalcCM: mov rax,-1                           ;j = -1
        vcvtsi2sd xmm2,xmm2,r8              ;xmm2 = nrows (DPFP)

Loop3:  add rax,1                           ;j += 1
        vmovsd xmm0,real8 ptr [rdi+rax*8]   ;col_means[j]
        vdivsd xmm1,xmm0,xmm2               ;mean = col_means[j] / nrows
        vmovsd real8 ptr [rdi+rax*8],xmm1   ;save result

        sub r9,1                            ;ncols -= 1
        jnz Loop3                           ;repeat until done

Done:   vzeroupper
        pop rdi
        pop rsi
        ret
CalcColMeansF64_avx endp
        end
```

To calculate the column means, function CalcColumnMeansF64_avx() must sum the elements of each column and then divide each column sum by the number of rows. The summing calculations are performed in the nested for-loops Loop1 and Loop2. The outer for-loop Loop1 simply cycles through each row of the matrix. Note that prior to the start of Loop2, CalcColumnMeansF64_avx() employs an xor r11,r11 instruction to initialize j = 0.

The summing code in for-loop Loop2 is partitioned to three code blocks. If four or more columns are available, CalcColumnMeansF64_avx() uses the instruction triplet vmovupd ymm0,ymmword ptr [rdx], vaddpd ymm1,ymm0,ymmword ptr [rsi], and vmovupd ymmword ptr [rdx],ymm1 to calculate col_means[j:j+3] += x[i][j:j+3]. The vmovupd (Move Unaligned Packed DPFP Values) instruction is used here since for most matrices, elements x[i][j:j+3] will not be aligned on a 32-byte boundary. If two or more columns are available, the same instruction triplet with XMM register operands is used to calculate col_means[j:j+1] += x[i][j:j+1]. The final code block uses scalar double-precision arithmetic to compute col_means[j] += x[i][j].

Following calculation of the column sums, CalcColMeansF64_avx() executes for-loop Loop3, which utilizes floating-point scalar arithmetic to calculate the column means. SIMD arithmetic could have been used here to calculate the final column means, but this is a one-time calculation so simpler scalar arithmetic is used instead. The extra code complexity of SIMD arithmetic would be warranted if CalcColMeansF64_avx()'s expected use case were to include matrices containing hundreds or thousands of columns. Note the use of the vcvtsi2sd xmm2,xmm2,r8 instruction, which converts nrows from a 64-bit integer to a double-precision floating-point value.

Listing 9-6c shows the NASM code for example Ch09_06. Unlike its MASM counterpart, the NASM version of CalcColMeansF64_avx() doesn't employ a formal function prologue and epilogue since it doesn't need to preserve any non-volatile general-purpose or XMM registers.

Listing 9-6c. Example Ch09_06 NASM Code

```
;------------------------------------------------------------------------
; Ch09_06_fasm.s
;------------------------------------------------------------------------

        %include "ModX86Asm3eNASM.inc"

;------------------------------------------------------------------------
; void CalcColMeansF64_avx(double* col_means, const double* x,
;    size_t nrows, size_t ncols);
;------------------------------------------------------------------------


NSE     equ 4                           ;num_simd_elements
NSE2    equ 2                           ;num_simd_elements2

        section .text

        global CalcColMeansF64_avx
CalcColMeansF64_avx:

; Load args in registers to match use in Ch09_06_fasm.asm
        mov r9,rcx                      ;r9 = ncols
        mov r8,rdx                      ;r8 = nrows
        mov rdx,rsi                     ;rdx = x
        mov rcx,rdi                     ;rcx = col_means

; Validate nrows and ncols
        test r8,r8
        jz Done                         ;jump if nrows == 0
        test r9,r9
        jz Done                         ;jump if ncols == 0

; Initialize all elements in col_means to 0.0
        mov r10,rcx                     ;save col_means for later
        mov rdi,rcx                     ;rdi = col_means
        mov rcx,r9                      ;number of elements in ncol_means
        xor eax,eax                     ;rax = fill value
        rep stosq                       ;fill col_means with 0

;------------------------------------------------------------------------
; Registers used in code below:
;
; rsi = &x[i][j]          r8  = nrows      rax = scratch register
; rcx = &x[0][0]          r9  = ncols
; rdx = &col_means[j]     r10 = i
; rdi = &col_means[0]     r11 = j
;------------------------------------------------------------------------
```

```
; Initialize
        mov rcx,rdx                     ;rcx = &x[0][0]
        mov rdi,r10                     ;rdi = &col_means[0]
        xor r10,r10                     ;i = 0

; Repeat Loop1 while i < nrows
Loop1:  cmp r10,r8
        jae CalcCM                      ;jump if i >= nrows

        xor r11,r11                     ;j = 0

; Repeat Loop2 while j < ncols
Loop2:  cmp r11,r9
        jb F1                           ;jump if j < ncols

        add r10,1                       ;i += 1
        jmp Loop1

; Calculate &x[i][j] and &col_means[j]
F1:     mov rax,r10                     ;rax = i
        mul r9                          ;rax = i * ncols
        add rax,r11                     ;rax = i * ncols + j
        lea rsi,[rcx+rax*8]             ;rsi = &x[i][j]
        lea rdx,[rdi+r11*8]             ;rdx = &col_means[j]

        mov rax,r11                     ;rax = j
        add rax,NSE                     ;rax = j + NSE
        cmp rax,r9
        ja F2                           ;jump if j + NSE > ncols

; Update sums (4 columns)
        vmovupd ymm0,[rdx]              ;ymm0 = col_means[j:j+3]
        vaddpd ymm1,ymm0,[rsi]          ;col_means[j:j+3] += x[i][j:j+3]
        vmovupd [rdx],ymm1              ;save result

        add r11,NSE                     ;j += NSE
        jmp Loop2

F2:     mov rax,r11                     ;rax = j
        add rax,NSE2                    ;rax = j + NSE2
        cmp rax,r9
        ja F3                           ;jump if j + NSE2 > ncols

; Update sums (2 columns)
        vmovupd xmm0,[rdx]              ;xmm0 = col_means[j:j+1]
        vaddpd xmm1,xmm0,[rsi]          ;col_means[j:j+1] += x[i][j:j+1]
        vmovupd [rdx],xmm1              ;save result

        add r11,NSE2                    ;j += NSE2
        jmp Loop2
```

```
; Update sums (1 column)
F3:     vmovsd xmm0,[rdx]                ;xmm0 = col_means[j]
        vaddsd xmm1,xmm0,[rsi]           ;col_means[j] += x[i][j]
        vmovsd [rdx],xmm1                ;save result

        add r11,1                        ;j += 1
        jmp Loop2

; Calculate column means
CalcCM: mov rax,-1                       ;j = -1
        vcvtsi2sd xmm2,xmm2,r8           ;xmm2 = nrows (DPFP)

Loop3:  add rax,1                        ;j += 1
        vmovsd xmm0,[rdi+rax*8]          ;col_means[j]
        vdivsd xmm1,xmm0,xmm2            ;mean = col_means[j] / nrows
        vmovsd [rdi+rax*8],xmm1          ;save result

        sub r9,1                         ;ncols -= 1
        jnz Loop3                        ;repeat until done

Done:   vzeroupper
        ret
```

The other item of note in Listing 9-6c is the opening code block of CalcColMeansF64_avx(), which contains four mov instructions. These instructions copy argument values ncols, nrows, x, and col_means from registers RCX, RDX, RSI, and RDI to R9, R8, RDX, and RCX. Note that the destination registers match the ones used by the Visual C++ calling convention. This was done to minimize code differences between the NASM and MASM versions of CalcColMeansF64_avx(). The same AVX instruction sequences and registers are used after the mov code block. One scenario where this is potentially useful is when developing x86-64 assembly language code that needs to be compatible with both Windows and Linux, although other factors need to be considered. In later chapters, this technique will be used to streamline the source code examples that perform more complicated SIMD calculations. Here are the results for source code example Ch09_06:

```
----- Results for Ch09_06 -----
 54.8 26.4  13.3  48.4  74.0  63.2  61.3  56.5 66.9  64.4  15.1  37.4  56.1  70.0  41.5
 19.9  3.9  11.5  32.3  58.2  41.0  55.0  45.9 34.4  20.4  56.1   9.7  56.3  75.9  50.2
 26.7  7.1  44.2  37.9  61.3  16.3  38.2  62.0 47.7  61.7  72.9  70.0   8.9  55.7  44.4
 30.3  5.3  64.4   7.8  33.8  51.6  20.4  30.3 61.3  14.1  50.0  37.8  14.4  43.0  63.0
 20.8 51.8   7.2  12.1  38.8  38.4  27.7  46.5 66.0  61.9  11.2  11.4  41.1  59.7  77.5
 54.6 62.5  59.7  61.8  18.3  34.0  60.6  68.8 78.4  33.1  74.9  50.0   7.8  29.4  35.2
 11.9 41.3   7.7  19.9  31.5  37.8  35.8  19.4 32.6  56.4  27.3   5.3  27.5  10.5  53.1
 32.5 23.3  14.7  19.1  69.2   8.2  65.0  42.6 27.8  30.8  36.1  29.9  37.5  78.0  10.8
 75.7 43.1  16.5  77.1  17.6  72.3  35.1  17.6 27.9  46.7  72.3  68.0  72.3  44.4  38.3
 68.8 46.8  32.0  36.8  43.7  66.8  45.7  77.1 15.9  33.5  59.2  76.0  15.4  32.4  56.1
 64.0 56.1  39.8  74.0  31.6  43.6   4.1  29.1 42.8  27.7  41.7   6.2  43.5  29.0  61.5
 31.0 33.6  62.9  58.9  30.4  66.2  63.6  27.1 64.7  11.6   3.5  77.1  75.3  25.5  53.2
 22.9 48.4  35.7   6.8   7.3  33.5  40.8  20.5 61.5   3.4  76.4   9.3  69.9  62.4  78.8
 71.5 13.6  55.1  15.7  79.7  63.9  40.0  66.5 39.0  75.3  63.1  51.8  10.1  25.5   4.1
 68.3 34.4  44.7  69.5  39.4  13.9   6.0  78.6 52.4  20.3  62.1  22.4  44.9  48.1  14.2
 75.6 77.4  24.9  16.7  12.5  61.4  59.2  65.7 34.4  21.9  77.8  45.6  13.3  57.7  56.8
```

```
66.1 48.6  57.7  77.4  11.9  53.2  50.6  24.4 58.1  58.9  29.7  19.1  57.0   9.5  42.4
61.7 68.2  21.5  52.3  43.1  25.3  37.3  77.9 67.1  11.6  30.9  21.8  74.5  34.9  76.0
55.0 42.5   8.8   3.6  72.3  48.6  26.8  62.8 24.7  42.6  22.9  19.7   7.0  45.5  11.6
23.1 37.2  21.6  77.1  16.4  59.3  60.4  46.7 43.5  61.2  10.6  68.9  23.7  41.6  24.2
22.3 20.9  36.8  17.4  30.8  24.8   4.3  21.2 55.6  20.2  40.1  51.5  78.4  13.1  26.0

45.6 37.7  32.4  39.2  39.1  44.0  39.9  47.0 47.8  37.0  44.5  37.6  39.8  42.5  43.8
45.6 37.7  32.4  39.2  39.1  44.0  39.9  47.0 47.8  37.0  44.5  37.6  39.8  42.5  43.8
```

Summary

Here are the key learning points for Chapter 9:

- The vaddp[d|s], vsubp[d|s], vmulp[d|s], vdivp[d|s], and vsqrtp[d|s] instructions carry out common arithmetic operation using packed double-precision and packed single-precision floating-point operands.

- The absolute value of a packed floating-point value can be calculated using a vpand instruction and a packed mask of elements containing 0x7FFFFFFF (single-precision) or 0x7FFFFFFFFFFFFFFF (double-precision).

- The vcmpp[d|s] instructions perform packed compare operations. The result of each SIMD element compare is all zeros (compare predicate false) or all ones (compare predicate true).

- The vcvtp[d|s]2dq and vcvtdq2p[d|s] instructions perform conversions between packed floating-point and packed signed doubleword operands. The vcvtps2pd and vcvtpd2ps perform conversions between packed single-precision and double-precision operands.

- The vminp[d|s] and vmaxp[d|s] instructions perform packed minimum and maximum value calculations using double-precision and single-precision floating-point operands.

- The vbroadcasts[d|s] instructions broadcast (i.e., copy) a scalar double-precision or single-precision value to all element positions of an x86-AVX SIMD register.

- Assembly language functions can use the vhaddp[d|s] instructions to perform data reductions of packed floating-point values.

- Memory operands referenced by the vmovap[d|s] instructions must be properly aligned on a 16-byte (XMM register), 32-byte (YMM register), or 64-byte (ZMM register) boundary. The vmovup[d|s] instructions can be used for unaligned operands in memory.

- When working with arrays or matrices, a SIMD calculating for-loop can utilize packed AVX instructions to carry out its computations when the number of available elements is greater than or equal to the register size (e.g., eight or more single-precision elements for a YMM register operand). Scalar AVX instructions can be employed to process any residual elements.

- A floating-point SIMD ternary operator can be implemented using the packed compare instructions vcmpp[d|s] and Boolean bitwise logical instructions vandp[d|s], vandnp[d|s], and vorp[d|s].

- An assembly language function that performs calculations using registers YMM0–YMM15 (or ZMM0–ZMM15) should employ a vzeroupper (or vzeroall) instruction before executing any instruction that crosses a function boundary (e.g., call or ret) to avoid potential performance delays that can occur when the processor transitions from executing x86-AVX instructions to x86-SSE instructions.

CHAPTER 10

■ ■ ■

AVX2 Programming – Packed Integers

In Chapter 8, you learned how to use AVX instructions to perform packed integer operations using 128-bit wide operands and the XMM register set. In this chapter, you'll learn how to carry out similar operations using AVX2 instructions using 256-bit wide operands and the YMM register set. This chapter's source code examples are divided into two major sections. The first section contains elementary examples that illustrate elementary packed integer operations using AVX2 instructions. The second section is a continuation of the SIMD image processing techniques first presented in Chapter 8. This section also spotlights a simple method that you can use to benchmark the performance of an assembly language function.

Using AVX2 instructions with 256-bit wide packed integer operands is not much different than using AVX instructions with 128-bit wide packed integer operands. The primary reason for this is that the same assembly language mnemonics are used for both operand types. AVX2 contains some new packed integer instructions that are not available on processors that only support AVX. However, on processors that support AVX2, most packed integer instructions can be used with either XMM or YMM register operands as you'll soon see.

Before continuing, a couple of remarks regarding future source code listings are necessary. Starting with this chapter, most source code examples will include a listing only for the MASM code unless there are significant differences between this code and the NASM code. If any noteworthy differences exist between the MASM and NASM code, they'll be mentioned in the text. Also, the C++ listing for some source code examples will only contain the *principal* C++ code. Principal C++ code is the primary code that's required to understand the purpose of the example and its central algorithm or function. It excludes the C++ code that performs test case initialization, formatting of results for output, and other miscellaneous tasks. As a reminder, all C++ and x86-64 assembly language code not shown in a listing is included with the software download package.

The source code examples in this chapter require a processor and an operating system that support AVX2. You can use one of the free utilities listed in Appendix B to verify the processing capabilities of your computer.

Integer Arithmetic

In this section, you'll learn how to perform fundamental integer arithmetic using AVX2 instructions and 256-bit wide integer operands. The first source code example highlights basic packed integer math. This is followed by an example that demonstrates packed integer size promotions. The source code examples surveyed in this section are designed to provide you with the necessary foundation for understanding the more sophisticated AVX2 source code examples presented later in this and subsequent chapters.

© Daniel Kusswurm 2023
D. Kusswurm, *Modern X86 Assembly Language Programming*,
https://doi.org/10.1007/978-1-4842-9603-5_10

Elementary Operations

The first source code example of this chapter is named Ch10_01. This example demonstrates how to perform packed integer arithmetic using AVX2 instructions and 256-bit wide SIMD operands. Listing 10-1a shows the C++ source code for example Ch10_01.

Listing 10-1a. Example Ch10_01 C++ Code

```
//----------------------------------------------------------------------------
// Ch10_01.h
//----------------------------------------------------------------------------

#pragma once
#include "YmmVal.h"

// Ch10_01_fasm.asm, Ch10_01_fasm.s
extern "C" void MathI16_avx2(YmmVal* c, const YmmVal* a, const YmmVal* b);
extern "C" void MathI32_avx2(YmmVal* c, const YmmVal* a, const YmmVal* b);


//----------------------------------------------------------------------------
// Ch10_01.cpp
//----------------------------------------------------------------------------

#include <iostream>
#include <iomanip>
#include <string>
#include <cstddef>
#include "Ch10_01.h"

static const std::string c_Line(75, '-');

static void MathI16(void)
{
    YmmVal a, b, c[6];

    a.m_I16[0] = 10;        b.m_I16[0] = 1000;
    a.m_I16[1] = 20;        b.m_I16[1] = 2000;
    a.m_I16[2] = 3000;      b.m_I16[2] = 30;
    a.m_I16[3] = 4000;      b.m_I16[3] = 40;

    a.m_I16[4] = 30000;     b.m_I16[4] = 3000;      // add overflow
    a.m_I16[5] = 6000;      b.m_I16[5] = 32000;     // add overflow
    a.m_I16[6] = 2000;      b.m_I16[6] = -31000;    // sub overflow
    a.m_I16[7] = 4000;      b.m_I16[7] = -30000;    // sub overflow

    a.m_I16[8] = 4000;      b.m_I16[8] = -2500;
    a.m_I16[9] = 3600;      b.m_I16[9] = -1200;
    a.m_I16[10] = 6000;     b.m_I16[10] = 9000;
    a.m_I16[11] = -20000;   b.m_I16[11] = -20000;

    a.m_I16[12] = -25000;   b.m_I16[12] = -27000;   // add overflow
    a.m_I16[13] = 8000;     b.m_I16[13] = 28700;    // add overflow
```

```
        a.m_I16[14] = 3;        b.m_I16[14] = -32766;      // sub overflow
        a.m_I16[15] = -15000;   b.m_I16[15] = 24000;       // sub overflow

        MathI16_avx2(c, &a, &b);

        constexpr char sp = ' ';
        constexpr char nl = '\n';
        constexpr int w1 = 2, w2 = 8;

        std::cout << "\nMathI16_avx2() results:\n\n";
        std::cout << " i        a         b        add      adds       sub       ";
        std::cout << "subs       min       max\n" << c_Line << nl;

        for (size_t i = 0; i < 16; i++)
        {
            std::cout << std::setw(w1) << i << sp;
            std::cout << std::setw(w2) << a.m_I16[i] << sp;
            std::cout << std::setw(w2) << b.m_I16[i] << sp;
            std::cout << std::setw(w2) << c[0].m_I16[i] << sp;
            std::cout << std::setw(w2) << c[1].m_I16[i] << sp;
            std::cout << std::setw(w2) << c[2].m_I16[i] << sp;
            std::cout << std::setw(w2) << c[3].m_I16[i] << sp;
            std::cout << std::setw(w2) << c[4].m_I16[i] << sp;
            std::cout << std::setw(w2) << c[5].m_I16[i] << nl;
        }
}

static void MathI32(void)
{
    YmmVal a, b, c[6];

    a.m_I32[0] = 64;        b.m_I32[0] = 4;
    a.m_I32[1] = 1024;      b.m_I32[1] = 5;
    a.m_I32[2] = -2048;     b.m_I32[2] = 2;
    a.m_I32[3] = 8192;      b.m_I32[3] = 5;
    a.m_I32[4] = -256;      b.m_I32[4] = 8;
    a.m_I32[5] = 4096;      b.m_I32[5] = 7;
    a.m_I32[6] = 16;        b.m_I32[6] = 3;
    a.m_I32[7] = 512;       b.m_I32[7] = 6;

    MathI32_avx2(c, &a, &b);

    constexpr char sp = ' ';
    constexpr char nl = '\n';
    constexpr int w1 = 2, w2 = 7, w3 = 8;

    std::cout << "\nMathI32_avx2() results:\n\n";
    std::cout << " i       a        b        add       sub       mull       ";
    std::cout << "sll        sra       abs a\n" << c_Line << nl;
```

```cpp
    for (size_t i = 0; i < 8; i++)
    {
        std::cout << std::setw(w1) << i << sp;
        std::cout << std::setw(w2) << a.m_I32[i] << sp;
        std::cout << std::setw(w2) << b.m_I32[i] << sp;
        std::cout << std::setw(w3) << c[0].m_I32[i] << sp;
        std::cout << std::setw(w3) << c[1].m_I32[i] << sp;
        std::cout << std::setw(w3) << c[2].m_I32[i] << sp;
        std::cout << std::setw(w3) << c[3].m_I32[i] << sp;
        std::cout << std::setw(w3) << c[4].m_I32[i] << sp;
        std::cout << std::setw(w3) << c[5].m_I32[i] << nl;
    }
}

int main(void)
{
    std::cout << "----- Results for Ch10_01 -----\n";

    MathI16();
    MathI32();
    return 0;
}
```

In Listing 10-1a, note that the declarations of assembly language functions MathI16_avx2() and MathU32_avx2() in file Ch10_01.h make use of the C++ structure YmmVal. This is the same data structure that you learned about in Chapter 9 (see example Ch09_01). File Ch10_01.cpp includes two functions named MathI16() and MathU32(). These static functions perform test case initialization for assembly language functions MathI16_avx2() and MathU32_avx2(), respectively. They also stream the results to std::cout.

Listing 10-1b shows the MASM source code for example Ch10_01. The first function in this listing, MathI16_avx2(), begins its execution with a vmovdqa ymm0,ymmword ptr [rdx] instruction that loads argument value a into register YMM0. The next instruction, vmovdqa ymm1,ymmword ptr [r8], loads argument value b into register YMM1. Note that registers RDX and R8 both point to buffers of type YmmVal, which means the target instances are aligned on a 32-byte boundary. The ensuing instruction pair, vpaddw ymm2,ymm0,ymm1 and vmovdqa ymmword ptr [rcx],ymm2, performs packed integer addition using 16-bit wide elements and saves the calculated sums to c[0]. This is followed by the instruction pair vpaddsw ymm2,ymm0,ymm1 and vmovdqa ymmword ptr [rcx+32],ymm2, which carries out packed saturated addition using 16-bit signed integer elements. The resultant sums are saved to c[1]. The remaining code blocks in MathI16_avx2() illustrate the use of the vpsubw, vpsubsw, vpminsw, and vpmaxsw instructions using 256-bit wide SIMD operands and 16-bit integer elements. Note that the displacements used in the vmovdqa instructions that save results to array c are integral multiples of 32 since the size of a YmmVal is 32 bytes.

Listing 10-1b. Example Ch10_01 MASM Code

```
;-------------------------------------------------------------------------
; Ch10_01_fasm.asm
;-------------------------------------------------------------------------


;-------------------------------------------------------------------------
; void MathI16_avx2(YmmVal* c, const YmmVal* a, const YmmVal* b);
;-------------------------------------------------------------------------
```

```asm
        .code
MathI16_avx2 proc
        vmovdqa ymm0,ymmword ptr [rdx]          ;ymm0 = a
        vmovdqa ymm1,ymmword ptr [r8]           ;ymm1 = b

        vpaddw ymm2,ymm0,ymm1                    ;packed addition - wraparound
        vmovdqa ymmword ptr [rcx],ymm2

        vpaddsw ymm2,ymm0,ymm1                   ;packed addition - saturated
        vmovdqa ymmword ptr [rcx+32],ymm2

        vpsubw ymm2,ymm0,ymm1                    ;packed subtraction - wraparound
        vmovdqa ymmword ptr [rcx+64],ymm2

        vpsubsw ymm2,ymm0,ymm1                   ;packed subtraction - saturated
        vmovdqa ymmword ptr [rcx+96],ymm2

        vpminsw ymm2,ymm0,ymm1                   ;packed minimum
        vmovdqa ymmword ptr [rcx+128],ymm2

        vpmaxsw ymm2,ymm0,ymm1                   ;packed maximum
        vmovdqa ymmword ptr [rcx+160],ymm2

        vzeroupper
        ret
MathI16_avx2 endp

;-----------------------------------------------------------------------------
; void MathI32_avx2(YmmVal* c, const YmmVal* a, const YmmVal* b);
;-----------------------------------------------------------------------------

MathI32_avx2 proc
        vmovdqa ymm0,ymmword ptr [rdx]          ;ymm0 = a
        vmovdqa ymm1,ymmword ptr [r8]           ;ymm1 = b

        vpaddd ymm2,ymm0,ymm1                    ;packed addition
        vmovdqa ymmword ptr [rcx],ymm2

        vpsubd ymm2,ymm0,ymm1                    ;packed subtraction
        vmovdqa ymmword ptr [rcx+32],ymm2

        vpmulld ymm2,ymm0,ymm1                   ;packed multiplication (low result)
        vmovdqa ymmword ptr [rcx+64],ymm2

        vpsllvd ymm2,ymm0,ymm1                   ;packed shift left logical
        vmovdqa ymmword ptr [rcx+96],ymm2

        vpsravd ymm2,ymm0,ymm1                   ;packed shift right arithmetic
        vmovdqa ymmword ptr [rcx+128],ymm2

        vpabsd ymm2,ymm0                         ;packed absolute value
        vmovdqa ymmword ptr [rcx+160],ymm2
```

```
        vzeroupper
        ret
MathI32_avx2 endp
        end
```

Also shown in Listing 10-1b is function MathI32_avx2(), which spotlights common packed operations using 256-bit wide operands and 32-bit integer elements. In this function, the vpsllvd ymm2,ymm0,ymm1 (Variable Bit Shift Left Logical) instruction left shifts each 32-bit wide (doubleword) element of YMM0 using the bit count of the corresponding element in YMM1. The vpsravd ymm2,ymm0,ymm1 (Variable Bit Shift Right Arithmetic) instruction performs arithmetic right shifts using the 32-bit wide integer elements in YMM0 and the corresponding element bit counts in YMM1. The vpabsd ymm2,ymm0 (Packed Absolute Value) instruction calculates absolute values of the 32-bit wide integer elements in YMM0. Note that both MathI16_avx2() and MathI32_avx2() include a vzeroupper instruction just before their respective ret instructions since they employ YMM registers to carry out their calculations.

Like many of the examples that you have already seen, the primary difference between the MASM and NASM code for example Ch10_01 is the use of different argument registers. Also recall that NASM doesn't require the use of a size operator with the vmovdqa instruction. Here are the results for source code example Ch10_01:

```
----- Results for Ch10_01 -----

MathI16_avx2() results:

 i       a       b     add    adds     sub    subs     min     max
 ------------------------------------------------------------------
 0      10    1000    1010    1010    -990    -990      10    1000
 1      20    2000    2020    2020   -1980   -1980      20    2000
 2    3000      30    3030    3030    2970    2970      30    3000
 3    4000      40    4040    4040    3960    3960      40    4000
 4   30000    3000  -32536   32767   27000   27000    3000   30000
 5    6000   32000  -27536   32767  -26000  -26000    6000   32000
 6    2000  -31000  -29000  -29000  -32536   32767  -31000    2000
 7    4000  -30000  -26000  -26000  -31536   32767  -30000    4000
 8    4000   -2500    1500    1500    6500    6500   -2500    4000
 9    3600   -1200    2400    2400    4800    4800   -1200    3600
10    6000    9000   15000   15000   -3000   -3000    6000    9000
11  -20000  -20000   25536  -32768       0       0  -20000  -20000
12  -25000  -27000   13536  -32768    2000    2000  -27000  -25000
13    8000   28700  -28836   32767  -20700  -20700    8000   28700
14       3  -32766  -32763  -32763  -32767   32767  -32766       3
15  -15000   24000    9000    9000   26536  -32768  -15000   24000


MathI32_avx2() results:

 i       a       b     add     sub    mull     sll     sra   abs a
 ------------------------------------------------------------------
 0      64       4      68      60     256    1024       4      64
 1    1024       5    1029    1019    5120   32768      32    1024
 2   -2048       2   -2046   -2050   -4096   -8192    -512    2048
 3    8192       5    8197    8187   40960  262144     256    8192
 4    -256       8    -248    -264   -2048  -65536      -1     256
```

5	4096	7	4103	4089	28672	524288	32	4096
6	16	3	19	13	48	128	2	16
7	512	6	518	506	3072	32768	8	512

Size Promotions

In Chapter 8, you learned how to use the vpunpckl[bw|wd] and vpunpckh[bw|wd] instructions to size-promote packed integers (see example Ch08_06). The next source code example, entitled Ch10_02, demonstrates how to perform packed integer size promotions using the instructions vpmovzx[bw|bd] (Packed Move with Zero Extend) and vpmovsx[wd|wq] (Packed Move with Sign Extend). Listing 10-2a shows the C++ source code for example Ch10_02.

Listing 10-2a. Example Ch10_02 C++ Code

```
//-----------------------------------------------------------------------------
// Ch10_02.h
//-----------------------------------------------------------------------------

#pragma once
#include "YmmVal.h"

// Ch10_02_fasm.asm, Ch10_02_fasm.s
extern "C" void ZeroExtU8_U16_avx2(YmmVal* c, const YmmVal* a);
extern "C" void ZeroExtU8_U32_avx2(YmmVal* c, const YmmVal* a);
extern "C" void SignExtI16_I32_avx2(YmmVal* c, const YmmVal* a);
extern "C" void SignExtI16_I64_avx2(YmmVal* c, const YmmVal* a);


//-----------------------------------------------------------------------------
// Ch10_02.cpp
//-----------------------------------------------------------------------------

#include <iostream>
#include <cstddef>
#include <cstdint>
#include "Ch10_02.h"

static void ZeroExtU8_U16(void)
{
    YmmVal a, c[2];

    for (size_t i = 0; i < 32; i++)
        a.m_U8[i] = (uint8_t)(i * 8);

    // Zero-extend U8 integers to U16
    ZeroExtU8_U16_avx2(c, &a);

    constexpr char nl = '\n';
    std::cout << "\nZeroExtU8_U16_avx2() results:\n";
```

```
    std::cout << "a (0:15):   " << a.ToStringU8(0) << nl;
    std::cout << "a (16:31):  " << a.ToStringU8(1) << nl;
    std::cout << nl;
    std::cout << "c (0:7):    " << c[0].ToStringU16(0) << nl;
    std::cout << "c (8:15):   " << c[0].ToStringU16(1) << nl;
    std::cout << "c (16:23):  " << c[1].ToStringU16(0) << nl;
    std::cout << "c (24:31):  " << c[1].ToStringU16(1) << nl;
}

static void ZeroExtU8_U32(void)
{
    YmmVal a, c[4];

    for (size_t i = 0; i < 32; i++)
        a.m_U8[i] = (uint8_t)(255 - i * 8);

    // Zero-extend U8 integers to U32
    ZeroExtU8_U32_avx2(c, &a);

    constexpr char nl = '\n';
    std::cout << "\nZeroExtU8_U32_avx2() results:\n";

    std::cout << "a (0:15):   " << a.ToStringU8(0) << nl;
    std::cout << "a (16:31):  " << a.ToStringU8(1) << nl;
    std::cout << nl;
    std::cout << "c (0:3):    " << c[0].ToStringU32(0) << nl;
    std::cout << "c (4:7):    " << c[0].ToStringU32(1) << nl;
    std::cout << "c (8:11):   " << c[1].ToStringU32(0) << nl;
    std::cout << "c (12:15):  " << c[1].ToStringU32(1) << nl;
    std::cout << "c (16:19):  " << c[2].ToStringU32(0) << nl;
    std::cout << "c (20:23):  " << c[2].ToStringU32(1) << nl;
    std::cout << "c (24:27):  " << c[3].ToStringU32(0) << nl;
    std::cout << "c (28:31):  " << c[3].ToStringU32(1) << nl;
}

static void SignExtI16_I32(void)
{
    YmmVal a, c[2];

    for (size_t i = 0; i < 16; i++)
        a.m_I16[i] = (int16_t)(-32768 + i * 4000);

    // Sign-extend I16 integers to I32
    SignExtI16_I32_avx2(c, &a);

    constexpr char nl = '\n';
    std::cout << "\nSignExtI16_I32_avx2() results:\n";

    std::cout << "a (0:7):    " << a.ToStringI16(0) << nl;
    std::cout << "a (8:15):   " << a.ToStringI16(1) << nl;
    std::cout << nl;
```

```cpp
    std::cout << "c (0:3):    " << c[0].ToStringI32(0) << nl;
    std::cout << "c (4:7):    " << c[0].ToStringI32(1) << nl;
    std::cout << "c (8:11):   " << c[1].ToStringI32(0) << nl;
    std::cout << "c (12:15):  " << c[1].ToStringI32(1) << nl;
}

static void SignExtI16_I64(void)
{
    YmmVal a, c[4];

    for (size_t i = 0; i < 16; i++)
        a.m_I16[i] = (int16_t)(32767 - i * 4000);

    // Sign-extend I16 integers to I64
    SignExtI16_I64_avx2(c, &a);

    constexpr char nl = '\n';
    std::cout << "\nSignExtI16_I64_avx2() results:\n";

    std::cout << "a (0:7):    " << a.ToStringI16(0) << nl;
    std::cout << "a (8:15):   " << a.ToStringI16(1) << nl;
    std::cout << nl;
    std::cout << "c (0:1):    " << c[0].ToStringI64(0) << nl;
    std::cout << "c (2:3):    " << c[0].ToStringI64(1) << nl;
    std::cout << "c (4:5):    " << c[1].ToStringI64(0) << nl;
    std::cout << "c (6:7):    " << c[1].ToStringI64(1) << nl;
    std::cout << "c (8:9):    " << c[2].ToStringI64(0) << nl;
    std::cout << "c (10:11):  " << c[2].ToStringI64(1) << nl;
    std::cout << "c (12:13):  " << c[3].ToStringI64(0) << nl;
    std::cout << "c (14:15):  " << c[3].ToStringI64(1) << nl;
}

int main(void)
{
    std::cout << "----- Results for Ch10_02 -----\n";

    ZeroExtU8_U16();
    ZeroExtU8_U32();
    SignExtI16_I32();
    SignExtI16_I64();
    return 0;
}
```

The C++ code in Listing 10-2a contains four functions that initialize test cases for various packed size promotion operations. The first function, ZeroExtU8_U16(), starts by initializing the unsigned byte elements of YmmVal a. It then calls assembly language function ZeroExtU8_U16_avx2() to size-promote the packed unsigned bytes into packed unsigned words. The function ZeroExtU8_U32() performs a similar set of initializations to demonstrate packed unsigned byte to packed unsigned doubleword promotions. Finally, functions SignExtI16_I32() and SignExtI16_I64() perform test case initialization for packed signed word to packed signed doubleword and packed signed quadword size promotions.

Listing 10-2b shows the MASM code for example Ch10_02. Toward the top of this listing is a function named ZeroExtU8_U16_avx2(), which zero-extends packed 8-bit integer elements to 16 bits. This function commences with a vmovdqa ymm0,ymmword ptr [rdx] instruction that loads argument value a into register YMM0. The next instruction, vextracti128 xmm1,ymm0,1 (Extract Packed Integer Values), copies the high-order 128 bits of register YMM0 into register XMM1. Note that the immediate operand of the vextracti128 instruction specifies which 128-bit lane (0 = lower, 1 = upper) to copy. The next two instructions, vpmovzxbw ymm2,xmm0 and vpmovzxbw ymm3,xmm1, zero-extend the 16-byte values in registers XMM0 (a[0:15]) and XMM1 (a[16:31]); the resultant 16-word values are saved in registers YMM2 and YMM3, respectively. Function ZeroExtU8_U16_avx2() then employs two vmovdqa instructions, which save the packed words to c[0:15] and c[16:31].

Listing 10-2b. Example Ch10_02 MASM Code

```
;------------------------------------------------------------------------
; Ch10_02_fasm.asm
;------------------------------------------------------------------------


;------------------------------------------------------------------------
; void ZeroExtU8_U16_avx2(YmmVal* c], const YmmVal* a);
;------------------------------------------------------------------------

        .code
ZeroExtU8_U16_avx2 proc
        vmovdqa ymm0,ymmword ptr [rdx]      ;ymm0 = a (32 byte values)
        vextracti128 xmm1,ymm0,1            ;xmm1 = high-order byte values

        vpmovzxbw ymm2,xmm0                 ;zero extend a[0:15] to word
        vpmovzxbw ymm3,xmm1                 ;zero extend a[16:31] to words

        vmovdqa ymmword ptr [rcx],ymm2      ;save words c[0:15]
        vmovdqa ymmword ptr [rcx+32],ymm3   ;save words c[16:31]

        vzeroupper
        ret
ZeroExtU8_U16_avx2 endp


;------------------------------------------------------------------------
; void ZeroExtU8_U32_avx2(YmmVal* c, const YmmVal* a);
;------------------------------------------------------------------------

ZeroExtU8_U32_avx2 proc
        vmovdqa ymm0,ymmword ptr [rdx]      ;ymm0 = a (32 bytes values)
        vextracti128 xmm1,ymm0,1            ;xmm1 = high-order byte values

        vpmovzxbd ymm2,xmm0                 ;zero extend a[0:7] to dword
        vpsrldq xmm0,xmm0,8                 ;xmm0[63:0] = a[8:15]
        vpmovzxbd ymm3,xmm0                 ;zero extend a[8:15] to dword

        vpmovzxbd ymm4,xmm1                 ;zero extend a[16:23] to dword
        vpsrldq xmm1,xmm1,8                 ;xmm1[63:0] = a[24:31]
        vpmovzxbd ymm5,xmm1                 ;zero extend a[24:31] to dword
```

```
        vmovdqa ymmword ptr [rcx],ymm2        ;save dwords c[0:7]
        vmovdqa ymmword ptr [rcx+32],ymm3     ;save dwords c[8:15]
        vmovdqa ymmword ptr [rcx+64],ymm4     ;save dwords c[16:23]
        vmovdqa ymmword ptr [rcx+96],ymm5     ;save dwords c[24:31]

        vzeroupper
        ret
ZeroExtU8_U32_avx2 endp

;-----------------------------------------------------------------------
; void SignExtI16_I32_avx2(YmmVal* c, const YmmVal* a);
;-----------------------------------------------------------------------

SignExtI16_I32_avx2 proc
        vmovdqa ymm0,ymmword ptr [rdx]        ;ymm0 = a (16 word values)
        vextracti128 xmm1,ymm0,1              ;xmm1 = high-order word values

        vpmovsxwd ymm2,xmm0                   ;sign extend a[0:7] to dword
        vpmovsxwd ymm3,xmm1                   ;sign extend a[8:15] to dwords

        vmovdqa ymmword ptr [rcx],ymm2        ;save dwords c[0:7]
        vmovdqa ymmword ptr [rcx+32],ymm3     ;save dwords c[8:15]

        vzeroupper
        ret
SignExtI16_I32_avx2 endp

;-----------------------------------------------------------------------
; void SignExtI16_I64_avx2(YmmVal* c, const YmmVal* a);
;-----------------------------------------------------------------------

SignExtI16_I64_avx2 proc
        vmovdqa ymm0,ymmword ptr [rdx]        ;ymm0 = a (16 word values)
        vextracti128 xmm1,ymm0,1              ;xmm1 = high-order word values

        vpmovsxwq ymm2,xmm0                   ;sign extend a[0:3] to qword
        vpsrldq xmm0,xmm0,8                   ;xmm0[63:0] = a[4:7]
        vpmovsxwq ymm3,xmm0                   ;sign extend a[4:7] to qword

        vpmovsxwq ymm4,xmm1                   ;sign extend a[8:11] to qword
        vpsrldq xmm1,xmm1,8                   ;xmm1[63:0] = a[12:15]
        vpmovsxwq ymm5,xmm1                   ;sign extend a[12:15] to 2word

        vmovdqa ymmword ptr [rcx],ymm2        ;save qwords c[0:3]
        vmovdqa ymmword ptr [rcx+32],ymm3     ;save qwords c[4:7]
        vmovdqa ymmword ptr [rcx+64],ymm4     ;save qwords c[8:11]
        vmovdqa ymmword ptr [rcx+96],ymm5     ;save qwords c[12:16]

        vzeroupper
        ret
SignExtI16_I64_avx2 endp
        end
```

The next function in Listing 10-2b, ZeroExtU8_U32_avx2(), illustrates the zero extension of packed byte elements to packed doublewords. This function uses sequences of the vpmovzxbd and vpsrldq instructions to carry out its operations as shown in Figure 10-1. Note that execution of each vpmovzxbd instruction zero-extends the eight low-order byte values in the specified XMM register. The final two functions in Listing 10-2b, SignExtI16_I32_avx2() and SignExtI16_I64_avx2(), use instructions vpmovsxwd (word to doubleword) and vpmovsxwq (word to quadword) to carry out signed integer size promotions.

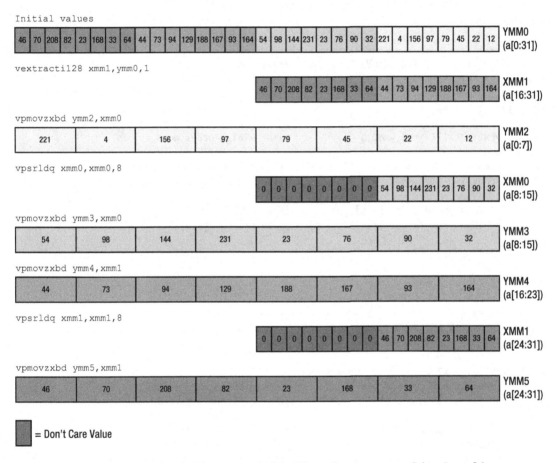

Figure 10-1. *Zero extension of packed bytes to packed doublewords using* vpmovzxbd *and* vpsrldq

It is often more expedient to use the explicit size promotion instructions vpmovzx[bw|bd|bq|wd|wq|dq] and vpmovsx[bw|bd|bq|wd|wq|dq] instead of sequences of vpunpckl[bw|wd|dq|] and vpunpckh[bw|wd|dq]. You'll see other examples of the vpmovzx and vpmovsx instructions later in this and subsequent chapters. Here are the results for example Ch10_02:

```
----- Results for Ch10_02 -----

ZeroExtU8_U16_avx2() results:
a (0:15):     0   8  16  24  32  40  48  56  |  64  72  80  88  96 104 112 120
a (16:31):  128 136 144 152 160 168 176 184  | 192 200 208 216 224 232 240 248
```

```
c (0:7):              0        8       16       24  |       32       40       48       56
c (8:15):            64       72       80       88  |       96      104      112      120
c (16:23):          128      136      144      152  |      160      168      176      184
c (24:31):          192      200      208      216  |      224      232      240      248

ZeroExtU8_U32_avx2() results:
a (0:15):     255 247 239 231 223 215 207 199  | 191 183 175 167 159 151 143 135
a (16:31):    127 119 111 103  95  87  79  71  |  63  55  47  39  31  23  15   7

c (0:3):                   255              247  |              239              231
c (4:7):                   223              215  |              207              199
c (8:11):                  191              183  |              175              167
c (12:15):                 159              151  |              143              135
c (16:19):                 127              119  |              111              103
c (20:23):                  95               87  |               79               71
c (24:27):                  63               55  |               47               39
c (28:31):                  31               23  |               15                7

SignExtI16_I32_avx2() results:
a (0:7):     -32768   -28768   -24768   -20768  |   -16768   -12768    -8768    -4768
a (8:15):      -768     3232     7232    11232  |    15232    19232    23232    27232

c (0:3):              -32768            -28768  |            -24768            -20768
c (4:7):              -16768            -12768  |             -8768             -4768
c (8:11):               -768              3232  |              7232             11232
c (12:15):             15232             19232  |             23232             27232

SignExtI16_I64_avx2() results:
a (0:7):      32767    28767    24767    20767  |    16767    12767     8767     4767
a (8:15):       767    -3233    -7233   -11233  |   -15233   -19233   -23233   -27233

c (0:1):                                 32767  |                              28767
c (2:3):                                 24767  |                              20767
c (4:5):                                 16767  |                              12767
c (6:7):                                  8767  |                               4767
c (8:9):                                   767  |                              -3233
c (10:11):                               -7233  |                             -11233
c (12:13):                              -15233  |                             -19233
c (14:15):                              -23233  |                             -27233
```

Image Processing

The source code examples presented in this section demonstrate a few common image processing techniques using AVX2 instructions and 256-bit wide SIMD operands. The first example explains how to clip the pixel values of a grayscale image. The second example employs AVX2 instructions to convert an RGB image to grayscale. This is followed by a source code example that performs unsigned 8-bit integer to single-precision floating-point pixel conversions. The final example exploits AVX2 instructions to construct an image histogram.

As mentioned in Chapter 8, SIMD techniques are suitable for many types of image processing algorithms. While the focus of this section is image processing, you should keep in mind that the same methods can also be employed to carry out similar operations in many algorithms that process large arrays or matrices of integer data.

Pixel Clipping

Pixel clipping is an image processing technique that bounds the intensity values of each pixel in an image between two threshold limits. This technique is often used to reduce the dynamic range of an image by eliminating its extremely dark and light pixels. Source code example Ch10_03 illustrates how to use the AVX2 instruction set to clip the pixels of an 8-bit grayscale image. Listing 10-3a shows the C++ source code for example Ch10_03.

Listing 10-3a. Example Ch10_03 C++ Code

```
//------------------------------------------------------------------------------
// Ch10_03.h
//------------------------------------------------------------------------------

#pragma once
#include <cstddef>
#include <cstdint>

// The members of ClipData must match the corresponding structure
// that's declared in the assembly langage files.

struct ClipData
{
    uint8_t* m_PbSrc;           // source buffer pointer
    uint8_t* m_PbDes;           // destination buffer pointer
    size_t m_NumPixels;         // number of pixels
    size_t m_NumClippedPixels;  // number of clipped pixels
    uint8_t m_ThreshLo;         // low threshold
    uint8_t m_ThreshHi;         // high threshold
};

// Ch10_03_fasm.asm, Ch10_03_fasm.s
extern "C" void ClipPixels_avx2(ClipData * clip_data);

// Ch10_03_fcpp.cpp
extern void ClipPixels_cpp(ClipData* clip_data);

// Ch10_03_misc.cpp
extern void InitPixelBuffer(uint8_t* pb, size_t num_pixels);

// Ch10_03_bm.cpp
extern void ClipPixels_bm(void);

// Miscellaneous constants
constexpr size_t c_Alignment = 32;
constexpr int c_RngMinVal = 0;
```

```cpp
constexpr int c_RngMaxVal = 255;
constexpr unsigned int c_RngSeed = 157;
constexpr uint8_t c_ThreshLo = 10;
constexpr uint8_t c_ThreshHi = 245;
constexpr size_t c_NumPixels = 8 * 1024 * 1024 + 31;
constexpr size_t c_NumPixelsBM = 10000000;


//------------------------------------------------------------------------
// Ch10_03_misc.cpp
//------------------------------------------------------------------------

#include "Ch10_03.h"
#include "MT.h"

void InitPixelBuffer(uint8_t* pb, size_t num_pixels)
{
    // Fill array pb with random values
    MT::FillArray(pb, num_pixels, c_RngMinVal, c_RngMaxVal, c_RngSeed);

    // Insert known values for test & debug
    if (num_pixels >= 31)
    {
        pb[7] = (c_ThreshLo > 0) ? c_ThreshLo - 1 : 0;
        pb[30] = (c_ThreshHi < 255) ? c_ThreshHi + 1 : 255;

        if (num_pixels >= 64)
        {
            pb[33] = (c_ThreshLo > 2) ? c_ThreshLo - 1 : 2;
            pb[35] = (c_ThreshHi < 254) ? c_ThreshHi + 1 : 254;
            pb[62] = 0;
            pb[63] = 255;
        }
    }
}


//------------------------------------------------------------------------
// Ch10_03_fcpp.cpp
//------------------------------------------------------------------------

#include "Ch10_03.h"
#include "AlignedMem.h"

static bool CheckArgs(const ClipData* clip_data)
{
    if (clip_data->m_NumPixels == 0)
        return false;

    if (!AlignedMem::IsAligned(clip_data->m_PbSrc, c_Alignment))
        return false;
```

```cpp
    if (!AlignedMem::IsAligned(clip_data->m_PbDes, c_Alignment))
        return false;

    return true;
}

void ClipPixels_cpp(ClipData* clip_data)
{
    if (!CheckArgs(clip_data))
        throw std::runtime_error("ClipPixels_cpp() - CheckArgs() failed");

    uint8_t* pb_src = clip_data->m_PbSrc;
    uint8_t* pb_des = clip_data->m_PbDes;
    size_t num_pixels = clip_data->m_NumPixels;
    size_t num_clipped_pixels = 0;
    uint8_t thresh_lo = clip_data->m_ThreshLo;
    uint8_t thresh_hi = clip_data->m_ThreshHi;

    for (size_t i = 0; i < num_pixels; i++)
    {
        uint8_t pixel = pb_src[i];

        if (pixel < thresh_lo)
        {
            pb_des[i] = thresh_lo;
            num_clipped_pixels++;
        }
        else if (pixel > thresh_hi)
        {
            pb_des[i] = thresh_hi;
            num_clipped_pixels++;
        }
        else
            pb_des[i] = pb_src[i];
    }

    clip_data->m_NumClippedPixels = num_clipped_pixels;
}

//-------------------------------------------------------------------------
// Ch10_03.cpp
//-------------------------------------------------------------------------

#include <iostream>
#include <cstring>
#include <limits>
#include <stdexcept>
#include "Ch10_03.h"
#include "AlignedMem.h"
```

```cpp
static void ClipPixels(void)
{
    constexpr char nl = '\n';
    constexpr uint8_t thresh_lo = c_ThreshLo;
    constexpr uint8_t thresh_hi = c_ThreshHi;
    constexpr size_t num_pixels = c_NumPixels;
    constexpr size_t ncp_init = std::numeric_limits<size_t>::max();

    AlignedArray<uint8_t> pb_src(num_pixels, c_Alignment);
    AlignedArray<uint8_t> pb_des0(num_pixels, c_Alignment);
    AlignedArray<uint8_t> pb_des1(num_pixels, c_Alignment);

    InitPixelBuffer(pb_src.Data(), num_pixels);

    ClipData cd0;
    cd0.m_PbSrc = pb_src.Data();
    cd0.m_PbDes = pb_des0.Data();
    cd0.m_NumPixels = num_pixels;
    cd0.m_NumClippedPixels = ncp_init;
    cd0.m_ThreshLo = thresh_lo;
    cd0.m_ThreshHi = thresh_hi;

    ClipData cd1;
    cd1.m_PbSrc = pb_src.Data();
    cd1.m_PbDes = pb_des1.Data();
    cd1.m_NumPixels = num_pixels;
    cd1.m_NumClippedPixels = ncp_init;
    cd1.m_ThreshLo = thresh_lo;
    cd1.m_ThreshHi = thresh_hi;

    ClipPixels_cpp(&cd0);
    ClipPixels_avx2(&cd1);

    std::cout << "----- Results for Ch10_03 -----\n";
    std::cout << "num_pixels (test case): " << num_pixels << nl;
    std::cout << "cd0.m_NumClippedPixels: " << cd0.m_NumClippedPixels << nl;
    std::cout << "cd1.m_NumClippedPixels: " << cd1.m_NumClippedPixels << nl;

    bool ncp_check = cd0.m_NumClippedPixels == cd1.m_NumClippedPixels;
    bool mem_check = memcmp(pb_des0.Data(), pb_des1.Data(), num_pixels) == 0;

    if (ncp_check && mem_check)
        std::cout << "\nCompare checks passed\n";
    else
        std::cout << "\nCompare checks failed!\n";
}

int main(void)
{
    try
    {
```

```
        ClipPixels();
        ClipPixels_bm();
    }

    catch (std::exception& ex)
    {
        std::cout << "Ch10_03 exception: " << ex.what() << '\n';
    }

    return 0;
}
```

The C++ code in Listing 10-3a begins with the declaration of a structure named ClipData. This structure (and its assembly language counterpart that you'll see later) contains the data that's required for the pixel clipping algorithm. Note in file Ch10_03.h that the declarations of both ClipPixels_avx2() and ClipPixels_cpp() expect a pointer to an instance of type ClipData. Also note the miscellaneous constant definitions in file Ch10_03.h, especially c_ThreshLo and c_ThreshHi. These values define the threshold limits used by the clipping functions. File Ch10_03_misc.cpp contains a function named InitPixelBuffer(), which fills the specified uint8_t pixel buffer with random values.

In Listing 10-3a, function ClipPixels_cpp() implements the pixel clipping algorithm using standard C++ statements. During execution of its for-loop, ClipPixels_cpp() checks each pixel to see if its intensity value is below c_ThreshLo or above c_ThreshHi. If a pixel intensity value exceeds one of these limits, it's clipped. Note that ClipPixels_cpp() updates num_clipped_pixels each time it clips a pixel. The final value of num_clipped_pixels is saved in the ClipData structure and used later to compare results.

Also shown in Listing 10-3a is file Ch10_03.cpp, which includes test function ClipPixels(). This function performs test case initialization and calls the pixel clipping functions ClipPixels_cpp() and ClipPixels_avx2(). Note that ClipPixels() employs C++ template class AlignedArray<uint8_t> to instantiate pixel buffers that are aligned on a c_Alignment (32-byte) boundary. Near the bottom of file Ch10_03.cpp is main(). This function calls ClipPixels() and ClipPixel_bm(). The latter function is a benchmarking function that measures the run-time performance of ClipPixels_cpp() and ClipPixels_avx2(). You'll learn more about this later.

Listing 10-3b shows the MASM code for example Ch10_03. File Ch10_03_fasm.asm opens with the definition of a structure named CD, which is the MASM counterpart of the C++ structure ClipData. Following its prologue, function ClipPixels_avx2() performs its requisite initializations. Note that pointers PbSrc (R8) and PbDes (R9) are tested to ensure that both pixel buffers are aligned on a 32-byte boundary. Also note the use of the two vpbroadcastb (Load Integer and Broadcast) instructions to initialize packed versions of ThreshLo (YMM4) and ThreshHi (YMM5).

Listing 10-3b. Example Ch10_03 MASM Code

```
;-------------------------------------------------------------------------
; Ch10_03_fasm.asm
;-------------------------------------------------------------------------


; The members of CD must match the corresponding structure
; that's declared in Ch10_03.h

CD                  struct
PbSrc               qword ?
PbDes               qword ?
NumPixels           qword ?
NumClippedPixels    qword ?
```

```
ThreshLo          byte ?
ThreshHi          byte ?
CD                ends


;-------------------------------------------------------------------------
; void ClipPixels_avx2(ClipData* clip_data);
;-------------------------------------------------------------------------


NSE       equ 32                              ;num_simd_elements


          .code
ClipPixels_avx2 proc frame

; Function prologue
          push rbx
          .pushreg rbx
          push rsi
          .pushreg rsi
          push rdi
          .pushreg rdi
          .endprolog


; Initialize
          xor r11,r11                         ;r11 = NumClippedPixels

          mov r8,[rcx+CD.PbSrc]               ;r8 = PbSrc
          test r8,1fh
          jnz Done                            ;jump if PbSrc not 32b aligned

          mov r9,[rcx+CD.PbDes]               ;r9 = PbDes
          test r9,1fh
          jnz Done                            ;jump if PbDes not 32b aligned

          mov r10,[rcx+CD.NumPixels]          ;r10 = NumPixels
          test r10,r10                        ;NumPixels == 0?
          jz Done                             ;jump if yes

          vpbroadcastb ymm4,[rcx+CD.ThreshLo] ;packed ThreshLo
          vpbroadcastb ymm5,[rcx+CD.ThreshHi] ;packed ThreshHi

          mov rax,-1                          ;rax = index (i) for Loop2
          cmp r10,NSE                         ;NumPixels >= NSE?
          jb Init2                            ;jump if no
          mov rax,-NSE                        ;rax = index (i) for Loop1

; First pixel clipping for-loop using SIMD arithmetic
Loop1:    add rax,NSE                         ;i += NSE
          vmovdqa ymm0,ymmword ptr [r8+rax]   ;load PbSrc[i:i+31]
          vpmaxub ymm1,ymm0,ymm4              ;clip to ThreshLo
          vpminub ymm2,ymm1,ymm5              ;clip to ThreshHi
          vmovdqa ymmword ptr [r9+rax],ymm2   ;save PbDes[i:i+31] (clipped pixels)
```

359

```
        vpcmpeqb ymm3,ymm2,ymm0              ;compare clipped to original
        vpmovmskb edx,ymm3                   ;edx = mask of non-clipped pixels
        not edx                              ;edx = mask of clipped pixels
        popcnt esi,edx                       ;esi = num clipped this iteration
        add r11,rsi                          ;update NumClippedPixels

        sub r10,NSE                          ;NumPixels -= NSE
        cmp r10,NSE                          ;NumPixels >= NSE?
        jae Loop1                            ;jump if yes

        test r10,r10                         ;NumPixels == 0?
        jz Done                              ;jump if yes

; Perform initializations for Loop2
        add rax,NSE-1                        ;adjust i for Loop2

Init2:  movzx esi,byte ptr [rcx+CD.ThreshLo] ;esi = ThreshLo
        movzx edi,byte ptr [rcx+CD.ThreshHi] ;edi = ThreshHi
        xor ebx,ebx                          ;rbx = temp clipped count

; Second for-loop for residual pixels (if any) using scalar instructions
Loop2:  add rax,1                            ;i += 1
        movzx edx,byte ptr [r8+rax]          ;load next PbSrc[i]
        cmp edx,esi                          ;PbSrc[i] < ThreshLo?
        cmovb edx,esi                        ;edx = min(PbSrc[i], ThreshLo)
        setb bl                              ;rbx = 1 if pixel clipped else 0
        jb Save2

        cmp edx,edi                          ;PbSrc[i] > ThreshHi?
        cmova edx,edi                        ;edx = max(PbSrc[i], ThreshHi)
        seta bl                              ;rbx = 1 if pixel clipped else 0

Save2:  mov byte ptr [r9+rax],dl             ;save pixel to PbDes[i]
        add r11,rbx                          ;update clipped pixel count

        sub r10,1                            ;NumPixels -= 1
        jnz Loop2                            ;repeat until done

Done:   mov [rcx+CD.NumClippedPixels],r11    ;save NumClippedPixels

; Function epilogue
        vzeroupper
        pop rdi
        pop rsi
        pop rbx
        ret

ClipPixels_avx2 endp
        end
```

In function ClipPixels_avx2(), for-loop Loop1 begins each iteration with an add rax,NSE instruction that updates register RAX for the next group of NSE (32) pixels in PbSrc and PbDes. The next instruction, vmovdqa ymm0,ymmword ptr [r8+rax], loads pixels PbSrc[i:i+31] into register YMM0. This is followed by the instruction pair vpmaxub ymm1,ymm0,ymm4 and vpminub ymm2,ymm1,ymm5, which clips pixel values pbSrc[i:i+31] to ThreshLo and ThreshHi, respectively. The ensuing vmovdqa ymmword ptr [r9+rax],ymm2 instruction saves the clipped pixels to PbDes[i:i+31].

The next code block in ClipPixels_avx2() counts the number of pixels that were clipped during the current iteration of Loop1. This block begins with a vpcmpeqb ymm3,ymm2,ymm0 instruction that compares the original pixel values in YMM0 to the clipped values in YMM2 for equality. The vpcmpeqb instruction sets each corresponding byte element in YMM3 to 0xFF if the pixel values match (i.e., the pixel was not clipped); otherwise, the byte element in YMM3 is set to 0x00. The next instruction, vpmovmskb edx,ymm3 (Move Byte Mask), copies the most significant bit of each byte element in YMM3 to its corresponding bit position in register EDX. This is followed by a not edx instruction whose execution yields a mask of clipped pixels. The next instruction, popcnt esi,edx (Return the Count of Number of Bits Set to 1),[1] counts the number of bits set to 1 in EDX, which equals the number of pixels clipped during the current iteration of Loop1. The ensuing add r11,rsi instruction adds this value to NumClippedPixels in register R11.

Following execution of Loop1, ClipPixels_avx2() employs a simple for-loop named Loop2 to process any residual pixels. Note that Loop2 uses x86 byte registers to carry out its compare operations. Also note the use of the mov qword ptr [rcx+CD.NumClippedPixels],r11 instruction that follows Loop2, which saves the total number of clipped pixels.

Listing 10-3c shows a portion of the NASM code for example Ch10_03. This listing displays the NASM declaration of assembly language structure CD, which is syntactically different than the counterpart MASM structure declaration shown in Listing 10-3b.

Listing 10-3c. Example Ch10_03 NASM Code

```
; --------------------------------------------------------------------
; Ch10_03_fasm.s
; --------------------------------------------------------------------

        %include "ModX86Asm3eNASM.inc"

; The members of CD must match the corresponding structure
; that's declared in Ch10_03.h

struc CD
.PbSrc:            resq 1
.PbDes             resq 1
.NumPixels         resq 1
.NumClippedPixels  resq 1
.ThreshLo          resb 1
.ThreshHi          resb 1
endstruc
```

---

[1] A program should verify processor support for popcnt using the cpuid instruction as explained in Chapter 16.

Here are the results for source code example Ch10_03:

```
----- Results for Ch10_03 -----
num_pixels (test case): 8388639
cd0.m_NumClippedPixels: 654924
cd1.m_NumClippedPixels: 654924

Compare checks passed

Running benchmark function ClipPixels_bm() - please wait
Benchmark times save to file @Ch10_03_ClipPixels_bm_HELIUM.csv
```

Benchmarking

As mentioned earlier in this section, source code example Ch10_03 incorporates a benchmarking function named ClipPixels_bm(). This function, whose source code is shown in Listing 10-3d, measures execution times of pixel clipping functions ClipPixels_cpp() and ClipPixels_avx2(). Most of the timing measurement code is encapsulated in a C++ class named BmThreadTimer. This class includes two member functions, BmThreadTimer::Start() and BmThreadTimer::Stop(), that implement a simple software stopwatch. Class BmThreadTimer also includes a member function named BmThreadTimer::SaveElapsedTimes(), which saves the timing measurements to a comma-separated value (.csv) text file. This function also saves summary statistics to a text file. The source code for class BmThreadTimer is not shown in Listing 10-3d but is included as part of the software download package.

Listing 10-3d. Example Ch10_03 C++ Benchmarking Code

```cpp
//------------------------------------------------------------------------------
// Ch10_03_bm.cpp
//------------------------------------------------------------------------------

#include <iostream>
#include <string>
#include <cstring>
#include "AlignedMem.h"
#include "BmThreadTimer.h"
#include "Ch10_03.h"

void ClipPixels_bm(void)
{
    std::cout << "\nRunning benchmark function ClipPixels_bm() - please wait\n";

    constexpr uint8_t thresh_lo = c_ThreshLo;
    constexpr uint8_t thresh_hi = c_ThreshHi;
    constexpr size_t num_pixels = c_NumPixelsBM;

    AlignedArray<uint8_t> pb_src(num_pixels, c_Alignment);
    AlignedArray<uint8_t> pb_des0(num_pixels, c_Alignment);
    AlignedArray<uint8_t> pb_des1(num_pixels, c_Alignment);
```

```
    InitPixelBuffer(pb_src.Data(), num_pixels);

    ClipData cd0;
    cd0.m_PbSrc = pb_src.Data();
    cd0.m_PbDes = pb_des0.Data();
    cd0.m_NumPixels = num_pixels;
    cd0.m_NumClippedPixels = (std::numeric_limits<size_t>::max)();
    cd0.m_ThreshLo = thresh_lo;
    cd0.m_ThreshHi = thresh_hi;

    ClipData cd1;
    cd1.m_PbSrc = pb_src.Data();
    cd1.m_PbDes = pb_des1.Data();
    cd1.m_NumPixels = num_pixels;
    cd1.m_NumClippedPixels = (std::numeric_limits<size_t>::max)();
    cd1.m_ThreshLo = thresh_lo;
    cd1.m_ThreshHi = thresh_hi;

    constexpr size_t num_alg = 2;
    constexpr size_t num_iter = BmThreadTimer::NumIterDef;
    BmThreadTimer bmtt(num_iter, num_alg);

    for (size_t i = 0; i < num_iter; i++)
    {
        bmtt.Start(i, 0);
        ClipPixels_cpp(&cd0);
        bmtt.Stop(i, 0);

        bmtt.Start(i, 1);
        ClipPixels_avx2(&cd1);
        bmtt.Stop(i, 1);
    }

    bool ncp_check = cd0.m_NumClippedPixels == cd1.m_NumClippedPixels;
    bool mem_check = memcmp(pb_des0.Data(), pb_des1.Data(), num_pixels) == 0;

    if (!ncp_check || !mem_check)
        std::cout << "\nBenchmark compare checks failed!\n";

    std::string fn = bmtt.BuildCsvFilenameString("@Ch10_03_ClipPixels_bm");
    bmtt.SaveElapsedTimes(fn, BmThreadTimer::EtUnit::MicroSec, 2);
    std::cout << "Benchmark times save to file " << fn << '\n';
}
```

Table 10-1 presents benchmark timing measurements for the functions ClipPixels_cpp() and ClipPixels_avx2() using an Intel Core i5-11600K (Debian 11, GNU C++ 10.2.1), Intel Core Intel i7-11700K (Windows 11 22H2, Visual C++ 2022), and AMD Ryzen 7 7700X (Ubuntu 22.10, GNU C++ 12.2.0). These measurements were made using executable files compiled for maximum speed: /O2 for Visual C++ and -O3 for GNU C++. In addition, the C++ compiler code generation options were set to match the x86-AVX instruction set used in the assembly language code. For the current example, the switches /arch:AVX2 and -mavx2 were utilized for Visual C++ and GNU C++, respectively. Doing this facilitates "apples-to-apples" comparisons between the C++ coded function and the assembly language counterparts. All timing measurements were made using ordinary desktop PCs that are also used for other purposes. No attempt was made to mitigate the effects of any hardware, software, operating system, BIOS, or other configuration differences between the PCs prior to running the benchmark executable file. The benchmarking test conditions described in this section are also used in subsequent source code examples.

Table 10-1. *Benchmark Timing Measurements (Microseconds) for Pixel Clipping Functions (10,000,000 Pixels)*

Function	i5-11600K	i7-11700K	7700X
ClipPixels_cpp()	9477 (153)	9231 (199)	6968 (10)
ClipPixels_avx2()	643 (15)	606 (28)	183 (6)

The mean (standard deviation) measurements shown in Table 10-1 are truncated statistics. Each function was executed 1000 times; the 25 smallest and 25 largest timing measurements were discarded before calculating the mean and standard deviation. This was done to minimize the effect of outliers that sometimes occur during function execution, especially when the host operating system preempts an executing thread and transfers it to another processor core. Class BmThreadTimer contains the source code for these statistical calculations.

The measurements in Table 10-1 demonstrate that function ClipPixels_avx2() outperforms ClipPixels_cpp() by a wide margin. It should be noted that the degree of performance gains in this example is somewhat atypical; however, it is not uncommon to achieve significant speed improvements when using assembly language, especially in code that can fully exploit the SIMD capabilities of x86-AVX. You'll see additional examples of accelerated performance throughout the remainder of this book.

The purpose of the benchmark timing measurements cited in this book is to provide constructive insights regarding the performance of a function coded using conventional C++ statements vs. an explicitly coded x86-64 assembly language counterpart. The software stopwatch technique of benchmarking is simple to perform (it doesn't require any special drivers or compiler switches) and provides a reasonable approximation of execution time. However, it also has weaknesses. For example, it may not accurately replicate real-world processor cache usage.

Like many other types of benchmarking, software performance benchmarking is not an exact science and subject to a variety of factors, both controllable and uncontrollable. It is important to keep mind that this book is a primer about x86 assembly language programming and not benchmarking. The source code examples are structured to hasten the study of x86-64 assembly language programming. Both Visual C++ and GNU C++ include a plethora of code generation options that can affect performance. It is also important to keep in mind that benchmark timing measurements should always be construed in a context that correlates with the software's purpose. Finally, it would be foolish to draw any general conclusions regarding the performance of AMD vs. Intel processors, Visual C++ vs. GNU C++ code efficiency, or Windows vs. Linux execution speed based solely on the type and small number of benchmark timing measurements published in this book. Comparisons should only be made using a C++ function and its counterpart assembly language function *on the same processor*. Appendix A contains additional information about the software tools used to develop the source code examples.

RGB to Grayscale

The next source example, named Ch10_04, explains how to use AVX2 instructions to convert an RGB color image to an 8-bit grayscale image. It also demonstrates the intermixing of packed integer and packed floating-point instructions in the same calculating function. Unlike the previous image processing examples, source code example Ch10_04 uses a PNG image file instead of an array of randomly generated pixel values.

A variety of algorithms exist to convert an RGB image into a grayscale image. One frequently used technique calculates grayscale pixel values using a weighted sum of the RGB color components. In this source code example, RGB pixel values are converted to grayscale values using the following equation:

$$GS(x,y) = R(x,y)W_r + G(x,y)W_g + B(x,y)W_b$$

In the conversion equation, each RGB color conversion coefficient is a floating-point number between 0.0 and 1.0. The sum of these coefficients normally equals 1.0. The exact values used for the coefficients are based on published standards that reflect a multitude of visual factors including properties of the target color space, display device characteristics, and perceived image quality. Appendix B lists some references that you can consult if you're interested in learning more about RGB to grayscale image conversion.

Listing 10-4a shows the principal C++ source code for example Ch10_04. This listing opens with the declaration of a structure named RGB32, which is in header file ImageMisc.h. Structure RGB32 defines an RGB component ordering scheme for a color pixel. Note that in this example, RGB32 structure member m_A (alpha channel) is not used. Header file ImageMisc.h includes several enum classes that are used to support the loading and saving of image files. Next in Listing 10-4a is the header file Ch10_04.h. This file contains function declarations and a few miscellaneous constants. In file Ch10_04_fcpp.cpp, function ConvertRgbToGs_cpp() includes code that converts the RGB pixel values in pb_rgb to grayscale. This function includes a simple for-loop that implements the previously defined RGB to grayscale conversion equation.

Listing 10-4a. Example Ch10_04 C++ Code

```
//-----------------------------------------------------------------------------
// ImageMisc.h
//-----------------------------------------------------------------------------

#pragma once
#include <cstdint>

struct RGB32
{
    // Do not change order of elements below
    uint8_t m_R;
    uint8_t m_G;
    uint8_t m_B;
    uint8_t m_A;
};

enum class PixelType : unsigned int
{
    Undefined,
    Gray8,
    Rgb32
};

enum class ImageFileType : unsigned int
{
    Undefined,
    BMP,
    PNG,
```

```
    JPEG,
    TIFF
};

enum class Channel : unsigned int
{
    // Do not change order of R, G, B, A
    R, G, B, A,
    None
};

//----------------------------------------------------------------------
// Ch10_04.h
//----------------------------------------------------------------------

#pragma once
#include <cstddef>
#include <cstdint>
#include "ImageMisc.h"

// Ch10_04_fasm.asm, Ch10_04_fasm.s
extern "C" void ConvertRgbToGs_avx2(uint8_t* pb_gs, const RGB32* pb_rgb,
    size_t num_pixels, const float coef[4]);

// Ch10_04_fcpp.cpp
extern void ConvertRgbToGs_cpp(uint8_t* pb_gs, const RGB32* pb_rgb,
    size_t num_pixels, const float coef[4]);

// Ch10_04_misc.cpp
extern void ConvertRgbToGs_bm(void);
extern bool CompareGsPixelBuffers(const uint8_t* pb_gs1, const uint8_t* pb_gs2,
    size_t num_pixels);

// Ch15_04.cpp
extern const float c_Coef[4];
extern const char* c_TestImageFileName;

// Ch10_04_bm.cpp
void ConvertRgbToGs_bm(void);

// Miscellaneous constants
constexpr size_t c_Alignment = 32;

//----------------------------------------------------------------------
// Ch10_04_fcpp.cpp
//----------------------------------------------------------------------

#include "Ch10_04.h"

#include <iostream>
#include <stdexcept>
```

```cpp
#include "Ch10_04.h"
#include "AlignedMem.h"
#include "ImageMisc.h"

static bool CheckArgs(const uint8_t* pb_gs, const RGB32* pb_rgb,
    size_t num_pixels, const float coef[4])
{
    if (num_pixels == 0)
        return false;

    if (num_pixels % 8 != 0)
        return false;

    if (!AlignedMem::IsAligned(pb_gs, c_Alignment))
        return false;

    if (!AlignedMem::IsAligned(pb_rgb, c_Alignment))
        return false;

    if (coef[0] < 0.0f || coef[1] < 0.0f || coef[2] < 0.0f)
        return false;

    return true;
}

void ConvertRgbToGs_cpp(uint8_t* pb_gs, const RGB32* pb_rgb, size_t num_pixels,
    const float coef[4])
{
    if (!CheckArgs(pb_gs, pb_rgb, num_pixels, coef))
        throw std::runtime_error("ConvertRgbToGs_cpp() - CheckArgs failed");

    for (size_t i = 0; i < num_pixels; i++)
    {
        uint8_t r = pb_rgb[i].m_R;
        uint8_t g = pb_rgb[i].m_G;
        uint8_t b = pb_rgb[i].m_B;

        float gs_temp = r * coef[0] + g * coef[1] + b * coef[2] + 0.5f;

        if (gs_temp > 255.0f)
            gs_temp = 255.0f;

        pb_gs[i] = (uint8_t)gs_temp;
    }
}
```

Listing 10-4b shows the MASM code for example Ch10_04. In this listing, file Ch10_04.asm starts with a .const section that defines the floating-point and integer constants needed for this example. Function ConvertRgbToGs_avx2() begins its execution with a prologue that preserves non-volatile SIMD registers XMM12–XMM15 on the stack using the macro SaveXmmRegs_M. Following its prologue, function

367

ConvertRgbToGs_avx2() validates num_pixels (R8) for size. It also ensures that argument pointers pb_gs (RCX) and pb_rgb (RDX) are properly aligned on a 32-byte boundary. Following the pixel buffer pointer checks, ConvertRgbToGs_avx2() verifies that the color coefficients in array coef[ ] are positive values.

Listing 10-4b. Example Ch10_04 MASM Code

```
;-----------------------------------------------------------------------
; Ch10_04_fasm.asm
;-----------------------------------------------------------------------

        include <MacrosX86-64-AVX.asmh>

            .const
F32_0p5     real4   0.5
F32_255p0   real4   255.0
I32_0xff    dd      0ffh


;-----------------------------------------------------------------------
; void ConvertRgbToGs_avx2(uint8_t* pb_gs, const RGB32* pb_rgb,
;   size_t num_pixels, const float coef[4]);
;-----------------------------------------------------------------------

NSE     equ 8                           ;num_simd_elements

        .code
ConvertRgbToGs_avx2 proc frame
        CreateFrame_M CV_,0,64
        SaveXmmRegs_M xmm12,xmm13,xmm14,xmm15
        EndProlog_M

; Validate argument values
        test r8,r8
        jz Done                         ;jump if num_pixels == 0
        test r8,07h
        jnz Done                        ;jump if num_pixels not multiple of 8

        test rcx,1fh
        jnz Done                        ;jump if pb_gs not 32b aligned
        test rdx,1fh
        jnz Done                        ;jump if pb_rgb not 32b aligned

        vxorps xmm0,xmm0,xmm0           ;xmm0 = 0.0

        vmovss xmm13,real4 ptr [r9]     ;xmm13 = coef[0]
        vcomiss xmm13,xmm0
        jb Done                         ;jump if coef[0] < 0.0

        vmovss xmm14,real4 ptr [r9+4]   ;xmm14 = coef[1]
        vcomiss xmm14,xmm0
        jb Done                         ;jump if coef[1] < 0.0
```

```
        vmovss xmm15,real4 ptr [r9+8]          ;xmm15 = coef[2]
        vcomiss xmm15,xmm0
        jb  Done                               ;jump if coef[2] < 0.0

; Perform required initializations
        vbroadcastss ymm4,real4 ptr [F32_0p5]     ;packed 0.5
        vbroadcastss ymm5,real4 ptr [F32_255p0]   ;packed 255.0

        vpbroadcastd ymm12,[I32_0xff]          ;packed 0x000000ff

        vbroadcastss ymm13,xmm13               ;packed coef[0]
        vbroadcastss ymm14,xmm14               ;packed coef[1]
        vbroadcastss ymm15,xmm15               ;packed coef[2]

        mov rax,-NSE                           ;rax = common pixel buffer offset

; Convert pixels from RGB to gray scale
Loop1:  add rax,NSE                            ;update pixel buffer offset
        vmovdqa ymm0,ymmword ptr [rdx+rax*4]   ;load next block of 8 RGB32 pixels

        vpand ymm1,ymm0,ymm12                  ;ymm1 = r values (dwords)
        vpsrld ymm0,ymm0,8
        vpand ymm2,ymm0,ymm12                  ;ymm2 = g values (dwords)
        vpsrld ymm0,ymm0,8
        vpand ymm3,ymm0,ymm12                  ;ymm3 = b values (dwords)

        vcvtdq2ps ymm1,ymm1                    ;ymm1 = r values (F32)
        vcvtdq2ps ymm2,ymm2                    ;ymm2 = g values (F32)
        vcvtdq2ps ymm3,ymm3                    ;ymm3 = b values (F32)

        vmulps ymm1,ymm1,ymm13                 ;ymm1 = r values * coef[0]
        vmulps ymm2,ymm2,ymm14                 ;ymm2 = g values * coef[1]
        vmulps ymm3,ymm3,ymm15                 ;ymm3 = b values * coef[2]

        vaddps ymm0,ymm1,ymm2                  ;ymm0 = sum of r and g values
        vaddps ymm1,ymm3,ymm4                  ;ymm1 = sum of b values and 0.5
        vaddps ymm0,ymm0,ymm1                  ;ymm0 = sum of r, g, b, and 0.5

        vminps ymm1,ymm0,ymm5                  ;clip grayscale values to 255.0

        vcvtps2dq ymm0,ymm1                    ;convert F32 values to dword
        vpackusdw ymm1,ymm0,ymm0               ;convert dwords to words
        vpermq ymm2,ymm1,10001000b             ;ymm2[127:0] = 8 grayscale words
        vpackuswb ymm3,ymm2,ymm2               ;ymm3[63:0] = 8 grayscale bytes
```

```
        vmovq qword ptr [rcx+rax],xmm3        ;save pb_gs[i:i+7]

        sub r8,NSE                            ;num_pixels -= NSE
        jnz Loop1                             ;jump if num_pixels != 0

Done:   vzeroupper
        RestoreXmmRegs_M xmm12,xmm13,xmm14,xmm15
        DeleteFrame_M
        ret

ConvertRgbToGs_avx2 endp
        end
```

Following argument validation, ConvertRgbToGs_avx2() employs the instruction pair vbroadcastss ymm4,real4 ptr [F32_Op5] and vbroadcastss ymm5,real4 ptr [F32_255p0] to create packed versions of the floating-point constants 0.5 and 255.0, respectively. The next instruction, vpbroadcastd ymm12,[I32_0xff], sets each doubleword element in YMM12 to 0x000000FF. This packed mask will be used during RGB de-interleaving as you'll soon see. The ensuing instruction triplet, vbroadcastss ymm13,xmm13, vbroadcastss ymm14,xmm14, and vbroadcastss ymm15,xmm15, creates packed versions of the color conversion coefficients. Note that the source operand for these vbroadcastss instructions is an XMM register. Unlike AVX, the source operand for the AVX2 version of vbroadcasts[d|s] can be a memory value or an XMM register.

Each iteration of for-loop Loop1 begins with an add rax,NSE instruction that updates RAX for the next block of pixels. The ensuing vmovdqa ymm0,ymmword ptr [rdx+rax*4] instruction loads a block of eight RGB32 pixels into register YMM0. The next code block uses a series of vpand and vpsrld instructions to de-interleave the 8-bit color components of each RGB32 pixel as shown in Figure 10-2. These values are then converted to single-precision floating-point using the vcvtdq2ps instruction, also shown in Figure 10-2.

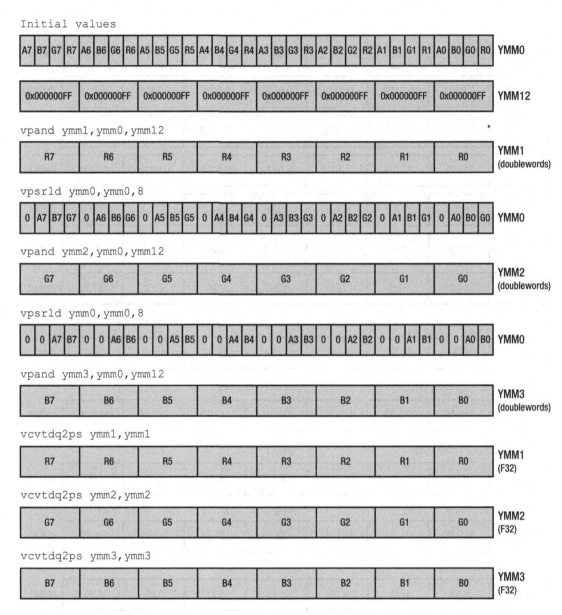

Figure 10-2. *RGB32 pixel de-interleaving and conversion to floating-point*

Following the conversion operation, `ConvertRgbToGs_avx2()` uses a series of `vmulps` instructions to multiply each color component by its corresponding color conversion coefficient. This is followed by a series of `vaddps` instructions that sum the color component values as shown in Figure 10-3. The `vminps ymm1,ymm0,ymm5` instruction that follows the summing operation ensures that each grayscale pixel value is not greater than 255.0.

Initial values

0.5	0.5	0.5	0.5	0.5	0.5	0.5	0.5	YMM4

0.2126	0.2126	0.2126	0.2126	0.2126	0.2126	0.2126	0.2126	YMM13

0.7152	0.7152	0.7152	0.7152	0.7152	0.7152	0.7152	0.7152	YMM14

0.0722	0.0722	0.0722	0.0722	0.0722	0.0722	0.0722	0.0722	YMM15

222.0	218.0	212.0	202.0	199.0	224.0	227.0	229.0	YMM1

162.0	158.0	156.0	165.0	155.0	159.0	161.0	164.0	YMM2

88.0	84.0	83.0	79.0	82.0	86.0	89.0	87.0	YMM3

```
vmulps ymm1,ymm1,ymm13          ;ymm1 = r values * coef[0]
```

47.20	46.35	45.07	42.95	42.31	47.62	48.26	48.69	YMM1

```
vmulps ymm2,ymm2,ymm14          ;ymm2 = g values * coef[1]
```

115.86	113.00	111.57	118.01	110.86	113.72	115.15	117.29	YMM2

```
vmulps ymm3,ymm3,ymm15          ;ymm3 = b values * coef[2]
```

6.35	6.06	5.99	5.70	5.92	6.21	6.43	6.28	YMM3

```
vaddps ymm0,ymm1,ymm2           ;ymm0 = sum of r and g values
```

163.06	159.35	156.64	160.96	153.17	161.34	163.41	165.98	YMM0

```
vaddps ymm1,ymm3,ymm4           ;ymm1 = sum of b values and 0.5
```

6.85	6.56	6.49	6.20	6.42	6.71	6.93	6.78	YMM1

```
vaddps ymm0,ymm0,ymm1           ;ymm0 = sum of r, g, b, and 0.5
```

169.91	165.91	163.13	167.16	159.59	168.05	170.34	172.76	YMM0

Figure 10-3. *SIMD RGB to grayscale calculation*

Figure 10-4 illustrates the final sequence of instructions used by ConvertRgbToGs_avx2() in for-loop Loop1. The vcvtps2dq ymm0,ymm1 (Convert Packed SPFP Values to Packed Signed Doubleword Values) instruction converts each single-precision floating-point element in YMM1 to a doubleword integer. Note that vcvtps2dq performs its conversions using rounding mode specified in MXCSR.RC (the default

MXCSR.RC rounding mode for both Visual C++ and GNU C++ is round to nearest). The ensuing vpackusdw ymm1,ymm0,ymm0 (Pack with Unsigned Saturation) instruction size-reduces the doubleword values in YMM0 to words. Note that vpackusdw performs two independent operations using the upper and lower lanes of YMM0. The next instruction, vpermq ymm2,ymm1,10001000b (Qwords Element Permutation), reorders the word elements of YMM1 as shown in Figure 10-4. In this instruction, bit positions 0 and 1 of the immediate operand 10001000b select the quadword that gets copied into YMM2[63:0] (00 = YMM1[63:0]; a function can also use 01 = YMM1[127:64], 10 = YMM1[191:128], 11 = YMM1[255:192]). Similarly, bit positions 2 and 3 of the immediate operand select the quadword that gets copied into YMM2[127:64]. Following execution of the vpermq instruction, ConvertRgbToGs_avx2() employs a vpackuswb ymm3,ymm2,ymm2 instruction to size-reduce the word elements of YMM2 to bytes.

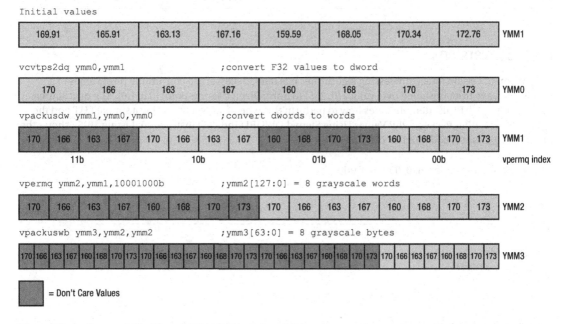

Figure 10-4. *Grayscale floating-point to 8-bit unsigned integer conversion*

Following the floating-point to unsigned integer conversion, ConvertRgbToGs_avx2() employs a vmovq qword ptr [rcx+rax],xmm3 (Move Quadword) instruction to save the converted pixel values to pb_des[i:i+7]. More specifically, the vmovq instruction copies XMM3[63:0] to the memory location specified by its destination operand. Execution of for-loop Loop1 continues until all pixels have been converted.

The NASM implementation of ConvertRgbToGs_avx2() resembles its MASM counterpart except for the use of different argument registers. Here are the results for source code example Ch10_04:

```
----- Results for Ch10_04 -----
Converting RGB image ../../Data/TestImageA.png
im_h = 2592 pixels
im_w = 1728 pixels
Saving grayscale image #0 - @Ch10_04_TestImageA_gs0_HELIUM.png
Saving grayscale image #1 - @Ch10_04_TestImageA_gs1_HELIUM.png
Grayscale pixel buffer compare OK

Running benchmark function ConvertRgbToGs_bm() - please wait
Benchmark times save to file @Ch10_04_ConvertRgbToGs_bm_HELIUM.csv
```

Table 10-2 shows the benchmark timing measurements for example Ch10_04. Like the previous example, the assembly language coded functions outperform the C++ counterpart function by a meaningful margin.

Table 10-2. *Benchmark Timing Measurements (Microseconds) for RGB to Grayscale Functions Using* `TestImageA.png`

Function	i5-11600K	i7-11700K	7700X
ConvertRgbToGs_cpp()	5694 (8)	5616 (85)	5884 (8)
ConvertRgbToGs_avx2()	1148 (4)	1076 (24)	728 (4)

Pixel Conversions

To implement certain image processing algorithms, it is often necessary to convert the pixel values of a grayscale image from unsigned byte values [0, 255] to normalized floating-point [0.0, 1.0]. The next source code example, Ch10_05, demonstrates how to perform this type of conversion using a simple LUT and the vgatherdps (Gather Packed SPFP Values Using Signed DWORD Indices) instruction. Listing 10-5a shows the principal C++ source code for this example.

Listing 10-5a. Example Ch10_05 C++ Code

```
//-------------------------------------------------------------------------
// Ch10_05.h
//-------------------------------------------------------------------------

#pragma once
#include <cstddef>
#include <cstdint>

// Ch10_05_fasm.asm, Ch10_05_fasm.s
extern "C" void ConvertU8ToF32_avx2(float* pb_des, const uint8_t * pb_src,
    size_t num_pixels);

// Ch10_05_fcpp.cpp
extern void ConvertU8ToF32_cpp(float* pb_des, const uint8_t* pb_src,
    size_t num_pixels);

// Ch10_05_misc.cpp
extern void BuildLUT_U8ToF32(void);
extern size_t CompareArraysF32(const float* pb_src1, const float* pb_src2,
    size_t num_pixels);
extern void InitArray(uint8_t* pb, size_t num_pixels);

extern "C" float g_LUT_U8ToF32[];

// Ch10_05_bm.cpp
extern void ConvertU8ToF32_bm(void);
```

```
// Miscellaneous constants
constexpr size_t c_Alignment = 32;
constexpr size_t c_NumPixels = 1024 * 1024 + 19;
constexpr size_t c_NumPixelsBM = 10000000;
constexpr int c_FillMinVal = 0;
constexpr int c_FillMaxVal = 255;
constexpr unsigned int c_RngSeed = 71;


//-----------------------------------------------------------------------------
// Ch10_05_fcpp.cpp
//-----------------------------------------------------------------------------

#include <stdexcept>
#include "Ch10_05.h"
#include "AlignedMem.h"

static bool CheckArgs(const void* pb1, const void* pb2, size_t num_pixels)
{
    if (num_pixels == 0)
        return false;

    if (!AlignedMem::IsAligned(pb1, c_Alignment))
        return false;

    if (!AlignedMem::IsAligned(pb2, c_Alignment))
        return false;

    return true;
}

void ConvertU8ToF32_cpp(float* pb_des, const uint8_t* pb_src, size_t num_pixels)
{
    if (!CheckArgs(pb_des, pb_src, num_pixels))
        throw std::runtime_error("ConvertU8ToF32_cpp() CheckArgs failed");

    for (size_t i = 0; i < num_pixels; i++)
        pb_des[i] = g_LUT_U8ToF32[pb_src[i]];
}
```

Listing 10-5a begins with the file Ch10_05.h, which contains the function declarations for this example. Note in this file that global array g_LUT_U8ToF32[] is declared using the "C" modifier since it is referenced in the assembly language code. Each entry in g_LUT_U8ToF32[] is used to translate an unsigned 8-bit grayscale pixel value to its normalized single-precision floating-point equivalent (i.e., 0 = 0.0, 1 = 0.0039215, 2 = 0.0078431, ... 255 = 1.0).

Also shown in Listing 10-5a is a file named Ch10_05_fcpp.cpp, which includes a conversion function named ConvertU8ToF32_cpp(). This function converts a pixel buffer of uint8_t values to normalized single-precision floating-point values. Following argument validation, function ConvertU8ToF32_cpp() employs a simple two-statement for-loop that converts each pixel from uint8_t to single-precision floating-point.

Listing 10-5b shows the MASM code for function ConvertU8ToF32_avx2(). This function begins its execution with a code block that validates argument value num_pixels (R8) for size. It then checks pixel buffer pointers pb_des (RCX) and pb_src (RDX) for proper alignment. Following argument validation, ConvertU8ToF32_avx2() performs its requisite initializations. Note that the lea r9,[g_LUT_U8ToF32] instruction loads the address of the pixel conversion LUT g_LUT_U8ToF32 into register R9.

Listing 10-5b. Example Ch10_05 MASM Code

```
;-----------------------------------------------------------------------
; Ch10_05_fasm.asm
;-----------------------------------------------------------------------


;-----------------------------------------------------------------------
; void ConvertU8ToF32_avx2(float* pb_des, const uint8_t* pb_src,
;    size_t num_pixels);
;-----------------------------------------------------------------------

NSE     equ 32                          ;num_simd_elements

        extern g_LUT_U8ToF32:qword

        .code
ConvertU8ToF32_avx2 proc

; Validate arguments
        test r8,r8
        jz Done                         ;jump if num_pixels == 0

        test rcx,1fh
        jnz Done                        ;jump if pb_des not 32b aligned
        test rdx,1fh
        jnz Done                        ;jump if pb_src not 32b aligned

; Initialize
        lea r9,qword ptr [g_LUT_U8ToF32] ;r9 = pointer to LUT
        vpcmpeqb ymm5,ymm5,ymm5         ;ymm5 = all ones

        mov rax,-1                      ;rax = index (i) for Loop2
        cmp r8,NSE                      ;num_pixels >= NSE?
        jb Loop2                        ;jump if no
        mov rax,-NSE                    ;rax = index (i) for Loop1

; Convert pixels from U8 to F32 using LUT and gather operations
Loop1:  add rax,NSE                     ;i += NSE
        vpmovzxbd ymm0,qword ptr [rdx+rax] ;ymm0 = pb_src[i:i+7] (U32)
        vmovdqa ymm1,ymm5               ;ymm1 = vgatherdps load mask
        vgatherdps ymm2,[r9+ymm0*4],ymm1 ;ymm2 = pb_src[i:i+7] (F32)
        vmovaps ymmword ptr [rcx+rax*4],ymm2 ;save pb_des[i:i+7]
```

```
        vpmovzxbd ymm0,qword ptr [rdx+rax+8]    ;ymm0 = pb_src[i+8:i+15] (U32)
        vmovdqa ymm1,ymm5                        ;ymm1 = vgatherdps load mask
        vgatherdps ymm2,[r9+ymm0*4],ymm1         ;ymm2 = pb_src[i_8:i+15] (F32)
        vmovaps ymmword ptr [rcx+rax*4+32],ymm2 ;save pb_des[i+8:i+15]

        vpmovzxbd ymm0,qword ptr [rdx+rax+16]    ;ymm0 = pb_src[i+16:i+23] (U32)
        vmovdqa ymm1,ymm5                        ;ymm1 = vgatherdps load mask
        vgatherdps ymm2,[r9+ymm0*4],ymm1         ;ymm2 = pb_src[i+16:i+23] (F32)
        vmovaps ymmword ptr [rcx+rax*4+64],ymm2 ;save pb_des[i+16:i+23]

        vpmovzxbd ymm0,qword ptr [rdx+rax+24]    ;ymm0 = pb_src[i+24:i+31] (U32)
        vmovdqa ymm1,ymm5                        ;ymm1 = vgatherdps load mask
        vgatherdps ymm2,[r9+ymm0*4],ymm1         ;ymm2 = pb_src[i+24:i+31] (F32)
        vmovaps ymmword ptr [rcx+rax*4+96],ymm2 ;save pb_des[i+24:i+31]

        sub r8,NSE                               ;num_pixels -= NSE
        cmp r8,NSE                               ;num_pixels >= NSE?
        jae Loop1                                ;jump if yes

; Convert any residual pixels using scalar instructions
        test r8,r8                               ;num_pixels == 0?
        jz Done                                  ;jump if yes
        add rax,NSE-1                            ;adjust i for Loop2

Loop2:  add rax,1                                ;i += 1
        movzx r10,byte ptr [rdx+rax]             ;load pb_src[i]
        vmovss xmm0,real4 ptr [r9+r10*4]         ;convert to F32 using LUT
        vmovss real4 ptr [rcx+rax*4],xmm0        ;save pb_des[i]

        sub r8,1                                 ;num_pixels -= 1
        jnz Loop2                                ;jump if num_pixels != 0

Done:   vzeroupper
        ret
ConvertU8ToF32_avx2 endp
        end
```

Each iteration of for-loop Loop1 begins with an add rax,NSE instruction that updates the common pixel buffer displacement value in register RAX for the next group of pixels. Next, ConvertU8ToF32_avx2() employs a vpmovzxbd ymm0,qword ptr [rdx+rax] instruction to load pixel values pb_src[i:i+7] into register YMM0. Recall that the vpmovzxbd instruction zero-extends each source operand pixel byte to a doubleword. The ensuing vmovdqa ymm1,ymm5 instruction loads register YMM1 with a mask. The most significant bit of each doubleword element in YMM1 is used by the subsequent vgatherdps instruction to perform conditional loads. More on this in a moment. The vgatherdps ymm2,[r9+ymm0*4],ymm1 instruction loads single-precision floating-point elements from the array pointed to by R9 (g_LUT_U8ToF32) into register YMM1. The elements loaded into YMM2 are designated by the signed doubleword indices in register YMM0 as illustrated in Figure 10-5.

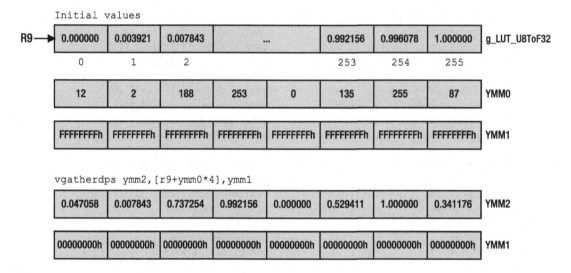

Figure 10-5. *Execution of vgatherdps instruction*

It is important to note that the vgatherdps ymm2,[r9+ymm0*4],ymm1 instruction will load an element from the array specified by R9 into YMM2 only if the most significant bit of the corresponding doubleword element in YMM1 (the mask operand) is set to 1. If this bit is set to 0, the doubleword element in destination operand YMM2 is not altered. Following each successful element gather, vgatherdps zeroes the corresponding doubleword element in the mask operand (YMM1); otherwise, the doubleword mask element remains unaltered. This mask operand zeroing scheme facilitates resumption of an executing vgatherdps instruction should a page fault occur when gathering elements from the specified array.

The next three code blocks employ the same sequence of instructions to convert pixels pb_src[i+8:i+15], pb_src[i+16:i+23], and pb_src[i+24:i+31]. Note that ConvertU8ToF32_avx2() uses a vmovdqa ymm1,ymm5 instruction prior to each vgatherdps instruction, which reloads the mask operand since execution of the previous vgatherdps instruction zeroed all doubleword elements in YMM1. Following execution of Loop1, for-loop Loop2 processes any residual pixels using scalar AVX instructions.

The NASM implementation of ConvertU8ToF32_avx2() utilizes the same instruction sequences as its MASM counterpart, but with different general-purpose argument registers. Here are the results for source code example Ch10_05:

```
----- Results for Ch10_05 -----
num_pixels (test case): 1048595
num_diff:               0
Pixel buffer compare test passed

Running benchmark function ConvertU8ToF32_bm() - please wait
Benchmark times save to file @Ch10_05_ConvertU8ToF32_bm_HELIUM.csv
```

Table 10-3 shows the benchmark timing measurements for example Ch10_05. In this example, the assembly language coded functions modestly outperform their C++ counterparts.

Table 10-3. *Benchmark Timing Measurements (Microseconds) for LUT Conversion Functions (10,000,000 Pixels)*

Function	i5-11600K	i7-11700K	7700X
ConvertU8ToF32_cpp()	3017 (10)	2669 (66)	2452 (62)
ConvertU8ToF32_avx2()	2419 (9)	2315 (65)	2327 (6)

It is important to mention that the vgatherdps instruction does not perform any checks for invalid indices. The use of an invalid index will cause the processor to load an erroneous data value or generate an exception if vgatherdps references an illegal memory address. The AVX2 instruction set extension also includes additional gather instructions including vgatherdpd and vgatherqp[d|s]. The latter two instructions require quadword indices. For integer doubleword and quadword gathers, you can use the instruction vpgatherd[d|q] or vpgatherq[d|q]. The next source code example demonstrates the use of the vpgatherdd instruction.

Image Histogram

One of the most informative statistical representations of a grayscale image is a histogram of its pixel intensity values. Image histograms are frequently generated in real time immediately following image capture or during the initial stages of a more sophisticated image processing algorithm. Figure 10-6 shows an example grayscale image with eight bits of intensity resolution per pixel and its histogram.

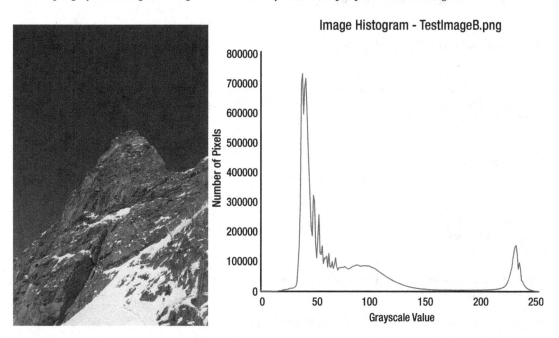

Figure 10-6. *Example grayscale image and its histogram*

Source code example Ch10_06 explains how to construct an image histogram using AVX2 instructions. Listing 10-6a shows the principal C++ code for this example.

Listing 10-6a. Example Ch10_06 C++ Code

```
//-----------------------------------------------------------------------
// Ch10_06.h
//-----------------------------------------------------------------------

#pragma once
#include <cstddef>
#include <cstdint>

// Ch10_06_fasm.asm, Ch10_06_fasm.s
extern "C" bool BuildHistogram_avx2(uint32_t * histo, const uint8_t * pixel_buff,
    size_t num_pixels);

// Ch10_06_fcpp.cpp
extern bool BuildHistogram_cpp(uint32_t* histo, const uint8_t* pixel_buff,
    size_t num_pixels);

// Ch10_06_misc.cpp
extern void SaveHistograms(const uint32_t* histo0, const uint32_t* histo1,
    size_t histo_size, bool rc0, bool rc1);

// Ch10_06_bm.cpp
extern void BuildHistogram_bm(void);

// Miscellaneous globals and constants
extern const char* g_ImageFileName;
constexpr size_t c_HistoSize = 256;       // Number of histogram bins
constexpr size_t c_Alignment = 32;

//-----------------------------------------------------------------------
// Ch10_06_fcpp.cpp
//-----------------------------------------------------------------------

#include <cstring>
#include <stdexcept>
#include "Ch10_06.h"
#include "AlignedMem.h"

static bool CheckArgs(uint32_t* histo, const uint8_t* pixel_buff,
    size_t num_pixels)
{
    if (!AlignedMem::IsAligned(histo, c_Alignment))
        return false;
    if (!AlignedMem::IsAligned(pixel_buff, c_Alignment))
        return false;
```

```
    if (num_pixels == 0)
        return false;
    if (num_pixels % 32 != 0)
        return false;

    return true;
}

bool BuildHistogram_cpp(uint32_t* histo, const uint8_t* pixel_buff,
    size_t num_pixels)
{
    if (!CheckArgs(histo, pixel_buff, num_pixels))
        throw std::runtime_error("BuildHistogram_cpp() CheckArgs failed");

    memset(histo, 0x00, c_HistoSize * sizeof(uint32_t));

    for (size_t i = 0; i < num_pixels; i++)
        histo[pixel_buff[i]]++;

    return true;
}
```

In Listing 10-6a, the file Ch10_06.h includes a constant named c_HistoSize that denotes the number of histogram bins. Each histogram bin represents a single grayscale intensity value in the range [0, 255]. File Ch10_06_fcpp.cpp contains a function named BuildHistogram_cpp(), which constructs an image histogram for a grayscale image. Note that following argument checking and initialization tasks, BuildHistogram_cpp() uses a simple two-statement for-loop to build the histogram. During execution of this for-loop, each pixel value in pixel_buff is used as an index into the histogram buffer histo. The entries in array histo maintain occurrence counts for each pixel intensity value.

The assembly language code for BuildHistogram_avx2() also uses pixel values in pixel_buff to select histogram bin counts. However, the primary difference between BuildHistogram_avx2() and its C++ counterpart BuildHistogram_cpp() is that the former exploits AVX2 SIMD instructions to construct eight intermediate histograms (named Histo0–Histo7) in unison. The bin counts in these eight intermediate histograms are then summed to create the final image histogram. Listing 10-6b shows the MASM code for example Ch10_06.

Listing 10-6b. Example Ch10_06 MASM Code

```
;-----------------------------------------------------------------------------
; Ch10_06_fasm.asm
;-----------------------------------------------------------------------------

        include <MacrosX86-64-AVX.asmh>

; Offsets for local histograms on stack
ConstVals       segment readonly align(32) 'const'
HistoOffsets    dword   256 * 0, 256 * 1, 256 * 2, 256 * 3
                dword   256 * 4, 256 * 5, 256 * 6, 256 * 7
```

```
;------------------------------------------------------------------
; void BuildHistogram_avx2(uint32_t* histo, const uint8_t* pixel_buff,
;    size_t num_pixels);
;------------------------------------------------------------------

HS       equ     256 * 4                       ;size of each local histogram

         .code
BuildHistogram_avx2 proc frame
         CreateFrame_M BH_,0,0,rdi
         EndProlog_M

; Validate arguments
         mov r10,rcx                           ;save histo (rcx used below)

         test r10,1fh
         jnz BadArg                            ;jump if histo not 32b aligned
         test rdx,1fh
         jnz BadArg                            ;jump if pixel_buff not 32b aligned

         test r8,r8
         jz BadArg                             ;jump if num_pixels == 0
         test r8,1fh
         jnz BadArg                            ;jump if (num_pixels % 32) != 0

; Allocate stack space for temp histograms
         and rsp,0ffffffffffffffe0h            ;align rsp to 32-byte boundary
         sub rsp,HS*8                          ;allocate local histogram space

; Initialize local histograms to zero
         xor eax,eax                           ;rax = fill value
         mov rdi,rsp                           ;rdi = ptr to local histograms
         mov rcx,HS*8/8                        ;rcx = size in qwords
         rep stosq                             ;zero local histograms

; Initialize
         mov eax,1
         vmovd xmm0,eax
         vpbroadcastd ymm0,xmm0                ;ymm0 = packed dwords of 1
         vmovdqa ymm1,ymmword ptr [HistoOffsets] ;ymm1 = local histogram offsets

         mov rax,-8                            ;pixel_buffer (pb) array offset

; Build local histograms
Loop1:   add rax,8                             ;i += 8

; Gather entries from local histograms (i.e., histo0[pb[i]] - histo7[pb[i+7]])
         vpmovzxbd ymm2,qword ptr [rdx+rax]    ;load pb[i:i+7] as dwords
         vpaddd ymm2,ymm2,ymm1                 ;add offsets of local histograms
         vpcmpeqd ymm3,ymm3,ymm3               ;set vpgatherdd mask to all ones
         vpgatherdd ymm4,[rsp+ymm2*4],ymm3     ;gather local histogram entries
```

```
; Update local histograms
        vpaddd ymm4,ymm4,ymm0                   ;histoX[pb[i+X]]+=1 (X=0,1,...7)

; Extract histo4[pb[i+4]] - histo7[pb[i+7]] for later use
        vextracti128 xmm3,ymm2,1                ;histo4 - histo7 offsets
        vextracti128 xmm5,ymm4,1                ;histo4[pb[i+4]] - histo7[pb[i+7]]

; Save histo0[pb[i]] - histo3[pb[i+3]]
        vmovd r9d,xmm2
        vmovd dword ptr [rsp+r9*4],xmm4         ;save histo0[pb[i+0]]

        vpsrldq xmm2,xmm2,4
        vpsrldq xmm4,xmm4,4
        vmovd r9d,xmm2
        vmovd dword ptr [rsp+r9*4],xmm4         ;save histo1[pb[i+1]]

        vpsrldq xmm2,xmm2,4
        vpsrldq xmm4,xmm4,4
        vmovd r9d,xmm2
        vmovd dword ptr [rsp+r9*4],xmm4         ;save histo3[pb[i+2]]

        vpsrldq xmm2,xmm2,4
        vpsrldq xmm4,xmm4,4
        vmovd r9d,xmm2
        vmovd dword ptr [rsp+r9*4],xmm4         ;save histo3[pb[i+3]]

; Save histo4[pb[i+4]] - histo7[pb[i+7]]
        vmovd r9d,xmm3
        vmovd dword ptr [rsp+r9*4],xmm5         ;save histo4[pb[i+4]]

        vpsrldq xmm3,xmm3,4
        vpsrldq xmm5,xmm5,4
        vmovd r9d,xmm3
        vmovd dword ptr [rsp+r9*4],xmm5         ;save histo5[pb[i+5]]

        vpsrldq xmm3,xmm3,4
        vpsrldq xmm5,xmm5,4
        vmovd r9d,xmm3
        vmovd dword ptr [rsp+r9*4],xmm5         ;save histo6[pb[i+6]]

        vpsrldq xmm3,xmm3,4
        vpsrldq xmm5,xmm5,4
        vmovd r9d,xmm3
        vmovd dword ptr [rsp+r9*4],xmm5         ;save histo7[pb[i+7]]

        sub r8,8                                ;num_pixels -= 8
        jnz Loop1                               ;repeat until done

; Reduce 8 local histograms to final histogram
        mov rax,-8                                      ;rax = array offset
```

```
Loop2:  add rax,8                                           ;i + 8
        vmovdqa ymm0,ymmword ptr [rsp+rax*4 + HS*0]         ;load histo0[i:i+7]
        vmovdqa ymm1,ymmword ptr [rsp+rax*4 + HS*1]         ;load histo1[i:i+7]
        vpaddd ymm0,ymm0,ymmword ptr [rsp+rax*4 + HS*2]     ;add histo2[i:i+7]
        vpaddd ymm1,ymm1,ymmword ptr [rsp+rax*4 + HS*3]     ;add histo3[i:i+7]
        vpaddd ymm0,ymm0,ymmword ptr [rsp+rax*4 + HS*4]     ;add histo4[i:i+7]
        vpaddd ymm1,ymm1,ymmword ptr [rsp+rax*4 + HS*5]     ;add histo5[i:i+7]
        vpaddd ymm0,ymm0,ymmword ptr [rsp+rax*4 + HS*6]     ;add histo6[i:i+7]
        vpaddd ymm1,ymm1,ymmword ptr [rsp+rax*4 + HS*7]     ;add histo7[i:i+7]
        vpaddd ymm2,ymm0,ymm1                               ;ymm2 = histo[i:i+7]

        vmovdqa ymmword ptr [r10+rax*4],ymm2     ;save histo[i:i+7]

        cmp rax,248                              ;i < 248?
        jb Loop2                                 ;jump if yes

        mov eax,1                                ;set success return code

Done:   vzeroupper
        DeleteFrame_M rdi
        ret

BadArg: xor eax,eax                              ;set bad argument return code
        jmp Done

BuildHistogram_avx2 endp
        end
```

Listing 10-6b opens with a custom section of constant values. The MASM statement ConstVals segment readonly align(32) 'const' defines the start of a read-only section of constant values that is aligned on a 32-byte boundary. The reason for using a custom section in this example is that MASM does not support 32-byte alignment for a standard .const section. In section ConstVals, table HistoOffsets contains offsets (in units of doublewords) that define the start position of each intermediate histogram. More on this shortly. The statement HS equ 256 * 4 defines the size (in bytes) of each intermediate histogram and the final histogram; each histogram bin is a doubleword.

Following its prologue, function BuildHistogram_avx2() verifies that argument values histo and pixel_buff are properly aligned on a 32-byte boundary. Argument value num_pixels is also validated for size. Note that num_pixels must be an integral multiple of 32.

Following argument validation, BuildHistogram_avx2() uses an and rsp,0ffffffffffffffe0h instruction to align RSP downward to the nearest 32-byte boundary. Note that even though MASM accepts a 64-bit immediate value in this instruction, the machine encoding of the and instruction contains the 8-bit value 0xE0, which is sign-extended to 64 bits (0xFFFFFFFFFFFFFFE0) during execution. Recall that mov is the only x86-64 instruction that supports 64-bit immediate values. The next instruction, sub rsp,HS*8, allocates space for the eight intermediate histograms on the stack as shown in Figure 10-7.

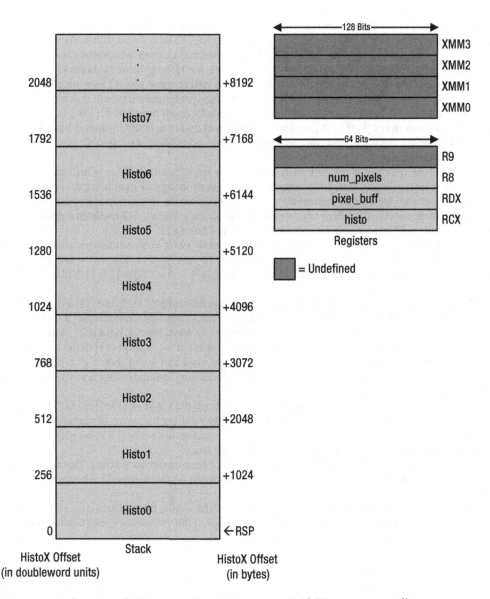

Figure 10-7. Stack allocation of eight intermediate histograms in BuildHistogram_avx2()

Following allocation of the intermediate histograms, BuildHistogram_avx2() exploits the stosq instruction to initialize the histogram bins to zero. In the initialization code block that follows, the vpbroadcastd ymm0,xmm0 instruction broadcasts the doubleword element in XMM0[31:0], which contains the value one, to each doubleword element in register YMM0. This register is used to update histogram count bins. The vmovdqa ymm1,[HistoOffsets] that follows loads the offsets for the eight intermediate histograms into register YMM1. Keep in mind that these offset values are in units of doublewords as shown in Figure 10-7 and are used to carry out a pixel gather operation as you'll soon see.

Execution of for-loop Loop1 begins with an add rax,8 instruction that calculates i += 8. The next instruction, vpmovzxbd ymm2,qword ptr [rdx+rax], loads pixel_buff[i:i+7] into register YMM2. Recall that during execution of a vpmovzxbd instruction, the byte values are zero-extended to doublewords

385

before being saved in the destination register. The next instruction, vpaddd ymm2,ymm2,ymm1, adds the histogram offsets in register YMM1 to the pixel values in register YMM2. This is followed by the instruction pair vpcmpeqb ymm3,ymm3,ymm3 and vpgatherdd ymm4,[rsp+ymm2*4],ymm3, which loads histogram bins histo0[pixel_buff[i+0]] into YMM4[31:0], histo1[pixel_buff[i+1]] into YMM4[63:32], etc.

The histogram bin loading technique employed in BuildHistogram_avx2() replicates the method that's used in C++ function BuildHistogram_cpp(), but processes eight histogram bins in unison. In for-loop Loop1, intermediate histogram Histo0 maintains bin counts for pixels pixel_buff[i+0], Histo1 maintains bin counts for pixels pixel_buff[i+1], and so on. The actual updating of the histogram bin counts is performed by the vpaddd ymm4,ymm4,ymm0 instruction, which adds one to each doubleword element register YMM4.

The use of the vpgatherdd instruction in Loop1 greatly simplifies the loading of histogram bin counts from the intermediate histograms. Following each SIMD bin count update operation, the revised values need to be "scattered" back to the intermediate histograms before the next group of 8 pixels can be processed. Unfortunately, AVX2 does not support scatter operations; AVX-512 includes a vpscatterdd instruction, and you'll learn more about this instruction in Chapter 13.

To simulate a scatter operation, function BuildHistogram_avx2() uses sequences of vmovd and vpsrldq instructions. It begins with the instruction pair vextracti128 xmm3,ymm2,1 (Extract Packed Integer Values) and vextracti128 xmm5,ymm4,1 that extracts histo4[pb[i+4]] - histo7[pb[i+7]] (XMM5) and their offsets (XMM3) for later use.

The next instruction, vmovd r9d,xmm2, copies the offset for histo0[pixel_buff[i+0]] to register R9. This is followed by a vmovd dword ptr [rsp+r9*4],xmm4 instruction that saves histo0[pixel_buff[i+0]]. The next two instructions, vpsrldq xmm2,xmm2,4 and vpsrldq xmm4,xmm4,4, right shift XMM2 and XMM4 by four bytes. This positions the offset and bin count for histo1[pixel_buff[i+1]] in the low-order doublewords of XMM2 and XMM4. The ensuing vmovd r9d,xmm2 and vmovd dword ptr [rsp+r9*4],xmm4 instructions save histo1[pb[i+1]]. The next two code blocks use the same instruction sequences to save histo2[pb[i+2]] and histo3[pb[i+3]].

The remaining code blocks in for-loop Loop1 save histo4[pb[i+4]] – histo7[pb[i+7]] using identical sequences of vmovd and vpsrldq instructions. The reason for splitting the saving of histo0[pb[i+0]] – histo7[pb[i+7]] into two distinct operations is that vpsrldq does not support 256-bit wide shifts; it carries out its shift operations using two independent 128-bit wide lanes.

Following execution of Loop1, BuildHistogram_avx2() executes for-loop Loop2. This second for-loop uses sequences of vmovdqa and vpaddd instructions to reduce the eight intermediate histograms to the final histogram.

The NASM code for example Ch10_06 employs an .rdata section that is aligned on a 32-byte boundary for HistoOffsets. It also uses register R11 to preserve a copy of RSP before allocating stack space for the intermediate histograms. Here are the results for source code example Ch10_06:

```
----- Results for Ch10_06 -----
Histograms are identical
Histograms saved to file @Ch10_06_Histograms_HELIUM.csv

Running benchmark function BuildHistogram_bm() - please wait
.......................
Benchmark times save to file @Ch10_06_BuildHistogram_bm_HELIUM.csv
```

Table 10-4 shows the benchmark timing measurements for example Ch10_06. On the Intel processors, the AVX2 assembly language coded histogram build functions are modestly faster than their C++ counterparts. However, the C++ coded function is somewhat faster than the assembly language function on the AMD 7700X processor. The reason for this is that vpgatherdd is a very slow executing instruction on the AMD 7700X processor. To be fair, AVX2 (and AVX-512) gather instruction executions often take a long time to complete on processors from both AMD and Intel, and these instructions should be employed judiciously. It is important to keep in mind that x86-64 instruction latency[2] and throughput can vary, sometimes considerably, depending on the processor's underlying microarchitecture (processor microarchitecture is reviewed in Chapter 17). It's not uncommon to obtain dissimilar timing measurements like those shown in Table 10-4 when benchmarking processors based on different microarchitectures. Appendix B contains a list of AMD and Intel programming reference manuals that you can consult for more information regarding x86-64 instruction latency and throughput.

Table 10-4. *Benchmark Timing Measurements (Microseconds) for Histogram Build Functions Using* `TestImageB.png`

Function	i5-11600K	i7-11700K	7700X
BuildHistogram_cpp()	8181 (10)	8216 (179)	6557 (7)
BuildHistogram_avx2()	6749 (12)	6663 (122)	7767 (8)

Summary

Here are the key learning points for Chapter 10:

- AVX2 extends the packed integer capabilities of AVX. Most x86-AVX packed integer instructions can be used with either 128- or 256-bit wide operands. SIMD memory operands should be properly aligned.

- The vpadd[b|w|d|q] and vpsub[b|w|d|q] instructions can be used to perform addition and subtraction using 128- or 256-bit wide packed integer values.

- The vpadds[b|w] and vpsubs[b|w] instructions can be used to perform signed saturated addition and subtraction using 128- or 256-bit packed integer values. Unsigned saturated addition and subtraction can be carried out using the vpaddus[b|w] and vpsubus[b|w] instructions.

- The vpmins[b|w|d|q] and vpmaxs[b|w|d|q] instructions can be used to calculate packed signed integer minimums and maximums. Packed unsigned integer minimums and maximums can be calculated using vpminus[b|w|d|q] and vpmaxus[b|w|d|q].

- The vpsllv[w|d|q], vpsrlv[w|d|q], and vpsrav[w|d|q] instructions can be used to perform packed left logical, right logical, and right arithmetic shifts using different bit counts for each SIMD element.

- The vpabs[b|w|d|q] instructions can be used to compute packed absolute values.

- The vpbroadcast[b|w|d|q] instructions can be used to broadcast an integer value to each element of a packed integer operand. The source operand can be a memory location or the low-order bits of an XMM register.

---

[2] Latency is the number of clock cycles required to complete execution of an instruction's micro-ops. Throughput is the number of clock cycles that the processor must wait before the execution unit issue ports can accept the same instruction.

- The vpmovmskb instruction generates a mask using the most significant bit of each byte element in a packed integer operand.

- The popcnt instruction returns the number of bits set to "1" in the specified source operand.

- The vperm[w|d|q] instructions can be used to permute the elements of a packed integer operand.

- Assembly language functions can use the vpackss[dw|wb] and vpackus[dw|wb] instructions to pack 128-bit or 256-bit wide integer operands using signed or unsigned saturation.

- Assembly language functions can use the vmovzx[bw|bd|bq|wd|wq|dq] and vmovsx[bw|bd|bq|wd|wq|dq] instructions to perform zero- or sign-extended packed integer size promotions.

- Assembly language functions can use the vgatherdp[d|s] and vgatherqp[d|s] instructions to perform floating-point gather operations using doubleword or quadword indices.

- Assembly language functions can use the vpgatherd[d|q] and vgatherq[d|q] instructions to perform integer gather operations using doubleword or quadword indices.

- The vextracti128 instruction can be used to extract 128 bits of integer values from a packed operand.

CHAPTER 11

■ ■ ■

AVX2 Programming – Packed Floating-Point – Part 1

In Chapter 9, you learned how to carry out elementary arithmetic using packed floating-point operands and AVX instructions. You also learned how to code simple SIMD functions that performed computations using the elements of a floating-point array or matrix. In this chapter, you'll study source code examples that perform more sophisticated floating-point calculations using AVX2 and fused-multiply-add (FMA) instructions. The first section highlights an array-based algorithm that demonstrates a least-squares calculation using packed double-precision floating-point values. The second section contains several examples that carry out calculations using single-precision and double-precision floating-point matrices including matrix-matrix and matrix-vector multiplication. As you'll soon see, SIMD techniques are ideal for accelerating these types of computations.

As a reminder, the source code examples in this chapter require a processor and an operating system that support AVX2. You can use one of the free utilities listed in Appendix B to verify that your computer meets this requirement.

Floating-Point Arrays

Source code examples Ch09_04 and Ch09_05 illustrated the use of AVX instructions to perform SIMD arithmetic calculations using floating-point arrays. In this section, you'll study another algorithm that uses AVX2 instructions to carry out packed floating-point array calculations. The source example presented in this section differs from the examples you saw in Chapter 9 in that it uses FMA instructions. Before looking at the source code for example Ch11_01, a few words about FMA arithmetic and instructions are warranted.

During the execution of a floating-point arithmetic (e.g., addition, subtraction, multiplication, etc.) or a conversion instruction, an x86 processor performs a distinct rounding operation. Rounding operations are defined as part of the IEEE 754 standard for floating-point arithmetic. Recall from the discussions in Chapters 1 and 5 that x86 processors support several different floating-point rounding modes (see Table 1-5 and example Ch05_06). An x86 FMA instruction combines multiplication and addition (or subtraction) into a single operation. More specifically, a fused-multiply-add (or fused-multiply-subtract) instruction performs a multiplication followed by an addition (or subtraction) using a single rounding operation instead of two.

Consider, for example, the expression $a = b * c + d$. Using standard floating-point arithmetic, the processor initially calculates the product $b * c$, and this calculation includes a rounding step. It then performs the floating-point addition, which also includes a rounding step. If the expression $a = b * c + d$ is evaluated using FMA arithmetic, the processor does not round the intermediate product $b * c$. Rounding is carried out only once using the product-sum $b * c + d$. FMA operations are often used to improve the performance and accuracy of multiply-accumulate computations such as dot products, matrix-vector

© Daniel Kusswurm 2023
D. Kusswurm, *Modern X86 Assembly Language Programming*,
https://doi.org/10.1007/978-1-4842-9603-5_11

multiplications, and convolutions. On x86 processors, the FMA instruction set is a distinct feature extension just like AVX or AVX2. This means that a program should never assume a processor supports FMA just because it also supports AVX or AVX2. It should always test for the presence of the FMA instruction set extension. You'll learn how to do this in Chapter 16.

Least Squares

Simple linear regression is a statistical technique that models a linear relationship between two variables. One popular method of simple linear regression is called least-squares fitting. This method uses a set of sample data points to determine a best-fit curve between the two variables. When used with a simple linear regression model, the curve is a straight line whose equation is $y = mx + b$. In this equation, x denotes the independent variable, y denotes the dependent (or measured) variable, m is the line's slope, and b is the line's y-axis intercept point. The slope and intercept point of a least-squares line are determined using a series of computations that minimize the sum of the squared deviations between the line and the sample data points. Following calculation of its slope and intercept, a least-squares line is often used to predict an unknown y value using a known x value. Appendix B contains some references that you can consult if you are interested in learning more about the mathematics of linear regression and least-squares fitting.

The following equations are used to calculate the slope and intercept point of a least-squares line:

$$m = \frac{n\sum_i x_i y_i - \sum_i x_i \sum_i y_i}{n\sum_i x_i^2 - \left(\sum_i x_i\right)^2}$$

$$b = \frac{\sum_i x_i^2 \sum_i y_i - \sum_i x_i \sum_i x_i y_i}{n\sum_i x_i^2 - \left(\sum_i x_i\right)^2}$$

At first glance, the slope and intercept equations may appear a little daunting. However, upon closer examination, a couple of simplifications become apparent. First, the slope and intercept denominators are the same, which means that this value only needs to be computed once. Second, it is only necessary to calculate four simple summation values (or sum variables) as shown in the following equations:

$$sum_x = \sum_i x_i$$

$$sum_y = \sum_i y_i$$

$$sum_{xy} = \sum_i x_i y_i$$

$$sum_{xx} = \sum_i x_i^2$$

Following calculation of the sum of these variables, the least-squares line slope and intercept point are easily derived using scalar floating-point arithmetic.

Listing 11-1a shows the principal C++ code for example Ch11_01. This example illustrates how to perform a least-squares calculation using double-precision floating-point arrays, AVX2 instructions, and FMA instructions.

Listing 11-1a. Example Ch11_01 C++ Code

```
//-----------------------------------------------------------------------------
// Ch11_01.h
//-----------------------------------------------------------------------------

#pragma once
#include <cstddef>

// Ch11_01_fasm.asm, Ch11_01_fasm.s
extern "C" void CalcLeastSquares_avx2(double* m, double* b, const double* x,
    const double* y, size_t n, double epsilon);

// Ch11_01_fcpp.cpp
extern void CalcLeastSquares_cpp(double* m, double* b, const double* x,
    const double* y, size_t n, double epsilon);

// Ch11_01_misc.cpp
extern void InitArrays(double* x, double* y, size_t n);

// Ch11_02_bm.cpp
extern void CalcLeastSquares_bm(void);

// Miscellaneous constants
constexpr size_t c_Alignment = 32;
constexpr double c_LsEpsilon = 1.0e-12;
constexpr unsigned int c_RngSeed1 = 73;
constexpr unsigned int c_RngSeed2 = 83;
constexpr double c_RngMinVal = -25.0;
constexpr double c_RngMaxVal = 25.0;

//-----------------------------------------------------------------------------
// Ch11_01_fcpp.cpp
//-----------------------------------------------------------------------------

#include <cmath>
#include <stdexcept>
#include "Ch11_01.h"
#include "AlignedMem.h"

static bool CheckArgs(const double* x, const double* y, size_t n)
{
    if (n < 2)
        return false;

    if (!AlignedMem::IsAligned(x, c_Alignment))
        return false;
```

```
    if (!AlignedMem::IsAligned(y, c_Alignment))
        return false;

    return true;
}

void CalcLeastSquares_cpp(double* m, double* b, const double* x,
    const double* y, size_t n, double epsilon)
{
    *m = 0.0;
    *b = 0.0;

    if (!CheckArgs(x, y, n))
        throw std::runtime_error("CalcLeastSquares_cpp() - CheckArgs() failed");

    double sum_x = 0.0, sum_y = 0.0, sum_xx = 0.0, sum_xy = 0.0;

    for (size_t i = 0; i < n; i++)
    {
        sum_x += x[i];
        sum_y += y[i];
        sum_xx += x[i] * x[i];
        sum_xy += x[i] * y[i];
    }

    double denom = n * sum_xx - sum_x * sum_x;

    if (fabs(denom) >= epsilon)
    {
        *m = (n * sum_xy - sum_x * sum_y) / denom;
        *b = (sum_xx * sum_y - sum_x * sum_xy) / denom;
    }
}
```

Listing 11-1a opens with header file Ch11_01.h, which contains the function declarations for this example. Note that the two least-squares calculating functions, CalcLeastSquares_avx2() and CalcLeastSquares_cpp(), require double-precision floating-point arrays (arguments x and y). These functions calculate the slope (m) and intercept point (b) using the previously defined equations.

Function CalcLeastSquares_cpp() computes a least-squares slope and intercept point using standard C++ statements and is included for result comparison and benchmarking purposes. Note that the for-loop in CalcLeastSquares_cpp() contains only four executable code statements. These statements correspond to the equations for the previously defined sum variables. Following execution of the for-loop, CalcLeastSquares_cpp() verifies that fabs(denom) >= c_LsEpsilon is true before calculating the final slope and intercept point. If this expression is false, the variable denom is considered too close to zero to be valid.

Listing 11-1b shows the MASM code for function CalcLeastSquares_avx2(). This listing begins with the definition of a macro named ReducePD_M. This macro sums the four double-precision floating-point values in YMM register YmmSrc and saves this sum in XMM register XmmDes. Note that macro arguments YmmSrc and XmmSrc must reference the same register number. Also note that macro ReducePD_M requires a temporary XMM register named XmmTmp whose number must be different than both YmmSrc and XmmDes.

Listing 11-1b. Example Ch11_01 MASM Code

```
;-------------------------------------------------------------------------------
; Ch11_01_fasm.asm
;-------------------------------------------------------------------------------

        include <MacrosX86-64-AVX.asmh>


;-------------------------------------------------------------------------------
; ReducePD_M macro
;
; Description:  This macro sums the double-precision elements in register YmmSrc.
;               The result is saved in register XmmDes.
;
; Macro Parameters (use complete register names):
;   XmmDes      xmm destination register
;   YmmSrc      ymm source register
;   XmmSrc      xmm source register (must be same number as YmmSrc)
;   XmmTmp      xmm temp register (must be different than XmmDes and YmmSrc)
;-------------------------------------------------------------------------------

ReducePD_M macro XmmDes,YmmSrc,XmmSrc,XmmTmp
        vextractf128 XmmTmp,YmmSrc,1    ;extract two high-order F64 values
        vaddpd XmmDes,XmmTmp,XmmSrc     ;reduce to two F64 values
        vhaddpd XmmDes,XmmDes,XmmDes    ;reduce to one F64 value
        endm


;-------------------------------------------------------------------------------
; void CalcLeastSquares_avx2(double* m, double* b, const double* x,
;   const double* y, size_t n, double epsilon);
;-------------------------------------------------------------------------------

NSE     equ 8                                   ;num_simd_elements

        .code
CalcLeastSquares_avx2 proc frame
        CreateFrame_M LS_,0,80
        SaveXmmRegs_M xmm11,xmm12,xmm13,xmm14,xmm15
        EndProlog_M

; Set m and b to zero (error values)
        xor eax,eax
        mov [rcx],rax                   ;m = 0.0
        mov [rdx],rax                   ;b = 0.0

; Validate arguments
        mov r10,[rbp+LS_OffsetStackArgs]        ;r10 = n
        cmp r10,2                               ;n < 2?
        jl Done                                 ;jump if yes
```

```
        test r8,1fh
        jnz Done                                ;jump if x not 32b aligned
        test r9,1fh
        jnz Done                                ;jump if y not 32b aligned

; Initialize
        vmovsd xmm11,real8 ptr [rbp+LS_OffsetStackArgs+8] ;xmm11 = epsilon

        vxorpd ymm12,ymm12,ymm12                ;packed sum_x = 0
        vxorpd ymm13,ymm13,ymm13                ;packed sum_y = 0
        vxorpd ymm14,ymm14,ymm14                ;packed sum_xx = 0
        vxorpd ymm15,ymm15,ymm15                ;packed sum_xy = 0
        mov r11,r10                             ;save copy of n for later

        mov rax,-8                              ;rax = array offset for Loop2
        cmp r10,NSE                             ;n >= NSE?
        jb Loop2                                ;jump if no
        mov rax,-NSE*8                          ;rax = array offset for Loop1

; Calculate sum vars using SIMD arithmetic
Loop1:  add rax,NSE*8                           ;update offset for current iteration
        vmovapd ymm0,ymmword ptr [r8+rax]       ;load x[i:i+3]
        vmovapd ymm1,ymmword ptr [r9+rax]       ;load y[i:i+3]
        vaddpd ymm12,ymm12,ymm0                 ;update packed sum_x
        vaddpd ymm13,ymm13,ymm1                 ;update packed sum_y
        vfmadd231pd ymm14,ymm0,ymm0             ;update packed sum_xx
        vfmadd231pd ymm15,ymm0,ymm1             ;update packed_sum_xy

        vmovapd ymm0,ymmword ptr [r8+rax+32]    ;load x[i+4:i+7]
        vmovapd ymm1,ymmword ptr [r9+rax+32]    ;load y[i+4:i+7]
        vaddpd ymm12,ymm12,ymm0                 ;update packed sum_x
        vaddpd ymm13,ymm13,ymm1                 ;update packed sum_y
        vfmadd231pd ymm14,ymm0,ymm0             ;update packed sum_xx
        vfmadd231pd ymm15,ymm0,ymm1             ;update packed_sum_xy

        sub r10,NSE                             ;n -= NSE
        cmp r10,NSE                             ;n >= NSE?
        jae Loop1                               ;jump if yes

; Reduce packed sum vars to scalars
        ReducePD_M xmm12,ymm12,xmm12,xmm0       ;xmm12 = sum_x
        ReducePD_M xmm13,ymm13,xmm13,xmm0       ;xmm13 = sum_y
        ReducePD_M xmm14,ymm14,xmm14,xmm0       ;xmm14 = sum_xx
        ReducePD_M xmm15,ymm15,xmm15,xmm0       ;xmm15 = sum_xy

        test r10,r10                            ;n == 0?
        jz CalcLS                               ;jump if yes

        add rax,NSE*8-8                         ;adjust array offset for Loop2
```

```
; Process any residual elements using scalar arithmetic
Loop2:   add rax,8                           ;update offset
         vmovsd xmm0,real8 ptr [r8+rax]      ;load x[i]
         vmovsd xmm1,real8 ptr [r9+rax]      ;load y[i]

         vaddsd xmm12,xmm12,xmm0             ;update sum_x
         vaddsd xmm13,xmm13,xmm1             ;update sum_y
         vfmadd231sd xmm14,xmm0,xmm0         ;update sum_xx
         vfmadd231sd xmm15,xmm0,xmm1         ;update sum_xy

         sub r10,1                           ;n -= 1
         jnz Loop2                           ;repeat until done

CalcLS:  vcvtsi2sd xmm5,xmm5,r11             ;xmm5 = n
         vmulsd xmm0,xmm5,xmm14              ;xmm0 = n * sum_xx
         vmulsd xmm1,xmm12,xmm12             ;xmm1 = sum_x * sum_x
         vsubsd xmm0,xmm0,xmm1               ;xmm0 = denom

         mov rax,7fffffffffffffffh           ;rax = F64 abs mask
         vmovq xmm1,rax
         vandpd xmm4,xmm0,xmm1               ;xmm4 = fabs(denom)
         vcomisd xmm4,xmm11                  ;fabs(denom) < epsilon ?
         jb Done                             ;jump if yes

; Compute and save slope
         vmulsd xmm0,xmm5,xmm15              ;n * sum_xy
         vmulsd xmm1,xmm12,xmm13             ;sum_x * sum_y
         vsubsd xmm2,xmm0,xmm1               ;n * sum_xy - sum_x * sum_y
         vdivsd xmm3,xmm2,xmm4               ;xmm3 = slope
         vmovsd real8 ptr [rcx],xmm3         ;save slope

; Compute and save intercept
         vmulsd xmm0,xmm14,xmm13             ;sum_xx * sum_y
         vmulsd xmm1,xmm12,xmm15             ;sum_x * sum_xy
         vsubsd xmm2,xmm0,xmm1               ;sum_xx * sum_y - sum_x _ sum_xy
         vdivsd xmm3,xmm2,xmm4               ;xmm3 = intercept
         vmovsd real8 ptr [rdx],xmm3         ;save intercept

Done:    vzeroupper
         RestoreXmmRegs_M xmm11,xmm12,xmm13,xmm14,xmm15
         DeleteFrame_M
         ret
CalcLeastSquares_avx2 endp
         end
```

The first executable instruction of macro ReducePD_M, vextractf128 XmmTmp,YmmSrc,1, copies the two high-order double-precision floating-point elements of register YmmSrc to register XmmTmp. The next instruction, vaddpd XmmDes,XmmTmp,XmmSrc, sums the double-precision floating-point elements in registers XmmTmp and XmmSrc. This is followed by a vhaddpd XmmDes,XmmDes,XmmDes instruction that yields the final sum in the low-order double-precision element of XmmDes.

Following its prologue, function CalcLeastSquares_avx2() sets the slope m (RCX) and intercept b (RDX) to 0.0. Setting these values to 0.0 allows the caller to determine if an error occurred during execution of CalcLeastSquares_avx2(). The next block of code validates argument value n for size and array pointers x and y for proper alignment on a 32-byte boundary. This is followed by a code block that initializes the elements of packed sum variables sum_x (YMM12), sum_y (YMM13), sum_xx (YMM14), and sum_xy (YMM15) to 0.0. The remaining code in the initialization code block sets register RAX as a common array offset register and ensures that n >= NSE is true. If n >= NSE is false, for-loop Loop1 is skipped.

Each iteration of Loop1 begins with an add rax,NSE*8 instruction that updates RAX so that it contains the proper offset for the next group of elements in arrays x and y. Function CalcLeastSquares_cpp() then employs the instruction pair vmovapd ymm0,ymmword ptr [r8+rax] and vmovapd ymm1,ymmword ptr [r9+rax] to load array elements x[i:i+3] and y[i:i+3] into registers YMM0 and YMM1, respectively. The next two instructions, vaddpd ymm12,ymm12,ymm0 and vaddpd ymm13,ymm13,ymm1, update sum_x and sum_y. This is followed by a vfmadd231pd ymm14,ymm0,ymm0 (Fused-Multiply-Add of Packed DPFP Values) instruction that updates sum_xx. More specifically, this instruction calculates sum_xx[0:3] += x[i:i+3] * x[i:i+3] by first multiplying the double-precision floating-point elements in the second operand (YMM0) by the third operand (YMM0); it then adds these products to the elements in the first operand (YMM14) and saves the result in the destination operand (YMM14). The ensuing vfmadd231pd ymm15,ymm0,ymm1 instruction updates sum_xy.

Before continuing with the source code in Listing 11-1b, a few words regarding x86 FMA instruction mnemonics are necessary. The standard x86 FMA instruction[1] mnemonic employs a three-digit operand ordering scheme that specifies which operands to use for multiplication and addition (or subtraction). The first digit specifies the operand to use as the multiplicand; the second digit specifies the operand to use as the multiplier; and the third digit specifies the operand that the product is added to (or subtracted from). Like other x86-64 assembly language instructions, the execution result of an FMA instruction is always saved in the leftmost (or destination) operand. Consider, for example, the instruction vfmadd132sd xmm10,xmm11,xmm12 (Fused-Multiply-Add of Scalar DPFP Values). In this example, operand 1 is XMM10, operand 2 is XMM11, and operand 3 is XMM12. During execution of this instruction, the processor calculates XMM10[63:0] * XMM12[63:0] + XMM11[63:0]; it then saves this result in XMM10[63:0]. All FMA operations support multiple instruction operand orderings. For example, a function also can use vfmadd213sd and vfmadd231sd to perform scalar FMA arithmetic using double-precision floating-point values. For some algorithms, having multiple instruction mnemonics for the same FMA operation is advantageous since it reduces the number of register-to-register transfers. Appendix B contains a list of reference manuals published by AMD and Intel that you can consult for more information regarding other x86 FMA instructions.

Back to the code in Listing 11-1b. Following execution of Loop1, CalcLeastSquares_avx2() uses macro ReducePD_M to reduce sum_x, sum_y, sum_xx, and sum_xy to scalar values. For-loop Loop2 handles any residual elements using scalar versions of the same instructions that Loop1 used. The first code block that follows label CalcLS calculates the common denominator for the least-squares slope and intercept. The ensuing code block contains assembly language instructions that verify the value of the denominator (denom). This block begins with a mov rax,7fffffffffffffffh instruction that loads register RAX with the mask value needed to compute a double-precision floating-point absolute value. The next two instructions, vmovq xmm1,rax and vandpd xmm4,xmm0,xmm1, calculate fabs(denom). The ensuing instruction pair, vcomisd xmm4,xmm11 and jb Done, skips over the remaining least-squares calculating code if denom < fabs(g_LsEpsilon) is true.

The remaining code in the MASM version of CalcLeastSquares_avx2() is straightforward scalar double-precision floating-point arithmetic that calculates the final least-squares slope and intercept point. These values are then saved to the buffers pointed to by RCX and RDX.

---

[1] Some AMD processors include FMA instructions that employ four operands. These instructions are not discussed in this book.

Listing 11-1c shows a portion of the NASM code for example Ch11_01. Like its MASM counterpart, the NASM code opens with the definition of a macro named ReducePD_M. Recall from the discussions in Chapter 5 that a NASM macro must specify the number of arguments as part of the %macro directive statement (see example Ch05_06). Also recall that a NASM macro uses %x for macro arguments where x signifies the macro parameter number (i.e., %1 is the first macro argument, %2 is the second argument, etc.). The actual AVX2 instructions used in the NASM version of macro ReducePD_M match the ones used in the MASM version.

Listing 11-1c. Example Ch11_01 NASM Code

```
;-----------------------------------------------------------------------
; Ch11_01_fasm.s
;-----------------------------------------------------------------------

        %include "ModX86Asm3eNASM.inc"

;-----------------------------------------------------------------------
; ReducePD_M macro
;
; Description:   This macro sums the double-precision elements in register YmmSrc.
;                The result is saved in register XmmDes.
;
; Macro Parameters (use complete register names):
;    %1 = XmmDes     xmm destination register
;    %2 = YmmSrc     ymm source register
;    %3 = XmmSrc     xmm source register (must be same number as YmmSrc)
;    %4 = XmmTmp     xmm temp register (must be different than XmmDes and YmmSrc)
;-----------------------------------------------------------------------

%macro ReducePD_M 4
        vextractf128 %4,%2,1            ;extract two high-order F64 values
        vaddpd %1,%4,%3                 ;reduce to two F64 values
        vhaddpd %1,%1,%1               ;reduce to one F64 value
%endmacro
```

The NASM version of function CalcLeastSquares_avx() uses the same sequences of AVX2 and FMA instructions that the MASM version employed to carry out the required least-squares calculation. Here are the results for source code example Ch11_01:

```
----- Results for Ch11_01 -----
slope m1:      -1.00874909
intercept b1:  196.22610714
slope m2:      -1.00874909
intercept b2:  196.22610714

Running benchmark function CalcLeastSquares_bm() - please wait
Benchmark times save to file @Ch11_01_CalcLeastSquares_bm_HELIUM.csv
```

Table 11-1 shows the benchmark timing measurements for example Ch11_01. As you can see, the assembly language implementations of the least-squares calculating functions significantly outperform their C++ counterpart functions.

Table 11-1. *Benchmark Timing Measurements (Microseconds) for Least-Squares Calculating Functions (n = 5,000,000)*

Function	i5-11600K	i7-11700K	7700X
CalcLeastSquares_cpp()	4562 (24)	4579 (84)	3089 (3)
CalcLeastSquares_avx2()	2259 (19)	2214 (60)	1116 (6)

Floating-Point Matrices

In this section, you will study several examples that demonstrate how to perform common matrix operations using AVX2 and FMA instructions. The first set of examples spotlights matrix multiplication. This is followed by two source code examples that explicate matrix-vector multiplication. The final source code example of this section explains how to calculate a covariance matrix.

Matrix Multiplication

The product of two matrices is defined as follows. Let **A** be an $m \times p$ matrix where m and p denote the number of rows and columns, respectively. Let **B** be a $p \times n$ matrix. The matrix product $\mathbf{C} = \mathbf{AB}$ is an $m \times n$ matrix where the value of each $c(i, j)$ in **C** is calculated using the following equation:

$$c_{ij} = \sum_{k=0}^{p-1} a_{ik} b_{kj} \quad i = 0, \ldots, m-1; \quad j = 0, \ldots, n-1$$

Note that the matrix multiplication equation uses zero-based subscripts since this simplifies translating the equation into C++ source code; most mathematical texts use one-based subscripts.

According to the definition of matrix multiplication, the number of columns in **A** must equal the number of rows in **B**. For example, if **A** is a 3×4 (rows × columns) matrix and **B** is a 4×2 matrix, the product **AB** is a 3×2 matrix, but the product **BA** is undefined. Note that each element $c(i, j)$ in **C** is simply the dot (inner) product of row i in matrix **A** and column j in matrix **B**. Dot product calculations are easy to implement using FMA instructions.

The archetypal procedure for calculating the product of two matrices using scalar arithmetic employs three nested for-loops to implement the previously defined matrix equation. The same technique can be utilized when employing SIMD techniques but with some minor modifications. The reason for this is that depending on the matrix sizes, a subset of the calculations may need to be carried out using partially filled SIMD data types. Figure 11-1 shows a block diagram of matrix **C** ($m \times n$), which is the product of matrix **A** ($m \times p$) and matrix **B** ($p \times n$). Note that the SIMD element groups in each row of **C**, except for the far right one, contain eight elements. If the number of columns in matrix **C** is not an integral multiple of eight, each row in matrix **C** will also contain a residual SIMD element group that contains between one and seven elements.

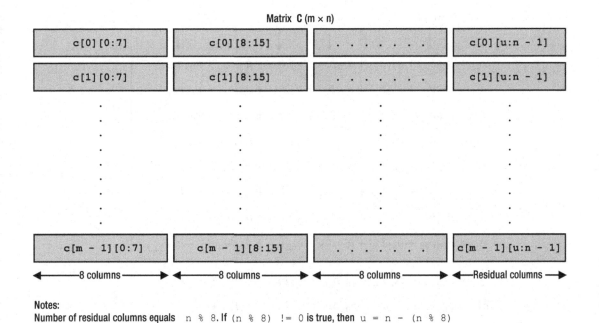

Matrix **C** (m × n)

Notes:
Number of residual columns equals `n % 8`. If `(n % 8) != 0` is true, then `u = n - (n % 8)`

Figure 11-1. *SIMD element groups for matrix **C** (m × n)*

Figure 11-2 underscores the handling of residual elements when using SIMD arithmetic to calculate a matrix product. In this figure, assume that matrix **A** is 5 × 6 and matrix **B** is 6 × 10. The first row of **C = AB**, where matrix **C** is 5 × 10, can be calculated using the equations shown in Figure 11-2. Note that the computations for matrix elements $c(0, 0)$ through $c(0, 7)$ can be carried out using 256-bit wide (i.e., eight single-precision floating-point values) SIMD operands. The two residual elements in the first row, $c(0, 8)$ and $c(0, 9)$, must be computed differently since there are fewer than eight elements. These elements can be calculated using masked load and store operations as you'll soon see.

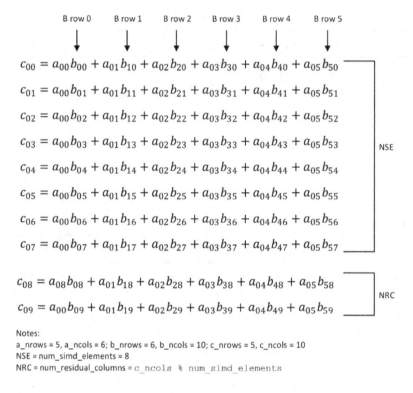

Figure 11-2. *SIMD equations for a matrix product (one row)*

Single-Precision

Source code example Ch11_02 demonstrates how to perform single-precision matrix multiplication using AVX2 and FMA instructions. Listing 11-2a shows the principal C++ code for this example.

Listing 11-2a. Example Ch11_02 C++ Code

```
//-------------------------------------------------------------------------
// Ch11_02.h
//-------------------------------------------------------------------------

#pragma once
#include <cstddef>
#include "MatrixF32.h"

// Ch11_02_fasm.asm, Ch11_02_fasm.s
extern "C" void MatrixMulF32_avx2(float* c, const float* a, const float* b,
    const size_t* sizes);

// Ch11_02_fcpp.cpp
extern void MatrixMulF32_cpp(MatrixF32& c, const MatrixF32& a, const MatrixF32& b);
```

```
// Ch11_02_misc.cpp
extern void InitMat(MatrixF32& c1, MatrixF32& c2, MatrixF32& a, MatrixF32& b);
extern void SaveResults(const MatrixF32& c1, const MatrixF32& c2,
    const MatrixF32& a, const MatrixF32& b, const char* s = nullptr);

// Ch11_02_bm.cpp
extern void MatrixMulF32_bm(void);

// Ch11_02_test.cpp (test code using intrinsics)
extern void MatrixMulF32_test(MatrixF32& c, const MatrixF32& a,
    const MatrixF32& b);

// Miscellaneous constants
constexpr float c_Epsilon = 1.0e-9f;

//------------------------------------------------------------------------------
// Ch11_02_fcpp.cpp
//------------------------------------------------------------------------------

#include "Ch11_02.h"

void MatrixMulF32_cpp(MatrixF32& c, const MatrixF32& a, const MatrixF32& b)
{
    // Code for MatrixF32::Mul() located in MatrixF32.h
    MatrixF32::Mul(c, a, b);
}
```

Listing 11-2a opens with the header file Ch11_02.h. Note that the declaration statement for calculating function MatrixMulF32_cpp() requires an argument of type MatrixF32. Class MatrixF32 is a simple wrapper class for a matrix of single-precision floating-point values. The internal buffer allocated by MatrixF32 is aligned on a 64-byte boundary, which means that it is properly aligned for use with AVX, AVX2, and AVX-512 instructions that require aligned operands. Class MatrixF32 is used in this and several other subsequent source code examples to handle matrix buffer management. It also contains a few calculating functions to facilitate performance benchmarking.

Next in Listing 11-2a is file Ch11_02_fcpp.cpp. This file contains the function MatrixMulF32_cpp(), which is used for result comparison and benchmarking purposes. Note that the actual matrix multiplication is performed by function MatrixF32::Mul(), which employs three nested for-loops to calculate the matrix product.

Recall from earlier source code examples that the address of an element in a C++ matrix can be calculated using integer multiplication and addition. For example, to calculate the address of matrix element a[i][j], one can use the expression &a[i * a_ncols + j]. The inner for-loop of source code example Ch09_06 exploited this technique since it's simple to code and easy to understand. Another alternative is to use pointers and pointer arithmetic in the for-loops for matrix element addresses. The advantage of this approach is that one can exploit the fact that constant offsets exist between matrix elements in different rows but in the same column (constant offsets also exist between consecutive elements in the same row). For example, the address of matrix element a[i+1][j] is &a[(i + 1) * a_ncols + j] and the index offset difference between element a[i][j] and element a[i+1][j] is a_ncols. When emitting code for a for-loop that references matrix elements using indices, a C++ compiler will often utilize pointer addition instead of integer multiplications and additions since eliminating the multiplications often yields faster code. The MASM assembly language code for example Ch11_02, shown in Listing 11-2b, employs this technique.

Listing 11-2b. Example Ch11_02 MASM Code

```
;----------------------------------------------------------------------
; Ch11_02_fasm.asm
;----------------------------------------------------------------------

        include <MacrosX86-64-AVX.asmh>

; Data for vmaskmovps masks

        .const
MaskMovLUT  equ $
mask0       dd  8 dup(0)
mask1       dd  1 dup(80000000h), 7 dup(0)
mask2       dd  2 dup(80000000h), 6 dup(0)
mask3       dd  3 dup(80000000h), 5 dup(0)
mask4       dd  4 dup(80000000h), 4 dup(0)
mask5       dd  5 dup(80000000h), 3 dup(0)
mask6       dd  6 dup(80000000h), 2 dup(0)
mask7       dd  7 dup(80000000h), 1 dup(0)

;----------------------------------------------------------------------
; void MatrixMulF32_avx2(float* c, const float* a, const float* b,
;    const size_t* sizes);
;----------------------------------------------------------------------

NSE         equ 8                           ;num_simd_elements
NSE_MOD     equ 07h                         ;mask to calculate num_residual_cols
SIZE_F32    equ 4                           ;scale factor for F32 elements

        .code
MatrixMulF32_avx2 proc frame
        CreateFrame_M MM_,0,0,rbx,rsi,rdi,r12,r13,r14,r15
        EndProlog_M

; Load matrix sizes
        mov r13,[r9]                        ;r13 = c_nrows
        mov r14,[r9+8]                      ;r14 = c_ncols (also b_ncols)
        mov r15,[r9+16]                     ;r15 = a_ncols

; Load mask for vmaskmovps instruction
        mov r12,r14                         ;r12 = c_ncols
        and r12,NSE_MOD                     ;num_residual_cols = c_ncols % NSE

        mov rax,r12                         ;rax = num_residual_cols
        shl rax,5                           ;rax = num_residual_cols * 32
        lea r11,[MaskMovLUT]                ;r11 = address of MaskMovLUT
        add rax,r11                         ;rax = address of maskX
        vmovdqu ymm5,ymmword ptr [rax]      ;ymm5 = maskX for vmaskmovps

        mov rax,-1                          ;rax = i
```

```
;----------------------------------------------------------------------------
; General-purpose registers used in code below:
;
;   rax     i                                       r9      j
;   rbx     matrix a element pointer (p_aa)         r10     k
;   rcx     matrix c                                r11     scratch
;   rdx     matrix a                                r12     num_residual_cols
;   rsi     matrix b element pointer (p_bb)         r13     c_nrows
;   rdi     &a[i][0]                                r15     a_ncols
;   r8      matrix b
;----------------------------------------------------------------------------

; Repeat for each row in c
        align 16
Loop1:  add rax,1                       ;i += 1
        cmp rax,r13
        jae Done                        ;jump if i >= c_nrows

        mov rdi,rdx                     ;rdi = &a[i][0]
        lea rdx,[rdx+r15*SIZE_F32]      ;rdx = &a[i+1][0]
        xor r9,r9                       ;r9 = j

; Repeat while there are at least NSE columns in current row of c
        align 16
Loop2:  lea r11,[r9+NSE]                ;r11 = j + NSE
        cmp r11,r14
        ja ChkRes                       ;jump if j + NSE > c_ncols

        mov rbx,rdi                     ;rbx = &a[i][0]
        lea rsi,[r8+r9*SIZE_F32]        ;rsi = &b[0][j]
        vxorps ymm2,ymm2,ymm2           ;initialize packed c_vals
        mov r10,r15                     ;r10 = a_ncols

; Calculate c[i][j:j+NSE-1]
        align 16
Loop3a: vbroadcastss ymm0,real4 ptr [rbx]   ;broadcast a[i][k]
        vfmadd231ps ymm2,ymm0,[rsi]         ;ymm2 += a[i][k] * b[k][j:j+NSE-1]

        add rbx,SIZE_F32                ;rbx = &a[i][k+1]
        lea rsi,[rsi+r14*SIZE_F32]      ;rsi = &b[k+1][j]
        sub r10,1                       ;k -= 1
        jnz Loop3a                      ;repeat until done

; Save c[i][j:j+NSE-1]
        vmovups ymmword ptr[rcx],ymm2   ;save c[i][j:j+NSE-1]

        add r9,NSE                      ;j += num_simd_elements
        add rcx,NSE*SIZE_F32            ;rcx = &c[i][j+NSE] (next group)
        jmp Loop2

ChkRes: test r12,r12                    ;num_residual_cols == 0?
        jz Loop1                        ;jump if yes
```

```
        mov rbx,rdi                          ;rbx = &a[i][0]
        lea rsi,[r8+r9*SIZE_F32]             ;rsi = &b[0][j]
        vxorps ymm2,ymm2,ymm2                ;initialize packed c_vals
        mov r10,r15                          ;r10 = a_ncols

; Calculate c[i][j:j+NRC] (NRC is num_residual_cols)
        align 16
Loop3b: vbroadcastss ymm0,real4 ptr [rbx]    ;broadcast a[i][k]
        vmaskmovps ymm1,ymm5,[rsi]           ;load b[k][j:j+NRC]
        vfmadd231ps ymm2,ymm1,ymm0           ;update product sums

        add rbx,SIZE_F32                     ;rbx = &a[i][k+1]
        lea rsi,[rsi+r14*SIZE_F32]           ;rsi = &b[k+1][j]
        sub r10,1                            ;k -= 1
        jnz Loop3b                           ;repeat until done

; Save c[i][j:j+NRC]
        vmaskmovps [rcx],ymm5,ymm2           ;save c[i][j:j+NRC]
        lea rcx,[rcx+r12*SIZE_F32]           ;rcx = &c[i][j+NRC+1] (next group)
        jmp Loop1

Done:   vzeroupper
        DeleteFrame_M rbx,rsi,rdi,r12,r13,r14,r15
        ret

MatrixMulF32_avx2 endp
        end
```

Listing 11-2b begins with a .const section that contains mask values for the vmaskmovps (Conditional SIMD Packed Loads and Stores) instruction. The operation performed by this instruction is explained later. Each maskX definition in the .const section contains eight doubleword values. The text dup is a MASM operator that performs both storage allocation and data initialization. For example, the statement mask0 dword 8 dup(0) defines a storage location named mask0 and allocates space for eight doubleword values; it also initializes each doubleword value to zero. The next statement, mask1 dword 1 dup(80000000h), 7 dup(0), allocates storage space for one doubleword and initializes it to 0x80000000; this statement also allocates storage space for seven doubleword values and initializes these values to zero.

Function MatrixMulF32_avx2() begins its execution with a formal function prologue that saves all non-volatile general-purpose registers on the stack. Following its prologue, a series of mov instructions loads matrix size values c_nrows, c_ncols (which equals b_ncols), and a_ncols into registers R13, R14, and R15. The next code block begins with the instruction pair mov r12,r14 and and r12,NSE_MOD, which calculates num_residual_cols = c_ncols % NSE. The ensuing code block that starts with the mov rax,r12 instruction loads the mask needed for the vmaskmovps instruction into register YMM5. Note that a vmovdqu instruction is used to perform the actual mask load since the mask values in MaskMovLUT may not be aligned in a 32-byte boundary.

Immediately before the label Loop1 is the statement align 16. This MASM directive positions the ensuing add rax,1 instruction on a 16-byte boundary. The reason for doing this is that execution of a for-loop is often faster when the target of an x86-64 jump instruction is aligned on a 16-byte boundary. The drawback of using the align directive in this manner is a slight increase in code size since the assembler must insert one or more "no operation" instructions to perform the alignment. Immediately following the add rax,1 instruction is the instruction pair cmp rax,r13 and jae Done, which terminates Loop1 when i >= c_nrows is true. The subsequent code block begins with a mov rdi,rdx instruction that loads &a[i][0] into register RDI to preserve this value for later use. This is followed by a lea rdx,[rdx+r15*SIZE_F32] instruction that loads &a[i+1][0] into register RDX for the next iteration of Loop1. Note that R15 contains a_ncols; multiplying this value by SIZE_F32 (four) and adding it to RDX yields the address of &a[i+1][0]. Following the lea instruction is an xor r9,r9 instruction that initializes Loop2 index variable j to zero.

For-loop Loop2 begins each iteration with a lea r11,[r9+NSE] instruction that loads j + NSE into register R11. On x86 processors, the lea instruction is often used to perform additions like this since it is usually faster than using two distinct instructions (e.g., mov r11,r9 and add r11,NSE). If j + NSE > c_ncols is false, the ensuing code block performs several requisite initializations for Loop3a. Note that registers RBX and RSI are initialized with the addresses of matrix elements a[i][0] and b[0][j], respectively. For-loop Loop3a, which repeats c_ncols times, calculates products for matrix elements c[i][j:j+7]. This for-loop begins each iteration with a vbroadcastss ymm0,real4 ptr [rbx] instruction that broadcasts a[i][k] to each single-precision element position in YMM0. The next instruction, vfmadd231ps ymm2,ymm0,ymmword ptr [rsi], calculates c[i][j:j+7] += a[i][k] * b[k][j:j+7]. Following the FMA operation, the add rbx,SIZE_F32 instruction updates RBX so that it points to element &a[i][k+1]. Execution of the ensuing lea rsi,[rsi+r14*SIZE_F32] instruction sets RSI to &b[k+1][j]. The vmovups ymmword ptr[rcx],ymm2 instruction that follows Loop3a saves matrix elements c[i][j:j+7].

Following completion of Loop2, MatrixMulF32_avx2() uses the instruction pair test r12,r12 and jz Loop1 to skip Loop3b if num_residual_cols == 0 is true. For-loop Loop3b computes products for matrix elements c[i][j:j+NRC] (NRC is num_residual_columns) using the same basic technique as used in Loop3a. Note that this for-loop uses a vmaskmovps ymm1,ymm5,ymmword ptr [rsi] instruction to load matrix elements b[k][j:j+NRC]. This vmaskmovps instruction only loads an element into register YMM1 if the most significant bit of the corresponding element in YMM5 is set to 1; otherwise, zero is loaded. For-loop Loop3a also uses a vmaskmovps ymmword ptr[rcx],ymm5,ymm2 instruction to save matrix elements c[i][j:j+NRC]. Note that when using vmaskmovps to perform a store, element positions in the destination memory buffer are not altered if the corresponding element mask bit is set to zero. Figure 11-3 illustrates utilization of the vmaskmovps to perform masked load and store operations.

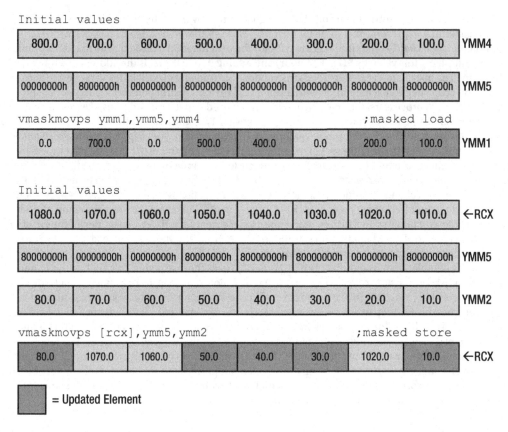

Figure 11-3. Representative masked load and store operations using vmaskmovps

The NASM code for source example Ch11_02 is similar to the MASM code that's shown in Listing 11-2b. Differences include the use of an .rdata section for the vmaskmovps instruction mask values. A series of mov instructions is also employed to rearrange the argument values passed via registers RCX, RDX, RSI, and RDI to match the general-purpose registers used in Listing 11-2b. Here are the results for source code example Ch11_02:

```
----- Results for Ch11_02 -----
Matrix compare passed
Matrix multiplication results saved to file @Ch11_02_MatrixMulF32_HELIUM.txt

Running benchmark function MatrixMulF32_bm() - please wait
.........................................
Matrix compare passed
Benchmark times save to file @Ch11_02_MatrixMulF32_bm_HELIUM.csv
```

Table 11-2 shows the benchmark timing measurements for example Ch11_02.

Table 11-2. *Benchmark Timing Measurements (Microseconds) for Single-Precision Matrix Multiplication Functions Using a 100 × 100 Matrix (100 Matrix Products)*

Function	i5-11600K	i7-11700K	7700X
MatrixMulF32_cpp()	54373 (82)	50220 (1670)	34839 (39)
MatrixMulF32_avx2()	7032 (18)	6929 (111)	5862 (8)

Double-Precision

The next source code example, named Ch11_03, also performs matrix multiplication but uses double-precision instead of single-precision floating-point elements. The C++ source code for example Ch11_03 is not shown since it's analogous to the code in Listing 11-2a. The only differences are the use of the C++ floating-point type double instead of float and class MatrixF64 instead of MatrixF32. Listing 11-3 shows the MASM code for example Ch11_03.

Listing 11-3. Example Ch11_03 MASM Code

```
;-----------------------------------------------------------------------------
; Ch11_03_fasm.asm
;-----------------------------------------------------------------------------

        include <MacrosX86-64-AVX.asmh>

; Data for vmaskmovpd masks

            .const
MaskMovLUT  equ $
mask0       dq  4 dup(0)
mask1       dq  1 dup(8000000000000000h), 3 dup(0)
mask2       dq  2 dup(8000000000000000h), 2 dup(0)
mask3       dq  3 dup(8000000000000000h), 1 dup(0)

;-----------------------------------------------------------------------------
; void MatrixMulF64_Aavx2(double* c, const double* a, const double* b,
;    const size_t* sizes);
;-----------------------------------------------------------------------------

NSE         equ 4                           ;num_simd_elements
NSE_MOD     equ 03h                         ;mask to calculate num_residual_cols
SIZE_F64    equ 8                           ;scale factor for F64 elements

            .code
MatrixMulF64_avx2 proc frame
        CreateFrame_M MM_,0,0,rbx,rsi,rdi,r12,r13,r14,r15
        EndProlog_M
```

```
; Load matrix sizes
        mov r13,qword ptr [r9]                  ;r13 = c_nrows
        mov r14,qword ptr [r9+8]                ;r14 = c_ncols (also b_ncols)
        mov r15,qword ptr [r9+16]               ;r15 = a_ncols

; Load mask for vmaskmovpd instruction
        mov r12,r14                             ;r12 = c_ncols
        and r12,NSE_MOD                         ;num_residual_cols = c_ncols % NSE

        mov rax,r12                             ;rax = num_residual_cols
        shl rax,5                               ;rax = num_residual_cols * 32
        lea r11,[MaskMovLUT]                    ;r11 = address of MaskMovLUT
        add rax,r11                             ;rax = address of maskX
        vmovdqu ymm5,ymmword ptr [rax]          ;ymm5 = maskX for vmaskmovpd

        mov rax,-1                              ;rax = i

;-------------------------------------------------------------------------
; General-purpose registers used in code below:
;
;    rax     i                                       r9      j
;    rbx     matrix a element pointer (p_aa)         r10     k
;    rcx     matrix c                                r11     scratch
;    rdx     matrix a                                r12     num_residual_cols
;    rsi     matrix b element pointer (p_bb)         r13     c_nrows
;    rdi     &a[i][0]                                r15     a_ncols
;    r8      matrix b
;-------------------------------------------------------------------------

; Repeat for each row in c
        align 16
Loop1:  add rax,1                               ;i += 1
        cmp rax,r13
        jae Done                                ;jump if i >= c_nrows

        mov rdi,rdx                             ;rdi = &a[i][0]
        lea rdx,[rdx+r15*SIZE_F64]              ;rdx = &a[i+1][0]
        xor r9,r9                               ;r9 = j

; Repeat while there are at least NSE columns in current row of c
        align 16
Loop2:  lea r11,[r9+NSE]                        ;r11 = j + NSE
        cmp r11,r14
        ja ChkRes                               ;jump if j + NSE > c_ncols

        mov rbx,rdi                             ;rbx = &a[i][0]
        lea rsi,[r8+r9*SIZE_F64]                ;rsi = &b[0][j]
        vxorpd ymm2,ymm2,ymm2                   ;initialize packed c_vals
        mov r10,r15                             ;r10 = a_ncols
```

```
        ; Calculate c[i][j:j+NSE-1]
                align 16
        Loop3a: vbroadcastsd ymm0,real8 ptr [rbx]          ;broadcast a[i][k]
                vfmadd231pd ymm2,ymm0,[rsi]                ;ymm2 += a[i][k] * b[k][j:j+NSE-1]

                add rbx,SIZE_F64                           ;rbx = &a[i][k+1]
                lea rsi,[rsi+r14*SIZE_F64]                 ;rsi = &b[k+1][j]
                sub r10,1                                  ;k -= 1
                jnz Loop3a                                 ;repeat until done

        ; Save c[i][j:j+NSE-1]
                vmovupd ymmword ptr[rcx],ymm2              ;save c[i][j:j+NSE-1]

                add r9,NSE                                 ;j += num_simd_elements
                add rcx,NSE*SIZE_F64                       ;rcx = &c[i][j+NSE] (next SIMD group)
                jmp Loop2

        ChkRes: test r12,r12                               ;num_residual_cols == 0?
                jz Loop1                                   ;jump if yes

                mov rbx,rdi                                ;rbx = &a[i][0]
                lea rsi,[r8+r9*SIZE_F64]                   ;rsi = &b[0][j]
                vxorpd ymm2,ymm2,ymm2                      ;initialize packed c_vals
                mov r10,r15                                ;r10 = a_ncols

        ; Calculate c[i][j:j+NRC] (NRC is num_residual_cols)
                align 16
        Loop3b: vbroadcastsd ymm0,real8 ptr [rbx]          ;broadcast a[i][k]
                vmaskmovpd ymm1,ymm5,[rsi]                 ;load b[k][j:j+NRC]
                vfmadd231pd ymm2,ymm1,ymm0                 ;update product sums

                add rbx,SIZE_F64                           ;rbx = &a[i][k+1]
                lea rsi,[rsi+r14*SIZE_F64]                 ;rsi = &b[k+1][j]
                sub r10,1                                  ;k -= 1
                jnz Loop3b                                 ;repeat until done

        ; Save c[i][j:j+NRC]
                vmaskmovpd [rcx],ymm5,ymm2                 ;save c[i][j:j+NRC]
                lea rcx,[rcx+r12*SIZE_F64]                 ;rcx = &c[i][j+NRC+1] (next SIMD group)
                jmp Loop1

        Done:   vzeroupper
                DeleteFrame_M rbx,rsi,rdi,r12,r13,r14,r15
                ret

        MatrixMulF64_avx2 endp
                end
```

The layout of function MatrixMulF64_avx2() in Listing 11-3 mostly parallels function MatrixMulF32_avx2() that's shown in Listing 11-2b. Differences include the use of quadword values in MaskMovLUT and the values for equates NSE (4 instead of 8) and NSE_MOD (03h instead of 07h). Also note that the value for equate SIZE_F64 is set to 8 instead of 4. The other notable difference is the use of double-precision AVX2 and FMA instructions instead of single-precision. These instructions incorporate the suffix pd in their mnemonics instead of ps. The NASM version of MatrixMulF64_avx2() (source code not shown) also includes these same changes. One important takeaway point from example Ch11_03 is that with a little forethought, it's usually a straightforward coding exercise to develop dual x86-AVX assembly language functions that carry out calculations using both single-precision and double-precision values. The output for example Ch11_03 is the same as the output for example Ch11_02.

Table 11-3 shows the benchmark timing measurements for example Ch11_03.

Table 11-3. *Benchmark Timing Measurements (Microseconds) for Double-Precision Matrix Multiplication Functions Using a 100 × 100 Matrix (100 Matrix Products)*

Function	i5-11600K	i7-11700K	7700X
MatrixMulF64_cpp()	55404 (457)	51300 (1812)	33649 (21)
MatrixMulF64_avx2()	13621 (1111)	13229 (342)	13013 (10)

Matrix (4 × 4) Multiplication

The matrix multiplication code in examples Ch11_02 and Ch11_03 works best when calculating a matrix product that contains at least eight (single-precision) or four (double-precision) columns. For smaller matrix products, especially 4 × 4 matrices, it is often advantageous to code size-optimized multiplication functions for improved performance. In this section, you will learn how to code AVX2 matrix multiplication functions that have been optimized for 4 × 4 matrices.

If the matrix multiplication equation shown earlier in this chapter is expanded for 4 × 4 matrix multiplication, the equations shown in Figure 11-4 are obtained. Just like the previous two examples, these equations are easy to implement using FMA instructions.

$$\begin{bmatrix} c_{00} & c_{01} & c_{02} & c_{03} \\ c_{10} & c_{11} & c_{12} & c_{13} \\ c_{20} & c_{21} & c_{22} & c_{23} \\ c_{30} & c_{31} & c_{32} & c_{33} \end{bmatrix} = \begin{bmatrix} a_{00} & a_{01} & a_{02} & a_{03} \\ a_{10} & a_{11} & a_{12} & a_{13} \\ a_{20} & a_{21} & a_{22} & a_{23} \\ a_{30} & a_{31} & a_{32} & a_{33} \end{bmatrix} \begin{bmatrix} b_{00} & b_{01} & b_{02} & b_{03} \\ b_{10} & b_{11} & b_{12} & b_{13} \\ b_{20} & b_{21} & b_{22} & b_{23} \\ b_{30} & b_{31} & b_{32} & b_{33} \end{bmatrix}$$

$$c_{00} = a_{00}b_{00} + a_{01}b_{10} + a_{02}b_{20} + a_{03}b_{30}$$

$$c_{01} = a_{00}b_{01} + a_{01}b_{11} + a_{02}b_{21} + a_{03}b_{31}$$

$$c_{02} = a_{00}b_{02} + a_{01}b_{12} + a_{02}b_{22} + a_{03}b_{32}$$

$$c_{03} = a_{00}b_{03} + a_{01}b_{13} + a_{02}b_{23} + a_{03}b_{33}$$

$$c_{10} = a_{10}b_{00} + a_{11}b_{10} + a_{12}b_{20} + a_{13}b_{30}$$

$$c_{11} = a_{10}b_{01} + a_{11}b_{11} + a_{12}b_{21} + a_{13}b_{31}$$

$$c_{12} = a_{10}b_{02} + a_{11}b_{12} + a_{12}b_{22} + a_{13}b_{32}$$

$$c_{13} = a_{10}b_{03} + a_{11}b_{13} + a_{12}b_{23} + a_{13}b_{33}$$

$$c_{20} = a_{20}b_{00} + a_{21}b_{10} + a_{22}b_{20} + a_{23}b_{30}$$

$$c_{21} = a_{20}b_{01} + a_{21}b_{11} + a_{22}b_{21} + a_{23}b_{31}$$

$$c_{22} = a_{20}b_{02} + a_{21}b_{12} + a_{22}b_{22} + a_{23}b_{32}$$

$$c_{23} = a_{20}b_{03} + a_{21}b_{13} + a_{22}b_{23} + a_{23}b_{33}$$

$$c_{30} = a_{30}b_{00} + a_{31}b_{10} + a_{32}b_{20} + a_{33}b_{30}$$

$$c_{31} = a_{30}b_{01} + a_{31}b_{11} + a_{32}b_{21} + a_{33}b_{31}$$

$$c_{32} = a_{30}b_{02} + a_{31}b_{12} + a_{32}b_{22} + a_{33}b_{32}$$

$$c_{33} = a_{30}b_{03} + a_{31}b_{13} + a_{32}b_{23} + a_{33}b_{33}$$

Figure 11-4. *Matrix multiplication equations using 4 × 4 matrices*

Single-Precision

Listing 11-4a shows the principal C++ code for example Ch11_04. This example illustrates 4 × 4 matrix multiplication using single-precision floating-point values.

Listing 11-4a. Example Ch11_04 C++ Code

```
//-----------------------------------------------------------------------------
// Ch11_04.h
//-----------------------------------------------------------------------------
```

```
#pragma once
#include "MatrixF32.h"

// Ch11_04_fasm.asm, Ch11_04_fasm.s
extern "C" void MatrixMul4x4F32a_avx2(float* c, const float* a, const float* b);
extern "C" void MatrixMul4x4F32b_avx2(float* c, const float* a, const float* b);

// Ch11_04_fcpp.cpp
extern void MatrixMul4x4F32_cpp(MatrixF32& c, const MatrixF32& a,
    const MatrixF32& b);

// Ch11_04_misc.cpp
extern void InitMat(MatrixF32& c1, MatrixF32& c2, MatrixF32& c3, MatrixF32& a,
    MatrixF32& b);

// Ch11_04_bm.cpp
extern void MatrixMul4x4F32_bm(void);

// Miscellaneous constants
constexpr float c_Epsilon = 1.0e-9f;

//---------------------------------------------------------------------------
// Ch11_04_fcpp.cpp
//---------------------------------------------------------------------------

#include "Ch11_04.h"

void MatrixMul4x4F32_cpp(MatrixF32& c, const MatrixF32& a, const MatrixF32& b)
{
    // Code for MatrixF32::Mul4x4() located in MatrixF32.h
    MatrixF32::Mul4x4(c, a, b);
}
```

The organization of the C++ code for example Ch11_04 closely resembles the previous two examples, but a few items warrant some discussion. In Listing 11-4a, note that header file Ch11_04.h contains declarations for two assembly language functions: MatrixMul4x4F32a_avx2() and MatrixMul4x4F32b_avx2(). The former function employs FMA instructions to carry out its matrix product calculations, while the latter uses distinct multiply and add operations. Both methods are used in this example to demonstrate the performance benefits of using FMA instructions vs. individual multiply and add instructions. Also shown in Listing 11-4a is function MatrixMul4x4F32_cpp(), which is included for result comparison and benchmarking purposes.

Listing 11-4b shows the MASM code for example Ch11_04. This listing opens with the definition of a macro named Mat4x4MulCalcRowF32a_M, which calculates one row of a 4 × 4 matrix multiplication using FMA instructions. Note that macro Mat4x4MulCalcRowF32a_M requires a single argument named disp. This argument corresponds to the displacement for row i of matrix a. The code emitted by macro Mat4x4MulCalcRowF32a_M employs a series of vbroadcastss and vfmadd231ps instructions to calculate matrix elements c[i][0:3]. Note that a vmovaps xmmword ptr [rcx+disp],xmm4 is used to save each row in matrix c. Unlike the matrix multiplication code in example Ch11_02 (Listing 11-2b), each matrix row in this example is properly aligned on a double quadword (16-byte) boundary.

Listing 11-4b. Example Ch11_04 MASM Code

```
;-------------------------------------------------------------------------------
; Ch11_04_fasm.asm
;-------------------------------------------------------------------------------


;-------------------------------------------------------------------------------
; Mat4x4MulCalcRowF32a_M macro
;
; Description:  This macro is used to compute one row of a 4x4 matrix
;               multiply using packed FMA instructions.
;
; Parameters:   disp = displacement for row a[i][], c[i][]
;
; Registers:    xmm0 = row b[0][]
;               xmm1 = row b[1][]
;               xmm2 = row b[2][]
;               xmm3 = row b[3][]
;               rcx = matrix c pointer
;               rdx = matrix a pointer
;               xmm4, xmm5 = scratch registers
;-------------------------------------------------------------------------------

Mat4x4MulCalcRowF32a_M macro disp
        vbroadcastss xmm5,real4 ptr [rdx+disp]      ;broadcast a[i][0]
        vmulps xmm4,xmm5,xmm0                        ;xmm4  = a[i][0] * b[0][]

        vbroadcastss xmm5,real4 ptr [rdx+disp+4]    ;broadcast a[i][1]
        vfmadd231ps xmm4,xmm5,xmm1                   ;xmm4 += a[i][1] * b[1][]

        vbroadcastss xmm5,real4 ptr [rdx+disp+8]    ;broadcast a[i][2]
        vfmadd231ps xmm4,xmm5,xmm2                   ;xmm4 += a[i][2] * b[2][]

        vbroadcastss xmm5,real4 ptr [rdx+disp+12]   ;broadcast a[i][3]
        vfmadd231ps xmm4,xmm5,xmm3                   ;xmm4 += a[i][3] * b[3][]

        vmovaps xmmword ptr [rcx+disp],xmm4          ;save row c[i][]
        endm


;-------------------------------------------------------------------------------
; Mat4x4MulCalcRowF32b_M macro
;
; Description:  This macro is used to compute one row of a 4x4 matrix
;               multiply using packed multiply and add instructions.
;
; Parameters:   disp = displacement for row a[i][], c[i][]
;
; Registers:    xmm0 = row b[0][]
;               xmm1 = row b[1][]
;               xmm2 = row b[2][]
;               xmm3 = row b[3][]
;               rcx = matrix c pointer
```

```
;                rdx = matrix a pointer
;                xmm4, xmm5 = scratch registers
;-------------------------------------------------------------------------

Mat4x4MulCalcRowF32b_M macro disp
        vbroadcastss xmm5,real4 ptr [rdx+disp]      ;broadcast a[i][0]
        vmulps xmm4,xmm5,xmm0                        ;xmm5 = a[i][0] * b[0][]

        vbroadcastss xmm5,real4 ptr [rdx+disp+4]    ;broadcast a[i][1]
        vmulps xmm5,xmm5,xmm1                        ;xmm5 = a[i][1] * b[1][]
        vaddps xmm4,xmm5,xmm4                        ;xmm4 += a[i][1] * b[1][]

        vbroadcastss xmm5,real4 ptr [rdx+disp+8]    ;broadcast a[i][2]
        vmulps xmm5,xmm5,xmm2                        ;xmm5 = a[i][2] * b[2][]
        vaddps xmm4,xmm5,xmm4                        ;xmm4 += a[i][2] * b[2][]

        vbroadcastss xmm5,real4 ptr [rdx+disp+12]   ;broadcast a[i][3]
        vmulps xmm5,xmm5,xmm3                        ;xmm5 = a[i][3] * b[3][]
        vaddps xmm4,xmm5,xmm4                        ;xmm4 += a[i][3] * b[3][]

        vmovaps xmmword ptr [rcx+disp],xmm4         ;save row c[i][]
        endm

;-------------------------------------------------------------------------
; void MatrixMul4x4F32a_avx2(float* c, const float* a, const float* b);
;-------------------------------------------------------------------------

        .code
MatrixMul4x4F32a_avx2 proc

; Load matrix b into xmm0 - xmm3
        vmovaps ymm0,ymmword ptr [r8]       ;xmm0 = row b[0][]
        vextractf128 xmm1,ymm0,1            ;xmm1 = row b[1][]
        vmovaps ymm2,ymmword ptr [r8+32]    ;xmm2 = row b[2][]
        vextractf128 xmm3,ymm2,1            ;xmm3 = row b[3][]

; Calculate matrix product c = a * b
        Mat4x4MulCalcRowF32a_M 0            ;calculate row c[0][]
        Mat4x4MulCalcRowF32a_M 16           ;calculate row c[1][]
        Mat4x4MulCalcRowF32a_M 32           ;calculate row c[2][]
        Mat4x4MulCalcRowF32a_M 48           ;calculate row c[3][]

        vzeroupper
        ret
MatrixMul4x4F32a_avx2 endp

;-------------------------------------------------------------------------
; void MatrixMul4x4F32b_avx2(float* c, const float* a, const float* b);
;-------------------------------------------------------------------------
```

```
MatrixMul4x4F32b_avx2 proc

; Load matrix b into xmm0 - xmm3
        vmovaps ymm0,ymmword ptr [r8]        ;xmm0 = row b[0][]
        vextractf128 xmm1,ymm0,1             ;xmm1 = row b[1][]
        vmovaps ymm2,ymmword ptr [r8+32]     ;xmm2 = row b[2][]
        vextractf128 xmm3,ymm2,1             ;xmm3 = row b[3][]

; Calculate matrix product c = a * b
        Mat4x4MulCalcRowF32b_M 0             ;calculate row c[0][]
        Mat4x4MulCalcRowF32b_M 16            ;calculate row c[1][]
        Mat4x4MulCalcRowF32b_M 32            ;calculate row c[2][]
        Mat4x4MulCalcRowF32b_M 48            ;calculate row c[3][]

        vzeroupper
        ret
MatrixMul4x4F32b_avx2 endp
        end
```

Following the definition of macro Mat4x4MulCalcRowF32a_M is another macro definition named Mat4x4MulCalcRowF32b_M. The code emitted by this macro differs from Mat4x4MulCalcRowF32a_M in that it uses distinct vmulps and vaddps instructions instead of a single vfmadd231ps instruction. The purpose of this macro is to compare the execution performance of distinct vmulps and vaddps instructions vs. a single vfmadd231ps instruction.

The next item in Listing 11-4b is the assembly language code for function MatrixMul4x4F32a_avx2(), which calculates the product of two 4 × 4 matrices. This function begins with a vmovaps ymm0,ymmword ptr [r8] instruction that loads rows 0 and 1 of matrix b into register YMM0. The ensuing vextractf128 xmm1,ymm0,1 instruction copies the four high-order single-precision elements in YMM0 (matrix b row 1) to register XMM1. Execution of this instruction does not alter the four low-order single-precision elements of YMM0 (i.e., register XMM0), which holds matrix b row 0. Rows 2 and 3 of matrix b are then loaded into registers XMM2 and XMM3 using a similar sequence of instructions. Following the loading of matrix b, function MatrixMul4x4F32a_avx2() utilizes macro Mat4x4MulCalcRowF32a_M four times to calculate the matrix product c = a * b. Note that each use of macro Mat4x4MulCalcRowF32a_M uses a different displacement value, which corresponds to a row offset of matrix a.

The final function in Listing 11-4b is named MatrixMul4x4F32b_avx2(). This function is almost identical to the previous function but utilizes macro Mat4x4MulCalcRowF32b_M to perform the 4 × 4 matrix multiplication.

The NASM code for example Ch11_04 mimics the MASM code in Listing 11-4b, but uses NASM directives and syntax for the definitions of macros Mat4x4MulCalcRowF32a_M and Mat4x4MulCalcRowF32b_M. It also utilizes different argument registers. Here are the results for source code example Ch11_04:

```
----- Results for Ch11_04 -----
Matrix a
        10.0        11.0        12.0        13.0
        20.0        21.0        22.0        23.0
        30.0        31.0        32.0        33.0
        40.0        41.0        42.0        43.0
```

```
Matrix b
        100.0       101.0       102.0       103.0
        200.0       201.0       202.0       203.0
        300.0       301.0       302.0       303.0
        400.0       401.0       402.0       403.0

Matrix c1
      12000.0     12046.0     12092.0     12138.0
      22000.0     22086.0     22172.0     22258.0
      32000.0     32126.0     32252.0     32378.0
      42000.0     42166.0     42332.0     42498.0

Matrix c2
      12000.0     12046.0     12092.0     12138.0
      22000.0     22086.0     22172.0     22258.0
      32000.0     32126.0     32252.0     32378.0
      42000.0     42166.0     42332.0     42498.0

Matrix c3
      12000.0     12046.0     12092.0     12138.0
      22000.0     22086.0     22172.0     22258.0
      32000.0     32126.0     32252.0     32378.0
      42000.0     42166.0     42332.0     42498.0

Matrix compare passed

Running benchmark function MatrixMul4x4F32_bm() - please wait
.................................................
Benchmark times save to file @Ch11_04_MatrixMul4x4F32_bm_HELIUM.csv
```

Table 11-4 shows the benchmark timing measurements for example Ch11_04. Note that there are meaningful performance gains between functions MatrixMul4x4F32a_avx2() (which utilized FMA instructions) and MatrixMul4x4F32b_avx2() (which exercised distinct multiply and add instructions).

Table 11-4. *Benchmark Timing Measurements (Microseconds) for 4 × 4 Matrix Multiplication Functions (1,000,000 Multiplications)*

Function	i5-11600K	i7-11700K	7700X
MatrixMul4x4F32_cpp()	5035 (10)	20814 (735)	4209 (7)
MatrixMul4x4F32a_avx2() (FMA)	2412 (3)	2423 (81)	1930 (12)
MatrixMul4x4F32b_avx2() (no FMA)	3021 (8)	2892 (98)	2104 (5)

Double-Precision

Listing 11-5 shows the MASM code for example Ch11_05, which performs 4 × 4 matrix multiplication using double-precision floating-point elements. The primary difference between the code in Listing 11-5 and the single-precision 4 × 4 matrix multiplication code in Listing 11-4b is that the former utilizes double-precision AVX2 and FMA instructions.

Listing 11-5. Example Ch11_05 MASM Code

```
;------------------------------------------------------------------------------
; Ch11_05_fasm.asm
;------------------------------------------------------------------------------


;------------------------------------------------------------------------------
; Mat4x4MulCalcRowF64a_M macro
;
; Description:   This macro is used to compute one row of a 4x4 matrix
;                multiply using packed FMA instructions.
;
; Parameters:    disp = displacement for row a[i][], c[i][]
;
; Registers:     ymm0 = row b[0][]
;                ymm1 = row b[1][]
;                ymm2 = row b[2][]
;                ymm3 = row b[3][]
;                rcx = matrix c pointer
;                rdx = matrix a pointer
;                ymm4, ymm5 = scratch registers
;------------------------------------------------------------------------------

Mat4x4MulCalcRowF64a_M macro disp
        vbroadcastsd ymm5,real8 ptr [rdx+disp]      ;broadcast a[i][0]
        vmulpd ymm4,ymm5,ymm0                        ;ymm4  = a[i][0] * b[0][]

        vbroadcastsd ymm5,real8 ptr [rdx+disp+8]    ;broadcast a[i][1]
        vfmadd231pd ymm4,ymm5,ymm1                   ;ymm4 += a[i][1] * b[1][]

        vbroadcastsd ymm5,real8 ptr [rdx+disp+16]   ;broadcast a[i][2]
        vfmadd231pd ymm4,ymm5,ymm2                   ;ymm4 += a[i][2] * b[2][]

        vbroadcastsd ymm5,real8 ptr [rdx+disp+24]   ;broadcast a[i][3]
        vfmadd231pd ymm4,ymm5,ymm3                   ;ymm4 += a[i][3] * b[3][]

        vmovapd ymmword ptr [rcx+disp],ymm4         ;save row c[i][]
        endm

;------------------------------------------------------------------------------
; Mat4x4MulCalcRowF64b_M macro
;
; Description:   This macro is used to compute one row of a 4x4 matrix
;                multiply using packed multiply and add instructions.
;
; Parameters:    disp = displacement for row a[i][], c[i][]
;
; Registers:     ymm0 = row b[0][]
;                ymm1 = row b[1][]
;                ymm2 = row b[2][]
;                ymm3 = row b[3][]
```

```
;             rcx = matrix c pointer
;             rdx = matrix a pointer
;             ymm4, ymm5 = scratch registers
;-------------------------------------------------------------------------

Mat4x4MulCalcRowF64b_M macro disp
        vbroadcastsd ymm5,real8 ptr [rdx+disp]        ;broadcast a[i][0]
        vmulpd ymm4,ymm5,ymm0                          ;ymm5  = a[i][0] * b[0][]

        vbroadcastsd ymm5,real8 ptr [rdx+disp+8]      ;broadcast a[i][1]
        vmulpd ymm5,ymm5,ymm1                          ;ymm5  = a[i][1] * b[1][]
        vaddpd ymm4,ymm5,ymm4                          ;ymm4 += a[i][1] * b[1][]

        vbroadcastsd ymm5,real8 ptr [rdx+disp+16]     ;broadcast a[i][2]
        vmulpd ymm5,ymm5,ymm2                          ;ymm5  = a[i][2] * b[2][]
        vaddpd ymm4,ymm5,ymm4                          ;ymm4 += a[i][2] * b[2][]

        vbroadcastsd ymm5,real8 ptr [rdx+disp+24]     ;broadcast a[i][3]
        vmulpd ymm5,ymm5,ymm3                          ;ymm5  = a[i][3] * b[3][]
        vaddpd ymm4,ymm5,ymm4                          ;ymm4 += a[i][3] * b[3][]

        vmovapd ymmword ptr [rcx+disp],ymm4            ;save row c[i][]
        endm

;-------------------------------------------------------------------------
; void MatrixMul4x4F64a_avx2(double* c, const double* a, const double* b);
;-------------------------------------------------------------------------


        .code
MatrixMul4x4F64a_avx2 proc

; Load matrix b into ymm0 - ymm3
        vmovapd ymm0,ymmword ptr [r8]        ;ymm0 = row b[0][]
        vmovapd ymm1,ymmword ptr [r8+32]     ;ymm1 = row b[1][]
        vmovapd ymm2,ymmword ptr [r8+64]     ;ymm2 = row b[2][]
        vmovapd ymm3,ymmword ptr [r8+96]     ;ymm3 = row b[3][]

; Calculate matrix product c = a * b
        Mat4x4MulCalcRowF64a_M 0             ;calculate row c[0][]
        Mat4x4MulCalcRowF64a_M 32            ;calculate row c[1][]
        Mat4x4MulCalcRowF64a_M 64            ;calculate row c[2][]
        Mat4x4MulCalcRowF64a_M 96            ;calculate row c[3][]

        vzeroupper
        ret
MatrixMul4x4F64a_avx2 endp

;-------------------------------------------------------------------------
; void MatrixMul4x4F64b_avx2(double* c, const double* a, const double* b);
;-------------------------------------------------------------------------
```

```
MatrixMul4x4F64b_avx2 proc

; Load matrix b into ymm0 - ymm3
        vmovapd ymm0,ymmword ptr [r8]          ;ymm0 = row b[0][]
        vmovapd ymm1,ymmword ptr [r8+32]       ;ymm1 = row b[1][]
        vmovapd ymm2,ymmword ptr [r8+64]       ;ymm2 = row b[2][]
        vmovapd ymm3,ymmword ptr [r8+96]       ;ymm3 = row b[3][]

; Calculate matrix product c = a * b
        Mat4x4MulCalcRowF64b_M 0               ;calculate row c[0][]
        Mat4x4MulCalcRowF64b_M 32              ;calculate row c[1][]
        Mat4x4MulCalcRowF64b_M 64              ;calculate row c[2][]
        Mat4x4MulCalcRowF64b_M 96              ;calculate row c[3][]

        vzeroupper
        ret
MatrixMul4x4F64b_avx2 endp
        end
```

Like the previous example, the NASM code for example Ch11_05 uses NASM directives and syntax for the definitions of macros Mat4x4MulCalcRowF64a_M and Mat4x4MulCalcRowF64b_M. The results for source code example Ch11_05 are the same as the results for Ch11_04.

Table 11-5 shows the benchmark timing measurements for example Ch11_05. Note that there are modest performance gains between the FMA and non-FMA versions of the double-precision 4 × 4 matrix multiplication functions.

Table 11-5. *Benchmark Timing Measurements (Microseconds) for 4 × 4 Matrix Multiplication Functions (1,000,000 Multiplications)*

Function	i5-11600K	i7-11700K	7700X
MatrixMul4x4F64_cpp()	6058 (21)	20766 (469)	4895 (8)
MatrixMul4x4F64a_avx2() (FMA)	2685 (11)	2706 (69)	2151 (72)
MatrixMul4x4F64b_avx2() (no FMA)	3137 (12)	2898 (71)	2196 (38)

Matrix (4 × 4) Vector Multiplication

Another common matrix operation is calculating the product of a 4 × 4 matrix and 4 × 1 vector. In 3D computer graphics, these types of calculations are universally employed to perform affine transformations (e.g., translation, rotation, and scaling) using homogeneous coordinates. Figure 11-5 shows the equations required to calculate the product of a 4 × 4 matrix and 4 × 1 vector. Note that the equations in Figure 11-5 utilize the columns of the specified matrix.

$$\begin{bmatrix} b_w \\ b_x \\ b_y \\ b_z \end{bmatrix} = \begin{bmatrix} m_{00} & m_{01} & m_{02} & m_{03} \\ m_{10} & m_{11} & m_{12} & m_{13} \\ m_{20} & m_{21} & m_{22} & m_{23} \\ m_{30} & m_{31} & m_{32} & m_{33} \end{bmatrix} \begin{bmatrix} a_w \\ a_x \\ a_y \\ a_z \end{bmatrix}$$

$$b_w = m_{00}a_w + m_{01}a_x + m_{02}a_y + m_{03}a_z$$

$$b_x = m_{10}a_w + m_{11}a_x + m_{12}a_y + m_{13}a_z$$

$$b_y = m_{20}a_w + m_{21}a_x + m_{22}a_y + m_{23}a_z$$

$$b_z = m_{30}a_w + m_{31}a_x + m_{32}a_y + m_{33}a_z$$

$$\uparrow \qquad \uparrow \qquad \uparrow \qquad \uparrow$$

M col 0   M col 1   M col 2   M col 3

Figure 11-5. *Matrix (4 × 4) vector multiplication equations*

Single-Precision

Listing 11-6a shows the principal C++ code for source code example Ch11-06, which demonstrates matrix-vector (4 × 4 and 4 × 1) multiplication using single-precision floating-point values.

Listing 11-6a. Example Ch11_06 C++ Code

```
//-----------------------------------------------------------------------
// Ch11_06.h
//-----------------------------------------------------------------------

#pragma once
#include <cstddef>
#include "MatrixF32.h"

// Simple 4x1 vector structure
struct Vec4x1_F32
{
    float W, X, Y, Z;
};

// Ch11_06_fasm.asm, Ch11_06_fasm.s
extern "C" void MatVecMulF32_avx2(Vec4x1_F32* vec_b, const float* m,
    const Vec4x1_F32* vec_a, size_t num_vec);

// Ch11_06_fcpp.cpp
extern void MatVecMulF32_cpp(Vec4x1_F32* vec_b, const MatrixF32& m,
    const Vec4x1_F32* vec_a, size_t num_vec);
```

```cpp
// Ch11_06_misc.cpp
extern void InitData(MatrixF32& m, Vec4x1_F32* va, size_t num_vec);
extern bool VecCompare(const Vec4x1_F32* v1, const Vec4x1_F32* v2);

// Ch11_06_bm.cpp
extern void MatrixVecMulF32_bm(void);

// Miscellaenous constants
constexpr size_t c_Alignment = 32;
constexpr int c_RngMinVal = 1;
constexpr int c_RngMaxVal = 500;
constexpr unsigned int c_RngSeedVal = 187;
constexpr float c_Epsilon = 1.0e-12f;

//-----------------------------------------------------------------------------
// Ch11_06_fcpp.cpp
//-----------------------------------------------------------------------------

#include <stdexcept>
#include "Ch11_06.h"
#include "MatrixF32.h"
#include "AlignedMem.h"

static bool CheckArgs(const Vec4x1_F32* vec_b, const MatrixF32& m,
    const Vec4x1_F32* vec_a, size_t num_vec)
{
    if (num_vec == 0)
        return false;

    if (m.GetNumRows() != 4 || m.GetNumCols() != 4)
        return false;

    if (!AlignedMem::IsAligned(m.Data(), c_Alignment))
        return false;

    if (!AlignedMem::IsAligned(vec_a, c_Alignment))
        return false;

    if (!AlignedMem::IsAligned(vec_b, c_Alignment))
        return false;

    return true;
}

void MatVecMulF32_cpp(Vec4x1_F32* vec_b, const MatrixF32& m,
    const Vec4x1_F32* vec_a, size_t num_vec)
{
    if (!CheckArgs(vec_b, m, vec_a, num_vec))
        throw std::runtime_error("MatVecMulF32_cpp() - CheckArgs failed");

    const float* mm = m.Data();
```

```
    // Calculate matrix-vector products
    for (size_t i = 0; i < num_vec; i++)
    {
        vec_b[i].W = mm[0] * vec_a[i].W + mm[1] * vec_a[i].X;
        vec_b[i].W += mm[2] * vec_a[i].Y + mm[3] * vec_a[i].Z;

        vec_b[i].X = mm[4] * vec_a[i].W + mm[5] * vec_a[i].X;
        vec_b[i].X += mm[6] * vec_a[i].Y + mm[7] * vec_a[i].Z;

        vec_b[i].Y = mm[8] * vec_a[i].W + mm[9] * vec_a[i].X;
        vec_b[i].Y += mm[10] * vec_a[i].Y + mm[11] * vec_a[i].Z;

        vec_b[i].Z = mm[12] * vec_a[i].W + mm[13] * vec_a[i].X;
        vec_b[i].Z += mm[14] * vec_a[i].Y + mm[15] * vec_a[i].Z;
    }
}
```

Near the top of Listing 11-6a is the declaration of a structure named Vec4x1_F32. This structure contains the components of a 4 × 1 column vector. Also shown in Listing 11-6a is function MatVecMulF32_cpp(), which performs matrix (4 × 4) vector (4 × 1) multiplication code using standard C++ statements. Note that the statements inside the for-loop implement the equations shown in Figure 11-5.

Listing 11-6b shows the MASM code for example Ch11_06, which begins with the definition of a macro named Mat4x4TransposeF32_M. This macro emits code that calculates the transpose of a 4 × 4 matrix of single-precision values. Macro Mat4x4TransposeF32_M requires rows 0–3 of the original matrix to be loaded in registers XMM0–XMM3, respectively, prior to its use. Following the transpose operation, registers XMM0–XMM3 contain the transposed matrix. Note that macro Mat4x4TransposeF32_M includes instructions that utilize registers XMM4 and XMM5 to hold intermediate results.

Listing 11-6b. Example Ch11_06 MASM Code

```
;-------------------------------------------------------------------------------
; Ch11_06_fasm.asm
;-------------------------------------------------------------------------------


;-------------------------------------------------------------------------------
; Mat4x4TransposeF32_M macro
;
; Description:   This macro transposes a 4x4 matrix of single-precision
;                floating-point values.
;
;  Input Matrix                    Output Matrix
;  -------------------------------------------------
;  xmm0     a3 a2 a1 a0            xmm0     d0 c0 b0 a0
;  xmm1     b3 b2 b1 b0            xmm1     d1 c1 b1 a1
;  xmm2     c3 c2 c1 c0            xmm2     d2 c2 b2 a2
;  xmm3     d3 d2 d1 d0            xmm3     d3 c3 b3 a3
;
; Scratch registers: xmm4, xmm5
;-------------------------------------------------------------------------------
```

```
Mat4x4TransposeF32_M macro
        vunpcklps xmm4,xmm0,xmm1                ;xmm4 = b1 a1 b0 a0
        vunpckhps xmm0,xmm0,xmm1                ;xmm0 = b3 a3 b2 a2
        vunpcklps xmm5,xmm2,xmm3                ;xmm5 = d1 c1 d0 c0
        vunpckhps xmm1,xmm2,xmm3                ;xmm1 = d3 c3 d2 c2

        vmovlhps xmm2,xmm0,xmm1                 ;xmm2 = d2 c2 b2 a2
        vmovhlps xmm3,xmm1,xmm0                 ;xmm3 = d3 c3 b3 a3
        vmovlhps xmm0,xmm4,xmm5                 ;xmm0 = d0 c0 b0 a0
        vmovhlps xmm1,xmm5,xmm4                 ;xmm1 = d1 c1 b1 a1
        endm


;-------------------------------------------------------------------------
; void MatVecMulF32_avx2(Vec4x1_F32* vec_b, const float* m,
;   const Vec4x1_F32* vec_a, size_t num_vec);
;-------------------------------------------------------------------------


        .code
MatVecMulF32_avx2 proc

; Validate arguments
        test r9,r9
        jz Done                                 ;jump if num_vec == 0

        test rcx,1fh
        jnz Done                                ;jump if vec_b not 32b aligned

        test rdx,1fh
        jnz Done                                ;jump if m not 32b aligned

        test r8,1fh
        jnz Done                                ;jump if vec_a 32b aligned

; Initialize
        mov rax,-16                             ;array offset
        vmovaps ymm0,ymmword ptr [rdx]          ;xmm0 = m row 0
        vextractf128 xmm1,ymm0,1                 ;xmm1 = m ro1 1
        vmovaps ymm2,ymmword ptr [rdx+32]       ;xmm2 = m row 2
        vextractf128 xmm3,ymm2,1                 ;xmm3 = m row 3

; Transpose m
        Mat4x4TransposeF32_M

; Calculate matrix-vector products
        align 16
Loop1:  add rax,16

        vbroadcastss xmm5,real4 ptr [r8+rax]    ;xmm5 = vec_a[i].W
        vmulps xmm4,xmm0,xmm5                    ;xmm4  = m_T row 0 * W vals
```

```
            vbroadcastss xmm5,real4 ptr [r8+rax+4]   ;xmm5 = vec_a[i].X
            vfmadd231ps xmm4,xmm1,xmm5               ;xmm4 += m_T row 1 * X vals

            vbroadcastss xmm5,real4 ptr [r8+rax+8]   ;xmm5 = vec_a[i].Y
            vfmadd231ps xmm4,xmm2,xmm5               ;xmm4 += m_T row 2 * Y vals

            vbroadcastss xmm5,real4 ptr [r8+rax+12]  ;xmm5 = vec_a[i].Z
            vfmadd231ps xmm4,xmm3,xmm5               ;xmm4 += m_T row 3 * Z vals

            vmovaps xmmword ptr [rcx+rax],xmm4        ;save vec_b[i]

            sub r9,1                                  ;num_vec -= 1
            jnz Loop1                                 ;repeat until done

Done:   vzeroupper
        ret


MatVecMulF32_avx2 endp
        end
```

Figure 11-6 illustrates the sequence of instructions used to calculate the matrix transpose. The first instruction, vunpcklps xmm4,xmm0,xmm1 (Unpack and Interleave Low Packed SPFP Values), interleaves the low-order single-precision floating-point elements of source operands XMM0 and XMM1 and saves the result in register XMM4. The next instruction, vunpckhps xmm0,xmm0,xmm1 (Unpack and Interleave High Packed SPFP Values), interleaves the high-order elements of registers XMM0 and XMM1. The ensuing instruction pair, vunpcklps xmm5,xmm2,xmm3 and vunpckhps xmm1,xmm2,xmm3, performs the same interleave operation using the elements for rows 2 and 3.

$$\mathbf{A} = \begin{bmatrix} 2 & 7 & 8 & 3 \\ 11 & 14 & 16 & 10 \\ 24 & 21 & 27 & 29 \\ 31 & 34 & 38 & 33 \end{bmatrix} \qquad \mathbf{A}^{\mathrm{T}} = \begin{bmatrix} 2 & 11 & 24 & 31 \\ 7 & 14 & 21 & 34 \\ 8 & 16 & 27 & 38 \\ 3 & 10 & 29 & 33 \end{bmatrix}$$

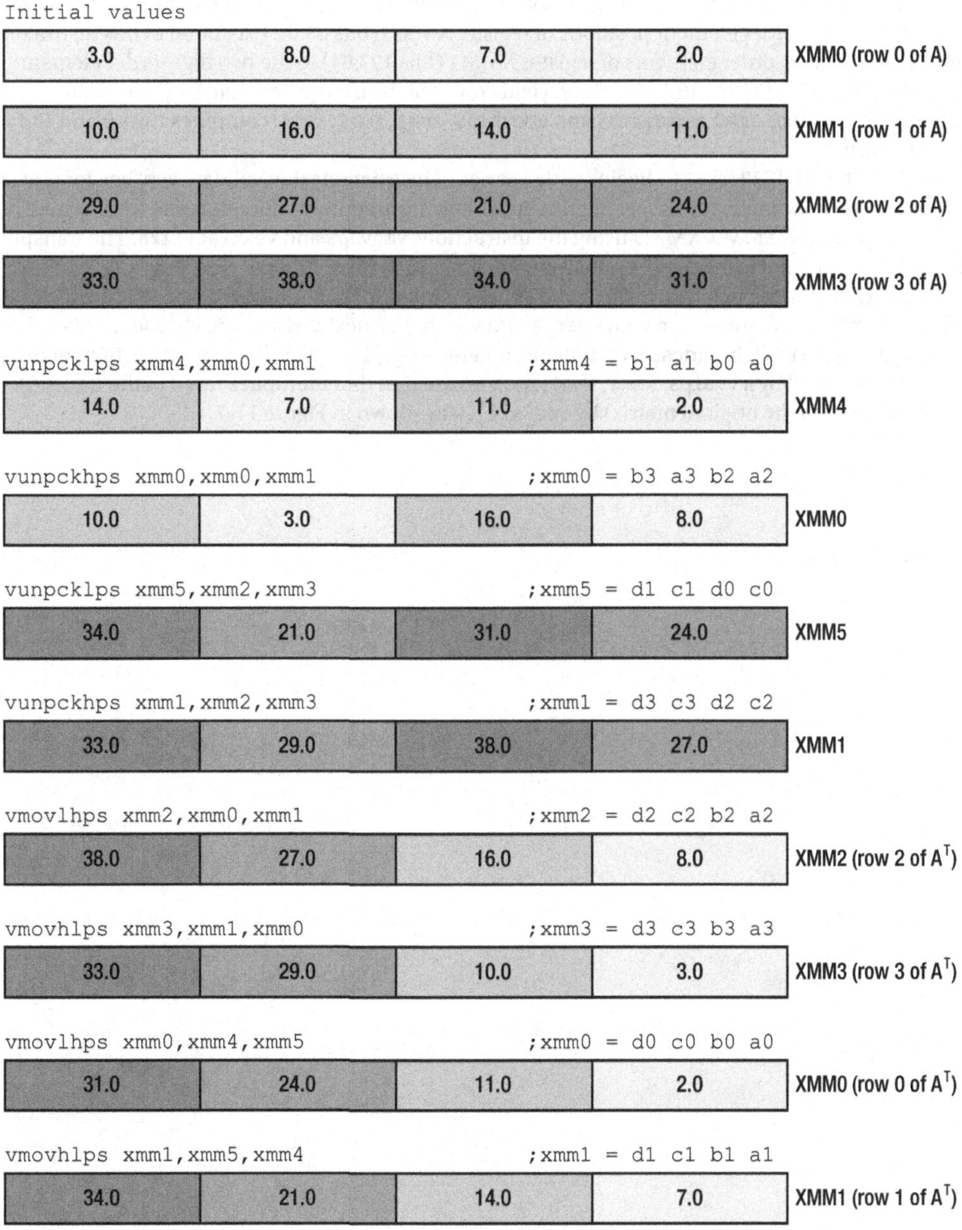

```
Initial values
```

3.0	8.0	7.0	2.0	XMM0 (row 0 of A)
10.0	16.0	14.0	11.0	XMM1 (row 1 of A)
29.0	27.0	21.0	24.0	XMM2 (row 2 of A)
33.0	38.0	34.0	31.0	XMM3 (row 3 of A)

```
vunpcklps xmm4,xmm0,xmm1                    ;xmm4 = b1 a1 b0 a0
```

14.0	7.0	11.0	2.0	XMM4

```
vunpckhps xmm0,xmm0,xmm1                    ;xmm0 = b3 a3 b2 a2
```

10.0	3.0	16.0	8.0	XMM0

```
vunpcklps xmm5,xmm2,xmm3                    ;xmm5 = d1 c1 d0 c0
```

34.0	21.0	31.0	24.0	XMM5

```
vunpckhps xmm1,xmm2,xmm3                    ;xmm1 = d3 c3 d2 c2
```

33.0	29.0	38.0	27.0	XMM1

```
vmovlhps xmm2,xmm0,xmm1                     ;xmm2 = d2 c2 b2 a2
```

38.0	27.0	16.0	8.0	XMM2 (row 2 of A^T)

```
vmovhlps xmm3,xmm1,xmm0                     ;xmm3 = d3 c3 b3 a3
```

33.0	29.0	10.0	3.0	XMM3 (row 3 of A^T)

```
vmovlhps xmm0,xmm4,xmm5                     ;xmm0 = d0 c0 b0 a0
```

31.0	24.0	11.0	2.0	XMM0 (row 0 of A^T)

```
vmovhlps xmm1,xmm5,xmm4                     ;xmm1 = d1 c1 b1 a1
```

34.0	21.0	14.0	7.0	XMM1 (row 1 of A^T)

Figure 11-6. Transposition of a 4 × 4 single-precision floating-point matrix using vunpcklps, vunpckhps, vmovlhps, *and* vmovhlps

Following the interleave instructions are a series of vmovlhps (Move Packed SPFP Values Low to High) and vmovhlps (Move Packed SPFP Values High to Low) instructions. Execution of the vmovlhps xmm2,xmm0,xmm1 instruction copies the two low-order single-precision floating-point elements of XMM0 (bits 63:0) to the same element positions of register XMM2 (bits 63:0) as shown in Figure 11-6. This instruction also copies the two low-order elements of XMM1 (bits 63:0) to the two high-order element positions of XMM2 (bits 127:64). Following execution of the vmovlhps xmm2,xmm0,xmm1 instruction, register XMM2 contains row 2 of the transposed matrix.

The next instruction, vmovhlps xmm3,xmm1,xmm0, copies the two high-order elements of XMM0 (bits 127:64) to the two low-order element positions of register XMM3 (bits 63:0). Execution of this instruction also copies the two high-order elements of register XMM1 (bits 127:64) to the two high-order element positions of register XMM3 (bits 127:64), which yields row 3 of the transposed matrix. The ensuing instruction pair, vmovlhps xmm0,xmm4,xmm5 and vmovhlps xmm1,xmm5,xmm4, computes rows 0 and 1 of the transposed matrix.

Function MatVecMulF32_avx2() begins with a series of instructions that validate num_vec for size and the various argument pointers for proper alignment. Following argument validation, the rows of matrix m are loaded into registers XMM0–XMM3 using the instructions vmovaps and vextractf128. The transpose of matrix m is then calculated using the previously defined macro Mat4x4TransposeF32_M.

Each iteration of Loop1 begins with an add rax,16 instruction that updates register RAX, which contains the displacement for vector arrays vec_a and vec_b. The next instruction, vbroadcastss xmm5,real4 ptr [r8+rax], broadcasts vector component vec_a[i].W to each element position of register XMM5. This is followed by a vmulps xmm4,xmm0,xmm5 instruction that multiplies row 0 of the transposed matrix (or column 0 of the original matrix) by vec_a[i].W as shown in Figure 11-7.

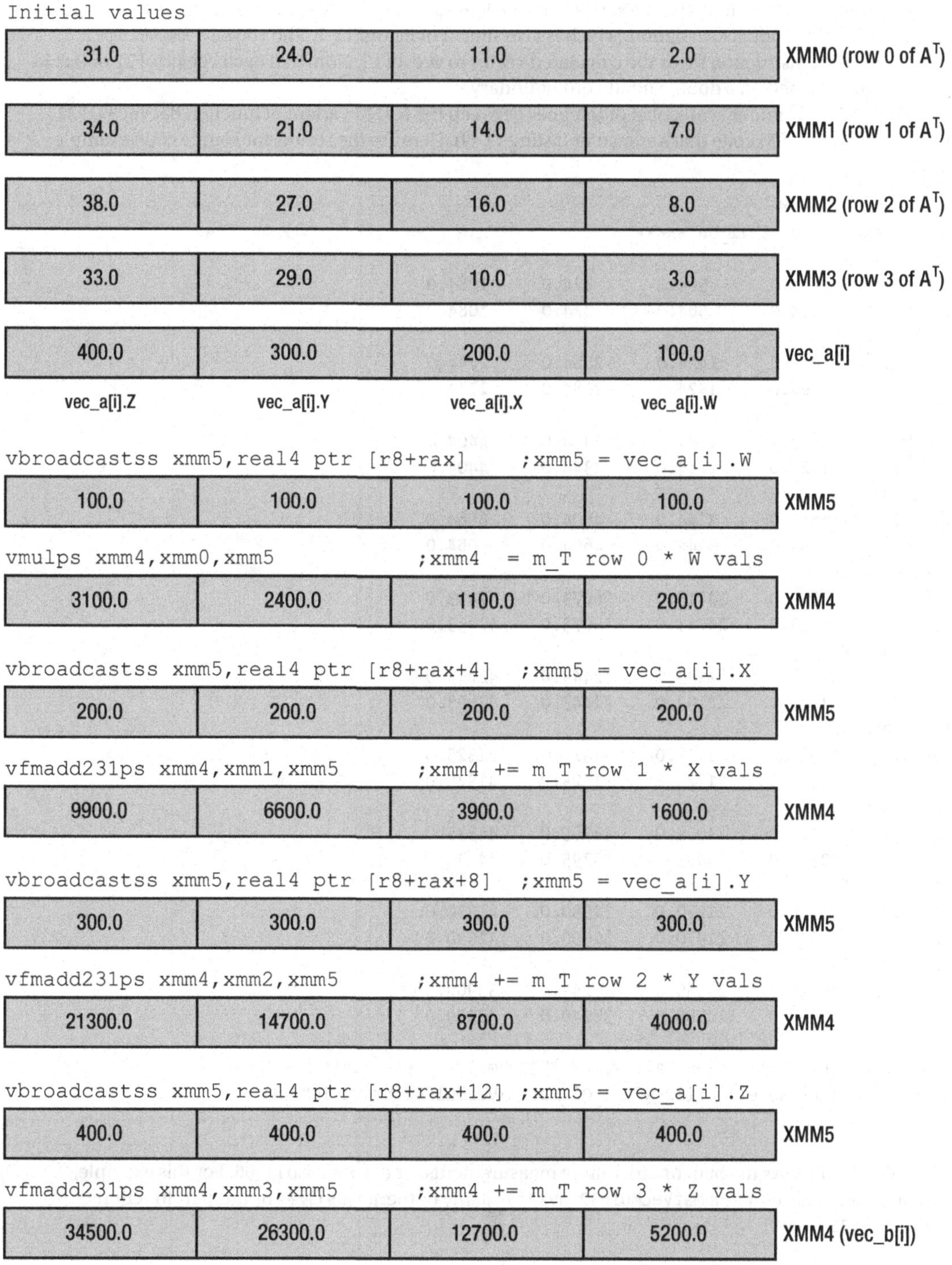

Initial values

31.0	24.0	11.0	2.0	XMM0 (row 0 of A^T)

34.0	21.0	14.0	7.0	XMM1 (row 1 of A^T)

38.0	27.0	16.0	8.0	XMM2 (row 2 of A^T)

33.0	29.0	10.0	3.0	XMM3 (row 3 of A^T)

400.0	300.0	200.0	100.0	vec_a[i]
vec_a[i].Z	vec_a[i].Y	vec_a[i].X	vec_a[i].W	

```
vbroadcastss xmm5,real4 ptr [r8+rax]      ;xmm5 = vec_a[i].W
```

100.0	100.0	100.0	100.0	XMM5

```
vmulps xmm4,xmm0,xmm5              ;xmm4  = m_T row 0 * W vals
```

3100.0	2400.0	1100.0	200.0	XMM4

```
vbroadcastss xmm5,real4 ptr [r8+rax+4]   ;xmm5 = vec_a[i].X
```

200.0	200.0	200.0	200.0	XMM5

```
vfmadd231ps xmm4,xmm1,xmm5        ;xmm4 += m_T row 1 * X vals
```

9900.0	6600.0	3900.0	1600.0	XMM4

```
vbroadcastss xmm5,real4 ptr [r8+rax+8]   ;xmm5 = vec_a[i].Y
```

300.0	300.0	300.0	300.0	XMM5

```
vfmadd231ps xmm4,xmm2,xmm5        ;xmm4 += m_T row 2 * Y vals
```

21300.0	14700.0	8700.0	4000.0	XMM4

```
vbroadcastss xmm5,real4 ptr [r8+rax+12]  ;xmm5 = vec_a[i].Z
```

400.0	400.0	400.0	400.0	XMM5

```
vfmadd231ps xmm4,xmm3,xmm5        ;xmm4 += m_T row 3 * Z vals
```

34500.0	26300.0	12700.0	5200.0	XMM4 (vec_b[i])

Figure 11-7. Calculation of matrix-vector (4 × 4, 4 × 1) product using vbroadcastss, vmulps, and vfmadd231ps

For-loop Loop1 concludes with a series of vbroadcastss and vfmadd231ps instructions that complete the matrix-vector product calculation, which is also shown in Figure 11-7. The vmovaps xmmword ptr [rcx+rax],xmm4 instruction saves the calculated vector to vec_b[i]. Note that each Vec4x1_F32 object in array vec_b is aligned on a double quadword boundary.

There are only minor syntactical differences between the NASM variant of function MatVecMulF32_avx2() and the MASM code that's shown in Listing 11-6b. Here are the results for source code example Ch11_06:

```
----- Results for Ch11_06 -----
Test case #0
vec_b1:      304.0      564.0      824.0      1084.0
vec_b2:      304.0      564.0      824.0      1084.0
Test case #1
vec_b1:      764.0     1424.0     2084.0      2744.0
vec_b2:      764.0     1424.0     2084.0      2744.0
Test case #2
vec_b1:     1224.0     2284.0     3344.0      4404.0
vec_b2:     1224.0     2284.0     3344.0      4404.0
Test case #3
vec_b1:     1684.0     3144.0     4604.0      6064.0
vec_b2:     1684.0     3144.0     4604.0      6064.0
Test case #4
vec_b1:    13353.0    24713.0    36073.0     47433.0
vec_b2:    13353.0    24713.0    36073.0     47433.0
Test case #5
vec_b1:    11943.0    22193.0    32443.0     42693.0
vec_b2:    11943.0    22193.0    32443.0     42693.0
Test case #6
vec_b1:    11925.0    21725.0    31525.0     41325.0
vec_b2:    11925.0    21725.0    31525.0     41325.0
Test case #7
vec_b1:    12315.0    23055.0    33795.0     44535.0
vec_b2:    12315.0    23055.0    33795.0     44535.0
Test case #8
vec_b1:    11990.0    21970.0    31950.0     41930.0
vec_b2:    11990.0    21970.0    31950.0     41930.0
Test case #9
vec_b1:    10929.0    20589.0    30249.0     39909.0
vec_b2:    10929.0    20589.0    30249.0     39909.0

Running benchmark function MatrixVecMulF32_bm() - please wait
Benchmark times save to file @Ch11_06_MatrixVecMulF32_bm_HELIUM.csv
```

Table 11-6 shows the benchmark timing measurements for example Ch11_06. For this example, assembly language function MatVecMulF32_avx2() clearly outperforms C++ counterpart function MatVecMulF32_cpp().

Table 11-6. *Benchmark Timing Measurements (Microseconds) for Matrix-Vector Multiplication Functions (5,000,000 Products)*

Function	i5-11600K	i7-11700K	7700X
MatrixVecMulF32_cpp()	19355 (89)	25729 (750)	11501 (11)
MatrixVecMulF32_avx2()	6738 (43)	6191 (102)	3854 (8)

Double-Precision

Source code example Ch11_07 demonstrates matrix (4 × 4) vector (4 × 1) multiplication using double-precision floating-point values. The principal C++ code for this example (not shown) closely resembles the C++ code that's shown in Listing 11-6a. For source code example Ch11_07, data type double is used instead of float; class MatrixF64 also replaces class MatrixF32. Listing 11-7 shows the MASM code for example Ch11_07.

Listing 11-7. Example Ch11_07 MASM Code

```
;-----------------------------------------------------------------------------
; Ch11_07_fasm.asm
;-----------------------------------------------------------------------------

        include <MacrosX86-64-AVX.asmh>

;-----------------------------------------------------------------------------
; Mat4x4TransposeF64_M macro
;
; Description:  This macro transposes a 4x4 matrix of double-precision
;               floating-point values.
;
;  Input Matrix                    Output Matrix
;  ------------------------------------------------
;  ymm0    a3 a2 a1 a0             ymm0    d0 c0 b0 a0
;  ymm1    b3 b2 b1 b0             ymm1    d1 c1 b1 a1
;  ymm2    c3 c2 c1 c0             ymm2    d2 c2 b2 a2
;  ymm3    d3 d2 d1 d0             ymm3    d3 c3 b3 a3
;
; Scratch registers: ymm4, ymm5, ymm6, ymm7
;-----------------------------------------------------------------------------

Mat4x4TransposeF64_M macro
        vunpcklpd ymm4,ymm0,ymm1            ;ymm4 = b2 a2 b0 a0
        vunpckhpd ymm5,ymm0,ymm1            ;ymm5 = b3 a3 b1 a1
        vunpcklpd ymm6,ymm2,ymm3            ;ymm6 = d2 c2 d0 c0
        vunpckhpd ymm7,ymm2,ymm3            ;ymm7 = d3 c3 d1 c1

        vperm2f128 ymm0,ymm4,ymm6,20h       ;ymm0 = d0 c0 b0 a0
        vperm2f128 ymm1,ymm5,ymm7,20h       ;ymm1 = d1 c1 b1 a1
        vperm2f128 ymm2,ymm4,ymm6,31h       ;ymm2 = d2 c2 b2 a2
        vperm2f128 ymm3,ymm5,ymm7,31h       ;ymm3 = d3 c3 b3 a3
        endm
```

```
;-----------------------------------------------------------------------------
; void MatVecMulF64_avx2(Vec4x1_F64* vec_b, const float* m,
;    const Vec4x1_F64* vec_a, size_t num_vec);
;-----------------------------------------------------------------------------

        .code
MatVecMulF64_avx2 proc frame
        CreateFrame_M MVMUL_,0,32
        SaveXmmRegs_M xmm6,xmm7
        EndProlog_M

; Validate arguments
        test r9,r9
        jz Done                         ;jump if num_vec == 0

        test rcx,1fh
        jnz Done                        ;jump if vec_b not 32b aligned

        test rdx,1fh
        jnz Done                        ;jump if m not 32b aligned

        test r8,1fh
        jnz Done                        ;jump if vec_a 32b aligned

; Initialize
        mov rax,-32                     ;array offset
        vmovapd ymm0,ymmword ptr [rdx]      ;ymm0 = m row 0
        vmovapd ymm1,ymmword ptr [rdx+32]   ;ymm1 = m row 1
        vmovapd ymm2,ymmword ptr [rdx+64]   ;ymm2 = m row 2
        vmovapd ymm3,ymmword ptr [rdx+96]   ;ymm3 = m row 3

; Transpose m
        Mat4x4TransposeF64_M

; Calculate matrix-vector products
        align 16
Loop1:  add rax,32

        vbroadcastsd ymm5,real8 ptr [r8+rax]     ;ymm5 = vec_a[i].W
        vmulpd ymm4,ymm0,ymm5                    ;ymm4 = m_T row 0 * W vals

        vbroadcastsd ymm5,real8 ptr [r8+rax+8]   ;ymm5 = vec_a[i].X
        vfmadd231pd ymm4,ymm1,ymm5               ;ymm4 += m_T row 1 * X vals

        vbroadcastsd ymm5,real8 ptr [r8+rax+16]  ;ymm5 = vec_a[i].Y
        vfmadd231pd ymm4,ymm2,ymm5               ;ymm4 += m_T row 2 * Y vals

        vbroadcastsd ymm5,real8 ptr [r8+rax+24]  ;ymm5 = vec_a[i].Z
        vfmadd231pd ymm4,ymm3,ymm5               ;ymm4 += m_T row 3 * Z vals
```

```
        vmovapd ymmword ptr [rcx+rax],ymm4        ;save vec_b[i]

        sub r9,1                                  ;num_vec -= 1
        jnz Loop1                                 ;repeat until done

Done:   vzeroupper
        RestoreXmmRegs_M xmm6,xmm7
        DeleteFrame_M
        ret

MatVecMulF64_avx2 endp
        end
```

There are two noteworthy differences between the double-precision floating-point code in Listing 11-7 and the single-precision version in Listing 11-6b. The first difference is that macro Mat4x4TransposeF64_M and function MatVecMulF64_avx2() utilize double-precision instead of single-precision AVX2 and FMA instructions. The other important modification is in macro Mat4x4TransposeF64_M. Note that this macro uses a series of vperm2f128 (Permute Floating-Point Values) instructions instead of vmovlhps and vmovhlps to transpose the 4 × 4 matrix that's loaded in registers YMM0–YMM3 as shown in Figure 11-8.

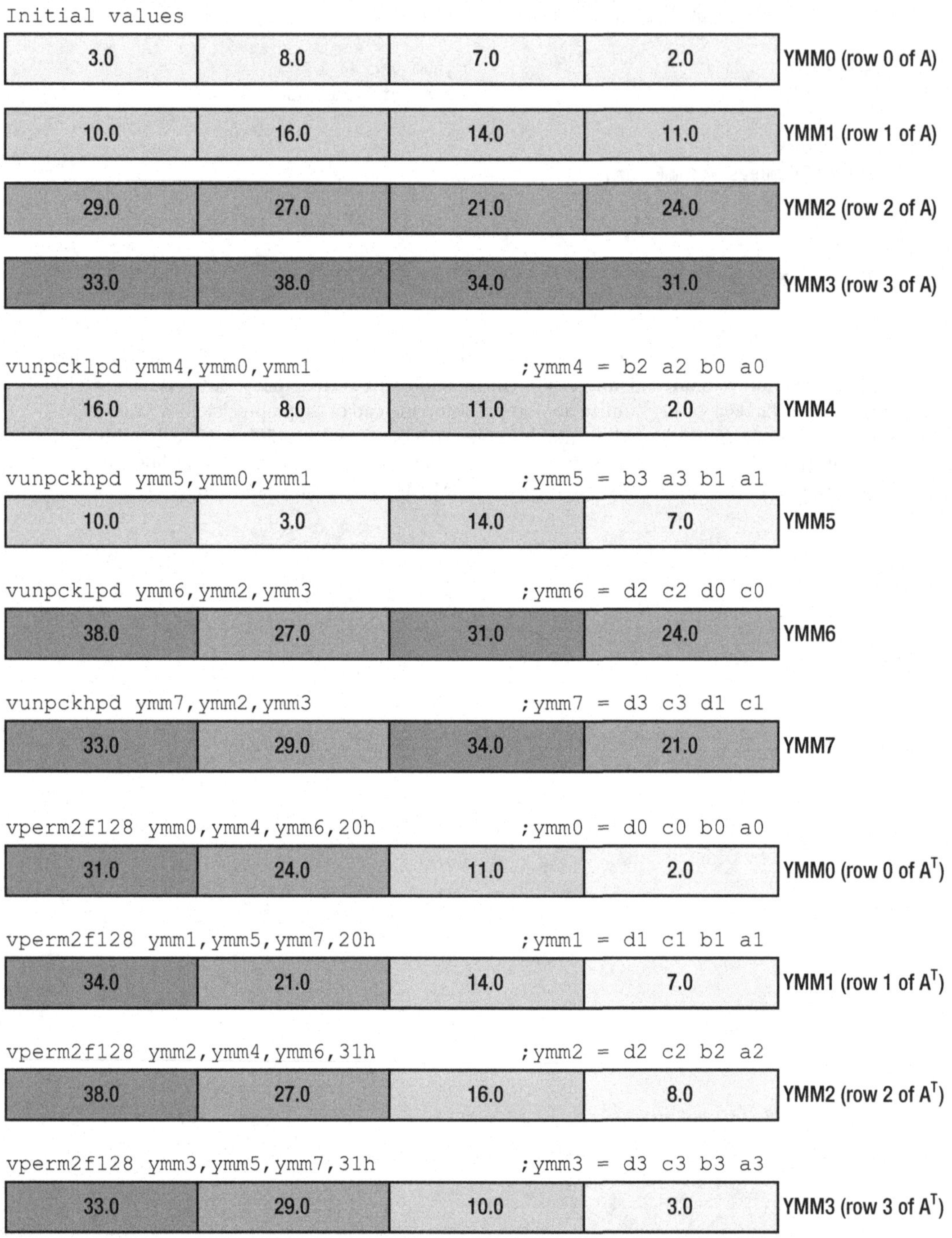

Initial values

3.0	8.0	7.0	2.0	YMM0 (row 0 of A)

10.0	16.0	14.0	11.0	YMM1 (row 1 of A)

29.0	27.0	21.0	24.0	YMM2 (row 2 of A)

33.0	38.0	34.0	31.0	YMM3 (row 3 of A)

```
vunpcklpd ymm4,ymm0,ymm1          ; ymm4 = b2 a2 b0 a0
```
16.0	8.0	11.0	2.0	YMM4

```
vunpckhpd ymm5,ymm0,ymm1          ; ymm5 = b3 a3 b1 a1
```
10.0	3.0	14.0	7.0	YMM5

```
vunpcklpd ymm6,ymm2,ymm3          ; ymm6 = d2 c2 d0 c0
```
38.0	27.0	31.0	24.0	YMM6

```
vunpckhpd ymm7,ymm2,ymm3          ; ymm7 = d3 c3 d1 c1
```
33.0	29.0	34.0	21.0	YMM7

```
vperm2f128 ymm0,ymm4,ymm6,20h     ; ymm0 = d0 c0 b0 a0
```
31.0	24.0	11.0	2.0	YMM0 (row 0 of A^T)

```
vperm2f128 ymm1,ymm5,ymm7,20h     ; ymm1 = d1 c1 b1 a1
```
34.0	21.0	14.0	7.0	YMM1 (row 1 of A^T)

```
vperm2f128 ymm2,ymm4,ymm6,31h     ; ymm2 = d2 c2 b2 a2
```
38.0	27.0	16.0	8.0	YMM2 (row 2 of A^T)

```
vperm2f128 ymm3,ymm5,ymm7,31h     ; ymm3 = d3 c3 b3 a3
```
33.0	29.0	10.0	3.0	YMM3 (row 3 of A^T)

Figure 11-8. *Transposition of a 4 × 4 double-precision floating-point matrix using vunpcklpd, vunpckhpd, and vperm2f128*

The immediate operand that's used with a vperm2f128 instruction specifies which 128-bit wide element group to copy from the two 256-bit wide source operands. Bits 1:0 of the immediate operand select a 128-bit wide source operand field to copy to the low-order 128 bits of the destination operand. Bits 5:4 of the immediate operand select the source operand field for the high-order 128 bits of the destination operand. Using the vperm2f128 ymm0,ymm4,ymm6,20h instruction as an example, immediate operand bit patterns 00b, 01b, 10b, and 11b can be used to select source operand bits YMM4[127:0], YMM4[255:128], YMM6[127:0], or YMM6[255:128], respectively. Bits 1:0 of immediate operand 20h copies bits YMM4[127:0] to YMM0[127:0]; bits 5:4 of immediate operand 20h copies bits YMM6[127:0] to YMM4[255:128]. Setting bit 3 (bit 7) of the immediate operand to 1 will zero the low-order (high-order) 128 bits of the destination operand.

Like the previous examples of this chapter, the NASM code for example Ch11_07 closely resembles the MASM code in Listing 11-7 except for a few minor syntactical differences. The results for source code example Ch11_07 match the results for Ch11_06. Table 11-7 shows the benchmark timing measurements for Ch11_07. Like single-precision matrix-vector multiplication function MatVecMulF32_avx2(), the double-precision matrix-vector multiplication functions outperform their C++ counterpart functions.

Table 11-7. *Benchmark Timing Measurements (Microseconds) for Matrix-Vector Multiplication Functions (5,000,000 Products)*

Function	i5-11600K	i7-11700K	7700X
MatrixVecMulF64_cpp()	21652 (42)	26578 (1115)	12303 (32)
MatrixVecMulF64_avx2()	13182 (30)	12391 (485)	7733 (12)

Covariance Matrix

Mathematicians often use a statistical measure called covariance to quantify the extent that two random variables vary together. When multiple random variables are being analyzed, it is common to calculate a matrix of all possible covariances. This matrix is called, unsurprisingly, a covariance matrix. Once calculated, a covariance matrix can be employed to perform a wide variety of advanced statistical analyses. Appendix B contains several references that you can consult if you're interested in learning more about covariance and covariance matrices.

The calculation of a covariance matrix begins with a sample data matrix as shown in Figure 11-9. In this figure, the rows of matrix **X** represent one random variable (or feature). Each column in **X** is a multivariate observation. Element c_{ij} of covariance matrix **C** is calculated using the following equation:

$$c_{ij} = \frac{\sum_{k=0}^{n_{obv}-1}\left(x_{ik}-\overline{x}_i\right)\left(x_{jk}-\overline{x}_j\right)}{n_{obv}-1}$$

where $i = 0, 1, \cdots, n_{var} - 1$ and $j = 0, 1, \cdots, n_{var} - 1$. In this equation, the symbols n_{obv} and n_{var} signify the number of observations and variables, respectively. A covariance matrix is always a square ($n_{var} \times n_{var}$) symmetric ($c_{ij} = c_{ji}$) matrix as shown in Figure 11-8. Each covariance matrix element c_{ij} represents the covariance between random variables x_i and x_j, and each main diagonal element c_{ii} is the variance for variable x_i.

Observations

Variables

$$\begin{matrix} x_0 \\ x_1 \\ x_2 \\ x_3 \end{matrix} \begin{bmatrix} 10.75 & 6.39 & 6.60 & \cdots & 21.37 & 1.86 & 13.17 \\ 8.30 & 7.46 & 8.32 & \cdots & 24.99 & 16.70 & 4.12 \\ 21.73 & 22.89 & 14.32 & \cdots & 9.65 & 0.40 & 6.40 \\ 15.65 & 22.62 & 2.34 & \cdots & 15.02 & 16.10 & 12.18 \end{bmatrix}$$

Data matrix **X** (4 × N)

$$\begin{bmatrix} 49.33 & 14.69 & 4.28 & 7.37 \\ 14.69 & 64.62 & -4.54 & 9.24 \\ 4.28 & -4.54 & 46.54 & 7.27 \\ 7.37 & 9.24 & 7.27 & 34.70 \end{bmatrix}$$

Covariance matrix **C** (4 × 4)

Figure 11-9. *Example data matrix and its covariance matrix*

The final source code example of this chapter, named Ch11_08, demonstrates how to calculate a covariance matrix using AVX2 instructions and double-precision arithmetic. Listing 11-8a shows the principal C++ source code for this example.

Listing 11-8a. Example Ch11_08 C++ Code

```
//------------------------------------------------------------------------------
// Ch11_08.h
//------------------------------------------------------------------------------

#pragma once
#include <vector>
#include "MatrixF64.h"

// Covariance matrix data (CMD) structure
struct CMD
{
    MatrixF64 m_X;                          // Data matrix (n_vars x n_obvs)
    MatrixF64 m_CovMat;                     // Covariance matrix (n_vars x n_vars)
    std::vector<double> m_VarMeans;         // Variable means (n_vars)

    CMD(size_t n_vars, size_t n_obvs) :
        m_X(n_vars, n_obvs), m_CovMat(n_vars, n_vars), m_VarMeans(n_vars) { }
};

// Ch11_08_fasm.asm, Ch11_08_fasm.s
extern "C" void CalcCovMatF64_avx2(double* cov_mat, double* var_means,
    const double* x, size_t n_vars, size_t n_obvs);

// Ch11_08_fcpp.cpp
extern bool CheckArgs(const CMD& cmd);
extern void CalcCovMatF64_cmd0(CMD& cmd);
extern void CalcCovMatF64_cmd1(CMD& cmd);
extern void CalcCovMatF64_cpp(double* cov_mat, double* var_means,
    const double* x, size_t n_vars, size_t n_ovbs);
```

```cpp
// Ch11_08_misc.cpp
extern bool CompareResults(CMD& cmd1, CMD& cmd2);
extern void DisplayData(const CMD& cmd);
extern void InitCMD(CMD& cmd1, CMD& cmd2);

// Ch11_08_bm.cpp
void CalcCovMatF64_bm(void);

//-----------------------------------------------------------------------------
// Ch11_08_fcpp.cpp
//-----------------------------------------------------------------------------

#include <stdexcept>
#include "Ch11_08.h"

bool CheckArgs(const CMD& cmd)
{
    size_t n_vars = cmd.m_X.GetNumRows();
    size_t n_obvs = cmd.m_X.GetNumCols();

    if (n_vars < 2 || n_obvs < 2)
        return false;

    if (cmd.m_CovMat.GetNumRows() != n_vars)
        return false;

    if (cmd.m_CovMat.GetNumCols() != n_vars)
        return false;

    if (cmd.m_VarMeans.size() != n_vars)
        return false;

    return true;
}

void CalcCovMatF64_cmd0(CMD& cmd)
{
    if (!CheckArgs(cmd))
        throw std::runtime_error("CalcCovMatrixF64_cmd0() - CheckArgs() failed");

    size_t n_vars = cmd.m_X.GetNumRows();
    size_t n_obvs = cmd.m_X.GetNumCols();
    double* cov_mat = cmd.m_CovMat.Data();
    double* x = cmd.m_X.Data();
    double* var_means = cmd.m_VarMeans.data();

    CalcCovMatF64_cpp(cov_mat, var_means, x, n_vars, n_obvs);
}
```

```
void CalcCovMatF64_cmd1(CMD& cmd)
{
    if (!CheckArgs(cmd))
        throw std::runtime_error("CalcCovMatrixF64_cmd1() - CheckArgs() failed");

    size_t n_vars = cmd.m_X.GetNumRows();
    size_t n_obvs = cmd.m_X.GetNumCols();
    double* cov_mat = cmd.m_CovMat.Data();
    double* x = cmd.m_X.Data();
    double* var_means = cmd.m_VarMeans.data();

    CalcCovMatF64_avx2(cov_mat, var_means, x, n_vars, n_obvs);
}

void CalcCovMatF64_cpp(double* cov_mat, double* var_means, const double* x,
    size_t n_vars, size_t n_obvs)
{
    // Calculate variable means (rows of cmd.m_X)
    for (size_t i = 0; i < n_vars; i++)
    {
        var_means[i] = 0.0;

        for (size_t j = 0; j < n_obvs; j++)
            var_means[i] += x[i * n_obvs + j];

        var_means[i] /= n_obvs;
    }

    // Calculate covariance matrix
    for (size_t i = 0; i < n_vars; i++)
    {
        for (size_t j = 0; j < n_vars; j++)
        {
            if (i <= j)
            {
                double sum = 0.0;

                for (size_t k = 0; k < n_obvs; k++)
                {
                    double temp1 = x[i * n_obvs + k] - var_means[i];
                    double temp2 = x[j * n_obvs + k] - var_means[j];
                    sum += temp1 * temp2;
                }

                cov_mat[i * n_vars + j] = sum / (n_obvs - 1);
            }
            else
                cov_mat[i * n_vars + j] = cov_mat[j * n_vars + i];
        }
    }
}
```

The first file in Listing 11-8a, Ch11_08.h, begins with the definition of a C++ structure named CMD (Covariance Matrix Data). This structure contains three container objects: a data matrix, a variable mean vector, and a covariance matrix. Note that structure CMD also defines a simple constructor that allocates space for the three container objects using the specified values for n_vars and n_obvs. Files not shown in Listing 11-8a include Ch11_08_misc.cpp and Ch11_08.cpp. The former file contains the definitions of helper functions CompareResults(), DisplayData(), and InitCMD(); the latter file includes code that instantiates the required CMD data structures, exercises the covariance matrix calculating functions, and streams results to std::cout.

The other file in Listing 11-8a is Ch11_08_fcpp.cpp. This file includes a function named CalcCovMatF64_cpp(), which computes a covariance matrix using standard C++ statements. The code in CalcCovMatF64_cpp() is split into two major sections. The first section calculates the mean for each variable (row) in data matrix x. The second section calculates the covariances. Note that function CalcCovMatF64_cpp() exploits the fact that a covariance matrix is symmetric and only carries out a complete calculation when i <= j is true. If i <= j is false, CalcCovMatF64_cpp() executes cov_mat[i][j] = cov_mat[j][j]. Also note in file Ch11_08_fcpp.cpp the definitions of function CalcCovMatF64_cmd0() and CalcCovMatF64_cmd1(). These functions perform argument validation and C++ raw pointer extraction; they also call the covariance matrix calculating functions CalcCovMatF64_cpp() and CalcCovMatF64_avx2(), respectively.

Listing 11-8b shows the MASM code for example Ch11_08. Before continuing, make sure you understand the particulars of Figure 11-9 and the covariance matrix equation presented earlier in this section. The assembly language code conveyed in Listing 11-8b is somewhat more complicated and marginally longer than what you've seen in previous examples. Having a solid understanding of the underlying covariance matrix arithmetic will be helpful when perusing the assembly language code in Listing 11-8b.

Listing 11-8b. Example Ch11_08 MASM Code

```
;-------------------------------------------------------------------------
; Ch11_08_fasm.asm
;-------------------------------------------------------------------------

        include <MacrosX86-64-AVX.asmh>


;-------------------------------------------------------------------------
; void CalcCovMatF64_avx2(double* cov_mat, double* var_means,
;   const double* x, size_t n_vars, size_t n_obvs);
;-------------------------------------------------------------------------

NSE     equ 4                           ;num_simd_elements
SF      equ 8                           ;scale factor for F64 elements

        .code
CalcCovMatF64_avx2 proc frame
        CreateFrame_M COV_,0,48,rbx,rsi,rdi,r12,r13
        SaveXmmRegs_M xmm6,xmm7,xmm8
        EndProlog_M

; Initialize
        mov r10,[rbp+COV_OffsetStackArgs]    ;r10 = n_obvs

        vcvtsi2sd xmm5,xmm5,r10              ;convert n_obvs to F64
        mov rax,r10
        sub rax,1                           ;rax = n_obvs - 1
        vcvtsi2sd xmm6,xmm6,rax             ;convert n_obvs - 1 to F64
```

```
        xor eax,eax                             ;i = 0
        jmp L1                                  ;begin execution of Loop1


;-----------------------------------------------------------------
; General-purpose register use for var_means[i] calculation:
;   rax     i                       r10     n_obvs
;   rbx     j                       r11     scratch register
;   rcx     cov_mat                 r12     -----
;   rdx     var_means               r13     -----
;   r8      x                       rsi     i * n_obvs
;   r9      n_vars                  rdi     -----
;-----------------------------------------------------------------


; Calculate var_means[i] (mean of row i in matrix x)
Loop1:  mov rsi,rax                             ;rsi = i
        imul rsi,r10                            ;rsi = i * n_obvs

        xor ebx,ebx                             ;j = 0
        vxorpd ymm0,ymm0,ymm0                   ;sums[0:NSE-1] = 0
        jmp L2                                  ;begin execution of Loop2

; Sum elements in row x[i] using SIMD addition
        align 16
Loop2:  lea r11,[rsi+rbx]                       ;r11 = i * n_obvs + j
        vaddpd ymm0,ymm0,[r8+r11*SF]            ;sums[0:NSE-1] += x[i][j:j+NSE-1]

        add rbx,NSE                             ;j += NSE
L2:     mov r11,rbx                             ;r11 = j
        add r11,NSE                             ;r11 = j + NSE
        cmp r11,r10                             ;j + NSE <= n_obvs?
        jbe Loop2                               ;jump if yes

; Reduce packed sums to scalar
        vextractf128 xmm1,ymm0,1                ;extract high-order F64 values (2)
        vaddpd xmm0,xmm1,xmm0
        vhaddpd xmm0,xmm0,xmm0                  ;scalar sum in xmm0[63:0]
        jmp L3                                  ;begin execution of Loop3

; Sum remaining elements in current row using scalar arithmetic
Loop3:  lea r11,[rsi+rbx]                       ;r11 = i * n_obvs + j
        vaddsd xmm0,xmm0,real8 ptr [r8+r11*SF]  ;sum += x[i][j]

        add rbx,1                               ;j += 1
L3:     cmp rbx,r10                             ;j < n_obvs?
        jb Loop3                                ;jump if yes

; Calculate var_means[i]
        vdivsd xmm1,xmm0,xmm5                   ;var_means[i] = sum / n_obvs
        vmovsd real8 ptr [rdx+rax*SF],xmm1      ;save var_means[i]
```

```
            add rax,1                         ;i += 1
L1:         cmp rax,r9                        ;i < n_vars?
            jb Loop1                          ;jump if yes


;-------------------------------------------------------------------
; General-purpose register use for cov_mat[i][j] calculation:
;    rax    i                  r10     n_obvs
;    rbx    j                  r11     scratch register
;    rcx    cov_mat            r12     i * n_vars
;    rdx    var_means          r13     k
;    r8     x                  rsi     i * n_obvs
;    r9     n_vars             rdi     j * n_obvs
;-------------------------------------------------------------------


; Calculate covariance matrix
            xor eax,eax                       ;i = 0
            jmp L4


Loop4:  mov r12,rax                           ;r12 = i
        imul r12,r9                           ;r12 = i * n_vars
        mov rsi,rax                           ;rsi = i
        imul rsi,r10                          ;rsi = i * n_obvs
        xor ebx,ebx                           ;j = 0
        jmp L5                                ;begin execution of Loop5


Loop5:  cmp rax,rbx                           ;i > j?
        ja NoCalc                             ;jump if yes

        mov rdi,rbx                           ;rdi = j
        imul rdi,r10                          ;rdi = j * n_obvs
        xor r13,r13                           ;k = 0

        vxorpd ymm0,ymm0,ymm0                 ;cov_mat[i][j] product sums = 0
        vbroadcastsd ymm7,real8 ptr [rdx+rax*SF] ;ymm7 = var_means[i]
        jmp L6                                ;begin execution of Loop6

; Calculate product sums for cov_mat[i][j] using SIMD arithmetic
        align 16
Loop6:  vbroadcastsd ymm8,real8 ptr [rdx+rbx*SF] ;ymm8 = var_means[j]
        lea r11,[rsi+r13]                     ;r11 = i * n_obvs + k
        vmovupd ymm1,[r8+r11*SF]              ;load x[i][k:k+NSE-1]
        lea r11,[rdi+r13]                     ;r11 = j * n_obvs + k
        vmovupd ymm2,[r8+r11*SF]              ;load x[j][k:k+NSE-1]
        vsubpd ymm3,ymm1,ymm7                 ;x[i][k:k+NSE-1] - var_means[i]
        vsubpd ymm4,ymm2,ymm8                 ;x[j][k:k+NSE-1] - var_means[j]
        vfmadd231pd ymm0,ymm3,ymm4            ;update cov_mat[i][j] product sums

        add r13,NSE                           ;k += NSE
L6:     lea r11,[r13+NSE]                     ;r11 = k + NSE
        cmp r11,r10                           ;k + NSE <= n_obvs?
        jbe Loop6                             ;jump if yes
```

439

```
; Reduce packed product sums for cov_mat[i][j] to scalar value
        vextractf128 xmm1,ymm0,1            ;extract high-order F64 values (2)
        vaddpd xmm0,xmm1,xmm0
        vhaddpd xmm0,xmm0,xmm0              ;scalar product sum in xmm0[63:0]
        jmp L7                             ;begin execution of Loop7

; Complete calculation of product sums for cov_mat[i][j] using scalar arithmetic
Loop7:  lea r11,[rsi+r13]                   ;r11 = i * n_obvs + k
        vmovsd xmm1,real8 ptr [r8+r11*SF]   ;load x[i][k]
        lea r11,[rdi+r13]                   ;r11 = j * n_obvs + k
        vmovsd xmm2,real8 ptr [r8+r11*SF]   ;load x[j][k]
        vsubsd xmm3,xmm1,xmm7               ;x[i][j] - var_means[i]
        vsubsd xmm4,xmm2,xmm8               ;x[j][i] - var_means[j]
        vfmadd231sd xmm0,xmm3,xmm4          ;update cov_mat[i][j] product sums

        add r13,1                          ;k += 1
L7:     cmp r13,r10                        ;k < n_obvs?
        jb Loop7                           ;jump if yes

; Calculate and save cov_mat[i][j]
        vdivsd xmm1,xmm0,xmm6               ;calc cov_mat[i][j]
        lea r11,[r12+rbx]                   ;r11 = i * n_vars + j
        vmovsd real8 ptr [rcx+r11*SF],xmm1  ;save cov_mat[i][j]
        jmp F1

; No calculation needed, set cov_mat[i][j] = cov_mat[j][i]
NoCalc: mov r11,rbx                         ;r11 = j
        imul r11,r9                         ;r11 = j * n_vars
        add r11,rax                         ;r11 = j * n_vars + i
        vmovsd xmm0,real8 ptr [rcx+r11*SF]  ;load cov_mat[j][i]
        lea r11,[r12+rbx]                   ;r11 = i * n_vars + j
        vmovsd real8 ptr [rcx+r11*SF],xmm0  ;save cov_mat[i][j]

F1:     add rbx,1                          ;j += 1
L5:     cmp rbx,r9                          ;j < n_vars?
        jb Loop5                           ;jump if yes

        add rax,1                          ;i += 1
L4:     cmp rax,r9                          ;i < n_vars?
        jb Loop4                           ;jump if yes

Done:   vzeroupper
        RestoreXmmRegs_M xmm6,xmm7,xmm8
        DeleteFrame_M rbx,rsi,rdi,r12,r13
        ret
CalcCovMatF64_avx2 endp
        end
```

The sole function in Listing 11-8b is named CalcCovMatF64_avx2(). Following its prologue is a code block that performs the requisite initializations for the covariance matrix calculating code. Note that argument n_obvs is passed to CalcCovMatF64_avx2() via the stack. The assembly language code in

Listing 11-8b consists of two major sections. The first section calculates the mean values (var_means) for each variable (or row) in data matrix x. The second section computes covariance matrix cov_mat. Recall from the discussions earlier in this section that a covariance matrix is always symmetrical. The calculating code in CalcCovMatF64_avx2() exploits this fact to reduce the number of performed calculations as you will soon see.

Each row of matrix x (R8) contains the values (or observations) for a single variable (see Figure 11-8). Function CalcCovMatF64_avx2() employs two nested for-loops to calculate the mean of each row in matrix x. For-loop Loop1 is the outermost for-loop. Each iteration of Loop1 begins with the instruction pair mov rsi,rax and imul rsi,r10 that sets RSI equal to i * n_obvs, which represents the index of data matrix element x[i][0]. The xor ebx,ebx instruction sets j = 0, while the vxorpd ymm0,ymm0,ymm0 instruction initializes sums[0:NSE-1] to zero (NSE equals four).

For-loop Loop2 sums elements in row x[i] using packed double-precision floating-point arithmetic. Note that Loop2 continues to execute until j + NSE <= n_obvs is false. Following execution of Loop2, the instruction triplet vextractf128 xmm1,ymm0,1, vaddpd xmm0,xmm1,xmm0, and vhaddpd xmm0,xmm0,xmm0 reduces the packed sums in YMM0 to a scalar value. Execution continues with for-loop Loop3, which adds any residual elements in row x[i] to the row sum in register XMM0. Following calculation of the row sum, the instruction pair vdivsd xmm1,xmm0,xmm5 and vmovsd real8 ptr [rdx+rax*SF],xmm1 calculate and save var_means[i].

The covariance calculating code in CalcCovMatF64_avx2() uses three nested for-loops to calculate each cov_mat[i][j] value. Each iteration of for-loop Loop4 begins with a series of instructions that calculate i * n_vars (R12) and i * n_obvs (RSI). Execution of the xor ebx,ebx instruction sets j = 0.

The first instruction of for-loop Loop5, cmp rax,rbx, checks if i > j is true. If yes, the ensuing ja NoCalc instruction skips over the covariance calculating code. The code that follows label NoCalc implements the expression cov_mat[i][j] = cov_mat[j][i]. If i > j is false, the ensuing mov rdi,rbx and imul rdi,r10 instructions calculate j * n_obvs. This is followed by an xor r13,r13 instruction that sets k = 0. The vxorpd ymm0,ymm0,ymm0 instruction initializes the product sums for cov_mat[i][j] to zero, while the vbroadcastsd ymm7,real8 ptr [rdx+rax*SF] instruction sets each double-precision floating-point element in YMM7 to var_means[i].

Each iteration of for-loop Loop6 begins with a vbroadcastsd ymm8,real8 ptr [rdx+rbx*SF] instruction that broadcasts var_means[j] to each double-precision element of YMM8. Next is a series of instructions that calculate x[i][k:k+NSE-1] - var_means[i] and x[j][k:k+NSE-1] - var_means[j]. Execution of the ensuing vfmadd231pd ymm0,ymm3,ymm4 instruction updates the product sums in register YMM0. For-loop Loop6 continues its execution until k + NSE <= n_obvs is false. Following completion of Loop6, the packed product sums in YMM0 are reduced to a scalar value using the instruction triplet vextractf128 xmm1,ymm0,1, vaddpd xmm0,xmm1,xmm0, and vhaddpd xmm0,xmm0,xmm0. For-loop Loop7 completes the calculation of the product sums for cov_mat[i][j] using scalar arithmetic.

Following execution of for-loop Loop7, CalcCovMatF64_avx2() employs the instruction triplet vdivsd xmm1,xmm0,xmm6, lea r11,[r12+rbx], and vmovsd real8 ptr [rcx+r11*SF],xmm1 to calculate and save cov_mat[i][j].

The NASM code for example Ch11_08 (not shown) closely resembles the MASM code. In the NASM code, the prologue for function CalcCovMatF64_avx2() only needs to preserve general-purpose registers RBX, R12, and R13. The other noteworthy difference is a series of mov instructions that reorder the argument values in the general-purpose registers to match those used in the MASM code. The covariance matrix calculating code is identical in both the MASM and NASM implementations of function CalcCovMatF64_avx2(). Here are the results for source code example Ch11_08:

```
----- Results for Ch11_08 -----
n_vars = 12, n_obvs = 103
Variable means
    0:     13.29      13.29
    1:     12.19      12.19
```

```
 2:     13.23     13.23
 3:     12.81     12.81
 4:     12.21     12.21
 5:     11.94     11.94
 6:     11.61     11.61
 7:     12.14     12.14
 8:     12.17     12.17
 9:     12.75     12.75
10:     11.57     11.57
11:     13.48     13.48

cmd0.m_CovMat
51.47  -5.44  -4.02  -7.40   9.38   9.54   3.78  -4.88  -0.13  -5.57  -3.05  -0.13
-5.44  46.43   0.65   3.14   6.77   5.55   7.53 -10.10   3.28  -9.78   2.20  -2.67
-4.02   0.65  47.41  -3.05   8.95   0.26  -3.35   1.96   7.56   1.05   5.73  14.40
-7.40   3.14  -3.05  49.82  -1.64   4.03  -0.29   6.52  -3.84  -0.89  -0.43   0.61
 9.38   6.77   8.95  -1.64  58.12   4.29   5.73 -15.49 -10.73   0.43  -1.55   3.88
 9.54   5.55   0.26   4.03   4.29  54.11   4.26  -2.84  -5.88  -1.29  -2.37  -4.08
 3.78   7.53  -3.35  -0.29   5.73   4.26  57.93  -2.79  -4.37   8.29  -0.89   0.75
-4.88 -10.10   1.96   6.52 -15.49  -2.84  -2.79  52.06   4.30  -3.24  -0.22  -0.53
-0.13   3.28   7.56  -3.84 -10.73  -5.88  -4.37   4.30  54.63  -7.42  -0.98   2.74
-5.57  -9.78   1.05  -0.89   0.43  -1.29   8.29  -3.24  -7.42  50.77  -9.46   0.80
-3.05   2.20   5.73  -0.43  -1.55  -2.37  -0.89  -0.22  -0.98  -9.46  44.26   1.52
-0.13  -2.67  14.40   0.61   3.88  -4.08   0.75  -0.53   2.74   0.80   1.52  55.52

cmd1.m_CovMat
51.47  -5.44  -4.02  -7.40   9.38   9.54   3.78  -4.88  -0.13  -5.57  -3.05  -0.13
-5.44  46.43   0.65   3.14   6.77   5.55   7.53 -10.10   3.28  -9.78   2.20  -2.67
-4.02   0.65  47.41  -3.05   8.95   0.26  -3.35   1.96   7.56   1.05   5.73  14.40
-7.40   3.14  -3.05  49.82  -1.64   4.03  -0.29   6.52  -3.84  -0.89  -0.43   0.61
 9.38   6.77   8.95  -1.64  58.12   4.29   5.73 -15.49 -10.73   0.43  -1.55   3.88
 9.54   5.55   0.26   4.03   4.29  54.11   4.26  -2.84  -5.88  -1.29  -2.37  -4.08
 3.78   7.53  -3.35  -0.29   5.73   4.26  57.93  -2.79  -4.37   8.29  -0.89   0.75
-4.88 -10.10   1.96   6.52 -15.49  -2.84  -2.79  52.06   4.30  -3.24  -0.22  -0.53
-0.13   3.28   7.56  -3.84 -10.73  -5.88  -4.37   4.30  54.63  -7.42  -0.98   2.74
-5.57  -9.78   1.05  -0.89   0.43  -1.29   8.29  -3.24  -7.42  50.77  -9.46   0.80
-3.05   2.20   5.73  -0.43  -1.55  -2.37  -0.89  -0.22  -0.98  -9.46  44.26   1.52
-0.13  -2.67  14.40   0.61   3.88  -4.08   0.75  -0.53   2.74   0.80   1.52  55.52

CompareResults - passed

Running benchmark function CalcCovMatF64_bm() - please wait
.........................................
Benchmark times save to file @Ch11_08_CalcCovMatF64_bm_HELIUM.csv
```

Table 11-8 shows the benchmark timing measurements for source example Ch11_08. As you can see from the benchmark timing measurements, the AVX2 assembly language code is considerably faster than the C++ code.

Table 11-8. *Benchmark Timing Measurements (Microseconds) for Covariance Matrix Calculation Functions (n_vars = 10, n_obvs = 250,000)*

Function	i5-11600K	i7-11700K	7700X
CalcCovMatF64_cpp()	14382 (26)	13688 (381)	9049 (15)
CalcCovMatF64_avx2()	5053 (19)	4573 (156)	2997 (14)

Summary

Here are the key learning points for Chapter 11:

- Nearly all AVX2 and FMA packed single-precision and double-precision floating-point instructions support 128-bit or 256-bit wide operands. Packed floating-point operands should always be properly aligned whenever possible.

- X86 FMA instructions perform product-sum additions or subtractions. Using FMA instructions instead of distinct multiply and add instructions often results in better performance and accuracy.

- The vextractf128 instruction extracts 128 bits of packed floating-point data from a 256-bit wide floating-point operand.

- A function can employ a sequence of vextractf128, vaddpd, and vhaddpd instructions to reduce the double-precision floating-point elements of a 256-bit wide operand to a scalar value.

- The vperm2f128 instruction can be utilized to rearrange the elements of a 256-bit wide packed floating-point operand.

- The vmovlhps and vmovhlps instructions rearrange the lower and upper quadwords of 128-bit wide packed single-precision floating-point operand.

- The vunpcklp[d|s] and vunpckhp[d|s] instructions interleave elements of packed floating-point operands.

- The vmaskmovp[d|s] instructions perform conditional loads and stores of individual elements in a packed floating-point operand.

- The align directive can be used to align the start of a performance-critical for-loop on a 16-byte boundary, which often yields improved performance.

- The lea instruction calculates the address of an object in memory. It can also be used to perform simple integer arithmetic (e.g., lea rax,[RCX+100] or lea rax,[RCX+RDX*8]).

■ ■ ■

## CHAPTER 12

AVX2 Programming – Packed Floating-Point – Part 2

In the previous chapter, you discovered how to exploit the AVX2 and FMA instruction sets to carry out accelerated computations using floating-point arrays and matrices. In this chapter, you'll learn how to code more sophisticated functions using the same instruction sets and data structures. The first section of this chapter contains two source code examples that illustrate how to calculate the inverse of a 4 × 4 matrix. The second section focuses on source code examples that perform 1D discrete convolutions.

This chapter accentuates floating-point algorithms that are somewhat more specialized than those examined in previous chapters. I encourage you to peruse this chapter thoroughly since it discusses practical particulars regarding the coding of assembly language functions that perform complex floating-point calculations. It also exemplifies how to minimize differences between assembly language functions that carry out calculations using single-precision and double-precision floating-point instructions. However, if your programming interests reside elsewhere, feel free to either skim or skip this chapter.

Matrix Inversion

In the previous chapter, you studied several source code examples that demonstrated arithmetic operations using matrices including matrix-matrix multiplication and matrix-vector multiplication. Another common matrix operation is the calculation of an inverse. The inverse of a matrix is defined as follows: let $\mathbf{M}$ and $\mathbf{X}$ represent $n \times n$ matrices. Matrix $\mathbf{X}$ is an inverse of $\mathbf{M}$ if $\mathbf{MX} = \mathbf{XM} = \mathbf{I}$, where $\mathbf{I}$ denotes an $n \times n$ identity matrix (i.e., a matrix of all zeros except for the main diagonal elements, which are equal to one). Figure 12-1 shows an example of an inverse matrix. It is important to note that not every $n \times n$ matrix has an inverse. A matrix without an inverse is called a singular matrix. Inverse matrices are sometimes employed to solve a system of linear equations. Many computer graphics applications also use inverse matrices to perform transformation operations.

$$
\begin{bmatrix} 6.0 & 2.0 & 2.0 \\ 2.0 & -2.0 & 2.0 \\ 0.0 & 4.0 & 2.0 \end{bmatrix} \begin{bmatrix} 0.1875 & -0.0625 & -0.125 \\ 0.0625 & -0.1875 & 0.125 \\ -0.125 & 0.375 & 0.25 \end{bmatrix} = \begin{bmatrix} 1.0 & 0.0 & 0.0 \\ 0.0 & 1.0 & 0.0 \\ 0.0 & 0.0 & 1.0 \end{bmatrix}
$$
$$\quad\;\;\mathbf{M} \qquad\qquad\qquad\qquad \mathbf{X} \qquad\qquad\qquad\qquad\quad \mathbf{I}$$

Figure 12-1. *Matrix **M** and its inverse matrix **X***

© Daniel Kusswurm 2023
D. Kusswurm, *Modern X86 Assembly Language Programming*,
https://doi.org/10.1007/978-1-4842-9603-5_12

The inverse of a matrix can be calculated using a variety of mathematical techniques. The source code that you'll examine later in this section uses a computational method based on the Cayley-Hamilton theorem. This theorem employs ordinary matrix arithmetic operations that are straightforward to implement using SIMD instructions. The following equations can be used to calculate the inverse of a 4 × 4 matrix:

$$\mathbf{M}^1 = \mathbf{M}; \mathbf{M}^2 = \mathbf{MM}; \mathbf{M}^3 = \mathbf{MMM}; \mathbf{M}^4 = \mathbf{MMMM}$$

$$trace(\mathbf{M}) = \sum_i m_{ii}$$

$$t_n = trace(\mathbf{M}^n)$$

$$c_0 = 1$$

$$c_1 = -t_1$$

$$c_2 = -\frac{1}{2}(c_1 t_1 + t_2)$$

$$c_3 = -\frac{1}{3}(c_2 t_1 + c_1 t_2 + t_3)$$

$$c_4 = -\frac{1}{4}(c_3 t_1 + c_2 t_2 + c_1 t_3 + t_4)$$

$$\mathbf{M}^{-1} = -\frac{1}{c_4}(\mathbf{M}^3 + c_1 \mathbf{M}^2 + c_2 \mathbf{M}^3 + c_3 \mathbf{I})$$

In these equations, note that the trace of a matrix is simply the sum of its main diagonal elements. Also note that coefficients c_1 - c_4 are scalar values.

Single-Precision

Listing 12-1a shows the principal C++ code for function Mat4x4InvF32_cpp(), which calculates the inverse of a 4 × 4 matrix of single-precision floating-point elements.

Listing 12-1a. Example Ch12_01 C++ Code

```
//-------------------------------------------------------------------------
// Ch12_01_fcpp.cpp
//-------------------------------------------------------------------------

#include <stdexcept>
#include <cmath>
#include "Ch12_01.h"
```

```
bool Mat4x4InvF32_cpp(MatrixF32& m_inv, const MatrixF32& m, float epsilon)
{
    constexpr size_t nrows = 4;
    constexpr size_t ncols = 4;

    if (m_inv.GetNumRows() != nrows || m_inv.GetNumCols() != ncols)
        throw std::runtime_error("Mat4x4InvF32_cpp() - invalid matrix size (m_inv)");

    if (m.GetNumRows() != nrows || m.GetNumCols() != ncols)
        throw std::runtime_error("Mat4x4InvF32_cpp() - invalid matrix size (m)");

    // Note: Local matrices in this function are declared static to avoid
    //        MatrixF32 constructor/destructor overhead during benchmarking.
    static MatrixF32 m2(nrows, ncols);
    static MatrixF32 m3(nrows, ncols);
    static MatrixF32 m4(nrows, ncols);
    static MatrixF32 I = MatrixF32::I(nrows);
    static MatrixF32 temp_a(nrows, ncols);
    static MatrixF32 temp_b(nrows, ncols);
    static MatrixF32 temp_c(nrows, ncols);
    static MatrixF32 temp_d(nrows, ncols);

    // Calculate matrix product and trace values
    MatrixF32::Mul(m2, m, m);
    MatrixF32::Mul(m3, m2, m);
    MatrixF32::Mul(m4, m3, m);

    float t1 = m.Trace();
    float t2 = m2.Trace();
    float t3 = m3.Trace();
    float t4 = m4.Trace();

    // Calculate coefficients
    float c1 = -t1;
    float c2 = -1.0f / 2.0f * (c1 * t1 + t2);
    float c3 = -1.0f / 3.0f * (c2 * t1 + c1 * t2 + t3);
    float c4 = -1.0f / 4.0f * (c3 * t1 + c2 * t2 + c1 * t3 + t4);

    // Make sure matrix is not singular
    bool is_singular = (fabs(c4) < epsilon);

    if (!is_singular)
    {
        // Calculate inverse = -1.0 / c4 * (m3 + c1 * m2 + c2 * m + c3 * I)
        MatrixF32::MulScalar(temp_a, I, c3);
        MatrixF32::MulScalar(temp_b, m, c2);
        MatrixF32::MulScalar(temp_c, m2, c1);
        MatrixF32::Add(temp_d, temp_a, temp_b);
        MatrixF32::Add(temp_d, temp_d, temp_c);
```

```
        MatrixF32::Add(temp_d, temp_d, m3);
        MatrixF32::MulScalar(m_inv, temp_d, -1.0f / c4);
    }

    return !is_singular;
}
```

Function Mat4x4InvF32_cpp() calculates the inverse of a 4×4 matrix of single-precision floating-point elements using the aforementioned Cayley-Hamilton equations. Note that this function utilizes several member functions provided by class MatrixF32 to calculate the inverse matrix. Also note that some of the intermediate matrices are declared using the C++ static qualifier. This is done to avoid constructor and destructor overhead when performing benchmark timing measurements. The drawback of using the static qualifier here means that function Mat4x4InvF32_cpp() is not thread-safe (a thread-safe function can be executed simultaneously by multiple threads). Following calculation of trace values t_1, t_2, t_3, and t_4, function Mat4x4InvF32_cpp() computes c_1, c_2, c_3, and c_4 using scalar arithmetic. It then checks to see if matrix m is singular. If fabs(c4) < epsilon is true, matrix m is singular, and the remaining executable statements are skipped. Otherwise, the final inverse matrix is computed.

Listing 12-1b shows the MASM assembly language code for example Ch12_01. This file begins with a custom section of floating-point constants named ConstVals. Note the use of the align(32) attribute, which ensures that identity matrix Mat4x4I is aligned in a 32-byte boundary. For function Mat4x4InvF32_avx2(), 16-byte alignment is also suitable, but 32-byte alignment is used here to minimize differences between this example and the assembly language code for example Ch12_02, which is presented in the next section.

Listing 12-1b. Example Ch12_01 MASM Code

```
;-------------------------------------------------------------------------------
; Ch12_01_fasm.asm
;-------------------------------------------------------------------------------

        include <MacrosX86-64-AVX.asmh>

ConstVals       segment readonly align(32) 'const'
Mat4x4I         real4 1.0, 0.0, 0.0, 0.0
                real4 0.0, 1.0, 0.0, 0.0
                real4 0.0, 0.0, 1.0, 0.0
                real4 0.0, 0.0, 0.0, 1.0

F32_SignBitMask dd 4 dup (80000000h)
F32_AbsMask     dd 4 dup (7fffffffh)

F32_1p0         real4  1.0
F32_N1p0        real4 -1.0
F32_N0p5        real4 -0.5
F32_N0p333      real4 -0.33333333333333
F32_N0p25       real4 -0.25


;-------------------------------------------------------------------------------
; Mat4x4TraceF32_M macro
;
; Description:  This macro emits instructions that calculate the trace of a
;               4x4 F32 matrix.
;
```

```
; Registers:    rcx      pointer to matrix
;               xmm0     calculated trace value
;               xmm1     scratch register
;-----------------------------------------------------------------------------


Mat4x4TraceF32_M macro
        vmovss  xmm0,real4 ptr [rcx]            ;xmm0 = m[0][0]
        vmovss  xmm1,real4 ptr [rcx+20]         ;xmm1 = m[1][1]
        vaddss  xmm0,xmm0,real4 ptr [rcx+40]    ;xmm0 = m[0][0] + m[2][2]
        vaddss  xmm1,xmm1,real4 ptr [rcx+60]    ;xmm1 = m[1][1] + m[3][3]
        vaddss  xmm0,xmm0,xmm1                  ;xmm0 = trace(m)
        endm



;-----------------------------------------------------------------------------
; Mat4x4MulCalcRowF32_M macro
;
; Description:   This macro emits instructions that calculates one row of a
;                4x4 F32 matrix multiplication (c = a * b).
;
; Parameters:    disp         displacement for row a[i][], c[i][]
;
; Registers:     rcx          matrix c pointer
;                rdx          matrix a pointer
;                xmm0         row b[0][]
;                xmm1         row b[1][]
;                xmm2         row b[2][]
;                xmm3         row b[3][]
;                xmm4, xmm5   scratch registers
;-----------------------------------------------------------------------------


Mat4x4MulCalcRowF32_M macro disp
        vbroadcastss xmm5,real4 ptr [rdx+disp]      ;broadcast a[i][0]
        vmulps  xmm4,xmm5,xmm0                      ;xmm4  = a[i][0] * b[0][]

        vbroadcastss xmm5,real4 ptr [rdx+disp+4]    ;broadcast a[i][1]
        vfmadd231ps xmm4,xmm5,xmm1                  ;xmm4 += a[i][1] * b[1][]

        vbroadcastss xmm5,real4 ptr [rdx+disp+8]    ;broadcast a[i][2]
        vfmadd231ps xmm4,xmm5,xmm2                  ;xmm4 += a[i][2] * b[2][]

        vbroadcastss xmm5,real4 ptr [rdx+disp+12]   ;broadcast a[i][3]
        vfmadd231ps xmm4,xmm5,xmm3                  ;xmm4 += a[i][3] * b[3][]

        vmovaps [rcx+disp],xmm4                     ;save row c[i][]
        endm


;-----------------------------------------------------------------------------
; void Mat4x4MulF32_avx2(float* c, const float* a, const float* b)
;-----------------------------------------------------------------------------
```

```
        .code
Mat4x4MulF32_avx2 proc
        vmovaps xmm0,[r8]                       ;xmm0 = b[0][]
        vmovaps xmm1,[r8+16]                    ;xmm1 = b[1][]
        vmovaps xmm2,[r8+32]                    ;xmm2 = b[2][]
        vmovaps xmm3,[r8+48]                    ;xmm3 = b[3][]

        Mat4x4MulCalcRowF32_M 0                 ;calculate c[0][]
        Mat4x4MulCalcRowF32_M 16                ;calculate c[1][]
        Mat4x4MulCalcRowF32_M 32                ;calculate c[2][]
        Mat4x4MulCalcRowF32_M 48                ;calculate c[3][]
        ret
Mat4x4MulF32_avx2 endp

;-------------------------------------------------------------------------
; bool Mat4x4InvF32_avx2(float* m_inv, const float* m, float epsilon)
;
; Returns    true    matrix m_inv calculated
;            false   matrix m_inv not calculated (m is singular)
;-------------------------------------------------------------------------

; Stack offsets and sizes (see figure in text)
OffsetM2        equ 32          ;offset of m2 relative to rsp
OffsetM3        equ 96          ;offset of m3 relative to rsp
OffsetM4        equ 160         ;offset of m4 relative to rsp
StkSizeLocal    equ 192         ;stack space (bytes) for temp matrices

Mat4x4InvF32_avx2 proc frame
        CreateFrame_M MI_,0,160
        SaveXmmRegs_M xmm6,xmm7,xmm8,xmm9,xmm10,xmm11,xmm12,xmm13,xmm14,xmm15
        EndProlog_M

; Save args to home area for later use
        mov [rbp+MI_OffsetHomeRCX],rcx          ;save m_inv ptr
        mov [rbp+MI_OffsetHomeRDX],rdx          ;save m ptr
        vmovss real4 ptr [rbp+MI_OffsetHomeR8],xmm2 ;save epsilon

; Allocate stack space for temp matrices + 32 bytes for function calls
        and rsp,0ffffffffffffffe0h              ;align rsp to 32-byte boundary
        sub rsp,StkSizeLocal+32                 ;alloc stack space

; Calculate m2
        lea rcx,[rsp+OffsetM2]                  ;rcx = m2 ptr
        mov r8,rdx                              ;r8 = rdx = m ptr
        call Mat4x4MulF32_avx2                  ;calculate and save m2

; Calculate m3
        lea rcx,[rsp+OffsetM3]                  ;rcx = m3 ptr
        lea rdx,[rsp+OffsetM2]                  ;rdx = m2 ptr
        mov r8,[rbp+MI_OffsetHomeRDX]           ;r8 = m
        call Mat4x4MulF32_avx2                  ;calculate and save m3
```

```
; Calculate m4
        lea rcx,[rsp+OffsetM4]              ;rcx = m4 ptr
        lea rdx,[rsp+OffsetM3]              ;rdx = m3 ptr
        mov r8,[rbp+MI_OffsetHomeRDX]       ;r8 = m ptr
        call Mat4x4MulF32_avx2             ;calculate and save m4

; Calculate trace of m, m2, m3, and m4
        mov rcx,[rbp+MI_OffsetHomeRDX]
        Mat4x4TraceF32_M
        vmovss xmm8,xmm0,xmm0               ;xmm8 = t1

        lea rcx,[rsp+OffsetM2]
        Mat4x4TraceF32_M
        vmovss xmm9,xmm0,xmm0               ;xmm9 = t2

        lea rcx,[rsp+OffsetM3]
        Mat4x4TraceF32_M
        vmovss xmm10,xmm0,xmm0              ;xmm10 = t3

        lea rcx,[rsp+OffsetM4]
        Mat4x4TraceF32_M
        vmovss xmm11,xmm0,xmm0              ;xmm11 = t4

;----------------------------------------------------------------------------
; Calculate the required coefficients
; c1 = -t1;
; c2 = -1.0f / 2.0f * (c1 * t1 + t2);
; c3 = -1.0f / 3.0f * (c2 * t1 + c1 * t2 + t3);
; c4 = -1.0f / 4.0f * (c3 * t1 + c2 * t2 + c1 * t3 + t4);
;
; Registers used:
;   t1 - t4 = xmm8 - xmm11
;   c1 - c4 = xmm12 - xmm15
;----------------------------------------------------------------------------

        vxorps xmm12,xmm8,[F32_SignBitMask]    ;c1 = -t1

        vmulss xmm13,xmm12,xmm8            ;c1 * t1
        vaddss xmm13,xmm13,xmm9            ;c1 * t1 + t2
        vmulss xmm13,xmm13,[F32_NOp5]      ;c2

        vmulss xmm14,xmm13,xmm8            ;c2 * t1
        vmulss xmm0,xmm12,xmm9             ;c1 * t2
        vaddss xmm14,xmm14,xmm0            ;c2 * t1 + c1 * t2
        vaddss xmm14,xmm14,xmm10           ;c2 * t1 + c1 * t2 + t3
        vmulss xmm14,xmm14,[F32_NOp333]    ;c3

        vmulss xmm15,xmm14,xmm8            ;c3 * t1
        vmulss xmm0,xmm13,xmm9             ;c2 * t2
        vmulss xmm1,xmm12,xmm10            ;c1 * t3
        vaddss xmm2,xmm0,xmm1              ;c2 * t2 + c1 * t3
```

```
        vaddss xmm15,xmm15,xmm2         ;c3 * t1 + c2 * t2 + c1 * t3
        vaddss xmm15,xmm15,xmm11        ;c3 * t1 + c2 * t2 + c1 * t3 + t4
        vmulss xmm15,xmm15,[F32_N0p25]  ;c4

; Make sure matrix is not singular
        vandps xmm0,xmm15,real4 ptr [F32_AbsMask]    ;compute fabs(c4)
        vcomiss xmm0,real4 ptr [rbp+MI_OffsetHomeR8];compare against epsilon
        setp al                             ;set al if unordered
        setb ah                             ;set ah if fabs(c4) < epsilon
        or al,ah                            ;is input matrix is_singular?
        jnz IsSing                          ;jump if yes

; Calculate m_inv = -1.0 / c4 * (m3 + c1 * m2 + c2 * m + c3 * I)
        vbroadcastss xmm14,xmm14                    ;xmm14 = packed c3
        lea rcx,[Mat4x4I]                           ;rcx = I ptr
        vmulps xmm0,xmm14,[rcx]
        vmulps xmm1,xmm14,[rcx+16]
        vmulps xmm2,xmm14,[rcx+32]
        vmulps xmm3,xmm14,[rcx+48]                  ;c3 * I

        vbroadcastss xmm13,xmm13                    ;xmm13 = packed c2
        mov rcx,[rbp+MI_OffsetHomeRDX]              ;rcx = m ptr
        vfmadd231ps xmm0,xmm13,[rcx]
        vfmadd231ps xmm1,xmm13,[rcx+16]
        vfmadd231ps xmm2,xmm13,[rcx+32]
        vfmadd231ps xmm3,xmm13,[rcx+48]             ;c2 * m + c3 * I

        vbroadcastss xmm12,xmm12                    ;xmm12 = packed c1
        lea rcx,[rsp+OffsetM2]                      ;rcx = m2 ptr
        vfmadd231ps xmm0,xmm12,[rcx]
        vfmadd231ps xmm1,xmm12,[rcx+16]
        vfmadd231ps xmm2,xmm12,[rcx+32]
        vfmadd231ps xmm3,xmm12,[rcx+48]             ;c1 * m2 + c2 * m + c3 * I

        lea rcx,[rsp+OffsetM3]                      ;rcx = m3 ptr
        vaddps xmm0,xmm0,[rcx]
        vaddps xmm1,xmm1,[rcx+16]
        vaddps xmm2,xmm2,[rcx+32]
        vaddps xmm3,xmm3,[rcx+48]                   ;m3 + c1 * m2 + c2 * m + c3 * I

        vmovss xmm4,[F32_N1p0]
        vdivss xmm4,xmm4,xmm15                      ;xmm4 = -1.0 / c4
        vbroadcastss xmm4,xmm4
        vmulps xmm0,xmm0,xmm4
        vmulps xmm1,xmm1,xmm4
        vmulps xmm2,xmm2,xmm4
        vmulps xmm3,xmm3,xmm4                       ;xmm0:xmm3 = m_inv
```

```
; Save m_inv
        mov rcx,[rbp+MI_OffsetHomeRCX]
        vmovaps [rcx],xmm0                              ;save m_inv[0][]
        vmovaps [rcx+16],xmm1                           ;save m_inv[1][]
        vmovaps [rcx+32],xmm2                           ;save m_inv[2][]
        vmovaps [rcx+48],xmm3                           ;save m_inv[3][]

        mov eax,1                                       ;set non-singular return code

Done:   RestoreXmmRegs_M xmm6,xmm7,xmm8,xmm9,xmm10,xmm11,xmm12,xmm13,xmm14,xmm15
        DeleteFrame_M
        ret

IsSing: xor eax,eax                                     ;set singular return code
        jmp Done


Mat4x4InvF32_avx2 endp
        end
```

Following declaration of the requisite constants is the definition of macro Mat4x4TraceF32_M. This macro emits code that computes the trace of a 4 × 4 matrix of single-precision floating-point elements. Note that prior to using this macro, register RCX must contain the address of the target matrix.

Next in Listing 12-1b is the definition of macro Mat4x4MulCalcRowF32_M and function Mat4x4MulF32_avx2(). Function Mat4x4MulF32_avx2() uses macro Mat4x4MulCalcRowF32_M to calculate the product of two 4 × 4 matrices (C = AB) of single-precision floating-point elements. The assembly language code in function Mat4x4MulF32_avx2() is basically the same code that was used in example Ch11_04 to perform 4 × 4 matrix multiplication. Note that macro Mat4x4MulCalcRowF32_M requires registers RCX and RDX to be loaded with pointers to matrices C and A, respectively. Also note that this macro expects the rows of matrix B to be loaded in registers XMM0–XMM3.

Immediately after the definition of function Mat4x4MulF32_avx2() is a series of equate statements that define offsets relative to RSP for intermediate matrix products m2, m3, and m4. The equate StkSizeLocal signifies how much stack space is needed to store these intermediate matrix products.

Function Mat4x4InvF32_avx2() begins its execution with a formal prologue that utilizes macros CreateFrame_M and SaveXmmRegs_m to create a stack frame and preserve the values of non-volatile registers XMM6–XMM15. The ensuing code block saves argument values m_inv, m, and epsilon on the stack for later use. Note that these values are saved in the home area for function Mat4x4InvF32_avx2(). The next instruction, and rsp,0fffffffffffffe0h, aligns the value in register RSP downward to the nearest 32-byte boundary. This is followed by a sub rsp,StkSizeLocal+32 instruction that allocates stack space for the previously mentioned intermediate matrix products plus 32 bytes of home area for function calls. Figure 12-2 illustrates organization of the stack following execution of the sub rsp,StkSizeLocal+32 instruction. In this figure, numbers appearing within parentheses are offsets or sizes for source code example Ch12_02 function Mat4x4InvF64_avx2(). More on this later.

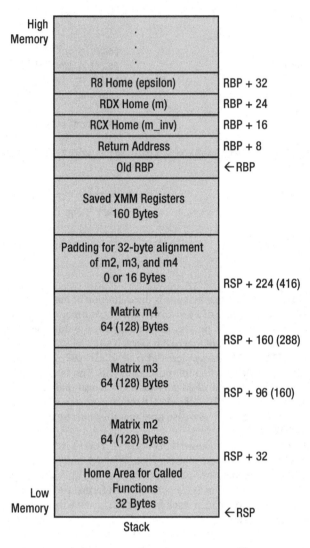

Figure 12-2. *Organization of stack following execution of the* sub rsp, StkSizeLocal+32 *instruction in function* Mat4x4InvF32_avx2() *and* Mat4x4InvF64_avx2() *(MASM version)*

Following allocation of the requisite stack space, function Mat4x4InvF32_avx2() employs a series of calls to Mat4x4MulF32_avx2() to calculate intermediate matrix products m2, m3, and m4. Next is a series of four code blocks that calculate matrix trace values t1, t2, t3, and t4 using macro Mat4x4TraceF32_M.

After the computation of the matrix trace values, Mat4x4InvF32_avx2() uses AVX scalar single-precision floating-point instructions to calculate coefficients c1, c2, c3, and c4. The ensuing instruction pair, vandps xmm0,xmm15,real4 ptr [F32_AbsMask] and vcomiss xmm0,real4 ptr [rbp+MI_OffsetHomeR8], compares fabs(c4) and epsilon. If fabs(c4) < epsilon is true (or if the compare is unordered), input matrix m is singular and execution of the jnz IsSing instruction skips over the remaining calculating code in Mat4x4InvF32_avx2().

If matrix m is not singular, the ensuing code blocks in Mat4x4InvF32_avx2() calculate m_inv = -1.0 / c4 * (m3 + c1 * m2 + c2 * m + c3 * I). While this expression may appear slightly unnerving, the parenthetical expression simply sums several scalar-matrix products. To calculate a scalar-matrix product, Mat4x4InvF32_avx2() multiplies each element of the target matrix by the specified scalar value. Following calculation of m_inv, Mat4x4InvF32_avx2() employs a series of vmovaps instructions to save m_inv.

Listing 12-1c shows the NASM code for example Ch12_01. There are a few minor differences between this code and the MASM code that's shown in Listing 12-1b. First, the appropriate NASM directives are used for the section of constants. Second, macros Mat4x4TraceF32_M and Mat4x4MulCalcRowF32_M are defined using NASM directives and syntax. Finally, different general-purpose registers are employed.

Listing 12-1c. Example Ch12_01 NASM Code

```
;-------------------------------------------------------------------------------
; Ch12_01_fasm.s
;-------------------------------------------------------------------------------

        %include "ModX86Asm3eNASM.inc"

        section .rdata align = 32
Mat4x4I         dd 1.0, 0.0, 0.0, 0.0
                dd 0.0, 1.0, 0.0, 0.0
                dd 0.0, 0.0, 1.0, 0.0
                dd 0.0, 0.0, 0.0, 1.0

F32_SignBitMask dd 4 dup (80000000h)
F32_AbsMask     dd 4 dup (7fffffffh)

F32_1p0         dd  1.0
F32_N1p0        dd -1.0
F32_N0p5        dd -0.5
F32_N0p333      dd -0.33333333333333
F32_N0p25       dd -0.25


;-------------------------------------------------------------------------------
; Mat4x4TraceF32_M macro
;
; Description:  This macro emits instructions that calculate the trace of a
;               4x4 F32 matrix.
;
; Registers:    rdi     pointer to matrix
;               xmm0    calculated trace value
;               xmm1    scratch register
;-------------------------------------------------------------------------------

%macro  Mat4x4TraceF32_M 0
        vmovss xmm0,[rdi]                       ;xmm0 = m[0][0]
        vmovss xmm1,[rdi+20]                    ;xmm1 = m[1][1]
        vaddss xmm0,xmm0,[rdi+40]               ;xmm0 = m[0][0] + m[2][2]
        vaddss xmm1,xmm1,[rdi+60]               ;xmm1 = m[1][1] + m[3][3]
        vaddss xmm0,xmm0,xmm1                    ;xmm0 = trace(m)
%endmacro
```

```
;-------------------------------------------------------------------------
; Mat4x4MulCalcRowF32_M macro
;
; Description:   This macro emits instructions that calculates one row of a
;                4x4 F32 matrix multiplication (c = a * b).
;
; Parameters:    %1              displacement for row a[i][], c[i][]
;
; Registers:     rdi             matrix c pointer
;                rsi             matrix a pointer
;                xmm0            row b[0][]
;                xmm1            row b[1][]
;                xmm2            row b[2][]
;                xmm3            row b[3][]
;                xmm4, xmm5      scratch registers
;-------------------------------------------------------------------------

%macro   Mat4x4MulCalcRowF32_M 1
         vbroadcastss xmm5,[rsi+%1]              ;broadcast a[i][0]
         vmulps xmm4,xmm5,xmm0                   ;xmm4  = a[i][0] * b[0][]

         vbroadcastss xmm5,[rsi+%1+4]            ;broadcast a[i][1]
         vfmadd231ps xmm4,xmm5,xmm1              ;xmm4 += a[i][1] * b[1][]

         vbroadcastss xmm5,[rsi+%1+8]            ;broadcast a[i][2]
         vfmadd231ps xmm4,xmm5,xmm2              ;xmm4 += a[i][2] * b[2][]

         vbroadcastss xmm5,[rsi+%1+12]           ;broadcast a[i][3]
         vfmadd231ps xmm4,xmm5,xmm3              ;xmm4 += a[i][3] * b[3][]

         vmovaps [rdi+%1],xmm4                   ;save row c[i][]
%endmacro

;-------------------------------------------------------------------------
; void Mat4x4MulF32_avx2(float* c, const float* a, const float* b)
;-------------------------------------------------------------------------

         section .text

         global Mat4x4MulF32_avx2
Mat4x4MulF32_avx2:
         vmovaps xmm0,[rdx]                      ;xmm0 = b[0][]
         vmovaps xmm1,[rdx+16]                   ;xmm1 = b[1][]
         vmovaps xmm2,[rdx+32]                   ;xmm2 = b[2][]
         vmovaps xmm3,[rdx+48]                   ;xmm3 = b[3][]

         Mat4x4MulCalcRowF32_M 0                 ;calculate c[0][]
         Mat4x4MulCalcRowF32_M 16                ;calculate c[1][]
         Mat4x4MulCalcRowF32_M 32                ;calculate c[2][]
         Mat4x4MulCalcRowF32_M 48                ;calculate c[3][]
         ret
```

```
;-------------------------------------------------------------------------
; bool Mat4x4InvF32_avx2(float* m_inv, const float* m, float epsilon)
;
; Returns    true     matrix m_inv calculated
;            false    matrix m_inv not calculated (m is singular)
;-------------------------------------------------------------------------


; Stack storage offsets relative to rsp (see figure in text)
OffsetM2         equ  0         ;offset of m2
OffsetM3         equ  64        ;offset of m3
OffsetM4         equ  128       ;offset of m4
Offset_m_inv     equ  192       ;offset for m_inv ptr
Offset_m         equ  200       ;offset for m ptr
Offset_epsilon   equ  208       ;offset for epsilon
OffsetExtra      equ  216       ;extra qword for StkSizeLocal % 32 == 0
StkSizeLocal     equ  224       ;stack space (bytes) for temp matrices, local vars


         global Mat4x4InvF32_avx2
Mat4x4InvF32_avx2:
         push rbp                          ;save caller's rbp
         mov rbp,rsp                       ;save caller's rsp
         and rsp,0ffffffffffffffe0h        ;align rsp to 32b boundary
         sub rsp,StkSizeLocal              ;allocate local storage space

; Save args on stack for later use
         mov [rsp+Offset_m_inv],rdi        ;save m_inv ptr
         mov [rsp+Offset_m],rsi            ;save m ptr
         vmovss [rsp+Offset_epsilon],xmm0  ;save epsilon

; Calculate m2
         lea rdi,[rsp+OffsetM2]            ;rdi = m2 ptr
         mov rdx,rsi                       ;rdx = rsi = m ptr
         call Mat4x4MulF32_avx2            ;calculate and save m2

; Calculate m3
         lea rdi,[rsp+OffsetM3]            ;rdi = m3 ptr
         lea rsi,[rsp+OffsetM2]            ;rsi = m2 ptr
         mov rdx,[rsp+Offset_m]            ;rdx = m ptr
         call Mat4x4MulF32_avx2            ;calculate and save m3

; Calculate m4
         lea rdi,[rsp+OffsetM4]            ;rdi = m4 ptr
         lea rsi,[rsp+OffsetM3]            ;rsi = m3 ptr
         mov rdx,[rsp+Offset_m]            ;rdx = m ptr
         call Mat4x4MulF32_avx2            ;calculate and save m4

; Calculate trace of m, m2, m3, and m4
         mov rdi,[rsp+Offset_m]
         Mat4x4TraceF32_M
         vmovss xmm8,xmm0,xmm0             ;xmm8 = t1
```

457

```
        lea rdi,[rsp+OffsetM2]
        Mat4x4TraceF32_M
        vmovss xmm9,xmm0,xmm0                    ;xmm9 = t2

        lea rdi,[rsp+OffsetM3]
        Mat4x4TraceF32_M
        vmovss xmm10,xmm0,xmm0                   ;xmm10 = t3

        lea rdi,[rsp+OffsetM4]
        Mat4x4TraceF32_M
        vmovss xmm11,xmm0,xmm0                   ;xmm11 = t4

;-------------------------------------------------------------------------
; Calculate the required coefficients
; c1 = -t1;
; c2 = -1.0f / 2.0f * (c1 * t1 + t2);
; c3 = -1.0f / 3.0f * (c2 * t1 + c1 * t2 + t3);
; c4 = -1.0f / 4.0f * (c3 * t1 + c2 * t2 + c1 * t3 + t4);
;
; Registers used:
;    t1 - t4 = xmm8 - xmm11
;    c1 - c4 = xmm12 - xmm15
;-------------------------------------------------------------------------

        vxorps xmm12,xmm8,[F32_SignBitMask] ;c1 = -t1

        vmulss xmm13,xmm12,xmm8                  ;c1 * t1
        vaddss xmm13,xmm13,xmm9                  ;c1 * t1 + t2
        vmulss xmm13,xmm13,[F32_NOp5]            ;c2

        vmulss xmm14,xmm13,xmm8                  ;c2 * t1
        vmulss xmm0,xmm12,xmm9                   ;c1 * t2
        vaddss xmm14,xmm14,xmm0                  ;c2 * t1 + c1 * t2
        vaddss xmm14,xmm14,xmm10                 ;c2 * t1 + c1 * t2 + t3
        vmulss xmm14,xmm14,[F32_NOp333]          ;c3

        vmulss xmm15,xmm14,xmm8                  ;c3 * t1
        vmulss xmm0,xmm13,xmm9                   ;c2 * t2
        vmulss xmm1,xmm12,xmm10                  ;c1 * t3
        vaddss xmm2,xmm0,xmm1                    ;c2 * t2 + c1 * t3
        vaddss xmm15,xmm15,xmm2                  ;c3 * t1 + c2 * t2 + c1 * t3
        vaddss xmm15,xmm15,xmm11                 ;c3 * t1 + c2 * t2 + c1 * t3 + t4
        vmulss xmm15,xmm15,[F32_NOp25]           ;c4

; Make sure matrix is not singular
        vandps xmm0,xmm15,[F32_AbsMask]          ;compute fabs(c4)
        vcomiss xmm0,[rsp+Offset_epsilon]        ;compare against epsilon
        setp al                                  ;set al if unordered
        setb ah                                  ;set ah if fabs(c4) < epsilon
        or al,ah                                 ;is input matrix is_singular?
        jnz IsSing                               ;jump if yes
```

```
; Calculate m_inv = -1.0 / c4 * (m3 + c1 * m2 + c2 * m + c3 * I)
        vbroadcastss xmm14,xmm14                ;xmm14 = packed c3
        lea rdi,[Mat4x4I]                       ;rdi = I ptr
        vmulps xmm0,xmm14,[rdi]
        vmulps xmm1,xmm14,[rdi+16]
        vmulps xmm2,xmm14,[rdi+32]
        vmulps xmm3,xmm14,[rdi+48]              ;c3 * I

        vbroadcastss xmm13,xmm13                ;xmm13 = packed c2
        mov rdi,[rsp+Offset_m]                  ;rdi = m ptr
        vfmadd231ps xmm0,xmm13,[rdi]
        vfmadd231ps xmm1,xmm13,[rdi+16]
        vfmadd231ps xmm2,xmm13,[rdi+32]
        vfmadd231ps xmm3,xmm13,[rdi+48]         ;c2 * m + c3 * I

        vbroadcastss xmm12,xmm12                ;xmm12 = packed c1
        lea rdi,[rsp+OffsetM2]                  ;rdi = m2 ptr
        vfmadd231ps xmm0,xmm12,[rdi]
        vfmadd231ps xmm1,xmm12,[rdi+16]
        vfmadd231ps xmm2,xmm12,[rdi+32]
        vfmadd231ps xmm3,xmm12,[rdi+48]         ;c1 * m2 + c2 * m + c3 * I

        lea rdi,[rsp+OffsetM3]                  ;rdi = m3 ptr
        vaddps xmm0,xmm0,[rdi]
        vaddps xmm1,xmm1,[rdi+16]
        vaddps xmm2,xmm2,[rdi+32]
        vaddps xmm3,xmm3,[rdi+48]               ;m3 + c1 * m2 + c2 * m + c3 * I

        vmovss xmm4,[F32_N1p0]
        vdivss xmm4,xmm4,xmm15                  ;xmm4 = -1.0 / c4
        vbroadcastss xmm4,xmm4
        vmulps xmm0,xmm0,xmm4
        vmulps xmm1,xmm1,xmm4
        vmulps xmm2,xmm2,xmm4
        vmulps xmm3,xmm3,xmm4                   ;xmm0:xmm3 = m_inv

; Save m_inv
        mov rdi,[rsp+Offset_m_inv]
        vmovaps [rdi],xmm0                      ;save m_inv[0][]
        vmovaps [rdi+16],xmm1                   ;save m_inv[1][]
        vmovaps [rdi+32],xmm2                   ;save m_inv[2][]
        vmovaps [rdi+48],xmm3                   ;save m_inv[3][]

        mov eax,1                               ;set non-singular return code

Done:   mov rsp,rbp
        pop rbp
        ret

IsSing: xor eax,eax                             ;set singular return code
        jmp Done
```

The NASM version of function Mat4x4InvF32_avx2() employs a different stack layout, which is shown in Figure 12-3. Note in this figure and in the code, register RSP is used as a base pointer for all local items on the stack. Also note that function Mat4x4InvF32_avx2() employs a simple prologue using the instruction pair push rbp and mov rbp,rsp. These instructions safeguard the contents of register RSP for use in the epilogue. The epilogue for function Mat4x4InvF32_avx2() utilizes instructions mov rsp,rbp and pop rbp to release local stack space and restore register RBP prior to execution of the ret instruction. In Figure 12-3, numbers appearing within parentheses are offsets or sizes for NASM function Mat4x4InvF64_avx2() in source code example Ch12_02.

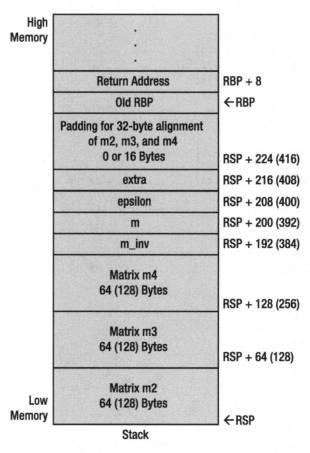

Figure 12-3. *Organization of stack following execution of prologue code in function* Mat4x4InvF32_avx2() *and* Mat4x4InvF64_avx2() *(NASM version)*

Prior to the definition of function Mat4x4InvF32_avx2() in Listing 12-1c, there are several equate statements that define offsets for all local stack variables. The matrix inverse calculating code in Listing 12-1c is basically the same as the code in Listing 12-1b, except for the use of different general-purpose registers. Here are the results for source code example Ch12_01:

```
----- Results for Ch12_01 -----

Test #1 - Source test matrix
     2.000000      7.000000      3.000000      4.000000
     5.000000      9.000000      6.000000      4.750000
     6.500000      3.000000      4.000000     10.000000
     7.000000      5.250000      8.125000      6.000000

Test #1 - Mat4x4InvF32_cpp() - Inverse matrix
    -0.943926      0.916570      0.197547     -0.425579
    -0.056882      0.251148      0.003028     -0.165952
     0.545399     -0.647656     -0.213597      0.505123
     0.412456     -0.412053      0.056125      0.124363

Test #1 - Mat4x4InvF32_cpp() - Verification matrix
     1.000000      0.000000      0.000000      0.000000
     0.000000      1.000000      0.000000      0.000000
     0.000000      0.000000      1.000000      0.000000
     0.000000      0.000000      0.000000      1.000000

Test #1 - Mat4x4InvF32_avx2() - Inverse matrix
    -0.943926      0.916570      0.197547     -0.425579
    -0.056882      0.251148      0.003028     -0.165952
     0.545399     -0.647656     -0.213597      0.505123
     0.412456     -0.412053      0.056125      0.124363

Test #1 - Mat4x4InvF32_avx2() - Verification matrix
     1.000000      0.000000      0.000000      0.000000
     0.000000      1.000000      0.000000      0.000000
     0.000000      0.000000      1.000000      0.000000
     0.000000      0.000000      0.000000      1.000000


---------------------------------------------------------------------------

Test #2 - Source test matrix
     0.500000     12.000000     17.250000      4.000000
     5.000000      2.000000      6.750000      8.000000
    13.125000      1.000000      3.000000      9.750000
    16.000000      1.625000      7.000000      0.250000

Test #2 - Mat4x4InvF32_cpp() - Inverse matrix
     0.001652     -0.069024      0.054959      0.038935
     0.135369     -0.359846      0.242038     -0.090325
    -0.035010      0.239298     -0.183964      0.077221
    -0.005335      0.056194      0.060361     -0.066908

Test #2 - Mat4x4InvF32_cpp() - Verification matrix
     1.000000      0.000000      0.000000      0.000000
     0.000000      1.000000      0.000000      0.000000
     0.000000      0.000000      1.000000      0.000000
     0.000000      0.000000      0.000000      1.000000
```

```
Test #2 - Mat4x4InvF32_avx2() - Inverse matrix
     0.001652     -0.069024      0.054959      0.038935
     0.135369     -0.359845      0.242037     -0.090325
    -0.035010      0.239297     -0.183964      0.077221
    -0.005335      0.056194      0.060361     -0.066908

Test #2 - Mat4x4InvF32_avx2() - Verification matrix
     1.000000      0.000000      0.000000      0.000000
     0.000000      1.000000      0.000000      0.000000
     0.000000      0.000000      1.000000      0.000000
     0.000000      0.000000      0.000000      1.000000


-----------------------------------------------------------------------


Test #3 - Source test matrix
     2.000000      0.000000      0.000000      1.000000
     0.000000      4.000000      5.000000      0.000000
     0.000000      0.000000      0.000000      7.000000
     0.000000      0.000000      0.000000      6.000000

Test #3 - Mat4x4InvF32_cpp() - Matrix is singular
Test #3 - Mat4x4InvF32_avx2() - Matrix is singular
-----------------------------------------------------------------------


Running benchmark function Mat4x4InvF32_bm() - please wait
Benchmark times save to file @Ch12_01_Mat4x4InvF32_bm_HELIUM.csv
```

Table 12-1 shows the benchmark timing measurements for example Ch12_01. As you can see, the assembly language implementations of the 4 × 4 matrix inversion functions significantly outperform their C++ counterpart functions.

Table 12-1. *Benchmark Timing Measurements (Microseconds) for Matrix (4 × 4) Inverse Functions (100,000 Inverse Operations)*

Function	i5-11600K	i7-11700K	7700X
Mat4x4InvF32_cpp()	9909 (83)	17575 (486)	6695 (49)
Mat4x4InvF32_avx2()	1679 (6)	2010 (39)	1666 (6)

Double-Precision

Listing 12-2a shows the principal C++ code for function Mat4x4InvF64_cpp(), which is the double-precision counterpart of Mat4x4InvF32_cpp(). Note that function Mat4x4InvF64_cpp() uses C++ data type double and class MatrixF64 instead of float and MatrixF32.

Listing 12-2a. Example Ch12_02 C++ Code

```
//-------------------------------------------------------------------------
// Ch12_02_fcpp.cpp
//-------------------------------------------------------------------------
```

```
#include <stdexcept>
#include <cmath>
#include "Ch12_02.h"

bool Mat4x4InvF64_cpp(MatrixF64& m_inv, const MatrixF64& m, double epsilon)
{
    constexpr size_t nrows = 4;
    constexpr size_t ncols = 4;

    if (m_inv.GetNumRows() != nrows || m_inv.GetNumCols() != ncols)
        throw std::runtime_error("Mat4x4InvF64_cpp() - invalid matrix size (m_inv)");

    if (m.GetNumRows() != nrows || m.GetNumCols() != ncols)
        throw std::runtime_error("Mat4x4InvF64_cpp() - invalid matrix size (m)");

    // Note: Local matrices in this function are declared static to avoid
    //        MatrixF64 constructor/destructor overhead during benchmarking.
    static MatrixF64 m2(nrows, ncols);
    static MatrixF64 m3(nrows, ncols);
    static MatrixF64 m4(nrows, ncols);
    static MatrixF64 I = MatrixF64::I(nrows);
    static MatrixF64 temp_a(nrows, ncols);
    static MatrixF64 temp_b(nrows, ncols);
    static MatrixF64 temp_c(nrows, ncols);
    static MatrixF64 temp_d(nrows, ncols);

    // Calculate matrix product and trace values
    MatrixF64::Mul(m2, m, m);
    MatrixF64::Mul(m3, m2, m);
    MatrixF64::Mul(m4, m3, m);

    double t1 = m.Trace();
    double t2 = m2.Trace();
    double t3 = m3.Trace();
    double t4 = m4.Trace();

    // Calculate coefficients
    double c1 = -t1;
    double c2 = -1.0 / 2.0 * (c1 * t1 + t2);
    double c3 = -1.0 / 3.0 * (c2 * t1 + c1 * t2 + t3);
    double c4 = -1.0 / 4.0 * (c3 * t1 + c2 * t2 + c1 * t3 + t4);

    // Make sure matrix is not singular
    bool is_singular = (fabs(c4) < epsilon);

    if (!is_singular)
    {
        // Calculate inverse = -1.0 / c4 * (m3 + c1 * m2 + c2 * m + c3 * I)
        MatrixF64::MulScalar(temp_a, I, c3);
        MatrixF64::MulScalar(temp_b, m, c2);
        MatrixF64::MulScalar(temp_c, m2, c1);
```

```
            MatrixF64::Add(temp_d, temp_a, temp_b);
            MatrixF64::Add(temp_d, temp_d, temp_c);
            MatrixF64::Add(temp_d, temp_d, m3);
            MatrixF64::MulScalar(m_inv, temp_d, -1.0 / c4);
    }

    return !is_singular;
}
```

Listing 12-2b shows the MASM code for example Ch12_02. The code in this listing opens with a custom MASM constant memory segment named ConstVals that is aligned on a 32-byte boundary. This ensures that identity matrix Mat4x4I is properly aligned. Next in Listing 12-2b is the definition of macros Mat4x4TraceF64_M and Mat4x4MulCalcRowF64_M. Note that these macros contain double-precision AVX and FMA instructions instead of single-precision instructions.

Listing 12-2b. Example Ch12_02 MASM Code

```
;-----------------------------------------------------------------------------
; Ch12_02_fasm.asm
;-----------------------------------------------------------------------------

        include <MacrosX86-64-AVX.asmh>

ConstVals       segment readonly align(32) 'const'
Mat4x4I         real8 1.0, 0.0, 0.0, 0.0
                real8 0.0, 1.0, 0.0, 0.0
                real8 0.0, 0.0, 1.0, 0.0
                real8 0.0, 0.0, 0.0, 1.0

F64_SignBitMask dq 2 dup (8000000000000000h)
F64_AbsMask     dq 2 dup (7fffffffffffffffh)

F64_1p0         real8  1.0
F64_N1p0        real8 -1.0
F64_N0p5        real8 -0.5
F64_N0p333      real8 -0.33333333333333
F64_N0p25       real8 -0.25
ConstVals       ends


;-----------------------------------------------------------------------------
; Mat4x4TraceF64_M macro
;
; Description:  This macro emits instructions that calculate the trace of a
;               4x4 F64 matrix.
;
; Registers:    rcx     pointer to matrix
;               xmm0    calculated trace value
;               xmm1    scratch register
;-----------------------------------------------------------------------------
```

```
Mat4x4TraceF64_M macro
        vmovsd xmm0,real8 ptr [rcx]               ;xmm0 = m[0][0]
        vmovsd xmm1,real8 ptr [rcx+40]            ;xmm1 = m[1][1]
        vaddsd xmm0,xmm0,real8 ptr [rcx+80]       ;xmm0 = m[0][0] + m[2][2]
        vaddsd xmm1,xmm1,real8 ptr [rcx+120]      ;xmm1 = m[1][1] + m[3][3]
        vaddsd xmm0,xmm0,xmm1                     ;xmm0 = trace(m)
        endm


;-----------------------------------------------------------------------------
; Mat4x4MulCalcRowF64_M macro
;
; Description:   This macro emits instructions that calculates one row of a
;                4x4 F64 matrix multiplication (c = a * b).
;
; Parameters:    disp            displacement for row a[i][], c[i][]
;
; Registers:     rcx             matrix c pointer
;                rdx             matrix a pointer
;                ymm0            row b[0][]
;                ymm1            row b[1][]
;                ymm2            row b[2][]
;                ymm3            row b[3][]
;                ymm4, ymm5      scratch registers
;-----------------------------------------------------------------------------


Mat4x4MulCalcRowF64_M macro disp
        vbroadcastsd ymm5,real8 ptr [rdx+disp]       ;broadcast a[i][0]
        vmulpd ymm4,ymm5,ymm0                        ;ymm4  = a[i][0] * b[0][]

        vbroadcastsd ymm5,real8 ptr [rdx+disp+8]     ;broadcast a[i][1]
        vfmadd231pd ymm4,ymm5,ymm1                   ;ymm4 += a[i][1] * b[1][]

        vbroadcastsd ymm5,real8 ptr [rdx+disp+16]    ;broadcast a[i][2]
        vfmadd231pd ymm4,ymm5,ymm2                   ;ymm4 += a[i][2] * b[2][]

        vbroadcastsd ymm5,real8 ptr [rdx+disp+24]    ;broadcast a[i][3]
        vfmadd231pd ymm4,ymm5,ymm3                   ;ymm4 += a[i][3] * b[3][]

        vmovapd [rcx+disp],ymm4                      ;save row c[i][]
        endm


;-----------------------------------------------------------------------------
; void Mat4x4MulF64_avx2(double* c, const double* a, const double* b)
;-----------------------------------------------------------------------------


        .code
Mat4x4MulF64_avx2 proc
        vmovapd ymm0,[r8]              ;ymm0 = b[0][]
        vmovapd ymm1,[r8+32]          ;ymm1 = b[1][]
        vmovapd ymm2,[r8+64]          ;ymm2 = b[2][]
        vmovapd ymm3,[r8+96]          ;ymm3 = b[3][]
```

465

```
          Mat4x4MulCalcRowF64_M 0              ;calculate c[0][]
          Mat4x4MulCalcRowF64_M 32             ;calculate c[1][]
          Mat4x4MulCalcRowF64_M 64             ;calculate c[2][]
          Mat4x4MulCalcRowF64_M 96             ;calculate c[3][]
          vzeroupper
          ret
Mat4x4MulF64_avx2 endp


;-------------------------------------------------------------------------
; bool Mat4x4InvF64_avx2(double* m_inv, const double* m, double epsilon)
;
; Returns   true    matrix m_inv calculated
;           false   matrix m_inv not calculated (m is singular)
;-------------------------------------------------------------------------

; Stack storage offsets and sizes (see figure in text)
OffsetM2        equ 32          ;offset of m2 relative to rsp
OffsetM3        equ 160         ;offset of m3 relative to rsp
OffsetM4        equ 288         ;offset of m4 relative to rsp
StkSizeLocal    equ 384         ;stack space (bytes) for temp matrices

Mat4x4InvF64_avx2 proc frame
        CreateFrame_M MI_,0,160
        SaveXmmRegs_M xmm6,xmm7,xmm8,xmm9,xmm10,xmm11,xmm12,xmm13,xmm14,xmm15
        EndProlog_M

; Save args to home area for later use
        mov [rbp+MI_OffsetHomeRCX],rcx          ;save m_inv ptr
        mov [rbp+MI_OffsetHomeRDX],rdx          ;save m ptr
        vmovsd real8 ptr [rbp+MI_OffsetHomeR8],xmm2 ;save epsilon

; Allocate stack space for temp matrices + 32 bytes for function calls
        and rsp,0fffffffffffffe0h               ;align rsp to 32-byte boundary
        sub rsp,StkSizeLocal+32                 ;alloc stack space

; Calculate m2
        lea rcx,[rsp+OffsetM2]                  ;rcx = m2 ptr
        mov r8,rdx                              ;r8 = rdx = m ptr
        call Mat4x4MulF64_avx2                  ;calculate and save m2

; Calculate m3
        lea rcx,[rsp+OffsetM3]                  ;rcx = m3 ptr
        lea rdx,[rsp+OffsetM2]               ·  ;rdx = m2 ptr
        mov r8,[rbp+MI_OffsetHomeRDX]           ;r8 = m ptr
        call Mat4x4MulF64_avx2                  ;calculate and save m3

; Calculate m4
        lea rcx,[rsp+OffsetM4]                  ;rcx = m4 ptr
        lea rdx,[rsp+OffsetM3]                  ;rdx = m3 ptr
        mov r8,[rbp+MI_OffsetHomeRDX]           ;r8 = m ptr
        call Mat4x4MulF64_avx2                  ;calculate and save m4
```

```
; Calculate trace of m, m2, m3, and m4
        mov rcx,[rbp+MI_OffsetHomeRDX]
        Mat4x4TraceF64_M
        vmovsd xmm8,xmm0,xmm0                ;xmm8 = t1

        lea rcx,[rsp+OffsetM2]
        Mat4x4TraceF64_M
        vmovsd xmm9,xmm0,xmm0                ;xmm9 = t2

        lea rcx,[rsp+OffsetM3]
        Mat4x4TraceF64_M
        vmovsd xmm10,xmm0,xmm0               ;xmm10 = t3

        lea rcx,[rsp+OffsetM4]
        Mat4x4TraceF64_M
        vmovsd xmm11,xmm0,xmm0               ;xmm11 = t4

;------------------------------------------------------------------------------
; Calculate the required coefficients
; c1 = -t1;
; c2 = -1.0f / 2.0f * (c1 * t1 + t2);
; c3 = -1.0f / 3.0f * (c2 * t1 + c1 * t2 + t3);
; c4 = -1.0f / 4.0f * (c3 * t1 + c2 * t2 + c1 * t3 + t4);
;
; Registers used:
;    t1 - t4 = xmm8 - xmm11
;    c1 - c4 = xmm12 - xmm15
;------------------------------------------------------------------------------

        vxorpd xmm12,xmm8,real8 ptr [F64_SignBitMask]     ;c1 = -t1

        vmulsd xmm13,xmm12,xmm8              ;c1 * t1
        vaddsd xmm13,xmm13,xmm9              ;c1 * t1 + t2
        vmulsd xmm13,xmm13,[F64_NOp5]        ;c2

        vmulsd xmm14,xmm13,xmm8              ;c2 * t1
        vmulsd xmm0,xmm12,xmm9               ;c1 * t2
        vaddsd xmm14,xmm14,xmm0              ;c2 * t1 + c1 * t2
        vaddsd xmm14,xmm14,xmm10             ;c2 * t1 + c1 * t2 + t3
        vmulsd xmm14,xmm14,[F64_NOp333]      ;c3

        vmulsd xmm15,xmm14,xmm8              ;c3 * t1
        vmulsd xmm0,xmm13,xmm9               ;c2 * t2
        vmulsd xmm1,xmm12,xmm10              ;c1 * t3
        vaddsd xmm2,xmm0,xmm1                ;c2 * t2 + c1 * t3
        vaddsd xmm15,xmm15,xmm2              ;c3 * t1 + c2 * t2 + c1 * t3
        vaddsd xmm15,xmm15,xmm11             ;c3 * t1 + c2 * t2 + c1 * t3 + t4
        vmulsd xmm15,xmm15,[F64_NOp25]       ;c4
```

467

```
; Make sure matrix is not singular
        vandpd xmm0,xmm15,[F64_AbsMask]             ;compute fabs(c4)
        vcomisd xmm0,real8 ptr [rbp+MI_OffsetHomeR8];compare against epsilon
        setp al                                     ;set al if unordered
        setb ah                                     ;set ah if fabs(c4) < epsilon
        or al,ah                                    ;is mat m singular?
        jnz IsSing                                  ;jump if yes

; Calculate m_inv = -1.0 / c4 * (m3 + c1 * m2 + c2 * m + c3 * I)
        vbroadcastsd ymm14,xmm14                    ;ymm14 = packed c3
        lea rcx,[Mat4x4I]                           ;rcx = I ptr
        vmulpd ymm0,ymm14,[rcx]
        vmulpd ymm1,ymm14,[rcx+32]
        vmulpd ymm2,ymm14,[rcx+64]
        vmulpd ymm3,ymm14,[rcx+96]                  ;c3 * I

        vbroadcastsd ymm13,xmm13                    ;ymm13 = packed c2
        mov rcx,[rbp+MI_OffsetHomeRDX]              ;rcx = m ptr
        vfmadd231pd ymm0,ymm13,[rcx]
        vfmadd231pd ymm1,ymm13,[rcx+32]
        vfmadd231pd ymm2,ymm13,[rcx+64]
        vfmadd231pd ymm3,ymm13,[rcx+96]             ;c2 * m + c3 * I

        vbroadcastsd ymm12,xmm12                    ;xmm12 = packed c1
        lea rcx,[rsp+OffsetM2]                      ;rcx = m2 ptr
        vfmadd231pd ymm0,ymm12,[rcx]
        vfmadd231pd ymm1,ymm12,[rcx+32]
        vfmadd231pd ymm2,ymm12,[rcx+64]
        vfmadd231pd ymm3,ymm12,[rcx+96]             ;c1 * m2 + c2 * m + c3 * I

        lea rcx,[rsp+OffsetM3]                      ;rcx = m3 ptr
        vaddpd ymm0,ymm0,[rcx]
        vaddpd ymm1,ymm1,[rcx+32]
        vaddpd ymm2,ymm2,[rcx+64]
        vaddpd ymm3,ymm3,[rcx+96]                   ;m3 + c1 * m2 + c2 * m + c3 * I

        vmovsd xmm4,[F64_N1p0]
        vdivsd xmm4,xmm4,xmm15                      ;xmm4 = -1.0 / c4
        vbroadcastsd ymm4,xmm4
        vmulpd ymm0,ymm0,ymm4
        vmulpd ymm1,ymm1,ymm4
        vmulpd ymm2,ymm2,ymm4
        vmulpd ymm3,ymm3,ymm4                       ;ymm0:ymm3 = m_inv

; Save m_inv
        mov rcx,[rbp+MI_OffsetHomeRCX]
        vmovapd [rcx],ymm0                          ;save m_inv[0][]
        vmovapd [rcx+32],ymm1                       ;save m_inv[1][]
        vmovapd [rcx+64],ymm2                       ;save m_inv[2][]
        vmovapd [rcx+96],ymm3                       ;save m_inv[3][]

        mov eax,1                                   ;set non-singular return code
```

```
Done:    vzeroupper
         RestoreXmmRegs_M xmm6,xmm7,xmm8,xmm9,xmm10,xmm11,xmm12,xmm13,xmm14,xmm15
         DeleteFrame_M
         ret

IsSing: xor eax,eax                                ;set singular return code
         jmp Done

Mat4x4InvF64_avx2 endp
         end
```

The remaining code in Listing 12-2b closely resembles the code in Listing 12-1b, but with a few minor differences. First, take note of the numeric values in the equate statements, which are different since a double-precision value occupies eight bytes of storage instead of four. Second, the stack layout for function Mat4x4InvF64_avx2() is identical to the one used for function Mat4x4InvF32_avx2() in Listing 12-1b, except for the actual offset values. These values appear within the parentheses in Figure 12-2. Finally, function Mat4x4InvF64_avx2() utilizes double-precision instead of single-precision instructions.

Listing 12-2c shows the NASM version of Mat4x4InvF32_avx2(). Like its MASM counterpart, the primary differences between the code in Listings 12-2c and 12-1c are the equate statement values and the use of double-precision instead of single-precision instructions.

Listing 12-2c. Example Ch12_02 NASM Code

```
;-------------------------------------------------------------------------------
; Ch12_02_fasm.s
;-------------------------------------------------------------------------------

         %include "ModX86Asm3eNASM.inc"

                  section .rdata align=32
Mat4x4I           dq 1.0, 0.0, 0.0, 0.0
                  dq 0.0, 1.0, 0.0, 0.0
                  dq 0.0, 0.0, 1.0, 0.0
                  dq 0.0, 0.0, 0.0, 1.0

F64_SignBitMask dq 2 dup (8000000000000000h)
F64_AbsMask     dq 2 dup (7fffffffffffffffh)

F64_1p0           dq  1.0
F64_N1p0          dq -1.0
F64_N0p5          dq -0.5
F64_N0p333        dq -0.33333333333333
F64_N0p25         dq -0.25


;-------------------------------------------------------------------------------
; Mat4x4TraceF64_M macro
;
; Description:   This macro emits instructions that calculate the trace of a
;                4x4 F64 matrix.
;
```

```
; Registers:    rdi     pointer to matrix
;               xmm0    calculated trace value
;               xmm1    scratch register
;---------------------------------------------------------------

%macro  Mat4x4TraceF64_M 0
        vmovsd xmm0,[rdi]                   ;xmm0 = m[0][0]
        vmovsd xmm1,[rdi+40]                ;xmm1 = m[1][1]
        vaddsd xmm0,xmm0,[rdi+80]           ;xmm0 = m[0][0] + m[2][2]
        vaddsd xmm1,xmm1,[rdi+120]          ;xmm1 = m[1][1] + m[3][3]
        vaddsd xmm0,xmm0,xmm1               ;xmm0 = trace(m)
%endmacro


;---------------------------------------------------------------
; Mat4x4MulCalcRowF64_M macro
;
; Description:  This macro emits instructions that calculates one row of a
;               4x4 F64 matrix multiplication (c = a * b).
;
; Parameters:   %1              displacement for row a[i][], c[i][]
;
; Registers:    rdi             matrix c pointer
;               rsi             matrix a pointer
;               ymm0            row b[0][]
;               ymm1            row b[1][]
;               ymm2            row b[2][]
;               ymm3            row b[3][]
;               ymm4, ymm5      scratch registers
;---------------------------------------------------------------

%macro  Mat4x4MulCalcRowF64_M 1
        vbroadcastsd ymm5,[rsi+%1]          ;broadcast a[i][0]
        vmulpd ymm4,ymm5,ymm0               ;ymm4  = a[i][0] * b[0][]

        vbroadcastsd ymm5,[rsi+%1+8]        ;broadcast a[i][1]
        vfmadd231pd ymm4,ymm5,ymm1          ;ymm4 += a[i][1] * b[1][]

        vbroadcastsd ymm5,[rsi+%1+16]       ;broadcast a[i][2]
        vfmadd231pd ymm4,ymm5,ymm2          ;ymm4 += a[i][2] * b[2][]

        vbroadcastsd ymm5,[rsi+%1+24]       ;broadcast a[i][3]
        vfmadd231pd ymm4,ymm5,ymm3          ;ymm4 += a[i][3] * b[3][]

        vmovapd [rdi+%1],ymm4               ;save row c[i][]
%endmacro


;---------------------------------------------------------------
; void Mat4x4MulF64_avx2(double* c, const double* a, const double* b)
;---------------------------------------------------------------
```

```
        section .text

        global Mat4x4MulF64_avx2
Mat4x4MulF64_avx2:

        vmovapd ymm0,[rdx]                  ;ymm0 = b[0][]
        vmovapd ymm1,[rdx+32]               ;ymm1 = b[1][]
        vmovapd ymm2,[rdx+64]               ;ymm2 = b[2][]
        vmovapd ymm3,[rdx+96]               ;ymm3 = b[3][]

        Mat4x4MulCalcRowF64_M 0             ;calculate c[0][]
        Mat4x4MulCalcRowF64_M 32            ;calculate c[1][]
        Mat4x4MulCalcRowF64_M 64            ;calculate c[2][]
        Mat4x4MulCalcRowF64_M 96            ;calculate c[3][]
        vzeroupper
        ret


;------------------------------------------------------------------------
; bool Mat4x4InvF64_avx2(double* m_inv, const double* m, double epsilon)
;
; Returns    true    matrix m_inv calculated
;            false   matrix m_inv not calculated (m is singular)
;------------------------------------------------------------------------

; Stack storage offsets relative to rsp (see figure in text)
OffsetM2        equ  0         ;offset of m2
OffsetM3        equ  128       ;offset of m3
OffsetM4        equ  256       ;offset of m4
Offset_m_inv    equ  384       ;offset for m_inv ptr
Offset_m        equ  392       ;offset for m ptr
Offset_epsilon  equ  400       ;offset for epsilon
OffsetExtra     equ  408       ;extra qword for StkSizeLocal % 32 == 0
StkSizeLocal    equ  416       ;stack space (bytes) for temp matrices, local vars

        global Mat4x4InvF64_avx2
Mat4x4InvF64_avx2:
        push rbp                            ;save caller's rbp
        mov rbp,rsp                         ;save caller's rsp
        and rsp,0fffffffffffffe0h           ;align rsp to 32b boundary
        sub rsp,StkSizeLocal                ;allocate local storage space

; Save args on stack for later use
        mov [rsp+Offset_m_inv],rdi          ;save m_inv ptr
        mov [rsp+Offset_m],rsi              ;save m ptr
        vmovsd [rsp+Offset_epsilon],xmm0    ;save epsilon

; Calculate m2
        lea rdi,[rsp+OffsetM2]              ;rdi = m2 ptr
        mov rdx,rsi                         ;rdx = rsi = m ptr
        call Mat4x4MulF64_avx2              ;calculate and save m2
```

```
; Calculate m3
        lea rdi,[rsp+OffsetM3]              ;rdi = m3 ptr
        lea rsi,[rsp+OffsetM2]              ;rsi = m2 ptr
        mov rdx,[rsp+Offset_m]             ;rdx = m ptr
        call Mat4x4MulF64_avx2             ;calculate and save m3

; Calculate m4
        lea rdi,[rsp+OffsetM4]              ;rdi = m4 ptr
        lea rsi,[rsp+OffsetM3]              ;rsi = m3 ptr
        mov rdx,[rsp+Offset_m]             ;rdx = m ptr
        call Mat4x4MulF64_avx2             ;calculate and save m4

; Calculate trace of m, m2, m3, and m4
        mov rdi,[rsp+Offset_m]
        Mat4x4TraceF64_M
        vmovsd xmm8,xmm0,xmm0               ;xmm8 = t1

        lea rdi,[rsp+OffsetM2]
        Mat4x4TraceF64_M
        vmovsd xmm9,xmm0,xmm0               ;xmm9 = t2

        lea rdi,[rsp+OffsetM3]
        Mat4x4TraceF64_M
        vmovsd xmm10,xmm0,xmm0              ;xmm10 = t3

        lea rdi,[rsp+OffsetM4]
        Mat4x4TraceF64_M
        vmovsd xmm11,xmm0,xmm0              ;xmm11 = t4

;-------------------------------------------------------------------------
; Calculate the required coefficients
; c1 = -t1;
; c2 = -1.0f / 2.0f * (c1 * t1 + t2);
; c3 = -1.0f / 3.0f * (c2 * t1 + c1 * t2 + t3);
; c4 = -1.0f / 4.0f * (c3 * t1 + c2 * t2 + c1 * t3 + t4);
;
; Registers used:
;   t1 - t4 = xmm8 - xmm11
;   c1 - c4 = xmm12 - xmm15
;-------------------------------------------------------------------------

        vxorpd xmm12,xmm8,[F64_SignBitMask] ;c1 = -t1

        vmulsd xmm13,xmm12,xmm8             ;c1 * t1
        vaddsd xmm13,xmm13,xmm9             ;c1 * t1 + t2
        vmulsd xmm13,xmm13,[F64_NOp5]       ;c2

        vmulsd xmm14,xmm13,xmm8             ;c2 * t1
        vmulsd xmm0,xmm12,xmm9              ;c1 * t2
        vaddsd xmm14,xmm14,xmm0             ;c2 * t1 + c1 * t2
        vaddsd xmm14,xmm14,xmm10            ;c2 * t1 + c1 * t2 + t3
        vmulsd xmm14,xmm14,[F64_NOp333]     ;c3
```

```
        vmulsd  xmm15,xmm14,xmm8            ;c3 * t1
        vmulsd  xmm0,xmm13,xmm9             ;c2 * t2
        vmulsd  xmm1,xmm12,xmm10            ;c1 * t3
        vaddsd  xmm2,xmm0,xmm1              ;c2 * t2 + c1 * t3
        vaddsd  xmm15,xmm15,xmm2            ;c3 * t1 + c2 * t2 + c1 * t3
        vaddsd  xmm15,xmm15,xmm11           ;c3 * t1 + c2 * t2 + c1 * t3 + t4
        vmulsd  xmm15,xmm15,[F64_NOp25]     ;c4

; Make sure matrix is not singular
        vandpd  xmm0,xmm15,[F64_AbsMask]    ;compute fabs(c4)
        vcomisd xmm0,[rsp+Offset_epsilon]   ;compare against epsilon
        setp    al                          ;set al if unordered
        setb    ah                          ;set ah if fabs(c4) < epsilon
        or      al,ah                       ;is mat m singular?
        jnz     IsSing                      ;jump if yes

; Calculate m_inv = -1.0 / c4 * (m3 + c1 * m2 + c2 * m + c3 * I)
        vbroadcastsd ymm14,xmm14            ;ymm14 = packed c3
        lea     rdi,[Mat4x4I]               ;rcx = I ptr
        vmulpd  ymm0,ymm14,[rdi]
        vmulpd  ymm1,ymm14,[rdi+32]
        vmulpd  ymm2,ymm14,[rdi+64]
        vmulpd  ymm3,ymm14,[rdi+96]         ;c3 * I

        vbroadcastsd ymm13,xmm13            ;ymm13 = packed c2
        mov     rdi,[rsp+Offset_m]          ;rcx = m ptr
        vfmadd231pd ymm0,ymm13,[rdi]
        vfmadd231pd ymm1,ymm13,[rdi+32]
        vfmadd231pd ymm2,ymm13,[rdi+64]
        vfmadd231pd ymm3,ymm13,[rdi+96]     ;c2 * m + c3 * I

        vbroadcastsd ymm12,xmm12            ;xmm12 = packed c1
        lea     rdi,[rsp+OffsetM2]          ;rcx = m2 ptr
        vfmadd231pd ymm0,ymm12,[rdi]
        vfmadd231pd ymm1,ymm12,[rdi+32]
        vfmadd231pd ymm2,ymm12,[rdi+64]
        vfmadd231pd ymm3,ymm12,[rdi+96]     ;c1 * m2 + c2 * m + c3 * I

        lea     rdi,[rsp+OffsetM3]          ;rcx = m3 ptr
        vaddpd  ymm0,ymm0,[rdi]
        vaddpd  ymm1,ymm1,[rdi+32]
        vaddpd  ymm2,ymm2,[rdi+64]
        vaddpd  ymm3,ymm3,[rdi+96]          ;m3 + c1 * m2 + c2 * m + c3 * I

        vmovsd  xmm4,[F64_N1p0]
        vdivsd  xmm4,xmm4,xmm15             ;xmm4 = -1.0 / c4
        vbroadcastsd ymm4,xmm4
        vmulpd  ymm0,ymm0,ymm4
        vmulpd  ymm1,ymm1,ymm4
        vmulpd  ymm2,ymm2,ymm4
        vmulpd  ymm3,ymm3,ymm4              ;ymm0:ymm3 = m_inv
```

473

```
; Save m_inv
        mov rdi,[rsp+Offset_m_inv]
        vmovapd [rdi],ymm0                  ;save m_inv[0][]
        vmovapd [rdi+32],ymm1               ;save m_inv[1][]
        vmovapd [rdi+64],ymm2               ;save m_inv[2][]
        vmovapd [rdi+96],ymm3               ;save m_inv[3][]

        mov eax,1                           ;set non-singular return code

Done:   vzeroupper
        mov rsp,rbp
        pop rbp
        ret

IsSing: xor eax,eax                         ;set singular return code
        jmp Done
```

Source code examples Ch12_01 and Ch12_02 exemplify that with a little forethought, you can create single-precision and double-precision variants of the same calculating function with minimal differences. The results for example Ch12_02 are the same as the results for example Ch12_01.

Table 12-2 shows the benchmark timing measurements for example Ch12_02. Like example Ch12_01, the assembly language double-precision 4 × 4 matrix inverse functions significantly outperform their C++ counterpart functions.

Table 12-2. *Benchmark Timing Measurements (Microseconds) for Matrix (4 × 4) Inverse Functions (100,000 Inverse Operations)*

Function	i5-11600K	i7-11700K	7700X
Mat4x4InvF64_cpp()	10603 (119)	18124 (570)	6823 (38)
Mat4x4InvF64_avx2()	1771 (18)	1818 (33)	1723 (9)

Signal Processing – Convolutions

A convolution is a mathematical operation that blends an input signal with a response signal to produce an output signal. Convolutions are used extensively in a wide variety of scientific and engineering applications. Convolution theory forms the basis for many signal processing and image processing methods. In this section, you'll learn the essentials of 1D convolution mathematics. The purpose of this section is to provide just enough background math to understand the convolution source code examples presented later in this chapter. Numerous books have been published that explain convolution, signal processing, and image processing theory in significantly greater detail. Appendix B contains a list of references that you can consult for additional information regarding these topics.

1D Convolution Arithmetic

The 1D convolution of an input signal x and a response signal g is defined as follows:

$$y(t) = \int_{-\infty}^{\infty} x(t-\tau)g(\tau)\,d\tau$$

where y represents the output signal. The notation $x * g$ is commonly used to denote the convolution of signals (or functions) x and g.

In computer software, an array of sampled data points is frequently employed to represent the input, response, and output signals. A 1D discrete convolution can be calculated using the following equation:

$$y[i] = \sum_{k=-M}^{M} x[i-k]g[k]$$

where $i = 0, 1, \cdots, N-1$ and $M = floor(N_g/2)$. In the preceding equations, N denotes the number of elements in the input and output signal arrays, and N_g symbolizes the number of elements in the response array. The discussions and source code examples in this chapter assume that N_g is an odd integer greater than or equal to three. If you examine the 1D discrete convolution equation carefully, you'll notice that each element of the output signal array y is computed using a basic sum-of-products calculation that encompasses the input signal x and the response signal g. As you have already seen, these types of operations are easy to implement using FMA instructions.

In digital signal processing, many applications use smoothing operators to reduce the amount of noise present in a raw data signal. For example, the top plot of Figure 12-4 shows a raw data signal that contains a fair amount of noise. The bottom plot of Figure 12-4 shows the same signal following the application of a smoothing operator. In this example, the smoothing operator convolved the original raw signal array with a set of discrete coefficients that approximate a low-pass (or Gaussian) filter. These coefficients correspond to the response signal array g that's shown in the discrete 1D convolution equation. The response signal array is often called a convolution kernel or convolution mask. This book uses the term convolution kernel to avoid any potential confusion with a Boolean or SIMD programming mask.

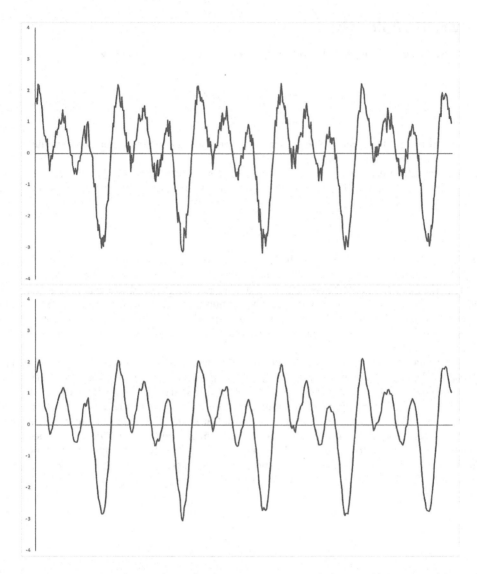

Figure 12-4. *Raw data signal (top plot) and its smoothed counterpart (bottom plot)*

The 1D discrete convolution equation can be implemented in source code using a couple of nested for-loops. During each outer loop iteration, the convolution kernel center point g[0] is superimposed over the current input signal array element x[i]. The inner for-loop calculates the intermediate products as shown in Figure 12-5. These intermediate products are then summed and saved to output signal array element y[i].

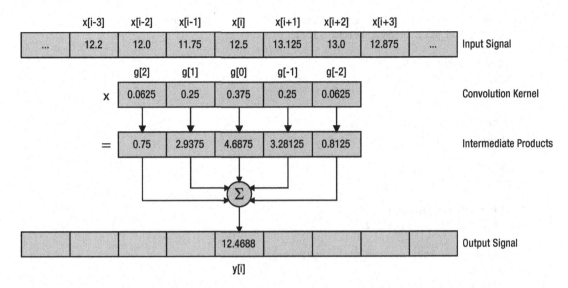

Figure 12-5. *Calculation of 1D discrete convolution output signal element*

The remaining sections of this chapter contain source code examples that illustrate 1D convolutions. The first two examples cover 1D convolutions using variable-size kernels. The next two examples are similar but employ fixed-size kernels, which often yield better performance as you'll soon see.

1D Convolution Using Variable-Size Kernel

In this section, you'll examine two source code examples that carry out 1D discrete convolution calculations. The first example performs a 1D discrete convolution using single-precision AVX2 and FMA instructions, while the second example uses double-precision instructions.

Single-Precision

Listing 12-3a shows the principal C++ code for example Ch12_03. In this listing, function Convolve1D_F32_cpp() computes a 1D discrete convolution using input signal x and convolution kernel signal kernel. Function Convolve1D_F32_cpp() begins its execution with a series of statements that validate kernel_size and num_pts. Recall from the earlier discussions that kernel_size must be an odd integer greater than or equal to three. Also, num_pts must be greater than or equal to kernel_size. Note that for many real-world signal processing applications, arrays x and y often contain thousands or millions of elements, while the size of the convolution kernel is often much smaller.

Listing 12-3a. Example Ch12_03 C++ Code

```
//-----------------------------------------------------------------------------
// Ch12_03_fcpp.cpp
//-----------------------------------------------------------------------------

#include "Ch12_03.h"
```

```
bool Convolve1D_F32_cpp(float* y, const float* x, const float* kernel,
        int64_t num_pts, int64_t kernel_size)
{
    // Validate arguments
    if (kernel_size < 3)
        return false;

    if ((kernel_size & 1) == 0)
        return false;

    if (num_pts < kernel_size)
        return false;

    // Perform 1D convolution
    int64_t ks2 = kernel_size / 2;

    for (int64_t i = ks2; i < num_pts - ks2; i++)
    {
        float y_val = 0.0f;

        for (int64_t k = -ks2; k <= ks2; k++)
            y_val += x[i - k] * kernel[k + ks2];

        y[i] = y_val;
    }

    return true;
}
```

The remaining code in Listing 12-3a computes a 1D convolution using a pair of nested for-loops. In the inner for-loop, note that index variable k ranges from -ks2 to ks2. This is the index variable of the 1D discrete convolution equation imparted earlier in this chapter.

Listing 12-3b shows the MASM code for example Ch12_03. The code in this listing opens with a series of equate statements that define symbolic names for assembly language function Convolve1D_F32_avx2(). The symbols NSE (eight) and NSE2 (four) represent sizes for SIMD arithmetic, while SF (four) is the scale factor for a single-precision floating-point element. Using equates for these values minimizes code differences between function Convolve1D_F32_avx2() and its double-precision floating-point counterpart that you'll see later in this chapter.

Listing 12-3b. Example Ch12_03 MASM Code

```
;-----------------------------------------------------------------------------
; Ch12_03_fasm.asm
;-----------------------------------------------------------------------------

            include <MacrosX86-64-AVX.asmh>

;-----------------------------------------------------------------------------
; bool Convolve1D_F32_avx2(float* y, const float* x, const float* kernel,
;   int64_t num_pts, int64_t kernel_size);
;-----------------------------------------------------------------------------
```

```
NSE       equ 8                           ;num_simd_elements
NSE2      equ 4                           ;num_simd_elements2
SF        equ 4                           ;scale factor for F32 elements


          .code
Convolve1D_F32_avx2 proc frame
          CreateFrame_M CV_,0,0,rbx,rsi,rdi,r12,r13
          EndProlog_M

; Validate arguments
          mov r10,[rbp+CV_OffsetStackArgs]      ;r10 = kernel_size (ks)
          cmp r10,3
          jl BadArg                             ;jump if ks < 3
          test r10,1
          jz BadArg                             ;jump if ks is even
          cmp r9,r10
          jl BadArg                             ;jump if num_pts < ks

; Initialize
          mov r11,r10                           ;r11 = ks
          shr r11,1                             ;r11 = ks2
          mov rsi,r9                            ;rsi = num_pts
          sub rsi,r11                           ;rsi = num_pts - ks2
          mov rdi,r11
          neg rdi                               ;rdi = -ks2
          mov rax,r11                           ;i = ks2

          jmp F1                                ;begin execution of Loop1a

;-----------------------------------------------------------------------------
; General-purpose registers used in code below:
;    rax    i                    r8     kernel
;    rbx    k                    r9     num_pts
;    rcx    y array              r10    kernel_size
;    rdx    x array              r11    ks2
;    rsi    num_pts - ks2        r12    scratch
;    rdi    -ks2                 r13    scratch
;-----------------------------------------------------------------------------

; Calculate y[i:i+NSE-1]
Loop1a: mov rbx,rdi                             ;k = -ks2
        vxorps ymm0,ymm0,ymm0                   ;y[i:i+NSE-1] = 0

        align 16
Loop1b: mov r12,rax                             ;r12 = i
        sub r12,rbx                             ;r12 = i - k
        lea r13,[rbx+r11]                       ;r13 = k + ks2

        vbroadcastss ymm2,real4 ptr [r8+r13*SF] ;ymm2 = kernel[k+ks2]
        vfmadd231ps ymm0,ymm2, [rdx+r12*SF]     ;update y[i:i+NSE-1]
```

```
        add rbx,1                               ;k += 1
        cmp rbx,r11
        jle Loop1b                              ;jump if k <= ks2

        vmovups [rcx+rax*SF],ymm0               ;save y[i:i+NSE-1]
        add rax,NSE                             ;i += NSE

F1:     lea r12,[rax+NSE]                       ;r12 = i + NSE
        cmp r12,rsi
        jle Loop1a                              ;jump if i + NSE <= num_pts - ks2

        jmp F2                                  ;begin execution of Loop2a

; Calculate y[i:i+NSE2-1]
Loop2a: mov rbx,rdi                             ;k = -ks2
        vxorps xmm0,xmm0,xmm0                   ;y[i:i+NSE2-1] = 0

        align 16
Loop2b: mov r12,rax                             ;r12 = i
        sub r12,rbx                             ;r12 = i - k
        lea r13,[rbx+r11]                       ;r13 = k + ks2

        vbroadcastss xmm2,real4 ptr [r8+r13*SF] ;xmm2 = kernel[k+ks2]
        vfmadd231ps xmm0,xmm2,[rdx+r12*SF]      ;update y[i:i+NSE2-1]

        add rbx,1                               ;k += 1
        cmp rbx,r11
        jle Loop2b                              ;jump if k <= ks2

        vmovups [rcx+rax*SF],xmm0               ;save y[i:i+NSE2-1]
        add rax,NSE2                            ;i += NSE2

F2:     lea r12,[rax+NSE2]                      ;r12 = i + NSE2
        cmp r12,rsi
        jle Loop2a                              ;jump if i + NSE2 <= num_pts - ks2

        jmp F3                                  ;begin execution of Loop3a

; Calculate y[i]
Loop3a: mov rbx,rdi                             ;k = -ks2
        vxorps xmm0,xmm0,xmm0                   ;y[i] = 0

        align 16
Loop3b: mov r12,rax                             ;r12 = i
        sub r12,rbx                             ;r12 = i - k
        lea r13,[rbx+r11]                       ;r13 = k + ks2

        vmovss xmm2,real4 ptr [r8+r13*SF]       ;xmm2 = kernel[k+ks2]
        vfmadd231ss xmm0,xmm2,[rdx+r12*SF]      ;update y[i]
```

```
        add rbx,1                           ;k += 1
        cmp rbx,r11
        jle Loop3b                          ;jump if k <= ks2

        vmovss real4 ptr [rcx+rax*SF],xmm0   ;save y[i]
        add rax,1                           ;i += 1

F3:     cmp rax,rsi
        jl Loop3a                           ;jump if i < num_pts - ks2

        mov eax,1                           ;set success return code

Done:   vzeroupper
        DeleteFrame_M rbx,rsi,rdi,r12,r13
        ret

BadArg: xor eax,eax                         ;set error return code
        jmp Done


Convolve1D_F32_avx2 endp
        end
```

Following its prologue, Convolve1D_F32_avx2() performs the same argument validation checks that were performed in function Convolve1D_F32_cpp(). Note that argument value kernel_size (ks) was passed via the stack. Following argument validation is a code block that performs the requisite register initializations.

Function Convolve1D_F32_avx2() computes a 1D discrete convolution using FMA instructions. Recall that a YMM register can hold eight single-precision floating-point values. This facilitates a SIMD implementation of the convolution algorithm that can process eight input signal points simultaneously. Figure 12-6 contains a graphic that illustrates a five-element convolution kernel along with an arbitrary segment of an input signal. Shown below the graphic are the equations that calculate output signal elements y[i:i+NSE-1]. These equations are a simple expansion of the 1D discrete convolution equation that you saw earlier in this chapter. Note that each column of the SIMD convolution equation set includes a single kernel value and eight consecutive elements from the input signal array. These equations can be implemented in code using FMA instructions that you have already seen.

Convolution kernel

g[-2]	g[-1]	g[0]	g[1]	g[2]

Input signal array

...	x[i-2]	x[i-1]	x[i]	x[i+1]	x[i+2]	x[i+3]	x[i+4]	x[i+5]	x[i+6]	x[i+7]	x[i+8]	x[i+9]	...

SIMD convolution equations (8 signal points)

```
y[i+0] = g[-2]x[i+2] + g[-1]x[i+1] + g[0]x[i+0] + g[1]x[i-1] + g[2]x[i-2]
y[i+1] = g[-2]x[i+3] + g[-1]x[i+2] + g[0]x[i+1] + g[1]x[i+0] + g[2]x[i-1]
y[i+2] = g[-2]x[i+4] + g[-1]x[i+3] + g[0]x[i+2] + g[1]x[i+1] + g[2]x[i+0]
y[i+3] = g[-2]x[i+5] + g[-1]x[i+4] + g[0]x[i+3] + g[1]x[i+2] + g[2]x[i+1]
y[i+4] = g[-2]x[i+6] + g[-1]x[i+5] + g[0]x[i+4] + g[1]x[i+3] + g[2]x[i+2]
y[i+5] = g[-2]x[i+7] + g[-1]x[i+6] + g[0]x[i+5] + g[1]x[i+4] + g[2]x[i+3]
y[i+6] = g[-2]x[i+8] + g[-1]x[i+7] + g[0]x[i+6] + g[1]x[i+5] + g[2]x[i+4]
y[i+7] = g[-2]x[i+9] + g[-1]x[i+8] + g[0]x[i+7] + g[1]x[i+6] + g[2]x[i+5]
```

Consecutive input signal array elements

Figure 12-6. *SIMD 1D discrete convolution equations for a five-element convolution kernel*

The convolution calculating code in function Convolve1D_F32_avx2() is partitioned into three distinct sections. The first section consists of outer for-loop Loop1a and inner for-loop Loop1b. These two for-loops carry out the same calculation that you saw in function Convolve1D_F32_cpp(). Note that Loop1b employs packed FMA arithmetic and 256-bit wide (YMM register) operands to calculate output signal elements y[i:i+NSE-1] using input signal elements x[i:i+NSE-1]. Execution of for-loop pair Loop1a and Loop1b continues until i + NSE <= num_pts - ks2 is false.

The second calculating section of function Convolve1D_F32_avx2() mimics the first section but carries out its calculations using 128-bit wide (XMM register) operands. Note that for-loops Loop2a and Loop2b calculate output signal elements y[i:i+NSE2-1]. Also note that Convolve1D_F32_avx2() utilizes the vmovups instruction to perform packed floating-point loads and stores since proper alignment of each SIMD element group is not guaranteed. Execution of for-loop pair Loop2a and Loop2b continues until i + NSE2 <= num_pts - ks2 is false. The final calculation section of function Convolve1D_F32_avx2() employs scalar FMA arithmetic to process any remaining convolution signal points.

The NASM code for function Convolve1D_F32_avx2() closely resembles the MASM code that's shown in Listing 12-3a except for minor differences in the function prologue and epilogue. Here are the results for source code example Ch12_03:

```
----- Results for Ch12_03 -----

Executing Convolve1D_F32()
Calculated results saved to file @Ch12_03_Convolve1D_F32_Output_HELIUM.csv

Running benchmark function Convolve1D_F32_bm() - please wait
Benchmark times saved to file @Ch12_03_Convolve1D_F32_bm_HELIUM.csv
```

Table 12-3 shows the benchmark timing measurements for example Ch12_03. These measurements were made using an input signal array containing 2,500,000 elements and a five-element convolution kernel.

Table 12-3. *Benchmark Timing Measurements (Microseconds) for 1D Discrete Convolution Functions (Single-Precision)*

Function	i5-11600K	i7-11700K	7700X
Convolve1D_F32_cpp()	4765 (8)	5726 (95)	3169 (6)
Convolve1D_F32_avx2()	1034 (8)	890 (26)	482 (3)

Double-Precision

The next source code example, named Ch12_04, demonstrates a 1D discrete convolution using double-precision floating-point elements. The C++ code for function Convolve1D_F64_cpp() is basically the same as the code that's shown for function Convolve1D_F32_cpp() in Listing 12-3a, except that the former utilizes the C++ data type double instead of float.

Listing 12-4 shows the MASM code for function Convolve1D_F64_avx2(). There are only a few minor variances between this function and its single-precision counterpart function that's shown in Listing 12-3b. The first item of note are values for equates NSE, NSE2, and SF. These values have been changed to support signal arrays containing double-precision floating-point values. The second modification is the use of double-precision instead of single-precision AVX2 and FMA instructions.

Listing 12-4. Example Ch12_04 MASM Code

```
;------------------------------------------------------------------------
; Ch12_04_fasm.asm
;------------------------------------------------------------------------

        include <MacrosX86-64-AVX.asmh>


;------------------------------------------------------------------------
; bool Convolve1D_F64_avx2(double* y, const double* x, const double* kernel,
;   int64_t num_pts, int64_t kernel_size);
;------------------------------------------------------------------------

NSE     equ 4                           ;num_simd_elements
NSE2    equ 2                           ;num_simd_elements2
SF      equ 8                           ;scale factor for F64 elements

        .code
Convolve1D_F64_avx2 proc frame
        CreateFrame_M CV_,0,0,rbx,rsi,rdi,r12,r13
        EndProlog_M

; Validate arguments
        mov r10,[rbp+CV_OffsetStackArgs]        ;r10 = kernel_size (ks)
        cmp r10,3
        jl BadArg                               ;jump if ks < 3
        test r10,1
```

```
            jz BadArg                               ;jump if ks is even
            cmp r9,r10
            jl BadArg                               ;jump if num_pts < ks

; Initialize
            mov r11,r10                             ;r11 = ks
            shr r11,1                               ;r11 = ks2
            mov rsi,r9                              ;rsi = num_pts
            sub rsi,r11                             ;rsi = num_pts - ks2
            mov rdi,r11
            neg rdi                                 ;rdi = -ks2
            mov rax,r11                             ;i = ks2

            jmp F1                                  ;begin execution of Loop1a

;-------------------------------------------------------------------------
; General-purpose registers used in code below:
;    rax     i                   r8      kernel
;    rbx     k                   r9      num_pts
;    rcx     y array             r10     kernel_size
;    rdx     x array             r11     ks2
;    rsi     num_pts - ks2       r12     scratch
;    rdi     -ks2                r13     scratch
;-------------------------------------------------------------------------

; Calculate y[i:i+NSE-1]
Loop1a: mov rbx,rdi                                 ;k = -ks2
            vxorpd ymm0,ymm0,ymm0                   ;y[i:i+NSE-1] = 0

            align 16
Loop1b: mov r12,rax                                 ;r12 = i
            sub r12,rbx                             ;r12 = i - k
            lea r13,[rbx+r11]                       ;r13 = k + ks2

            vbroadcastsd ymm2,real8 ptr [r8+r13*SF] ;ymm2 = kernel[k+ks2]
            vfmadd231pd ymm0,ymm2,[rdx+r12*SF]      ;update y[i:i+NSE-1]

            add rbx,1                               ;k += 1
            cmp rbx,r11
            jle Loop1b                              ;jump if k <= ks2

            vmovupd [rcx+rax*SF],ymm0               ;save y[i:i+NSE-1]
            add rax,NSE                             ;i += NSE

F1:         lea r12,[rax+NSE]                       ;r12 = i + NSE
            cmp r12,rsi
            jle Loop1a                              ;jump if i + NSE <= num_pts - ks2

            jmp F2                                  ;begin execution of Loop2a
```

```
; Calculate y[i:i+NSE2-1]
Loop2a: mov rbx,rdi                              ;k = -ks2
        vxorpd xmm0,xmm0,xmm0                     ;y[i:i+NSE2-1] = 0

        align 16
Loop2b: mov r12,rax                               ;r12 = i
        sub r12,rbx                               ;r12 = i - k
        lea r13,[rbx+r11]                         ;r13 = k + ks2

        vmovddup xmm2,real8 ptr [r8+r13*SF]       ;xmm2 = kernel[k+ks2]
        vfmadd231pd xmm0,xmm2,[rdx+r12*SF]        ;update y[i:i+NSE2-1]

        add rbx,1                                 ;k += 1
        cmp rbx,r11
        jle Loop2b                                ;jump if k <= ks2

        vmovupd [rcx+rax*SF],xmm0                 ;save y[i:i+NSE2-1]
        add rax,NSE2                              ;i += NSE2

F2:     lea r12,[rax+NSE2]                        ;r12 = i + NSE2
        cmp r12,rsi
        jle Loop2a                                ;jump if i + NSE2 <= num_pts - ks2

        jmp F3                                    ;begin execution of Loop3a

; Calculate y[i]
Loop3a: mov rbx,rdi                               ;k = -ks2
        vxorpd xmm0,xmm0,xmm0                     ;y[i] = 0

        align 16
Loop3b: mov r12,rax                               ;r12 = i
        sub r12,rbx                               ;r12 = i - k
        lea r13,[rbx+r11]                         ;r13 = k + ks2

        vmovsd xmm2,real8 ptr [r8+r13*SF]         ;xmm2 = kernel[k+ks2]
        vfmadd231sd xmm0,xmm2,[rdx+r12*SF]        ;update y[i]

        add rbx,1                                 ;k += 1
        cmp rbx,r11
        jle Loop3b                                ;jump if k <= ks2

        vmovsd real8 ptr [rcx+rax*SF],xmm0        ;save y[i]
        add rax,1                                 ;i += 1

F3:     cmp rax,rsi
        jl Loop3a                                 ;jump if i < num_pts - ks2

        mov eax,1                                 ;set success return code
```

485

```
Done:   vzeroupper
        DeleteFrame_M rbx,rsi,rdi,r12,r13
        ret

BadArg: xor eax,eax                              ;set error return code
        jmp Done

Convolve1D_F64_avx2 endp
        end
```

The final code modification is located in for-loop Loop2b. Note the use of the instruction vmovddup xmm2,real8 ptr [r8+r13*SF] (Replicate Double-Precision Floating-Point Values). Execution of this instruction broadcasts convolution kernel element kernel[k+ks2] to both double-precision element positions of register XMM2. The vmovddup instruction is used here since the AVX2 vbroadcastsd instruction does not support an XMM register destination operand.

Except for a few mov instructions that rearrange argument register values, the NASM code for function Convolve1D_F64_avx2() is fundamentally the same as the MASM code that's shown in Listing 12-4. Source code examples Ch12_03 and Ch12_04 exemplify again that with a little planning, you can create single-precision and double-precision variants of the same assembly language calculating function with minimal code differences. This strategy also applies to the coding of both MASM and NASM variants. The results for example Ch12_04 are the same as the results for example Ch12_03, albeit with a little extra precision.

Table 12-4 shows the benchmark timing measurements for example Ch12_04. These measurements were made using an input signal array containing 2,500,000 elements and a five-element convolution kernel.

Table 12-4. Benchmark Timing Measurements (Microseconds) for 1D Discrete Convolution Functions (Double-Precision)

Function	i5-11600K	i7-11700K	7700X
Convolve1D_F64_cpp()	4499 (9)	5769 (102)	2751 (6)
Convolve1D_F64_avx2()	2124 (23)	1770 (40)	1023 (4)

1D Convolution Using Fixed-Size Kernel

The convolution functions of examples Ch12_03 and Ch12_04 carry out their calculations using a variable-size convolution kernel. Many real-world signal processing libraries include convolution functions that are optimized for specific kernel sizes. Size-optimized convolution functions are often faster than their variable-size counterparts as you'll soon see. The first source code example of this section explains how to code a single-precision 1D discrete convolution for a fixed five-element kernel. The second source code example elucidates a double-precision 1D discrete convolution using a five-element convolution kernel.

Single-Precision

Listing 12-5a shows the principal C++ code for example Ch12_05. This listing contains the source code for function Convolve1D_Ks5_F32_cpp(), which computes a 1D discrete convolution using a five-element convolution kernel. Note that function Convolve1D_Ks5_F32_cpp() employs C++ specifier constexpr in the definitions of variables kernel_size and ks2. Using the constexpr specifier (when appropriate) often enables a C++ compiler to generate more efficient code.

Listing 12-5a. Example Ch12_05 C++ Code

```cpp
//------------------------------------------------------------------------------
// Ch12_05_fcpp.cpp
//------------------------------------------------------------------------------

#include "Ch12_05.h"

bool Convolve1D_Ks5_F32_cpp(float* y, const float* x, const float* kernel,
    int64_t num_pts)
{
    constexpr int64_t kernel_size = 5;
    constexpr int64_t ks2 = kernel_size / 2;

    if (num_pts < kernel_size)
        return false;

    // Perform 1D convolution
    for (int64_t i = ks2; i < num_pts - ks2; i++)
    {
        float y_val = 0.0f;

        for (int64_t k = -ks2; k <= ks2; k++)
            y_val += x[i - k] * kernel[k + ks2];

        y[i] = y_val;
    }

    return true;
}
```

Listing 12-5b shows the MASM code for function Convolve1D_Ks5_F32_avx2(). The primary difference between this code and the code for function Convolve1D_F32_avx2() in Listing 12-3b is that the inner for-loops (Loop1b, Loop2b, and Loop3b) of the latter have been removed and replaced with explicit sequences of vmulps and vfmadd231ps instructions. This complete unrolling of the inner for-loops in Convolve1D_Ks5_F32_avx2() is possible since it always performs its calculations using a five-element convolution kernel.

Listing 12-5b. Example Ch12_05 MASM Code

```asm
;------------------------------------------------------------------------------
; Ch12_05_fasm.asm
;------------------------------------------------------------------------------

            include <MacrosX86-64-AVX.asmh>

;------------------------------------------------------------------------------
; bool Convolve1D_Ks5_F32_avx2(float* y, const float* x, const float* kernel,
;    int64_t num_pts);
;------------------------------------------------------------------------------
```

```
NSE        equ      8                          ;num_simd_elements
NSE2       equ      4                          ;num_simd_elements2
KS         equ      5                          ;kernel_size
KS2        equ      2                          ;floor(kernel_size / 2)
SF         equ      4                          ;scale factor for F32 elements

           .code
Convolve1D_Ks5_F32_avx2 proc frame
           CreateFrame_M CV5_,0,0,rsi
           EndProlog_M

; Validate arguments
           cmp r9,KS
           jl BadArg                           ;jump if num_pts < KS

; Initialize
           mov rax,KS2                         ;i = ks2
           mov r10,r9                          ;r10 = num_pts
           sub r10,KS2                         ;r10 = num_pts - KS2

           vbroadcastss ymm0,real4 ptr [r8]     ;ymm0 = packed kernel[0]
           vbroadcastss ymm1,real4 ptr [r8+4]   ;ymm1 = packed kernel[1]
           vbroadcastss ymm2,real4 ptr [r8+8]   ;ymm2 = packed kernel[2]
           vbroadcastss ymm3,real4 ptr [r8+12]  ;ymm3 = packed kernel[3]
           vbroadcastss ymm4,real4 ptr [r8+16]  ;ymm4 = packed kernel[4]

           jmp F1                              ;begin execution of Loop1

;------------------------------------------------------------------------------
; General-purpose registers used in code below:
;    rax      i                  r8       kernel
;    rcx      y array            r9       num_pts
;    rdx      x array            r10      num_pts - KS2
;    rsi      scratch            r11      k
;------------------------------------------------------------------------------

; Calculate y[i:i+NSE-1]
           align 16
Loop1:     lea r11,[rax+KS2]                   ;k = i + KS2

           vmulps ymm5,ymm0,[rdx+r11*SF]        ;kernel[0] * x[k:k+NSE-1]
           vfmadd231ps ymm5,ymm1,[rdx+r11*SF-4] ;kernel[1] * x[k-1:k-1+NSE-1]
           vfmadd231ps ymm5,ymm2,[rdx+r11*SF-8] ;kernel[2] * x[k-2:k-2+NSE-1]
           vfmadd231ps ymm5,ymm3,[rdx+r11*SF-12];kernel[3] * x[k-3:k-3+NSE-1]
           vfmadd231ps ymm5,ymm4,[rdx+r11*SF-16];kernel[4] * x[k-4:k-4+NSE-1]

           vmovups [rcx+rax*SF],ymm5            ;save y[i:i+NSE-1]
           add rax,NSE                          ;i += NSE
```

```
F1:     lea rsi,[rax+NSE]                       ;rsi = i + NSE
        cmp rsi,r10                             ;i + NSE <= num_pts - ks2?
        jle Loop1                               ;jump if yes

        jmp F2                                  ;begin execution of Loop2

; Calculate y[i:i+NSE2-1]
Loop2:  lea r11,[rax+KS2]                       ;k = i + KS2

        vmulps xmm5,xmm0,[rdx+r11*SF]           ;kernel[0] * x[k:k+NSE2-1]
        vfmadd231ps xmm5,xmm1,[rdx+r11*SF-4]    ;kernel[1] * x[k-1:k-1+NSE2-1]
        vfmadd231ps xmm5,xmm2,[rdx+r11*SF-8]    ;kernel[2] * x[k-2:k-2+NSE2-1]
        vfmadd231ps xmm5,xmm3,[rdx+r11*SF-12]   ;kernel[3] * x[k-3:k-3+NSE2-1]
        vfmadd231ps xmm5,xmm4,[rdx+r11*SF-16]   ;kernel[4] * x[k-4:k-4+NSE2-1]

        vmovups [rcx+rax*SF],xmm5               ;save y[i:i+NSE2-1]
        add rax,NSE2                            ;i += NSE2

F2:     lea rsi,[rax+NSE2]                      ;rsi = i + NSE2
        cmp rsi,r10                             ;i + NSE2 <= num_pts - KS2?
        jle Loop2                               ;jump if yes

        jmp F3                                  ;begin execution of Loop3

; Calculate y[i]
Loop3:  lea r11,[rax+KS2]                       ;k = i + KS2

        vmulss xmm5,xmm0,real4 ptr [rdx+r11*SF] ;kernel[0] * x[k]
        vfmadd231ss xmm5,xmm1,[rdx+r11*SF-4]    ;kernel[1] * x[k-1]
        vfmadd231ss xmm5,xmm2,[rdx+r11*SF-8]    ;kernel[2] * x[k-2]
        vfmadd231ss xmm5,xmm3,[rdx+r11*SF-12]   ;kernel[3] * x[k-3]
        vfmadd231ss xmm5,xmm4,[rdx+r11*SF-16]   ;kernel[4] * x[k-4]

        vmovss real4 ptr [rcx+rax*SF],xmm5      ;save y[i]
        add rax,1                               ;i += 1

F3:     cmp rax,r10                             ;i < num_pts - KS2?
        jl Loop3                                ;jump if yes

        mov eax,1                               ;set success return code

Done:   vzeroupper
        DeleteFrame_M rsi
        ret

BadArg: xor eax,eax                             ;set error return code
        jmp Done

Convolve1D_Ks5_F32_avx2 endp
        end
```

The NASM code for example Ch12_05 corresponds to the MASM code except for a series of mov instructions that perform argument register rearrangement. The results for source code example Ch12_05 are identical to the results for example Ch12_03. Table 12-5 shows the benchmark timing measurements for example Ch12_05. Like example Ch12_03, these measurements were made using a 2,500,000-element input signal array. If you compare the benchmark timing measurements in Table 12-3 with those in Table 12-5, you'll notice that the fixed-size kernel functions (both C++ and assembly language) are appreciably faster than their variable-length counterparts.

Table 12-5. *Benchmark Timing Measurements (Microseconds) for 1D Discrete Convolution Functions (Single-Precision, Five-Element Convolution Kernel)*

Function	i5-11600K	i7-11700K	7700X
Convolve1D_Ks5_F32_cpp()	742 (4)	3618 (75)	272 (2)
Convolve1D_Ks5_F32_avx2()	657 (4)	623 (29)	268 (2)

Double-Precision

The final code example of this chapter, named Ch12_06, is the double-precision floating-point counterpart of example Ch12_05. Listing 12-6a shows the principal C++ code for this example. Note that in this listing, function Convolve1D_Ks5_F64_cpp() performs a 1D discrete convolution using double-precision floating-point signal arrays and a fixed five-element convolution kernel.

Listing 12-6a. Example Ch12_06 C++ Code

```
//------------------------------------------------------------------------
// Ch12_06_fcpp.cpp
//------------------------------------------------------------------------

#include "Ch12_06.h"

bool Convolve1D_Ks5_F64_cpp(double* y, const double* x, const double* kernel,
    int64_t num_pts)
{
    constexpr int64_t kernel_size = 5;
    constexpr int64_t ks2 = kernel_size / 2;

    if (num_pts < kernel_size)
        return false;

    // Perform 1D convolution
    for (int64_t i = ks2; i < num_pts - ks2; i++)
    {
        double y_val = 0.0;

        for (int64_t k = -ks2; k <= ks2; k++)
            y_val += x[i - k] * kernel[k + ks2];
```

```
        y[i] = y_val;
    }

    return true;
}
```

Listing 12-6b shows the MASM code for example Ch12_06. Note that the values for equate symbols NSE, NSE2, and SF have been adjusted for double-precision floating-point values.

Listing 12-6b. Example Ch12_06 MASM Code

```
;-------------------------------------------------------------------------------
; Ch12_06_fasm.asm
;-------------------------------------------------------------------------------

            include <MacrosX86-64-AVX.asmh>

;-------------------------------------------------------------------------------
; bool Convolve1D_Ks5_F64_avx2(double* y, const double* x, const double* kernel,
;    int64_t num_pts);
;-------------------------------------------------------------------------------

NSE     equ     4                       ;num_simd_elements
NSE2    equ     2                       ;num_simd_elements2
KS      equ     5                       ;kernel_size
KS2     equ     2                       ;floor(kernel_size / 2)
SF      equ     8                       ;scale factor for F64 elements

        .code
Convolve1D_Ks5_F64_avx2 proc frame
        CreateFrame_M CV5_,0,0,rsi
        EndProlog_M

; Validate arguments
        cmp r9,KS
        jl BadArg                       ;jump if num_pts < KS

; Initialize
        mov rax,KS2                     ;i = ks2
        mov r10,r9                      ;r10 = num_pts
        sub r10,KS2                     ;r10 = num_pts - KS2

        vbroadcastsd ymm0,real8 ptr [r8]        ;ymm0 = packed kernel[0]
        vbroadcastsd ymm1,real8 ptr [r8+8]      ;ymm1 = packed kernel[1]
        vbroadcastsd ymm2,real8 ptr [r8+16]     ;ymm2 = packed kernel[2]
        vbroadcastsd ymm3,real8 ptr [r8+24]     ;ymm3 = packed kernel[3]
        vbroadcastsd ymm4,real8 ptr [r8+32]     ;ymm4 = packed kernel[4]

        jmp F1                          ;begin execution of Loop1
```

```
;-------------------------------------------------------------------------------
; General-purpose registers used in code below:
;   rax     i                       r8      kernel
;   rcx     y array                 r9      num_pts
;   rdx     x array                 r10     num_pts - KS2
;   rsi     scratch                 r11     k
;-------------------------------------------------------------------------------

; Calculate y[i:i+NSE-1]
        align 16
Loop1:  lea r11,[rax+KS2]                        ;k = i + KS2

        vmulpd ymm5,ymm0,[rdx+r11*SF]            ;kernel[0] * x[k:k+NSE-1]
        vfmadd231pd ymm5,ymm1,[rdx+r11*SF-8]     ;kernel[1] * x[k-1:k-1+NSE-1]
        vfmadd231pd ymm5,ymm2,[rdx+r11*SF-16]    ;kernel[2] * x[k-2:k-2+NSE-1]
        vfmadd231pd ymm5,ymm3,[rdx+r11*SF-24]    ;kernel[3] * x[k-3:k-3+NSE-1]
        vfmadd231pd ymm5,ymm4,[rdx+r11*SF-32]    ;kernel[4] * x[k-4:k-4+NSE-1]

        vmovupd [rcx+rax*SF],ymm5                ;save y[i:i+NSE-1]
        add rax,NSE                              ;i += NSE

F1:     lea rsi,[rax+NSE]                        ;rsi = i + NSE
        cmp rsi,r10                              ;i + NSE <= num_pts - ks2?
        jle Loop1                                ;jump if yes

        jmp F2                                   ;begin execution of Loop2

; Calculate y[i:i+NSE2-1]
Loop2:  lea r11,[rax+KS2]                        ;k = i + KS2

        vmulpd xmm5,xmm0,[rdx+r11*SF]            ;kernel[0] * x[k:k+NSE2-1]
        vfmadd231pd xmm5,xmm1,[rdx+r11*SF-8]     ;kernel[1] * x[k-1:k-1+NSE2-1]
        vfmadd231pd xmm5,xmm2,[rdx+r11*SF-16]    ;kernel[2] * x[k-2:k-2+NSE2-1]
        vfmadd231pd xmm5,xmm3,[rdx+r11*SF-24]    ;kernel[3] * x[k-3:k-3+NSE2-1]
        vfmadd231pd xmm5,xmm4,[rdx+r11*SF-32]    ;kernel[4] * x[k-4:k-4+NSE2-1]

        vmovupd [rcx+rax*SF],xmm5                ;save y[i:i+NSE2-1]
        add rax,NSE2                             ;i += NSE2

F2:     lea rsi,[rax+NSE2]                       ;rsi = i + NSE2
        cmp rsi,r10                              ;i + NSE2 <= num_pts - KS2?
        jle Loop2                                ;jump if yes

        jmp F3                                   ;begin execution of Loop3

; Calculate y[i]
Loop3:  lea r11,[rax+KS2]                        ;k = i + KS2

        vmulsd xmm5,xmm0,real8 ptr [rdx+r11*SF]  ;kernel[0] * x[k]
        vfmadd231sd xmm5,xmm1,[rdx+r11*SF-8]     ;kernel[1] * x[k-1]
        vfmadd231sd xmm5,xmm2,[rdx+r11*SF-16]    ;kernel[2] * x[k-2]
```

```
        vfmadd231sd xmm5,xmm3,[rdx+r11*SF-24]    ;kernel[3] * x[k-3]
        vfmadd231sd xmm5,xmm4,[rdx+r11*SF-32]    ;kernel[4] * x[k-4]

        vmovsd real8 ptr [rcx+rax*SF],xmm5       ;save y[i]
        add rax,1                                 ;i += 1

F3:     cmp rax,r10                              ;i < num_pts - KS2?
        jl Loop3                                  ;jump if yes

        mov eax,1                                ;set success return code

Done:   vzeroupper
        DeleteFrame_M rsi
        ret

BadArg: xor eax,eax                              ;set error return code
        jmp Done

Convolve1D_Ks5_F64_avx2 endp
        end
```

Like the other source examples of this chapter, there are only minor differences between the MASM code for function Convolve1D_Ks5_F64_avx2() in Listing 12-6b and its NASM counterpart. The results for source code example Ch12_06 are the same as the results for example Ch12_04. Table 12-6 shows the benchmark timing measurements for example Ch12_06. These measurements were made using a 2,500,000-element input signal array. If you compare the benchmark timing measurements in Tables 12-4 and 12-6, you'll notice again that the fixed-size kernel functions are faster than their variable-length counterparts.

Table 12-6. *Benchmark Timing Measurements (Microseconds) for 1D Discrete Convolution Functions (Double-Precision, Five-Element Convolution Kernel)*

Function	i5-11600K	i7-11700K	7700X
Convolve1D_Ks5_F64_cpp()	1568 (21)	3718 (71)	766 (5)
Convolve1D_Ks5_F64_avx2()	1519 (20)	1408 (47)	759 (6)

Summary

Here are the key learning points for Chapter 12:

- X86-AVX instructions and SIMD programming techniques are often employed synergistically to accelerate the performance of algorithms that carry out complex operations using floating-point arrays and matrices.

- With a little bit of forethought and coding savvy, it is possible to minimize source code differences between assembly language functions that carry out computations using either single-precision or double-precision floating-point values.

- Source code differences between MASM and NASM calculating functions can be lessened by including a code block that exercises mov instructions to rearrange argument register values.

- The performance of signal processing (and similar) calculations can be improved by unrolling a for-loop that supports variable-length convolution kernels and replacing it with a series of instructions that implement a fixed-length convolution kernel.

CHAPTER 13

■ ■ ■

AVX-512 Programming – Packed Integers

AVX-512 is undoubtedly the largest and perhaps the most consequential extension of the x86 platform to date. It doubles the number of available SIMD registers and broadens the width of each register from 256 to 512 bits. AVX-512 also extends the instruction syntax of AVX and AVX2 to support additional capabilities not available in these earlier extensions including mask merging, zero merging, embedded broadcasts, and instruction-level rounding control for floating-point operations.

The chapter you are about to read introduces AVX-512 SIMD programming using packed integers. It begins with a brief overview of AVX-512 including its execution environment and extended instruction capabilities. This is followed by a section that explains basic packed integer arithmetic using 512-bit wide operands. The chapter concludes with a section that demonstrates a few integer-based image processing techniques using AVX-512.

AVX-512 Overview

AVX-512 is a collection of interrelated but distinct instruction set extensions. An AVX-512-compliant processor must minimally support the AVX-512 foundation (AVX512F) instruction set extension. This extension includes instructions that perform fundamental arithmetic using 512-bit wide operands of packed floating-point (single-precision or double-precision) or packed integer (32-bit or 64-bit) elements. The AVX512F extension also includes instructions that perform permutations, data conversions, and scatter operations (a scatter operation is the inverse of a gather operation).

Table 13-1 lists the AVX-512 instruction set extensions that have been incorporated into mainstream server, workstation, and high-end desktop processors from both AMD and Intel. Not listed in Table 13-1 are the AVX-512 instruction set extensions that are exclusive to specialized processors such as the Intel Xeon Phi. Like other x86 instruction set extensions such as AVX, AVX2, and FMA, a program must never assume that its host processor supports any of the AVX-512 instruction set extensions shown in Table 13-1 based on processor name, model number, or underlying microarchitecture. To ensure software compatibility with future processors, a program should always verify at run-time that any required AVX-512 instruction set extensions are available. You'll learn how to do this in Chapter 16.

© Daniel Kusswurm 2023
D. Kusswurm, *Modern X86 Assembly Language Programming*,
https://doi.org/10.1007/978-1-4842-9603-5_13

Table 13-1. *Overview of AVX-512 Instruction Set Extensions*

Extension Name (CPUID Flag)	Description
AVX512F	Foundation instructions
AVX512CD	Conflict detect instructions
AVX512DQ	Doubleword and quadword instructions
AVX512BW	Byte and word instructions
AVX512VL	128-bit and 256-bit vector length instructions
AVX512_IFMA	Integer fused-multiply-add
AVX512_VBMI	Vector byte manipulation instructions
AVX512_VNNI	Vector neural net instructions
AVX512_VPOPCNTDQ	Vector bit count instructions
AVX512_VBMI2	Vector byte manipulation instructions
AVX512_BITALG	Vector bit manipulation instructions
AVX512_BF16	Vector neural net instructions (BFLOAT16 format)
AVX512_VP2INTERSECT	Vector pair intersection instructions
AVX512_FP16	Vector and scalar half-precision floating-point (IEEE 754 format)

Execution Environment

AVX-512 augments the execution environments AVX and AVX2 with the addition of new registers and data types. It also extends the assembly language instruction syntax of AVX and AVX2 to support enhanced operations such as merging, embedded broadcasts, and instruction-level rounding control.

Figure 13-1 illustrates the AVX-512 register sets. AVX-512 extends the width of each AVX SIMD register from 256 bits to 512 bits. The 512-bit wide registers are known as the ZMM register set. AVX-512 conforming processors include 32 ZMM registers named ZMM0–ZMM31. The YMM and XMM register sets are aliased to the low-order 256 bits and 128 bits of each ZMM register, respectively. AVX-512 processors also include eight new opmask registers named K0–K7. These registers are primarily used as masks to perform merge masking and zero masking, which are described in the next section. They can also be employed as destination operands for SIMD compares and other instructions that generate mask results.

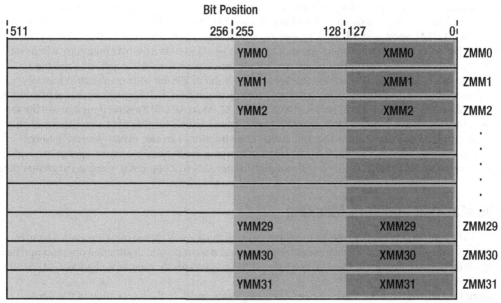

AVX-512 Register Set

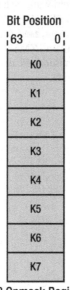

AVX-512 Opmask Register Set

Figure 13-1. *AVX-512 register sets*

The alignment requirements for 512-bit wide operands in memory are the same as the ones for 128-bit and 256-bit wide operands. Except for instructions that explicitly require an aligned operand (e.g., vmovdqa[32|64], vmovap[d|s], etc.), proper alignment of a 512-bit wide operand in memory is not mandatory. However, 512-bit wide operands should *always* be aligned on a 64-byte boundary whenever possible to avoid processing delays that might occur if the processor is forced to access an unaligned operand in memory. AVX-512 instructions that reference 128-bit or 256-bit wide operands in memory should also ensure that these SIMD value types are properly aligned on their respective natural boundaries.

AVX-512 extends the instruction syntax of AVX and AVX2. Most AVX-512 instructions can use the same three-operand instruction syntax as AVX and AVX2 instructions, which consists of two non-destructive source operands and one destination operand. AVX-512 instructions can also exploit several optional operands. These new operands facilitate SIMD element merging, embedded broadcast operations, and floating-point rounding control. The next few sections discuss AVX-512's optional operands in greater detail.

Merge Masking and Zero Masking

Most AVX-512 instructions support merge masking and zero masking. A merge masking operation uses the bits of an opmask register as a mask to control instruction execution and destination operand updates on a per-element basis. An instruction can use zero masking to set specific elements of an AVX-512 SIMD destination operand to zero.

Figure 13-2 illustrates these masking operations in greater detail. In the top portion of this figure, registers ZMM0, ZMM1, and ZMM2 each contain 16 single-precision floating-point values. Figure 13-2 also shows the 16 low-order bits of opmask register K1. Below opmask register K1 are three distinct executions of the AVX-512 instruction vaddps (Add Packed Single-Precision Floating-Point Values) using the displayed initial values. In the first example, the vaddps zmm2,zmm0,zmm1 instruction performs a packed single-precision floating-point add of the elements in ZMM0 and ZMM1 and saves the resultant sums in register ZMM2. Execution of this AVX-512 vaddps instruction is identical to the AVX vaddps instruction except that the former utilizes 512-bit wide ZMM register operands.

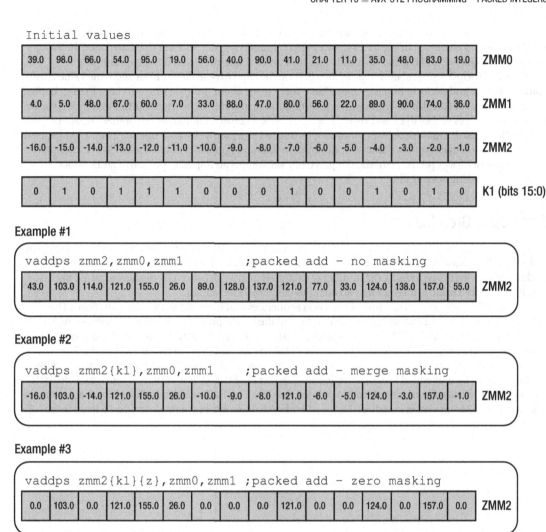

Figure 13-2. *Execution examples of the* vaddps *instruction using no masking, merge masking, and zero masking*

The next instruction in Figure 13-1, vaddps zmm2{k1},zmm0,zmm1, illustrates how the bits of opmask register K1 are used to perform conditional adds and updates of the destination operand on a per-element basis. More specifically, an element sum is calculated and saved in the destination operand only if the corresponding bit position of the opmask register is set to one; otherwise, the destination operand element position remains unchanged. This is called merge masking. The final example instruction in Figure 13-2, vaddps zmm2{k1}{z},zmm0,zmm1, is similar to the previous instruction. The extra {z} operand instructs the processor to perform zero masking instead of merge masking. Zero masking sets a destination operand element to zero if its corresponding bit position in the opmask register is set to zero; otherwise, the sum is calculated and saved.

At this point, a few more words about the opmask registers are necessary. The eight opmask registers are somewhat like the general-purpose registers. On processors that support AVX-512, each opmask register is 64 bits wide. However, when employed as a mask operand, only the low-order bits are used during instruction execution. The exact number of used low-order bits varies depending on the number of SIMD operand elements. In Figure 13-2, bits 0–15 of opmask register K1 form the mask since the vaddps instruction employs ZMM register operands that contain 16 single-precision floating-point values.

AVX-512 includes several new instructions that can be used to read values from and write values to an opmask register and perform Boolean operations. You'll learn about these instructions later in this chapter. An opmask register can also be employed as a destination operand with instructions that generate a vector mask result such as vcmpp[d|s] and vpcmp[b|w|d|q]. AVX-512 instructions can use opmask registers K1–K7 as a predicate mask. Opmask register K0 cannot be utilized as a predicate mask operand, but it can be used in any instruction that requires a source or destination operand opmask register. If an AVX-512 instruction attempts to use K0 as a predicate mask, the processor substitutes an implicit operand of all 1s, which disables all masking operations.

Embedded Broadcasts

Many AVX-512 instructions can carry out a SIMD computation using an embedded broadcast operand. An embedded broadcast operand is a memory-based scalar value that is replicated N times into a temporary packed value, where N represents the number of vector elements referenced by the instruction. This temporary packed value is then used as an operand in a SIMD calculation.

Figure 13-3 contains two example instruction sequences that illustrate broadcast operations. The first example uses the vbroadcastss instruction to load the single-precision floating-point constant 2.0 into each element position of ZMM1. The ensuing vmulps zmm2,zmm0,zmm1 instruction multiplies each single-precision floating-point element in register ZMM0 by 2.0 and saves the results to ZMM2. The second example instruction in Figure 13-3, vmulps zmm2,zmm0,real4 bcst [rax], carries out this same operation using an embedded broadcast operand. The text real4 bcst is a MASM directive that instructs the assembler to treat the memory location pointed to by register RAX as an embedded broadcast operand. NASM uses a different syntax and directive for an embedded broadcast operand, and you'll learn more about this later.

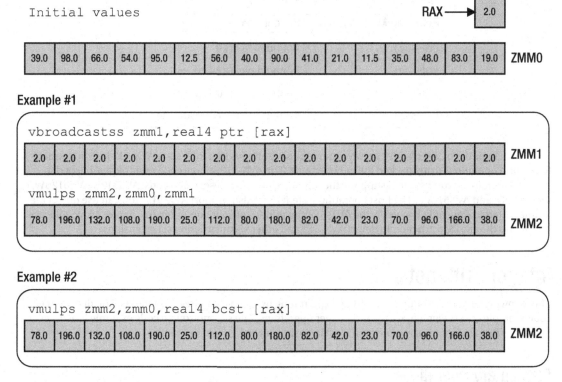

Figure 13-3. *Packed single-precision floating-point multiplication using the vbroadcastss and vmulps instructions vs. a vmulps instruction with an embedded broadcast operand*

AVX-512 supports embedded broadcast operations using 32-bit or 64-bit wide elements, both integer and floating-point. Embedded broadcasts cannot be performed using 8-bit or 16-bit wide elements.

Instruction-Level Rounding

The final AVX-512 instruction syntax enhancement involves instruction-level rounding control for floating-point operations. In Chapter 5, you learned how to use the vldmxcsr and vstmxcsr instructions to change the processor's global rounding mode for floating-point operations (see example Ch05_06). AVX-512 allows some instructions to specify a floating-point rounding mode operand that overrides the current rounding mode in MXCSR.RC. Table 13-2 shows the supported rounding mode operands, which are also called static rounding modes. The -sae suffix that's appended to each static rounding mode operand string is an acronym for suppress all exceptions. This suffix serves as a reminder that floating-point exceptions are always masked whenever a static rounding mode operand is specified; MXCSR flag updates are also disabled.

Table 13-2. *AVX-512 Instruction-Level Static Rounding Modes*

Rounding Mode Operand	Description
{rn-sae}	Round to nearest
{rd-sae}	Round down (toward $-\infty$)
{ru-sac}	Round up (toward $+\infty$)
{rz-sae}	Round toward zero (truncate)

The remainder of this chapter surveys source code examples that utilize the AVX-512 instruction set to perform operations using packed integer operands. The AVX-512 source code examples published in this book require a processor that supports the following instruction set extensions: AVX512F, AVX512BW, AVX512DQ, and AVX512VL. The host operating system must also support AVX-512. You can use one of the utilities listed in Appendix B to verify the AVX-512 capabilities of your computer. In Chapter 16, you'll learn how to use the cpuid instruction to detect AVX-512 and other x86 instruction set extensions.

Integer Arithmetic

The following section introduces AVX-512 programming using packed integer operands. The first source code example covers elementary packed integer operations. The second source code example illustrates how to perform merge masking and zero masking using packed integer operands.

Elementary Operations

Listing 13-1a shows the C++ source code for example Ch13_01. This example demonstrates basic packed integer arithmetic using AVX-512 instructions and 512-bit wide operands. Source code example Ch13_01 also highlights some minor differences between AVX/AVX2 and AVX-512 assembly language programming.

Listing 13-1a. Example Ch13_01 C++ Code

```
//-------------------------------------------------
//               ZmmVal.h
//-------------------------------------------------

#pragma once
#include <string>
#include <cstdint>
#include <sstream>
#include <iomanip>

struct alignas(64) ZmmVal
{
public:
    union
    {
        int8_t m_I8[64];
        int16_t m_I16[32];
        int32_t m_I32[16];
        int64_t m_I64[8];
```

```
        uint8_t m_U8[64];
        uint16_t m_U16[32];
        uint32_t m_U32[16];
        uint64_t m_U64[8];
        float m_F32[16];
        double m_F64[8];
    };

// ...

//----------------------------------------------------------------------
// Ch13_01.h
//----------------------------------------------------------------------

#pragma once
#include "ZmmVal.h"

// Ch13_01_fasm.asm, Ch13_01_fasm.s
extern "C" void MathI16_avx512(ZmmVal* c, const ZmmVal* a, const ZmmVal* b);
extern "C" void MathI64_avx512(ZmmVal* c, const ZmmVal* a, const ZmmVal* b);

//----------------------------------------------------------------------
// Ch13_01.cpp
//----------------------------------------------------------------------

#include <iostream>
#include <iomanip>
#include <string>
#include <cstddef>
#include "Ch13_01.h"

static void MathI16(void)
{
    ZmmVal a, b, c[6];

    a.m_I16[0] = 10;        b.m_I16[0] = 100;
    a.m_I16[1] = 20;        b.m_I16[1] = 200;
    a.m_I16[2] = 30;        b.m_I16[2] = 300;
    a.m_I16[3] = 40;        b.m_I16[3] = 400;
    a.m_I16[4] = 50;        b.m_I16[4] = 500;
    a.m_I16[5] = 60;        b.m_I16[5] = 600;
    a.m_I16[6] = 70;        b.m_I16[6] = 700;
    a.m_I16[7] = 80;        b.m_I16[7] = 800;

    a.m_I16[8] = 1000;      b.m_I16[8] = -100;
    a.m_I16[9] = 2000;      b.m_I16[9] = 200;
    a.m_I16[10] = 3000;     b.m_I16[10] = -300;
    a.m_I16[11] = 4000;     b.m_I16[11] = 400;
    a.m_I16[12] = 5000;     b.m_I16[12] = -500;
    a.m_I16[13] = 6000;     b.m_I16[13] = 600;
    a.m_I16[14] = 7000;     b.m_I16[14] = -700;
    a.m_I16[15] = 8000;     b.m_I16[15] = 800;
```

```cpp
    a.m_I16[16] = -1000;     b.m_I16[16] = 100;
    a.m_I16[17] = -2000;     b.m_I16[17] = -200;
    a.m_I16[18] = 3000;      b.m_I16[18] = 303;
    a.m_I16[19] = 4000;      b.m_I16[19] = -400;
    a.m_I16[20] = -5000;     b.m_I16[20] = 500;
    a.m_I16[21] = -6000;     b.m_I16[21] = -600;
    a.m_I16[22] = -7000;     b.m_I16[22] = 700;
    a.m_I16[23] = -8000;     b.m_I16[23] = 800;

    a.m_I16[24] = 30000;     b.m_I16[24] = 3000;      // add overflow
    a.m_I16[25] = 6000;      b.m_I16[25] = 32000;     // add overflow
    a.m_I16[26] = -25000;    b.m_I16[26] = -27000;    // add overflow
    a.m_I16[27] = 8000;      b.m_I16[27] = 28700;     // add overflow
    a.m_I16[28] = 2000;      b.m_I16[28] = -31000;    // sub overflow
    a.m_I16[29] = 4000;      b.m_I16[29] = -30000;    // sub overflow
    a.m_I16[30] = -3000;     b.m_I16[30] = 32000;     // sub overflow
    a.m_I16[31] = -15000;    b.m_I16[31] = 24000;     // sub overflow

    MathI16_avx512(c, &a, &b);

    std::cout << "\nMathI16_avx512() results:\n\n";
    std::cout << " i        a        b        add       adds       sub       subs";
    std::cout << "         min       max\n";
    std::cout << std::string(74, '-') << '\n';

    for (size_t i = 0; i < 32; i++)
    {
        std::cout << std::setw(2) << i << ' ';
        std::cout << std::setw(8) << a.m_I16[i] << ' ';
        std::cout << std::setw(8) << b.m_I16[i] << ' ';
        std::cout << std::setw(8) << c[0].m_I16[i] << ' ';
        std::cout << std::setw(8) << c[1].m_I16[i] << ' ';
        std::cout << std::setw(8) << c[2].m_I16[i] << ' ';
        std::cout << std::setw(8) << c[3].m_I16[i] << ' ';
        std::cout << std::setw(8) << c[4].m_I16[i] << ' ';
        std::cout << std::setw(8) << c[5].m_I16[i] << '\n';
    }
}

static void MathI64(void)
{
    ZmmVal a, b, c[6];

    a.m_I64[0] = 64;         b.m_I64[0] = 4;
    a.m_I64[1] = 1024;       b.m_I64[1] = 5;
    a.m_I64[2] = -2048;      b.m_I64[2] = 2;
    a.m_I64[3] = 8192;       b.m_I64[3] = 5;
    a.m_I64[4] = -256;       b.m_I64[4] = 8;
    a.m_I64[5] = 4096;       b.m_I64[5] = 7;
    a.m_I64[6] = 16;         b.m_I64[6] = 3;
    a.m_I64[7] = 512;        b.m_I64[7] = 6;
```

```
    MathI64_avx512(c, &a, &b);

    std::cout << "\nMathI64_avx512() results:\n\n";
    std::cout << " i     a      b     add     sub     mul     sll     sra";
    std::cout << "     abs\n";
    std::cout << std::string(70, '-') << '\n';

    for (size_t i = 0; i < 8; i++)
    {
        std::cout << std::setw(2) << i << ' ';
        std::cout << std::setw(6) << a.m_I64[i] << ' ';
        std::cout << std::setw(6) << b.m_I64[i] << ' ';
        std::cout << std::setw(8) << c[0].m_I64[i] << ' ';
        std::cout << std::setw(8) << c[1].m_I64[i] << ' ';
        std::cout << std::setw(8) << c[2].m_I64[i] << ' ';
        std::cout << std::setw(8) << c[3].m_I64[i] << ' ';
        std::cout << std::setw(8) << c[4].m_I64[i] << ' ';
        std::cout << std::setw(8) << c[5].m_I64[i] << '\n';
    }
}

int main(void)
{
    std::cout << "----- Results for Ch13_01 -----\n";

    MathI16();
    MathI64();
    return 0;
}
```

Listing 13-1a opens with the definition of a C++ structure named ZmmVal, which is defined in the header file ZmmVal.h. This structure is the 512-bit wide counterpart of the XmmVal and YmmVal structures you saw in earlier chapters. Like structures XmmVal and YmmVal, structure ZmmVal contains an anonymous public union that facilitates SIMD data exchange between functions. It also includes several string formatting member functions. These functions are not shown in Listing 13-1a but are included in the software download package. The alignas(64) specifier that's used in the definition of ZmmVal instructs the C++ compiler to align each ZmmVal instance on a 64-byte boundary.

Following the definition of ZmmVal in Listing 13-1a is header file Ch13_01.h. This file incorporates the required function declarations for this source code example. Note that the function declarations make use of structure ZmmVal. The next file in Listing 13-1a, Ch13_01.cpp, contains functions MathI16() and MathI64(). Function MathI16() performs test case initialization for the AVX-512 assembly language function MathI16_avx512(), which carries out SIMD arithmetic operations using 16-bit wide integer elements. The function MathI64() is akin to MathI16() except that it uses 64-bit wide integer elements and calls MathI64_avx512().

Listing 13-1b shows the MASM code for example Ch13_01, which begins with the definition of a function named MathI16_avx512(). The first instruction of function MathI16_avx512(), vmovdqa64 zmm0,zmmword ptr [rdx], loads 512 bits of packed integer data from the memory location pointed to by register RDX (argument value a) into register ZMM0. Unlike the AVX/AVX2 packed integer move instructions vmovdqa and vmovdqu, the AVX-512 packed integer move instructions vmovdqa[32|64] (Move Aligned Packed Integer Values) and vmovdqu[8|16|32|64] (Move Unaligned Packed Integer Values) contain a size suffix. The size suffixes facilitate merge masking and zero masking. You'll see examples of these operations later in this chapter. When merge masking and zero masking are not utilized, as in this example, a function can use a vmovdqa[32|64] or vmovdqu[8|16|32|64] instruction to perform packed integer loads or stores of 512-bit wide operands. These AVX-512 instructions also can be used to perform packed integer loads or stores using 128- or 256-bit wide SIMD operands.

Listing 13-1b. Example Ch13_01 MASM Code

```
;------------------------------------------------------------------------------
; Ch13_01_fasm.asm
;------------------------------------------------------------------------------


;------------------------------------------------------------------------------
; void MathI16_Aavx512(ZmmVal* c, const ZmmVal* a, const ZmmVal* b);
;------------------------------------------------------------------------------

        .code
MathI16_avx512 proc
        vmovdqa64 zmm0,zmmword ptr [rdx]        ;load a values
        vmovdqa64 zmm1,zmmword ptr [r8]         ;load b values

        vpaddw zmm2,zmm0,zmm1                    ;packed addition - wraparound
        vmovdqa64 zmmword ptr [rcx],zmm2         ;save result

        vpaddsw zmm2,zmm0,zmm1                   ;packed addition - saturated
        vmovdqa64 zmmword ptr [rcx+64],zmm2      ;save result

        vpsubw zmm2,zmm0,zmm1                    ;packed subtraction - wraparound
        vmovdqa64 zmmword ptr [rcx+128],zmm2     ;save result

        vpsubsw zmm2,zmm0,zmm1                   ;packed subtraction - saturated
        vmovdqa64 zmmword ptr [rcx++192],zmm2    ;save result

        vpminsw zmm2,zmm0,zmm1                   ;packed min values
        vmovdqa64 zmmword ptr [rcx+256],zmm2     ;save result

        vpmaxsw zmm2,zmm0,zmm1                   ;packed max values
        vmovdqa64 zmmword ptr [rcx+320],zmm2     ;save result

        vzeroupper                              ;clear upper YMM/ZMM bits
        ret
MathI16_avx512 endp

;------------------------------------------------------------------------------
; void MathI64_avx512(ZmmVal* c, const ZmmVal* a, const ZmmVal* b);
;------------------------------------------------------------------------------

MathI64_avx512 proc
        vmovdqa64 zmm16,zmmword ptr [rdx]        ;load a values
        vmovdqa64 zmm17,zmmword ptr [r8]         ;load b values
```

```
        vpaddq  zmm18,zmm16,zmm17            ;packed qword addition
        vmovdqa64 zmmword ptr [rcx],zmm18    ;save result

        vpsubq  zmm18,zmm16,zmm17            ;packed qword subtraction
        vmovdqa64 zmmword ptr [rcx+64],zmm18 ;save result

        vpmullq zmm18,zmm16,zmm17            ;packed qword multiplication
        vmovdqa64 zmmword ptr [rcx+128],zmm18 ;save products (low 64-bits)

        vpsllvq zmm18,zmm16,zmm17            ;packed qword shift left
        vmovdqa64 zmmword ptr [rcx+192],zmm18 ;save result

        vpsravq zmm18,zmm16,zmm17            ;packed qword shift right
        vmovdqa64 zmmword ptr [rcx+256],zmm18 ;save result

        vpabsq  zmm18,zmm16                  ;packed qword abs (a values)
        vmovdqa64 zmmword ptr [rcx+320],zmm18 ;save result

        ret                                 ;vzeroupper not needed
MathI64_avx512 endp
        end
```

The next instruction in Listing 13-1b, vmovdqa64 zmm1,zmmword ptr [r8], loads argument value b into register ZMM1. This is followed by a vpaddw zmm2,zmm0,zmm1 instruction that performs packed integer addition using 16-bit wide integer elements. The ensuing vmovdqa64 zmmword ptr [rcx],zmm2 instruction saves the calculated sums to c[0]. The next instruction, vpaddsw zmm2,zmm0,zmm1, performs packed integer addition using 16-bit wide elements and saturated arithmetic. The subsequent vmovdqa64 zmmword ptr [rcx+64],zmm2 instruction saves this result to c[1]. Note that except for the ZMM register operands, MathI16_avx512() uses instructions vpaddw and vpaddsw just like they were used in AVX2 source example Ch10_01.

The ensuing code blocks in MathI16_avx512() illustrate the use of the vpsubw, vpsubsw, vpminsw, and vpmaxsw instructions using 512-bit wide operands and 16-bit wide integer elements. Note that the displacements on the vmovdqa64 save instructions are integral multiples of 64 since each ZMM register (and ZmmVal instance) is 64 bytes wide. The penultimate instruction of MathI16_avx512() is vzeroupper. Proper use of this instruction in functions that modify a ZMM register will be explained shortly.

In Listing 13-1b, function MathI64_avx512() begins its execution with the instruction pair vmovdqa64 zmm16,zmmword ptr [rdx] and vmovdqa64 zmm17,zmmword ptr [r8] that loads registers ZMM16 and ZMM17 with argument values a and b, respectively. The ensuing vpaddq zmm18,zmm16,zmm17 performs packed integer addition using quadword elements. The next instruction, vmovdqa64 zmmword ptr [rcx],zmm18, saves the calculated quadword sums to c[0]. The remaining instructions in function MathI64_avx512() perform other packed integer operations using quadword elements including subtraction (vpsubq), multiplication (vpmullq), shift left logical (vpsllvq), shift right arithmetic (vpsravq), and absolute value (vpabsq).

You may have noticed that function MathI64_avx512() does not include a vzeroupper instruction prior to its ret instruction. Recall from the discussions in Chapter 9 that execution of a vzeroupper (or vzeroall) instruction prevents potential performance delays from occurring whenever the processor transitions from executing x86-AVX instructions to executing x86-SSE instructions. A vzeroupper instruction should always be used prior to returning from any function that modifies the upper 128 bits of registers YMM0–YMM15. This rule also applies if a function calls another function that might use x86-SSE instructions such as a C++ math library function. On processors that support AVX-512, the vzeroupper usage rule is extended to include the upper 384 bits of registers ZMM0–ZMM15. It is not necessary for a function to use vzeroupper if it only modifies registers YMM16–YMM31 or ZMM16–ZMM31.

Listing 13-1c shows the NASM code for example Ch13_01. This code mimics the MASM code in Listing 13-1b, except for the use of different argument registers. Also note that the vmovdqa64 instructions do not require a size operator.

Listing 13-1c. Example Ch13_01 NASM Code

```
;-----------------------------------------------------------------------------
; Ch13_01_fasm.s
;-----------------------------------------------------------------------------

        %include "ModX86Asm3eNASM.inc"

;-----------------------------------------------------------------------------
; void MathI16_Aavx512(ZmmVal* c, const ZmmVal* a, const ZmmVal* b);
;-----------------------------------------------------------------------------

        section .text

        global MathI16_avx512
MathI16_avx512:

        vmovdqa64 zmm0,[rsi]             ;load a values
        vmovdqa64 zmm1,[rdx]             ;load b values

        vpaddw zmm2,zmm0,zmm1            ;packed addition - wraparound
        vmovdqa64 [rdi],zmm2             ;save result

        vpaddsw zmm2,zmm0,zmm1           ;packed addition - saturated
        vmovdqa64 [rdi+64],zmm2          ;save result

        vpsubw zmm2,zmm0,zmm1            ;packed subtraction - wraparound
        vmovdqa64 [rdi+128],zmm2         ;save result

        vpsubsw zmm2,zmm0,zmm1           ;packed subtraction - saturated
        vmovdqa64 [rdi++192],zmm2        ;save result

        vpminsw zmm2,zmm0,zmm1           ;packed min values
        vmovdqa64 [rdi+256],zmm2         ;save result

        vpmaxsw zmm2,zmm0,zmm1           ;packed max values
        vmovdqa64 [rdi+320],zmm2         ;save result

        vzeroupper                       ;clear upper YMM/ZMM bits
        ret


;-----------------------------------------------------------------------------
; void MathI64_avx512(ZmmVal* c, const ZmmVal* a, const ZmmVal* b);
;-----------------------------------------------------------------------------
```

```
        global MathI64_avx512
MathI64_avx512:

        vmovdqa64 zmm16,[rsi]                ;load a values
        vmovdqa64 zmm17,[rdx]                ;load b values

        vpaddq zmm18,zmm16,zmm17             ;packed qword addition
        vmovdqa64 [rdi],zmm18                ;save result

        vpsubq zmm18,zmm16,zmm17             ;packed qword subtraction
        vmovdqa64 [rdi+64],zmm18             ;save result

        vpmullq zmm18,zmm16,zmm17            ;packed qword multiplication
        vmovdqa64 [rdi+128],zmm18            ;save products (low 64-bits)

        vpsllvq zmm18,zmm16,zmm17            ;packed qword shift left
        vmovdqa64 [rdi+192],zmm18            ;save result

        vpsravq zmm18,zmm16,zmm17            ;packed qword shift right
        vmovdqa64 [rdi+256],zmm18            ;save result

        vpabsq zmm18,zmm16                   ;packed qword abs (a values)
        vmovdqa64 [rdi+320],zmm18            ;save result

        ret                                  ;vzeroupper not needed
```

Here are the results for source code example Ch13_01:

```
----- Results for Ch13_01 -----

MathI16_avx512() results:

i       a       b      add     adds     sub    subs     min     max
--------------------------------------------------------------------
0      10     100     110     110     -90     -90      10     100
1      20     200     220     220    -180    -180      20     200
2      30     300     330     330    -270    -270      30     300
3      40     400     440     440    -360    -360      40     400
4      50     500     550     550    -450    -450      50     500
5      60     600     660     660    -540    -540      60     600
6      70     700     770     770    -630    -630      70     700
7      80     800     880     880    -720    -720      80     800
8    1000    -100     900     900    1100    1100    -100    1000
9    2000     200    2200    2200    1800    1800     200    2000
10   3000    -300    2700    2700    3300    3300    -300    3000
11   4000     400    4400    4400    3600    3600     400    4000
12   5000    -500    4500    4500    5500    5500    -500    5000
13   6000     600    6600    6600    5400    5400     600    6000
14   7000    -700    6300    6300    7700    7700    -700    7000
15   8000     800    8800    8800    7200    7200     800    8000
16  -1000     100    -900    -900   -1100   -1100   -1000     100
```

17	-2000	-200	-2200	-2200	-1800	-1800	-2000	-200
18	3000	303	3303	3303	2697	2697	303	3000
19	4000	-400	3600	3600	4400	4400	-400	4000
20	-5000	500	-4500	-4500	-5500	-5500	-5000	500
21	-6000	-600	-6600	-6600	-5400	-5400	-6000	-600
22	-7000	700	-6300	-6300	-7700	-7700	-7000	700
23	-8000	800	-7200	-7200	-8800	-8800	-8000	800
24	30000	3000	-32536	32767	27000	27000	3000	30000
25	6000	32000	-27536	32767	-26000	-26000	6000	32000
26	-25000	-27000	13536	-32768	2000	2000	-27000	-25000
27	8000	28700	-28836	32767	-20700	-20700	8000	28700
28	2000	-31000	-29000	-29000	-32536	32767	-31000	2000
29	4000	-30000	-26000	-26000	-31536	32767	-30000	4000
30	-3000	32000	29000	29000	30536	-32768	-3000	32000
31	-15000	24000	9000	9000	26536	-32768	-15000	24000

MathI64_avx512() results:

i	a	b	add	sub	mul	sll	sra	abs
0	64	4	68	60	256	1024	4	64
1	1024	5	1029	1019	5120	32768	32	1024
2	-2048	2	-2046	-2050	-4096	-8192	-512	2048
3	8192	5	8197	8187	40960	262144	256	8192
4	-256	8	-248	-264	-2048	-65536	-1	256
5	4096	7	4103	4089	28672	524288	32	4096
6	16	3	19	13	48	128	2	16
7	512	6	518	506	3072	32768	8	512

One critique of AVX-512 is the confusion that's sometimes triggered by the numerous instruction extensions listed in Table 13-1. In Listings 13-1b and 13-1c, the vmovdqa64 instruction requires a processor that supports AVX512F. However, the SIMD arithmetic instructions in function MathI16_avx512() (vpaddw, vpaddsw, etc.) will only execute on a processor that supports AVX512VL and AVX512BW. In function MathI64_avx512(), the vpmulldq instruction requires a processor that supports AVX512VL and AVX512DQ. Mainstream server, workstation, and high-end desktop processors marketed by both AMD and Intel that support AVX-512 have included all four of these instruction set extensions, and this is unlikely to change in future processors that support AVX-512. Nevertheless, as mentioned earlier in this chapter, a program should always verify at run-time that any required AVX-512 instruction set extensions are supported by both the processor and host OS.

Masked Operations

Perhaps the most distinguishing feature between AVX-512 and its predecessor SIMD instruction set extensions is the former's support for zero masking and merge masking. The next source code example, named Ch13_02, explains how to perform zero masking and merge masking using an AVX-512 opmask register. It also illustrates how to implement a SIMD ternary operation using packed quadword integers and 512-bit wide operands. Listing 13-2a shows the C++ code for example Ch13_02.

Listing 13-2a. Example Ch13_02 C++ Code

```
//-------------------------------------------------------------------------------
// Ch13_02.h
//-------------------------------------------------------------------------------

#pragma once
#include <cstdint>
#include "ZmmVal.h"

// Ch13_02_fasm.asm, Ch13_02_fasm.s
extern "C" void MaskOpI64a_avx512(ZmmVal* c, uint8_t mask, const ZmmVal* a,
    const ZmmVal* b);
extern "C" void MaskOpI64b_avx512(ZmmVal* c, uint8_t mask, const ZmmVal* a,
    const ZmmVal* b1, const ZmmVal* b2);
extern "C" void MaskOpI64c_avx512(ZmmVal* c, const ZmmVal* a, int64_t x1,
    int64_t x2);

//-------------------------------------------------------------------------------
// Ch13_02.cpp
//-------------------------------------------------------------------------------

#include <iostream>
#include <iomanip>
#include <cstdint>
#include <cstddef>
#include "Ch13_02.h"

static void MaskOpI64a(void)
{
    ZmmVal a, b, c[5];
    constexpr uint8_t mask = 0x7b;

    a.m_I64[0] = 64;        b.m_I64[0] = 4;
    a.m_I64[1] = 1024;      b.m_I64[1] = 5;
    a.m_I64[2] = -2048;     b.m_I64[2] = 2;
    a.m_I64[3] = 8192;      b.m_I64[3] = 5;
    a.m_I64[4] = -256;      b.m_I64[4] = 8;
    a.m_I64[5] = 4096;      b.m_I64[5] = 7;
    a.m_I64[6] = 16;        b.m_I64[6] = 3;
    a.m_I64[7] = 512;       b.m_I64[7] = 6;

    MaskOpI64a_avx512(c, mask, &a, &b);

    std::cout << "\nMaskOpI64a_avx512() results ";
    std::cout << "(mask = 0x" << std::hex << (int)mask << std::dec;
    std::cout << "):\n\n";
    std::cout << " i      a       b       add     sub     mul     sll     sra\n";
    std::cout << std::string(61, '-') << '\n';
```

```cpp
    for (size_t i = 0; i < 8; i++)
    {
        std::cout << std::setw(2) << i << ' ';
        std::cout << std::setw(6) << a.m_I64[i] << ' ';
        std::cout << std::setw(6) << b.m_I64[i] << ' ';
        std::cout << std::setw(8) << c[0].m_I64[i] << ' ';
        std::cout << std::setw(8) << c[1].m_I64[i] << ' ';
        std::cout << std::setw(8) << c[2].m_I64[i] << ' ';
        std::cout << std::setw(8) << c[3].m_I64[i] << ' ';
        std::cout << std::setw(8) << c[4].m_I64[i] << '\n';
    }
}

static void MaskOpI64b(void)
{
    ZmmVal a, b1, b2, c[5];
    constexpr uint8_t mask = 0xb6;

    a.m_I64[0] = 111111;   b1.m_I64[0] = 64;     b2.m_I64[0] = 4;
    a.m_I64[1] = 222222;   b1.m_I64[1] = 1024;   b2.m_I64[1] = 5;
    a.m_I64[2] = 333333;   b1.m_I64[2] = -2048;  b2.m_I64[2] = 2;
    a.m_I64[3] = 444444;   b1.m_I64[3] = 8192;   b2.m_I64[3] = 5;
    a.m_I64[4] = 555555;   b1.m_I64[4] = -256;   b2.m_I64[4] = 8;
    a.m_I64[5] = 666666;   b1.m_I64[5] = 4096;   b2.m_I64[5] = 7;
    a.m_I64[6] = 777777;   b1.m_I64[6] = 16;     b2.m_I64[6] = 3;
    a.m_I64[7] = 888888;   b1.m_I64[7] = 512;    b2.m_I64[7] = 6;

    MaskOpI64b_avx512(c, mask, &a, &b1, &b2);

    std::cout << "\nMaskOpI64b_avx512() results ";
    std::cout << "(mask = 0x" << std::hex << (int)mask << std::dec;
    std::cout << "):\n\n";
    std::cout << " i        a      b1      b2      add      sub      mul      sll";
    std::cout << "      sra\n";
    std::cout << std::string(68, '-') << '\n';

    for (size_t i = 0; i < 8; i++)
    {
        std::cout << std::setw(2) << i << ' ';
        std::cout << std::setw(6) << a.m_I64[i] << ' ';
        std::cout << std::setw(6) << b1.m_I64[i] << ' ';
        std::cout << std::setw(6) << b2.m_I64[i] << ' ';
        std::cout << std::setw(8) << c[0].m_I64[i] << ' ';
        std::cout << std::setw(8) << c[1].m_I64[i] << ' ';
        std::cout << std::setw(8) << c[2].m_I64[i] << ' ';
        std::cout << std::setw(8) << c[3].m_I64[i] << ' ';
        std::cout << std::setw(8) << c[4].m_I64[i] << '\n';
    }
}
```

```cpp
static void MaskOpI64c(void)
{
    ZmmVal a, c;
    constexpr int64_t x1 = 0;
    constexpr int64_t x2 = 42;

    a.m_I64[0] = -100;
    a.m_I64[1] = 200;
    a.m_I64[2] = 300;
    a.m_I64[3] = -400;
    a.m_I64[4] = -500;
    a.m_I64[5] = 600;
    a.m_I64[6] = 700;
    a.m_I64[7] = -800;

    MaskOpI64c_avx512(&c, &a, x1, x2);

    std::cout << "\nMaskOpI64c_avx512() results ";
    std::cout << "(x1 = " << x1 << ", x2 = " << x2 << "):\n\n";
    std::cout << " i        a         c\n";
    std::cout << std::string(20, '-') << "\n";

    for (size_t i = 0; i < 8; i++)
    {
        std::cout << std::setw(2) << i << ' ';
        std::cout << std::setw(8) << a.m_I64[i] << ' ';
        std::cout << std::setw(8) << c.m_I64[i] << '\n';
    }
}

int main(void)
{
    std::cout << "----- Results for Ch13_02 -----\n";

    MaskOpI64a();
    MaskOpI64b();
    MaskOpI64c();
    return 0;
}
```

Listing 13-2a includes header file Ch13_02.h. This file contains the mandatory function declarations for this example. Also shown in Listing 13-2a is file Ch13_02.cpp, which defines three static test functions that exercise the AVX-512 assembly language functions MaskOpI64a_avx512(), MaskOpI64b_avx512(), and MaskOpI64c_avx512(). Note that each test function initializes instances of ZmmVal using 64-bit wide integer elements.

Listing 13-2b shows the MASM code for example Ch13_02. This listing opens with an assembly language header file named cmpequ_int.asmh, which contains equ statements for AVX-512 packed integer compare predicates. More on this later.

Listing 13-2b. Example Ch13_02 MASM Code

```
;-------------------------------------------------------------------------
; cmpequ_int.asmh
;-------------------------------------------------------------------------

; Compare predicates for AVX-512 vpcmp* packed integer instructions
CMP_EQ          equ 00h
CMP_LT          equ 01h
CMP_LE          equ 02h
CMP_FALSE       equ 03h
CMP_NEQ         equ 04h
CMP_NLT         equ 05h
CMP_GE          equ 05h
CMP_NLE         equ 06h
CMP_GT          equ 06h
CMP_TRUE        equ 07h


;-------------------------------------------------------------------------
; Ch13_02_fasm.asm
;-------------------------------------------------------------------------

        include <cmpequ_int.asmh>

;-------------------------------------------------------------------------
; void MaskOpI64a_avx512(ZmmVal c[5], uint8_t mask, const ZmmVal* a,
;   const ZmmVal* b);
;-------------------------------------------------------------------------

        .code
MaskOpI64a_avx512 proc
        vmovdqa64 zmm0,zmmword ptr [r8]         ;load a values
        vmovdqa64 zmm1,zmmword ptr [r9]         ;load b values

        kmovb k1,edx                            ;k1 = opmask

        vpaddq zmm2{k1}{z},zmm0,zmm1            ;masked qword addition
        vmovdqa64 zmmword ptr [rcx],zmm2        ;save result

        vpsubq zmm2{k1}{z},zmm0,zmm1            ;masked qword subtraction
        vmovdqa64 zmmword ptr [rcx+64],zmm2     ;save result

        vpmullq zmm2{k1}{z},zmm0,zmm1           ;masked qword multiplication
        vmovdqa64 zmmword ptr [rcx+128],zmm2    ;save products (low 64-bits)

        vpsllvq zmm2{k1}{z},zmm0,zmm1           ;masked qword shift left
        vmovdqa64 zmmword ptr [rcx+192],zmm2    ;save result

        vpsravq zmm2{k1}{z},zmm0,zmm1           ;masked qword shift right
        vmovdqa64 zmmword ptr [rcx+256],zmm2    ;save result
```

```
        vzeroupper
        ret
MaskOpI64a_avx512 endp

;-----------------------------------------------------------------------------
; void MaskOpI64b_avx512(ZmmVal c[5], uint8_t mask, const ZmmVal* a,
;   const ZmmVal* b1, const ZmmVal* b2);
;-----------------------------------------------------------------------------

MaskOpI64b_avx512 proc
        vmovdqa64 zmm0,zmmword ptr [r8]         ;load a values
        vmovdqa64 zmm1,zmmword ptr [r9]         ;load b1 values
        mov rax,[rsp+40]                        ;rax = b2
        vmovdqa64 zmm2,zmmword ptr [rax]        ;load b2 values

        kmovb k1,edx                            ;k1 = opmask

        vpaddq zmm0{k1},zmm1,zmm2               ;masked qword addition
        vmovdqa64 zmmword ptr [rcx],zmm0        ;save result

        vpsubq zmm0{k1},zmm1,zmm2               ;masked qword subtraction
        vmovdqa64 zmmword ptr [rcx+64],zmm0     ;save result

        vpmullq zmm0{k1},zmm1,zmm2              ;masked qword multiplication
        vmovdqa64 zmmword ptr [rcx+128],zmm0    ;save products (low 64-bits)

        vpsllvq zmm0{k1},zmm1,zmm2              ;masked qword shift left
        vmovdqa64 zmmword ptr [rcx+192],zmm0    ;save result

        vpsravq zmm0{k1},zmm1,zmm2              ;masked qword shift right
        vmovdqa64 zmmword ptr [rcx+256],zmm0    ;save result

        vzeroupper
        ret
MaskOpI64b_avx512 endp

;-----------------------------------------------------------------------------
; void MaskOpI64c_avx512(ZmmVal* c, const ZmmVal* a, int64_t x1, int64_t x2);
;-----------------------------------------------------------------------------

MaskOpI64c_avx512 proc
        vmovdqa64 zmm0,zmmword ptr [rdx]        ;load a values
        vpbroadcastq zmm1,r8                    ;broadcast x1 to zmm1
        vpbroadcastq zmm2,r9                    ;broadcast x2 to zmm2

; c[i] = (a[i] >= x1) ? a[i] + x2 : a[i]
        vpcmpq k1,zmm0,zmm1,CMP_GE              ;k1 = a[i] >= x1 mask
        vpaddq zmm0{k1},zmm0,zmm2               ;masked qword addition
        vmovdqa64 zmmword ptr [rcx],zmm0        ;save result
```

●

```
        vzeroupper
        ret
MaskOpI64c_avx512 endp
        end
```

The first function in Listing 13-2b, MaskOpI64a_avx512(), begins its execution with two vmovdqa64 instructions that load ZmmVal arguments a and b into registers ZMM0 and ZMM1, respectively. The next instruction, kmovb k1,edx (Move from and to Mask Register), copies the low-order eight bits of register EDX (argument value mask) to the low-order eight bits of opmask register K1; the high-order bits of register K1 are set to zero. Recall from the discussions earlier in this chapter that AVX-512 includes eight opmask registers named K0–K7 (see Figure 13-1). Most AVX-512 instructions can be used with an opmask register to perform either zero masking or merge masking. Beside the kmovb instruction, AVX-512 includes additional instructions that a function can use to perform opmask register addition, bitwise logical operations, and shifts. You'll see examples of these instructions in this and later chapters.

Before continuing with the code of example Ch13_02, a few more words regarding opmask registers and their instruction mnemonics are required. The width of an AVX-512 opmask register is 64 bits; however, an AVX-512 instruction will only use or modify the exact number of low-order bits needed to carry out an operation. The high-order bits are either zeroed or ignored. The last letter of most opmask register instruction mnemonics signifies the size of the data value (b = byte, w = word, d = doubleword, q = quadword). In the current example, function MaskOpI64a_avx512() uses the kmovb instruction since subsequent instructions manipulate quadword elements and each ZMM register can hold eight quadword values, which means only eight opmask register bits are needed. AVX-512 instructions can use registers K1–K7 to perform merge masking or zero masking. Opmask register K0 cannot be specified for these operations since AVX-512 instruction encodings use the encoding pattern for register K0 to implement unconditional processing.

Returning to the code in Listing 13-2b, the first instruction that follows the kmovb k1,edx instruction is vpaddq zmm2{k1}{z},zmm0,zmm1. This instruction performs conditional adds of the quadword elements in registers ZMM0 and ZMM1. The elements in these source operand registers are summed only if the corresponding bit position in opmask register K1 is set to 1. If the corresponding bit position in K1 is set to 0, the element in destination register ZMM2 is set to 0 as illustrated in Figure 13-4. Note that opmask register K1 in the vpaddq instruction is surrounded by curly braces; these are required. The {z} operand enables zero masking. Using an AVX-512 instruction with an opmask register sans the {z} operand selects merge masking as you'll soon see. Most AVX-512 instructions support both zero masking and merge masking.

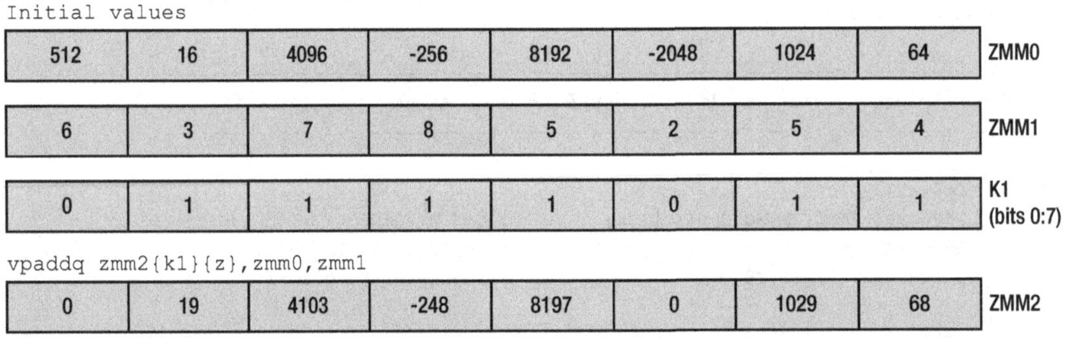

Initial values

512	16	4096	-256	8192	-2048	1024	64	ZMM0

6	3	7	8	5	2	5	4	ZMM1

0	1	1	1	1	0	1	1	K1 (bits 0:7)

vpaddq zmm2{k1}{z},zmm0,zmm1

0	19	4103	-248	8197	0	1029	68	ZMM2

Figure 13-4. *Execution of the vpaddq zmm2{k1}{z},zmm0,zmm1 instruction using zero masking*

Following the vpaddq instruction is a vmovdqa64 zmmword ptr [rcx],zmm0 instruction that saves the 512-bit wide result to c[0]. It should be noted that AVX-512 load/store instructions like vmovdqa64 also support merge masking and zero masking. The remaining code in function MaskOpI64a_avx512() illustrates the use of additional AVX-512 instructions using packed quadword elements and zero masking.

The next function in Listing 13-2b, MaskOpI64b_avx512(), demonstrates how to perform merge masking. The first code block in this function contains a series of vmovdqa64 instructions that load argument values a, b1, and b2 into registers ZMM0, ZMM1, and ZMM2, respectively. This is followed by a kmovb k1,edx instruction that loads argument value mask into opmask register K1. The next instruction, vpaddq zmm0{k1},zmm1,zmm2, performs conditional adds of the quadword elements in registers ZMM1 and ZMM2. The quadword elements of ZMM1 and ZMM2 are summed only if the corresponding bit position in opmask register K1 is set to 1. If this bit is set to 0, the quadword element in destination operand ZMM0 remains unaltered as shown in Figure 13-5. Like the previous function, the subsequent code in MaskOpI64b_avx512() highlights the use of additional AVX-512 instructions using packed quadword elements and merge masking.

Initial values

888888	777777	666666	555555	444444	333333	222222	111111	ZMM0

512	16	4096	-256	8192	-2048	1024	64	ZMM1

6	3	7	8	5	2	5	4	ZMM2

1	0	1	1	0	1	1	0	K1 (bits 0:7)

vpaddq zmm0{k1},zmm1,zmm2

518	777777	4103	-248	444444	-2046	1029	111111	ZMM0

Figure 13-5. Execution of the vpaddq zmm0{k1},zmm1,zmm2 instruction using merge masking

The final function in Listing 13-2b is named MaskOpI64c_avx512(). This function demonstrates how to implement a SIMD ternary operator using an opmask register. The first instruction of this function, vmovdqa64 zmm0,zmmword ptr [rdx], loads argument value a into register ZMM0. This is followed by a vpbroadcastq zmm1,r8 instruction that broadcasts the quadword value in register R8 (argument value x1) to each quadword element position in ZMM1. Unlike AVX2, the AVX-512 vpbroadcast[b|w|d|q] instructions can use a general-purpose register as a source operand. Execution of the ensuing vpbroadcastq zmm2,r9 instruction sets each quadword element in ZMM2 to the value in register R9 (argument value x2).

The next code block contains instructions that implement the SIMD ternary expression c[i] = (a[i] >= x1) ? a[i] + x2 : a[i]. Note that in this expression, indices within the brackets signify SIMD quadword element positions. The first instruction of this code block, vpcmpq k1,zmm0,zmm1,CMP_GE (Compare Packed Integer Values into Mask), compares each quadword element in register ZMM0 to its counterpart element in register ZMM1, which contains x1. If the specified compare predicate CMP_GE is true, the corresponding bit position in opmask register K1 is set to 1; otherwise, it is set to 0. The next instruction, vpaddq zmm0{k1},zmm0,zmm2, sums counterpart quadword elements in ZMM0 and ZMM2 whose corresponding bit in opmask register K1 is set to 1. This quadword element sum is then saved in ZMM0 as illustrated in Figure 13-6. If the corresponding bit in opmask register K1 is set to 0, the quadword element in ZMM0 is not changed.

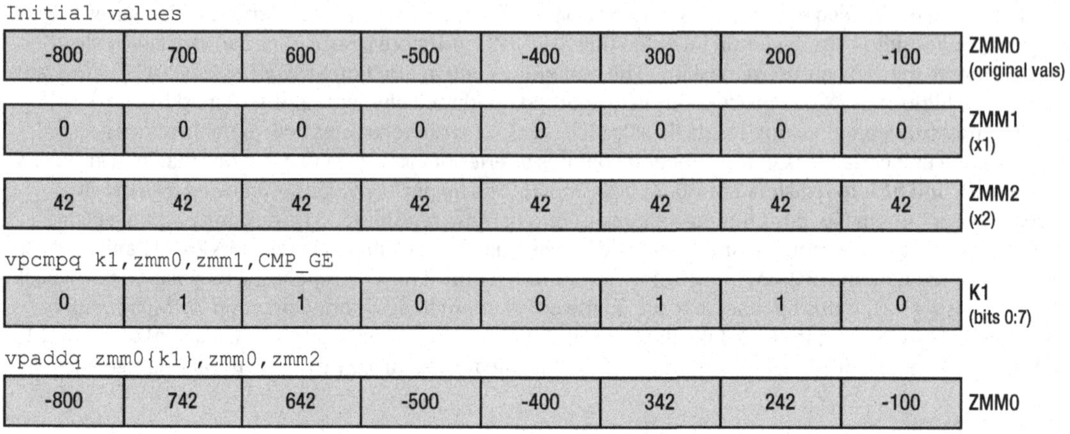

Initial values

-800	700	600	-500	-400	300	200	-100	ZMM0 (original vals)

0	0	0	0	0	0	0	0	ZMM1 (x1)

42	42	42	42	42	42	42	42	ZMM2 (x2)

vpcmpq k1,zmm0,zmm1,CMP_GE

0	1	1	0	0	1	1	0	K1 (bits 0:7)

vpaddq zmm0{k1},zmm0,zmm2

-800	742	642	-500	-400	342	242	-100	ZMM0

Figure 13-6. *Execution of a SIMD ternary operation using AVX-512 merge masking*

Listing 13-2c shows the NASM code for example Ch13_02. The primary difference between this code and the MASM code shown in Listing 13-2b is the use of different argument registers.

Listing 13-2c. Example Ch13_02 NASM Code

```
;-----------------------------------------------------------------------------
; Ch13_02_fasm.s
;-----------------------------------------------------------------------------

        %include "ModX86Asm3eNASM.inc"
        %include "cmpequ_int.inc"


;-----------------------------------------------------------------------------
; void MaskOpI64a_avx512(ZmmVal c[5], uint8_t mask, const ZmmVal* a,
;   const ZmmVal* b);
;-----------------------------------------------------------------------------

        section .text

        global MaskOpI64a_avx512
MaskOpI64a_avx512:

        vmovdqa64 zmm0,[rdx]            ;load a values
        vmovdqa64 zmm1,[rcx]            ;load b values

        kmovb k1,esi                   ;k1 = opmask

        vpaddq zmm2{k1}{z},zmm0,zmm1    ;masked qword addition
        vmovdqa64 [rdi],zmm2            ;save result

        vpsubq zmm2{k1}{z},zmm0,zmm1    ;masked qword subtraction
        vmovdqa64 [rdi+64],zmm2         ;save result
```

```
        vpmullq zmm2{k1}{z},zmm0,zmm1        ;masked qword multiplication
        vmovdqa64 [rdi+128],zmm2             ;save products (low 64-bits)

        vpsllvq zmm2{k1}{z},zmm0,zmm1        ;masked qword shift left
        vmovdqa64 [rdi+192],zmm2             ;save result

        vpsravq zmm2{k1}{z},zmm0,zmm1        ;masked qword shift right
        vmovdqa64 [rdi+256],zmm2             ;save result

        vzeroupper
        ret

;-----------------------------------------------------------------------------
; void MaskOpI64b_avx512(ZmmVal c[5], uint8_t mask, const ZmmVal* a,
;    const ZmmVal* b1, const ZmmVal* b2);
;-----------------------------------------------------------------------------

        global MaskOpI64b_avx512
MaskOpI64b_avx512:

        vmovdqa64 zmm0,[rdx]                 ;load a values
        vmovdqa64 zmm1,[rcx]                 ;load b1 values
        vmovdqa64 zmm2,[r8]                  ;load b2 values

        kmovb k1,esi                         ;k1 = opmask

        vpaddq zmm0{k1},zmm1,zmm2            ;masked qword addition
        vmovdqa64 [rdi],zmm0                 ;save result

        vpsubq zmm0{k1},zmm1,zmm2            ;masked qword subtraction
        vmovdqa64 [rdi+64],zmm0              ;save result

        vpmullq zmm0{k1},zmm1,zmm2           ;masked qword multiplication
        vmovdqa64 [rdi+128],zmm0             ;save products (low 64-bits)

        vpsllvq zmm0{k1},zmm1,zmm2           ;masked qword shift left
        vmovdqa64 [rdi+192],zmm0             ;save result

        vpsravq zmm0{k1},zmm1,zmm2           ;masked qword shift right
        vmovdqa64 [rdi+256],zmm0             ;save result

        vzeroupper
        ret

;-----------------------------------------------------------------------------
; void MaskOpI64c_avx512(ZmmVal* c, const ZmmVal* a, int64_t x1, int64_t x2);
;-----------------------------------------------------------------------------

        global MaskOpI64c_avx512
MaskOpI64c_avx512:
```

```
        vmovdqa64 zmm0,[rsi]              ;load a values
        vpbroadcastq zmm1,rdx            ;broadcast x1 to zmm1
        vpbroadcastq zmm2,rcx            ;broadcast x2 to zmm2

; c[i] = (a[i] >= x1) ? a[i] + x2 : a[i]
        vpcmpq k1,zmm0,zmm1,CMP_GE        ;k1 = a[i] >= x1 mask
        vpaddq zmm0{k1},zmm0,zmm2         ;masked qword addition
        vmovdqa64 [rdi],zmm0              ;save result


        vzeroupper
        ret
```

Compared to AVX and AVX2, AVX-512's incorporation of distinct opmask registers and its support for merge masking and zero masking provides software developers with a significant amount of algorithmic flexibility. You'll see additional examples of AVX-512 masking later in this and subsequent chapters. Here are the results for source code example Ch13_02:

```
----- Results for Ch13_02 -----

MaskOpI64a_avx512() results (mask = 0x7b):

i       a       b      add      sub      mul      sll      sra
-------------------------------------------------------------------
0      64       4       68       60      256     1024        4
1    1024       5     1029     1019     5120    32768       32
2   -2048       2        0        0        0        0        0
3    8192       5     8197     8187    40960   262144      256
4    -256       8     -248     -264    -2048   -65536       -1
5    4096       7     4103     4089    28672   524288       32
6      16       3       19       13       48      128        2
7     512       6        0        0        0        0        0


MaskOpI64b_avx512() results (mask = 0xb6):

i       a      b1      b2      add      sub      mul      sll      sra
----------------------------------------------------------------------
0 111111      64       4   111111   111111   111111   111111   111111
1 222222    1024       5     1029     1019     5120    32768       32
2 333333   -2048       2    -2046    -2050    -4096    -8192     -512
3 444444    8192       5   444444   444444   444444   444444   444444
4 555555    -256       8     -248     -264    -2048   -65536       -1
5 666666    4096       7     4103     4089    28672   524288       32
6 777777      16       3   777777   777777   777777   777777   777777
7 888888     512       6      518      506     3072    32768        8

MaskOpI64c_avx512() results (x1 = 0, x2 = 42):

i        a        c
--------------------
0     -100     -100
1      200      242
```

2	300	342
3	-400	-400
4	-500	-500
5	600	642
6	700	742
7	-800	-800

Image Processing

The following section contains three source code examples that exemplify image processing techniques using AVX-512 instructions and packed integer operands. The first example spotlights image thresholding. This is followed by an example that calculates grayscale image statistics including mean and standard deviation. The final example demonstrates how to construct a grayscale image histogram.

Image Thresholding

Image thresholding is an image processing technique that creates a mask image[1] from a grayscale image. The mask image often signifies which pixels in the original image are greater than a predetermined or algorithmically derived intensity threshold value. Other relational operators such as less than, equal, and not equal can also be used to create a mask image. The next source code example, named Ch13_03, uses AVX-512 packed integer instructions to implement a general-purpose image thresholding function. Listing 13-3a shows the principal C++ code for this example.

Listing 13-3a. Example Ch13_03 C++ Code

```
//----------------------------------------------------------------------------
// Ch13_03.h
//----------------------------------------------------------------------------

#pragma once
#include <cstddef>
#include <cstdint>

// Note: any changes to CmpOp must also be reflected in the assembly
// language files.
enum class CmpOp : uint64_t { EQ, NE, LT, LE, GT, GE };

// Ch13_03_fasm.asm, Ch13_03_fasm.s
extern "C" void ComparePixels_avx512(uint8_t * des, const uint8_t * src,
    size_t num_pixels, CmpOp cmp_op, uint8_t cmp_val);

// Ch13_03_fcpp.cpp
extern void ComparePixels_cpp(uint8_t* des, const uint8_t* src, size_t num_pixels,
    CmpOp cmp_op, uint8_t cmp_val);
```

---

[1] In an 8-bit per pixel mask image, each pixel value is either 0 or 255.

```cpp
// Ch13_03_misc.cpp
extern bool CheckArgs(const uint8_t* des, const uint8_t* src, size_t num_pixels);
extern void DisplayResults(const uint8_t* des1, const uint8_t* des2,
    size_t num_pixels, CmpOp cmp_op, uint8_t cmp_val, size_t test_id);
extern void InitArray(uint8_t* x, size_t n, unsigned int seed);

// Miscellaneous constants
const size_t c_Alignment = 64;

//-----------------------------------------------------------------------------
// Ch13_03_fcpp.cpp
//-----------------------------------------------------------------------------

#include <iostream>
#include <stdexcept>
#include "Ch13_03.h"

void ComparePixels_cpp(uint8_t* des, const uint8_t* src, size_t num_pixels,
    CmpOp cmp_op, uint8_t cmp_val)
{
    if (!CheckArgs(des, src, num_pixels))
        throw std::runtime_error("ComparePixels_Cpp() - CheckArgs failed");

    constexpr uint8_t cmp_false = 0x00;
    constexpr uint8_t cmp_true = 0xff;

    switch (cmp_op)
    {
        case CmpOp::EQ:
            for (size_t i = 0; i < num_pixels; i++)
                des[i] = (src[i] == cmp_val) ? cmp_true : cmp_false;
            break;

        case CmpOp::NE:
            for (size_t i = 0; i < num_pixels; i++)
                des[i] = (src[i] != cmp_val) ? cmp_true : cmp_false;
            break;

        case CmpOp::LT:
            for (size_t i = 0; i < num_pixels; i++)
                des[i] = (src[i] < cmp_val) ? cmp_true : cmp_false;
            break;

        case CmpOp::LE:
            for (size_t i = 0; i < num_pixels; i++)
                des[i] = (src[i] <= cmp_val) ? cmp_true : cmp_false;
            break;

        case CmpOp::GT:
            for (size_t i = 0; i < num_pixels; i++)
                des[i] = (src[i] > cmp_val) ? cmp_true : cmp_false;
            break;
```

```
        case CmpOp::GE:
            for (size_t i = 0; i < num_pixels; i++)
                des[i] = (src[i] >= cmp_val) ? cmp_true : cmp_false;
            break;

        default:
            throw std::runtime_error("ComparePixels_cpp() - invalid cmp_op");
    }
}
```

Listing 13-3a begins with the declaration of enum CmpOp, which defines symbolic names for the relational operators by the pixel compare functions. Note that CmpOp is declared using C++ type uint64_t. The assembly language function ComparePixels_avx512() uses its cmp_op argument as an index into a jump table, so using type uint64_t for enum CmpOp simplifies the assembly language code a tiny bit.

The most important code in Listing 13-3a is function ComparePixels_cpp(), which is located in file Ch13_03_fcpp.cpp. This function compares each value in pixel buffer src to cmp_val using relational operator cmp_op. Note that distinct cases inside the C++ switch statement are employed for each relational operator. The assembly language code that you'll soon see emulates this construct. File Ch13_03.cpp (not shown in Listing 13-3a) contains the code that allocates and initializes the test pixel buffers. In this file, template class AlignedArray<uint8_t> is exploited to ensure that the pixel buffers are aligned on a 64-byte boundary.

Listing 13-3b shows the MASM code for function example Ch13_03. Near the top of this listing is the definition of a macro named PixelCmp_M. This macro emits instructions that implement a thresholding for-loop for the compare predicate specified by the macro parameter CmpOp. Supported compare predicates, which are defined in the assembly language header file cmpequ_int.asmh, include CMP_EQ, CMP_NEQ, CMP_LT, CMP_LE, CMP_GT, and CMP_GE. The first instruction of macro PixelCmp_M, add rax,NSE, updates for-loop index variable i so that it indexes the next block of 64 pixels in both the source and mask (destination) images. In this example, all source and mask image pixel values are 8-bit unsigned integers. The next instruction, vmovdqa64 zmm2,zmmword ptr [rdx+rax], loads pixel values src[i:i+63] into register ZMM2. Note that the use of the vmovdqa64 instruction means that each pixel block in source image src must be properly aligned on a 64-byte boundary. It should also be noted that it is acceptable to use the instruction vmovdqa64 to load 8-bit wide elements since neither merge masking nor zero masking are used here (AVX-512 does not include a vmovdqa8 instruction).

Listing 13-3b. Example Ch13_03 MASM Code

```
;-------------------------------------------------------------------------------
; Ch13_03_fasm.asm
;-------------------------------------------------------------------------------

        include <cmpequ_int.asmh>

NSE     equ     64                            ;num_simd_elements


;-------------------------------------------------------------------------------
; Macro PixelCmp_M
;-------------------------------------------------------------------------------

PixelCmp_M macro CmpOp
        align 16
@@:     add rax,NSE                           ;i += NSE
        vmovdqa64 zmm2,zmmword ptr [rdx+rax]  ;load src[i:i+63]
```

```
        vpcmpub k1,zmm2,zmm1,CmpOp          ;packed compare using CmpOp
        vmovdqu8 zmm3{k1}{z},zmm0            ;create pixel mask
        vmovdqa64 zmmword ptr [rcx+rax],zmm3 ;save des[i:i+63]
        sub r8,NSE                          ;num_pixels -= NSE
        jnz @B                              ;repeat until done
        jmp Done
        endm
```

```
;-------------------------------------------------------------------------------
; void ComparePixels_avx512(uint8_t* des, const uint8_t* src, size_t num_pixels,
;   CmpOp cmp_op, uint8_t cmp_val);
;-------------------------------------------------------------------------------

        .code
ComparePixels_avx512 proc

; Validate arguments
        mov eax,1                           ;load error return code

        test r8,r8
        jz Done                             ;jump if num_pixels == 0

        test r8,3fh
        jnz Done                            ;jump if num_pixels % 64 != 0

        test rcx,3fh
        jnz Done                            ;jump if des not 64b aligned

        test rdx,3fh
        jnz Done                            ;jump if src not 64b aligned

        cmp r9,CmpOpTableCount
        jae Done                            ;jump if cmp_op is invalid

; Initialize
        mov eax,0ffh
        vpbroadcastb zmm0,eax               ;zmm0 = packed 0xff
        vpbroadcastb zmm1,byte ptr [rsp+40] ;zmm1 = packed cmp_val
        mov rax,-NSE                        ;i = -NSE

; Jump to target compare code
        lea r10,[CmpOpTable]                ;r10 = address of CmpOpTable
        mov r11,[r10+r9*8]                  ;r11 = address of compare code block
        jmp r11                             ;jump to specified compare code block

; Compare code blocks using macro PixelCmp_M
CmpEQ:  PixelCmp_M CMP_EQ
CmpNE:  PixelCmp_M CMP_NEQ
CmpLT:  PixelCmp_M CMP_LT
```

```
CmpLE:   PixelCmp_M CMP_LE
CmpGT:   PixelCmp_M CMP_GT
CmpGE:   PixelCmp_M CMP_GE

Done:    vzeroupper
         ret

; The order of values in following table must match enum CmpOp
; that's defined in Ch03_03.h.

         align 8
CmpOpTable equ $
         qword CmpEQ
         qword CmpNE
         qword CmpLT
         qword CmpLE
         qword CmpGT
         qword CmpGE
CmpOpTableCount equ ($ - CmpOpTable) / size qword

ComparePixels_avx512 endp
         end
```

Following the vmovdqa64 instruction is the AVX-512 instruction vpcmpub k1,zmm2,zmm1,CmpOp (Compare Packed Byte Values into Mask). This instruction compares each unsigned byte element in ZMM2 to its corresponding element position in ZMM1 using compare predicate CmpOp. Prior to using macro PixelCmp_M, a function must broadcast the desired compare value to each byte element in register ZMM1 as you'll soon see. Execution of vpcmpub sets each bit in opmask register K1 to 1 (compare predicate true) or 0 (compare predicate false). The next instruction, vmovdqu8 zmm3{k1}{z},zmm0, employs zero masking to create the required pixel mask as shown in Figure 13-7. Note that this figure uses compare predicate CMP_GE for macro argument CmpOp. The ensuing vmovdqa64 zmmword ptr [rcx+rax],zmm3 instruction saves the calculated pixel mask to des[i:i+63]. The remaining instructions in macro PixelCmp_M are required to complete the for-loop.

Initial values

0xFF	0xFF	0xFF	0xFF	0xFF	0xFF	0xFF	...	0xFF	0xFF	0xFF	0xFF	0xFF	0xFF	0xFF	ZMM0

100	100	100	100	100	100	100	...	100	100	100	100	100	100	100	ZMM1 (cmp_val)

229	232	36	127	144	12	45	...	235	72	77	240	68	21	100	ZMM2 (src[i:i+63])

vpcmpub k1,zmm2,zmm1,CMP_GE

1	1	0	1	1	0	0	...	1	0	0	1	0	0	1	K1

vmovdqu8 zmm3{k1}{z},zmm0

0xFF	0xFF	0x00	0xFF	0xFF	0x00	0x00	...	0xFF	0x00	0x00	0xFF	0x00	0x00	0xFF	ZMM3

Figure 13-7. *Generation of a pixel mask using AVX-512 instructions vpcmpub and vmovdqu8*

The next item in Listing 13-3b is the definition of assembly language function ComparePixels_
avx512(). This function uses macro PixelCmp_M and an assembly language jump table to implement a
general-purpose image thresholding function. Function ComparePixels_avx512() begins its execution with
a code block that validates num_pixels for size. Note that in this example, num_pixels must be an integral
multiple of 64. The next code block verifies that pixel buffers src and des are properly aligned on a 64-byte
boundary. The final argument check validates cmp_op. This check is important since ComparePixels_
avx512() uses cmp_op as an index into a jump table. Using an invalid value for cmp_op could cause the
program to crash. Subsequent to argument validation, ComparePixels_avx512() employs the instruction
pair mov eax,0ffh and vpbroadcastb zmm0,eax to set each byte element in register ZMM0 to 0xFF. The next
instruction, vpbroadcastb zmm1,byte ptr [rsp+40], loads cmp_val into each byte element of ZMM1.

Following initialization, function ComparePixels_avx512() loads the address of CmpOpTable into
register R10 using a lea r10,[CmpOpTable] instruction. The next instruction, mov r11,[r10+r9*8], loads
the address of the compare code block specified by cmp_op (R9) into register R11. This is followed by a jmp
r11 instruction that transfers program control to code block specified by cmp_op. Toward the end of
Listing 13-3b is an assembly language jump table named CmpOpTable. This table contains addresses of labels
in ComparePixels_avx512() that use macro PixelCmp_M to implement a for-loop for the specific compare
predicate. It is important to note that the order of the quadword label values in CmpOpTable must match the
enumerated type CmpOp that's defined in header file Ch13_03.h.

Listing 13-3c shows the NASM code for example Ch13_03. In the definition of macro PixelCmp_M, note
the use of the symbol %%L1. This symbol instructs NASM to generate a unique label name with each use of
PixelCmp_M. This is important since macro PixelCmp_M is used multiple times. Using a standard label name
such as L1 in macro PixelCmp_M will produce an assembly error since there would be multiple definitions of
label L1.

Listing 13-3c. Example Ch13_03 NASM Code

```
;-------------------------------------------------------------------------------
; Ch13_03_fasm.asm
;-------------------------------------------------------------------------------

        %include "ModX86Asm3eNASM.inc"
        %include "cmpequ_int.asmh"

NSE     equ     64                              ;num_simd_elements


;-------------------------------------------------------------------------------
; Macro PixelCmp_M
;-------------------------------------------------------------------------------

%macro  PixelCmp_M 1
        align 16
%%L1:   add rax,NSE                             ;i += NSE
        vmovdqa64 zmm2,[rsi+rax]                ;load src[i:i+63]
        vpcmpub k1,zmm2,zmm1,%1                 ;packed compare using CmpOp
        vmovdqu8 zmm3{k1}{z},zmm0               ;create pixel mask
        vmovdqa64 [rdi+rax],zmm3                ;save des[i:i+63]
        sub rdx,NSE                             ;num_pixels -= NSE
        jnz %%L1                                ;repeat until done
        jmp Done
%endmacro


;-------------------------------------------------------------------------------
; void ComparePixels_avx512(uint8_t* des, const uint8_t* src, size_t num_pixels,
;   CmpOp cmp_op, uint8_t cmp_val);
;-------------------------------------------------------------------------------

        section .text

        global ComparePixels_avx512
ComparePixels_avx512:

; Validate arguments
        mov eax,1                               ;load error return code

        test rdx,rdx
        jz Done                                 ;jump if num_pixels == 0

        test rdx,3fh
        jnz Done                                ;jump if num_pixels % 64 != 0

        test rdi,3fh
        jnz Done                                ;jump if des not 64b aligned
```

```
        test rsi,3fh
        jnz Done                            ;jump if src not 64b aligned

        cmp rcx,CmpOpTableCount
        jae Done                            ;jump if cmp_op is invalid

; Initialize
        mov eax,0ffh
        vpbroadcastb zmm0,eax               ;zmm0 = packed 0xff
        vpbroadcastb zmm1,r8b               ;zmm1 = packed cmp_val
        mov rax,-NSE                        ;i = -NSE

; Jump to target compare code
        lea r10,[CmpOpTable]                ;r10 = address of CmpOpTable
        mov r11,[r10+rcx*8]                 ;r11 = address of compare code block
        jmp r11                             ;jump to specified compare code block

; Compare code blocks using macro PixelCmp_M
CmpEQ:   PixelCmp_M CMP_EQ
CmpNE:   PixelCmp_M CMP_NEQ
CmpLT:   PixelCmp_M CMP_LT
CmpLE:   PixelCmp_M CMP_LE
CmpGT:   PixelCmp_M CMP_GT
CmpGE:   PixelCmp_M CMP_GE

Done:   vzeroupper
        ret

; The order of values in following table must match enum CmpOp
; that's defined in Ch03_03.h.

        section .data align = 8
CmpOpTable equ $
        dq CmpEQ
        dq CmpNE
        dq CmpLT
        dq CmpLE
        dq CmpGT
        dq CmpGE
CmpOpTableCount equ ($ - CmpOpTable) / 8
```

The NASM code for function ComparePixels_avx512() in Listing 13-3c is basically the same as the MASM code shown in Listing 13-3b except for different argument registers. Here are the results for source code example Ch13_03.

```
----- Results for Ch13_03 -----

Test #1
  num_pixels: 4194304
  cmp_op:     EQ
  cmp_val:    197
  Pixel masks are identical
  Number of non-zero mask pixels = 16371

Test #2
  num_pixels: 4194304
  cmp_op:     NE
  cmp_val:    222
  Pixel masks are identical
  Number of non-zero mask pixels = 4178047

Test #3
  num_pixels: 4194304
  cmp_op:     LT
  cmp_val:    43
  Pixel masks are identical
  Number of non-zero mask pixels = 703907

Test #4
  num_pixels: 4194304
  cmp_op:     LE
  cmp_val:    43
  Pixel masks are identical
  Number of non-zero mask pixels = 720312

Test #5
  num_pixels: 4194304
  cmp_op:     GT
  cmp_val:    129
  Pixel masks are identical
  Number of non-zero mask pixels = 2064045

Test #6
  num_pixels: 4194304
  cmp_op:     GE
  cmp_val:    222
  Pixel masks are identical
  Number of non-zero mask pixels = 557260
```

Image Statistics

The next source code example, entitled Ch13_04, illustrates how to calculate the mean and standard deviation of a grayscale image. The C++ and assembly language functions in this example use the following equations to calculate the mean and standard deviation:

$$\bar{x} = \frac{1}{n}\sum_i x_i$$

$$s = \sqrt{\frac{n\sum_i x_i^2 - \left(\sum_i x_i\right)^2}{n(n-1)}}$$

In this equation, the symbol x_i represents an image pixel and n denotes the total number of pixels. If you study these equations carefully, you'll notice that two sums must be calculated: the sum of all pixels and the sum of pixel values squared. Once these sums are calculated, the mean and standard deviation can be derived using scalar floating-point arithmetic. It should be noted that the standard deviation equation defined here is suitable for this source code example since integer arithmetic is employed to calculate the required sums. However, this same equation is often unsuitable for other standard deviation calculations, especially those that involve floating-point values. You may want to consult one of the statistical variance references listed in Appendix B before using this equation in your own programs.

To make the source code in example Ch13_04 a bit more interesting, the mean and standard deviation calculating functions only use pixel values that reside between two threshold limits.

Listing 13-4a shows the principal C++ code for example Ch13_04. This listing starts with the declaration of a structure named ImageStats, which is located in header file Ch13_04.h. This structure contains the required data for the mean and standard deviation calculating functions. In file Ch13_04.cpp (not shown in Listing 13-4a), the function CalcImageStats() uses the C++ class ImageMatrix to load a test PNG image file. This function also invokes the statistical calculating functions CalcImageStats_cpp() and CalcImageStats_avx512(). Note that both functions require an argument of type ImageStats.

Listing 13-4a. Example Ch13_04 C++ Code

```
//-----------------------------------------------------------------------------
// Ch13_04.h
//-----------------------------------------------------------------------------

#pragma once
#include <cstddef>
#include <cstdint>

// Simple image statistics structure. This must match the structure that's
// defined in Ch13_04_fasm.asm

struct ImageStats
{
    uint8_t* m_PixelBuffer;
    uint32_t m_PixelMinVal;
    uint32_t m_PixelMaxVal;
    size_t m_NumPixels;
    size_t m_NumPixelsInRange;
    uint64_t m_PixelSum;
```

```cpp
        uint64_t m_PixelSumSquares;
        double m_PixelMean;
        double m_PixelStDev;
};

// Ch13_04_fasm.cpp, Ch13_04_fasm.s
extern "C" void CalcImageStats_avx512(ImageStats& im_stats);

// Ch13_04_fcpp.cpp
extern void CalcImageStats_cpp(ImageStats& im_stats);

// Ch13_04_misc.cpp
extern "C" bool CheckArgs(const ImageStats& im_stats);

// Ch13_04_bm.cpp
extern void CalcImageStats_bm(void);

// Miscellaneous globals and constants
extern const char* g_ImageFileName;
constexpr size_t c_Alignment = 64;
constexpr uint32_t c_PixelMinVal = 40;
constexpr uint32_t c_PixelMaxVal = 230;

//-----------------------------------------------------------------------------
// Ch13_04_fcpp.cpp
//-----------------------------------------------------------------------------

#include <iostream>
#include <stdexcept>
#include <cmath>
#include "Ch13_04.h"

void CalcImageStats_cpp(ImageStats& im_stats)
{
    if (!CheckArgs(im_stats))
        throw std::runtime_error("CalcImageStats_cpp() - CheckArgs failed");

    // Perform required initializations
    im_stats.m_PixelSum = 0;
    im_stats.m_PixelSumSquares = 0;
    im_stats.m_NumPixelsInRange = 0;
    size_t num_pixels = im_stats.m_NumPixels;
    const uint8_t* pb = im_stats.m_PixelBuffer;

    // Calculate intermediate sums
    for (size_t i = 0; i < num_pixels; i++)
    {
        uint32_t pval = pb[i];
```

```
        if (pval >= im_stats.m_PixelMinVal && pval <= im_stats.m_PixelMaxVal)
        {
            im_stats.m_PixelSum += pval;
            im_stats.m_PixelSumSquares += (uint64_t)pval * pval;
            im_stats.m_NumPixelsInRange++;
        }
    }

    // Calculate image stats
    double temp0 = (double)im_stats.m_NumPixelsInRange * im_stats.m_PixelSumSquares;
    double temp1 = (double)im_stats.m_PixelSum * im_stats.m_PixelSum;
    double temp2 = (double)(im_stats.m_NumPixelsInRange - 1);
    double var_num = temp0 - temp1;
    double var_den = (double)im_stats.m_NumPixelsInRange * temp2;
    double var = var_num / var_den;

    im_stats.m_PixelMean = (double)im_stats.m_PixelSum / im_stats.m_NumPixelsInRange;
    im_stats.m_PixelStDev = sqrt(var);
}
```

Also shown in Listing 13-4a is file Ch13_04_fcpp.cpp. This file contains the definition of function CalcImageStats_cpp(), which calculates the image mean and standard deviation using standard C++ statements. Note that the for-loop includes a block of code that tests each pixel value to ensure that it is in range before updating m_PixelSum, m_PixelSumSquares, and m_NumPixelsInRange. Following calculation of the required sums, it computes the final mean and standard deviation.

Listing 13-4b shows the MASM code for example Ch13_04. Toward the top of this listing is the definition of an assembly language structure named IS. This structure is the semantic equivalent of the C++ structure ImageStats that's shown in Listing 13-4a.

Listing 13-4b. Example Ch13_04 MASM Code

```
;-----------------------------------------------------------------------------
; Ch13_04_fasm.asm
;-----------------------------------------------------------------------------

            include <cmpequ_int.asmh>
            include <MacrosX86-64-AVX.asmh>

; Image statistics structure. This must match the structure that's
; defined in Ch13_04.h

IS                  struct
PixelBuffer         qword ?
PixelMinVal         dword ?
PixelMaxVal         dword ?
NumPixels           qword ?
NumPixelsInRange    qword ?
PixelSum            qword ?
PixelSumSquares     qword ?
PixelMean           real8 ?
PixelStDev          real8 ?
IS                  ends
```

```
;-------------------------------------------------------------------------------
; UpdateSumVars_M - update pixel_sums (zmm16) and pixel_sum_sqs (zmm17)
;
; Macro Parameters:
;   EI                 pixel block extract index
;
; Registers:
;   zmm5               pixel buffer values pb[i:i+63]
;   zmm16              pixel_sums (16 dwords)
;   zmm17              pixel_sum_sqs (16 dwords)
;   zmm18/xmm18        scratch registers
;-------------------------------------------------------------------------------

UpdateSumVars_M macro EI
        vextracti64x2 xmm18,zmm5,EI          ;extract pixels pb[i+EI*16:i+EI*16+15]
        vpmovzxbd zmm18,xmm18                ;promote to dwords
        vpaddd zmm16,zmm16,zmm18             ;update pixel_sums
        vpmulld zmm18,zmm18,zmm18
        vpaddd zmm17,zmm17,zmm18             ;update pixel_sum_sqs
        endm


;-------------------------------------------------------------------------------
; UpdateQwords_M - add dword elements in ZmmSrc to qword sums in ZmmDes
;
; Macro Parameters:
;   ZmmDes             zmm destination register
;   ZmmSrc             zmm source register
;   YmmSrc             ymm source register (must be same number as ZmmSrc)
;
; Registers:
;   zmm31/ymm31        scratch registers
;-------------------------------------------------------------------------------

UpdateQwords_M macro ZmmDes,ZmmSrc,YmmSrc
        vextracti32x8 ymm31,ZmmSrc,1         ;extract ZmmSrc dwords 8:15
        vpaddd ymm31,ymm31,YmmSrc            ;add ZmmSrc dwords 8:15 and 0:7
        vpmovzxdq zmm31,ymm31                ;promote to qwords
        vpaddq ZmmDes,ZmmDes,zmm31           ;update ZmmDes qwords 0:7
        endm


;-------------------------------------------------------------------------------
; SumQwords_M  - sum qword elements in ZmmSrc
;
; Macro Parameters:
;   GprDes             destination general-purpose register
;   GprTmp             temp general-purpose register (must be different than GprDes)
;   ZmmSrc             zmm source register
;   YmmSrc             ymm source register (must be same number as ZmmSrc)
;
```

```
; Registers:
;    ymm30/xmm30        scratch registers
;    xmm31             scratch register
;-------------------------------------------------------------------------------

SumQwords_M macro GprDes,GprTmp,ZmmSrc,YmmSrc
        vextracti64x4 ymm30,ZmmSrc,1        ;ymm30 = ZmmSrc qword elements 4:7
        vpaddq ymm30,ymm30,YmmSrc           ;sum ZmmSrc qwords 4:7 and 0:3
        vextracti64x2 xmm31,ymm30,1         ;xmm31 = ymm30 qwords 2:3
        vpaddq xmm31,xmm31,xmm30            ;xmm31 = sum of ymm30 qwords

        vpextrq GprTmp,xmm31,0              ;extract xmm31 qword 0
        vpextrq GprDes,xmm31,1              ;extract xmm31 qword 1
        add GprDes,GprTmp                   ;GprDes = scalar qword sum
        endm


;-------------------------------------------------------------------------------
; void CalcImageStats_avx512(ImageStats& im_stats);
;-------------------------------------------------------------------------------

NSE     equ 64                              ;num_simd_elements

        extern CheckArgs:proc

        .code
CalcImageStats_avx512 proc frame
        CreateFrame_M CIS_,0,0
        EndProlog_M

; Validate values in im_stats
        mov qword ptr [rbp+CIS_OffsetHomeRCX],rcx   ;save im_stats

        sub rsp,32                          ;allocate CheckArgs home area
        call CheckArgs                      ;validate values im_stats
        or eax,eax
        jz Done                             ;jump if CheckArgs failed

        mov rcx,qword ptr [rbp+CIS_OffsetHomeRCX]   ;rcx = im_stats

; Initialize
        mov rdx,qword ptr [rcx+IS.PixelBuffer]  ;rdx = pixel_buffer (pb)
        mov r8,qword ptr [rcx+IS.NumPixels]     ;r8 = num_pixels

        vpbroadcastb zmm0,byte ptr [rcx+IS.PixelMinVal]   ;pixel_min_vals
        vpbroadcastb zmm1,byte ptr [rcx+IS.PixelMaxVal]   ;pixel_max_vals

        vpxorq zmm2,zmm2,zmm2                ;zmm2 = pixel_sums (8 qwords)
        vpxorq zmm3,zmm3,zmm3                ;zmm3 = pixel_sum_sqs (8 qwords)

        xor r9,r9                           ;r9 = num_pixels_in_range
        lea rax,[rdx+r8-NSE]                ;rax = addr of final pixel block
        sub rdx,NSE                         ;adjust pb for Loop1
```

```
;------------------------------------------------------------------
; Registers used in code below:
;
;   rax      &pixel_buffer[num_pixels]   zmm0    pixel_min_vals
;   rcx      im_stats                    zmm1    pixel_max_vals
;   rdx      pixel_buffer                zmm2    pixel_sums (8 qwords)
;   r8       num_pixels                  zmm3    pixel_sum_sqs (8 qwords)
;   r9       num_pixels_in_range         zmm4    pixel values
;   r10      scratch register            zmm5    pixel values in range (or zero)
;   r11      scratch register            zmm16 - zmm18 scratch registers
;------------------------------------------------------------------


; Load next block of 64 pixels, calc in-range pixels
        align 16
Loop1:  add rdx,NSE                         ;rdx = &pb[i:i+63]
        vmovdqa64 zmm4,zmmword ptr [rdx]     ;load pb[i:i+63]
        vpcmpub k1,zmm4,zmm0,CMP_GE          ;k1 = mask of pixels GE PixelMinVal
        vpcmpub k2,zmm4,zmm1,CMP_LE          ;k2 = mask of pixels LE PixelMaxVal
        kandq k3,k1,k2                       ;k3 = mask of in-range pixels
        vmovdqu8 zmm5{k3}{z},zmm4            ;zmm5 = pixels in range (or zero)

        kmovq r10,k3                         ;r10 = in-range mask
        popcnt r10,r10                       ;r10 = number of in-range pixels
        add r9,r10                           ;update num_pixels_in_range

; Update pixel_sums and pixel_sums_sqs
        vpxord zmm16,zmm16,zmm16             ;loop pixel_sums (16 dwords)
        vpxord zmm17,zmm17,zmm17             ;loop pixel_sum_sqs (16 dwords)

        UpdateSumVars_M 0                    ;process pb[i:i+15]
        UpdateSumVars_M 1                    ;process pb[i+16:i+31]
        UpdateSumVars_M 2                    ;process pb[i+32:i+47]
        UpdateSumVars_M 3                    ;process pb[i+48:i+63]

        UpdateQwords_M zmm2,zmm16,ymm16      ;update pixel_sums
        UpdateQwords_M zmm3,zmm17,ymm17      ;update pixel_sum_sqs

        cmp rdx,rax                          ;more pixels?
        jb Loop1                             ;jump if yes

; Calculate final image statistics
        SumQwords_M r10,rax,zmm2,ymm2        ;r10 = pixel_sum
        SumQwords_M r11,rax,zmm3,ymm3        ;r11 = pixel_sum_sqs

        mov qword ptr [rcx+IS.NumPixelsInRange],r9  ;save num_pixels_in_range
        mov qword ptr [rcx+IS.PixelSum],r10         ;save pixel_sum
        mov qword ptr [rcx+IS.PixelSumSquares],r11  ;save pixel_sum_sqs
```

```
        vcvtusi2sd xmm16,xmm16,r9                ;num_pixels_in_range as F64
        sub r9,1                                 ;r9 = num_pixels_in_range - 1
        vcvtusi2sd xmm17,xmm16,r9                ;num_pixels_in_range - 1 as F64
        vcvtusi2sd xmm18,xmm18,r10               ;pixel_sum as F64
        vcvtusi2sd xmm19,xmm19,r11               ;pixel_sum_sqs as F64

        vmulsd xmm0,xmm16,xmm19                  ;num_pixels_in_range * pixel_sum_sqs
        vmulsd xmm1,xmm18,xmm18                  ;pixel_sum * pixel_sum
        vsubsd xmm2,xmm0,xmm1                    ;variance numerator
        vmulsd xmm3,xmm16,xmm17                  ;variance denominator
        vdivsd xmm4,xmm2,xmm3                    ;variance

        vdivsd xmm0,xmm18,xmm16                  ;calc mean
        vmovsd real8 ptr [rcx+IS.PixelMean],xmm0 ;save mean

        vsqrtsd xmm1,xmm1,xmm4                   ;calc st_dev
        vmovsd real8 ptr [rcx+IS.PixelStDev],xmm1 ;save st_dev

Done:   vzeroupper
        DeleteFrame_M
        ret

CalcImageStats_avx512 endp
        end
```

Following the declaration of structure IS are three macro definitions. The first macro, UpdateSumVars_M, emits code that updates pixel_sums and pixel_sum_sqs during execution of Loop1 in function CalcImageStats_avx512(). Note that macro UpdateSumVars_M requires an argument named EI (extract index), which specifies the 16-pixel block that UpdateSumVars_M should process. The first instruction of UpdateSumVars_M, vextracti64x2 xmm18,zmm5,EI (Extract Packed Integer Values), copies 128 bits of integer data from ZMM5 to register XMM18. More specifically, execution of this instruction extracts pixel values pb[i+EI*16:i+EI*16+15] from register ZMM5 and saves them in XMM18. The next instruction, vpmovzxbd zmm18,xmm18, size-extends the pixel values from bytes to doublewords. The ensuing instruction triplet, vpaddd zmm16,zmm16,zmm18, vpmulld zmm18,zmm18,zmm18, and vpaddd zmm17,zmm17,zmm18, updates pixel_sums (ZMM16) and pixel_sum_sqs (ZMM17).

The next macro in Listing 13-4b, UpdateQwords_M, adds the doubleword values in ZmmSrc to the quadword values in ZmmDes. This macro begins with a vextracti32x8 ymm31,ZmmSrc,1 instruction that extracts the eight high-order doublewords from ZmmSrc and saves them in register YMM31. The next macro instruction, vpaddd ymm31,ymm31,YmmSrc, sums the doubleword elements of YMM31 (ZmmSrc doublewords 8:15) and YmmSrc (ZmmSrc doublewords 0:7). The ensuing instruction pair, vpmovzxdq zmm31,ymm31 and vpaddq ZmmDes,ZmmDes,zmm31, size-promotes the doubleword elements of YMM31 to quadwords and then adds these values to the quadword elements of ZmmDes.

The final macro in Listing 13-4b, SumQwords_M, reduces the quadword elements of argument ZmmSrc to a scalar value and saves this result in general-purpose register Gpr. This macro begins with a vextracti64x4 ymm30,ZmmSrc,1 instruction that extracts the four high-order quadwords from ZmmSrc and saves these values in YMM30 (macro SumQwords_M uses YMM30 as a scratchpad register). The subsequent instruction, vpaddq ymm30,ymm30,YmmSrc, sums the just extracted quadword elements with the four quadwords in YmmSrc (i.e., the four low-order quadwords of ZmmSrc). The ensuing instruction pair, vextracti64x2 xmm31,ymm30,1 and vpaddq xmm31,xmm31,xmm30, reduces the number of quadwords to two. The final three instructions of SumQwords_M, vpextrq GprTmp,xmm31,0, vpextrq GprDes,xmm31,1, and add GprDes,GprTmp, calculate the final scalar quadword sum. Note that different general-purpose registers must be used for macro parameters GprTmp and GprDes.

Following its prologue, function CalcImageStats_avx512() begins its execution with a code block that validates the values in im_stats. In this function, argument validation is performed using the C++ function CheckArgs(). Using a C++ function to perform run-time argument validation is often convenient in applications that include both a C++ and x86-AVX assembly language implementation of the same calculating function. Note that prior to calling CheckArgs(), CalcImageStats_avx512() saves register RCX (im_stats) in its home area on the stack. The reason for this register save is that RCX is a volatile register that CheckArgs() might modify. The mov rcx,qword ptr [rbp+CIS_OffsetHomeRCX] instruction that occurs after the call to CheckArgs() reloads RCX with argument value im_stats.

Following argument validation in CalcImageStats_avx512() is a code block that performs the required initializations for Loop1. Note that the byte elements of registers ZMM0 and ZMM1 are loaded with IS. PixelMinVal and IS.PixelMaxVal, respectively. The vpxorq zmm2,zmm2,zmm2 instruction that follows initializes each quadword elements of ZMM2 (pixel_sums) to zero. Unlike AVX and AVX2, AVX-512 bitwise logical instructions incorporate a size suffix letter as part of the mnemonic, which facilitates masking operations. The ensuing vpxorq zmm3,zmm3,zmm3 instruction initializes each quadword element in pixel_sum_sqs to zero.

Each iteration of Loop1 commences with instruction pair add rdx,NSE and vmovdqa64 zmm4,zmmword ptr [rdx] that loads pixel values pb[i:i+63] into register ZMM4. The next instruction, vpcmpub k1,zmm4,zmm0,CMP_GE, loads the opmask register with a mask of all pixels in ZMM4 whose value is greater than or equal to PixelMinVal. This is followed by a vpcmpub k2,zmm4,zmm1,CMP_LE that loads K2 with a mask of all pixels in ZMM4 whose value is less than or equal to PixelMaxVal. The next instruction, kandq k3,k1,k2 (Bitwise Logical AND Masks), performs a bitwise logical AND of opmask registers K1 and K2. The result of this operation is a quadword mask of all pixels whose values reside between PixelMinVal and PixelMaxVal. The vmovdqu8 zmm5{k3}{z},zmm4 instruction that follows loads each byte element of ZMM5 with either an original pixel value (pixel is in range) or zero (pixel is out of range). Figure 13-8 illustrates execution of these instructions. After the vmovdqu8 instruction is the instruction triplet kmovq r10,k3, popcnt r10,r10, and add r9,r10, which updates num_pixels_in_range (R9).

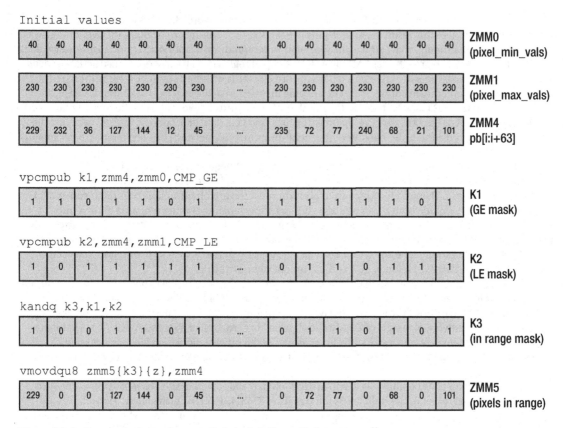

Figure 13-8. *Removal of out-of-range pixels in* CalcImageStats_avx512()

Following determination of in-range pixels, CalcImageStats_avx512() updates pixel_sums and pixel_sum_sqs. The code block that performs this action begins with the instruction pair vpxord zmm16,zmm16,zmm16 and vpxord zmm17,zmm17,zmm17. These instructions initialize registers ZMM16 and ZMM17 to hold intermediate doubleword results. Next is a series of UpdateSumVars_M usages that update ZMM16 (pixel_sums) and ZMM17 (pixel_sum_sqs) using the in-range pixel values from the current iteration of Loop1. The subsequent two instructions, UpdateQwords_M zmm2,zmm16,zmm16 and UpdateQwords_M zmm3,zmm17,zmm17, employ the just calculated intermediate results to update the quadword values in ZMM2 (pixel_sums) and ZMM3 (pixel_sum_sqs).

Upon completion of Loop1, CalcImageStats_avx512() exploits macro SumQwords_M twice to reduce packed quadword variables pixel_sum (ZMM2) and pixel_sum_sqs (ZMM3) to scalar values. Following this reduction, scalar double-precision floating-point arithmetic is used to calculate the final pixel mean and standard deviation. Note that the scalar code employs the AVX-512 instruction vcvtusi2sd (Convert Unsigned Integer to Scalar DPFP Value).

Listing 13-4c shows the NASM code for example Ch13_04. The first notable difference between this code and the MASM code is the directives used to define the assembly language structure IS. The second dissimilarity is the macro definitions. Recall that NASM uses the symbols %1, %2, etc., for macro parameters. Using numeric symbols instead of symbolic names means that the code in a NASM macro definition with multiple parameters might appear a little confusing. Adding a comment block that defines the purpose of each macro parameter, as exemplified in Listing 13-4c, usually precludes any confusion.

Listing 13-4c. Example Ch13_04 NASM Code

```
;-------------------------------------------------------------------------------
; Ch13_04_fasm.s
;-------------------------------------------------------------------------------

        %include "ModX86Asm3eNASM.inc"
        %include "cmpequ_int.asmh"

; Image statistics structure. This must match the structure that's
; defined in Ch13_04.h

struc IS
.PixelBuffer            resq 1
.PixelMinVal            resd 1
.PixelMaxVal            resd 1
.NumPixels              resq 1
.NumPixelsInRange       resq 1
.PixelSum               resq 1
.PixelSumSquares        resq 1
.PixelMean              resq 1
.PixelStDev             resq 1
endstruc


;-------------------------------------------------------------------------------
; UpdateSumVars_M - update pixel_sums (zmm16) and pixel_sum_sqs (zmm17)
;
; Macro Parameters:
;   EI (%1)         pixel block extract index
;
; Registers:
;   zmm5            pixel buffer values pb[i:i+63]
;   zmm16           pixel_sums (16 dwords)
;   zmm17           pixel_sum_sqs (16 dwords)
;   zmm18/xmm18     scratch registers
;-------------------------------------------------------------------------------

%macro  UpdateSumVars_M 1
        vextracti64x2 xmm18,zmm5,%1     ;extract pixels pb[i+EI*16:i+EI*16+15]
        vpmovzxbd zmm18,xmm18           ;promote to dwords
        vpaddd zmm16,zmm16,zmm18        ;update pixel_sums
        vpmulld zmm18,zmm18,zmm18
        vpaddd zmm17,zmm17,zmm18        ;update pixel_sum_sqs
%endmacro


;-------------------------------------------------------------------------------
; UpdateQwords_M - add dword elements in ZmmSrc to qword sums in ZmmDes
;
; Macro Parameters:
;   ZmmDes (%1)     zmm destination register
;   ZmmSrc (%2)     zmm source register
;   YmmSrc (%3)     ymm source register (must be same number as ZmmSrc)
```

```
;
; Registers:
;   zmm31/ymm31     scratch registers
;---------------------------------------------------------------------------

%macro  UpdateQwords_M 3
        vextracti32x8 ymm31,%2,1              ;extract ZmmSrc dwords 8:15
        vpaddd ymm31,ymm31,%3                 ;add ZmmSrc dwords 8:15 and 0:7
        vpmovzxdq zmm31,ymm31                 ;promote to qwords
        vpaddq %1,%1,zmm31                    ;update ZmmDes qwords 0:7
%endmacro


;---------------------------------------------------------------------------
; SumQwords_M  - sum qword elements in ZmmSrc
;
; Macro Parameters:
;   GprDes (%1)     destination general-purpose register
;   GprTmp (%2)     temp general-purpose register (must be different than GprDes)
;   ZmmSrc (%3)     zmm source register
;   YmmSrc (%4)     ymm source register (must be same number as ZmmSrc)
;
; Registers:
;   ymm30/xmm30     scratch registers
;   xmm31           scratch register
;---------------------------------------------------------------------------

%macro SumQwords_M 4
        vextracti64x4 ymm30,%3,1             ;ymm30 = ZmmSrc qword elements 4:7
        vpaddq ymm30,ymm30,%4                ;sum ZmmSrc qwords 4:7 and 0:3
        vextracti64x2 xmm31,ymm30,1          ;xmm31 = ymm30 qwords 2:3
        vpaddq xmm31,xmm31,xmm30             ;xmm31 = sum of ymm30 qwords

        vpextrq %2,xmm31,0                   ;extract xmm31 qword 0
        vpextrq %1,xmm31,1                   ;extract xmm31 qword 1
        add %1,%2                            ;GprDes = scalar qword sum
%endmacro

;---------------------------------------------------------------------------
; void CalcImageStats_avx512(ImageStats& im_stats);
;---------------------------------------------------------------------------

NSE     equ 64                               ;num_simd_elements

        section .text
        extern CheckArgs

        global CalcImageStats_avx512
CalcImageStats_avx512:
```

```
; Validate values in im_stats
        push rdi                            ;save im_stats
        call CheckArgs                      ;validate values im_stats
        pop rdi                             ;restore im_stats
        or eax,eax
        jz Done                             ;jump if CheckArgs failed

; Initialize
        mov rdx,[rdi+IS.PixelBuffer]        ;rdx = pixel_buffer (pb)
        mov r8,[rdi+IS.NumPixels]           ;r8 = num_pixels

        vpbroadcastb zmm0,[rdi+IS.PixelMinVal] ;pixel_min_vals
        vpbroadcastb zmm1,[rdi+IS.PixelMaxVal] ;pixel_max_vals

        vpxorq zmm2,zmm2,zmm2               ;zmm2 = pixel_sums (8 qwords)
        vpxorq zmm3,zmm3,zmm3               ;zmm3 = pixel_sum_sqs (8 qwords)

        xor r9,r9                           ;r9 = num_pixels_in_range
        lea rax,[rdx+r8-NSE]                ;rax = addr of final pixel block
        sub rdx,NSE                         ;adjust pb for Loop1

;-------------------------------------------------------------------------
; Registers used in code below:
;
;   rax     &pixel_buffer[num_pixels]   zmm0    pixel_min_vals
;   rdi     im_stats                    zmm1    pixel_max_vals
;   rdx     pixel_buffer                zmm2    pixel_sums (8 qwords)
;   r8      num_pixels                  zmm3    pixel_sum_sqs (8 qwords)
;   r9      num_pixels_in_range         zmm4    pixel values
;   r10     scratch register            zmm5    pixel values in range (or zero)
;   r11     scratch register            zmm16 - zmm18 scratch registers
;-------------------------------------------------------------------------

; Load next block of 64 pixels, calc in-range pixels
        align 16
Loop1:  add rdx,NSE                         ;rdx = &pb[i:i+63]
        vmovdqa64 zmm4,[rdx]                 ;load pb[i:i+63]
        vpcmpub k1,zmm4,zmm0,CMP_GE          ;k1 = mask of pixels GE PixelMinVal
        vpcmpub k2,zmm4,zmm1,CMP_LE          ;k2 = mask of pixels LE PixelMaxVal
        kandq k3,k1,k2                       ;k3 = mask of in-range pixels
        vmovdqu8 zmm5{k3}{z},zmm4            ;zmm5 = pixels in range (or zero)

        kmovq r10,k3                         ;r10 = in-range mask
        popcnt r10,r10                       ;r10 = number of in-range pixels
        add r9,r10                           ;update num_pixels_in_range

; Update pixel_sums and pixel_sums_sqs
        vpxord zmm16,zmm16,zmm16             ;loop pixel_sums (16 dwords)
        vpxord zmm17,zmm17,zmm17             ;loop pixel_sum_sqs (16 dwords)

        UpdateSumVars_M 0                    ;process pb[i:i+15]
        UpdateSumVars_M 1                    ;process pb[i+16:i+31]
```

541

```
        UpdateSumVars_M 2                       ;process pb[i+32:i+47]
        UpdateSumVars_M 3                       ;process pb[i+48:i+63]

        UpdateQwords_M zmm2,zmm16,ymm16         ;update pixel_sums
        UpdateQwords_M zmm3,zmm17,ymm17         ;update pixel_sum_sqs

        cmp rdx,rax                             ;more pixels?
        jb Loop1                                ;jump if yes

; Calculate final image statistics
        SumQwords_M r10,rax,zmm2,ymm2           ;r10 = pixel_sum
        SumQwords_M r11,rax,zmm3,ymm3           ;r11 = pixel_sum_sqs

        mov [rdi+IS.NumPixelsInRange],r9        ;save num_pixels_in_range
        mov [rdi+IS.PixelSum],r10               ;save pixel_sum
        mov [rdi+IS.PixelSumSquares],r11        ;save pixel_sum_sqs

        vcvtusi2sd xmm16,xmm16,r9               ;num_pixels_in_range as F64
        sub r9,1                                ;r9 = num_pixels_in_range - 1
        vcvtusi2sd xmm17,xmm16,r9               ;num_pixels_in_range - 1 as F64
        vcvtusi2sd xmm18,xmm18,r10              ;pixel_sum as F64
        vcvtusi2sd xmm19,xmm19,r11              ;pixel_sum_sqs as F64

        vmulsd xmm0,xmm16,xmm19                 ;num_pixels_in_range * pixel_sum_sqs
        vmulsd xmm1,xmm18,xmm18                 ;pixel_sum * pixel_sum
        vsubsd xmm2,xmm0,xmm1                   ;variance numerator
        vmulsd xmm3,xmm16,xmm17                 ;variance denominator
        vdivsd xmm4,xmm2,xmm3                   ;variance

        vdivsd xmm0,xmm18,xmm16                 ;calc mean
        vmovsd [rdi+IS.PixelMean],xmm0          ;save mean

        vsqrtsd xmm1,xmm1,xmm4                  ;calc st_dev
        vmovsd [rdi+IS.PixelStDev],xmm1         ;save st_dev

Done:   vzeroupper
        ret
```

The final difference of note in Listing 13-4c is that argument value im_stats is passed via register RDI. The image mean and standard deviation calculating code is the same. Here are the results for source code example Ch13_04:

```
----- Results for Ch13_04 -----
image_fn:               ../../Data/TestImageB.png
num_pixels:             15360000
c_PixelMinVal:          40
c_PixelMaxVal:          230

m_NumPixelsInRange:     11562072    | 11562072
m_PixelSum:             887533305   | 887533305
```

```
m_PixelSumSquares:    90086695723  |  90086695723
m_PixelMean:          76.762479    |  76.762479
m_PixelStDev:         43.578576    |  43.578576

Running benchmark function CalcImageStats_bm() - please wait
Benchmark times save to file @Ch13_04_CalcImageStats_bm_HELIUM.csv
```

Table 13-3 shows the benchmark timing measurements for example Ch13_04. As you can see, the assembly language implementations of the pixel mean and standard deviation calculating functions are significantly faster than their C++ counterparts.

Table 13-3. *Benchmark Timing Measurements (Microseconds) for Pixel Mean/SD Calculation Using* `TestImageB.png`

Function	i5-11600K	i7-11700K	7700X
CalcImageStats_cpp()	11817 (20)	20292 (724)	10002 (22)
CalcImageStats_avx512()	1199 (7)	1122 (22)	924 (5)

Image Histogram

In Chapter 10, you learned how to construct an image histogram using AVX2 instructions (see example Ch10_06). In this section, you'll learn how to build an image histogram using AVX-512 instructions. You'll also learn how to use the vpscatterdd (Scatter Packed Dwords using Dword Indices) instruction. The C++ source code for example Ch13_05 is the same as the C++ code for example Ch10_06 and is not shown. Before continuing with this section, you may want to review the C++ code in Listing 10-6a. You may also want to review the assembly language code in Listing 10-6b (or Listing 10-6c) and Figure 10-7 since a similar histogram construction technique is used in this example.

Recall from source code example Ch10_06 that assembly language function BuildHistogram_avx2() constructed eight intermediate histograms on the stack to facilitate the use of SIMD gather operations (see Figure 10-7). During each iteration of Loop1, BuildHistogram_avx2() utilized a vpgatherdd instruction to read bin values from the intermediate histograms. The histogram bin values were then updated and saved using a simulated scatter operation. The AVX-512 function BuildHistogram_avx512(), shown in Listing 13-5, utilizes the same technique except that it updates 16 intermediate histograms in unison. It also exploits the AVX-512 vpscatterdd instruction to carry out the scatter operation.

Listing 13-5. Example Ch13_05 MASM Code

```
;----------------------------------------------------------------------
; Ch13_05_fasm.asm
;----------------------------------------------------------------------

        include <MacrosX86-64-AVX.asmh>

; Offsets for local histograms on stack
ConstVals       segment readonly align(64) 'const'
HistoOffsets    dword   256 *  0, 256 *  1, 256 *  2, 256 *  3
                dword   256 *  4, 256 *  5, 256 *  6, 256 *  7
                dword   256 *  8, 256 *  9, 256 * 10, 256 * 11
                dword   256 * 12, 256 * 13, 256 * 14, 256 * 15
```

```
;-------------------------------------------------------------------
; void BuildHistogram_avx512(uint32_t* histo, const uint8_t* pixel_buff,
;    size_t num_pixels);
;-------------------------------------------------------------------

HS       equ     256 * 4                          ;size of histogram in bytes

         .code
BuildHistogram_avx512 proc frame
         CreateFrame_M BH_,0,0,rdi
         EndProlog_M

; Validate arguments
         mov r10,rcx                              ;save copy of histo

         test r10,3fh
         jnz BadArg                               ;jump if histo not 64b aligned
         test rdx,3fh
         jnz BadArg                               ;jump if pixel_buff not 64b aligned

         test r8,r8
         jz BadArg                                ;jump if num_pixels == 0
         test r8,3fh
         jnz BadArg                               ;jump if (num_pixels % 64) != 0

; Allocate stack space for temp histograms
         and rsp,0ffffffffffffffc0h               ;align rsp to 64-byte boundary
         sub rsp,HS*16                            ;allocate local histogram space

; Initialize local histograms to zero
         xor eax,eax                              ;rax = fill value
         mov rdi,rsp                              ;rdi = ptr to local histograms
         mov rcx,HS*16/8                          ;rcx = size in qwords
         rep stosq                                ;zero local histograms

; Initialize
         mov eax,1
         vpbroadcastd zmm16,eax                   ;packed dwords of 1
         vmovdqa32 zmm17,zmmword ptr [HistoOffsets]  ;zmm17 = local histogram offsets

         kxnord k0,k0,k0                          ;mask of all ones
         mov rax,-16                              ;pixel_buffer (pb) array offset

; Build local histograms
Loop1:   add rax,16                               ;i += 16

; Gather entries from local histograms (i.e., histo0[pb[i]] - histo15[pb[i+15]])
         vpmovzxbd zmm1,xmmword ptr [rdx+rax]     ;load pb[i:i+15] as dwords
         vpaddd zmm2,zmm1,zmm17                    ;add offsets of local histograms
         kmovd k1,k0                              ;set vpgatherdd mask to all ones
         vpgatherdd zmm3{k1},[rsp+zmm2*4]         ;zmm3 = histo entries
```

```
; Update local histograms
        vpaddd zmm4,zmm3,zmm16                          ;add ones

; Save updated histo0[pb[i]] - histo15[pb[i+15]]
        kmovd k2,k0                                     ;set vpscatterdd mask to all ones
        vpscatterdd [rsp+zmm2*4]{k2},zmm4               ;save updated histo entries

        sub r8,16                                       ;num_pixels -= 16
        jnz Loop1                                       ;repeat until done

; Reduce 16 local histograms to final histogram
        mov rax,-16                                     ;initialize array offset

Loop2:  add rax,16                                              ;rax += 16
        vmovdqa32 zmm0,zmmword ptr [rsp+rax*4 + HS*0]           ;load histo0[i:i+15]
        vmovdqa32 zmm1,zmmword ptr [rsp+rax*4 + HS*1]           ;load histo1[i:i+15]
        vpaddd zmm0,zmm0,zmmword ptr [rsp+rax*4 + HS*2]         ;add histo2[i:i+15]
        vpaddd zmm1,zmm1,zmmword ptr [rsp+rax*4 + HS*3]         ;add histo3[i:i+15]
        vpaddd zmm0,zmm0,zmmword ptr [rsp+rax*4 + HS*4]         ;add histo4[i:i+15]
        vpaddd zmm1,zmm1,zmmword ptr [rsp+rax*4 + HS*5]         ;add histo5[i:i+15]
        vpaddd zmm0,zmm0,zmmword ptr [rsp+rax*4 + HS*6]         ;add histo6[i:i+15]
        vpaddd zmm1,zmm1,zmmword ptr [rsp+rax*4 + HS*7]         ;add histo7[i:i+15]
        vpaddd zmm0,zmm0,zmmword ptr [rsp+rax*4 + HS*8]         ;add histo8[i:i+15]
        vpaddd zmm1,zmm1,zmmword ptr [rsp+rax*4 + HS*9]         ;add histo9[i:i+15]
        vpaddd zmm0,zmm0,zmmword ptr [rsp+rax*4 + HS*10]        ;add histo10[i:i+15]
        vpaddd zmm1,zmm1,zmmword ptr [rsp+rax*4 + HS*11]        ;add histo11[i:i+15]
        vpaddd zmm0,zmm0,zmmword ptr [rsp+rax*4 + HS*12]        ;add histo12[i:i+15]
        vpaddd zmm1,zmm1,zmmword ptr [rsp+rax*4 + HS*13]        ;add histo13[i:i+15]
        vpaddd zmm0,zmm0,zmmword ptr [rsp+rax*4 + HS*14]        ;add histo14[i:i+15]
        vpaddd zmm1,zmm1,zmmword ptr [rsp+rax*4 + HS*15]        ;add histo15[i:i+15]
        vpaddd zmm2,zmm0,zmm1                                   ;zmm2 = histo[i:i+15]

        vmovdqa32 zmmword ptr [r10+rax*4],zmm2                  ;save histo[i:i+15]

        cmp rax,240                                     ;i < 240
        jb Loop2                                        ;jump if yes

        mov eax,1                                       ;set success return code

Done:   vzeroupper
        DeleteFrame_M rdi
        ret

BadArg: xor eax,eax                                     ;set bad argument return code
        jmp Done

BuildHistogram_avx512 endp
        end
```

The assembly language code in Listing 13-5 resembles the code in Listing 10-6b. Listing 13-5 opens with a custom section of constant values. The MASM statement ConstVals segment readonly align(64) 'const' defines the start of a read-only section of constant values that is aligned on a 64-byte boundary.

In section ConstVals, table HistoOffsets contains offsets (in units of doublewords) that define the start position of each intermediate histogram on the stack. Note that HistoOffsets contains offsets for 16 intermediate histograms. The statement HS equ 256 * 4 defines the size (in bytes) of each intermediate histogram and the final histogram; each histogram entry is a doubleword value.

Following argument validation, BuildHistogram_avx512() uses the instruction pair and rsp,0ffffffffffffffc0h and sub rsp,HS*16 to allocate 16 intermediate histograms on the stack. The use of the and rsp,0ffffffffffffffc0h instruction ensures that each intermediate histogram is aligned on a 64-byte boundary. The subsequent code block uses the rep stosq instruction to initialize all intermediate histogram bins to zero. Also note that prior to the start of for-loop Loop1, each doubleword element of register ZMM16 is initialized to 1, and the intermediate histogram offsets from table HistoOffsets are loaded into register ZMM17.

Each iteration of for-loop Loop1 begins with an add rax,16 instruction that calculates i += 16. The next instruction, vpmovzxbd zmm1,xmmword ptr [rdx+rax], loads pixels pb[i:i+15] into register ZMM1. Recall that execution of the vpmovzxbd instruction zero-extends each source operand byte value to a doubleword. The ensuing vpaddd zmm2,zmm1,zmm17 instruction adds the histogram offsets in register ZMM17 to the pixel values in ZMM1. The next instruction, kmovd k1,k0, loads all ones into opmask register K1. The final instruction of the current code block, vpgatherdd zmm3{k1},[rsp+zmm2*4], loads Histo0[pb[i]] into ZMM3[31:0], Histo1[pb[i+1]] into ZMM3[63:32], Histo2[pb[i+2]] into ZMM3[95:64], and so on.

Subsequent to the gather operation, BuildHistogram_avx512() uses a vpaddd zmm4,zmm3,zmm16 instruction to update the histogram bin values in register ZMM3. The ensuing instruction pair, kmovd k2,k0 and vpscatterdd [rsp+zmm2*4]{k2},zmm4, saves the update histogram bin values. Recall that in example Ch10_06, function BuildHistogram_avx2() (Listing 10-6b) simulated a scatter operation using sequences of vmovd and vpsrldq instructions. Following execution of Loop1, the SIMD addition code in for-loop Loop2 reduces the intermediate histograms to the final histogram.

The NASM code for example Ch13_05 (not shown) is basically the same as the MASM code shown in Listing 13-5, except for different argument registers. Here are the results for source code example Ch13_05:

```
----- Results for Ch13_05 -----
Histograms are identical
Histograms saved to file @Ch13_05_Histograms_HELIUM.txt

Running benchmark function BuildHistogram_bm() - please wait
Benchmark times save to file @Ch13_05_BuildHistogram_bm_HELIUM.csv
```

Table 13-4 shows the benchmark timing measurements for example Ch13_05. The measurements for function BuildHistogram_avx2() were copied from Table 10-4. Note that on the two Intel processors, the AVX-512 implementation of the histogram build function outperformed its AVX2 counterpart by a meaningful margin. For the AMD processor, the AVX-512 histogram build function is slower than its AVX2 counterpart (the vpgatherdd and vpscatterdd instructions are slow executors on the AMD 7700X processor).

Table 13-4. *Benchmark Timing Measurements (Microseconds) for Histogram Build Functions Using* TestImageB.png

Function	i5-11600K	i7-11700K	7700X
BuildHistogram_cpp()	8202 (12)	8291 (323)	6639 (8)
BuildHistogram_avx2()	6749 (12)	6663 (122)	7767 (8)
BuildHistogram_avx512()	5132 (5)	5069 (218)	8552 (9)

Summary

Here are the key learning points for Chapter 13:

- AVX-512 is a collection of interrelated instruction set extensions. All AVX-512 conforming processors support AVX512F. A program should always perform a run-time check to detect the presence of AVX512F and any other AVX-512 instruction set extensions it requires.

- The AVX-512 register set includes 32 512-bit wide registers named ZMM0–ZMM31. The low-order 256 and 128 bits are aliased to registers YMM0–YMM31 and XMM0–XMM31, respectively.

- The AVX-512 register set also includes eight opmask registers named K0–K7. Opmask registers K1–K7 can be used to perform instruction-level merge masking or zero masking.

- Many AVX-512 instructions that require a packed operand of constant values can use an embedded broadcast operand instead of a separate broadcast instruction.

- A static rounding mode operand can be specified with many AVX-512 instructions that perform floating-point operations using 512-bit wide packed or scalar floating-point register operands.

- Assembly language functions can use AVX-512 promoted versions of most AVX and AVX2 packed integer instructions to perform operations using 512-, 256-, and 128-bit wide operands.

- Assembly language functions can use the vmovdqa[32|64] and vmovdqu[8|16|32|64] to perform aligned and unaligned moves of packed integer operands.

- The vpcmpu[b|w|d|q] instructions perform packed unsigned integer compare operations and save the resultant compare mask to an opmask register.

- The vpand[d|q], vpandn[d|q], vpor[d|q], and vpxor[d|q] instructions can be used with an opmask register to perform merge or zero masking using doubleword or quadword elements.

- The vextracti[32x4|32x8|64x2|64x4] instructions can be used to extract packed doubleword or quadword values from a packed integer operand.

- The kmov[b|w|d|q] instruction can be used to perform opmask register moves.

- The following instructions can be used to perform opmask register bitwise logical operations: kand[b|w|d|q], kandn[b|w|d|q], knot[b|w|d|q], kor[b|w|d|q], kxnor[b|w|d|q], and kxor[b|w|d|q].

- Functions that modify registers ZMM0–ZMM15 should include a vzeroupper instruction prior to crossing a function boundary to avoid potential x86-AVX to x86-SSE state transition performance penalties. It is not necessary for a function to use vzeroupper if it only modifies registers YMM16–YMM31 or ZMM16–ZMM31.

CHAPTER 14

■ ■ ■

AVX-512 Programming – Packed Floating-Point – Part 1

This chapter introduces AVX-512 programming using packed floating-point values. It begins with a section that illustrates fundamental packed floating-point operations using 512-bit wide operands. This is followed by a section that spotlights the use of AVX-512 with floating-point arrays and matrices. The source code examples in this section are AVX-512 implementations of AVX2 examples that you saw in earlier chapters.

As a reminder, the AVX-512 source code examples published in this book require a processor that supports the following instruction set extensions: AVX512F, AVX512BW, AVX512DQ, and AVX512VL. The host operating system must also support AVX-512. Examples of recent operating systems that support AVX-512 include Windows (version 10 and later), Debian (version 9 and later), and Ubuntu (version 18.04 LTS and later).

Floating-Point Arithmetic

In this section, you'll study two source code examples that demonstrate packed AVX-512 floating-point operations using single-precision and double-precision values. The first example explains basic packed floating-point arithmetic. This example also highlights new assembly language instruction operands that are exclusive to AVX-512. The second source code example demonstrates packed floating-point comparisons. Both source code examples in this section use 512-bit wide operands and the ZMM register set.

Elementary Operations

Source code example Ch14_01 elucidates how to perform packed floating-point arithmetic using AVX-512 instructions and the ZMM register set. It also spotlights other features unique to AVX-512 including instruction-level rounding control and broadcast operations. Listing 14-1a shows the C++ source code for example Ch14_01.

Listing 14-1a. Example Ch14_01 C++ Code

```
//-------------------------------------------------------------------------
// Ch14_01.h
//-------------------------------------------------------------------------

#pragma once
#include "ZmmVal.h"
```

© Daniel Kusswurm 2023
D. Kusswurm, *Modern X86 Assembly Language Programming*,
https://doi.org/10.1007/978-1-4842-9603-5_14

```cpp
// Ch14_01_fasm.asm, Ch14_01_fasm.s
extern "C" void PackedMathF32_avx512(ZmmVal* c, const ZmmVal* a, const ZmmVal* b);
extern "C" void PackedMathF64_avx512(ZmmVal* c, const ZmmVal* a, const ZmmVal* b);

//------------------------------------------------------------------------------
// Ch14_01.cpp
//------------------------------------------------------------------------------

#include <iostream>
#include <numbers>
#include "Ch14_01.h"

static void PackedMathF32(void)
{
    using namespace std::numbers;

    ZmmVal a, b, c[9];
    constexpr char nl = '\n';

    a.m_F32[0] = 36.333333f;            b.m_F32[0] = -0.1111111f;
    a.m_F32[1] = 0.03125f;              b.m_F32[1] = 64.0f;
    a.m_F32[2] = 2.0f;                  b.m_F32[2] = -0.0625f;
    a.m_F32[3] = 42.0f;                 b.m_F32[3] = 8.666667f;
    a.m_F32[4] = 7.0f;                  b.m_F32[4] = -18.125f;
    a.m_F32[5] = 20.5f;                 b.m_F32[5] = 56.0f;
    a.m_F32[6] = 36.125f;               b.m_F32[6] = 24.0f;
    a.m_F32[7] = 0.5f;                  b.m_F32[7] = -158.444444f;

    a.m_F32[8] = 136.77777f;            b.m_F32[8] = -9.1111111f;
    a.m_F32[9] = 2.03125f;              b.m_F32[9] = 864.0f;
    a.m_F32[10] = 32.0f;                b.m_F32[10] = -70.0625f;
    a.m_F32[11] = 442.0f;               b.m_F32[11] = 98.666667f;
    a.m_F32[12] = 57.0f;                b.m_F32[12] = -518.125f;
    a.m_F32[13] = 620.5f;               b.m_F32[13] = 456.0f;
    a.m_F32[14] = 736.125f;             b.m_F32[14] = (float)pi;
    a.m_F32[15] = (float)e;             b.m_F32[15] = -298.6f;

    PackedMathF32_avx512(c, &a, &b);

    std::cout << ("PackedMathF32_avx512() results:\n\n");

    for (size_t i = 0; i < 4; i++)
    {
        std::cout << "Group #" << i << nl;
        std::cout << "  a:              " << a.ToStringF32(i) << nl;
        std::cout << "  b:              " << b.ToStringF32(i) << nl;
        std::cout << "  addps:          " << c[0].ToStringF32(i) << nl;
        std::cout << "  addps {rd-sae}: " << c[1].ToStringF32(i) << nl;
        std::cout << "  subps:          " << c[2].ToStringF32(i) << nl;
        std::cout << "  mulps:          " << c[3].ToStringF32(i) << nl;
        std::cout << "  divps:          " << c[4].ToStringF32(i) << nl;
```

```
            std::cout << "  minps:          " << c[5].ToStringF32(i) << nl;
            std::cout << "  maxps:          " << c[6].ToStringF32(i) << nl;
            std::cout << "  sqrtps:         " << c[7].ToStringF32(i) << nl;
            std::cout << "  absps:          " << c[8].ToStringF32(i) << nl;
            std::cout << nl;
        }
    }

    static void PackedMathF64(void)
    {
        using namespace std::numbers;

        ZmmVal a, b, c[9];
        constexpr char nl = '\n';

        a.m_F64[0] = e;                 b.m_F64[0] = pi;
        a.m_F64[1] = log10e;            b.m_F64[1] = e / 2.0;
        a.m_F64[2] = sqrt2 / 5.0;       b.m_F64[2] = ln2;
        a.m_F64[3] = 7.0;               b.m_F64[3] = -pi;

        a.m_F64[4] = ln10;              b.m_F64[4] = pi / 3.0;
        a.m_F64[5] = 1.0 / pi;          b.m_F64[5] = 1.0 / e;
        a.m_F64[6] = inv_sqrtpi;        b.m_F64[6] = pi;
        a.m_F64[7] = sqrt2;             b.m_F64[7] = -pi / 2.0;

        PackedMathF64_avx512(c, &a, &b);

        std::cout << ("PackedMathF64_avx512() results:\n\n");

        for (size_t i = 0; i < 4; i++)
        {
            constexpr int p = 16;
            constexpr int w = 32;

            std::cout << "Group #" << i << nl;

            std::cout << "  a:              " << a.ToStringF64(i, w, p) << nl;
            std::cout << "  b:              " << b.ToStringF64(i, w, p) << nl;
            std::cout << "  addpd:          " << c[0].ToStringF64(i, w, p) << nl;
            std::cout << "  subpd:          " << c[1].ToStringF64(i, w, p) << nl;
            std::cout << "  mulpd:          " << c[2].ToStringF64(i, w, p) << nl;
            std::cout << "  divpd:          " << c[3].ToStringF64(i, w, p) << nl;
            std::cout << "  divpd {ru-sae}: " << c[4].ToStringF64(i, w, p) << nl;
            std::cout << "  minpd:          " << c[5].ToStringF64(i, w, p) << nl;
            std::cout << "  maxpd:          " << c[6].ToStringF64(i, w, p) << nl;
            std::cout << "  sqrtpd:         " << c[7].ToStringF64(i, w, p) << nl;
            std::cout << "  abspd:          " << c[8].ToStringF64(i, w, p) << nl;
            std::cout << nl;
        }
    }
```

```
int main(void)
{
    std::cout << "----- Results for Ch14_01 -----\n\n";

    PackedMathF32();
    PackedMathF64();
    return 0;
}
```

Listing 14-1a commences with the header file Ch14_01.h, which contains the requisite function declarations for this example. Note that the function declarations for both PackedMathF32_avx512() and PackedMathF64_avx512() require pointers to instances of a ZmmVal. Structure ZmmVal contains an anonymous union that facilitates data exchange between a C++ and assembly language function (see Listing 13-1a). File Ch14_01.cpp includes definitions for static functions PackedMathF32() and PackedMathF64(), which exercise the assembly functions for this example. These functions also format and stream the calculated results to std::cout.

Listing 14-1b shows the MASM code for example Ch14_01. This listing begins with a .const section that defines masks for single-precision and double-precision absolute values. Recall that the absolute value of a floating-point number can be calculated by setting its sign bit to zero. Following the .const section is the definition of function PackedMathF32_avx512(). This function illustrates the use of ordinary AVX-512 floating-point arithmetic instructions using 512-bit wide packed operands with single-precision elements. The first instruction of this function, vmovaps zmm0,zmmword ptr [rdx], loads ZmmVal a into register ZMM0. This is followed by a vmovaps zmm1,zmmword ptr [r8] instruction that loads ZmmVal b into register ZMM1. Following the two vmovaps instructions is a vaddps zmm2,zmm0,zmm1 instruction that performs packed single-precision floating-point addition. The next instruction, vmovaps zmmword ptr[rcx],zmm2, saves the resultant 16 sums to c[0].

Listing 14-1b. Example Ch14_01 MASM Code

```
;-----------------------------------------------------------------------------
; Ch14_01_fasm.asm
;-----------------------------------------------------------------------------

            .const
F64_AbsMask   dq   07fffffffffffffffh
F32_AbsMask   dd   07fffffffh


;-----------------------------------------------------------------------------
; void PackedMathF32_avx512(ZmmVal* c, const ZmmVal* a, const ZmmVal* b);
;-----------------------------------------------------------------------------

            .code
PackedMathF32_avx512 proc
        vmovaps zmm0,zmmword ptr [rdx]         ;zmm0 = a
        vmovaps zmm1,zmmword ptr [r8]          ;zmm1 = b

        vaddps zmm2,zmm0,zmm1                  ;F32 addition
        vmovaps zmmword ptr [rcx],zmm2

        vaddps zmm2,zmm0,zmm1{rd-sae}          ;F32 addition (round down toward -inf)
        vmovaps zmmword ptr [rcx+64],zmm2
```

```
        vsubps  zmm2,zmm0,zmm1              ;F32 subtraction
        vmovaps zmmword ptr [rcx+128],zmm2

        vmulps  zmm2,zmm0,zmm1              ;F32 multiplication
        vmovaps zmmword ptr [rcx+192],zmm2

        vdivps  zmm2,zmm0,zmm1              ;F32 division
        vmovaps zmmword ptr [rcx+256],zmm2

        vminps  zmm2,zmm0,zmm1              ;F32 min
        vmovaps zmmword ptr [rcx+320],zmm2

        vmaxps  zmm2,zmm0,zmm1              ;F32 max
        vmovaps zmmword ptr [rcx+384],zmm2

        vsqrtps zmm2,zmm0                   ;F32 sqrt(a)
        vmovaps zmmword ptr [rcx+448],zmm2

        vandps  zmm2,zmm1,real4 bcst [F32_AbsMask]   ;F32 abs(b)
        vmovaps zmmword ptr [rcx+512],zmm2

        vzeroupper
        ret
PackedMathF32_avx512 endp

;-------------------------------------------------------------------------------
; void PackedMathF64_avx512(ZmmVal* c, const ZmmVal* a, const ZmmVal* b);
;-------------------------------------------------------------------------------

PackedMathF64_avx512 proc
        vmovapd zmm0,zmmword ptr [rdx]      ;zmm0 = a
        vmovapd zmm1,zmmword ptr [r8]       ;zmm1 = b

        vaddpd  zmm2,zmm0,zmm1              ;F64 addition
        vmovapd zmmword ptr [rcx],zmm2

        vsubpd  zmm2,zmm0,zmm1              ;F64 subtraction
        vmovapd zmmword ptr [rcx+64],zmm2

        vmulpd  zmm2,zmm0,zmm1              ;F64 multiplication
        vmovapd zmmword ptr [rcx+128],zmm2

        vdivpd  zmm2,zmm0,zmm1              ;F64 division
        vmovapd zmmword ptr [rcx+192],zmm2

        vdivpd  zmm2,zmm0,zmm1{ru-sae}      ;F64 division (round up toward +inf)
        vmovapd zmmword ptr [rcx+256],zmm2

        vminpd  zmm2,zmm0,zmm1              ;F64 min
        vmovapd zmmword ptr [rcx+320],zmm2
```

```
        vmaxpd zmm2,zmm0,zmm1                    ;F64 max
        vmovapd zmmword ptr [rcx+384],zmm2

        vsqrtpd zmm2,zmm0                        ;F64 sqrt(a)
        vmovapd zmmword ptr [rcx+448],zmm2

        vandpd zmm2,zmm1,real8 bcst [F64_AbsMask]    ;F64 abs(b)
        vmovapd zmmword ptr [rcx+512],zmm2

        vzeroupper
        ret
PackedMathF64_avx512 endp
        end
```

The subsequent vaddps zmm2,zmm0,zmm1{rd-sae} instruction also performs packed single-precision floating-point addition. The operand text {rd-sae} (see Table 13-2) that's included in this instruction specifies the rounding method that the processor should use during execution of vaddps. Recall from the discussions in earlier chapters that control bits MXCSR.RC specify the rounding mode for most x86-AVX floating-point arithmetic instructions. On processors that support AVX-512, some floating-point arithmetic and conversion instructions can specify a static (or per instruction) rounding mode that overrides the current rounding mode in MXCSR.RC.

In the current example, the rd-sae operand instructs the processor to use round down toward $-\infty$. Other static rounding mode options include round up toward $+\infty$ (ru-sae), round to nearest (rn-sae), and round toward zero (rz-sae). The text sae signifies "suppress all exceptions" and is required when using a static rounding mode. This means the processor will not generate any floating-point exceptions or set any status flags in MXCSR during execution of an AVX-512 instruction that specifies a static rounding mode. It is important to note that static rounding modes are restricted to AVX-512 instruction forms that use only 512-bit wide register operands (e.g., vaddps zmm2,zmm0,zmmword ptr [rax]{rd-sae} is invalid); scalar floating-point arithmetic instructions that use only register operands can also specify a static rounding mode.

The remaining code in PackedMathF32_avx512() illustrates the use of additional AVX-512 packed single-precision floating-point instructions including vsubps, vmulps, vdivps, vminps, vmaxps, and vsqrtps. Note that except for the 512-bit wide operands, the use of these instructions is basically the same as it was for AVX.

Toward the end of function PackedMathF32_avx512() is the AVX-512 instruction vandps zmm2,zmm1,real4 bcst [F32_AbsMask]. This is an example of an instruction that exploits AVX-512's embedded broadcast capabilities. During execution of the vandps zmm2,zmm1,real4 bcst [F32_AbsMask] instruction, the processor performs a bitwise logical AND using each single-precision floating-point element in register ZMM1 and memory operand F32_AbsMask (0x7FFFFFFF). Using an embedded broadcast simplifies the coding of SIMD operations that require a constant value since it eliminates the need for an explicit broadcast instruction; it also preserves SIMD registers for other uses. Embedded broadcasts can be used with some (but not all) AVX-512 instructions that support memory operands. The element size of an embedded broadcast value must be 32 or 64 bits wide; AVX-512 does not support embedded broadcasts using 8- or 16-bit wide elements.

The next function in Listing 14-1b is PackedMathF64_avx512(), which is the double-precision counterpart of PackedMathF32_avx512(). Note that PackedMathF64_avx512() uses vaddpd, vsubpd, vmulpd, etc., to perform packed double-precision floating-point arithmetic using 512-bit wide operands. Also note that in this function, the second vdivpd instruction specifies a static rounding mode of ru-sae.

Listing 14-1c shows the NASM code for example Ch14_01. This listing resembles the MASM code in Listing 14-1b, but with two noteworthy exceptions. First, note that a comma is required when an instruction specifies an AVX-512 rounding mode as demonstrated by the vaddps zmm2,zmm0,zmm1,{rd-sae} instruction.

Second, NASM uses the operand {1to16} instead of bcst to signify an embedded broadcast. Note the vandps zmm2,zmm1,[F32_AbsMask] {1to16} instruction, which calculates packed single-precision absolute values. The double-precision counterpart instruction in function PackedMathF64_avx512() is vandpd zmm2,zmm1,[F64_AbsMask] {1to8}.

Listing 14-1c. Example Ch14_01 NASM Code

```
;-----------------------------------------------------------------------------
; Ch14_01_fasm.s
;-----------------------------------------------------------------------------

        %include "ModX86Asm3eNASM.inc"

        section .rdata
F64_AbsMask  dq      07fffffffffffffffh
F32_AbsMask  dd      07fffffffh


;-----------------------------------------------------------------------------
; void PackedMathF32_avx512(ZmmVal* c], const ZmmVal* a, const ZmmVal* b);
;-----------------------------------------------------------------------------

        section .text

        global PackedMathF32_avx512
PackedMathF32_avx512:

        vmovaps zmm0,[rsi]              ;zmm0 = a
        vmovaps zmm1,[rdx]              ;zmm1 = b

        vaddps zmm2,zmm0,zmm1           ;F32 addition
        vmovaps [rdi],zmm2

        vaddps zmm2,zmm0,zmm1,{rd-sae}  ;F32 addition (round down toward -inf)
        vmovaps [rdi+64],zmm2

        vsubps zmm2,zmm0,zmm1           ;F32 subtraction
        vmovaps [rdi+128],zmm2

        vmulps zmm2,zmm0,zmm1           ;F32 multiplication
        vmovaps [rdi+192],zmm2

        vdivps zmm2,zmm0,zmm1           ;F32 division
        vmovaps [rdi+256],zmm2

        vminps zmm2,zmm0,zmm1           ;F32 min
        vmovaps [rdi+320],zmm2

        vmaxps zmm2,zmm0,zmm1           ;F32 max
        vmovaps [rdi+384],zmm2
```

```
        vsqrtps zmm2,zmm0                       ;F32 sqrt(a)
        vmovaps [rdi+448],zmm2

        vandps zmm2,zmm1,[F32_AbsMask] {1to16}  ;F32 abs(b)
        vmovaps [rdi+512],zmm2

        vzeroupper
        ret

;-----------------------------------------------------------------------
; void PackedMathF64_avx512(ZmmVal* c, const ZmmVal* a, const ZmmVal* b);
;-----------------------------------------------------------------------

        global PackedMathF64_avx512
PackedMathF64_avx512:

        vmovapd zmm0,[rsi]                       ;zmm0 = a
        vmovapd zmm1,[rdx]                       ;zmm1 = b

        vaddpd zmm2,zmm0,zmm1                     ;F64 addition
        vmovapd [rdi],zmm2

        vsubpd zmm2,zmm0,zmm1                     ;F64 subtraction
        vmovapd [rdi+64],zmm2

        vmulpd zmm2,zmm0,zmm1                     ;F64 multiplication
        vmovapd [rdi+128],zmm2

        vdivpd zmm2,zmm0,zmm1                     ;F64 division
        vmovapd [rdi+192],zmm2

        vdivpd zmm2,zmm0,zmm1,{ru-sae}           ;F64 division (round up toward +inf)
        vmovapd [rdi+256],zmm2

        vminpd zmm2,zmm0,zmm1                     ;F64 min
        vmovapd [rdi+320],zmm2

        vmaxpd zmm2,zmm0,zmm1                     ;F64 max
        vmovapd [rdi+384],zmm2

        vsqrtpd zmm2,zmm0                         ;F64 sqrt(a)
        vmovapd [rdi+448],zmm2

        vandpd zmm2,zmm1,[F64_AbsMask] {1to8}    ;F64 abs(b)
        vmovapd [rdi+512],zmm2

        vzeroupper
        ret
```

The results for source code example Ch14_01 follow this paragraph. Static rounding mode value dissimilarities are shown in bold (recall that the default rounding mode for both Visual C++ and GNU C++ programs is round to nearest).

```
----- Results for Ch14_01 -----

PackedMathF32_avx512() results:

Group #0
  a:                  36.333332      0.031250   |    2.000000     42.000000
  b:                  -0.111111     64.000000   |   -0.062500      8.666667
  addps:              36.222221     64.031250   |    1.937500     50.666668
  addps {rd-sae}:     36.222218     64.031250   |    1.937500     50.666664
  subps:              36.444443    -63.968750   |    2.062500     33.333332
  mulps:              -4.037036      2.000000   |   -0.125000    364.000000
  divps:            -327.000031      0.000488   |  -32.000000      4.846154
  minps:              -0.111111      0.031250   |   -0.062500      8.666667
  maxps:              36.333332     64.000000   |    2.000000     42.000000
  sqrtps:              6.027714      0.176777   |    1.414214      6.480741
  absps:               0.111111     64.000000   |    0.062500      8.666667

Group #1
  a:                   7.000000     20.500000   |   36.125000      0.500000
  b:                 -18.125000     56.000000   |   24.000000   -158.444443
  addps:             -11.125000     76.500000   |   60.125000   -157.944443
  addps {rd-sae}:    -11.125000     76.500000   |   60.125000   -157.944443
  subps:              25.125000    -35.500000   |   12.125000    158.944443
  mulps:            -126.875000   1148.000000   |  867.000000    -79.222221
  divps:              -0.386207      0.366071   |    1.505208     -0.003156
  minps:             -18.125000     20.500000   |   24.000000   -158.444443
  maxps:               7.000000     56.000000   |   36.125000      0.500000
  sqrtps:              2.645751      4.527693   |    6.010407      0.707107
  absps:              18.125000     56.000000   |   24.000000    158.444443

Group #2
  a:                 136.777771      2.031250   |   32.000000    442.000000
  b:                  -9.111111    864.000000   |  -70.062500     98.666664
  addps:             127.666656    866.031250   |  -38.062500    540.666687
  addps {rd-sae}:    127.666656    866.031250   |  -38.062500    540.666626
  subps:             145.888885   -861.968750   |  102.062500    343.333344
  mulps:           -1246.197388   1755.000000   | -2242.000000  43610.664062
  divps:             -15.012195      0.002351   |   -0.456735      4.479730
  minps:              -9.111111      2.031250   |  -70.062500     98.666664
  maxps:             136.777771    864.000000   |   32.000000    442.000000
  sqrtps:             11.695203      1.425219   |    5.656854     21.023796
  absps:               9.111111    864.000000   |   70.062500     98.666664

Group #3
  a:                  57.000000    620.500000   |  736.125000      2.718282
  b:                -518.125000    456.000000   |    3.141593   -298.600006
  addps:            -461.125000   1076.500000   |  739.266602   -295.881714
```

```
addps {rd-sae}:     -461.125000      1076.500000   |     739.266541      -295.881744
subps:               575.125000       164.500000   |     732.983398       301.318298
mulps:            -29533.125000    282948.000000   |    2312.604980      -811.678955
divps:                -0.110012         1.360746   |     234.315857        -0.009103
minps:              -518.125000       456.000000   |       3.141593      -298.600006
maxps:                57.000000       620.500000   |     736.125000         2.718282
sqrtps:                7.549834        24.909838   |      27.131624         1.648721
absps:               518.125000       456.000000   |       3.141593       298.600006
```

PackedMathF64_avx512() results:

Group #0
```
a:                   2.7182818284590451   |   0.4342944819032518
b:                   3.1415926535897931   |   1.3591409142295225
addpd:               5.8598744820488378   |   1.7934353961327743
subpd:              -0.4233108251307480   |  -0.9248464323262707
mulpd:               8.5397342226735660   |   0.5902673991788225
divpd:               0.8652559794322651   |   0.3195360226128187
divpd {ru-sae}:      0.8652559794322652   |   0.3195360226128187
minpd:               2.7182818284590451   |   0.4342944819032518
maxpd:               3.1415926535897931   |   1.3591409142295225
sqrtpd:              1.6487212707001282   |   0.6590102289822608
abspd:               3.1415926535897931   |   1.3591409142295225
```

Group #1
```
a:                   0.2828427124746190   |   7.0000000000000000
b:                   0.6931471805599453   |  -3.1415926535897931
addpd:               0.9759898930345643   |   3.8584073464102069
subpd:              -0.4103044680853263   |  10.1415926535897931
mulpd:               0.1960516286937094   | -21.9911485751285518
divpd:               0.4080557786387158   |  -2.2281692032865350
divpd {ru-sae}:      0.4080557786387158   |  -2.2281692032865346
minpd:               0.2828427124746190   |  -3.1415926535897931
maxpd:               0.6931471805599453   |   7.0000000000000000
sqrtpd:              0.5318295896944989   |   2.6457513110645907
abspd:               0.6931471805599453   |   3.1415926535897931
```

Group #2
```
a:                   2.3025850929940459   |   0.3183098861837907
b:                   1.0471975511965976   |   0.3678794411714423
addpd:               3.3497826441906433   |   0.6861893273552331
subpd:               1.2553875417974483   |  -0.0495695549876516
mulpd:               2.4112614708051550   |   0.1170996630486383
divpd:               2.1988067966382836   |   0.8652559794322651
divpd {ru-sae}:      2.1988067966382840   |   0.8652559794322652
minpd:               1.0471975511965976   |   0.3183098861837907
maxpd:               2.3025850929940459   |   0.3678794411714423
sqrtpd:              1.5174271293851465   |   0.5641895835477563
abspd:               1.0471975511965976   |   0.3678794411714423
```

Group #3
```
  a:                0.5641895835477563   |        1.4142135623730951
  b:                3.1415926535897931   |       -1.5707963267948966
  addpd:            3.7057822371375493   |       -0.1565827644218014
  subpd:           -2.5774030700420369   |        2.9850098891679915
  mulpd:            1.7724538509055159   |       -2.2214414690791831
  divpd:            0.1795871221251666   |       -0.9003163161571062
  divpd {ru-sae}:   0.1795871221251666   |       -0.9003163161571061
  minpd:            0.5641895835477563   |       -1.5707963267948966
  maxpd:            3.1415926535897931   |        1.4142135623730951
  sqrtpd:           0.7511255444649425   |        1.1892071150027210
  abspd:            3.1415926535897931   |        1.5707963267948966
```

Packed Comparisons

The next source code example, entitled Ch14_02, expounds single- and double-precision packed floating-point comparisons using AVX-512 instructions and 512-bit wide operands. This example closely resembles the AVX packed comparison example that you saw in Chapter 9 (see example Ch09_02). Listing 14-2a shows the C++ source code for example Ch14_02. In this listing, note that the ZmmVal initialization code in functions CompareF32() and CompareF64() utilizes a variety of floating-point constant values including QNaNs.

Listing 14-2a. Example Ch14_02 C++ Code

```
//------------------------------------------------------------------------------
// Ch14_02.h
//------------------------------------------------------------------------------

#pragma once
#include "ZmmVal.h"

// Ch14_02_fasm.asm, Ch14_02_fasm.s
extern "C" void PackedCompareF32_avx512(uint16_t* c, const ZmmVal* a,
    const ZmmVal* b);
extern "C" void PackedCompareF64_avx512(uint8_t* c, const ZmmVal* a,
    const ZmmVal* b);

//------------------------------------------------------------------------------
// Ch14_02.cpp
//------------------------------------------------------------------------------

#include <iostream>
#include <iostream>
#include <iomanip>
#include <limits>
#include <numbers>
#include "Ch14_02.h"
```

```
static const char* c_CmpStr[8] = { "EQ", "NE", "LT", "LE", "GT", "GE", "OD", "UO" };

static void CompareF32(void)
{
    using namespace std::numbers;

    ZmmVal a, b;
    uint16_t c[8];
    constexpr char nl = '\n';
    constexpr float qnan_f32 = std::numeric_limits<float>::quiet_NaN();

    a.m_F32[0] = 2.0f;                  b.m_F32[0] = 1.0f;
    a.m_F32[1] = 7.0f;                  b.m_F32[1] = 12.0f;
    a.m_F32[2] = -6.0f;                 b.m_F32[2] = -6.0f;
    a.m_F32[3] = 3.0f;                  b.m_F32[3] = 8.0f;
    a.m_F32[4] = -16.0f;                b.m_F32[4] = -36.0f;
    a.m_F32[5] = 3.5f;                  b.m_F32[5] = 3.5f;
    a.m_F32[6] = (float)pi;             b.m_F32[6] = -6.0f;
    a.m_F32[7] = (float)sqrt2;          b.m_F32[7] = qnan_f32;
    a.m_F32[8] = 102.0f;                b.m_F32[8] = 1.0f / (float)sqrt2;
    a.m_F32[9] = 77.0f;                 b.m_F32[9] = 77.0f;
    a.m_F32[10] = 187.0f;               b.m_F32[10] = 33.0f;
    a.m_F32[11] = -5.1f;                b.m_F32[11] = -87.0f;
    a.m_F32[12] = 16.0f;                b.m_F32[12] = 936.0f;
    a.m_F32[13] = 0.5f;                 b.m_F32[13] = 0.5f;
    a.m_F32[14] = 2.0f * (float)pi;     b.m_F32[14] = 66.6667f;
    a.m_F32[15] = 1.0f / (float)sqrt2;  b.m_F32[15] = 100.7f;

    PackedCompareF32_avx512(c, &a, &b);

    constexpr int w1 = 10;
    constexpr int w2 = 6;

    std::cout << ("\nPackedCompareF32_avx512() results:\n\n");
    std::cout << std::fixed << std::setprecision(4);
    std::cout << "        a            b       ";

    for (size_t j = 0; j < 8; j++)
        std::cout << std::setw(w2) << c_CmpStr[j];
    std::cout << nl << std::string(70, '-') << nl;

    for (size_t i = 0; i < 16; i++)
    {
        std::cout << std::setw(w1) << a.m_F32[i] << " ";
        std::cout << std::setw(w1) << b.m_F32[i];

        for (size_t j = 0; j < 8; j++)
            std::cout << std::setw(w2) << ((c[j] & (1 << i)) ? 1 : 0);

        std::cout << nl;
    }
}
```

```cpp
static void CompareF64(void)
{
    using namespace std::numbers;

    ZmmVal a, b;
    uint8_t c[8];
    constexpr char nl = '\n';
    constexpr double qnan_f64 = std::numeric_limits<double>::quiet_NaN();

    a.m_F64[0] = 2.0;            b.m_F64[0] = e;
    a.m_F64[1] = pi;             b.m_F64[1] = -inv_pi;
    a.m_F64[2] = 12.0;           b.m_F64[2] = 42.0;
    a.m_F64[3] = 33.3333333333;  b.m_F64[3] = sqrt2;
    a.m_F64[4] = 0.5;            b.m_F64[4] = e * 2.0;
    a.m_F64[5] = -pi;            b.m_F64[5] = -pi * 2.0;
    a.m_F64[6] = -24.0;          b.m_F64[6] = -24.0;
    a.m_F64[7] = qnan_f64;       b.m_F64[7] = 100.0;

    PackedCompareF64_avx512(c, &a, &b);

    constexpr int w1 = 10;
    constexpr int w2 = 6;

    std::cout << ("\nPackedCompareF64_avx512() results:\n\n");
    std::cout << std::fixed << std::setprecision(4);
    std::cout << "        a          b      ";

    for (size_t j = 0; j < 8; j++)
        std::cout << std::setw(w2) << c_CmpStr[j];
    std::cout << nl << std::string(70, '-') << nl;

    for (size_t i = 0; i < 8; i++)
    {
        std::cout << std::setw(w1) << a.m_F64[i] << " ";
        std::cout << std::setw(w1) << b.m_F64[i];

        for (size_t j = 0; j < 8; j++)
            std::cout << std::setw(w2) << ((c[j] & (1 << i)) ? 1 : 0);

        std::cout << nl;
    }
}

int main(void)
{
    std::cout << "----- Results for Ch14_02 -----\n";

    CompareF32();
    CompareF64();
    return 0;
}
```

Listing 14-2b shows the MASM code for example Ch14_02. This listing opens with the definition of a function named PackedCompareF32_avx512(), which demonstrates how to perform packed floating-point compare operations using single-precision elements. The first two instructions of this function, vmovaps zmm0,zmmword ptr [rdx] and vmovaps zmm1,zmmword ptr [r8], load ZmmVal arguments a and b into registers ZMM0 and ZMM1, respectively. The next instruction, vcmpps k1,zmm0,zmm1,CMP_EQ_OQ, compares corresponding single-precision floating-point elements in ZMM0 and ZMM1 for equality. If the elements are equal, the corresponding element bit position in opmask register K1 is set to 1; otherwise, it is set to 0. The compare predicate CMP_EQ_OQ that's used in the vcmpps instruction is defined in the assembly language header file cmpequ_fp.asmh (see Listing 5-5a). Following the vcmpps instruction is a kmovw word ptr[rcx],k1 instruction that saves the resultant compare mask to c[0]. The word variant of instruction kmov[b|w|d|q] is used here since each ZMM register operand contains 16 single-precision floating-point elements. The remaining instructions in PackedCompareF32_avx512() demonstrate the use of other common floating-point compare predicates.

Listing 14-2b. Example Ch14_02 MASM Code

```
;-----------------------------------------------------------------------------
; Ch14_02_fasm.asm
;-----------------------------------------------------------------------------

        include <cmpequ_fp.asmh>


;-----------------------------------------------------------------------------
; void PackedCompareF32_avx512(uint16_t* c, const ZmmVal* a, const ZmmVal* b);
;-----------------------------------------------------------------------------

        .code
PackedCompareF32_avx512 proc
        vmovaps zmm0,zmmword ptr [rdx]      ;zmm0 = a
        vmovaps zmm1,zmmword ptr [r8]       ;zmm1 = b

        vcmpps k1,zmm0,zmm1,CMP_EQ_OQ       ;packed compare for EQ
        kmovw word ptr [rcx],k1             ;save mask

        vcmpps k1,zmm0,zmm1,CMP_NEQ_OQ      ;packed compare for NEQ
        kmovw word ptr [rcx+2],k1           ;save mask

        vcmpps k1,zmm0,zmm1,CMP_LT_OQ       ;packed compare for LT
        kmovw word ptr [rcx+4],k1           ;save mask

        vcmpps k1,zmm0,zmm1,CMP_LE_OQ       ;packed compare for LE
        kmovw word ptr [rcx+6],k1           ;save mask

        vcmpps k1,zmm0,zmm1,CMP_GT_OQ       ;packed compare for GT
        kmovw word ptr [rcx+8],k1           ;save mask

        vcmpps k1,zmm0,zmm1,CMP_GE_OQ       ;packed compare for GE
        kmovw word ptr [rcx+10],k1          ;save mask

        vcmpps k1,zmm0,zmm1,CMP_ORD_Q       ;packed compare for ORD
        kmovw word ptr [rcx+12],k1          ;save mask
```

```
            vcmpps k1,zmm0,zmm1,CMP_UNORD_Q          ;packed compare for UNORD
            kmovw word ptr [rcx+14],k1               ;save mask


            vzeroupper
            ret
PackedCompareF32_avx512 endp


;-------------------------------------------------------------------------------
; void PackedCompareF64_avx512(uint8_t c[8], const ZmmVal* a, const ZmmVal* b);
;-------------------------------------------------------------------------------

PackedCompareF64_avx512 proc
            vmovapd zmm0,zmmword ptr [rdx]           ;zmm0 = a
            vmovapd zmm1,zmmword ptr [r8]            ;zmm1 = b

            vcmppd k1,zmm0,zmm1,CMP_EQ_OQ            ;packed compare for EQ
            kmovb byte ptr [rcx],k1                  ;save mask

            vcmppd k1,zmm0,zmm1,CMP_NEQ_OQ           ;packed compare for NEQ
            kmovb byte ptr [rcx+1],k1                ;save mask

            vcmppd k1,zmm0,zmm1,CMP_LT_OQ            ;packed compare for LT
            kmovb byte ptr [rcx+2],k1                ;save mask

            vcmppd k1,zmm0,zmm1,CMP_LE_OQ            ;packed compare for LE
            kmovb byte ptr [rcx+3],k1                ;save mask

            vcmppd k1,zmm0,zmm1,CMP_GT_OQ            ;packed compare for GT
            kmovb byte ptr [rcx+4],k1                ;save mask

            vcmppd k1,zmm0,zmm1,CMP_GE_OQ            ;packed compare for GE
            kmovb byte ptr [rcx+5],k1                ;save mask

            vcmppd k1,zmm0,zmm1,CMP_ORD_Q            ;packed compare for ORD
            kmovb byte ptr [rcx+6],k1                ;save mask

            vcmppd k1,zmm0,zmm1,CMP_UNORD_Q          ;packed compare for UNORD
            kmovb byte ptr [rcx+7],k1                ;save mask


            vzeroupper
            ret
PackedCompareF64_avx512 endp
            end
```

The next function in Listing 14-2b is named PackedCompareF64_avx512(). This function is the double-precision complement of PackedCompareF32_avx512(). Note that PackedCompareF64_avx512() utilizes the instructions vmovapd and vcmppd to perform packed double-precision floating-point loads and compares. Also note that PackedCompareF64_avx512() uses the kmovb instruction to save each compare result since each ZMM register contains eight double-precision floating-point values.

Listing 14-2c shows the NASM code for example Ch14_02. The code in this listing is the same as the MASM code in Listing 14-2b, except for the use of different general-purpose registers and the removal of size operators zmmword ptr and word ptr from the vmovaps and kmovw instructions, respectively.

Listing 14-2c. Example Ch14_02 NASM Code

```
;-----------------------------------------------------------------------------
; Ch14_02_fasm.s
;-----------------------------------------------------------------------------

        %include "ModX86Asm3eNASM.inc"
        %include "cmpequ_fp.inc"

;-----------------------------------------------------------------------------
; void PackedCompareF32_avx512(uint16_t* c, const ZmmVal* a, const ZmmVal* b);
;-----------------------------------------------------------------------------

        section .text

        global PackedCompareF32_avx512
PackedCompareF32_avx512:

        vmovaps zmm0,[rsi]                  ;zmm0 = a
        vmovaps zmm1,[rdx]                  ;zmm1 = b

        vcmpps k1,zmm0,zmm1,CMP_EQ_OQ       ;packed compare for EQ
        kmovw [rdi],k1                      ;save mask

        vcmpps k1,zmm0,zmm1,CMP_NEQ_OQ      ;packed compare for NEQ
        kmovw [rdi+2],k1                    ;save mask

        vcmpps k1,zmm0,zmm1,CMP_LT_OQ       ;packed compare for LT
        kmovw [rdi+4],k1                    ;save mask

        vcmpps k1,zmm0,zmm1,CMP_LE_OQ       ;packed compare for LE
        kmovw [rdi+6],k1                    ;save mask

        vcmpps k1,zmm0,zmm1,CMP_GT_OQ       ;packed compare for GT
        kmovw [rdi+8],k1                    ;save mask

        vcmpps k1,zmm0,zmm1,CMP_GE_OQ       ;packed compare for GE
        kmovw [rdi+10],k1                   ;save mask

        vcmpps k1,zmm0,zmm1,CMP_ORD_Q       ;packed compare for ORD
        kmovw [rdi+12],k1                   ;save mask

        vcmpps k1,zmm0,zmm1,CMP_UNORD_Q     ;packed compare for UNORD
        kmovw [rdi+14],k1                   ;save mask

        vzeroupper
        ret
```

```
;-----------------------------------------------------------------------------
; void PackedCompareF64_avx512(uint8_t c[8], const ZmmVal* a, const ZmmVal* b);
;-----------------------------------------------------------------------------

        global PackedCompareF64_avx512
PackedCompareF64_avx512:

        vmovapd zmm0,[rsi]                  ;zmm0 = a
        vmovapd zmm1,[rdx]                  ;zmm1 = b

        vcmppd  k1,zmm0,zmm1,CMP_EQ_OQ      ;packed compare for EQ
        kmovb   [rdi],k1                    ;save mask

        vcmppd  k1,zmm0,zmm1,CMP_NEQ_OQ     ;packed compare for NEQ
        kmovb   [rdi+1],k1                  ;save mask

        vcmppd  k1,zmm0,zmm1,CMP_LT_OQ      ;packed compare for LT
        kmovb   [rdi+2],k1                  ;save mask

        vcmppd  k1,zmm0,zmm1,CMP_LE_OQ      ;packed compare for LE
        kmovb   [rdi+3],k1                  ;save mask

        vcmppd  k1,zmm0,zmm1,CMP_GT_OQ      ;packed compare for GT
        kmovb   [rdi+4],k1                  ;save mask

        vcmppd  k1,zmm0,zmm1,CMP_GE_OQ      ;packed compare for GE
        kmovb   [rdi+5],k1                  ;save mask

        vcmppd  k1,zmm0,zmm1,CMP_ORD_Q      ;packed compare for ORD
        kmovb   [rdi+6],k1                  ;save mask

        vcmppd  k1,zmm0,zmm1,CMP_UNORD_Q    ;packed compare for UNORD
        kmovb   [rdi+7],k1                  ;save mask

        vzeroupper
        ret
```

Here are the results for source code example Ch14_02:

```
----- Results for Ch14_02 -----

PackedCompareF32_avx512() results:

       a          b        EQ    NE    LT    LE    GT    GE    OD    UO
-------------------------------------------------------------------------
    2.0000     1.0000      0     1     0     0     1     1     1     0
    7.0000    12.0000      0     1     1     1     0     0     1     0
   -6.0000    -6.0000      1     0     0     1     0     1     1     0
    3.0000     8.0000      0     1     1     1     0     0     1     0
  -16.0000   -36.0000      0     1     0     0     1     1     1     0
    3.5000     3.5000      1     0     0     1     0     1     1     0
```

3.1416	-6.0000	0	1	0	0	1	1	1	0
1.4142	nan	0	0	0	0	0	0	0	1
102.0000	0.7071	0	1	0	0	1	1	1	0
77.0000	77.0000	1	0	0	1	0	1	1	0
187.0000	33.0000	0	1	0	0	1	1	1	0
-5.1000	-87.0000	0	1	0	0	1	1	1	0
16.0000	936.0000	0	1	1	1	0	0	1	0
0.5000	0.5000	1	0	0	1	0	1	1	0
6.2832	66.6667	0	1	1	1	0	0	1	0
0.7071	100.7000	0	1	1	1	0	0	1	0

PackedCompareF64_avx512() results:

a	b	EQ	NE	LT	LE	GT	GE	OD	UO
2.0000	2.7183	0	1	1	1	0	0	1	0
3.1416	-0.3183	0	1	0	0	1	1	1	0
12.0000	42.0000	0	1	1	1	0	0	1	0
33.3333	1.4142	0	1	0	0	1	1	1	0
0.5000	5.4366	0	1	1	1	0	0	1	0
-3.1416	-6.2832	0	1	0	0	1	1	1	0
-24.0000	-24.0000	1	0	0	1	0	1	1	0
nan	100.0000	0	0	0	0	0	0	0	1

Floating-Point Arrays

In Chapter 9, you learned how to use AVX instructions to implement a double-precision floating-point SIMD ternary operator (see example Ch09_05). The next example of this chapter, named Ch14_03, also implements a SIMD ternary operator but utilizes AVX-512 instructions and opmask registers. The C++ source code for example Ch14_03 is not shown since it's basically the same code that was used in example Ch09_05 (see Listing 9-5a). You may want to review this code and its distance calculation equation before proceeding with the remainder of this section.

Listing 14-3a shows the MASM code for example Ch14_03. In this listing, function CalcDistances_ avx512() exploits macro CreateFrame_M to create a stack frame and perform non-volatile general-purpose register preservation. Following this is a series of mov instructions that copy argument values from volatile to non-volatile general-purpose registers. The reason for this copy operation is that CalcDistances_avx512() is a non-leaf function; it calls the C++ function CheckArgs() to perform argument validation.

Listing 14-3a. Example Ch14_03 MASM Code

```
;-------------------------------------------------------------------------------
; Ch14_03_fasm.asm
;-------------------------------------------------------------------------------

        include <cmpequ_fp.asmh>
        include <MacrosX86-64-AVX.asmh>


        .const
F64_minus1  real8 -1.0
```

```
;-------------------------------------------------------------------------------
; bool CalcDistances_avx512(double* d, const double* x1, const double* y1,
;     const double* x2, const double* y2, size_t n, double thresh);
;-------------------------------------------------------------------------------

NSE        equ 8                                        ;num_simd_elements

           extern CheckArgs:proc

           .code
CalcDistances_avx512 proc frame
           CreateFrame_M CD_,0,0,rbx,r12,r13,r14,r15
           EndProlog_M

; Copy arguments in volatile registers to non-volatile registers
           mov rbx,rcx                    ;rbx = d
           mov r12,rdx                    ;r12 = x1
           mov r13,r8                     ;r13 = y1
           mov r14,r9                     ;r14 = x2
           mov r15,[rbp+CD_OffsetStackArgs]   ;r15 = y2

; Make sure the arguments are valid. Note that arguments d, x1, y1, and x2 are
; already in the correct registers for CheckArgs().
           push [rbp+CD_OffsetStackArgs+8]     ;copy n to stack
           push r15                            ;copy y2 to stack
           sub rsp,32                          ;create home area
           call CheckArgs
           or eax,eax                          ;valid arguments?
           jz Err                              ;jump if CheckArgs() failed

;-------------------------------------------------------------------------------
; Registers used in code below:
;
; rax = array offset      rbx = d          r10 = n          r12 = x1
; r13 = y1                r14 = x2         r15 = y2
;
; zmm16 = packed thresh     zmm17 = packed -1.0
;-------------------------------------------------------------------------------

; Initialize
           mov rax,-NSE*8                                      ;array offset
           mov r10,[rbp+CD_OffsetStackArgs+8]                  ;r10 = n
           vbroadcastsd zmm16,real8 ptr [rbp+CD_OffsetStackArgs+16]   ;packed thresh
           vbroadcastsd zmm17,real8 ptr [f64_minus1]          ;packed -1.0

; Calculate distances using SIMD arithmetic
Loop1:    add rax,NSE*8                     ;rax = offset to next elements

           vmovapd zmm0,zmmword ptr [r12+rax]     ;zmm0 = x1[i:i+NSE-1]
           vsubpd zmm1,zmm0,[r14+rax]             ;zmm1 = x1 - x2
           vmulpd zmm1,zmm1,zmm1                  ;zmm1 = (x1 - x2) ** 2
```

```
        vmovapd zmm2,zmmword ptr [r13+rax]        ;zmm2 = y1[i:i+NSE-1]
        vsubpd zmm3,zmm2,[r15+rax]                ;zmm3 = y1 - y2
        vmulpd zmm3,zmm3,zmm3                      ;zmm3 = (y1 - y1) ** 2

        vaddpd zmm4,zmm1,zmm3                      ;(x1 - x2) ** 2 + (y1 - y1) ** 2
        vsqrtpd zmm0,zmm4                          ;dist (temp3 in C++ code)

; Calculate d = (temp3 >= thresh) ? temp3 * -1.0 : temp3; using SIMD arithmetic
        vcmppd k1,zmm0,zmm16,CMP_GE_OQ             ;compare raw dist to thresh
        vmovapd zmm2{k1}{z},zmm17                  ;zmm2 = -1.0 (compare true) or zero
        vmulpd zmm3,zmm2,zmm0                      ;zmm3 = -1.0 * dist or 0.0
        knotb k2,k1                                ;k2 = mask for dist < thresh
        vmovapd zmm4{k2}{z},zmm0                   ;zmm4 = dist or 0.0
        vorpd zmm5,zmm4,zmm3                       ;zmm5 = final result
        vmovapd zmmword ptr [rbx+rax],zmm5         ;save result to d[i:i+NSE-1]

        sub r10,NSE                                ;n -= NSE
        jnz Loop1                                  ;jump if yes

        mov eax,1                                  ;set success return code

Done:   vzeroupper
        DeleteFrame_M rbx,r12,r13,r14,r15          ;delete stack frame and restore regs
        ret

Err:    xor eax,eax                                ;set errror return code
        jmp Done

CalcDistances_avx512 endp
        end
```

Following argument validation, CalcDistances_avx512() carries out its required initializations. Next is for-loop Loop1. Each iteration of Loop1 begins with an add rax,NSE*8 instruction that updates the common offset value in register RAX for the next group of elements in arrays d, x1, x2, y1, and y2. The ensuing instruction triplet, vmovapd zmm0,zmmword ptr [r12+rax], vsubpd zmm1,zmm0,[r14+rax], and vmulpd zmm1,zmm1,zmm1, calculates (x1[i:i+NSE-1] - x2[i:i+NSE-1]) ** 2. The code block that follows performs the same calculation using y1[i:i+NSE-1] and y2[i:i+NSE-1]. Execution of instructions vaddpd zmm4,zmm1,zmm3 and vsqrtpd zmm0,zmm4 completes the calculation of dist.

Recall from example Ch09_05 that function CalcDistances_avx2() (Listing 9-5b) implemented an arbitrary SIMD ternary operator for demonstration purposes. Function CalcDistances_avx512() carries out this same calculation. If dist >= thresh is true, then d = dist * -1.0; otherwise, d = dist. The code block that performs this computation begins with a vcmppd k1,zmm0,zmm16,CMP_GE_OQ instruction that compares each double-precision dist value in ZMM0 to thresh. The next instruction, vmovapd zmm2{k1}{z},zmm17, sets each element in ZMM2 to -1.0 if dist >= thresh is true; otherwise, the element is set to 0.0. This is followed by a vmulpd zmm3,zmm2,zmm0 instruction that calculates -1.0 * dist or 0.0 * dist for each element in ZMM3 as shown in Figure 14-1.

Initial values

25.0	25.0	25.0	25.0	25.0	25.0	25.0	25.0	ZMM16 (thresh)

-1.0	-1.0	-1.0	-1.0	-1.0	-1.0	-1.0	-1.0	ZMM17

13.0	22.0	89.0	12.0	63.0	34.0	56.0	18.0	ZMM0 (dist[i:i+7])

`vcmppd k1,zmm0,zmm16,CMP_GE_OQ`

0	0	1	0	1	1	1	0	K1 (bits 0:7)

`vmovapd zmm2{k1}{z},zmm17`

0.0	0.0	-1.0	0.0	-1.0	-1.0	-1.0	0.0	ZMM2

`vmulpd zmm3,zmm2,zmm0`

0.0	0.0	-89.0	0.0	-63.0	-34.0	-56.0	0.0	ZMM3

`knotb k2,k1`

1	1	0	1	0	0	0	1	K2 (bits 0:7)

`vmovapd zmm4{k2}{z},zmm0`

13.0	22.0	0.0	12.0	0.0	0.0	0.0	18.0	ZMM4

`vorpd zmm5,zmm4,zmm3`

13.0	22.0	-89.0	12.0	-63.0	-34.0	-56.0	18.0	ZMM5

Figure 14-1. *SIMD ternary operation performed in* CalcDistances_avx512()

Execution of the instruction pair knotb k2,k1 and vmovapd zmm4{k2}{z},zmm0 sets each element in ZMM4 to 0.0 if dist >= thresh is true; otherwise, the element is set to dist. This operation is also shown in Figure 14-1. The vorpd zmm5,zmm4,zmm3 instruction merges the intermediate results in ZMM3 and ZMM4 to form the final SIMD ternary result. The ensuing vmovapd zmmword ptr [rbx+rax],zmm5 instruction saves this result to d[i:i+NSE-1]. Execution of for-loop Loop1 continues until n == 0 (R10) is true.

Listing 14-3b shows the NASM code for example Ch14_03. In this listing, note that the prologue for function CalcDistances_avx512() utilizes a sub rsp,16 instruction, which allocates stack storage space that's used to preserve argument values n and thresh on the stack. Function CalcDistances_avx512() can't use the red zone to preserve these values since it's a non-leaf function. The other argument values, d, x1, y1, x2, y2, are copied to non-volatile general-purpose registers prior to calling CheckArgs().

569

Listing 14-3b. Example Ch14_03 NASM Code

```nasm
;-------------------------------------------------------------------
; Ch14_03_fasm.s
;-------------------------------------------------------------------

        %include "ModX86Asm3eNASM.inc"
        %include "cmpequ_fp.inc"

            section .rdata
F64_minus1  dq -1.0


;-------------------------------------------------------------------
; bool CalcDistances_avx512(double* d, const double* x1, const double* y1,
;   const double* x2, const double* y2, size_t n, double thresh);
;-------------------------------------------------------------------

NSE     equ 8                           ;num_simd_elements

        section .text
        extern CheckArgs

        global CalcDistances_avx512
CalcDistances_avx512:
        push rbx                        ;save non-volatile GPRs
        push r12
        push r13
        push r14
        push r15
        sub rsp,16                      ;allocate stack space for arg saves

; Copy arguments in volatile registers to non-volatile registers.
; Also save args n and thresh on stack.
        mov rbx,rdi                     ;rbx = d
        mov r12,rsi                     ;r12 = x1
        mov r13,rdx                     ;r13 = y1
        mov r14,rcx                     ;r14 = x2
        mov r15,r8                      ;r15 = y2
        mov [rsp],r9                    ;save n on stack
        vmovsd [rsp+8],xmm0             ;save thresh on stack

; Make sure the arguments are valid. Note that arguments d, x1, y1, x2,
; n, and y2 are already in the correct registers for CheckArgs().
        call CheckArgs
        or eax,eax                      ;valid arguments?
        jz Err                          ;jump if CheckArgs() failed

;-------------------------------------------------------------------
; Registers used in code below:
;
; rax = array offset         rbx = d          r10 = n         r12 = x1
; r13 = y1                    r14 = x2         r15 = y2
```

```
;
; zmm16 = packed thresh      zmm17 = packed -1.0
;-------------------------------------------------------------------------------

; Initialize
        mov rax,-NSE*8                          ;array offset
        mov r10,[rsp]                           ;r10 = n
        vbroadcastsd zmm16,[rsp+8]              ;packed thresh
        vbroadcastsd zmm17,[F64_minus1]        ;packed -1.0

; Calculate distances using SIMD arithmetic
Loop1:  add rax,NSE*8                           ;rax = offset to next elements

        vmovapd zmm0,[r12+rax]                  ;zmm0 = x1[i:i+NSE-1]
        vsubpd zmm1,zmm0,[r14+rax]              ;zmm1 = x1 - x2
        vmulpd zmm1,zmm1,zmm1                   ;zmm1 = (x1 - x2) ** 2

        vmovapd zmm2,[r13+rax]                  ;zmm2 = y1[i:i+NSE-1]
        vsubpd zmm3,zmm2,[r15+rax]              ;zmm3 = y1 - y2
        vmulpd zmm3,zmm3,zmm3                   ;zmm3 = (y1 - y1) ** 2

        vaddpd zmm4,zmm1,zmm3                   ;(x1 - x2) ** 2 + (y1 - y1) ** 2
        vsqrtpd zmm0,zmm4                       ;dist (temp3 in C++ code)

; Calculate d = (temp3 >= thresh) ? temp3 * -1.0 : temp3; using SIMD arithmetic
        vcmppd k1,zmm0,zmm16,CMP_GE_OQ          ;compare raw dist to thresh
        vmovapd zmm2{k1}{z},zmm17               ;zmm2 = -1.0 (compare true) or zero
        vmulpd zmm3,zmm2,zmm0                   ;zmm3 = -1.0 * dist or 0.0
        knotb k2,k1                             ;k2 = mask for dist < thresh
        vmovapd zmm4{k2}{z},zmm0                ;zmm4 = dist or 0.0
        vorpd zmm5,zmm4,zmm3                    ;zmm5 = final result
        vmovapd [rbx+rax],zmm5                  ;save result to d[i:i+NSE-1]

        sub r10,NSE                             ;n -= NSE
        jnz Loop1                               ;jump if yes

        mov eax,1                               ;set success return code

Done:   vzeroupper
        add rsp,16                              ;release local stack space
        pop r15                                 ;restore non-volatile registers
        pop r14
        pop r13
        pop r12
        pop rbx
        ret

Err:    xor eax,eax                             ;set errror return code
        jmp Done
```

The SIMD ternary code in the NASM implementation of CalcDistances_avx512() employs the same AVX-512 instruction sequences as its MASM counterpart. Note that the epilogue of function CalcDistances_avx512() includes an add rsp,16 instruction, which releases the previously allocated local stack storage space and properly positions RSP for the ensuing pop and ret instructions. Here are the results for source code example Ch14_03:

```
----- Results for Ch14_03 (thresh = 25.0000) -----

      x1       y1       x2       y2 |      d1        d2
-----------------------------------------------------------
   1.4193   60.9381   28.1498   62.3203 |  -26.7662   -26.7662
  45.6211   31.3445   17.8668   52.2026 |  -34.7183   -34.7183
  19.3088   69.7241   40.1756   18.2590 |  -55.5345   -55.5345
  35.7644   74.3092   25.8307   19.3251 |  -55.8742   -55.8742
  26.5019   28.6746   27.3385   51.6712 |   23.0119    23.0119
  22.4397   68.9241    8.9053   19.0044 |  -51.7219   -51.7219
  64.0793   12.0018   37.2446   66.0294 |  -60.3248   -60.3248
  25.2135   24.3822   53.2614   18.4492 |  -28.6685   -28.6685
  33.6993   39.2796   15.6201   56.1528 |   24.7298    24.7298
  51.2222   26.2416   21.9895   17.1022 |  -30.6281   -30.6281
  49.3491   62.0335   37.7140   10.1119 |  -53.2093   -53.2093
  67.8222   21.8987   19.2436   59.0732 |  -61.1704   -61.1704
  38.9824   32.9499   34.2359   56.1616 |   23.6920    23.6920
  36.6898   63.5419   36.8821   74.6301 |   11.0899    11.0899
  26.4318    3.7547   40.6940   32.9107 |  -32.4574   -32.4574
  17.2157   29.4545   12.5259   29.1989 |    4.6967     4.6967
  17.4332   16.3869   58.3692   31.8759 |  -43.7684   -43.7684
  35.8889   17.8839   16.9624   65.8577 |  -51.5722   -51.5722
  50.4938   43.9717   61.8307   24.9722 |   22.1248    22.1248
  10.0090   42.7649   25.1586   61.5460 |   24.1297    24.1297
  24.4566   11.3373   43.9400   53.0586 |  -46.0464   -46.0464
  30.7898   59.3711   63.0179   26.2297 |  -46.2277   -46.2277
  48.9057   18.8767   40.9833   39.1118 |   21.7307    21.7307
  59.4277   44.6346   44.9898   35.3745 |   17.1522    17.1522
```

Floating-Point Matrices

The following section contains three examples that exemplify the use of AVX-512 instructions with floating-point matrices. The first example spotlights the calculation of a covariance matrix. This is followed by an example that explains how to perform matrix multiplication. The final example covers matrix-vector multiplication.

The source code examples presented in this section contain AVX-512 implementations of the same AVX2 functions that you scrutinized in Chapter 11. The reason for doing this is to provide helpful insights regarding some of the similarities and differences between AVX-512 and AVX2 programming.

Covariance Matrix

Source code example Ch11_08 elucidated the construction of a covariance matrix using AVX2 instructions. The source code example presented in this section, entitled Ch14_04, is the AVX-512 counterpart of example Ch11_08. Before perusing the content of this section, you may want to review both the C++ and assembly language code for example Ch11_08 in conjunction with the text that expounds covariance matrix arithmetic in Chapter 11.

Listing 14-4 shows the MASM code for example Ch14_04. The layout of this code closely resembles the MASM code that you saw in Listing 11-8b, but with a few important differences. Near the top of Listing 14-4, note that NSE is assigned a value eight instead of four since a ZMM register can hold eight double-precision floating-point elements. Also observe that function CalcCovMatF64_avx512() doesn't employ macro SaveXmmRegs_M in its prologue. The reason for this is that function CalcCovMatF64_avx512() utilizes volatile registers XMM16–XMM18 instead of non-volatile registers XMM6–XMM8.

Listing 14-4. Example Ch14_04 MASM Code

```
;-------------------------------------------------------------------------
; Ch14_04_fasm.asm
;-------------------------------------------------------------------------

        include <MacrosX86-64-AVX.asmh>

;-------------------------------------------------------------------------
; void CalcCovMatF64_avx512(double* cov_mat, double* var_means,
;   const double* x, size_t n_vars, size_t n_obvs);
;-------------------------------------------------------------------------

NSE     equ 8                           ;num_simd_elements
SF      equ 8                           ;scale factor for F64 elements

        .code
CalcCovMatF64_avx512 proc frame
        CreateFrame_M COV_,0,0,rbx,rsi,rdi,r12,r13
        EndProlog_M

; Initialize
        mov r10,[rbp+COV_OffsetStackArgs]       ;r10 = n_obvs
        vcvtusi2sd xmm5,xmm5,r10                 ;convert n_obvs to F64
        mov rax,r10
        sub rax,1                                ;rax = n_obvs - 1
        vcvtusi2sd xmm16,xmm16,rax               ;convert n_obvs - 1 to F64

        xor eax,eax                              ;i = 0
        jmp L1                                   ;begin execution of Loop1


;-------------------------------------------------------------------------
; General-purpose register use for var_means[i] calculation:
;   rax     i                       r10     n_obvs
;   rbx     j                       r11     scratch register
;   rcx     cov_mat                 r12     -----
;   rdx     var_means               r13     -----
```

```
;   r8      x                       rsi     i * n_obvs
;   r9      n_vars                  rdi     -----
;------------------------------------------------------------------

; Calculate var_means[i] (mean of row i in matrix x)
Loop1:  mov rsi,rax                         ;rsi = i
        imul rsi,r10                        ;rsi = i * n_obvs

        xor ebx,ebx                         ;j = 0
        vxorpd zmm0,zmm0,zmm0               ;sums[0:NSE-1] = 0
        jmp L2                              ;begin execution of Loop2

; Sum elements in row x[i] using SIMD addition
        align 16
Loop2:  lea r11,[rsi+rbx]                   ;r11 = i * n_obvs + j
        vaddpd zmm0,zmm0,[r8+r11*SF]        ;sums[0:NSE-1] += x[i][j:j+NSE-1]

        add rbx,NSE                         ;j += NSE
L2:     mov r11,rbx                         ;r11 = j
        add r11,NSE                         ;r11 = j + NSE
        cmp r11,r10                         ;j + NSE <= n_obvs?
        jbe Loop2                           ;jump if yes

; Reduce packed sums to scalar
        vextractf64x4 ymm1,zmm0,1           ;extract high-order F64 values (4)
        vaddpd ymm0,ymm1,ymm0               ;sum elements
        vextractf128 xmm1,ymm0,1            ;extract high-order F64 values (2)
        vaddpd xmm0,xmm1,xmm0               ;sum elements
        vhaddpd xmm0,xmm0,xmm0              ;scalar sum in xmm0[63:0]

        jmp L3                              ;begin execution of Loop3

; Sum remaining elements in current row using scalar arithmetic
Loop3:  lea r11,[rsi+rbx]                   ;r11 = i * n_obvs + j
        vaddsd xmm0,xmm0,real8 ptr [r8+r11*SF]  ;sum += x[i][j]

        add rbx,1                           ;j += 1
L3:     cmp rbx,r10                         ;j < n_obvs?
        jb Loop3                            ;jump if yes

; Calculate var_means[i]
        vdivsd xmm1,xmm0,xmm5               ;var_means[i] = sum / n_obvs
        vmovsd real8 ptr [rdx+rax*SF],xmm1  ;save var_means[i]

        add rax,1                           ;i += 1
L1:     cmp rax,r9                          ;i < n_vars?
        jb Loop1                            ;jump if yes

;------------------------------------------------------------------
; General-purpose register use for cov_mat[i][j] calculation:
;   rax     i                       r10     n_obvs
```

```
;   rbx     j                      r11     scratch register
;   rcx     cov_mat                r12     i * n_vars
;   rdx     var_means              r13     k
;   r8      x                      rsi     i * n_obvs
;   r9      n_vars                 rdi     j * n_obvs
;-------------------------------------------------------------------

; Calculate covariance matrix
        xor  eax,eax                      ;i = 0
        jmp  L4


Loop4:  mov  r12,rax                      ;r12 = i
        imul r12,r9                       ;r12 = i * n_vars
        mov  rsi,rax                      ;rsi = i
        imul rsi,r10                      ;rsi = i * n_obvs
        xor  ebx,ebx                      ;j = 0
        jmp  L5                           ;begin execution of Loop5


Loop5:  cmp  rax,rbx                      ;i > j?
        ja   NoCalc                       ;jump if yes

        mov  rdi,rbx                      ;rdi = j
        imul rdi,r10                      ;rdi = j * n_obvs
        xor  r13,r13                      ;k = 0

        vxorpd       zmm0,zmm0,zmm0                    ;cov_mat[i][j] product sums = 0
        vbroadcastsd zmm17,real8 ptr [rdx+rax*SF]      ;zmm17 = var_means[i]
        jmp  L6                           ;begin execution of Loop6

; Calculate product sums for cov_mat[i][j] using SIMD arithmetic
        align 16
Loop6:  vbroadcastsd zmm18,real8 ptr [rdx+rbx*SF] ;zmm18 = var_means[j]
        lea    r11,[rsi+r13]               ;r11 = i * n_obvs + k
        vmovupd zmm1,[r8+r11*SF]           ;load x[i][k:k+NSE-1]
        lea    r11,[rdi+r13]               ;r11 = j * n_obvs + k
        vmovupd zmm2,[r8+r11*SF]           ;load x[j][k:k+NSE-1]
        vsubpd zmm3,zmm1,zmm17             ;x[i][k:k+NSE-1] - var_means[i]
        vsubpd zmm4,zmm2,zmm18             ;x[j][k:k+NSE-1] - var_means[j]
        vfmadd231pd zmm0,zmm3,zmm4         ;update cov_mat[i][j] product sums

        add    r13,NSE                     ;k += NSE
L6:     lea    r11,[r13+NSE]               ;r11 = k + NSE
        cmp    r11,r10                     ;k + NSE <= n_obvs?
        jbe    Loop6                       ;jump if yes

; Reduce packed product sums for cov_mat[i][j] to scalar value
        vextractf64x4 ymm1,zmm0,1          ;extract high-order F64 values (4)
        vaddpd        ymm0,ymm1,ymm0       ;sum elements
        vextractf128  xmm1,ymm0,1          ;extract high-order F64 values (2)
        vaddpd        xmm0,xmm1,xmm0       ;sum elements
        vhaddpd       xmm0,xmm0,xmm0       ;scalar product sum in xmm0[63:0]
```

```
        jmp L7                                   ;begin execution of Loop7

; Complete calculation of product sums for cov_mat[i][j] using scalar arithmetic
Loop7:  lea r11,[rsi+r13]                        ;r11 = i * n_obvs + k
        vmovsd xmm1,real8 ptr [r8+r11*SF]        ;load x[i][k]
        lea r11,[rdi+r13]                        ;r11 = j * n_obvs + k
        vmovsd xmm2,real8 ptr [r8+r11*SF]        ;load x[j][k]
        vsubsd xmm3,xmm1,xmm17                    ;x[i][j] - var_means[i]
        vsubsd xmm4,xmm2,xmm18                    ;x[j][i] - var_means[j]
        vfmadd231sd xmm0,xmm3,xmm4                ;update cov_mat[i][j] product sums

        add r13,1                                ;k += 1
L7:     cmp r13,r10                              ;k < n_obvs?
        jb Loop7                                 ;jump if yes

; Calculate and save cov_mat[i][j]
        vdivsd xmm1,xmm0,xmm16                    ;calc cov_mat[i][j]
        lea r11,[r12+rbx]                         ;r11 = i * n_vars + j
        vmovsd real8 ptr [rcx+r11*SF],xmm1        ;save cov_mat[i][j]
        jmp F1

; No calculation needed, set cov_mat[i][j] = cov_mat[j][i]
NoCalc: mov r11,rbx                              ;r11 = j
        imul r11,r9                              ;r11 = j * n_vars
        add r11,rax                              ;r11 = j * n_vars + i
        vmovsd xmm0,real8 ptr [rcx+r11*SF]       ;load cov_mat[j][i]
        lea r11,[r12+rbx]                         ;r11 = i * n_vars + j
        vmovsd real8 ptr [rcx+r11*SF],xmm0        ;save cov_mat[i][j]

F1:     add rbx,1                                ;j += 1
L5:     cmp rbx,r9                               ;j < n_vars?
        jb Loop5                                 ;jump if yes

        add rax,1                                ;i += 1
L4:     cmp rax,r9                               ;i < n_vars?
        jb Loop4                                 ;jump if yes

Done:   vzeroupper
        DeleteFrame_M rbx,rsi,rdi,r12,r13
        ret
CalcCovMatF64_avx512 endp
        end
```

In Listing 14-4, for-loops Loop1, Loop2, and Loop3 compute the mean of each row in matrix x. Note that Loop2 uses 512-bit wide packed operands to calculate the row sums (in Listing 11-8b, 256-bit wide operands were employed). The code block that follows Loop2 reduces the eight double-precision floating-point values in register ZMM0 to a scalar value. This block begins with a vextractf64x4 ymm1,zmm0,1 instruction that copies the four double-precision floating-point values in ZMM0[511:256] to YMM1[255:0]. Note that the immediate operand of the vextractf64x4 instruction specifies which set of double-precision values (0 = bits 255:0, 1 = bits 511:256) to extract. The ensuing vaddpd ymm0,ymm1,ymm0 instruction reduces the number of intermediate sums to four. This is followed by the instruction triplet vextractf128 xmm1,ymm0,1, vaddpd xmm0,xmm1,xmm0, and vhaddpd xmm0,xmm0,xmm0, which completes the reduction operation. The for-loop Loop3 completes the summing of elements in row x[i][] using scalar arithmetic. The subsequent code block then calculates var_means[i].

The second part of function CalcCovMatF64_avx512() calculates covariance matrix cov_mat. In Listing 14-4, for-loops Loop4, Loop5, and Loop6 carry out this computation.

Execution of for-loop Loop4 opens with a code block that calculates offsets for matrix x, array var_ means, and matrix cov_mat. Recall from the discussions in Chapter 11 that a covariance matrix is symmetric (i.e., cov_mat[i][j] == cov_mat[j][i] is true). Near the top of Loop5, function CalcCovMatF64_avx512() uses the instruction pair cmp rax,rbx and ja NoCalc to skip over the calculating code for cov_mat[i][j] if i > j is true.

Once again, the primary difference in Loop6 between the AVX-512 covariance matrix code in Listing 14-4 and AVX2 code in Listing 11-8b is that the former uses 512-bit wide instead of 256-bit wide packed double-precision floating-point operands. For example, note that the vmovupd, vsubpd, and vfmadd231pd instructions in Loop6 use ZMM register operands. Following execution of Loop6, CalcCovMatF64_avx512() uses scalar double-precision floating-point arithmetic to complete the product-sum computation for cov_mat[i][j]. The code blocks in Listing 14-4 that update loop variable indices and perform loop termination checks are equivalent to those in Listing 11-8b.

The NASM code for example Ch14_04 (not shown) is identical to the code shown in Listing 14-4, except for the inclusion of a code block that rearranges the argument value registers. The results for example Ch14_04 are the same as example Ch11_08.

Table 14-1 shows the benchmark timing measurements for source example Ch14_04. As you can see from the benchmark timing measurements, the AVX-512 assembly language code is significantly faster than the C++ code. Table 14-1 also shows the benchmark timing measurements for function CalcCovMatF64_ avx2(), which were copied from Table 11-8. Note that the AVX-512 implementations of the covariance matrix algorithm are modestly faster than the AVX2 versions.

Table 14-1. *Benchmark Timing Measurements (Microseconds) for Covariance Matrix Calculation Functions (n_vars = 10, n_obvs = 250,000)*

Function	i5-11600K	i7-11700K	7700X
CalcCovMatF64_cpp()	14344 (23)	13959 (563)	9222 (17)
CalcCovMatF64_avx2()	5053 (19)	4573 (156)	2997 (14)
CalcCovMatF64_avx512()	4799 (19)	4292 (455)	1882 (8)

Matrix Multiplication

In Chapter 11, you learned how to code assembly language functions that performed matrix multiplication using AVX2 instructions (see examples Ch11_02 and Ch11_03). In this section, you'll learn how to code matrix multiplication functions using AVX-512 instructions. Before continuing, you may want to revisit the matrix multiplication equation and the accompanying explanatory text in Chapter 11. You also may want to review the C++ source code for examples Ch11_02 and Ch11_03 since the same code is used in examples Ch14_05 and Ch14_06.

Single-Precision

Listing 14-5 shows the MASM code for example Ch14_05. This listing opens with three equate statements that define NSE (num_simd_elements), NSE_MOD (num_residual_cols calculation mask), and SF (scale factor) for single-precision floating-point values. Following its prologue, function MatrixMulF32_avx2() uses a series of mov instructions that load c_nrows into R13, c_ncols into R14, and a_ncols into R15. The ensuing code block calculates num_residual_cols. Note that this code block also initializes opmask register K1 with a mask for residual column loads and stores. Recall that in example Ch11_02, function MatrixMulF32_avx2() consumed a YMM register to maintain the residual column load and store mask (see Listing 11-2b).

Listing 14-5. Example Ch14_05 MASM Code

```
;-----------------------------------------------------------------------------
; Ch14_05_fasm.asm
;-----------------------------------------------------------------------------

        include <MacrosX86-64-AVX.asmh>


;-----------------------------------------------------------------------------
; void MatrixMulF32_avx512(float* c, const float* a, const float* b,
;   const size_t* sizes);
;-----------------------------------------------------------------------------

NSE           equ 16                    ;num_simd_elements
NSE_MOD       equ 0fh                   ;mask to calculate num_residual_cols
SF            equ 4                     ;scale factor for F32 elements

        .code
MatrixMulF32_avx512 proc frame
        CreateFrame_M MM_,0,0,rbx,rsi,rdi,r12,r13,r14,r15
        EndProlog_M

; Load matrix sizes
        mov r13,[r9]                    ;r13 = c_nrows
        mov r14,[r9+8]                  ;r14 = c_ncols (also b_ncols)
        mov r15,[r9+16]                 ;r15 = a_ncols

; Calculate mask for residual column loads and stores
        mov r12,r14                     ;r12 = c_ncols
        and r12,NSE_MOD                 ;num_residual_cols = c_ncols % NSE
        mov r9,rcx                      ;save rcx
        mov rcx,r12                     ;rcx = num_residual_cols
        mov eax,1
        shl eax,cl                      ;eax = 2 ** num_residual_cols
        sub eax,1                       ;eax = 2 ** num_residual_cols - 1
        kmovw k1,eax                    ;k1 = mask for residual col load/store
        mov rcx,r9                      ;restore rcx

        mov rax,-1                      ;rax = i
```

```
;-----------------------------------------------------------------------------
; General-purpose registers used in code below:
;
;   rax     i                                       r9      j
;   rbx     matrix a element pointer (p_aa)         r10     k
;   rcx     matrix c                                r11     scratch
;   rdx     matrix a                                r12     num_residual_cols
;   rsi     matrix b element pointer (p_bb)         r13     c_nrows
;   rdi     &a[i][0]                                r15     a_ncols
;   r8      matrix b
;-----------------------------------------------------------------------------

; Repeat for each row in c
        align 16
Loop1:  add rax,1                               ;i += 1
        cmp rax,r13
        jae Done                                ;jump if i >= c_nrows

        mov rdi,rdx                             ;rdi = &a[i][0]
        lea rdx,[rdx+r15*SF]                    ;rdx = &a[i+1][0]
        xor r9,r9                               ;r9 = j

; Repeat while there are at least NSE columns in current row of c
        align 16
Loop2:  lea r11,[r9+NSE]                        ;r11 = j + NSE
        cmp r11,r14
        ja ChkRes                               ;jump if j + NSE > c_ncols

        mov rbx,rdi                             ;rbx = &a[i][0]
        lea rsi,[r8+r9*SF]                      ;rsi = &b[0][j]
        vxorps zmm2,zmm2,zmm2                   ;initialize packed c_vals
        mov r10,r15                             ;r10 = a_ncols

; Calculate c[i][j:j+NSE-1]
        align 16
Loop3a: vbroadcastss zmm0,real4 ptr [rbx]      ;broadcast a[i][k]
        vfmadd231ps zmm2,zmm0,[rsi]             ;zmm2 += a[i][k] * b[k][j:j+NSE-1]

        add rbx,SF                              ;rbx = &a[i][k+1]
        lea rsi,[rsi+r14*SF]                    ;rsi = &b[k+1][j]
        sub r10,1                               ;k -= 1
        jnz Loop3a                              ;repeat until done

; Save c[i][j:j+NSE-1]
        vmovups zmmword ptr [rcx],zmm2          ;save c[i][j:j+NSE-1]

        add r9,NSE                              ;j += num_simd_elements
        add rcx,NSE*SF                          ;rcx = &c[i][j+NSE] (next group)
        jmp Loop2
```

```
ChkRes: test r12,r12                              ;num_residual_cols == 0?
        jz Loop1                                  ;jump if yes

        mov rbx,rdi                               ;rbx = &a[i][0]
        lea rsi,[r8+r9*SF]                        ;rsi = &b[0][j]
        vxorps zmm2,zmm2,zmm2                      ;initialize packed c_vals
        mov r10,r15                               ;r10 = a_ncols

; Calculate c[i][j:j+NRC] (NRC is num_residual_cols)
        align 16
Loop3b: vbroadcastss zmm0,real4 ptr [rbx]         ;broadcast a[i][k]
        vmovups zmm1{k1},zmmword ptr [rsi]         ;load b[k][j:j+NRC]
        vfmadd231ps zmm2,zmm0,zmm1                 ;zmm2 += a[i][k] * b[k][j:j+NRC]

        add rbx,SF                                 ;rbx = &a[i][k+1]
        lea rsi,[rsi+r14*SF]                       ;rsi = &b[k+1][j]
        sub r10,1                                  ;k -= 1
        jnz Loop3b                                 ;repeat until done

; Save c[i][j:j+NRC]
        vmovups zmmword ptr [rcx]{k1},zmm2         ;save c[i][j:j+NRC]
        lea rcx,[rcx+r12*SF]                       ;rcx = &c[i][j+NRC+1] (next group)
        jmp Loop1

Done:   vzeroupper
        DeleteFrame_M rbx,rsi,rdi,r12,r13,r14,r15
        ret

MatrixMulF32_avx512 endp
        end
```

In Listing 14-5, the arrangement of for-loops Loop1, Loop2, Loop3a, and Loop3b in function MatrixMulF32_avx512() closely resembles the same for-loops in function MatrixMulF32_avx2() (see Listing 11-2b). However, there are two noteworthy divergences that warrant discussion. First, function MatrixMulF32_avx512() uses ZMM registers to perform the required SIMD arithmetic. This means that Loop3a calculates 16 matrix elements, c[i][j:j+NSE-1], during each iteration. Second, note in Loop3b that MatrixMulF32_avx512() employs an opmask register with the vmovups instructions to perform residual column loads and stores. In example Ch11_02, function MatrixMulF32_avx2() used vmaskmovps with a YMM register operand instruction to carry out this same operation.

The NASM code for example Ch14_05 (not shown) is basically the same as the MASM code except for a code block that rearranges values in the argument registers. The output for source code example Ch14_05 is the same as the output for example Ch11_02.

Table 14-2 shows the benchmark timing measurements for source example Ch14_05. Table 14-2 also shows the benchmark timing measurements for function MatrixMulF32_avx2(), which were copied from Table 11-2. Note that the AVX-512 implementations of the matrix multiplication algorithm are significantly faster than their AVX2 counterparts.

Table 14-2. *Benchmark Timing Measurements (Microseconds) for Matrix Multiplication Functions Using a 100 × 100 Matrix (100 Matrix Products)*

Function	i5-11600K	i7-11700K	7700X
MatrixMulF32_cpp()	54308 (31)	50615 (1601)	35126 (49)
MatrixMulF32_avx2()	7032 (18)	6929 (111)	5862 (8)
MatrixMulF32_avx512()	3808 (6)	3821 (127)	3513 (5)

Double-Precision

Listing 14-6 shows the MASM code for example Ch14_06. This listing shows the code for function MatrixMulF64_avx512(), which performs matrix multiplication using double-precision floating-point elements. Source code example Ch14_06 is the AVX-512 counterpart of AVX2 example Ch11_03.

Listing 14-6. Example Ch14_06 MASM Code

```
;-------------------------------------------------------------------------------
; Ch14_06_fasm.asm
;-------------------------------------------------------------------------------

        include <MacrosX86-64-AVX.asmh>

;-------------------------------------------------------------------------------
; void MatrixMulF64_avx512(float* c, const float* a, const float* b,
;    const size_t* sizes);
;-------------------------------------------------------------------------------

NSE         equ 8                       ;num_simd_elements
NSE_MOD     equ 07h                     ;mask to calculate num_residual_cols
SF          equ 8                       ;scale factor for F64 elements

        .code
MatrixMulF64_avx512 proc frame
        CreateFrame_M MM_,0,0,rbx,rsi,rdi,r12,r13,r14,r15
        EndProlog_M

; Load matrix sizes
        mov r13,[r9]                    ;r13 = c_nrows
        mov r14,[r9+8]                  ;r14 = c_ncols (also b_ncols)
        mov r15,[r9+16]                 ;r15 = a_ncols

; Calculate mask for residual column loads and stores
        mov r12,r14                     ;r12 = c_ncols
        and r12,NSE_MOD                 ;num_residual_cols = c_ncols % NSE
        mov r9,rcx                      ;save rcx
        mov rcx,r12                     ;rcx = num_residual_cols
        mov eax,1
        shl eax,cl                      ;eax = 2 ** num_residual_cols
        sub eax,1                       ;eax = 2 ** num_residual_cols - 1
```

```
        kmovb k1,eax                    ;k1 = mask for residual col load/store
        mov rcx,r9                      ;restore rcx

        mov rax,-1                      ;rax = i

;----------------------------------------------------------------------------
; General-purpose registers used in code below:
;
;   rax     i                                   r9      j
;   rbx     matrix a element pointer (p_aa)     r10     k
;   rcx     matrix c                            r11     scratch
;   rdx     matrix a                            r12     num_residual_cols
;   rsi     matrix b element pointer (p_bb)     r13     c_nrows
;   rdi     &a[i][0]                            r15     a_ncols
;   r8      matrix b
;----------------------------------------------------------------------------


; Repeat for each row in c
        align 16
Loop1:  add rax,1                       ;i += 1
        cmp rax,r13
        jae Done                        ;jump if i >= c_nrows

        mov rdi,rdx                     ;rdi = &a[i][0]
        lea rdx,[rdx+r15*SF]            ;rdx = &a[i+1][0]
        xor r9,r9                       ;r9 = j

; Repeat while there are at least NSE columns in current row of c
        align 16
Loop2:  lea r11,[r9+NSE]                ;r11 = j + NSE
        cmp r11,r14
        ja ChkRes                       ;jump if j + NSE > c_ncols

        mov rbx,rdi                     ;rbx = &a[i][0]
        lea rsi,[r8+r9*SF]              ;rsi = &b[0][j]
        vxorpd zmm2,zmm2,zmm2           ;initialize packed c_vals
        mov r10,r15                     ;r10 = a_ncols

; Calculate c[i][j:j+NSE-1]
        align 16
Loop3a: vbroadcastsd zmm0,real8 ptr [rbx]  ;broadcast a[i][k]
        vfmadd231pd zmm2,zmm0,[rsi]        ;zmm2 += a[i][k] * b[k][j:j+NSE-1]

        add rbx,SF                      ;rbx = &a[i][k+1]
        lea rsi,[rsi+r14*SF]            ;rsi = &b[k+1][j]
        sub r10,1                       ;k -= 1
        jnz Loop3a                      ;repeat until done

; Save c[i][j:j+NSE-1]
        vmovupd zmmword ptr [rcx],zmm2  ;save c[i][j:j+NSE-1]
```

```
        add  r9,NSE                              ;j += num_simd_elements
        add  rcx,NSE*SF                          ;rcx = &c[i][j+NSE] (next group)
        jmp  Loop2

ChkRes: test r12,r12                             ;num_residual_cols == 0?
        jz   Loop1                               ;jump if yes

        mov  rbx,rdi                             ;rbx = &a[i][0]
        lea  rsi,[r8+r9*SF]                      ;rsi = &b[0][j]
        vxorpd zmm2,zmm2,zmm2                     ;initialize packed c_vals
        mov  r10,r15                             ;r10 = a_ncols

; Calculate c[i][j:j+NRC] (NRC is num_residual_cols)
        align 16
Loop3b: vbroadcastsd zmm0,real8 ptr [rbx]        ;broadcast a[i][k]
        vmovupd zmm1{k1},zmmword ptr [rsi]        ;load b[k][j:j+NRC]
        vfmadd231pd zmm2,zmm0,zmm1                ;zmm2 += a[i][k] * b[k][j:j+NRC]

        add  rbx,SF                              ;rbx = &a[i][k+1]
        lea  rsi,[rsi+r14*SF]                    ;rsi = &b[k+1][j]
        sub  r10,1                               ;k -= 1
        jnz  Loop3b                              ;repeat until done

; Save c[i][j:j+NRC]
        vmovupd zmmword ptr [rcx]{k1},zmm2        ;save c[i][j:j+NRC]
        lea  rcx,[rcx+r12*SF]                    ;rcx = &c[i][j+NRC+1] (next group)
        jmp  Loop1

Done:   vzeroupper
        DeleteFrame_M rbx,rsi,rdi,r12,r13,r14,r15
        ret

MatrixMulF64_avx512 endp
        end
```

The code in Listing 14-6 for function MatrixMulF64_avx512() mostly parallels the code for function MatrixMulF32_avx512() that's shown in Listing 14-5. Modifications include different values for equates NSE (8 instead of 16), NSE_MOD (07h instead of 0fh), and SF (8 instead of 4). Also note that the mask initialization code uses a kmovb instead of a kmovw instruction to load the residual column load and store mask into register K1. Finally, the matrix multiplication calculating code in MatrixMulF64_avx512() utilizes double-precision instead of single-precision arithmetic instructions.

Like the previous example, the NASM source code for function MatrixMulF64_avx512() (not shown) is the basically the same as the MASM code, except for an extra code block that reorders the argument register values. The output for source code example Ch14_06 matches the output for example Ch11_03.

Table 14-3 shows the benchmark timing measurements for source example Ch14_06. Table 14-3 also shows the benchmark timing measurements for function MatrixMulF64_avx2(), which were copied from Table 11-3. Like the previous example, the AVX-512 implementations of the double-precision matrix multiplication algorithm are demonstrably faster than the AVX2 counterparts.

Table 14-3. *Benchmark Timing Measurements (Microseconds) for Matrix Multiplication Functions Using a 100 × 100 Matrix (100 Matrix Products)*

Function	i5-11600K	i7-11700K	7700X
MatrixMulF32_cpp()	55192 (47)	51065 (1734)	33641 (20)
MatrixMulF32_avx2()	13621 (1111)	13229 (342)	13013 (10)
MatrixMulF32_avx512()	8296 (11)	8263 (140)	7065 (12)

Matrix (4 × 4) Vector Multiplication

Source code examples Ch11_06 and Ch11_07 demonstrated matrix-vector (4 × 4, 4 × 1) product calculations using AVX2 single-precision and double-precision instructions. In this section, you'll learn how to perform these same calculations using AVX-512 instructions. You'll also learn how to use the vmovntp[d|s] (Store Packed Floating-Point Values Using Non-temporal Hint) instructions.

Single-Precision

Source code example Ch14_07 calculates matrix-vector (4 × 4, 4 × 1) products using single-precision elements and SIMD arithmetic. The C++ source code for this example is the same as the C++ code for example Ch11_06 (see Listing 11-6a). You may want to review this code, especially the definition of C++ structure Vec4x1_F32, before continuing with this section. You may also want to review the matrix-vector multiplication equations shown in Figure 11-5.

Listing 14-7 shows the MASM code for example Ch14_07. This listing opens with a custom MASM section named ConstVals that defines doubleword permutation indices. The first group of indices, MatIndCol0–MatIndCol3, contain the indices necessary to transpose a 4 × 4 matrix of single-precision floating-point values. The second group of indices, VecIndW–VecIndZ, are used to rearrange the components of four 4 × 1 vectors. Note that ConstVals is aligned on a 64-byte boundary. Next in Listing 14-7 are two equate statements. Symbol NVPI defines the number of vectors (four) that for-loop Loop1 processes during each iteration, while symbol SIZEVEC denotes the size in bytes (16) of a Vec4x1_F32 structure.

Listing 14-7. Example Ch14_07 MASM Code

```
;-----------------------------------------------------------------------
; Ch14_07_fasm.asm
;-----------------------------------------------------------------------

ConstVals    segment readonly align(64) 'const'

; Indices for matrix permutations
MatIndCol0   dword 0, 4,  8, 12, 0, 4,  8, 12, 0, 4,  8, 12, 0, 4,  8, 12
MatIndCol1   dword 1, 5,  9, 13, 1, 5,  9, 13, 1, 5,  9, 13, 1, 5,  9, 13
MatIndCol2   dword 2, 6, 10, 14, 2, 6, 10, 14, 2, 6, 10, 14, 2, 6, 10, 14
MatIndCol3   dword 3, 7, 11, 15, 3, 7, 11, 15, 3, 7, 11, 15, 3, 7, 11, 15

; Indices for vector permutations
VecIndW      dword 0, 0, 0, 0, 4, 4, 4, 4,  8,  8,  8,  8, 12, 12, 12, 12
VecIndX      dword 1, 1, 1, 1, 5, 5, 5, 5,  9,  9,  9,  9, 13, 13, 13, 13
VecIndY      dword 2, 2, 2, 2, 6, 6, 6, 6, 10, 10, 10, 10, 14, 14, 14, 14
```

584

```
VecIndZ     dword 3, 3, 3, 3, 7, 7, 7, 7, 11, 11, 11, 11, 15, 15, 15, 15
ConstVals   ends


;-------------------------------------------------------------------------
; void MatVecMulF32_avx512(Vec4x1_F32* vec_b, const float* m,
;   const Vec4x1_F32* vec_a, size_t num_vec);
;-------------------------------------------------------------------------


NVPI    equ   4                         ;num_vec_per_iteration
SIZEVEC equ   16                        ;size (bytes) of Vec4x1_F32 struct

        .code
MatVecMulF32_avx512 proc

; Validate arguments
        test r9,r9
        jz Done                         ;jump if num_vec == 0

        test rcx,3fh
        jnz Done                        ;jump if vec_b not 64b aligned
        test rdx,3fh
        jnz Done                        ;jump if m not 64b aligned
        test r8,3fh
        jnz Done                        ;jump if vec_a 64b aligned

; Load indices for matrix and vector permutations
        vmovdqa32 zmm16,zmmword ptr [MatIndCol0]    ;m col 0 indices
        vmovdqa32 zmm17,zmmword ptr [MatIndCol1]    ;m col 1 indices
        vmovdqa32 zmm18,zmmword ptr [MatIndCol2]    ;m col 2 indices
        vmovdqa32 zmm19,zmmword ptr [MatIndCol3]    ;m col 3 indices

        vmovdqa32 zmm24,zmmword ptr [VecIndW]       ;W component indices
        vmovdqa32 zmm25,zmmword ptr [VecIndX]       ;X component indices
        vmovdqa32 zmm26,zmmword ptr [VecIndY]       ;Y component indices
        vmovdqa32 zmm27,zmmword ptr [VecIndZ]       ;Z component indices

; Load source matrix m and permute NVPI copies of each column
        vmovaps zmm0,zmmword ptr [rdx]      ;zmm0  = matrix m
        vpermps zmm20,zmm16,zmm0            ;zmm20 = m col 0
        vpermps zmm21,zmm17,zmm0            ;zmm21 = m col 1
        vpermps zmm22,zmm18,zmm0            ;zmm22 = m col 2
        vpermps zmm23,zmm19,zmm0            ;zmm23 = m col 3

        mov rax,-SIZEVEC                    ;initialize offset for Loop2
        cmp r9,NVPI                         ;num_vec >= NVPI?
        jb Loop2                            ;jump if no
        mov rax,-SIZEVEC*NVPI               ;initialize offset for Loop1

; Calculate matrix-vector products using SIMD arithmetic
        align 16
Loop1:  add rax,SIZEVEC*NVPI                ;update offset
        vmovaps zmm4,zmmword ptr [r8+rax]   ;zmm4 = vec_a[i:i+NVPI-1]
```

```
        vpermps zmm0,zmm24,zmm4           ;zmm0 = vec_a W components
        vpermps zmm1,zmm25,zmm4           ;zmm1 = vec_a X components
        vpermps zmm2,zmm26,zmm4           ;zmm2 = vec_a Y components
        vpermps zmm3,zmm27,zmm4           ;zmm3 = vec_a Z components

; Perform matrix-vector multiplications (NVPI vectors)
        vmulps zmm4,zmm20,zmm0            ;zmm4  = m col 0 * W
        vfmadd231ps zmm4,zmm21,zmm1       ;zmm4 += m col 1 * X
        vfmadd231ps zmm4,zmm22,zmm2       ;zmm4 += m col 2 * Y
        vfmadd231ps zmm4,zmm23,zmm3       ;zmm4 += m col 3 * Z

; Save matrix-vector products (NVPI vectors)
        vmovntps zmmword ptr [rcx+rax],zmm4 ;save vec_b[i:i+NVPI-1]

        sub r9,NVPI                       ;num_vec -= NVPI
        cmp r9,NVPI                       ;num_vec >= NVPI?
        jae Loop1                         ;jump if yes

; Test for more vectors
        test r9,r9                        ;num_vec == 0?
        jz Done                           ;jump if yes

        add rax,SIZEVEC*NVPI-SIZEVEC      ;adjust i for Loop2

; Calculate remaining matrix-vector products
        align 16
Loop2:  add rax,SIZEVEC                            ;update offset
        vbroadcastss xmm0,real4 ptr [r8+rax]    ;xmm0 = vec_a[i] W components
        vbroadcastss xmm1,real4 ptr [r8+rax+4]  ;xmm1 = vec_a[i] X components
        vbroadcastss xmm2,real4 ptr [r8+rax+8]  ;xmm2 = vec_a[i] Y components
        vbroadcastss xmm3,real4 ptr [r8+rax+12] ;xmm3 = vec_a[i] Z components

        vmulps xmm4,xmm20,xmm0            ;xmm4  = m col 0 * W
        vfmadd231ps xmm4,xmm21,xmm1       ;xmm4 += m col 1 * X
        vfmadd231ps xmm4,xmm22,xmm2       ;xmm4 += m col 2 * Y
        vfmadd231ps xmm4,xmm23,xmm3       ;xmm4 += m col 3 * Z

        vmovntps xmmword ptr [rcx+rax],xmm4       ;save vec_b[i]

        sub r9,1                          ;num_vec -= 1
        jnz Loop2                         ;repeat until done

Done:   vzeroupper
        ret
MatVecMulF32_avx512 endp
        end
```

Following argument validation, function MatVecMulF32_avx512() uses four vmovdqa32 instructions to load matrix permutation indices MatIndCol0–MatIndCol3 into registers ZMM16–ZMM19. It then utilizes another set of four vmovdqa32 instructions to load vector permutation indices VecIndW–VecIndZ into registers ZMM24–ZMM27.

The next code block opens with a vmovaps zmm0,zmmword ptr [rdx] instruction that loads the elements of matrix m into register ZMM0. The ensuing instruction, vpermps zmm20,zmm16,zmm0 (Permute Single-Precision Floating-Point Elements), permutes the elements of matrix m in ZMM0 using the indices in register ZMM16. Following execution of this instruction, register ZMM20 contains four copies of matrix m column 0. The subsequent triplet of vpermps instructions loads four copies of matrix m columns 1, 2, and 3 into registers ZMM21, ZMM22, and ZMM23, respectively. Figure 14-2 illustrates these permutations in greater detail.

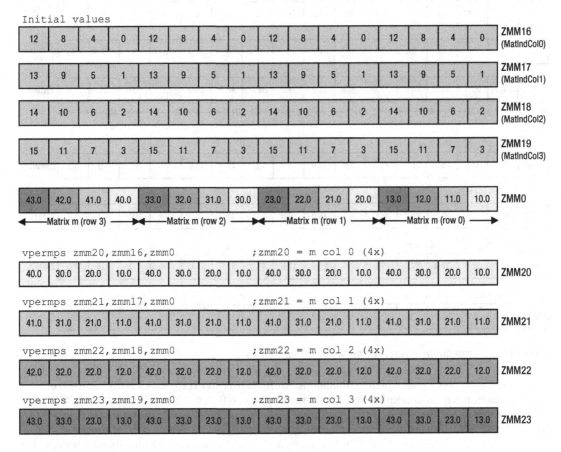

Figure 14-2. *Permutation of matrix columns using vpermps*

Each iteration of Loop1 begins with an add rax,NVPI instruction that calculates i += NVPI. The ensuing vmovaps zmm4,zmmword ptr [r8+rax] instruction loads vectors vec_a[i:i+NVPI-1] into register ZMM4. The X, Y, W, and Z components of these vectors are then reordered using a series of vpermps instructions. Figure 14-3 illustrates this operation in greater detail.

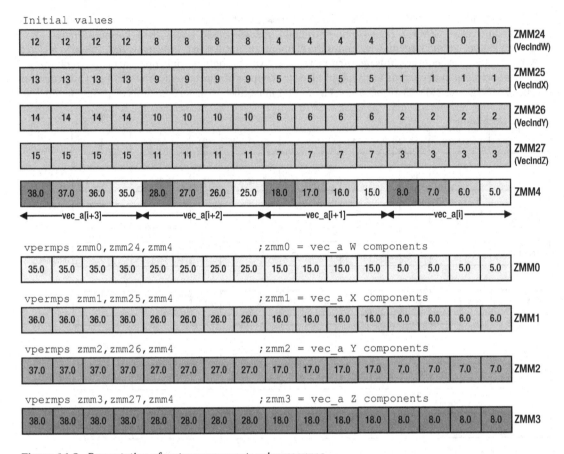

Figure 14-3. *Permutation of vector components using* vpermps

Following the vector component permutations, MatVecMulF32_avx512() uses a vmulps and three vfmadd231ps instructions to calculate four matrix-vector products (i.e., m * vec_a[i:i+NVPI-1]). The vmovntps zmmword ptr [rcx+r10],zmm4 that follows saves the calculated matrix-vector products to vec_b[i:i+NVPI-1]. Unlike the vmovaps instruction, the vmovntps instruction notifies the processor that the data being saved is non-temporal. Non-temporal data is data that will not be immediately reused, which means the processor can optionally bypass its normal memory cache hierarchy to perform the store. Doing this often improves performance since cache pollution is reduced. You'll learn more about non-temporal store instructions in Chapter 16.

Execution of Loop1 continues until fewer than NVPI vectors remain. Following execution of for-loop Loop1 is another for-loop named Loop2. This for-loop processes any residual vectors. Note that Loop2 uses a series of vbroadcastss instructions to create packed versions of vec_a[i].W, vec_a[i].X, vec_a[i].Y, and vec_a[i].Z. This loop also employs scalar instructions vmulps and vfmadd231ps to calculate m * vec_a[i].

The NASM code for example Ch14_07 (not shown) is basically the same as the MASM code, except for the use of different general-purpose registers.

The results for source code example Ch14_07 are the same as the results for example Ch11_06. Table 14-4 shows the benchmark timing measurements for source example Ch14_07. For this example, the AVX-512 implementations of the matrix-vector multiplication functions are considerably faster than the C++ versions.

Table 14-4. *Benchmark Timing Measurements (Microseconds) for Matrix-Vector (4 × 4, 4 × 1) Multiplications (5,000,000 Matrix-Vector Products)*

Function	i5-11600K	i7-11700K	7700X
MatrixVecMulF32_cpp()	19271 (18)	25822 (933)	11571 (15)
MatrixVecMulF32_avx512()	4377 (18)	3959 (64)	2914 (6)

Double-Precision

The next source code example, named Ch14_08, also calculates matrix-vector (4 × 4, 4 × 1) products but uses double-precision instead of single-precision values. Listing 14-8 shows the MASM code for this example.

Listing 14-8. Example Ch14_08 MASM Code

```
;-------------------------------------------------------------------------
; Ch14_08_fasm.asm
;-------------------------------------------------------------------------

ConstVals    segment readonly align(64) 'const'

; Indices for matrix permutations
MatIndCol0   qword 0, 4,   8, 12, 0, 4,   8, 12
MatIndCol1   qword 1, 5,   9, 13, 1, 5,   9, 13
MatIndCol2   qword 2, 6, 10, 14, 2, 6, 10, 14
MatIndCol3   qword 3, 7, 11, 15, 3, 7, 11, 15

; Indices for vector permutations
VecIndW      qword 0, 0, 0, 0, 4, 4, 4, 4
VecIndX      qword 1, 1, 1, 1, 5, 5, 5, 5
VecIndY      qword 2, 2, 2, 2, 6, 6, 6, 6
VecIndZ      qword 3, 3, 3, 3, 7, 7, 7, 7
ConstVals    ends

;-------------------------------------------------------------------------
; void MatVecMulF64_avx512(Vec4x1_F64* vec_b, const float* m,
;   const Vec4x1_F64* vec_a, size_t num_vec);
;-------------------------------------------------------------------------

NVPI    equ    2                       ;num_vec_per_iteration
SIZEVEC equ    32                      ;size (bytes) of Vec4x1_F64 struct

        .code
MatVecMulF64_avx512 proc

; Validate arguments
        test r9,r9
        jz Done                        ;jump if num_vec == 0

        test rcx,3fh
        jnz Done                       ;jump if vec_b not 64b aligned
```

```
        test rdx,3fh
        jnz Done                        ;jump if m not 64b aligned
        test r8,3fh
        jnz Done                        ;jump if vec_a 64b aligned

; Load indices for matrix and vector permutations
        vmovdqa64 zmm20,zmmword ptr [MatIndCol0]    ;m col 0 indices
        vmovdqa64 zmm21,zmmword ptr [MatIndCol1]    ;m col 1 indices
        vmovdqa64 zmm22,zmmword ptr [MatIndCol2]    ;m col 2 indices
        vmovdqa64 zmm23,zmmword ptr [MatIndCol3]    ;m col 3 indices

        vmovdqa64 zmm24,zmmword ptr [VecIndW]       ;W component indices
        vmovdqa64 zmm25,zmmword ptr [VecIndX]       ;X component indices
        vmovdqa64 zmm26,zmmword ptr [VecIndY]       ;Y component indices
        vmovdqa64 zmm27,zmmword ptr [VecIndZ]       ;Z component indices

; Load source matrix m and permute NVPI copies of each column
        vmovapd zmm0,zmmword ptr [rdx]      ;zmm0  = matrix m (rows 0 & 1)
        vmovapd zmm1,zmmword ptr [rdx+64]   ;zmm1  = matrix m (rows 2 & 3)
        vpermi2pd zmm20,zmm0,zmm1           ;zmm20 = m col 0
        vpermi2pd zmm21,zmm0,zmm1           ;zmm21 = m col 1
        vpermi2pd zmm22,zmm0,zmm1           ;zmm22 = m col 2
        vpermi2pd zmm23,zmm0,zmm1           ;zmm23 = m col 3

        xor eax,eax                        ;initialize offset for FinalV
        cmp r9,NVPI                        ;num_vec >= NVPI?
        jb FinalV                          ;jump if no
        mov rax,-SIZEVEC*NVPI              ;initialize offset for Loop1

; Calculate matrix-vector products using SIMD arithmetic
        align 16
Loop1:  add rax,SIZEVEC*NVPI               ;update offset
        vmovapd zmm4,zmmword ptr [r8+rax]  ;zmm4 = vec_a[i:i+NVPI-1]
        vpermpd zmm0,zmm24,zmm4            ;zmm0 = vec_a W components
        vpermpd zmm1,zmm25,zmm4            ;zmm1 = vec_a X components
        vpermpd zmm2,zmm26,zmm4            ;zmm2 = vec_a Y components
        vpermpd zmm3,zmm27,zmm4            ;zmm3 = vec_a Z components

; Perform matrix-vector multiplications (NVPI vectors)
        vmulpd zmm4,zmm20,zmm0             ;zmm4  = m col 0 * W
        vfmadd231pd zmm4,zmm21,zmm1        ;zmm4 += m col 1 * X
        vfmadd231pd zmm4,zmm22,zmm2        ;zmm4 += m col 2 * Y
        vfmadd231pd zmm4,zmm23,zmm3        ;zmm4 += m col 3 * Z

; Save matrix-vector products (NVPI vectors)
        vmovntpd zmmword ptr [rcx+rax],zmm4 ;save vec_b[i:i+NVPI-1]

        sub r9,NVPI                        ;num_vec -= NVPI
        cmp r9,NVPI                        ;num_vec >= NVPI?
        jae Loop1                          ;jump if yes
```

```
; Test for more vectors
        test r9,r9                      ;num_vec == 0?
        jz Done                         ;jump if yes

        add rax,SIZEVEC*NVPI            ;adjust offset for final vec

; Calculate final matrix-vector product
FinalV: vbroadcastsd ymm0,real8 ptr [r8+rax]    ;ymm0 = vec_a[i] W components
        vbroadcastsd ymm1,real8 ptr [r8+rax+8]  ;ymm1 = vec_a[i] X components
        vbroadcastsd ymm2,real8 ptr [r8+rax+16] ;ymm2 = vec_a[i] Y components
        vbroadcastsd ymm3,real8 ptr [r8+rax+24] ;ymm3 = vec_a[i] Z components

        vmulpd ymm4,ymm20,ymm0          ;ymm4  = m col 0 * W
        vfmadd231pd ymm4,ymm21,ymm1     ;ymm4 += m col 1 * X
        vfmadd231pd ymm4,ymm22,ymm2     ;ymm4 += m col 2 * Y
        vfmadd231pd ymm4,ymm23,ymm3     ;ymm4 += m col 3 * Z

        vmovntpd ymmword ptr [rcx+rax],ymm4     ;save vec_b[i]

Done:   vzeroupper
        ret
MatVecMulF64_avx512 endp
        end
```

Most of the code in Listing 14-8 resembles the code in Listing 14-7, but there are a few noteworthy differences to reflect the processing of double-precision instead of single-precision matrices and vectors. In section ConstVals, note that the permutation indices are quadwords instead of doublewords. Also note that the values for equate symbols NVPI and SIZEVEC have changed. NVPI now equals two, while SIZEVEC, which signifies the size in bytes of a Vec4x1_F64 structure, is set to 32.

Following argument validation, MatVecMulF64_avx512() utilizes multiple vmovdqa64 instructions to load matrix permutation indices MatIndCol0-MatIndCol3 into registers ZMM20-ZMM23. Next is another set of four vmovdqa64 instructions that load vector permutation indices VecIndW-VecIndZ into registers ZMM24-ZMM27. The ensuing code block opens with two vmovapd instructions that load matrix m into registers ZMM0 (rows 0 and 1) and ZMM1 (rows 2 and 3). The next instruction, vpermi2pd zmm20,zmm0,zmm1 (Full Permute from Two Tables Overwriting the Index), permutes the elements of matrix m in registers ZMM0 and ZMM1 using the indices in register ZMM20. Figure 14-4 illustrates execution of the vpermi2pd instruction in greater detail. Note that index values 0–7 select elements from the first source operand (ZMM0), while index values 8–15 select elements from the second source operand (ZMM1). The outcome of this permutation is two copies of matrix m column 0, which are saved in register ZMM20. Function MatVecMulF64_avx512() then utilizes three additional vpermi2pd instructions that perform similar permutation operations to obtain columns 1, 2, and 3 of matrix m.

Initial values

12	8	4	0	12	8	4	0	ZMM20 (MatIndCol0)

13	9	5	1	13	9	5	1	ZMM21 (MatIndCol1)

14	10	6	2	14	10	6	2	ZMM22 (MatIndCol2)

15	11	7	3	15	11	7	3	ZMM23 (MatIndCol3)

23.0	22.0	21.0	20.0	13.0	12.0	11.0	10.0	ZMM0

◄────────── Matrix m (row 1) ──────────►◄────────── Matrix m (row 0) ──────────►

43.0	42.0	41.0	40.0	33.0	32.0	31.0	30.0	ZMM1

◄────────── Matrix m (row 3) ──────────►◄────────── Matrix m (row 2) ──────────►

```
vpermi2pd zmm20,zmm0,zmm1          ;zmm20 = m col 0
```

40.0	30.0	20.0	10.0	40.0	30.0	20.0	10.0	ZMM20

```
vpermi2pd zmm21,zmm0,zmm1          ;zmm21 = m col 1
```

41.0	31.0	21.0	11.0	41.0	31.0	21.0	11.0	ZMM21

```
vpermi2pd zmm22,zmm0,zmm1          ;zmm22 = m col 2
```

42.0	32.0	22.0	12.0	42.0	32.0	22.0	12.0	ZMM22

```
vpermi2pd zmm23,zmm0,zmm1          ;zmm23 = m col 3
```

43.0	33.0	23.0	13.0	43.0	33.0	23.0	13.0	ZMM23

Figure 14-4. *Execution of* vpermi2pd *instructions in* MatVecMulF64_avx512()

Execution of for-loop Loop1 begins with an add rax,SIZEVEC*NVPI instruction that updates the offset value in register RAX for the next set of vectors. The subsequent instruction, vmovapd zmm4,zmmword ptr [r8+rax], loads vectors vec_a[i:i+NVPI-1] into register ZMM4. Recall that for this example, NVPI equals two. The ensuing group of four vpermpd instructions permutes the vector components in register ZMM4 using the indices in registers ZMM24–ZMM27 as shown in Figure 14-5. Following the permutation operation, MatVecMulF64_avx512() uses instructions vmulpd and vfmadd231pd to calculate NVPI matrix-vector products. It also utilizes the vmovntpd instruction to save the resultant vectors. Execution of Loop1 continues until fewer than NVPI vectors remain.

Initial values

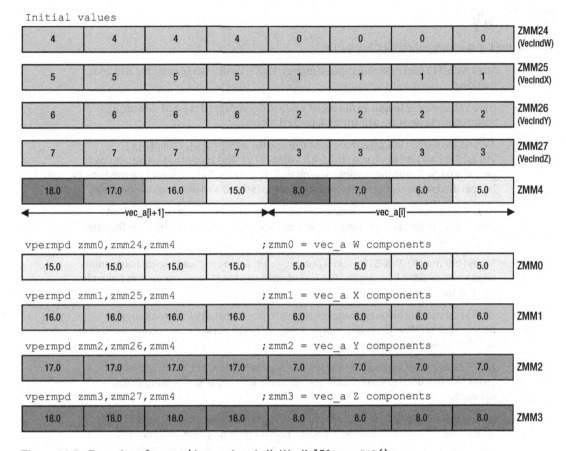

Figure 14-5. Execution of vpermpd instructions in MatVecMulF64_avx512()

Following execution of Loop1, MatVecMulF64_avx512() checks to see if there are any residual vectors. Note that since NVPI equals two, the number of residual vectors can equal only zero or one. If necessary, the code block that follows label FinalV calculates the final matrix-vector product.

The NASM code for example Ch14_08 (not shown) is basically the same as the MASM code shown in Listing 14-8, except for the use of different general-purpose registers.

The results for source code example Ch14_08 are the same as the results for example Ch11_07. Table 14-5 shows the benchmark timing measurements for source example Ch14_08. Like the previous example, the timing measurements for the AVX-512 matrix-vector product functions are significantly faster than the C++ versions.

Table 14-5. Benchmark Timing Measurements (Microseconds) for Matrix-Vector (4 × 4, 4 × 1) Multiplications (5,000,000 Matrix-Vector Products)

Function	i5-11600K	i7-11700K	7700X
MatrixVecMulF64_cpp()	21608 (25)	26214 (652)	12362 (34)
MatrixVecMulF64_avx512()	8537 (20)	7990 (114)	5850 (9)

Summary

Here are the key learning points for Chapter 14:

- Most AVX-512 packed floating-point instructions support merge masking and zero masking.

- AVX-512 assembly language functions can use the vmovap[d|s] and vmovup[d|s] instructions to perform 512-bit wide packed moves.

- AVX-512 assembly language functions can use the vaddp[d|s], vsubp[d|s], vmulp[d|s], vdivp[d|s], vsqrtp[d|s], vminp[d|s], and vmaxp[d|s] instructions to perform packed arithmetic using 512-bit wide operands. A static rounding mode can be specified when registers are used for both the source and destination operands.

- AVX-512 assembly language functions can use the vandp[d|s], vorp[d|s], and vxorp[d|s] instructions to perform Boolean operations using 512-bit wide floating-point operands.

- Many (but not all) AVX-512 packed floating-point arithmetic and logical instructions support embedded broadcasts. The size of an embedded broadcast operand must be 32 or 64 bits.

- AVX-512 assembly language functions can use the vcmpp[d|s] instructions to perform packed floating-point comparisons. AVX-512 packed comparison results are saved to an opmask register.

- AVX-512 assembly language functions can use the vextractf[32x4|32x8|64x2 |64x4] instructions to extract multiple elements from a packed floating-point operand.

- AVX-512 assembly language functions can use the vpermp[d|s] and vpermi2p[d|s] instructions to permute the elements of a packed floating-point operand. The vpermp[d|s] instructions can also be used on processors that support AVX2.

- AVX-512 functions should always ensure that packed 128-, 256-, and 512-bit wide floating-point operands are aligned on a proper boundary whenever possible.

CHAPTER 15

■ ■ ■

AVX-512 Programming – Packed Floating-Point – Part 2

In the previous chapter, you studied a variety of source code examples that explained how to exploit the AVX-512 instruction set to perform packed floating-point computations using the elements of an array or matrix. In this chapter, you'll learn how to code a few signal processing functions using AVX-512 instructions and SIMD arithmetic. The source code examples presented in this chapter are AVX-512 implementations of the same signal processing functions that you saw in Chapter 12.

Like the AVX2 source code examples in Chapter 12, the assembly language source code in this chapter is a bit more specialized than some of the other examples you've scrutinized. If your programming interests reside elsewhere, feel free to either browse or skip this chapter. However, reading this chapter is worthwhile since it accentuates constructive particulars regarding the development of assembly language code that performs SIMD floating-point calculations. It also expounds how to minimize differences between single-precision and double-precision AVX-512 code.

The NASM code for this chapter's examples is not shown in any listings since it's basically the same as the MASM code, except for the inclusion of a code block that rearranges argument register values. As a reminder, all source code files not shown in an explicit listing are included in the software download package.

Signal Processing

The section that you are about to read explains how to code 1D discrete convolution functions using the AVX-512 instruction set. It also illustrates some strategies that can be employed to minimize differences between AVX-512 and AVX2 coded functions. Before examining this section's examples, you may want to review the primer on convolution math that was presented in Chapter 12.

1D Convolution Using Variable-Size Kernel

In Chapter 12, you learned how to code 1D discrete convolution functions using AVX2 and FMA instructions. In this section, you'll learn how to code the same algorithms using AVX-512 instructions. The first example implements a 1D discrete convolution using a variable-size kernel with single-precision floating-point signal arrays. The second source code example realizes the same algorithm using double-precision floating-point signal arrays. Before continuing, it is recommended that you reexamine the C++ source code for examples Ch12_03 (Listing 12-3a) and Ch12_04 (Listing 12-4) since the assembly language functions of this section implement the same algorithms. You may also want to review the AVX2 assembly language code (Listings 12-3b and 12-4b) for these same examples.

© Daniel Kusswurm 2023
D. Kusswurm, *Modern X86 Assembly Language Programming*,
https://doi.org/10.1007/978-1-4842-9603-5_15

Single-Precision

Listing 15-1 shows the MASM source code for function Convolve1D_F32_avx512(). This function performs a 1D discrete convolution using input signal x and convolution kernel signal kernel. Near the top of Listing 15-1 is a series of equate statements that define symbolic names for assembly language function Convolve1D_F32_avx512(). The symbols NSE, NSE2, and NSE3 represent element size counts for SIMD arithmetic, while SF is the scale factor for a single-precision floating-point element. Using equates for these values helps to minimize code differences between function Convolve1D_F32_avx512() and its double-precision counterpart that you'll review in the next section.

Listing 15-1. Example Ch15_01 MASM Code

```
;-------------------------------------------------------------------
; Ch15_01_fasm.asm
;-------------------------------------------------------------------

            include <MacrosX86-64-AVX.asmh>


;-------------------------------------------------------------------
; bool Convolve1D_F32_avx512(float* y, const float* x, const float* kernel,
;   int64_t num_pts, int64_t kernel_size);
;-------------------------------------------------------------------

NSE     equ 16                          ;num_simd_elements
NSE2    equ 8                           ;num_simd_elements2
NSE3    equ 4                           ;num_simd_elements3
SF      equ 4                           ;scale factor for F32 elements

        .code
Convolve1D_F32_avx512 proc frame
        CreateFrame_M CV_,0,0,rbx,rsi,rdi,r12,r13
        EndProlog_M

; Validate arguments
        mov r10,[rbp+CV_OffsetStackArgs]        ;r10 = kernel_size (ks)
        cmp r10,3
        jl BadArg                               ;jump if ks < 3
        test r10,1
        jz BadArg                               ;jump if ks is even
        cmp r9,r10
        jl BadArg                               ;jump if num_pts < ks

; Initialize
        mov r11,r10                             ;r11 = ks
        shr r11,1                               ;r11 = ks2
        mov rsi,r9                              ;rsi = num_pts
        sub rsi,r11                             ;rsi = num_pts - ks2
        mov rdi,r11
        neg rdi                                 ;rdi = -ks2
        mov rax,r11                             ;i = ks2

        jmp F1                                  ;begin execution of Loop1a
```

```
;-------------------------------------------------------------------------
; General-purpose registers used in code below:
;    rax     i                  r8      kernel
;    rbx     k                  r9      num_pts
;    rcx     y array            r10     kernel_size
;    rdx     x array            r11     ks2
;    rsi     num_pts - ks2      r12     scratch
;    rdi     -ks2               r13     scratch
;-------------------------------------------------------------------------


; Calculate y[i:i+NSE-1]
Loop1a: mov rbx,rdi                              ;k = -ks2
        vxorps zmm0,zmm0,zmm0                     ;y[i:i+NSE-1] = 0

        align 16
Loop1b: mov r12,rax                               ;r12 = i
        sub r12,rbx                               ;r12 = i - k
        lea r13,[rbx+r11]                         ;r13 = k + ks2

        vbroadcastss zmm2,real4 ptr [r8+r13*SF]   ;zmm2 = kernel[k+ks2]
        vfmadd231ps zmm0,zmm2,[rdx+r12*SF]        ;update y[i:i+NSE-1]

        add rbx,1                                 ;k += 1
        cmp rbx,r11
        jle Loop1b                                ;jump if k <= ks2

        vmovups [rcx+rax*SF],zmm0                 ;save y[i:i+NSE-1]
        add rax,NSE                               ;i += NSE

F1:     lea r12,[rax+NSE]                         ;r12 = i + NSE
        cmp r12,rsi
        jle Loop1a                                ;jump if i + NSE <= num_pts - ks2

        jmp F2                                    ;begin execution of Loop2a

; Calculate y[i:i+NSE2-1]
Loop2a: mov rbx,rdi                               ;k = -ks2
        vxorps ymm0,ymm0,ymm0                     ;y[i:i+NSE2-1] = 0

        align 16
Loop2b: mov r12,rax                               ;r12 = i
        sub r12,rbx                               ;r12 = i - k
        lea r13,[rbx+r11]                         ;r13 = k + ks2

        vbroadcastss ymm2,real4 ptr [r8+r13*SF]   ;ymm2 = kernel[k+ks2]
        vfmadd231ps ymm0,ymm2,[rdx+r12*SF]        ;update y[i:i+NSE2-1]

        add rbx,1                                 ;k += 1
        cmp rbx,r11
        jle Loop2b                                ;jump if k <= ks2
```

```
        vmovups [rcx+rax*SF],ymm0              ;save y[i:i+NSE2-1]
        add rax,NSE2                           ;i += NSE2

F2:     lea r12,[rax+NSE2]                      ;r12 = i + NSE2
        cmp r12,rsi
        jle Loop2a                             ;jump if i + NSE2 <= num_pts - ks2

        jmp F3                                 ;begin execution of Loop3a

; Calculate y[i:i+NSE3-1]
Loop3a: mov rbx,rdi                            ;k = -ks2
        vxorps xmm0,xmm0,xmm0                   ;y[i:i+NSE3-1] = 0

        align 16
Loop3b: mov r12,rax                            ;r12 = i
        sub r12,rbx                            ;r12 = i - k
        lea r13,[rbx+r11]                      ;r13 = k + ks2

        vbroadcastss xmm2,real4 ptr [r8+r13*SF] ;xmm2 = kernel[k+ks2]
        vfmadd231ps xmm0,xmm2,[rdx+r12*SF]     ;update y[i:i+NSE3-1]

        add rbx,1                              ;k += 1
        cmp rbx,r11
        jle Loop3b                             ;jump if k <= ks2

        vmovups [rcx+rax*SF],xmm0              ;save y[i:i+NSE3-1]
        add rax,NSE3                           ;i += NSE3

F3:     lea r12,[rax+NSE3]                      ;r12 = i + NSE3
        cmp r12,rsi
        jle Loop3a                             ;jump if i + NSE3 <= num_pts - ks2

        jmp F4                                 ;begin execution of Loop4a

; Calculate y[i]
Loop4a: mov rbx,rdi                            ;k = -ks2
        vxorps xmm0,xmm0,xmm0                   ;y[i] = 0

        align 16
Loop4b: mov r12,rax                            ;r12 = i
        sub r12,rbx                            ;r12 = i - k
        lea r13,[rbx+r11]                      ;r13 = k + ks2

        vmovss xmm2,real4 ptr [r8+r13*SF]      ;xmm2 = kernel[k+ks2]
        vfmadd231ss xmm0,xmm2,[rdx+r12*SF]     ;update y[i]

        add rbx,1                              ;k += 1
        cmp rbx,r11
        jle Loop4b                             ;jump if k <= ks2

        vmovss real4 ptr [rcx+rax*SF],xmm0     ;save y[i]
        add rax,1                              ;i += 1
```

```
F4:     cmp rax,rsi
        jl Loop4a                       ;jump if i < num_pts - ks2

        mov eax,1                       ;set success return code

Done:   vzeroupper
        DeleteFrame_M rbx,rsi,rdi,r12,r13
        ret

BadArg: xor eax,eax                     ;set error return code
        jmp Done


Convolve1D_F32_avx512 endp
        end
```

Following execution of its prologue code, Convolve1D_F32_avx512() validates arguments kernel_size and num_pts. Recall from the discussions in Chapter 12 that kernel_size must be an odd integer greater than or equal to three. Also note that num_pts must be greater than or equal to kernel_size. Following argument validation is a code block that performs the requisite initializations for the convolution for-loops.

Function Convolve1D_F32_avx512() computes a 1D discrete convolution using AVX-512 instructions. Recall that a ZMM register can hold 16 single-precision floating-point values, which means that the SIMD calculating code in Convolve1D_F32_avx512() can process 16 input signal points simultaneously. This is a straightforward extension of the code used in function Convolve1D_F32_avx2() (see Listing 12-3b and Figure 12-6).

The convolution calculating code for Convolve1D_F32_avx512() is partitioned into four distinct sections. The first section consists of outer for-loop Loop1a and inner for-loop Loop1b. These two for-loops carry out the same calculation that you saw in function Convolve1D_F32_cpp() (see Listing 12-3a). Note that Loop1b employs packed FMA arithmetic and 512-bit wide operands to calculate output signal elements y[i:i+NSE-1] using input signal elements x[i:i+NSE-1]. Execution of for-loop pair Loop1a and Loop1b continues until i + NSE <= num_pts - ks2 is false. Also note that Convolve1D_F32_avx512() utilizes the vmovups instruction to perform packed floating-point stores since proper alignment of each SIMD element group is not guaranteed.

The second calculating section of function Convolve1D_F32_avx512() closely resembles the first section but utilizes 256-bit wide operands. Note that for-loops Loop2a and Loop2b calculate output signal elements y[i:i+NSE2-1]. Execution of for-loop pair Loop2a and Loop2b continues until i + NSE2 <= num_pts - ks2 is false. In the third calculating section, for-loops Loop3a and Loop3b calculate output signal elements y[i:i+NSE3-1] using 128-bit wide operands. This for-loop pair executes until i + NSE3 <= num_pts - ks2 is false. The final calculating section uses scalar single-precision floating-point arithmetic to process any residual signal points.

Before continuing with this section, carefully compare the code for function Convolve1D_F32_avx512() in Listing 15-1 and the code for function Convolve1D_F32_avx2() in Listing 12-3b. The primary difference between these two functions is that the former includes an extra section that exploits AVX-512 instructions. Source code examples Ch15_01 and Ch12_03 exemplify that with a little forethought, it's possible to minimize code differences between AVX2 and AVX-512 functions that perform the same calculation. The results for source code example Ch15_01 are the same as the results for source code example Ch12_03.

Table 15-1 shows the benchmark timing measurements for source example Ch15_01. This table also includes the benchmark timing measurements for function Convolve1D_F32_avx2(), which were copied from Table 12-3. These measurements were made using an input signal array containing 2,500,000 elements and a five-element convolution kernel. For this example, the AVX-512 1D discrete convolution functions modestly outperform their AVX2 counterparts.

Table 15-1. *Benchmark Timing Measurements (Microseconds) for 1D Discrete Convolution Functions (Single-Precision)*

Function	i5-11600K	i7-11700K	7700X
Convolve1D_F32_cpp()	6169 (11)	5735 (92)	3855 (12)
Convolve1D_F32_avx2()	1034 (8)	890 (26)	482 (3)
Convolve1D_F32_avx512()	783 (5)	742 (30)	405 (14)

Double-Precision

Listing 15-2 shows the MASM code for example Ch15_02. This listing contains the source code for function Convolve1D_F64_avx512(), which is the double-precision counterpart of function Convolve1D_F32_avx512().

Listing 15-2. Example Ch15_02 MASM Code

```
;-------------------------------------------------------------------------------
; Ch15_02_fasm.asm
;-------------------------------------------------------------------------------

            include <MacrosX86-64-AVX.asmh>

;-------------------------------------------------------------------------------
; bool Convolve1D_F64_avx512(float* y, const float* x, const float* kernel,
;   int64_t num_pts, int64_t kernel_size);
;-------------------------------------------------------------------------------

NSE     equ 8                           ;num_simd_elements
NSE2    equ 4                           ;num_simd_elements2
NSE3    equ 2                           ;num_simd_elements3
SF      equ 8                           ;scale factor for F64 elements

        .code
Convolve1D_F64_avx512 proc frame
        CreateFrame_M CV_,0,0,rbx,rsi,rdi,r12,r13
        EndProlog_M

; Validate arguments
        mov r10,[rbp+CV_OffsetStackArgs] ;r10 = kernel_size (ks)
        cmp r10,3
        jl BadArg                        ;jump if ks < 3
        test r10,1
        jz BadArg                        ;jump if ks is even
        cmp r9,r10
        jl BadArg                        ;jump if num_pts < ks

; Initialize
        mov r11,r10                      ;r11 = ks
        shr r11,1                        ;r11 = ks2
```

```
            mov rsi,r9                          ;rsi = num_pts
            sub rsi,r11                         ;rsi = num_pts - ks2
            mov rdi,r11
            neg rdi                             ;rdi = -ks2
            mov rax,r11                         ;i = ks2

            jmp F1                              ;begin execution of Loop1a


;-----------------------------------------------------------------------------
; General-purpose registers used in code below:
;   rax     i                   r8      kernel
;   rbx     k                   r9      num_pts
;   rcx     y array             r10     kernel_size
;   rdx     x array             r11     ks2
;   rsi     num_pts - ks2       r12     scratch
;   rdi     -ks2                r13     scratch
;-----------------------------------------------------------------------------


; Calculate y[i:i+NSE-1]
Loop1a: mov rbx,rdi                             ;k = -ks2
        vxorpd zmm0,zmm0,zmm0                   ;y[i:i+NSE-1] = 0

        align 16
Loop1b: mov r12,rax                             ;r12 = i
        sub r12,rbx                             ;r12 = i - k
        lea r13,[rbx+r11]                       ;r13 = k + ks2

        vbroadcastsd zmm2,real8 ptr [r8+r13*SF] ;zmm2 = kernel[k+ks2]
        vfmadd231pd zmm0,zmm2,[rdx+r12*SF]      ;update y[i:i+NSE-1]

        add rbx,1                               ;k += 1
        cmp rbx,r11
        jle Loop1b                              ;jump if k <= ks2

        vmovupd [rcx+rax*SF],zmm0               ;save y[i:i+NSE-1]
        add rax,NSE                             ;i += NSE

F1:     lea r12,[rax+NSE]                       ;r12 = i + NSE
        cmp r12,rsi
        jle Loop1a                              ;jump if i + NSE <= num_pts - ks2

        jmp F2                                  ;begin execution of Loop2a

; Calculate y[i:i+NSE2-1]
Loop2a: mov rbx,rdi                             ;k = -ks2
        vxorpd ymm0,ymm0,ymm0                   ;y[i:i+NSE2-1] = 0

        align 16
Loop2b: mov r12,rax                             ;r12 = i
        sub r12,rbx                             ;r12 = i - k
        lea r13,[rbx+r11]                       ;r13 = k + ks2
```

```
        vbroadcastsd ymm2,real8 ptr [r8+r13*SF]  ;ymm2 = kernel[k+ks2]
        vfmadd231pd ymm0,ymm2,[rdx+r12*SF]       ;update y[i:i+NSE2-1]

        add rbx,1                                ;k += 1
        cmp rbx,r11
        jle Loop2b                               ;jump if k <= ks2

        vmovupd [rcx+rax*SF],ymm0                 ;save y[i:i+NSE2-1]
        add rax,NSE2                             ;i += NSE2

F2:     lea r12,[rax+NSE2]                        ;r12 = i + NSE2
        cmp r12,rsi
        jle Loop2a                               ;jump if i + NSE2 <= num_pts - ks2

        jmp F3                                   ;begin execution of Loop3a

; Calculate y[i:i+NSE3-1]
Loop3a: mov rbx,rdi                              ;k = -ks2
        vxorpd xmm0,xmm0,xmm0                     ;y[i:i+NSE3-1] = 0

        align 16
Loop3b: mov r12,rax                              ;r12 = i
        sub r12,rbx                              ;r12 = i - k
        lea r13,[rbx+r11]                         ;r13 = k + ks2

        vmovddup xmm2,real8 ptr [r8+r13*SF]       ;xmm2 = kernel[k+ks2]
        vfmadd231pd xmm0,xmm2,[rdx+r12*SF]        ;update y[i:i+NSE3-1]

        add rbx,1                                ;k += 1
        cmp rbx,r11
        jle Loop3b                               ;jump if k <= ks2

        vmovupd [rcx+rax*SF],xmm0                 ;save y[i:i+NSE3-1]
        add rax,NSE3                             ;i += NSE3

F3:     lea r12,[rax+NSE3]                        ;r12 = i + NSE3
        cmp r12,rsi
        jle Loop3a                               ;jump if i + NSE3 <= num_pts - ks2

        jmp F4                                   ;begin execution of Loop4a

; Calculate y[i]
Loop4a: mov rbx,rdi                              ;k = -ks2
        vxorpd xmm0,xmm0,xmm0                     ;y[i] = 0

        align 16
Loop4b: mov r12,rax                              ;r12 = i
        sub r12,rbx                              ;r12 = i - k
        lea r13,[rbx+r11]                         ;r13 = k + ks2

        vmovsd xmm2,real8 ptr [r8+r13*SF]         ;xmm2 = kernel[k+ks2]
        vfmadd231sd xmm0,xmm2,[rdx+r12*SF]        ;update y[i]
```

```
        add rbx,1                               ;k += 1
        cmp rbx,r11
        jle Loop4b                              ;jump if k <= ks2

        vmovsd real8 ptr [rcx+rax*SF],xmm0       ;save y[i]
        add rax,1                               ;i += 1

F4:     cmp rax,rsi
        jl Loop4a                               ;jump if i < num_pts - ks2

        mov eax,1                               ;set success return code

Done:   vzeroupper
        DeleteFrame_M rbx,rsi,rdi,r12,r13
        ret

BadArg: xor eax,eax                             ;set error return code
        jmp Done


Convolve1D_F64_avx512 endp
        end
```

In Listing 15-2, the layout of function Convolve1D_F64_avx512() closely resembles its single-precision analog, but with a few important differences. First, note that the values for equate symbols NSE, NSE2, and NSE3 have been reduced by a factor of two. Also note that equate SF is assigned a value of eight instead of four. Finally, note that function Convolve1D_F64_avx512() uses double-precision AVX-512 arithmetic instructions instead of single-precision. The results for source example Ch15_02 are the same as the results for source code example Ch12_04.

Table 15-2 shows the benchmark timing measurements for source example Ch15_02. This table also includes the benchmark timing measurements for function Convolve1D_F64_avx2(), which were copied from Table 12-4. These measurements were made using an input signal array containing 2,500,000 elements and a five-element convolution kernel. As you can see from the numbers, the AVX-512 variants of the double-precision 1D discrete convolution functions are moderately faster than the AVX2 versions.

Table 15-2. *Benchmark Timing Measurements (Microseconds) for 1D Discrete Convolution Functions (Single-Precision)*

Function	i5-11600K	i7-11700K	7700X
Convolve1D_F64_cpp()	5445 (7)	5778 (85)	3480 (7)
Convolve1D_F64_avx2()	2124 (23)	1770 (40)	1023 (4)
Convolve1D_F64_avx512()	1679 (8)	1552 (31)	861 (8)

The layout of the assembly language code in examples Ch15_01 and Ch15_02 demonstrates again that with a little algorithmic prudence, you can create single-precision and double-precision variants of a calculating function with minimal variations. This strategy also applies to the coding of both MASM and NASM variants when developing assembly language code for both Windows and Linux.

1D Convolution Using Fixed-Size Kernel

In Chapter 12, you learned that many signal processing applications often exploit 1D discrete convolution functions that are optimized for specific kernel sizes since these types of functions are usually faster than their variable-size counterparts. Case in point, source code examples Ch12_05 and Ch12_06 used AVX2 instructions to perform 1D discrete convolutions using a five-element convolution kernel.

The next two source code examples use AVX-512 instructions to implement the same five-element convolution kernel algorithms. The first example implements a 1D discrete convolution using single-precision floating-point signal arrays, while the second example executes the same algorithm using double-precision arrays. Before studying these sections, you may want to review C++ and assembly language code for source code examples Ch12_05 (Listings 12-5a and 12-5b) and Ch12_06 (Listings 12-6a and 12-6b).

Single-Precision

Source code example Ch15_03 demonstrates how to use AVX-512 instructions to calculate a 1D discrete convolution using a single-precision five-element convolution kernel and input signal array. The C++ code for this example is identical to the C++ code that was used in example Ch12_05 (see Listing 12-5a). Listing 15-3 shows the MASM code for example Ch15_03.

Listing 15-3. Example Ch15_03 MASM Code

```
;-------------------------------------------------------------------------
; Ch15_03_fasm.asm
;-------------------------------------------------------------------------

            include <MacrosX86-64-AVX.asmh>


;-------------------------------------------------------------------------
; bool Convolve1D_Ks5_F32_avx512(float* y, const float* x, const float* kernel,
;     int64_t num_pts);
;-------------------------------------------------------------------------

NSE     equ     16                      ;num_simd_elements
NSE2    equ     8                       ;num_simd_elements2
NSE3    equ     4                       ;num_simd_elements3
KS      equ     5                       ;kernel_size
KS2     equ     2                       ;floor(kernel_size / 2)
SF      equ     4                       ;scale factor for F32 elements


        .code
Convolve1D_Ks5_F32_avx512 proc frame
        CreateFrame_M CV5_,0,0,rsi
        EndProlog_M

; Validate arguments
        cmp r9,KS
        jl BadArg                       ;jump if num_pts < KS

; Initialize
        mov rax,KS2                     ;i = ks2
        mov r10,r9                      ;r10 = num_pts
        sub r10,KS2                     ;r10 = num_pts - KS2
```

```
        vbroadcastss zmm0,real4 ptr [r8]          ;zmm0 = packed kernel[0]
        vbroadcastss zmm1,real4 ptr [r8+4]        ;zmm1 = packed kernel[1]
        vbroadcastss zmm2,real4 ptr [r8+8]        ;zmm2 = packed kernel[2]
        vbroadcastss zmm3,real4 ptr [r8+12]       ;zmm3 = packed kernel[3]
        vbroadcastss zmm4,real4 ptr [r8+16]       ;zmm4 = packed kernel[4]

        jmp F1                                    ;begin execution of Loop1


;-------------------------------------------------------------------------
; General-purpose registers used in code below:
;    rax     i                r8      kernel
;    rcx     y array          r9      num_pts
;    rdx     x array          r10     num_pts - KS2
;    rsi     scratch          r11     k
;-------------------------------------------------------------------------

; Calculate y[i:i+NSE-1]
        align 16
Loop1:  lea r11,[rax+KS2]                         ;k = i + KS2

        vmulps zmm5,zmm0,[rdx+r11*SF]             ;kernel[0] * x[k:k+NSE-1]
        vfmadd231ps zmm5,zmm1,[rdx+r11*SF-4]      ;kernel[1] * x[k-1:k-1+NSE-1]
        vfmadd231ps zmm5,zmm2,[rdx+r11*SF-8]      ;kernel[2] * x[k-2:k-2+NSE-1]
        vfmadd231ps zmm5,zmm3,[rdx+r11*SF-12]     ;kernel[3] * x[k-3:k-3+NSE-1]
        vfmadd231ps zmm5,zmm4,[rdx+r11*SF-16]     ;kernel[4] * x[k-4:k-4+NSE-1]

        vmovups [rcx+rax*SF],zmm5                 ;save y[i:i+NSE-1]
        add rax,NSE                               ;i += NSE

F1:     lea rsi,[rax+NSE]                         ;rsi = i + NSE
        cmp rsi,r10                               ;i + NSE <= num_pts - ks2?
        jle Loop1                                 ;jump if yes

        jmp F2                                    ;begin execution of Loop2

; Calculate y[i:i+NSE2-1]
Loop2:  lea r11,[rax+KS2]                         ;k = i + KS2

        vmulps ymm5,ymm0,[rdx+r11*SF]            ;kernel[0] * x[k:k+NSE2-1]
        vfmadd231ps ymm5,ymm1,[rdx+r11*SF-4]     ;kernel[1] * x[k-1:k-1+NSE2-1]
        vfmadd231ps ymm5,ymm2,[rdx+r11*SF-8]     ;kernel[2] * x[k-2:k-2+NSE2-1]
        vfmadd231ps ymm5,ymm3,[rdx+r11*SF-12]    ;kernel[3] * x[k-3:k-3+NSE2-1]
        vfmadd231ps ymm5,ymm4,[rdx+r11*SF-16]    ;kernel[4] * x[k-4:k-4+NSE2-1]

        vmovups [rcx+rax*SF],ymm5                 ;save y[i:i+NSE2-1]
        add rax,NSE2                              ;i += NSE2

F2:     lea rsi,[rax+NSE2]                        ;rsi = i + NSE2
        cmp rsi,r10                               ;i + NSE2 <= num_pts - KS2?
        jle Loop2                                 ;jump if yes

        jmp F3                                    ;begin execution of Loop3
```

```
; Calculate y[i:i+NSE3-1]
Loop3:  lea r11,[rax+KS2]                         ;k = i + KS2

        vmulps xmm5,xmm0,[rdx+r11*SF]             ;kernel[0] * x[k:k+NSE3-1]
        vfmadd231ps xmm5,xmm1,[rdx+r11*SF-4]      ;kernel[1] * x[k-1:k-1+NSE3-1]
        vfmadd231ps xmm5,xmm2,[rdx+r11*SF-8]      ;kernel[2] * x[k-2:k-2+NSE3-1]
        vfmadd231ps xmm5,xmm3,[rdx+r11*SF-12]     ;kernel[3] * x[k-3:k-3+NSE3-1]
        vfmadd231ps xmm5,xmm4,[rdx+r11*SF-16]     ;kernel[4] * x[k-4:k-4+NSE3-1]

        vmovups [rcx+rax*SF],xmm5                 ;save y[i:i+NSE3-1]
        add rax,NSE3                              ;i += NSE3

F3:     lea rsi,[rax+NSE3]                        ;rsi = i + NSE3
        cmp rsi,r10                               ;i + NSE3 <= num_pts - KS2?
        jle Loop3                                 ;jump if yes

        jmp F4                                    ;begin execution of Loop4

; Calculate y[i]
Loop4:  lea r11,[rax+KS2]                         ;k = i + KS2

        vmulss xmm5,xmm0,real4 ptr [rdx+r11*SF]   ;kernel[0] * x[k]
        vfmadd231ss xmm5,xmm1,[rdx+r11*SF-4]      ;kernel[1] * x[k-1]
        vfmadd231ss xmm5,xmm2,[rdx+r11*SF-8]      ;kernel[2] * x[k-2]
        vfmadd231ss xmm5,xmm3,[rdx+r11*SF-12]     ;kernel[3] * x[k-3]
        vfmadd231ss xmm5,xmm4,[rdx+r11*SF-16]     ;kernel[4] * x[k-4]

        vmovss real4 ptr [rcx+rax*SF],xmm5        ;save y[i]
        add rax,1                                 ;i += 1

F4:     cmp rax,r10                               ;i < num_pts - KS2?
        jl Loop4                                  ;jump if yes

        mov eax,1                                 ;set success return code

Done:   vzeroupper
        DeleteFrame_M rsi
        ret

BadArg: xor eax,eax                               ;set error return code
        jmp Done


Convolve1D_Ks5_F32_avx512 endp
        end
```

Near the top of Listing 15-3 is a series of equate statements. Note that the values for NSE, NSE2, NSE3, and SF match the ones used in Listing 15-1. Also note that equates are used to define symbolic names for the kernel sizes KS and KS2 since the size of the convolution kernel is fixed at five elements.

Function Convolve1D_Ks5_F32_avx512() opens with simple prologue and a quick validation check to ensure that num_pts < KS is false. Following its prologue, the instruction layout of function Convolve1D_Ks5_F32_avx512() resembles Convolve1D_F32_avx512(), but with one critical divergence. If you compare the code in Listing 15-3 with the code in Listing 15-1, you will notice that the code for inner for-loops Loop1b-Loop4b has been removed from Convolve1D_Ks5_F32_avx512() and replaced with explicit sequences of vmulps and vfmadd231ps instructions. The complete unrolling of these inner for-loops is possible since the size of the convolution kernel is fixed at five elements.

The results for source code example Ch15_03 are the same as the results for example Ch15_01. Table 15-3 shows the benchmark timing measurements for source code example Ch15_03. These measurements were made using an input signal array containing 2,500,000 elements. Table 15-3 also includes the benchmark timing measurements for function Convolve1D_Ks5_F32_avx2(), which were copied from Table 12-5. Note that on the Intel processors, the AVX-512 and AVX2 timing measurements are about the same. For the AMD processor, function Convolve1D_Ks5_F32_avx512() is a tad slower than Convolve1D_Ks5_F32_avx2(). Also note that for this example, the benchmark timing measurements for the C++ functions on the i5-11600K and 7700X test computers are comparable to their assembly language counterparts. The reason for this is that the GNU C++ compiler emitted sequences of AVX-512 FMA instructions analogous to those explicitly coded in function Convolve1D_Ks5_F32_avx512(). One very important takeaway point from this example is that you should always measure the performance of an explicitly coded assembly language function and its C++ counterpart function to substantiate any performance gains.

Table 15-3. *Benchmark Timing Measurements (Microseconds) for 1D Discrete Convolution Functions (Single-Precision)*

Function	i5-11600K	i7-11700K	7700X
Convolve1D_Ks5_F32_cpp()	636 (4)	3624 (52)	289 (2)
Convolve1D_Ks5_F32_avx2()	657 (4)	623 (29)	268 (2)
Convolve1D_Ks5_F32_avx512()	633 (4)	601 (26)	302 (2)

Double-Precision

Listing 15-4 shows the MASM code for function Convolve1D_Ks5_F64_avx512(), which is the double-precision counterpart of Convolve1D_Ks5_F32_avx512().

Listing 15-4. Example Ch15_04 MASM Code

```
;-------------------------------------------------------------------------
; Ch15_04_fasm.asm
;-------------------------------------------------------------------------

            include <MacrosX86-64-AVX.asmh>


;-------------------------------------------------------------------------
; bool Convolve1D_Ks5_F64_avx512(float* y, const float* x, const float* kernel,
;   int64_t num_pts);
;-------------------------------------------------------------------------

NSE     equ     8                       ;num_simd_elements
NSE2    equ     4                       ;num_simd_elements2
NSE3    equ     2                       ;num_simd_elements3
KS      equ     5                       ;kernel_size
```

```
KS2      equ    2                         ;floor(kernel_size / 2)
SF       equ    8                         ;scale factor for F64 elements

         .code
Convolve1D_Ks5_F64_avx512 proc frame
         CreateFrame_M CV5_,0,0,rsi
         EndProlog_M

; Validate arguments
         cmp r9,KS
         jl BadArg                        ;jump if num_pts < KS

; Initialize
         mov rax,KS2                      ;i = ks2
         mov r10,r9                       ;r10 = num_pts
         sub r10,KS2                      ;r10 = num_pts - KS2

         vbroadcastsd zmm0,real8 ptr [r8]      ;zmm0 = packed kernel[0]
         vbroadcastsd zmm1,real8 ptr [r8+8]    ;zmm1 = packed kernel[1]
         vbroadcastsd zmm2,real8 ptr [r8+16]   ;zmm2 = packed kernel[2]
         vbroadcastsd zmm3,real8 ptr [r8+24]   ;zmm3 = packed kernel[3]
         vbroadcastsd zmm4,real8 ptr [r8+32]   ;zmm4 = packed kernel[4]

         jmp F1                           ;begin execution of Loop1

;-------------------------------------------------------------------------
; General-purpose registers used in code below:
;    rax      i               r8       kernel
;    rcx      y array         r9       num_pts
;    rdx      x array         r10      num_pts - KS2
;    rsi      scratch         r11      k
;-------------------------------------------------------------------------

; Calculate y[i:i+NSE-1]
         align 16
Loop1:   lea r11,[rax+KS2]                ;k = i + KS2

         vmulpd zmm5,zmm0,[rdx+r11*SF]       ;kernel[0] * x[k:k+NSE-1]
         vfmadd231pd zmm5,zmm1,[rdx+r11*SF-8]   ;kernel[1] * x[k-1:k-1+NSE-1]
         vfmadd231pd zmm5,zmm2,[rdx+r11*SF-16]  ;kernel[2] * x[k-2:k-2+NSE-1]
         vfmadd231pd zmm5,zmm3,[rdx+r11*SF-24]  ;kernel[3] * x[k-3:k-3+NSE-1]
         vfmadd231pd zmm5,zmm4,[rdx+r11*SF-32]  ;kernel[4] * x[k-4:k-4+NSE-1]

         vmovupd [rcx+rax*SF],zmm5        ;save y[i:i+NSE-1]
         add rax,NSE                      ;i += NSE

F1:      lea rsi,[rax+NSE]                ;rsi = i + NSE
         cmp rsi,r10                      ;i + NSE <= num_pts - ks2?
         jle Loop1                        ;jump if yes

         jmp F2                           ;begin execution of Loop2
```

```
; Calculate y[i:i+NSE2-1]
Loop2:  lea r11,[rax+KS2]                       ;k = i + KS2

        vmulpd ymm5,ymm0,[rdx+r11*SF]           ;kernel[0] * x[k:k+NSE2-1]
        vfmadd231pd ymm5,ymm1,[rdx+r11*SF-8]    ;kernel[1] * x[k-1:k-1+NSE2-1]
        vfmadd231pd ymm5,ymm2,[rdx+r11*SF-16]   ;kernel[2] * x[k-2:k-2+NSE2-1]
        vfmadd231pd ymm5,ymm3,[rdx+r11*SF-24]   ;kernel[3] * x[k-3:k-3+NSE2-1]
        vfmadd231pd ymm5,ymm4,[rdx+r11*SF-32]   ;kernel[4] * x[k-4:k-4+NSE2-1]

        vmovupd [rcx+rax*SF],ymm5               ;save y[i:i+NSE2-1]
        add rax,NSE2                            ;i += NSE2

F2:     lea rsi,[rax+NSE2]                      ;rsi = i + NSE2
        cmp rsi,r10                             ;i + NSE2 <= num_pts - KS2?
        jle Loop2                               ;jump if yes

        jmp F3                                  ;begin execution of Loop3

; Calculate y[i:i+NSE3-1]
Loop3:  lea r11,[rax+KS2]                       ;k = i + KS2

        vmulpd xmm5,xmm0,[rdx+r11*SF]           ;kernel[0] * x[k:k+NSE3-1]
        vfmadd231pd xmm5,xmm1,[rdx+r11*SF-8]    ;kernel[1] * x[k-1:k-1+NSE3-1]
        vfmadd231pd xmm5,xmm2,[rdx+r11*SF-16]   ;kernel[2] * x[k-2:k-2+NSE3-1]
        vfmadd231pd xmm5,xmm3,[rdx+r11*SF-24]   ;kernel[3] * x[k-3:k-3+NSE3-1]
        vfmadd231pd xmm5,xmm4,[rdx+r11*SF-32]   ;kernel[4] * x[k-4:k-4+NSE3-1]

        vmovupd [rcx+rax*SF],xmm5               ;save y[i:i+NSE3-1]
        add rax,NSE3                            ;i += NSE3

F3:     lea rsi,[rax+NSE3]                      ;rsi = i + NSE3
        cmp rsi,r10                             ;i + NSE3 <= num_pts - KS2?
        jle Loop3                               ;jump if yes

        jmp F4                                  ;begin execution of Loop4

; Calculate y[i]
Loop4:  lea r11,[rax+KS2]                       ;k = i + KS2

        vmulsd xmm5,xmm0,real8 ptr [rdx+r11*SF] ;kernel[0] * x[k]
        vfmadd231sd xmm5,xmm1,[rdx+r11*SF-8]    ;kernel[1] * x[k-1]
        vfmadd231sd xmm5,xmm2,[rdx+r11*SF-16]   ;kernel[2] * x[k-2]
        vfmadd231sd xmm5,xmm3,[rdx+r11*SF-24]   ;kernel[3] * x[k-3]
        vfmadd231sd xmm5,xmm4,[rdx+r11*SF-32]   ;kernel[4] * x[k-4]

        vmovsd real8 ptr [rcx+rax*SF],xmm5      ;save y[i]
        add rax,1                               ;i += 1

F4:     cmp rax,r10                             ;i < num_pts - KS2?
        jl Loop4                                ;jump if yes

        mov eax,1                               ;set success return code
```

```
Done:    vzeroupper
         DeleteFrame_M rsi
         ret

BadArg:  xor eax,eax                        ;set error return code
         jmp Done

Convolve1D_Ks5_F64_avx512 endp
         end
```

The code in Listing 15-4 for function Convolve1D_Ks5_F64_avx512() exemplifies again that with a little forethought, it's possible to code both single-precision and double-precision variants of the same calculating function with minimal differences. In Listing 15-4, note that the values for equates NSE, NSE2, NSE3, and SF have been adjusted for a double-precision floating-point convolution kernel and input signal array. Also note that calculating for-loops Loop1–Loop4 use double-precision instead of single-precision arithmetic instructions.

The results for source code example Ch15_04 basically match the results for example Ch15_03, but with a little extra precision. Table 15-4 shows the benchmark timing measurements for source code example Ch15_04. These measurements were made using an input signal array containing 2,500,000 elements. Table 15-4 also contains the benchmark timing measurements for function Convolve1D_Ks5_F64_avx2(), which were copied from Table 12-6. For this example, the timing measurements for AVX-512 and AVX2 versions of the 1D discrete convolution functions are about the same. Like the previous example, the timing measurements for the C++ functions on the i5-11600K and 7700X test computers are roughly the same as their assembly language counterparts since the GNU C++ compiler emitted similar sequences of AVX-512 FMA instructions as those used in the assembly language code.

Table 15-4. Benchmark Timing Measurements (Microseconds) for 1D Discrete Convolution Functions (Single-Precision)

Function	i5-11600K	i7-11700K	7700X
Convolve1D_Ks5_F64_cpp()	1479 (7)	3737 (61)	771 (4)
Convolve1D_Ks5_F64_avx2()	1519 (20)	1408 (47)	759 (6)
Convolve1D_Ks5_F64_avx512()	1503 (7)	1373 (34)	776 (5)

Summary

Here are the key learning points for Chapter 15:

- With a bit of forethought and coding savvy, it is possible to minimize source code differences between single-precision and double-precision versions of an assembly language function.

- It is also possible to develop both AVX2 and AVX-512 variants of a function by employing a common arrangement for the assembly language source code.

- Source code differences between Windows (MASM) and Linux (NASM) functions can be minimized by including a code block that exercises mov instructions to rearrange argument value registers.

- The performance of an explicitly coded assembly language function and its C++ counterpart function should always be benchmarked to substantiate any performance gains.

CHAPTER 16

■ ■ ■

Advanced Assembly Language Programming

In this chapter, you'll review a few source code examples that demonstrate advanced x86 assembly language programming techniques. The first two source code examples describe how to use the cpuid instruction to query processor vendor information and detect x86-AVX instruction set extensions. This is followed by two source examples that illustrate how to accelerate SIMD calculating functions using non-temporal memory store instructions. The final source code example expounds a text processing function using SIMD techniques and AVX2 instructions.

CPUID Instruction

It has been mentioned several times in this book, but it bears repeating once more: a program should *never* assume that a specific instruction set extension such as AVX, AVX2, FMA, or AVX-512 is available on its host processor. To ensure software compatibility with both current and future x86 processors, a program should always verify that any required x86 instruction set extensions are available.

The following section contains two source code examples that demonstrate the use of the cpuid instruction. The first example uses cpuid to obtain processor vendor information. The second example employs cpuid to detect various instruction set extensions including AVX, AVX2, FMA, and AVX-512. The cpuid instruction can also be directed to obtain other processor configuration data including information regarding its memory caches, paging hardware, and on-chip monitors. If you're interested in learning how to use cpuid to identify these or other processor features, you can consult the AMD and Intel programming reference manuals listed in Appendix B.

Processor Vendor Information

Source code example Ch16_01 uses the cpuid instruction to obtain processor vendor and brand information. Listing 16-1a shows the C++ code for this example.

© Daniel Kusswurm 2023
D. Kusswurm, *Modern X86 Assembly Language Programming*,
https://doi.org/10.1007/978-1-4842-9603-5_16

Listing 16-1a. Example Ch16_01 C++ Code

```
//-----------------------------------------------------------------------------
// Ch16_01.h
//-----------------------------------------------------------------------------

#pragma once
#include <cstddef>

// Ch16_01_fasm.asm, Ch16_01_fasm.s
extern "C" int GetProcessorVendorInfo_a(char* vendor, size_t vendor_len,
    char* brand, size_t brand_len);

//-----------------------------------------------------------------------------
// Ch16_01.cpp
//-----------------------------------------------------------------------------

#include <iostream>
#include "Ch16_01.h"

int main(void)
{
    char vendor[13];
    char brand[49];
    constexpr size_t vendor_len = sizeof(vendor);
    constexpr size_t brand_len = sizeof(brand);

    std::cout << "----- Results for Ch16_01 -----\n\n";

    int max_leaf = GetProcessorVendorInfo_a(vendor, vendor_len, brand, brand_len);

    if (max_leaf >= 0)
    {
        constexpr char nl = '\n';

        std::cout << "max_leaf:         " << max_leaf << nl;
        std::cout << "Processor vendor: " << vendor << nl;
        std::cout << "Processor brand:  " << brand << nl;
    }
    else
        std::cout << "GetProcessorVendorInfo_a() failed!\n";

    return 0;
}
```

The C++ source code in Listing 16-1a is straightforward. Function main() includes code that calls the assembly language function GetProcessorVendorInfo_a(). This function uses the cpuid instruction to obtain processor vendor and brand information. The remaining code in function main() streams the results obtained from GetProcessorVendorInfo_a() to std::cout.

Listing 16-1b shows the MASM code for example Ch16_01. Before examining the source code in this listing, a few words regarding x86 registers and cpuid instruction usage are necessary. During cpuid instruction execution, the processor utilizes registers EAX, EBX, ECX, and EDX to query and return feature information. Prior to using the cpuid instruction, the calling function must load a "leaf" value into register EAX. The leaf value specifies what information the cpuid instruction should return. The function may also need to load a "sub-leaf" value into register ECX. The cpuid instruction returns its results in registers EAX, EBX, ECX, and EDX. The calling function must then decipher the values in these registers to ascertain processor feature information or instruction set availability. It is often necessary for a program to use cpuid multiple times. Most programs typically exercise cpuid during initialization and save the results for later use. The reason for this is that cpuid is a serializing instruction. A serializing instruction forces the processor to finish executing all previously fetched instructions and perform any pending memory writes before fetching and executing the next instruction. In other words, it takes the processor a long time to execute a cpuid instruction.

Listing 16-1b. Example Ch16_01 MASM Code

```
;-------------------------------------------------------------------------
; Ch16_01_fasm.asm
;-------------------------------------------------------------------------


;-------------------------------------------------------------------------
; int GetProcessorVendorInfo_asm(char* vendor, size_t vendor_len, char* brand,
;   size_t brand_len);
;-------------------------------------------------------------------------

VENDOR_LEN_MIN   equ 13
BRAND_LEN_MIN    equ 49


        .code
GetProcessorVendorInfo_a proc frame
        push rbx
        .pushreg rbx
        .endprolog

; Make sure string buffers are large enough
        cmp rdx,VENDOR_LEN_MIN
        jb BadArg
        cmp r9,BRAND_LEN_MIN
        jb BadArg

        mov r10,rcx                     ;save copy of arg vendor

; Query processor vendor information string
        xor eax,eax                     ;leaf value for vendor ID string
        cpuid
        mov r11d,eax                    ;save max leaf value

        mov [r10],ebx                   ;save vendor[0:3]
        mov [r10+4],edx                 ;save vendor[4:7]
        mov [r10+8],ecx                 ;save vendor[8:11]
        mov [r10+12],byte ptr 0         ;null terminate string

; Query processor brand information string
        mov eax,80000000h               ;request max leaf for extended info
        cpuid
```

```
        cmp eax,80000004h              ;processor brand string available?
        jb NoInfo                      ;jump if no

        mov eax,80000002h              ;request brand string chars 0 - 15
        cpuid
        mov [r8+0],eax                 ;save brand[0:3]
        mov [r8+4],ebx                 ;save brand[4:7]
        mov [r8+8],ecx                 ;save brand[8:11]
        mov [r8+12],edx                ;save brand[12:15]

        mov eax,80000003h              ;request brand string chars 16 - 31
        cpuid
        mov [r8+16],eax                ;save brand[16:19]
        mov [r8+20],ebx                ;save brand[20:23]
        mov [r8+24],ecx                ;save brand[24:27]
        mov [r8+28],edx                ;save brand[28:31]

        mov eax,80000004h              ;request brand string chars 32 - 47
        cpuid
        mov [r8+32],eax                ;save brand[32:35]
        mov [r8+36],ebx                ;save brand[36:39]
        mov [r8+40],ecx                ;save brand[40:43]
        mov [r8+44],edx                ;save brand[44:47]
        mov [r8+48],byte ptr 0         ;null terminate string
        jmp SetRC

NoInfo: mov eax,412F4eh               ;eax = "N/A\0"
        mov [r8],eax

SetRC:  mov eax,r11d                   ;set success return code

Done:   pop rbx
        ret

BadArg: mov eax,-1                     ;set error return code
        jmp Done


GetProcessorVendorInfo_a endp
        end
```

In Listing 16-1b, execution of function GetProcessorVendorInfo_a() commences with short prologue that preserves non-volatile register RBX on the stack. The ensuing code block utilizes two cmp instructions to validate argument values vendor_len and brand_len for size. The next instruction, mov r10,rcx, saves a copy of argument value vendor for later use.

The next code block in GetProcessorVendorInfo_a() opens with an xor eax,eax instruction that loads leaf value 00h into register EAX. This is followed by a cpuid instruction, which obtains the processor's vendor identification string. Following execution of the cpuid instruction, register EAX contains the maximum leaf value that's supported by the processor. The mov r11,eax instruction saves this value so that it can be returned to the caller. Subsequent uses of the cpuid instruction should avoid using leaf values greater than the maximum leaf value that's supported by the processor. The vendor identification string resides in registers EBX, ECX, and EDX. The ensuing code block utilizes a series of mov instructions to save the vendor identification string to the buffer pointed to by R10 (vendor). The mov [r10+12],byte ptr 0 instruction null-terminates the vendor identification string.

Function GetProcessorVendorInfo_a() then employs multiple cpuid instructions to obtain the processor's brand information string. This task begins with the instruction pair mov eax,80000000h and cpuid, which obtains the maximum leaf value for processor extended information. Execution of the instruction pair, cmp eax,80000004h and jb NoInfo, skips over the brand information query code if this data is not available. Next is a series of code blocks that utilize three cpuid instructions to obtain the processor's brand information string. Note that prior to each cpuid instruction, GetProcessorVendorInfo_a() uses a mov instruction to load an extended leaf value into register EAX. This extended leaf value specifies which characters of the brand information string the cpuid instruction should return. Following each brand information string query, a series of mov instructions saves the results to the buffer pointed to by register R8 (brand).

The NASM code for example Ch16_01 is basically the same as the MASM code, except for different argument registers. The results for source code example Ch16_01 follow this paragraph. These results were obtained using computers with the following processors: Intel Core i7-8700K, Intel Core i7-11700K, and AMD Ryzen 7 7700X. Note that the maximum leaf values for these processors are different.

```
----- Results for Ch16_01 -----

max_leaf:        22
Processor vendor: GenuineIntel
Processor brand:  Intel(R) Core(TM) i7-8700K CPU @ 3.70GHz


----- Results for Ch16_01 -----

max_leaf:        27
Processor vendor: GenuineIntel
Processor brand:  11th Gen Intel(R) Core(TM) i7-11700K @ 3.60GHz


----- Results for Ch16_01 -----

max_leaf:        16
Processor vendor: AuthenticAMD
Processor brand:  AMD Ryzen 7 7700X 8-Core Processor
```

As mentioned earlier, a function must load a leaf value into register EAX prior to each use of the cpuid instruction. For some cpuid leaf values, a sub-leaf value must also be loaded into register ECX, and you'll see an example of this in the next section. The number of valid leaf (and extended leaf) values that a specific processor supports is quite large, especially for newer processors. The information returned by a cpuid instruction query can also be substantial. The cpuid instruction source code examples presented in this chapter demonstrate only a small subset of its capabilities. Before incorporating cpuid into any production code, you should consult the AMD and Intel programming reference manuals listed in Appendix B for additional information regarding proper use of this instruction.

X86-AVX Detection

The next source code example, named Ch16_02, uses the cpuid instruction to detect various x86-AVX instruction set extensions including AVX, AVX2, FMA, and AVX-512. Listing 16-2a shows the C++ code for this example.

Listing 16-2a. Example Ch16_02 C++ Code

```cpp
//----------------------------------------------------------------------
// Ch16_02.h
//----------------------------------------------------------------------

#pragma once
#include <cstddef>
#include <cstdint>

// Values in namespace CpuFlags must match the equ statements
// in the assembly language files. Values must also be
// consecutively numbered starting from zero.

namespace CpuidFlags
{
    constexpr size_t POPCNT = 0;
    constexpr size_t AVX = 1;
    constexpr size_t AVX2 = 2;
    constexpr size_t FMA = 3;
    constexpr size_t AVX512F = 4;
    constexpr size_t AVX512VL = 5;
    constexpr size_t AVX512DQ = 6;
    constexpr size_t AVX512BW = 7;
    constexpr size_t AVX512_VMBI = 8;
    constexpr size_t AVX512_VMBI2 = 9;
    constexpr size_t AVX512_FP16 = 10;
    constexpr size_t AVX512_BF16 = 11;
    constexpr size_t NUM_FLAGS = 12;
};

// Ch16_02_fasm.asm, Ch16_02_fasm.s
extern "C" bool GetCpuidFlags_a(uint8_t* flags, size_t flags_len);

// Ch16_02_fasm2.asm, Ch16_02_fasm2.s
extern "C" int GetProcessorVendorInfo_a(char* vendor, size_t vendor_len,
    char* brand, size_t brand_len);

//----------------------------------------------------------------------
// Ch16_02.cpp
//----------------------------------------------------------------------

#include <iostream>
#include <iomanip>
#include <cstring>
#include "Ch16_02.h"

const char* s_FlagNames[CpuidFlags::NUM_FLAGS]
{
    "POPCNT",
    "AVX",
    "AVX2",
```

```cpp
    "FMA",
    "AVX512F",
    "AVX512VL",
    "AVX512DQ",
    "AVX512BW",
    "AVX512_VBMI",
    "AVX512_VBMI2",
    "AVX512_FP16",
    "AVX512_BF16"
};

int main(void)
{
    char vendor[13];
    char brand[49];
    constexpr size_t vendor_len = sizeof(vendor);
    constexpr size_t brand_len = sizeof(brand);

    std::cout << "----- Results for Ch16_02 -----\n\n";

    int max_leaf = GetProcessorVendorInfo_a(vendor, vendor_len, brand, brand_len);

    if (max_leaf >= 0)
    {
        constexpr char nl = '\n';
        constexpr size_t num_flags = CpuidFlags::NUM_FLAGS;
        uint8_t flags[num_flags];

        std::cout << "Processor vendor: " << vendor << nl;
        std::cout << "Processor brand:  " << brand << nl;

        bool rc = GetCpuidFlags_a(flags, num_flags);

        if (rc)
        {
            std::cout << "\nCPUID Feature Flags\n";
            std::cout << std::string(23, '-') << nl;

            for (size_t i = 0; i < num_flags; i++)
            {
                std::string s1 = std::string(s_FlagNames[i]);
                std::string s2 = s1 + std::string(":    ");

                std::cout << std::setw(20) << std::left << s2;
                std::cout << std::setw(2) << (unsigned)flags[i] << nl;
            }
        }
        else
            std::cout << "GetCpuidFlags_a() failed!\n";
    }
```

```
    else
        std::cout << "GetProcessorVendorInfo_a() failed!\n";

    return 0;
}
```

Listing 16-2a opens with a C++ namespace named CpuidFlags. This namespace contains a set of symbolic names for various x86-AVX instruction set extensions. The numeric values for the constants in namespace CpuidFlags must match the equate symbols that are defined in the assembly language code. File Ch16_02.cpp contains code that calls assembly language function GetCpuidFlags_a(). Note that the first argument for GetCpuidFlags_a() is an array of uint8_t values. Each flag entry in this array corresponds to an instruction set extension defined in namespace CpuidFlags. The code for function GetProcessorVendorInfo_a() is the same code that you saw in example Ch16_01. The remaining code in Ch16_02.cpp formats and streams the results to std::cout.

Listing 16-2b shows the MASM code for example Ch16_02. This file opens with a series of equates whose symbolic names and values match the names and values in namespace CpuidFlags. The next set of equates defines symbolic names for various x86-AVX instruction set extensions. The appended comment that follows each equ definition documents the leaf value, sub-leaf value, and the output register bit for each instruction set extension. For example, the comment text CPUID(EAX=07h,ECX=00h):EBX[bit 5] signifies that to detect the AVX2 instruction set, a function must load leaf value 07h into register EAX and sub-leaf value 00h into register ECX prior to using cpuid. Following execution of the cpuid instruction, bit 5 of register EBX can be tested to determine processor support AVX2. The expression that's assigned to symbolic name BIT_AVX2, equ 1 shl 5, ensures that the code in GetCpuidFlags_a() tests the correct bit in register EBX. The final two equates, STATE_AVX and STATE_AVX512, define processor state flags for the xgetbv (Get Value of Extended Control Register) instruction, which is used to ascertain host operating system support for AVX, AVX2, and AVX-512. More on this shortly.

Listing 16-2b. Example Ch16_02 MASM Code

```
;-----------------------------------------------------------------------------
; Ch16_02_fasm.asm
;-----------------------------------------------------------------------------

; Note: The equ statements below must match the values assigned
; in C++ namespace CpuFlags (see Ch16_02.h). Values must also be
; consecutively numbered starting from zero.
FL_POPCNT          equ 0
FL_AVX             equ 1
FL_AVX2            equ 2
FL_FMA             equ 3
FL_AVX512F         equ 4
FL_AVX512VL        equ 5
FL_AVX512DQ        equ 6
FL_AVX512BW        equ 7
FL_AVX512_VBMI     equ 8
FL_AVX512_VBMI2    equ 9
FL_AVX512_FP16     equ 10
FL_AVX512_BF16     equ 11
FL_NUM_FLAGS       equ 12
```

```
; CPUID flag bits.
; See cpuid instruction documentation for more information.
BIT_FMA              equ 1 shl 12        ;CPUID(EAX=01h):ECX[bit 12]
BIT_POPCNT           equ 1 shl 23        ;CPUID(EAX=01h):ECX[bit 23]
BIT_OSXSAVE          equ 1 shl 27        ;CPUID(EAX=01h):ECX[bit 27]
BIT_AVX              equ 1 shl 28        ;CPUID(EAX=01h):ECX[bit 28]
BIT_AVX2             equ 1 shl 5         ;CPUID(EAX=07h,ECX=00h):EBX[bit 5]
BIT_AVX512F          equ 1 shl 16        ;CPUID(EAX=07h,ECX=00h):EBX[bit 16]
BIT_AVX512DQ         equ 1 shl 17        ;CPUID(EAX=07h,ECX=00h):EBX[bit 17]
BIT_AVX512BW         equ 1 shl 30        ;CPUID(EAX=07h,ECX=00h):EBX[bit 30]
BIT_AVX512VL         equ 1 shl 31        ;CPUID(EAX=07h,ECX=00h):EBX[bit 31]
BIT_AVX512_VBMI      equ 1 shl 1         ;CPUID(EAX=07h,ECX=00h):ECX[bit 1]
BIT_AVX512_VBMI2     equ 1 shl 6         ;CPUID(EAX=07h,ECX=00h):ECX[bit 6]
BIT_AVX512_FP16      equ 1 shl 23        ;CPUID(EAX=07h,ECX=00h):EDX[bit 23]
BIT_AVX512_BF16      equ 1 shl 5         ;CPUID(EAX=07h,ECX=01h):EAX[bit 5]

; AVX/AVX-512 state flags.
; See xgetbv instruction documentation for more information.
STATE_AVX            equ 06h
STATE_AVX512         equ 0e0h


;-------------------------------------------------------------------------
; bool GetCpuidFlags(uint8_t* flags, size_t flags_len);
;-------------------------------------------------------------------------

        .code
GetCpuidFlags_a proc frame
        push rbx
        .pushreg rbx
        push rdi
        .pushreg rdi
        .endprolog

; Make sure flags buffer is large enough
        cmp rdx,FL_NUM_FLAGS                 ;flags_len >= FL_NUM_FLAGS?
        jb BadArg                            ;jump if no

; Initialize all flags to false
        xor eax,eax                          ;al = fill value
        mov r10,rcx                          ;save copy of arg flags
        mov rdi,rcx
        mov rcx,FL_NUM_FLAGS
        rep stosb                            ;set all flags to false

; Verify CPUID support for leaf value eax = 07h
        xor eax,eax
        cpuid                                ;get max leaf value
        cmp eax,7                            ;max leaf >= 7?
        jb Done                              ;jump if no
```

```
; Verify OS support for xgetbv instruction
        mov eax,1
        cpuid
        test ecx,BIT_OSXSAVE              ;OS enabled xgetbv?
        jz Done                           ;jump if no
        mov r8d,ecx                       ;save cpuid(eax=01h):ecx results

; Verify OS support for AVX/AVX2
        xor ecx,ecx                       ;select XCR0
        xgetbv                            ;result in edx:eax
        mov r9d,eax                       ;save AVX-512 state flags for later
        and eax,STATE_AVX
        cmp eax,STATE_AVX                 ;OS support for AVX/AVX2?
        jne Done                          ;jump if no

; Verify CPU support for AVX, FMA, and POPCNT
        test r8d,BIT_AVX
        setnz byte ptr [r10+FL_AVX]

        test r8d,BIT_FMA
        setnz byte ptr [r10+FL_FMA]

        test r8d,BIT_POPCNT
        setnz byte ptr [r10+FL_POPCNT]

; Verify CPU support for AVX2
        mov eax,7                         ;eax = leaf value
        xor ecx,ecx                       ;ecx = sub-leaf value
        cpuid

        test ebx,BIT_AVX2
        setnz byte ptr [r10+FL_AVX2]

; Verify OS support for AVX-512
        and r9d,STATE_AVX512
        cmp r9d,STATE_AVX512              ;OS support for AVX-512?
        jne Done                          ;jump if no

; Verify CPU support for AVX512F, AVX512VL, AVX512DQ, and AVX512BW
        test ebx,BIT_AVX512F
        setnz byte ptr [r10+FL_AVX512F]

        test ebx,BIT_AVX512VL
        setnz byte ptr [r10+FL_AVX512VL]

        test ebx,BIT_AVX512DQ
        setnz byte ptr [r10+FL_AVX512DQ]

        test ebx,BIT_AVX512BW
        setnz byte ptr [r10+FL_AVX512BW]
```

```
; Verify CPU support for AVX512_VBMI and AVX512_VBMI2
        test ecx,BIT_AVX512_VBMI
        setnz byte ptr [r10+FL_AVX512_VBMI]

        test ecx,BIT_AVX512_VBMI2
        setnz byte ptr [r10+FL_AVX512_VBMI2]

; Verify CPU support for AVX512_FP16
        test edx,BIT_AVX512_FP16
        setnz byte ptr [r10+FL_AVX512_FP16]

; Verify CPU support for AVX512_BF16
        mov eax,7
        mov ecx,1
        cpuid
        test eax,BIT_AVX512_BF16
        setnz byte ptr [r10+FL_AVX512_BF16]

Done:   mov eax,1                       ;set success return code
        pop rdi
        pop rbx
        ret

BadArg: xor eax,eax                     ;set error return code
        jmp Done

GetCpuidFlags_a endp
        end
```

Function GetCpuidFlags_a() begins its execution with a short prologue that preserves non-volatile registers RBX and RDI on the stack. It then validates argument value flags_len for size. The next code block uses a rep stosb instruction to initialize each flag in array flags to zero. Following initialization of array flags, GetCpuidFlags_a() employs a cpuid instruction with EAX equal to 00h to verify that the processor supports the use of the cpuid instruction using a leaf value of 07h. Recall from the previous example that following execution of cpuid with EAX equal to 00h, register EAX contains the maximum leaf value supported by the processor.

The subsequent code block uses another cpuid instruction with EAX equal to 01h to determine if GetCpuidFlags_a() can use the xgetbv instruction to read extended control register XCR0. This register contains status flags that signify OS support for processor AVX/AVX2 state information (i.e., the XMM and YMM registers are enabled and usable). Following execution of this cpuid instruction, the ensuing instruction pair test ecx,BIT_OSXSAVE and jz Done skips over the remaining processing code in GetCpuidFlags_a() if the host OS has not enabled the use of the xgetbv instruction to read XCR0. The mov r8d,ecx instruction that follows the jz Done instruction saves other cpuid results in register ECX for later use.

If xgetbv instruction use is permitted, function GetCpuidFlags_a() utilizes it to read extended control register XCR0. The mov r9d,eax instruction saves the current value of control register XCR0 in R9D for later use since XCR0 also contains status flags for AVX-512. The instruction triplet and eax,STATE_AVX, cmp eax,STATE_AVX, and jne Done skips over the remaining code in GetCpuidFlags_a() if the host OS does not support AVX/AVX2.

Following verification of OS support for AVX/AVX2, function GetCpuidFlags_a() employs the instruction pair test r8d,BIT_AVX and setnz byte ptr [r10+FL_AVX] to ascertain processor support for AVX. Recall that the setcc instruction sets its byte operand to one if the specified condition code is true;

otherwise, the byte operand is set to zero. The ensuing instruction pair, test r8d,BIT_FMA and setnz byte ptr [r10+FL_FMA], performs the same processor support check for FMA. It is important to keep in mind that FMA is a distinct x86 instruction set extension. A function should *never* assume processor support for FMA even if the processor supports AVX or AVX2. Function GetCpuidFlags_a() then employs the instruction pair test r8d,BIT_POPCNT and setnz byte [r10+FL_POPCNT] to confirm processor support for the popcnt instruction.

The remaining code blocks in GetCpuidFlags_a() also use the cpuid instruction (when necessary) and perform status flag tests to confirm support for other instruction set extensions including AVX2, AVX512F, AVX512VL, AVX512DQ, AVX512BW, AVX512_VBMI, and AVX512_VBMI2. The final two checks in GetCpuidFlags_a() are for instruction set extensions AVX512_BF16 and AVX512_FP16. The AVX512_BF16 instruction set extension includes instructions that carry out operations using bfloat16 values, which are used in machine learning applications. The AVX512_FP16 instruction set extension contains instructions that perform scalar and packed half-precision floating-point arithmetic per the IEEE 754-2019 standard.

The NASM code for function GetCpuidFlags_a() is almost identical to the MASM code, except for different argument registers. The results for source code example Ch16_02 follow this paragraph. These results were obtained using the same test computers as those used in example Ch16_01.

```
----- Results for Ch16_02 -----

Processor vendor: GenuineIntel
Processor brand:  Intel(R) Core(TM) i7-8700K CPU @ 3.70GHz

CPUID Feature Flags
----------------------
POPCNT:              1
AVX:                 1
AVX2:                1
FMA:                 1
AVX512F:             0
AVX512VL:            0
AVX512DQ:            0
AVX512BW:            0
AVX512_VBMI:         0
AVX512_VBMI2:        0
AVX512_FP16:         0
AVX512_BF16:         0

----- Results for Ch16_02 -----

Processor vendor: GenuineIntel
Processor brand:  11th Gen Intel(R) Core(TM) i7-11700K @ 3.60GHz

CPUID Feature Flags
----------------------
POPCNT:              1
AVX:                 1
AVX2:                1
FMA:                 1
AVX512F:             1
AVX512VL:            1
AVX512DQ:            1
AVX512BW:            1
```

```
AVX512_VBMI:        1
AVX512_VBMI2:       1
AVX512_FP16:        0
AVX512_BF16:        0


----- Results for Ch16_02 -----

Processor vendor: AuthenticAMD
Processor brand:  AMD Ryzen 7 7700X 8-Core Processor

CPUID Feature Flags
----------------------
POPCNT:             1
AVX:                1
AVX2:               1
FMA:                1
AVX512F:            1
AVX512VL:           1
AVX512DQ:           1
AVX512BW:           1
AVX512_VBMI:        1
AVX512_VBMI2:       1
AVX512_FP16:        0
AVX512_BF16:        1
```

The assembly language source code in example Ch16_02 detects only a small subset of possible instruction set extensions supported by modern x86 processors. I included this example since I think it's important for an assembly language programmer to have a basic understanding of the cpuid instruction and the data it returns. However, given the intricacies of cpuid instruction usage and the plethora of current (and potential future) x86 instruction set extensions, some programmers opt to use C++ compiler intrinsic functions or a third-party library to perform run-time instruction set detection. Appendix B contains a list of references that you can consult for more information regarding these options.

Non-temporal Memory Stores

The data in the processor's memory cache can be classified as either temporal or non-temporal. Temporal data is data that is accessed more than once within a short period of time. Examples of temporal data include the elements of an array or data structure that are referenced multiple times during execution of a for-loop. More importantly, it also includes the machine code of an executing program. Non-temporal data is any data value that is accessed once and not immediately reused. The destination arrays of many SIMD processing algorithms often contain non-temporal data. The differentiation between temporal and non-temporal data is important since processor performance often degrades if its memory caches contain excessive amounts of non-temporal data. This condition is commonly called cache pollution. Ideally, a processor's memory caches should contain only temporal data since it makes little sense to cache items that are only used once.

The source code examples in this section explain how to use several x86 non-temporal store instructions. The first example covers non-temporal integer SIMD stores using the vmovntdq (Store Packed Integers Using Non-temporal Hint) instruction. The second source code example demonstrates floating-point SIMD stores using the vmovntpd (Store Packed Double-Precision Floating-Point Values Using Non-temporal Hint) instruction.

Integer Non-temporal Memory Stores

Listing 16-3a shows the principal C++ source code for example Ch16_03. This example demonstrates the use of the non-temporal packed integer store instruction vmovntdq.

Listing 16-3a. Example Ch16_03 C++ Code

```
//-----------------------------------------------------------------------
// Ch16_03.h
//-----------------------------------------------------------------------

#pragma once
#include <cstddef>
#include <cstdint>

// Ch16_03_fasm.asm, Ch16_03_fasm.s
extern "C" bool AbsImage_avx2(uint8_t* pb_des, const uint8_t* pb_src0,
    const uint8_t* pb_src1, size_t num_pixels);

// Ch16_03_fasm2.asm, Ch16_03_fasm2.s
extern "C" bool AbsImageNT_avx2(uint8_t* pb_des, const uint8_t* pb_src0,
    const uint8_t* pb_src1, size_t num_pixels);

// Ch16_03_fcpp.cpp
extern bool AbsImage_cpp(uint8_t* pb_des, const uint8_t* pb_src0,
    const uint8_t* pb_src1, size_t num_pixels);

// Ch16_03_misc.cpp
extern "C" bool CheckArgs(const uint8_t* pb_des, const uint8_t* pb_src0,
    const uint8_t* pb_src1, size_t num_pixels);

// Ch16_03_bm.cpp
extern void AbsImage_bm();

// Miscellaneous globals
extern const char* g_ImageFileName0;
extern const char* g_ImageFileName1;

//-----------------------------------------------------------------------
// Ch16_03_fcpp.cpp
//-----------------------------------------------------------------------

#include <cmath>
#include "Ch16_03.h"

bool AbsImage_cpp(uint8_t* pb_des, const uint8_t* pb_src0,
    const uint8_t* pb_src1, size_t num_pixels)
{
    if (!CheckArgs(pb_des, pb_src0, pb_src1, num_pixels))
        return false;
```

```
        for (size_t i = 0; i < num_pixels; i++)
            pb_des[i] = (uint8_t)abs(pb_src0[i] - pb_src1[i]);

        return true;
}
```

In Listing 16-3a, note that file Ch16_03.h includes declarations for two assembly language functions: AbsImage_avx2() and AbsImageNT_avx2(). The code in function AbsImage_avx2() uses the vmovdqa instruction to perform SIMD integer (pixel) stores. Function AbsImageNT_avx2() uses the non-temporal instruction vmovntdq to perform this same operation. Listing 16-3a also shows the code for function AbsImage_cpp(), which implements the same image absolute value calculation as its assembly language counterparts.

Listing 16-3b shows the MASM code for function AbsImage_avx2(). Each iteration of for-loop Loop1 begins with an add rax,NSE instruction that calculates i += NSE. The next two instructions, vmovdqa ymm0,ymmword ptr [r13+rax] and vmovdqa ymm1,ymmword ptr [r14+rax], load pixel values pb_src0[i:i+NSE-1] and pb_src1[i:i+NSE-1] into registers YMM0 and YMM1, respectively. The ensuing code block utilizes sequences of vpunpcklbw and vpunpckhbw to size-promote the pixel values from bytes to words.

Listing 16-3b. Example Ch16_03 MASM Code

```
;-------------------------------------------------------------------------------
; Ch16_03_fasm.asm
;-------------------------------------------------------------------------------

        include <MacrosX86-64-AVX.asmh>

;-------------------------------------------------------------------------------
; bool AbsImage_avx2(uint8_t* pb_des, const uint8_t* pb_src0,
;    const uint8_t * pb_src1, size_t num_pixels);
;-------------------------------------------------------------------------------

NSE     equ 32                                  ;num_simd_elements

        extern CheckArgs:proc

        .code
AbsImage_avx2 proc frame
        CreateFrame_M TI_,0,16,r12,r13,r14,r15
        SaveXmmRegs_M xmm15
        EndProlog_M

; Copy args to non-volatile registers
        mov r12,rcx                             ;pb_des
        mov r13,rdx                             ;pb_src0
        mov r14,r8                              ;pb_src1
        mov r15,r9                              ;num_pixels

; Validate arguments
        sub rsp,32                              ;allocate home area
        call CheckArgs
```

```
        or eax,eax                              ;arguments valid?
        jz Done                                 ;jump if no

; Initialize
        vpxor ymm15,ymm15,ymm15                 ;packed zeros
        mov rax,-NSE                            ;rax = array index i

; Calculate pb_des[i] = abs(pb_src0[i] - pb_src2[i])
Loop1:  add rax,NSE                                    ;i += NSE
        vmovdqa ymm0,ymmword ptr [r13+rax]  ;load pb_src0[i:i+NSE-1]
        vmovdqa ymm1,ymmword ptr [r14+rax]  ;load pb_src1[i:i+NSE-1]

        vpunpcklbw ymm2,ymm0,ymm15          ;convert pb_src0 to words
        vpunpckhbw ymm3,ymm0,ymm15
        vpunpcklbw ymm4,ymm1,ymm15          ;convert pb_src1 to words
        vpunpckhbw ymm5,ymm1,ymm15

        vpsubw ymm0,ymm2,ymm4               ;calc pb_src0 - pb_src1
        vpsubw ymm1,ymm3,ymm5
        vpabsw ymm0,ymm0                    ;calc abs(pb_src0 - pb_src1)
        vpabsw ymm1,ymm1
        vpackuswb ymm2,ymm0,ymm1            ;convert result to bytes

; Note: AbsImageNT_avx2() uses vmovntdq instead of vmovdqa
        vmovdqa ymmword ptr [r12+rax],ymm2  ;save pb_des[i:i+NSE-1]

        sub r15,NSE                         ;num_pixels -= NSE
        jnz Loop1                           ;repeat until done

        mov eax,1                           ;set success return code

Done:   vzeroupper
        RestoreXmmRegs_M xmm15
        DeleteFrame_M r12,r13,r14,r15
        ret

AbsImage_avx2 endp
        end
```

Following the byte-to-word size promotions, AbsImage_avx2() uses instructions vpsubw and vpabs to calculate abs(pb_src0[i:i+NSE-1] - pb_src1[i:i+NSE-1]). The subsequent vpackuswb ymm2,ymm0,ymm1 instruction size-reduces the calculated absolute values from words to bytes. Execution of the vmovdqa ymmword ptr [r12+rax],ymm2 instruction saves these values to pb_des[i:i+NSE-1].

MASM function AbsImageNT_avx2() (source code not shown) is identical to AbsImage_avx2() except for the use of the non-temporal store instruction vmovntdq near the bottom of Loop1. This instruction replaces the vmovdqa instruction that was used in AbsImage_avx2(). The NASM code for functions AbsImage_avx2() and AbsImageNT_avx2() is the same as the MASM code, except for different argument registers. Here are the results for source code example Ch16_03:

```
----- Results for Ch16_03 -----

Loading source image #0: ../../Data/TestImageD0.png
Loading source image #1: ../../Data/TestImageD1.png
Number of pixels: 24000000
Saving destination image #0: @Ch16_03_AbsImage0_HELIUM.png
Saving destination image #1: @Ch16_03_AbsImage1_HELIUM.png
Saving destination image #2: @Ch16_03_AbsImage2_HELIUM.png
Destination image compare test passed

Running benchmark function AbsImage_bm() - please wait

Benchmark times saved to file @Ch16_03_AbsImage_bm_HELIUM.csv
```

Table 16-1 shows the benchmark timing measurements for example Ch16_03. As you can see from the timing measurements in this table, using vmovntdq instead of vmovdqa to save the calculated pixel values yielded meaningful performance gains on all three test computers.

Table 16-1. *Benchmark Timing Measurements (Microseconds) for Image Absolute Value Functions Using Test Images* TestImageD0.png *and* TestImageD1.png

Function	i5-11600K	i7-11700K	7700X
AbsImage_cpp()	2766 (8)	2986 (73)	1436 (6)
AbsImage_avx2()	2653 (8)	2289 (68)	1427 (6)
AbsImageNT_avx2()	2082 (8)	1688 (67)	1114 (7)

Floating-Point Non-temporal Memory Stores

The next source code example, named Ch16_04, demonstrates vector cross product calculations using arrays of three-dimensional vectors. It also illustrates the use of the non-temporal store instruction vmovntpd. Listing 16-4a shows the principal C++ code for example Ch16_04.

Listing 16-4a. Example Ch16_04 C++ Code

```
//------------------------------------------------------------------------------
// Ch16_04.h
//------------------------------------------------------------------------------

#pragma once
#include <cstddef>

// VecSOA structure. This structure must match the structures that
// are defined in the assembly language files.
struct VecSOA
{
    size_t NumVec = 0;        // number of vectors (must be even multiple of 4)
    double* X = nullptr;      // vector X components
    double* Y = nullptr;      // vector Y components
    double* Z = nullptr;      // vector Z components
};
```

627

```
// Ch16_04_fasm.asm, Ch16_04_fasm.s
extern "C" bool VecCrossProducts_avx2(VecSOA* c, const VecSOA* a,
    const VecSOA* b);

// Ch16_04_fasm2.asm, Ch16_04_fasm2.s
extern "C" bool VecCrossProductsNT_avx2(VecSOA* c, const VecSOA* a,
    const VecSOA* b);

// Ch16_04_fcpp.cpp
extern bool VecCrossProducts_cpp(VecSOA* c, const VecSOA* a, const VecSOA* b);

// Ch16_04_misc.cpp
extern void AllocateTestVectors(VecSOA* c1, VecSOA* c2, VecSOA* c3,
    VecSOA* a, VecSOA* b, size_t num_vec);
extern "C" bool CheckArgs(const VecSOA * c, const VecSOA * a, const VecSOA * b);
extern void DisplayResults(VecSOA* c1, VecSOA* c2, VecSOA* c3, VecSOA* a,
    VecSOA* b);
extern void ReleaseTestVectors(VecSOA* c1, VecSOA* c2, VecSOA* c3,
    VecSOA* a, VecSOA* b);

// Ch16_04_bm.cpp
extern void VecCrossProducts_bm(void);

// Miscellaneous constants
constexpr size_t c_Alignment = 32;
constexpr size_t c_NumVec = 16;
constexpr size_t c_NumVecBM = 2000000;

//-----------------------------------------------------------------------------
// Ch16_04_fcpp.cpp
//-----------------------------------------------------------------------------

#include "Ch16_04.h"

bool VecCrossProducts_cpp(VecSOA* c, const VecSOA* a, const VecSOA* b)
{
    if (!CheckArgs(c, a, b))
        return false;

    for (size_t i = 0; i < c->NumVec; i++)
    {
        c->X[i] = a->Y[i] * b->Z[i] - a->Z[i] * b->Y[i];
        c->Y[i] = a->Z[i] * b->X[i] - a->X[i] * b->Z[i];
        c->Z[i] = a->X[i] * b->Y[i] - a->Y[i] * b->X[i];
    }

    return true;
}
```

The cross product of two three-dimensional vectors **a** and **b** is a third vector **c** that is perpendicular to both **a** and **b**. Example Ch16_04 uses the following equations to calculate a vector cross product:

$$c_x = a_y b_z - a_z b_y$$

$$c_y = a_z b_x - a_x b_z$$

$$c_z = a_x b_y - a_y b_x$$

Near the top of Listing 16-4a is the declaration of a C++ structure named VecSOA. This structure includes pointers to three double-precision floating-point arrays that hold vector components x, y, and z. A "structure of arrays" construct is used in this example instead of an "array of structures" (e.g., struct Vec3D { double x; double y; double z; }; Vec3D VecArray[100];) since the former is often faster when performing SIMD arithmetic calculations on an x86 processor.[1] Also shown in Listing 16-4a is function VecCrossProducts_cpp(), which calculates cross products using VecSOA arguments a, b, and c.

Listing 16-4b shows the MASM code for example Ch16_04. Near the top of this listing is the declaration of MASM structure VecSOA, which is the semantic counterpart of the C++ structure VecSOA from Listing 16-4a. Following argument validation, VecCrossProducts_avx2() uses a series of mov instructions that load pointers to the various vector component arrays into general-purpose registers. A mov instruction is also employed to load the number of vector cross products into register R8.

Listing 16-4b. Example Ch16_04 MASM Code

```
;-------------------------------------------------------------------------
; Ch16_04_fasm.asm
;-------------------------------------------------------------------------

        include <MacrosX86-64-AVX.asmh>

; VecSOA structure. This structure must match the structure that's
; defined in Ch16_04.h

VecSOA      struct
NumVec      qword ?
X           qword ?
Y           qword ?
Z           qword ?
VecSOA      ends


;-------------------------------------------------------------------------
; bool VecCrossProducts_avx2(VecSOA* c, const VecSOA* a, const VecSOA* b);
;-------------------------------------------------------------------------

NSE     equ 4                       ;num_simd_elements
                                    ;(num CrossProds per iteration of Loop1)

        extern CheckArgs:proc
```

---
[1] For this example, utilizing an array of structures construct would necessitate the use of extra permutation instructions.

```
        .code
VecCrossProducts_avx2 proc frame
        CreateFrame_M CP_,0,48,r12,r13,r14,r15
        SaveXmmRegs_M xmm6,xmm7,xmm8
        EndProlog_M

; Preserve argument values in non-volatile GP registers
        mov r13,rcx                     ;arg c
        mov r14,rdx                     ;arg a
        mov r15,r8                      ;arg b

; Validate arguments
        sub rsp,32                      ;allocate home area
        call CheckArgs
        or eax,eax                      ;arguments valid?
        jz Done                         ;jump if no

; Perform required initializations
        mov r8,[r13+VecSOA.NumVec]      ;number of vector CPs to calculate

        mov r9,[r13+VecSOA.X]           ;c.X pointer
        mov rcx,[r13+VecSOA.Y]          ;c.Y pointer
        mov rdx,[r13+VecSOA.Z]          ;c.Z pointer

        mov r10,[r14+VecSOA.X]          ;a.X pointer
        mov r11,[r14+VecSOA.Y]          ;a.Y pointer
        mov r12,[r14+VecSOA.Z]          ;a.Z pointer

        mov r13,[r15+VecSOA.X]          ;b.X pointer
        mov r14,[r15+VecSOA.Y]          ;b.Y pointer
        mov r15,[r15+VecSOA.Z]          ;b.Z pointer

        mov rax,-NSE                    ;initialize i

; Load next block of vectors
Loop1:  add rax,NSE                     ;i += NSE

        vmovapd ymm0,ymmword ptr [r10+rax*8]    ;ymm0 = a.X[i:i+NSE-1]
        vmovapd ymm1,ymmword ptr [r11+rax*8]    ;ymm1 = a.Y[i:i+NSE-1]
        vmovapd ymm2,ymmword ptr [r12+rax*8]    ;ymm2 = a.Z[i:i+NSE-1]

        vmovapd ymm3,ymmword ptr [r13+rax*8]    ;ymm3 = b.X[i:i+NSE-1]
        vmovapd ymm4,ymmword ptr [r14+rax*8]    ;ymm4 = b.Y[i:i+NSE-1]
        vmovapd ymm5,ymmword ptr [r15+rax*8]    ;ymm5 = b.Z[i:i+NSE-1]

; Calculate cross products
        vmulpd ymm6,ymm1,ymm5
        vmulpd ymm7,ymm2,ymm4
        vsubpd ymm8,ymm6,ymm7           ;c.X = a.Y * b.Z - a.Z * b.Y
```

630

```
; Note: VecCrossProductsNT_avx2() uses vmovntpd instead of vmovapd
        vmovapd ymmword ptr [r9+rax*8],ymm8    ;save c.X[i:i+NSE-1]

        vmulpd ymm6,ymm2,ymm3
        vmulpd ymm7,ymm0,ymm5
        vsubpd ymm8,ymm6,ymm7                  ;c.Y = a.Z * b.X - a.X * b.Z

; Note: VecCrossProductsNT_avx2() uses vmovntpd instead of vmovapd
        vmovapd ymmword ptr [rcx+rax*8],ymm8   ;save c.Y[i:i+NSE-1]

        vmulpd ymm6,ymm0,ymm4
        vmulpd ymm7,ymm1,ymm3
        vsubpd ymm8,ymm6,ymm7                  ;c.Z = a.X * b.Y - a.Y * b.X

; Note: VecCrossProductsNT_avx2() uses vmovntpd instead of vmovapd
        vmovapd ymmword ptr [rdx+rax*8],ymm8   ;save c.Z[i:i+NSE-1]

        sub r8,NSE                             ;num_pixels -= NSE
        jnz Loop1                              ;repeat until done

        mov eax,1                              ;set success return code

Done:   vzeroupper
        RestoreXmmRegs_M xmm6,xmm7,xmm8
        DeleteFrame_M r12,r13,r14,r15
        ret
VecCrossProducts_avx2 endp
        end
```

Each iteration of for-loop Loop1 commences with an add RAX,NSE instruction that calculates i +=
NSE. Next is a sequence of three vmovapd instructions that load vector components a.X[i:i+NSE-1] into
YMM0, a.Y[i:i+NSE-1] into YMM1, and a.Z[i:i+NSE-1] into YMM2. The ensuing vmovapd triplet loads
vector components b.X[i:i+NSE-1] into YMM3, b.Y[i:i+NSE-1] into YMM4, and b.Z[i:i+NSE-1] into
register YMM5. Following these loads, registers YMM0–YMM2 contain the x, y, and z components of four
(NSE) vectors from array a; registers YMM3–YMM5 contain the x, y, and z components of four vectors from
array b.

After the vector component loads, VecCrossProducts_avx2() uses three vmulpd instructions and a
vsubpd instruction to calculate c.X[i:i+NSE-1]. It then utilizes a vmovapd ymmword ptr [r9+rax*8],ymm8
to save this result. The same instruction sequences are then employed to calculate and save c.Y[i:i+NSE-1]
and c.Z[i:i+NSE-1].

The MASM code for function VecCrossProductsNT_avx2() (not shown) is identical to code in
VecCrossProducts_avx2() except that the former uses vmovntpd instead of vmovapd in Loop1 to save
the calculated vector cross products. The vector cross product calculating code in the NASM versions of
VecCrossProducts_avx2() and VecCrossProductsNT_avx2() is identical to the MASM code that's shown in
Listing 16-4b. Here are the condensed results for example Ch16_04:

```
----- Results for Ch16_04 -----
Vector cross product #0
  a:       44        26        18
  b:       81        18         6
  c1:    -168      1194     -1314
```

631

```
c2:        -168        1194       -1314
c3:        -168        1194       -1314
Vector cross product #1
  a:          83          90          59
  b:          49          46           9
  c1:      -1904        2144        -592
  c2:      -1904        2144        -592
  c3:      -1904        2144        -592
Vector cross product #2
  a:          83           9          83
  b:          89          31          38
  c1:      -2231        4233        1772
  c2:      -2231        4233        1772
  c3:      -2231        4233        1772
                    .
                    .
                    .
Vector cross product #15
  a:          86          89          56
  b:          73           9          91
  c1:       7595       -3738       -5723
  c2:       7595       -3738       -5723
  c3:       7595       -3738       -5723


Running benchmark function VecCrossProducts_bm() - please wait

Benchmark times save to file @Ch16_04_VecCrossProducts_bm_HELIUM.csv
```

Table 16-2 shows the benchmark timing measurements for example Ch16_04. Note that the use of non-temporal store instruction vmovntpd instead of vmovapd yielded accelerated performance on all three test computers.

Table 16-2. *Benchmark Timing Measurements (Microseconds) for Vector Cross Product Functions (2,000,000 Cross Products)*

Function	i5-11600K	i7-11700K	7700X
VecCrossProducts_cpp()	6444 (15)	8886 (164)	4340 (9)
VecCrossProducts_avx2()	4962 (14)	4573 (93)	3292 (8)
VecCrossProductsNT_avx2()	3661 (12)	3345 (78)	2342 (7)

It should be noted that x86-AVX non-temporal store instructions such as vmovntdq and vmovntp[d|s] require proper alignment of the target memory operand. It is also important to mention that non-temporal store instructions merely provide a hint to the processor that the executing function does not expect to reuse the specified data anytime soon. Depending on the underlying microarchitecture, the processor might ignore the hint and perform a normal store that utilizes processor cache memory. Another factor to keep in mind is that non-temporal store instructions do not always improve performance. For some calculations, slower performance is possible, which means that it's imperative to benchmark any code that utilizes non-temporal store instructions. Finally, care must be exercised when using non-temporal store instructions to reference the same memory locations from multiple threads, especially from threads that execute on different physical processors. You are encouraged to consult the AMD and Intel programming reference manuals listed in Appendix B for more information regarding this topic.

SIMD Text Processing

Most of the x86-AVX source code examples presented in this book have emphasized numerically oriented functions and algorithms. X86-AVX assembly language code can also be used to accelerate the performance of text string processing functions. The final example of this chapter demonstrates the use of AVX2 instructions to perform character replacement in a text string. Listing 16-5a shows the principal C++ code for example Ch16_05. In this listing, function ReplaceChar_cpp() utilizes a simple for-loop to replace each occurrence of character char_old in text string s with character char_new. It also counts the number of character replacements performed.

Listing 16-5a. Example Ch16_05 C++ Code

```
//-----------------------------------------------------------------------------
// Ch16_05.h
//-----------------------------------------------------------------------------

#pragma once
#include <cstddef>

// Ch16_05_fasm.asm, Ch16_05_fasm.s
extern "C" size_t ReplaceChar_avx2(char* s, char char_old, char char_new);

// Ch16_05_fcpp.cpp
extern size_t ReplaceChar_cpp(char* s, char char_old, char char_new);

// Ch16_05_bm.cpp
extern void ReplaceChar_bm(void);

// Ch16_05_test.cpp
extern void TestStringGenerator(void);

// Miscellaneous constants
constexpr char c_CharMin = 'A';          // min char for test strings
constexpr char c_CharMax = 'K';          // max char for test strings
constexpr char c_CharOld = 'D';          // character to replace
constexpr char c_CharNew = '-';          // replacement character

constexpr size_t c_MinLen = 0;           // min test string len - ReplaceChar()
constexpr size_t c_MaxLen = 67;          // max test string len - ReplaceChar()
constexpr size_t c_NumTestStrings = 500;     // num test strings - ReplaceChar()
constexpr size_t c_NumTestStringsBM = 50000;// num test strings - ReplaceChar_bm()
```

```
//------------------------------------------------------------------------------
// Ch16_05_fcpp.cpp
//------------------------------------------------------------------------------

#include <cstring>
#include "Ch16_05.h"

size_t ReplaceChar_cpp(char* s, char char_old, char char_new)
{
    size_t num_replaced = 0;

    for (size_t i = 0; s[i] != '\0'; i++)
    {
        if (s[i] == char_old)
        {
            s[i] = char_new;
            num_replaced++;
        }
    }

    return num_replaced;
}
```

Listing 16-5b shows the MASM code for function ReplaceChar_avx2(). This function performs the same text string character replacement operation as its C++ counterpart function.

Listing 16-5b. Example Ch16_05 MASM Code

```
;------------------------------------------------------------------------------
; Ch16_05_fasm.asm
;------------------------------------------------------------------------------


;------------------------------------------------------------------------------
; size_t ReplaceChar_avx2(char* s, char char_old, char char_new);
;------------------------------------------------------------------------------

            .code
ReplaceChar_avx2 proc
            xor r9,r9                       ;num_replaced = 0
            sub rcx,1                       ;adjust pointer for Loop1

; Use GP registers to replace characters until string pointer is 16-byte aligned
Loop1:      add rcx,1                       ;rcx = &s[i]
            test rcx,0fh                    ;is rcx 16-byte aligned?
            jz Aln16                        ;jump if yes

            mov r10b,[rcx]                  ;r10b = s[i]
            or r10b,r10b                    ;null char?
            jz Done                         ;jump if yes

            cmp r10b,dl                     ;s[i] = char_old?
            jne Loop1                       ;jump if no
```

```
        mov [rcx],r8b                       ;s[i] = char_new
        add r9,1                            ;num_replaced += 1
        jmp Loop1

; Use XMM registers to replace characters
Aln16:  sub rcx,16                          ;adjust for Loop2
        vpxor xmm0,xmm0,xmm0                ;xmm0 = packed null chars

        vmovd xmm1,edx
        vpbroadcastb xmm1,xmm1              ;xmm1 = packed char_old

        vmovd xmm2,r8d
        vpbroadcastb xmm2,xmm2              ;xmm2 = packed char_new

Loop2:  add rcx,16                          ;update pointer

        vmovdqa xmm3,xmmword ptr [rcx]      ;xmm3 = s[i:i+15]

        vpcmpeqb xmm4,xmm3,xmm0             ;test for null char
        vpmovmskb r10,xmm4
        or r10,r10                          ;null char found?
        jnz NullCh                          ;jump if yes

        vpcmpeqb xmm4,xmm3,xmm1             ;compare s[i:i+15] to char_old
        vpmovmskb r10,xmm4
        popcnt r10,r10                      ;r10 = num_matches
        jz Loop2                            ;jump if no char_old matches

        add r9,r10                          ;num_replaced += num_matches
        vpandn xmm5,xmm4,xmm3               ;remove char_old (keeps non-matches)
        vpand xmm3,xmm4,xmm2               ;insert char_new (zeros non-matches)
        vpor xmm3,xmm3,xmm5                ;merge for final result
        vmovdqa xmmword ptr [rcx],xmm3     ;save s[i:i+15]
        jmp Loop2

; Use GP registers to process residual characters
NullCh: sub rcx,1                           ;adjust for Loop3

Loop3:  add rcx,1                           ;rcx points to s[i]
        mov r10b,[rcx]                      ;r10b = s[i]
        or r10b,r10b                        ;null char?
        jz Done                             ;jump if yes

        cmp r10b,dl                         ;s[i] == char_old?
        jne Loop3                           ;jump if no

        mov [rcx],r8b                       ;s[i] = char_new
        add r9,1                            ;num_replaced += 1
        jmp Loop3                           ;repeat until done
```

```
Done:    mov rax,r9                         ;return num_replaced to caller
         ret
ReplaceChar_avx2 endp
         end
```

In Listing 16-5b, function ReplaceChar_avx2() utilizes three distinct for-loops to carry out the character replacement operation. The first for-loop, Loop1, uses general-purpose registers to perform character replacements. Each iteration of this for-loop begins with an add rcx,1 instruction that loads &s[i] into register RCX. The next instruction, test rcx,0fh, checks to see if &s[i] is aligned on a 16-byte boundary. If true, execution of the ensuing jz Aln16 instruction terminates Loop1. Otherwise, ReplaceChar_avx2() uses the instruction triplet mov r10b,[rcx], or r10b,r10b, and jz Done to detect the end-of-string null terminator. If s[i] == 0x00 is false, the cmp r10b,dl instruction compares s[i] and char_old. If s[i] == old_char is true, execution of the mov [rcx],r8b instruction overwrites s[i] with new_char, and the subsequent add r9,1 instruction calculates num_replaced += 1.

Once the text string pointer in RCX is aligned on a 16-byte boundary, function ReplaceChar_avx2() switches to using SIMD instructions to perform character replacements. Prior to the start of for-loop Loop2, ReplaceChar_avx2() constructs packed versions of 0x00 (XMM0), char_old (XMM1), and char_new (XMM2). Near the top of Loop2 is a vmovdqa xmm3,xmmword ptr [rcx] instruction that loads text string fragment s[i:i+15] into register XMM3. The next instruction, vpcmpeqb xmm4,xmm3,xmm0, compares each character in XMM3 against 0x00. Recall that the vpcmpeqb sets each destination operand byte element to 0xFF if the corresponding source operand byte elements match; otherwise, the destination operand byte is set to 0x00. The vpmovmskb r10,xmm4 instruction that follows loads a mask into register R10 using the most significant bit of each byte element in XMM4. The instruction pair that follows, or r10,r10 and jnz NullCh, terminates Loop2 if one of the characters in s[i:i+15] is equal to 0x00.

The next code block in ReplaceChar_avx2() utilizes the instruction vpcmpeqb xmm4,xmm3,xmm1 to compare each character in XMM3 against char_old. The ensuing instruction triplet vpmovmskb r10,xmm4, popcnt r10,r10, and jz Loop2 bypasses the remaining code in Loop2 if no char_old matches are found. If a char_old match is found, the add r9,r10 instruction calculates num_replaced += num_matches. The next three instructions, vpandn xmm5,xmm4,xmm3 (Logical AND NOT), vpand xmm3,xmm4,xmm2, and vpor xmm3,xmm3,xmm5, replace all occurrences of char_old in XMM3 with char_new. Note that the vpandn xmm5,xmm4,xmm3 instruction calculates xmm5 = ~xmm4 & xmm3. The ensuing vmovdqa [rdi],xmm3 instruction saves the updated text string fragment to s[i:i+15].

The final for-loop in ReplaceChar_avx2(), Loop3, employs general-purpose registers to handle any residual character replacements in text string s. The mov rax,r9 instruction that precedes the ret instruction copies return value num_replaced into register RAX.

The NASM implementation of ReplaceChar_avx2() closely resembles the MASM version except for different argument value registers. Here are the condensed results for source code example Ch16_05:

```
----- Results for Ch16_05 -----

----- Test case #0 -----
s1 before:    HDAFDKHGDKKFBJEFGIFJBBCHHFCBEGABDCDBEIAFIEIAGAHCGAHHIHJFD
s1 after:     H-AF-KHG-KKFBJEFGIFJBBCHHFCBEGAB-C-BEIAFIEIAGAHCGAHHIHJF-
num_replaced1: 6
s2 before:    HDAFDKHGDKKFBJEFGIFJBBCHHFCBEGABDCDBEIAFIEIAGAHCGAHHIHJFD
s2 after:     H-AF-KHG-KKFBJEFGIFJBBCHHFCBEGAB-C-BEIAFIEIAGAHCGAHHIHJF-
num_replaced2: 6
```

```
----- Test case #1 -----
s1 before:      EDJGJEAJHHA
s1 after:       E-JGJEAJHHA
num_replaced1: 1
s2 before:      EDJGJEAJHHA
s2 after:       E-JGJEAJHHA
num_replaced2: 1

----- Test case #2 -----
s1 before:      EHJIAKFJBKJABKIBJKBBCCKHHCDEEJBBC
s1 after:       EHJIAKFJBKJABKIBJKBBCCKHHC-EEJBBC
num_replaced1: 1
s2 before:      EHJIAKFJBKJABKIBJKBBCCKHHCDEEJBBC
s2 after:       EHJIAKFJBKJABKIBJKBBCCKHHC-EEJBBC
num_replaced2: 1

----- Test case #3 -----
s1 before:      HCEJIHJBKDHGAADCBHDDEEKAHABCCAABHFCIGHHJBHJFCDBBAHAFAFDGIFDJJ
s1 after:       HCEJIHJBK-HGAA-CBH--EEKAHABCCAABHFCIGHHJBHJFC-BBAHAFAF-GIF-JJ
num_replaced1: 7
s2 before:      HCEJIHJBKDHGAADCBHDDEEKAHABCCAABHFCIGHHJBHJFCDBBAHAFAFDGIFDJJ
s2 after:       HCEJIHJBK-HGAA-CBH--EEKAHABCCAABHFCIGHHJBHJFC-BBAHAFAF-GIF-JJ
num_replaced2: 7

                        .
                        .
                        .

----- Test case #10 -----
s1 before:      EEA
s1 after:       EEA
num_replaced1: 0
s2 before:      EEA
s2 after:       EEA
num_replaced2: 0
```

Figure 16-1 shows benchmark timing measurements for ReplaceChar_cpp() and ReplaceChar_avx2() using 50,000 test strings for each length group. The benchmark timing measurements reveal that for shorter string lengths, ReplaceChar_cpp() outperforms ReplaceChar_avx2(). The opposite becomes true when the string length exceeds 23–27 bytes. The timing measurements shown in Figure 16-1 were obtained using the i5-11600K test computer; similar results were achieved using the i7-11700K and 7700X test computers.

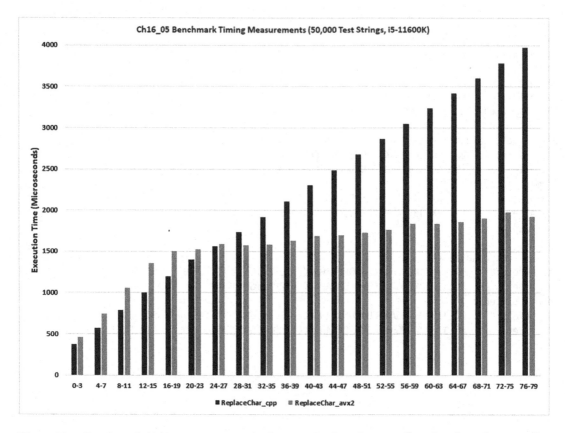

Figure 16-1. *Benchmark timing measurements for functions* ReplaceChar_cpp() *and* ReplaceChar_avx2()

Summary

Here are the key learning points for Chapter 16:

- An application program should always use the cpuid instruction to verify processor support for specific x86 instruction set extensions. This is extremely important for software compatibility with current and future processors from both AMD and Intel.

- An assembly language function can use a vmovntdq instruction instead of vmovdqa to perform a non-temporal packed integer memory store.

- An assembly language function can use the vmovntp[d|s] instruction instead of vmovap[d|s] to perform a non-temporal packed floating-point memory store.

- You should always benchmark any function that utilizes a non-temporal store instruction to confirm any expected performance gains.

- For some SIMD algorithms, organizing the data using a structure of arrays construct instead of an array of structures construct often improves performance. However, benchmarking should be performed to verify any projected performance improvements.

CHAPTER 17

■ ■ ■

Assembly Language Optimization and Development Guidelines

Congratulations if you have made it this far. I hope that your x86-64 assembly language journey has been informative and worthwhile. In this final chapter, you'll learn some practical techniques that can boost the performance of your x86-64 assembly language code. You'll also encounter a few helpful guidelines related to assembly language software development and workflow.

Assembly Language Optimization Guidelines

This section discusses guidelines and techniques that you can exploit to improve the performance of your x86-64 assembly language code. The guidelines and techniques covered in this section are suitable for use in code that targets processors based on microarchitectures from both AMD and Intel. A processor's microarchitecture is characterized by the organization and operation of its internal hardware components including instruction pipelines, decoders, schedulers, execution units, data buses, and memory caches. Contemporary AMD processor microarchitectures include Zen, Zen+, and Zen2 (Family 17h) along with Zen 3, Zen 3+, and Zen 4 (Family 19h). Modern Intel processor microarchitectures include Cypress Cove, Golden Cove, and Raptor Cove. Microarchitectures are often optimized for processors that target specific use cases such as notebook, desktop, workstation, and server computers.

It is important to recognize that different processor microarchitectures exhibit different performance characteristics. This means that it's possible for a recommended technique or a specific sequence of instructions to improve performance on one microarchitecture but not yield any performance gains on another. You should always benchmark your x86-64 assembly language code to confirm any performance gains. If you have the resources, try benchmarking your code using a variety of processors from both AMD and Intel.

It is also important to keep in mind that none of the recommendations mentioned in this chapter will ameliorate the performance of an inappropriate or poorly designed algorithm. The design of an algorithm is often the most critical component of its ultimate performance.

The content of this section is not intended to be a comprehensive examination of x86-64 assembly language optimization topics. Such an undertaking would minimally require several lengthy chapters or conceivably an entire book. You are encouraged to consult the AMD and Intel programming reference manuals listed in Appendix B for more information regarding the development of optimized x86-64 assembly language code.

© Daniel Kusswurm 2023
D. Kusswurm, *Modern X86 Assembly Language Programming*,
https://doi.org/10.1007/978-1-4842-9603-5_17

The remainder of this section presents x86-64 assembly language optimization guidelines and techniques. They are organized into the following five categories:

- Basic Techniques

- Floating-Point Arithmetic

- Branch Instructions

- Data Alignment

- SIMD Techniques

All optimization guidelines and techniques must be applied in a prudent manner. For example, it rarely makes sense to add extra mov, push, pop, or other instructions to a function just to use a recommended instruction form only once.

Basic Techniques

The following coding techniques are frequently employed to improve the performance of x86-64 assembly language code:

- Use an xor or sub instruction to zero a register instead of a mov instruction. For example, use xor r10,r10 or sub r10,r10 instead of mov r10,0. The mov instruction can be used when it's necessary to avoid modifying the status flags in RFLAGS.

- To reduce code size, use 32-bit forms of the xor or sub instructions to zero registers RAX, RBX, RCX, RDX, RSI, RDI, and RBP (e.g., use xor eax,eax instead of xor rax,rax). The machine encodings of the 32-bit forms are shorter.

- Use 32-bit instead of 64-bit instruction forms and general-purpose registers when possible. For example, if the maximum number of for-loop iterations does not exceed the range limits of a 32-bit integer, use a 32-bit instead of a 64-bit general-purpose register for the loop counter.

- When appropriate, use 32-bit instruction forms to load 64-bit registers with positive constants. For example, the instructions mov eax,16 and mov r8d,42 effectively set RAX to 16 and R8 to 42.

- When possible, use a test instruction instead of a cmp instruction. Also, use test instead of an and instruction when the bitwise logical result is not needed.

- Use a test instruction instead of a cmp instruction to carry out a simple less than, equal to, or greater than zero check (e.g., use test eax,eax instead of cmp eax,0).

- Avoid memory-immediate forms of the cmp and test instructions (e.g., cmp [RAX],42, test [RSP],01h, etc.). However, don't add extra instructions to eschew the memory-immediate form.

- Use the two- or three-operand form of the imul instruction to multiply two signed integers when the full-width product is not needed. For example, use imul rax,rcx when a 64-bit truncated product is sufficient instead of imul rcx, which returns a 128-bit product in RDX:RAX. This guideline also applies to 32-bit signed integer multiplication (e.g., imul eax,ecx instead of imul ecx).

- Use the two-operand form of the imul instruction instead of mul to perform unsigned integer multiplication when the full-width product is not needed.

- Minimize the use of the `inc` and `dec` instructions either before or after other instructions that modify the status flags in RFLAGS. Instead, use an `add` or `sub` instruction with an immediate value of one (e.g., use `add eax,1` instead of `inc eax`).

- In performance-critical for-loops, avoid use of a `lea` instruction that contains three effective address components (e.g., `lea rax,[rbx+rcx*8+Disp]`). The three-component form of the `lea` instruction can be used to perform one-time address loads prior to the start of a performance-critical for-loop.

- When possible, use the `lea` instruction to carry out simple integer arithmetic using multiple operands. For example, use `lea rax,[rbx+rcx*8]` to load RBX + RCX * 8 into register RAX.

- Exploit the `lea` instruction to multiply an unsigned integer by 3. For example, the `lea rax,[rcx+rcx*2]` calculates RAX = RCX * 3. Similarly, use the `lea rax,[rcx+rcx*4]` and `lea rax,[rcx+rcx*8]` instructions to calculate RAX = RCX * 5 and RAX = RCX * 9, respectively.

- Load memory values that are needed for multiple calculations into a register. If a memory value is needed only for a single calculation, use the register-memory instruction form (e.g., `add eax,[rcx]`, `cmp rax,[rdx]`, `vpaddd xmm0, xmm1,[r8]`, `vmulps ymm0,ymm1,[r9]`, etc.).

- Avoid declaring data values inside a code section. In situations where it's necessary to do this (e.g., when defining a read-only jump table), position the data after a `jmp` or `ret` instruction. Declaring data values in a code section may cause the processor to unnecessarily consume limited instruction cache memory. Positioning jump table data after a `jmp` or `ret` instruction prevents the jump table's data bytes from being accidentally executed as instructions.

- Arrange code in performance-critical for-loops, especially ones that utilize x86-AVX SIMD instructions, to preclude loop-carried data dependencies.

- Avoid using instructions that require an operand-size prefix to load a 16-bit register since these instructions take longer to decode. Use an equivalent 32-bit register instead. For example, use `mov edx,42` instead of `mov dx,42`.

- Create and use macros for recurrent arithmetic or other calculations (e.g., SIMD reductions) to avoid the run-time overhead of a function call.

- Use the `vmov[d|q]` instruction to spill a general-purpose register to an unused volatile XMM register. Use local stack space when a register (general-purpose or SIMD) spill to memory is required. (A register spill preserves the current value in a register so that the same register can be used for other calculations.)

Floating-Point Arithmetic

The following coding techniques can be employed to improve the performance of x86-64 assembly language code that performs floating-point operations. These guidelines apply to both scalar and packed floating-point calculations.

- Use x86-AVX instructions and the XMM register set to perform scalar floating-point arithmetic. Do not use the legacy x87 FPU to perform these types of calculations.

- When possible, use single-precision values instead of double-precision floating-point.

- Arrange floating-point instruction sequences to minimize data dependencies. Exploit multiple destination registers to save intermediate results.

- Partially unroll performance-critical for-loops that carry out arithmetic operations, especially for-loops that contain data-dependent sequences of floating-point addition, multiplication, FMA, or other arithmetic operations.

- Consider fully unrolling small for-loops when the iteration count is a known assembly-time constant.

- Avoid using floating-point denormal constants.

- When possible, prevent floating-point underflows and denormal values from occurring during arithmetic calculations.

- If excessive arithmetic underflows are expected, consider enabling the flush-to-zero (MXCSR.FTZ) and denormals-are-zero (MXCSR.DAZ) modes.

Branch Instructions

Assembly language branch instructions such as jmp, call, and ret are potentially time-consuming operations to perform since they can affect the contents of the processor's front-end pipelines and internal caches. The conditional jump instruction jcc is also a performance concern given its frequency of use. The following optimization techniques can be employed to minimize the adverse performance effects of branch instructions:

- Organize code to minimize the number of possible branch instructions.

- Partially unroll simple for-loops to reduce the number of executed conditional jump instructions. Avoid excessive loop unrolling since this may result in slower executing code.

- Eliminate unpredictable data-dependent branches using the setcc or cmovcc instructions.

- In performance-critical for-loops, align the target labels of conditional jump instructions (e.g., jz, jnz, jb, jbe, etc.) on a 16-byte boundary. To prevent large increases in code size, restrict the use of this technique to conditional jump instructions that regulate the number of times a for-loop executes.

- Move conditional code that is unlikely to execute (e.g., error handling code) to another program section or memory page.

Branch Prediction Unit

All modern x86 processors include a hardware component called the branch prediction unit (BPU). This component helps select the next set of instructions to execute by predicting which branch targets are most likely to execute based on recent code execution patterns. A branch target is simply the destination operand of a transfer control instruction such as jcc, jmp, call, or ret. The BPU enables a processor core to speculatively execute the micro-ops of other instructions before the outcome of a branch decision is known.

The BPU employs both static and dynamic techniques to predict the target of a conditional jump instruction. Incorrect branch predictions can be minimized if blocks of code containing conditional jump instructions are arranged such that they're consistent with the BPU's static prediction algorithm:

- Use forward conditional jumps when the fall-through code is more likely to execute.

- Use backward conditional jumps when the fall-through code is less likely to execute.

The forward conditional jump approach is frequently used in code blocks that perform argument checking. The backward conditional jump technique is often employed at the bottom of a calculating code block following a counter update or other for-loop terminating test decision. Listing 17-1 contains a short assembly language function that exemplifies these practices.

Listing 17-1. Example Ch17_01 MASM Code

```
;-------------------------------------------------------------------------
; Ch17_01_fasm.asm
;-------------------------------------------------------------------------


;-------------------------------------------------------------------------
; bool CalcResult_avx(double* y, const double* x, size_t n);
;-------------------------------------------------------------------------


NSE        equ        8                       ;num_simd_elements


           .const
F64_2p0    real8 2.0


           .code
CalcResult_avx proc

; Forward conditional jumps are used in this code block since
; the fall-through cases are more likely to occur
           test r8,r8
           jz Error                           ;jump if n == 0
           test r8,07h
           jnz Error                          ;jump if (n % NSE) != 0
           test rcx,1fh
           jnz Error                          ;jump if y not 32-byte aligned
           test rdx,1fh
           jnz Error                          ;jump if x not 32-byte aligned

; Initialize
           mov rax,-NSE*8                      ;rax = common array offset
           vbroadcastsd ymm5,[F64_2p0]        ;packed 2.0

; Simple array processing loop
           align 16
Loop1:     add rax,NSE*8                       ;update offset for x[] and y[]

           vmovapd ymm0,ymmword ptr [rdx+rax]  ;load x[i:i+3]
           vdivpd ymm1,ymm0,ymm5
           vsqrtpd ymm2,ymm1
           vmovapd ymmword ptr [rcx+rax],ymm2  ;save y[i:i+3]
```

```
        vmovapd ymm0,ymmword ptr [rdx+rax+32]    ;load x[i+4:i+7]
        vdivpd ymm1,ymm0,ymm5
        vsqrtpd ymm2,ymm1
        vmovapd ymmword ptr [rcx+rax+32],ymm2    ;save y[i+4:i+7]

; A backward conditional jump is used in this code block since
; the fall-through case is less likely to occur
        sub r8,NSE
        jnz Loop1

        mov eax,1                                ;set success return code
        vzeroupper
        ret

; Error handling code that's unlikely to execute
Error:  xor eax,eax                              ;set error return code
        ret
CalcResult_avx endp
        end
```

Data Alignment

It's been mentioned multiple times in this book, but the importance of using properly aligned data cannot be overemphasized. Functions that reference improperly aligned data values in memory are likely to trigger the processor into performing additional memory cycles, which can adversely affect overall performance. The following data alignment practices should be considered universal truths and always observed:

- Align multibyte integer and scalar floating-point values on their proper boundaries.

- Align 128-, 256-, and 512-bit wide packed integer and floating-point values on their proper boundaries.

- Exploit the C++ alignas specifier to ensure proper alignment of a data structure that contains packed integer or floating-point values.

- Pad assembly language data structures to ensure that each member is properly aligned.

- Arrange the members of a data structure to avoid cache line splits. A cache line split occurs when a structure member crosses a cache line (64-byte) boundary.

- Use the aligned memory allocation library functions _aligned_malloc() (Visual C++) or aligned_alloc() (GNU C++) to dynamically allocate arrays aligned on a specific boundary.

- Evaluate the performance effects of different data layouts such as a structure of arrays vs. an array of structures.

SIMD Techniques

The following techniques should be observed, when appropriate, by any function that performs SIMD computations using AVX, AVX2, or AVX-512 instructions:

- Do not code assembly language functions that intermix x86-AVX and x86-SSE instructions.

- Arrange sequences of x86-AVX assembly language instructions to reduce SIMD register dependencies.

- Load multiple-use variables or constants into a SIMD register.

- Use broadcast instructions to load an integer or floating-point constant into the elements of a SIMD register.

- On systems that support AVX-512, exploit the extra SIMD registers to reduce or eliminate data dependencies and register spills.

- Use vpxor (e.g., vpxor xmm0,xmm0,xmm0) to zero the integer elements of an x86-AVX SIMD register.

- Use vxorp[d|s] (e.g., vxorps ymm0,ymm0,ymm0) to zero the floating-point elements of an x86-AVX SIMD register.

- Use vcmpeq[b|w|d|q] (e.g., vcmpeqb xmm0,xmm0,xmm0) to load all ones into an x86-AVX SIMD register.

- Use x86-AVX masking and Boolean operations to implement data-dependent calculations (e.g., a SIMD ternary operation).

- Perform packed data loads and stores using the aligned move instructions (e.g., vmovdqa, vmovap[d|s], etc.).

- Process SIMD arrays using small data blocks to maximize reuse of resident cache data.

- Use the vzeroupper instruction when required to avoid potential x86-AVX to x86-SSE state transition penalties.

- Avoid the use of x86-AVX gather and scatter instructions with known array indices (i.e., indices that can be defined as assembly-time constants). Instead, use standard memory load and store instructions.

- Use x86-AVX gather instructions well ahead of when the data is needed.

- When possible, use the doubleword forms of the gather and scatter instructions instead of the quadword forms (e.g., use vgatherdp[d|s] instead of vgatherqp[d|s]).

- Consider the use of non-temporal load (e.g., vmovntdq) and store instructions (e.g., vmovntdqa, vmovntp[d|s], etc.) to minimize cache pollution. Always perform function benchmarking to verify the performance gains of any non-temporal instruction usage.

Assembly Language Development Guidelines

The discussions and source code examples imparted in this book were designed to help you understand x86-64 assembly language programming and the computational capabilities of x86-AVX. At this juncture, you may be asking yourself when it is appropriate to explicitly code a function using assembly language. As mentioned in the Introduction, software development using x86-64 assembly language to accelerate the performance of a computationally intense algorithm or function should be regarded as a specialized programming tool that must be sagaciously exploited. Assembly language coding typically requires extra effort, even for software developers who are well versed with the intricacies of the x86-64 instruction set and SIMD programming techniques. Explicit x86-64 assembly language coding is often a trade-off between development effort, performance gains, and future maintainability.

For the most part, the development of assembly language code is no different than other programming languages. When creating x86-64 assembly language code, you still need to perform normal software design, coding, and test activities. However, x86-64 assembly language coding typically requires additional testing and benchmarking to substantiate any performance gains.

The remainder of this section outlines a simple workflow for x86-64 assembly language software development. You are encouraged to scrutinize the suggested workflow and adapt it for a specific project or development environment. Here are the workflow steps:

- Identify Functions for x86-64 Assembly Language Coding
- Select Target x86-AVX Instruction Set
- Establish Benchmark Timing Objectives
- Code x86-64 Assembly Language Functions
- Benchmark x86-64 Assembly Language Code
- Optimize x86-64 Assembly Language Code
- Repeat Benchmarking and Optimization Steps

Identify Functions for x86-64 Assembly Language Coding

The first step of assembly language software development is to identify existing bottleneck functions that may benefit from x86-64 assembly language coding. Functions most likely to benefit from x86-64 assembly language coding are those that can exploit the x86-AVX instruction set to carry out calculations using large arrays or matrices. For example, coding an x86-AVX image processing function that enables the end user to see the resultant image appreciably sooner is something worth considering. If you are creating a new calculating algorithm or function, code a C++ variant first. There are two reasons for this. First, debugging a C++ function is generally easier than debugging an assembly language function. Second, once the C++ code is working, it can be used to verify the correctness of the assembly language code. It can also be used for benchmarking purposes.

Select Target x86-AVX Instruction Set

The next step is to determine which x86-AVX instruction set extension to use. What to select here depends mostly on your target users. If you are developing a mainstream application for Windows or Linux, you might want to select AVX or AVX2. If you are developing an application that targets processors in recently marketed workstations or servers, you could select AVX2 or AVX-512. Always verify that the host processor supports any required x86 instruction set extensions. For example, if your assembly language code utilizes AVX2 instructions, you should test for the presence of this instruction set extension during application startup, possibly inside function `main()`. It is also a good idea to include a test for AVX2 or any other required x86 instruction set extensions during program installation.

Establish Benchmark Timing Objectives

Following selection of the target x86-AVX instruction set, try to establish some benchmark timing objectives for your explicitly coded assembly language functions. If possible, use unambiguous and quantifiable objectives. For example, function `Foo_avx2()` must complete its calculations within x milliseconds (useful for functions with real-time constraints) or be y percent faster than baseline function `Foo_cpp()`.

Code x86-64 Assembly Language Functions

Once you have established your benchmark timing objectives, you can code your x86-64 assembly language functions. To minimize future maintenance activities, you may want to use a common library for a project's x86-64 assembly language coded functions. Doing this also simplifies code reuse on future projects.

Benchmark x86-64 Assembly Language Code

The next workflow step is to perform benchmark timing measurements of an x86-64 assembly language function and its counterpart C++ function. There are several ways of doing this. One method is to employ a simple software stopwatch like the C++ class `BmThreadTimer` that was used in many of this book's source code examples. The advantage of this approach is that it does not require any special drivers, compiler settings, or third-party tools to carry out the requisite timing measurements. For more precise timing measurements and/or insights into potential software bottlenecks, one of the AMD or Intel processor profiling tools listed in Appendix B may be helpful.

Optimize x86-64 Assembly Language Code

During this workflow phase, experiment with different x86-AVX assembly language instructions or different sequences of instructions. The reason for this is that different x86-AVX instructions or sequences of x86-AVX instructions sometimes yield different performance results, especially on different processor microarchitectures. You should also exploit the optimization techniques discussed earlier in this chapter. When performing x86-AVX assembly language function optimization, focus on the code blocks inside performance-critical for-loops. Optimizing a code block that performs a one-time data initialization or a single transformation operation is unlikely to result in a noticeable increase in performance.

Repeat Benchmarking and Optimization Steps

The last phase of the workflow is to repeat the benchmarking and optimization steps until you have achieved your benchmark timing objective or continued optimization attempts fail to yield any meaningful performance gains.

Summary

Here are the key learning points for Chapter 17:

- X86-64 assembly language programming is often a trade-off between development effort, performance gains, and future maintainability.

- Application of this chapter's assembly language optimization guidelines and techniques often yields in improved performance. However, it is not uncommon to encounter coding situations where a recommended guideline or technique is not the best approach.

- When developing assembly language code, don't spend an excessive amount of time trying to achieve maximum performance. Instead, focus on performance gains that are relatively easy to attain (e.g., implementing an algorithm using SIMD instead of scalar arithmetic).

- Always compare benchmark timing measurements of functions coded using x86-64 assembly language vs. baseline functions using C++ or another language. Always verify any expected performance gains.

- To achieve optimal performance for a specific algorithm or function, it may be necessary to code and benchmark multiple versions that utilize different sequences of x86-64 or x86-AVX instructions.

- None of the optimization guidelines and techniques presented in this chapter will ameliorate an inappropriate or poorly designed algorithm.

APPENDIX A

■ ■ ■

Source Code and Development Tools

Appendix A explains how to download and set up the source code. It also describes how to build and execute the source code examples on both Windows and Linux.

Source Code Download and Setup

Perform the following steps to download and set up the source code:

1. Create a source code master folder. Use `C:\Users\<UserName>\Documents\ModX86Asm3e` (Windows) or `~/Documents/ModX86Asm3e` (Linux). If you prefer, you can create the master folder at a different location. Note that if you do this, you'll also need to modify some subsequent instructions accordingly.

2. Using your favorite browser, navigate to the following GitHub website: `https://github.com/Apress/modern-x86-assembly-language-programming-3e`.

3. Click the **Code** button and select **Download ZIP**.

4. Save the ZIP file in the master folder that you created in Step 1.

5. Open a File Manager window and navigate to the master folder.

6. Right-click the downloaded ZIP file and select **Extract All...** (Windows) or **Extract Here** (Linux).

7. Windows Only: In the dialog box that appears, edit the folder name so that it matches the master folder name that was created in Step 1. Click **Extract**.

8. Open the master folder and rename subfolder `modern-x86-assembly-language-programming-3e-master` to Code.

9. Verify that subfolder Code matches the folder tree shown in Figure A-1. Note that subfolder Code may also contain several miscellaneous files besides the folders shown in Figure A-1.

© Daniel Kusswurm 2023
D. Kusswurm, *Modern X86 Assembly Language Programming*,
https://doi.org/10.1007/978-1-4842-9603-5

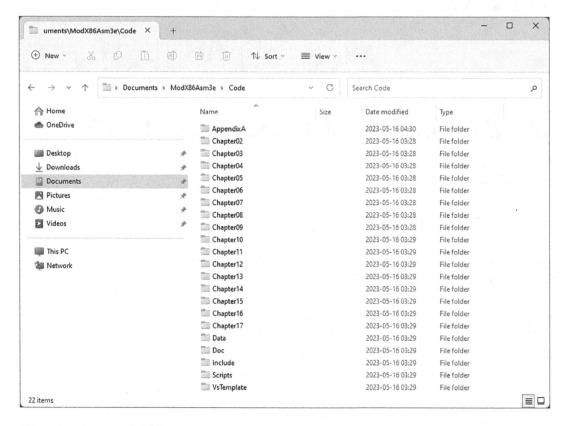

Figure A-1. *Source code folder tree*

Some source code examples use relative pathname strings (e.g., `../../Data/TestImageA.png`) to specify a test image file. You may need to change these pathname strings if you use a folder structure that differs from the default one created in this section.

Source Code Development Tools

The following section discusses the development tools that were used to create the source code examples. The content is partitioned into two subsections. The first subsection covers Windows, Visual Studio, and MASM. The second subsection details Linux, the GNU toolchain, and NASM. You can read one or both subsections depending on your interests.

Windows Development Tools

In this section, you'll learn how to use Microsoft's Visual Studio development IDE to run the source code examples. You'll also learn how to create a simple Visual Studio C++ project. The source code examples in this book were created using Visual Studio Professional 2022, but you can use any 2022 edition including the free Community edition. For more information regarding Visual Studio editions and usage, visit `https://visualstudio.microsoft.com/`.

Visual Studio uses logical entities called solutions and projects to help simplify application development. A solution is a collection of one or more projects that are used to build an application. A project is a container object that organizes an application's files. A Visual Studio project is usually created for each buildable component of an application (e.g., executable file, dynamic-linked library, static library, etc.).

A standard Visual Studio C++ project includes two solution configurations named Debug and Release. As implied by their names, these configurations support separate builds for initial development and final release. A standard Visual Studio C++ project also incorporates two solution platforms. The default solution platforms are named Win32 and x64. These solution platforms contain the necessary settings to build 32-bit and 64-bit executables, respectively. The Visual Studio solution and project files for this book's source code examples include only the x64 platform.

Running a Source Code Example

Perform the following steps to execute any of the book's source code examples:

1. Using File Explorer, double-click the chapter's Visual Studio solution (.sln) file. The .sln file for each chapter is in the chapter subfolder (e.g., C:\Users\<UserName>\Documents\Modx86Asm3e\Code\Chapter02).

2. Select menu item Build ➤ Configuration Manager. In the Configuration Manager dialog box, set Active Solution Configuration to **Release**. Then set Active Solution Platform to **x64**. Note that these options may already be selected.

3. If necessary, select menu item View ➤ Solution Explorer to open the Solution Explorer window.

4. In the Solution Explorer window, right-click a project to run (e.g., Ch02_01) and choose **Set as Startup Project**.

5. Select menu item Debug ➤ Start Without Debugging to run the program.

Creating a Visual Studio C++ Project

In this section, you'll learn how to create a simple Visual Studio project that includes both C++ and assembly language source code files. The ensuing paragraphs describe the same basic procedure that was used to create this book's source code examples and includes the following stages:

- Create a C++ project

- Enable MASM support

- Add an assembly language file

- Set project properties

- Edit the source code

- Build and run the project

You may need to adapt some of the subsequent instructions depending on your configuration of Visual Studio.

Create a C++ Project

Use the following steps to create a Visual Studio C++ solution and project:

1. Start Visual Studio.

2. Select File ➤ New ➤ Project.

3. In the Create a new project dialog box, adjust the three dropdown box selections (located just below the Search for templates textbox) to match those in Figure A-2. Then select **Console App** as shown in Figure A-2. Click **Next**.

4. In the Configure your new project dialog box, enter Example1 in the Project name text box.

5. Enter a location folder for the project in the Location text box or leave it unchanged to use the default location.

6. In the Solution name text box, enter TestSolution.

7. Verify that the Configure your new project dialog box matches Figure A-3 (the Location folder text can be different). Click **Create**.

8. Select Build ➤ Configuration Manager. In the Configuration Manager dialog box, choose <**Edit...**> under Active Solution Platforms (Figure A-4).

9. In the Edit Solution Platforms dialog box, select **x86** (Figure A-5). Click **Remove**.

10. Click **Close** to close the Edit Solution Platforms dialog box. Click **Close** to close the Configuration Manager dialog box.

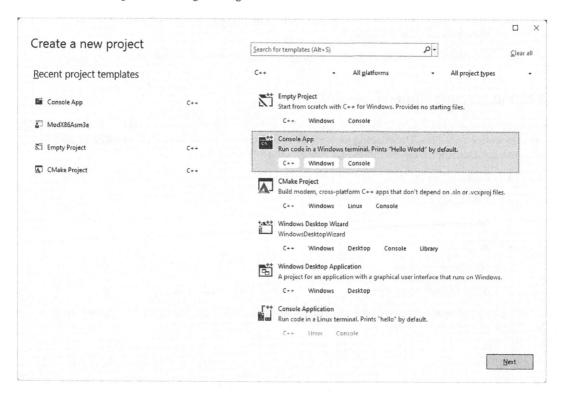

Figure A-2. *Create a new project dialog box*

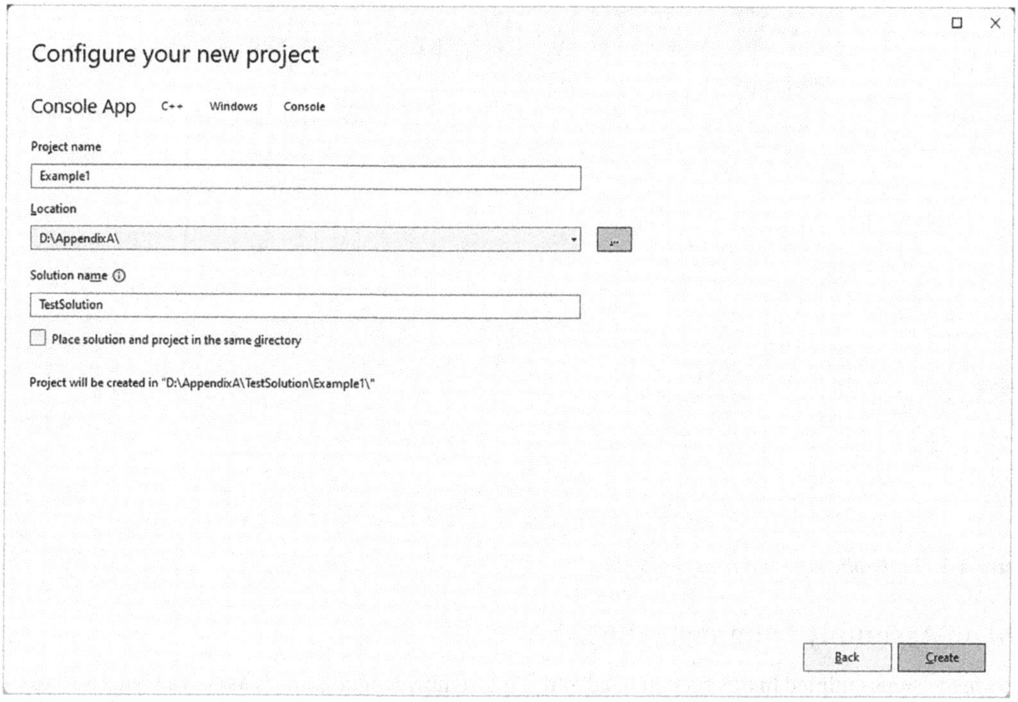

Figure A-3. *Configure your new project dialog box*

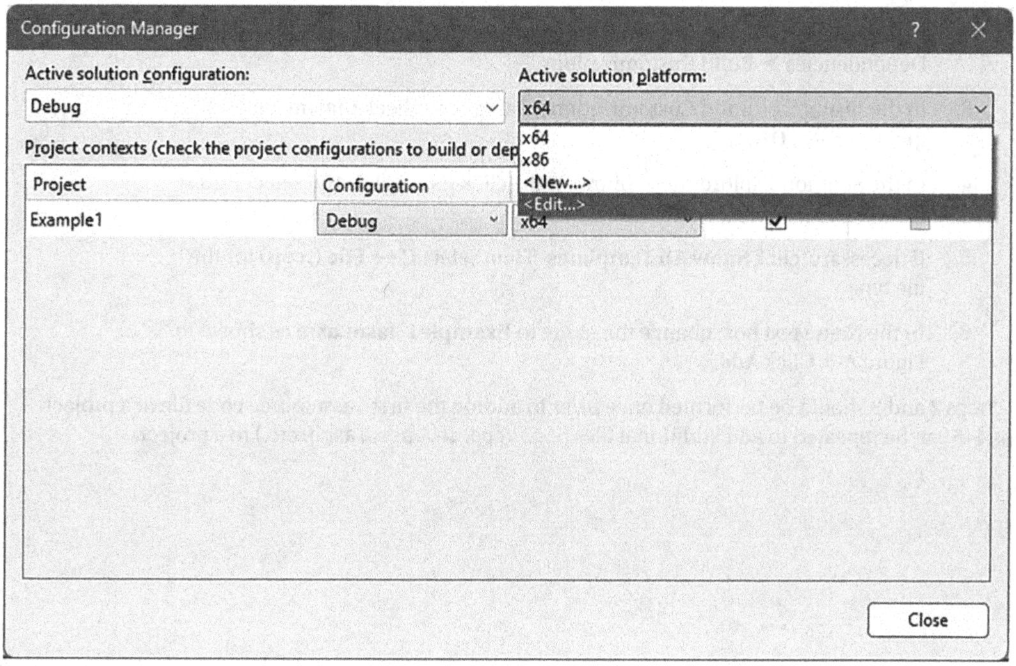

Figure A-4. *Configuration Manager dialog box*

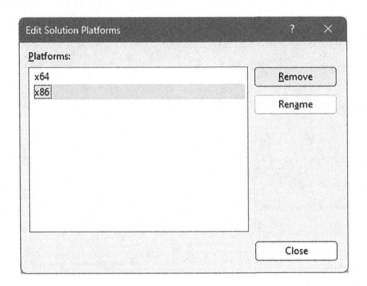

Figure A-5. Edit Solution Platforms dialog box

Add an Assembly Language File

Perform the steps outlined in this section to add an x86 assembly language file (.asm) to a Visual Studio C++ project:

1. Select View ➤ Solution Explorer to open the Solution Explorer tree control (if necessary).

2. In the Solution Explorer tree control, right-click **Example1** and select Build Dependencies ➤ Build Customizations.

3. In the Visual C++ Build Customizations dialog box, check **masm(.targets, .props)**. Click **OK**.

4. In the Solution Explorer tree control, right-click **Example1** and select Add ➤ New Item.

5. If necessary, click **Show All Templates**. Then select **C++ File (.cpp)** for the file type.

6. In the Name text box, change the name to **Example1_fasm.asm** as shown in Figure A-6. Click **Add**.

Steps 2 and 3 should be performed once *prior* to adding the first .asm source code file to a project. Steps 4–6 can be repeated to add additional files (e.g., .cpp, .h, .asm, .asmh, etc.) to a project.

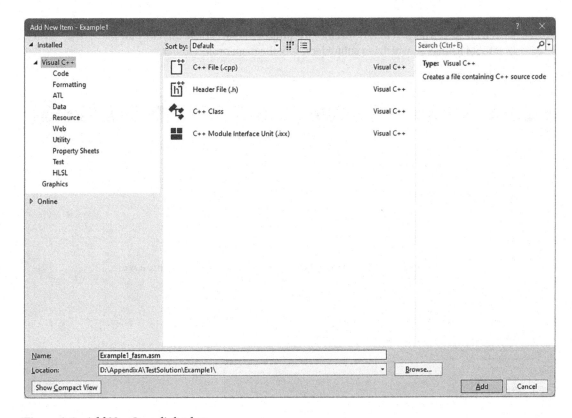

Figure A-6. *Add New Item dialog box*

Set Project Properties

Perform the steps in this section to set the project's properties. Note that the steps that enable listing files (Steps 4–6) are optional.

1. In the Solution Explorer tree control, right-click **Example1** and select **Properties**.

2. In the Property Pages dialog box, change the Configuration setting to **All Configurations** and the Platform setting to **All Platforms**. Note that one or both options may already be set.

3. Select Configuration Properties ➤ C/C++ ➤ Code Generation. Change the setting Enable Enhanced Instruction Set to **Advanced Vector Extensions (/arch:AVX)** (Figure A-7). You can also select **/arch:AVX2** or **/arch:AVX512**.

4. Select Configuration Properties ➤ C/C++ ➤ Output Files. Change the setting Assembler Output to **Assembly Machine and Source Code (/FAcs)** (Figure A-8).

5. Select Configuration Properties ➤ Microsoft Macro Assembler ➤ Listing File (you may need to adjust the vertical scroll bar downward to see this option). Change the setting Enable Assembly Generated Code Listing to **Yes (/Sg)** (Figure A-9).

6. Change the Assembled Code Listing File text field to **$(IntDir)\%(filename).lst** (Figure A-9). This macro text specifies the project's intermediate directory for the MASM listing file, which is a subfolder under the main project folder.

7. Click **OK**.

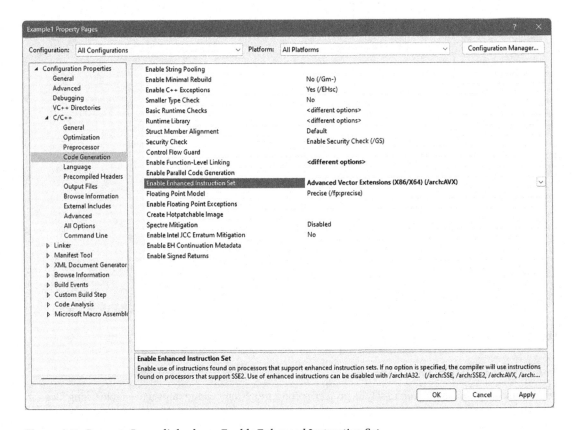

Figure A-7. *Property Pages dialog box – Enable Enhanced Instruction Set*

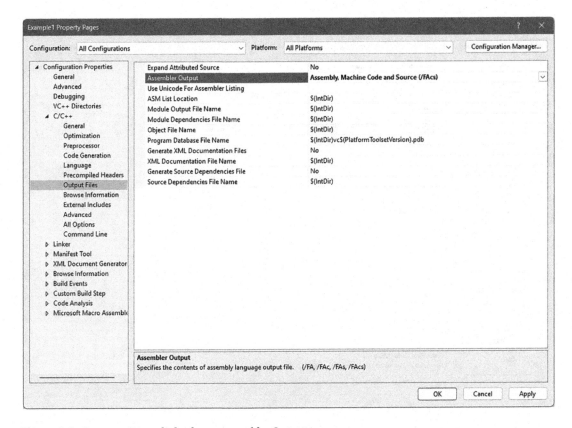

Figure A-8. *Property Pages dialog box – Assembler Output*

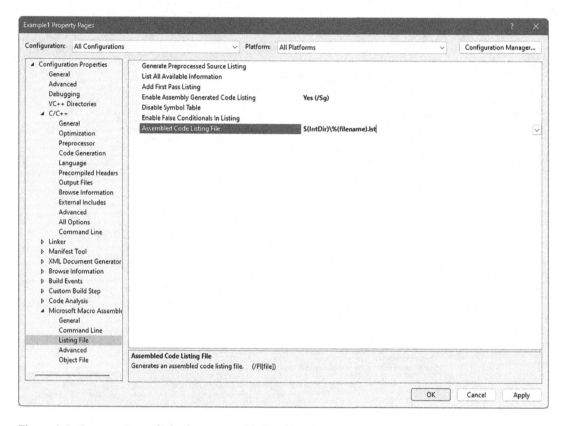

Figure A-9. *Property Pages dialog box – Assembled Code Listing File*

The default code optimization settings for the Visual C++ Debug and Release solution configurations are /0d (disable) and /02 (maximum optimization favor speed), respectively. The benchmark timing measurements published in this book were performed using the Release configuration as described in Chapter 10.

Edit the Source Code

Use the steps that follow this paragraph to edit the source code so that it matches the code in Listings A-1a and A-1b. Note that the source code shown in these listings is included in the master source code folder under subfolder AppendixA\TestSolution\Example1 (see Figure A-1). If you prefer, you can cut and paste the C++ and assembly language source code from the files in this folder instead of typing it.

1. In the Editor window, click the tab named Example1.cpp.

2. Edit the C++ source code to match the code for Example1.cpp that's shown in Listing A-1a.

3. Click the tab named Example1_fasm.asm.

4. Edit the assembly language source code to match the code for Example1_fasm. asm that's shown in Listing A-1b.

5. Select File ➤ Save All.

Listing A-1a. Appendix A Example1 C++ Code

```cpp
//----------------------------------------------------------------------------
// Example1.cpp
//----------------------------------------------------------------------------

#include <iostream>
#include <iomanip>
#include <string>
#include <cmath>

extern "C" void CalcZ_avx(float* z, const float* x, const float* y, size_t n);

static void CalcZ_cpp(float* z, const float* x, const float* y, size_t n)
{
    for (size_t i = 0; i < n; i++)
        z[i] = x[i] + y[i];
}

int main(void)
{
    constexpr size_t n = 20;
    float x[n], y[n], z1[n], z2[n];

    // Initialize the data arrays
    for (size_t i = 0; i < n; i++)
    {
        x[i] = i * 10.0f + 10.0f;
        y[i] = i * 1000.0f + 1000.0f;
        z1[i] = z2[i] = 0.0f;
    }

    // Exercise the calculating functions
    CalcZ_cpp(z1, x, y, n);
    CalcZ_avx(z2, x, y, n);

    // Display the results
    constexpr char nl = '\n';
    constexpr size_t w = 10;
    constexpr float eps = 1.0e-6f;

    std::cout << std::fixed << std::setprecision(1);

    std::cout << std::setw(w) << "i";
    std::cout << std::setw(w) << "x";
    std::cout << std::setw(w) << "y";
    std::cout << std::setw(w) << "z1";
    std::cout << std::setw(w) << "z2" << nl;
    std::cout << std::string(50, '-') << nl;
```

```cpp
    for (size_t i = 0; i < n; i++)
    {
        std::cout << std::setw(w) << i;
        std::cout << std::setw(w) << x[i];
        std::cout << std::setw(w) << y[i];
        std::cout << std::setw(w) << z1[i];
        std::cout << std::setw(w) << z2[i] << nl;

        if (fabs(z1[i] - z2[i]) > eps)
        {
            std::cout << "Compare error!\n";
            break;
        }
    }
}
```

Listing A-1b. Appendix A Example1 MASM Code

```asm
;-----------------------------------------------------------------------
; Example1_fasm.asm
;-----------------------------------------------------------------------


;-----------------------------------------------------------------------
; void CalcZ_avx(float* z, const float* x, const float* x, size_t n);
;-----------------------------------------------------------------------

NSE     equ 8                           ;num_simd_elements
SF      equ 4                           ;scale factor for F32

        .code
CalcZ_avx proc

; Validate arguments
        test r9,r9                      ;n == 0?
        jz Done                         ;jump if yes

; Initialize
        mov rax,-SF                     ;rax = array offset (Loop2)
        cmp r9,NSE                      ;n < NSE?
        jb Loop2                        ;jump if yes
        mov rax,-NSE*SF                 ;rax = array offset (Loop1)

; Calculate z[i:i+7] = x[i:i+7] + y[i:i+7]
Loop1:  add rax,NSE*SF                  ;update array offset
        vmovups ymm0,ymmword ptr [rdx+rax]   ;ymm0 = x[i:i+7]
        vmovups ymm1,ymmword ptr [r8+rax]    ;ymm1 = y[i:i+7]
        vaddps ymm2,ymm0,ymm1           ;z[i:i+7] = x[i:i+7] + y[i:i+7]
        vmovups ymmword ptr [rcx+rax],ymm2   ;save z[i:i+7]

        sub r9,NSE                      ;n -= NSE
        cmp r9,NSE                      ;n >= NSE?
        jae Loop1                       ;jump if yes
```

```
        test r9,r9                          ;n == 0?
        jz Done                             ;jump if yes
        add rax,NSE*SF-SF                    ;adjust array offset for Loop2

; Calculate z[i] = x[i] + y[i] for remaining elements
Loop2:  add rax,SF                          ;update array offset
        vmovss xmm0,real4 ptr [rdx+rax]     ;xmm0 = x[i]
        vmovss xmm1,real4 ptr [r8+rax]      ;xmm1 = y[i]
        vaddss xmm2,xmm0,xmm1               ;z[i] = x[i] + y[i]
        vmovss real4 ptr [rcx+rax],xmm2     ;save z[i]

        sub r9,1                            ;n -= 1
        jnz Loop2                           ;repeat until done

Done:   vzeroupper
        ret                                 ;return to caller
CalcZ_avx endp
        end
```

Build and Run the Project

Use the following steps to build and run the project:

1. Select Build ➤ Configuration Manager.

2. In the Configuration Manager dialog box, select the desired Active solution configuration. Choose **Debug** for a Visual Studio Debugger1 build or **Release** for a final production code build. Click **Close**.

3. Select Build ➤ Build Solution.

4. If necessary, fix any reported Visual C++ compiler or MASM errors and repeat Step 1.

5. Select Debug ➤ Start Without Debugging.

6. Verify that the output matches the console window shown in Figure A-10.

7. Press any key to close the console window.

---

[1] For information regarding Visual Studio debugger use, visit https://learn.microsoft.com/en-us/visualstudio/debugger/?view=vs-2022

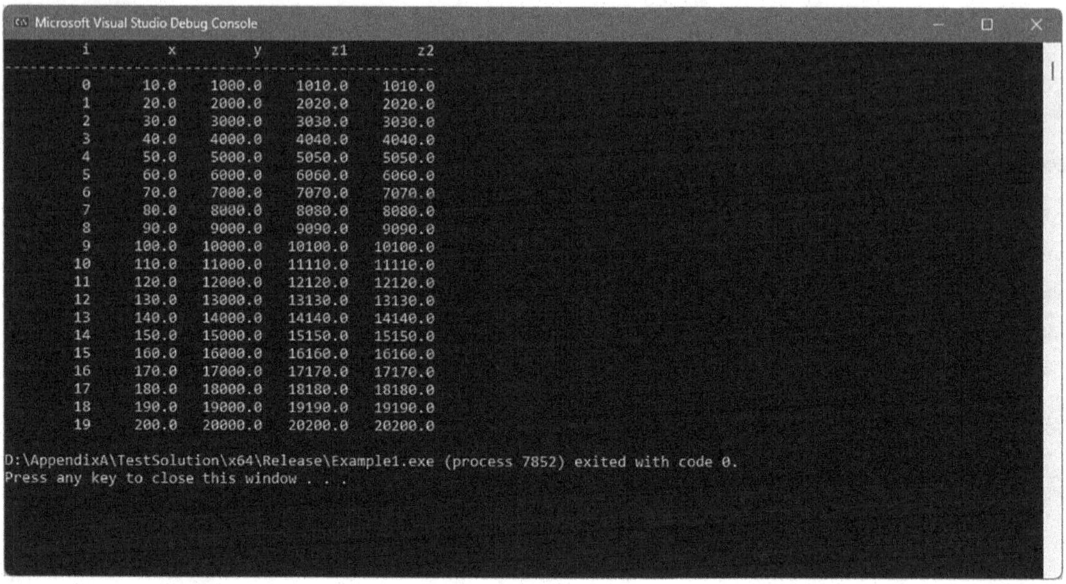

Figure A-10. Console window output for Example1

Linux Development Tools

You can also build and execute this book's source code examples using Linux. The examples were built and tested using 64-bit versions of Debian 11 and Ubuntu 22.10.

Additional Configuration

The Linux source code examples require nasm (www.nasm.us/) and libpng (www.libpng.org/pub/png) to be installed on the host computer. To install these packages on a computer running Debian or Ubuntu,[2] open a terminal window and enter the following commands:

1. `sudo apt update`

2. `sudo apt -y install nasm`

3. `sudo apt -y install libpng-dev`

Build and Run

Perform the following steps to build and run a source code example on Linux:

1. Open a terminal window in your home folder.

2. Using the cd command, change the current working directory to a source code example directory. For example, to build and execute source code example Ch02_01, type the following: `cd Documents/ModX86Asm3e/Code/Chapter02/Ch02_01`. Press **Enter**.

---

[2] To install nasm or libpng on other editions of Linux, consult the appropriate documentation.

3. Type make and press **Enter** to build source code example Ch02_01.

4. Type ./Ch02_01 and press **Enter** to run source code example Ch02_01.

Make Utility

GNU Make ("Make") is a software development utility that facilitates automated program builds. It is usually installed on computers that run Linux. Make uses dependency rules to specify the source code (e.g., .cpp and .h) and intermediate (e.g., .o) files needed to build a target. A target can be any type of file but is often an executable file. Dependency rules are defined in a special file called a makefile. Each dependency rule includes one or more shell commands that instruct Make how to build a target or intermediate file.

The primary advantage of using Make is its ability to selectively execute commands based on changes that occur to a target's dependencies. For example, Make will recompile only the source code files that have changed since it was last run. It uses the last modified datetime stamp of each dependent file to accomplish this.

The remainder of this section briefly discusses the makefiles that were created for this book's source code examples. It is important to note that the subsequent paragraphs are not intended to be a tutorial on Make or how to create makefiles. Comprehensive usage information for Make and makefile dependency rule creation is available at www.gnu.org/software/make/manual/.

Listing A-2 shows the makefile for source code example Ch02_01. Other source code examples use a makefile that is almost identical to the one discussed in this section except for the target name and the GNU C++ (CPPCODE) compiler switches.

Listing A-2. Example Ch02_01 makefile

```
# Target name, include dir, and object dir
TARGET = Ch02_01
INCDIR1 = .
INCDIR2 = ../../Include
OBJDIR = x64lin

# g++ code generation options
CPPCODE = -m64 -mavx

# include files
CPPINCFILES1 = $(wildcard $(INCDIR1)/*.h)
CPPINCFILES2 = $(wildcard $(INCDIR2)/*.h)
ASMINCFILES1 = $(wildcard $(INCDIR1)/*.inc)
ASMINCFILES2 = $(wildcard $(INCDIR2)/*.inc)

# .cpp files in current directory
CPPFILES = $(wildcard *.cpp)
CPPOBJFILES_ = $(CPPFILES:.cpp=.o)
CPPOBJFILES = $(patsubst %, $(OBJDIR)/%, $(CPPOBJFILES_))

# .s files in current directory
ASMFILES = $(wildcard *.s)
ASMOBJFILES_ = $(ASMFILES:.s=.o)
ASMOBJFILES = $(patsubst %, $(OBJDIR)/%, $(ASMOBJFILES_))
```

```
# Target object files
OBJFILES = $(CPPOBJFILES) $(ASMOBJFILES)

# g++ and NASM options - required
CPPOPT = $(CPPCODE) -O3 -std=c++20 -Wall -Wextra
ASMOPT = -f elf64

# g++ and NASM options - optional (comment out to disable)
CPPDEBUG = -g
ASMDEBUG = -g
CPPLISTFILE = -Wa,-aghl=$(OBJDIR)/$(basename $<).lst -save-temps=obj
ASMLISTFILE = -l $(OBJDIR)/$(basename $<).lst -Lm -Ls

# Create directory for object and temp files
MKOBJDIR := $(shell mkdir -p $(OBJDIR))

# Build rules
$(TARGET): $(OBJFILES)
        g++ $(CPPCODE) $(OBJFILES) -o $(TARGET)

# Note: full recompiles/assembles on any include file changes
$(OBJDIR)/%.o: %.cpp $(CPPINCFILES1) $(CPPINCFILES2)
        g++ -I$(INCDIR1) -I$(INCDIR2) $(CPPOPT) $(CPPDEBUG) $(CPPLISTFILE) -c -o $@ $<

$(OBJDIR)/%.o: %.s $(ASMINCFILES1) $(ASMINCFILES2)
        nasm -I$(INCDIR1) -I$(INCDIR2) $(ASMOPT) $(ASMDEBUG) $(ASMLISTFILE) -o $@ $<

.PHONY: clean

clean:
        rm -f $(TARGET)
        rm -rf $(OBJDIR)
```

The first non-comment line in Listing A-2, TARGET = Ch02_01, sets the makefile variable TARGET equal to the text string Ch02_01. Like most programming languages, a makefile can use variables (which are sometimes called macros) to streamline rule creation and eliminate duplication. The next three statements assign text strings to makefile variables INCDIR1, INCDIR2, and OBJDIR. The variables INCDIR1 and INCDIR2 define the directories that contain include files, while OBJDIR defines the directory that stores object modules and other temporary files.

The CPPCODE variable contains GNU C++ compiler code generation switches. The switch -m64 instructs the C++ compiler to generate x86-64 code. The next switch, -mavx, directs the C++ compiler to emit AVX instructions. Other source examples employ different C++ compiler code generation switches. The -mavx2 switch enables AVX2 code generation. The AVX-512 source code examples use the following compiler switches: -mavx512f, -mavx512vl, -mavx512bw, and -mavx512dq. The -mfma switch instructs the C++ compiler to emit FMA instructions. The GNU C++ compiler also supports many other x86 code generation options. For more information regarding these options, visit https://gcc.gnu.org/.

The remaining lines in Listing A-2 are the same for all source code example makefiles. The first few sections instruct Make to build lists of file names with extensions .h and .cpp. These sections also build lists of assembly language source code files with extensions .s and .inc. Having Make build lists of file names eliminates the need to manually create file dependency lists that would be different for each source code example.

Let's take a closer look at the makefile statements that build the file lists. The statement CPPINCFILES1 = $(wildcard $(INCDIR1)/*.h) builds a list of all .h files located in the directory INCDIR1 and assigns this list to variable CPPINCFILES1. This statement uses the variable INCDIR1 that was defined in the previous group of statements. Note that the variable name INCDIR1 is surrounded by parentheses and includes a leading $ symbol. This syntax is required when using a previously defined variable. The text wildcard is a Make function that performs file searches using a search pattern. In the current statement, wildcard searches directory INCDIR1 for all *.h files. The remaining statements in this block initialize variables CPPINCFILES2, ASMINCFILES1, and ASMINCFILES2 using the same wildcard technique.

The first statement of the next group, CPPFILES = $(wildcard *.cpp), builds a list of all .cpp files in the current directory and assigns this list to variable CPPFILES. The next two statements build a list of .o (object module) files that correspond to the .cpp files in the current directory and assign this list to CPPOBJFILES. The ensuing statement group uses the same technique to build a list of object modules that correspond to the .s (assembly language) files in the current directory and assigns this list to ASMOBJFILES. This is followed by the statement OBJFILES = $(CPPOBJFILES) $(ASMOBJFILES), which sets OBJFILES equal to a list of all object module files that are needed to build the executable file TARGET.

The next two makefile variables, CPPOPT and ASMOPT, contain option switches for the GNU C++ compiler and NASM assembler. These switches are required and should not be changed. The $(CPPCODE) option adds the C++ compiler switches that were defined earlier in the makefile. The -O3 option instructs the C++ compiler to generate the fastest possible code. The drawback of using this option is somewhat slower compile times. The -std=c++20 switch enables compilation of the C++ source code using ISO C++ 2020 features. The -Wall and -Wextra switches enable nearly all GNU C++ compiler warning messages.

The next variable group controls optional features. The CPPDEBUG and ASMDEBUG variables instruct the GNU C++ compiler and NASM assembler to generate debugging information for use with the GNU debugger (gdb). The variables CPPLISTFILE and ASMLISTFILE include switches that enable the generation of listing files. Note that the compiler and assembler listing files are saved in the OBJDIR directory.

Following the definition of ASMLISTFILE is the statement MKOBJDIR := $(shell mkdir -p $(OBJDIR)). This statement instructs Make to create the subdirectory OBJDIR. Recall that this directory contains the target's object module files, temporary files, and listing files.

The build rules group begins with a $(TARGET): $(OBJFILES) dependency rule. This rule informs Make that TARGET depends on the object module files defined by the variable OBJFILES. The ensuing statement, g++ $(CPPCODE) $(OBJFILES) -o $(TARGET), is the shell command[3] that Make runs to build the executable file TARGET. More specifically, this command links the object modules defined by OBJFILES into a single executable file. Note that this makefile statement is indented with a tab character, which is required.

The next dependency rule, $(OBJDIR)/%.o: %.cpp $(CPPINCFILES1) $(CPPINCFILES2), notifies Make that each .o file in OBJDIR depends on a corresponding .cpp file in the current directory. Each .o file also depends on the include files defined by the variables CPPINCFILES1 and CPPINCFILES2. Make uses the ensuing shell command g++ -I$(INCDIR1) -I$(INCDIR2) $(CPPOPT) $(CPPDEBUG) $(CPPLISTFILE) -c -o $@ $< to compile each C++ source code file. In this statement, Make replaces the automatic variable $< with the name of a C++ file. It also replaces the automatic variable $@ with the name of the corresponding object module file. The -c switch instructs the GNU C++ compiler to skip the link step, while the -o switch directs the compiler to save the output object module to file $@. A similar dependency rule and shell command pair are also used for NASM and the assembly language files.

The statement .PHONY: clean defines a fake (or non-file) target named clean. Typing make clean in a terminal window instructs Make to execute shell commands rm -f $(TARGET) and rm -rf $(OBJDIR). These commands delete the file TARGET and remove the subdirectory OBJDIR. The make clean command is typically employed to force a complete rebuild of a target executable the next time Make is used.

---

[3] Source code examples that utilize the libpng library also include the switch -lpng.

APPENDIX B

■ ■ ■

References and Resources

Appendix B lists the principal references that were consulted during the writing of this book. It also includes additional x86 assembly language programming references and resources that you might find useful or interesting.

X86 Assembly Language Programming References

The following list contains the principal references that were consulted during the writing of this book:

AMD64 Architecture Programmer's Manual: Volumes 1–5, Publication Number 40332, www.amd.com/system/files/TechDocs/40332.pdf

Software Optimization Guide for AMD Family 17h Processors, Publication Number 55723, www.amd.com/en/support/tech-docs?keyword=55723

Software Optimization Guide for AMD Family 17h Models 30h and Greater Processors, Publication Number 56305, www.amd.com/en/support/tech-docs?keyword=56305

Software Optimization Guide for the AMD Zen4 Microarchitecture, Publication Number 57647, www.amd.com/en/support/tech-docs?keyword=57647

Software Optimization Guide for AMD EPYC 7003 Processors, Publication Number 56665, www.amd.com/en/support/tech-docs?keyword=56665

Intel 64 and IA-32 Architectures Software Developer's Manual, Combined Volumes: 1, 2A, 2B, 2C, 2D, 3A, 3B, 3C, 3D, and 4, www.intel.com/content/www/us/en/processors/architectures-software-developer-manuals.html

Intel 64 and IA-32 Architectures Optimization Reference Manual, www.intel.com/content/www/us/en/processors/architectures-software-developer-manuals.html

Daniel Kusswurm, *Modern X86 Assembly Language Programming, Second Edition,* ISBN 978-1-4842-4062-5, Apress, 2018

Daniel Kusswurm, *Modern Parallel Programming with C++ and Assembly Language,* ISBN 978-1-4842-7917-5, Apress, 2022

© Daniel Kusswurm 2023
D. Kusswurm, *Modern X86 Assembly Language Programming,*
https://doi.org/10.1007/978-1-4842-9603-5

H.J. Lu, et. al, *System V Application Binary Interface – AMD64 Architecture Processor Supplement*, https://github.com/hjl-tools/x86-psABI/wiki/x86-64-psABI-1.0.pdf

Microsoft, *X64 Calling Convention*, https://learn.microsoft.com/en-us/cpp/build/x64-calling-convention?view=msvc-170

The following list contains supplemental x86 processor and programming resources that may be of interest:

Agner Fog, *The microarchitecture of Intel, AMD, and VIA CPUs: An optimization guide for assembly programmers and compiler makers*, https://agner.org/optimize/#manuals

Agner Fog, *Optimizing subroutines in assembly language: An optimization guide for x86 platforms*, https://agner.org/optimize/#manuals

Patrick Konsor, *Avoiding AVX-SSE Transition Penalties*, www.intel.com/content/dam/develop/external/us/en/documents/11mc12-avoiding-2bavx-sse-2btransition-2bpenalties-2brh-2bfinal-256953.pdf

James Reinders, *AVX-512 May Be a Hidden Gem in Intel Xeon Scalable Processors*, June 2017, www.hpcwire.com/2017/06/29/reinders-avx-512-may-hidden-gem-intel-xeon-scalable-processors

Advanced Vector Extensions, Wikipedia, https://en.wikipedia.org/wiki/Advanced_Vector_Extensions

AVX-512, Wikipedia, https://en.wikipedia.org/wiki/AVX-512

IEEE 754, Wikipedia, https://en.wikipedia.org/wiki/IEEE_754

List of AMD CPU Microarchitectures, Wikipedia, https://en.wikipedia.org/wiki/List_of_AMD_CPU_microarchitectures

List of AMD Processors, Wikipedia, https://en.wikipedia.org/wiki/List_of_AMD_processors

List of Intel CPU Microarchitectures, Wikipedia, https://en.wikipedia.org/wiki/List_of_Intel_CPU_microarchitectures

List of Intel Processors, Wikipedia, https://en.wikipedia.org/wiki/Intel_processor

List of Intel Xeon Processors, Wikipedia, https://en.wikipedia.org/wiki/List_of_Intel_Xeon_microprocessors

Loop-Level Parallelism, Wikipedia, https://en.wikipedia.org/wiki/Loop-level_parallelism

Loop Unrolling, Wikipedia, https://en.wikipedia.org/wiki/Loop_unrolling

Microarchitecture, Wikipedia, https://en.wikipedia.org/wiki/Microarchitecture

Algorithm References

The following resources were consulted to develop the algorithms used in the source code examples:

Forman S. Acton, *REAL Computing Made REAL – Preventing Errors in Scientific and Engineering Calculations*, ISBN 978-0486442211, Dover Publications, 2005

Tony Chan, Gene Golub, Randall LeVeque, *Algorithms for Computing the Sample Variance: Analysis and Recommendations*, The American Statistician, Volume 37 Number 3 (1983), p. 242–247

James F. Epperson, *An Introduction to Numerical Methods and Analysis, Second Edition*, ISBN 978-1-118-36759-9, Wiley, 2013

David Goldberg, *What Every Computer Scientist Should Know About Floating-Point Arithmetic*, ACM Computing Surveys, Volume 23 Issue 1 (March 1991), p. 5–48

Rafael C. Gonzalez and Richard E. Woods, *Digital Image Processing, Fourth Edition*, ISBN 978-0-133-35672-4, 2018

James E. Miller, David G. Moursund, Charles S. Duris, *Elementary Theory & Application of Numerical Analysis, Revised Edition*, ISBN 978-0486479064, Dover Publications, 2011

Anthony Pettofrezzo, *Matrices and Transformations*, ISBN 0-486-63634-8, Dover Publications, 1978

Hans Schneider and George Barker, *Matrices and Linear Algebra*, ISBN 0-486-66014-1, Dover Publications, 1989

Eric W. Weisstein, *Convolution*, MathWorld, http://mathworld.wolfram.com/Convolution.html

Eric W. Weisstein, *Correlation Coefficient*, MathWorld, http://mathworld.wolfram.com/CorrelationCoefficient.html

Eric W. Weisstein, *Cross Product*, MathWorld, http://mathworld.wolfram.com/CrossProduct.html

Eric W. Weisstein, *Least Squares Fitting*, MathWorld, http://mathworld.wolfram.com/LeastSquaresFitting.html

Eric W. Weisstein, *Matrix Multiplication*, MathWorld, http://mathworld.wolfram.com/MatrixMultiplication.html

David M. Young and Robert Todd Gregory, *A Survey of Numerical Mathematics, Volume 1*, ISBN 0-486-65691-8, Dover Publications, 1988

Algorithms for Calculating Variance, Wikipedia, https://en.wikipedia.org/wiki/Algorithms_for_calculating_variance

Associative Property, Wikipedia, https://en.wikipedia.org/wiki/Associative_property

Body Surface Area Calculator, www.globalrph.com/bsa2.htm

Convolution, Wikipedia, https://en.wikipedia.org/wiki/Convolution

Floating-Point Arithmetic, Wikipedia, https://en.wikipedia.org/wiki/Floating-point_arithmetic

Grayscale, Wikipedia, https://en.wikipedia.org/wiki/Grayscale

C++ References

The following resources contain valuable information about C++ programming and the C++ Standard Template Libraries:

J. Burton Browning and Bruce Sutherland, *C++ 20 Recipes*, Apress, ISBN 978-1-4842-5712-8, 2020

Ivor Horton, *Using the C++ Standard Template Libraries*, Apress, ISBN 978-1-4842-0005-6, 2015

Nicolai M. Josuttis, *The C++ Standard Library – A Tutorial and Reference, Second Edition*, Addison Wesley, ISBN 978-0-321-62321-8, 2012

Bjarne Stroustrup, *The C++ Programming Language, Fourth Edition*, Addison Wesley, ISBN 978-0-321-56384-2, 2013

Standard C++, https://isocpp.org/

cplusplus.com, www.cplusplus.com

C++ Reference, https://en.cppreference.com/w/

Software Development Tools

The following software development tools were used to create the source code examples in this book:

GNU Binutils, www.gnu.org/software/binutils/

GNU Compiler Collection, www.gnu.org/software/gcc/

GNU Make, www.gnu.org/software/make

NASM, The Netwide Assembler, www.nasm.us/

Portable Network Graphics, www.libpng.org/pub/png/libpng.html

Visual Studio, https://visualstudio.microsoft.com/

Miscellaneous Utilities, Tools, and Libraries

The following utilities, tools, and libraries may be of interest to readers of this book:

AMD µProf, https://developer.amd.com/amd-uprof/

cpuid, www.cpuid.com/

cpuid.h, https://gcc.gnu.org/git/?p=gcc.git;a=blob;f=gcc/config/i386/cpuid.h

__cpuid, __cpuidex, https://learn.microsoft.com/en-us/cpp/intrinsics/cpuid-cpuidex?view=msvc-170

gprof, https://sourceware.org/binutils/docs/gprof/

Intel VTune Profiler, www.intel.com/content/www/us/en/docs/vtune-profiler/get-started-guide/2023-1/overview.html

libcpuid, https://github.com/anrieff/libcpuid

Index

Printed in the United States
by Baker & Taylor Publisher Services